NASA's
DISCOVERY
PROGRAM

NASA's
DISCOVERY
PROGRAM

The First Twenty Years of Competitive
Planetary Exploration

By Susan M. Niebur with
David W. Brown (editor)

Foreword by Michael J. Neufeld and
Afterword by Curt Niebur

National Aeronautics and Space Administration

Office of Communications
NASA History Division
Washington, DC 20546

NASA SP-2023-4238

Library of Congress Cataloging-in-Publication Data

Names: Niebur, Susan M., 1973-2012, author. | Brown, David W., editor. | United States. NASA History Division, issuing body.

Title: NASA's Discovery Program: the first twenty years of competitive planetary exploration / by Susan M. Niebur with David W. Brown (ed.).

Other titles: First twenty years of competitive planetary exploration | NASA SP (Series); 2023-4238.

Description: Washington, DC: National Aeronautics and Space Administration, Office of Communications, NASA History Division, 2023. |

Series: NASA SP; 2023-4238 | In scope of the U.S. Government Publishing Office Cataloging and Indexing Program (C&I); Federal Depository Library Program (FDLP) distribution status to be determined upon publication. | Includes bibliographical references and index. | Summary: "Started in the early 1990s to provide opportunities for small, relatively simple planetary science missions, NASA's Discovery Program has funded a series of focused and innovative missions to investigate the planets and small bodies of our solar system. This book draws on interviews with program managers, engineers, and scientists and takes an in-depth look at the management techniques they used to design creative and cost-effective spacecraft that continue to yield valuable scientific data"— Provided by publisher.

Identifiers: LCCN 2023003999 (print) | LCCN 2023004000 (ebook) | ISBN 9781626830769 (paperback) | ISBN 9781626830776 (ebook)

Subjects: LCSH: Discovery Program (U.S.) | Planets. | Planetary Scientists—United States. | Astronomy—Observations. | Outer space—Exploration.

Classification: LCC QB500.262.N54 2023 (print) | LCC QB500.262 (ebook) | DDC 919.904--dc23/eng/20230623 | SUDOC NAS 1.21:4238

LC record available at https://lccn.loc.gov/2023003999

LC ebook record available at https://lccn.loc.gov/2023004000

ISBN 978-1-62683-076-9

TABLE OF

Contents

ACKNOWLEDGMENTS

This history manuscript took an unusual path, and as such, special thanks are due to a number of people. First, of course, to the late Susan Niebur, who did the initial research and writing before her untimely passing. Before Susan, thanks go to Harley Thronson, Ming-Ying Wei, and Jens Feeley, who conceptualized, funded, and implemented the original call for and selection of history of space and Earth science proposals. Next to David Brown, who did yeoman's work editing Susan's rough draft and notes into a more complete form. Thank you also to Michael Neufeld for his careful review and for writing an excellent foreword that contextualizes NASA's Discovery Program, brings the story up to date, and explains his and the other contributors' roles. Last but certainly not least, thank you to Curt Niebur for providing an eloquent afterword.

Special thanks go to Tom Wagner, former Discovery Program Scientist, who expressed interest in having Susan's unfinished manuscript completed and published and provided strong support along the way. In the NASA History Division, James Anderson, Steve Garber, and Michele Ostovar worked hard to get the manuscript ready for production. Intern Maddy Pollack carefully consolidated footnotes where it was warranted. She and interns Olivia Reste, Travis Frederick, and Joshua Schmidt assisted in the review and compiled the images reproduced in this book.

Many thanks to the outstanding production team in the NASA Headquarters Communications Support Services Center (CSSC). Lisa Jirousek skillfully copy-edited the manuscript, and Andrew Cooke performed careful quality assurance. Michael Chinn and Ronna Goldman skillfully laid out the elegant book design. Kristin Harley expertly prepared the index. Tun Hla, Vee Talbert, and Bill Keeter professionally managed the whole process. Thank you all for your skill, professionalism, and collegial attitudes in bringing this book to fruition.

Brian Odom
NASA Chief Historian

The Discovery Program, 1989–2022

By Michael J. Neufeld

The Discovery Program is the most important NASA robotic planetary spacecraft program you have never heard of—unless you are a space agency insider. Initiated in 1989 and legislated into existence in 1993, Discovery has funded a series of relatively small, focused, and innovative missions to the planets and small bodies of the solar system. Notable ones include Mars Pathfinder, which landed a miniature rover on Mars in 1997; NEAR Shoemaker, which orbited and landed on 433 Eros in 2000–2001; Deep Impact, which hit Comet Tempel 1 in 2005; MESSENGER, which orbited Mercury between 2011 and 2015; and the Kepler space telescope, which discovered thousands of exoplanets. If the public has heard of anything, it is the missions, not the program from which they sprang.

The Origins of the Discovery Program

At the end of the 1980s, there was growing discomfort in the science community with the planetary exploration program of the National Aeronautics and Space Administration (NASA). Almost the whole planetary budget went to a handful of large, expensive missions, which had been significantly delayed by the national policy of using only the Space Shuttle as a launch vehicle. An attempt to create a lower-cost Planetary Observer spacecraft series produced only one mission, Mars Observer, which significantly overran its budget, in part because it had to be redesigned for an expendable booster after the Challenger Shuttle accident of January 1986.[1] Opportunities for small, relatively simple missions were absent.

A new attempt to create a low-cost planetary program came primarily from two would-be reformers: Stamatios "Tom" Krimigis and Wesley T. Huntress. Krimigis was a prominent scientist in space physics/heliophysics at the Johns Hopkins Applied Physics Laboratory (APL) and the head of APL's Space Department from 1991 to 2004. Wes Huntress had been a distinguished cosmochemist at the Jet Propulsion Laboratory (JPL), a NASA planetary exploration center run by the California Institute of Technology. He became head of the Solar System Exploration Division at NASA Headquarters in 1990 and Associate Administrator for Space Science in 1993. Both were dissatisfied with the status quo in planetary exploration; both wanted competitive selections of mission proposals for smaller, less expensive spacecraft led by scientists as Principal Investigators (PIs). Both thought JPL's stranglehold on planetary projects, a product of NASA's attempt to streamline during the lean budget years of the 1970s and early 1980s, made it complacent and expensive. Huntress wanted to give JPL competition, and Krimigis was only too happy to supply it.

I have told the story of the origins of the Discovery Program elsewhere,[2] as does Susan Niebur at greater length in this book, so I will only summarize the key points here. In fall 1993, Congress authorized for Discovery a $132 million budget—double what NASA had asked for. Over the preceding two years, the agency had awarded the planned first mission, NEAR, to APL. But it was then displaced to second when the idea for an innovative, JPL-built Mars Pathfinder lander and mini-rover became popular at NASA Headquarters, notably with the new Administrator as of April 1992, Daniel Goldin. Thanks to the intervention of Senator Barbara Mikulski of Maryland, where APL was situated, both spacecraft were in the budget.

These two assigned missions would be followed by open competitions with projects proposed by PIs as part of a standing budget line. That model, as Krimigis had advo-

---

1   On Mars Observer, see Erik M. Conway, *Exploration and Engineering: The Jet Propulsion Laboratory and the Quest for Mars* (Baltimore: Johns Hopkins, 2015), chaps. 1 and 3.

2   Michael J. Neufeld, "Transforming Solar System Exploration: The Origins of the Discovery Program, 1989–1993," *Space Policy* 30 (2014), 5–12. For participant accounts of the early years, see Stamatios M. Krimigis and Joseph Veverka, "Foreword: Genesis of Discovery," *Journal of the Astronautical Sciences* 43 (Oct.–Dec. 1995), 345–47, and Robert W. Farquhar, *Fifty Years on the Space Frontier: Halo Orbits, Comets, Asteroids and More* (Denver: Outskirts Press, 2010), 137–42. For an overview of the program up to 2016, see Michael J. Neufeld, "The Discovery Program: Competition, Innovation, and Risk in Planetary Exploration," in *NASA Spaceflight: A History of Innovation*, edited by Roger D. Launius and Howard McCurdy (New York: Palgrave Macmillan, 2017), 267–90.

cated from the outset and Huntress pushed through, was based on NASA's Explorer Program. It had been launching heliophysics and astronomy satellites since the late 1950s. But Principal Investigators in Explorer were only responsible for the science and the scientific instruments, not the spacecraft engineering and overall leadership. Discovery would put scientist PIs at universities and other institutions in charge of leading the project, supported by a Project Manager (PM) focused on engineering, budget, and schedule.[3]

For the Solar System Exploration Division, this was a radical departure from the traditional model, where NASA HQ assigned a mission to JPL, after a laborious process of obtaining a budgetary line for a "new start" from the current presidential administration and Congress. With a "level of effort" program, there would be money in the federal budget every year to fund a steady stream of Discovery missions—the initial objective was a launch every 18 to 24 months—without having to seek permission for each project individually. (Congress formally approved that permanent line in 1995.) The PI would lead a "science investigation" to put the science at the forefront of the proposal and the project, inverting the traditional JPL approach, which was dominated by engineering considerations coming out of an era when it was a challenge just to get the spacecraft safely to the Moon or a planet.

There was one more important context for Discovery's emergence: it became the poster child for Dan Goldin's campaign to shake up NASA and institute a "faster, better, cheaper" (FBC) approach to robotic spacecraft development.[4] The perception of the space agency as bureaucratic, failure-prone, and expensive had risen quickly in the early 1990s, notably because of the flawed mirror of the Hubble Space Telescope. In early 1992, President George H. W. Bush replaced Administrator Richard Truly, an astronaut, with Goldin, who had worked as an executive at the mostly military aerospace contractor TRW. The fast, risk-taking methods of the Strategic Defense Initiative, created to fulfill President Ronald Reagan's vision of a defense against ballistic mis-

---

3   Niebur, Susan M., "Principal investigators and project managers: Insights from Discovery," *Space Policy* 28 (2012),174–84. See also her "Principal Investigators and mission leadership," *Space Policy* 25 (2009), 181–86, and "Women and mission leadership," *Space Policy* 25 (2009), 257–63.

4   Stephanie A. Roy, "The origin of the smaller, faster, cheaper approach in NASA's solar system exploration program," *Space Policy* 14 (1998), 153–71; Howard E. McCurdy, *Faster, Better, Cheaper: Low-Cost Innovation in the U.S. Space Program* (Baltimore: Johns Hopkins University Press, 2001), and "Learning from History: Low-cost Project Innovation in the U.S. National Aeronautics and Space Administration," *International Journal of Project Management* 31 (2013), 705–11; Amy Page Kaminski, "Faster, Better, Cheaper: A Sociotechnical Perspective on Programmatic Choice, Success, and Failure in NASA's Solar System Exploration Program," in *Exploring the Solar System: The History and Science of Planetary Exploration*, edited by Roger D. Launius (New York: Palgrave Macmillan, 2013), 77–101; and Jason W. Callahan, "Funding Planetary Science: History and Political Economy," in *50 Years of Planetary Exploration: Historical Perspectives*, edited by Linda Billings (Washington, DC: NASA, 2021), NASA SP-2021-4705, 35–88, 64–70 referenced here.

siles, were the model for a reform. Soon after arriving, Wes Huntress introduced Dan Goldin to Discovery, which neatly fit the Administrator's rhetoric about instituting FBC methods at NASA. Because of his reputation as a reformer, Goldin survived the transition to the Bill Clinton administration in 1993. Thus, for most of the nineties, his "faster, better, cheaper" methods would dominate the development of space science spacecraft. But FBC came to a sudden end in 1999, when two Mars spacecraft not part of Discovery failed upon reaching the Red Planet. The media and the political class heaped criticism on the agency, and Goldin became risk-averse.

Discovery's Rise, Crisis, and Renewal

Back in December 1992, NASA held its first workshop at San Juan Capistrano, California, to solicit mission ideas for Discovery. No fewer than 73 proposals were accepted from potential PIs, indicating that there was lively support in academia, the agency, and industry for the concept of competed small planetary missions. In early 1993, Huntress chose 11 to be funded for further development. A year later, NASA released the first Announcement of Opportunity (AO), leading to the selection of the first competed mission, Lunar Prospector, in February 1995, plus an ensuing competition among three proposals. The winner was Stardust, a spacecraft to retrieve a sample of particles from a comet's tail. Two more selections were made each in 1997, 1999, and 2001 (see "Discovery Missions" table). NEAR launched first, in early 1996, and flew by asteroid Mathilde before heading to a rendezvous with Eros; Mars Pathfinder made a spectacular landing on Independence Day, 1997, and deployed the mini-rover Sojourner. NEAR suffered an inflight crisis and missed Eros in 1999 but successfully orbited in 2000 and made a landing in 2001, something not originally planned. Thus, despite the political crisis of confidence that the 1999 Mars failures created, as well as Goldin's retreat from FBC rhetoric and methods, Discovery looked to be a great success. It adhered to the early goals of frequent competitive selections and launches of PI-led projects supported by a variety of centers.

The crisis of Discovery came after 2002, when one spacecraft, CONTOUR, blew up as it was leaving Earth orbit, followed by several projects getting into trouble with cost and schedule. In its original conception, missions were to come under a cost cap ($150 million in 1992 dollars, without the launch vehicle) and be terminated if they ran significantly over budget or behind schedule. As Goldin framed it, inflight failures were to be expected in a "faster, better, cheaper" framework. The political and public reaction to the 1999 Mars failures showed how difficult that was. NASA and the Administrator were harshly criticized and ridiculed for incompetence and wasting the taxpayers' money. Studies of those failures revealed weak management controls, technical compromises, and inadequate testing coming out of very lean budgets. Afterward, NASA imposed more stringent project management reviews and paperwork, which inevitably increased cost.

Discovery Missions

Name	Selection	Launch	PI/Institution	Lead Center	Spacecraft Manufacturer	Target
Mars Pathfinder	1992	1996	none/JPL (M. Golombek, PS)	JPL	JPL	Mars
NEAR	1992	1996	none/APL (A. Cheng, PS)	APL	APL	Mathilde, Eros
Lunar Prospector	1995	1998	A. Binder/Lunar Research Institute	ARC	LM Sunnyvale	Moon
Stardust	1995	1999	D. Brownlee/ U. Washington	JPL	LM Denver	Comet Wild 2
Genesis	1997	2001	D. Burnett/Caltech	JPL	LM Denver	solar wind/ Earth-Sun L1
CONTOUR	1997	2002	J. Veverka/Cornell	APL	APL	2 comets (failed)
MESSENGER	1999	2004	S. Solomon/CIW	APL	APL	Mercury
Deep Impact	1999	2005	M. A'Hearn/ U. Maryland	JPL	Ball Aerospace	Comet Tempel 1
Dawn	2001	2007	C. Russell/UCLA	JPL	Orbital Sciences	Vesta, Ceres
Kepler	2001	2009	W. Borucki/ARC	JPL/ ARC	Ball Aerospace	extrasolar planets
GRAIL	2007	2011	M. Zuber/MIT	JPL	LM Denver	Moon
InSight	2012	2018	W. B. Banerdt/JPL	JPL	LM Denver	Mars
Lucy	2017	2021	H. Levison/SwRI	GSFC	LM Denver	Jupiter's Trojan asteroids
Psyche	2017	2023	L. Elkins-Tanton/ ASU	JPL	JPL	Psyche
DAVINCI	2021	2029?	J. Garvin/GSFC	GSFC	LM Denver/ GSFC	Venus
VERITAS	2021	2031?	S. Smrekar/JPL	JPL	LM Denver	Venus

Terminating mission projects in the development phase, another expectation in Discovery's design and Goldin's rhetoric, was also much easier said than done. The sunk cost of tens of millions of dollars expended and hardware already built was difficult to discard, especially when a team was promising that X additional dollars would fix the problems. Deep Impact went through termination review twice and survived both. MESSENGER blew through the cost cap, and its launch was delayed by months, in part out of what the PI and APL thought was an excess of caution, but a formal termination review was never called. The Kepler telescope had major overruns and delays, due to factors including the extreme technical challenge of detecting Earth-size planets around other stars and NASA mandating the shift to full-cost accounting. Yet it was repeatedly extended. Finally, Dawn actually was cancelled in 2006 and then uncancelled a few months later. All four would go on to be groundbreaking missions.[5]

What emerged from the Mars failures of 1999 and Discovery's troubles of 2002–2005 was essentially version 2.0, in which missions could no longer be relatively cheap or risky. The cost cap was repeatedly raised such that, as of 2023, it is effectively more than double the original $150 million in 1992 dollars. The greatly increased emphasis on program reviews and documentation made development longer and more expensive. Realism also set in about the ambition of many of the proposals. After NEAR and Lunar Prospector, which were significantly under the cap, every proposal to 2001 was right up to it. The competitive process favored maximizing the science, which led to overly optimistic estimates of the cost of increasingly sophisticated instrumentation. That was a significant factor in the overruns and delays of the early 2000s. Combined with cuts in Space Science's overall budget, that meant that there was insufficient money in the budget of Solar System Exploration (after 2004, the Planetary Science Division of the Science Mission Directorate) to open new competitions, as already-chosen ones had to be funded years longer than originally budgeted. The resulting dearth in selections is visible in the preceding table. NASA chose only two new spacecraft proposals in the sixteen years between 2001 and 2017.[6]

One partial substitute was the awarding of "Missions of Opportunity," a budget line initiated in 1998. These cheaper proposals (originally capped at $35 million) were for instruments on other, usually foreign, spacecraft or for the creative reuse of NASA ones. See the table on the following page for a complete list. Notable is how the main spacecraft busses of both Deep Impact and Stardust were employed for new science after they fulfilled their original missions of dropping off a comet impactor and a sample return capsule, respectively.

---

5   For a more thorough account of these years, see Neufeld, "The Discovery Program," 276–80. The tables in this foreword are updated versions of the tables in that article.

6   Ibid., 280–83; Callahan, "Funding Planetary Science," 70–74.

Program management was also reorganized during the crisis years, in part due to Goldin's forced downsizing of NASA Headquarters. Contract administration and fulfillment were put into a separate Discovery office, first briefly at JPL, then at Marshall Space Flight Center in Huntsville, Alabama. That office soon added New Frontiers, a new competitive program for "medium-sized" planetary missions, beginning in 2003 with the New Horizons project to send a spacecraft to Pluto and the Kuiper Belt.[7] And in response to the new competition presented by APL, and later by Goddard Space Flight Center, Director Charles Elachi reorganized the Jet Propulsion Laboratory so that it could support multiple proposals. JPL often found Principal Investigators from within, or from the ranks of allied scientists in academia, reversing the early Discovery expectation that PIs would be academics who would ally with a center to advance their own idea. JPL's success in that endeavor is visible in the "Discovery Missions" table: almost all winning proposals after 2001 are from there.

Discovery Missions of Opportunity

Name	Selection	Launch	PI/Institution	Lead Center	Spacecraft	Target
Aspera-3 (instrument)	1998	2003	D. Winningham/SwRI	SwRI	Mars Express (ESA)	Mars
NetLander instruments	2001	cancelled	W. B. Banerdt/JPL	JPL	NetLander (France)	Mars
M^3 (instrument)	2005	2008	C. Pieters/Brown U.	JPL	Chandrayaan-1 (India)	Moon
EPOXI	2007	2005	M. A'Hearn/U. Maryland	JPL/Ball	Deep Impact bus	extrasolar planets/Comet Hartley 2
Stardust NExT	2007	1999	J. Veverka/Cornell	JPL	Stardust bus	Comet Tempel 1
Strofio (instrument)	2009	2018	S. Livi/SwRI	SwRI	BepiColombo (ESA)	Mercury
MEGANE (instrument)	2017	2024?	D. J. Lawrence/APL	APL	MMX (Japan)	Martian moons Phobos and Deimos

---

7   Michael J. Neufeld, "First Mission to Pluto: Policy, Politics, Science and Technology in the Origins of New Horizons, 1989–2003," *Historical Studies in the Natural Sciences* 44 (2014), 234–276, abridged and updated as "The Difficult Birth of NASA's Pluto Mission," *Physics Today* 69, no. 4 (April 2016), 40–47.

The creation of the New Frontiers mission line shows that, although the Discovery Program was no longer particularly fast or cheap, it was very successful in producing innovative and original proposals that maximized science return for focused planetary science projects. That success has continued. Beginning in 2017, Discovery was also able to restore the selection of two proposals at a time, if not at the every-other-year pace of the early years. A new mission line may be needed for cheap and risky missions, such as the CubeSats that have been launched to Mars and the Moon recently, but, without a doubt, Discovery has been a groundbreaking program that has revolutionized the NASA planetary program and gives every indication that it will be around for decades to come.

About This Book and Its Author

Dr. Susan M. Niebur was the Discovery Program Scientist at NASA Headquarters from 2002 to 2006. A PhD physicist who had written a dissertation on galactic cosmic rays, she had looked for a job at the space agency out of pure enthusiasm for it. She won a Presidential Management Internship there in 2001 and moved on to the Discovery position only one year later. As a young woman, she already stood out in a place dominated by aging, predominantly male civil servants. She had come with her husband, Curt Niebur, who came to Headquarters shortly after her and is still today a leading administrator in the Planetary Science Division. But when they began to have children, she found the work arrangements too inflexible. She quit and formed her own consulting company, as well as taking a leading role in encouraging young women who were planetary scientists, and early-career scientists generally, to organize and change the discipline. She founded the Women in Planetary Science website and the annual women's breakfast at the Lunar and Planetary Science Conference in Houston. Both continue to promote career advancement and networking today.[8]

In 2007, Susan Niebur won a NASA grant to write a history of the Discovery Program, the origin of this book. She also published several articles from her research and personal knowledge of the subject, focusing particularly on the role of the PI. Very unfortunately, she never finished the book manuscript, as she tragically died at age 38 in early 2012 after a five-year struggle with cancer. That story is told by this book's editor, David W. Brown, in his engrossing work on the origin of a mission to explore Jupiter's moon Europa. (Curt Niebur is one of his central characters.) Later that year,

---

8   David W. Brown, *The Mission* (New York: Custom House, 2021), 103–07; "Susan Niebur (1973–2012), Astrophysicist," *https://solarsystem.nasa.gov/people/1700/susan-niebur-1973-2012/*; Women in Planetary Science website, *https://womeninplanetaryscience.wordpress.com/*; Division for Planetary Sciences, American Astronomical Society, "2012 Prize Recipients," Susan Niebur citation, *https://dps.aas.org/prizes/2012*. All websites accessed 7 Sept. 2022. For her articles on PIs and Discovery, see n. 3. For a full list of her publications, see *https://susanniebur.wordpress.com/publication-list/*, accessed 9 Sept. 2022.

the American Astronomical Society posthumously awarded Susan Niebur the Harold Masursky Award for "outstanding service to planetary science and exploration." Asteroid 113394 Niebur was later named in her honor.[9]

She left behind a partially completed Discovery manuscript and a rich collection of materials and oral histories covering the first two decades of the program, up to about 2011. To complete this book, NASA hired David Brown to edit the chapters that were essentially finished—approximately the first sixty percent of the manuscript—and to complete the rest from a collection of drafts, notes, copied news articles, and oral history excerpts. It was a monumental task, but to the best of his ability, David has tried to write in her voice and finish the book the way she would have wanted to. It is by far the most comprehensive history yet written of Discovery's early years. It is a fitting tribute to a charismatic, energetic, and influential young scientist, someone who unfortunately did not live long enough to see her children grow up or hold this book in her hand.

---

9   Brown, *The Mission*, 183–85, 226–28, 334–36. For Susan Niebur's blog of her family and illness, see *https://toddlerplanet.wordpress.com/*, accessed 7 Sept. 2022.

CHAPTER 1

Discovery Begins

Prompted in part by the grounding of the Space Shuttle fleet due to fuel leaks, along with embarrassing revelations of a Hubble Space Telescope that was defective on launch, the George H. W. Bush administration requested in July 1990 that an independent group evaluate the long-term goals of the National Aeronautics and Space Administration (NASA). Five months later, the Advisory Committee on the Future of the United States Space Program released its much-anticipated report, declaring space science to be NASA's highest priority, above even the Space Shuttle, space station, and a return to the Moon.[1] The report came on the heels of a difficult decade for the field of planetary science, which had seen only a few large projects replace the robust series of Mariner, Pioneer, and Voyager spacecraft that had characterized American robotic space exploration since the 1960s. To correct for the dearth of mission launches and

---

1   Report of the Advisory Committee on the Future of the U.S. Space Program. (1990). U.S. Government Printing Office.

to fully address the newly prioritized science objectives of NASA, the agency's management and the planetary science community sought a new approach to the robotic exploration of the solar system.

LAUNCHING A MISSION LINE

Two of NASA's existing, high-priority planetary science missions had been previously delayed in the 1980s, in part by issues related to the Space Shuttle. The first of these projects was the Galileo mission to Jupiter, first selected in 1977. The billion-dollar "large strategic science mission" (colloquially known as a "flagship") was set for a 1984 Space Shuttle launch with a Centaur upper stage pushing it toward the outer planets. NASA's Jet Propulsion Laboratory (JPL), an agency research and development center in Pasadena, California, delivered the spacecraft to NASA's Kennedy Space Center in December 1985 as payload for the Space Shuttle. Before launch, however, tragedy struck with the loss of the Space Shuttle Challenger in January 1986. This grounded the Jupiter orbiter for years while NASA struggled to return to flight. NASA implemented additional safety regulations, which rendered the Centaur upper stage—fueled with liquid hydrogen—far too dangerous for flight aboard the Shuttle. Engineers determined that a solid-fueled inertial upper stage, however, would be permissible, though it would supply much less thrust to the spacecraft.

Galileo engineers went to work replacing the planned direct trajectory with a more complicated route that sent the spacecraft around Venus and Earth, using the gravity of each as a slingshot "assist." Galileo launched finally on 18 October 1989, on Space Shuttle Atlantis, using the integrated upper stage and three gravity assists to boost it toward the outer planets. Scientists, some of whom had been involved since the project's inception, awaited its December 1995 arrival at the Jupiter system.[2]

Meanwhile, NASA's Magellan radar mapper mission to Venus, also scheduled for launch on a Space Shuttle, was postponed in the post-Challenger standdown of 1986 through 1989. With the date of Shuttle flight resumption uncertain, the Magellan team worked toward its original May 1988 launch window, with a backup date of October 1989. Once Shuttle flights resumed, however, Galileo took precedence, and the Magellan team had to rework their planned trajectory to compensate for the reduced lift available at launch. Moreover, the delayed date of arrival invalidated the meticulously planned Venus mapping campaign. Engineers would now have to compensate for different relative positions of the spacecraft, Earth, and the Sun.

On 4 May 1989, NASA launched Magellan and its integrated upper stage on Space Shuttle Atlantis. After both stages of the integrated upper stage fired as planned, Magellan

---

2   Dick, S. (2007). *Why We Explore: Mission to Jupiter.* Retrieved 1 August 2011 from *http://www. nasa.gov/exploration/whyweexplore/Why_We_26.html.*

continued its journey, entering orbit around Venus on 10 August 1990, and executed a very successful mission. Magellan ended with a dramatic plunge into the Venusian atmosphere on 11 October 1994.

A Graying Organization

NASA might have attempted more missions, but an earlier effort to start a less-expensive, medium-class mission line called Planetary Observer had failed. The first in the series, Mars Observer, went so far over budget and schedule that the agency deemed future such missions unviable. Mars Observer suffered from what some in the planetary science community call the "last bus out" syndrome, in which researchers continue to add scientific instruments to the spacecraft in hopes of not missing the last trip to a planet for many years. This resulted in what detractors called "Christmas treeing" the mission, with instruments hung like ornaments on the spacecraft.

The continual expansion of the mission's scope, coupled with requisite engineering changes, caused Mars Observer to overrun its budget long before its completion. Then the spacecraft arrived at Mars and promptly vanished, never to be heard from again, possibly having exploded, crashed into the planet, missed Mars entirely, or some combination of the three. After the total developmental and operational failures of Mars Observer, the Planetary Observer line thus ended ignominiously.

Meanwhile, the flagship-class Cassini mission to Saturn, along with its twin, the Comet Rendezvous Asteroid Flyby (CRAF), both remained in the NASA budget approved by Congress for a New Start in 1989.[3] Due to budget restraints and dollars diverted by Congress to the burgeoning space station program, CRAF would be soon canceled.[4]

The 1980s were a quiet, vexing decade for planetary scientists and spacecraft engineers.[5] "JPL is a bit of a graying organization," commented Lew Allen, director of the Jet Propulsion Laboratory, in 1988.[6] "With the ten-year period in which no spacecraft have been launched, I'm concerned that the skills are not honed" to the extent that they must be to ensure the success of future missions.

---

3   Committee on Planetary and Lunar Exploration. (1985). *Assessment of Planned Scientific Content of the CRAF Mission.* Washington, DC: National Academy of Sciences; Weissman, P., and Marcia Neugebauer. (1991). *The Comet Rendezvous Asteroid Flyby Mission: A Status Report. Asteroids, Comets, Meteors 1991,* 629–632.

4   Broad, W. J. (1991, 8 June). "House Vote Sets Stage for Conflict Between Two Allies in Space Program." *New York Times,* A7.

5   Niebur, S. (2009, 24 September). Personal interview with T. Krimigis. Located in the "Discovery Program" file, NASA Historical Reference Collection, History Division, NASA Headquarters, Washington, DC.

6   Spotts, P. (1988, 6 January). "JPL's Allen Says US Must Soon Get Its Own Launchers off the Pads." *Christian Science Monitor. https://www.csmonitor.com/1988/0106/ajpl.html.*

Allen advocated less-expensive new missions that would include the miniaturization of technologies "to permit important scientific experiments to be done on very small vehicles," as well as the Lunar Observer—previous frontrunner as the next mission in the doomed Planetary Observer class—to circle the Moon's poles in search of water.[7] Small groups of scientists pushed NASA to find ways to explore the solar system in cost-effective, imaginative ways, but even low-cost, high-reward modifications of current missions, such as adding asteroid flybys to Galileo's trajectory or shifting the trajectory of the third International Sun–Earth Explorer (ISEE) to rendezvous with Halley's Comet, were met with resistance at the agency.[8] As NASA continued to cope with the devastating loss of Challenger, management chose to reduce risk significantly whenever possible on current and future missions.

This risk aversion, coupled with limited financial resources, left little room for NASA to even consider new missions, let alone large ones in the mold of Galileo, Magellan, or Mars Observer. Some planetary scientists supplemented their own dwindling mission resources by turning to studies of Earth, where funding opportunities were more certain because of higher launch cadences due to lower spacecraft cost and complexity, as well as reliable military dollars. Solar system exploration would continue, but glacially, one large institutional mission at a time. Scientists seeking new planetary missions were frustrated by the pace of plans for giant flagships and with NASA's faltering plans for the development and launch of smaller, focused missions.

One Zero Too Many

In the summer of 1989, scientists hand-picked by NASA management met for a series of workshops to define the future of planetary exploration in the next decade. The Small Mission Program Group, chaired by Robert Brown of the Space Telescope Science Institute, was tasked with identifying the next planetary science investigations that NASA should attempt using mission concepts smaller than flagships. At the second meeting of the Committee on Strategic Planning, held at the University of New Hampshire between 26 June and 30 June 1989, members of the planetary science community and NASA expected the group to return details supporting the Lunar Observer as the agency's top priority for flight. It soon became clear, however, that this committee was

---

7   Ibid.

8   Niebur, S. (2009, 10 September). Personal interview with J. Veverka. Located in the "CONTOUR" file, NASA Historical Reference Collection, History Division, NASA Headquarters, Washington, DC; Farquhar, R. (2011). *Fifty Years on the Space Frontier: Halo Orbits, Comets, Asteroids, and More*. Denver: Outskirts Press.

not going to rubber-stamp the "easy" choice. Several committee members felt strongly that other celestial bodies should take priority and refused to endorse the spacecraft. The committee, in other words, rebelled.[9]

MARS PATHFINDER

During one session, Tom Krimigis, then-head of the Space Physics and Instrumentation Group at Johns Hopkins University's Applied Physics Laboratory (APL), introduced an idea for Principal Investigator (PI)–led, low-cost, high-tempo planetary missions that he and several colleagues had advocated elsewhere. This intrigued the Committee on Strategic Planning, and when the subpanels gathered at a plenary session chaired by Joseph Veverka of Cornell University, Brown raised the idea of the new mission line. Scientists present did not believe it could be done, however, as NASA had just recently attempted an unsuccessful line of low-cost missions that aimed to provide frequent access to space. Mars Observer, the pilot project for Planetary Observers, demonstrated the weakness of the model.[10]

Krimigis was undeterred by the widespread skepticism. Citing the PI-led missions recently proposed and executed through the Explorer Program, a midsize mission line whose history dated back to the very first days of NASA, when Explorer 1 was launched in January 1958, he explained that a different paradigm could produce drastically different results from what had been revealed by Mars Observer. Some members of the panel were intrigued, though Don Hunten of the Lunar and Planetary Laboratory at the University of Arizona, as well as other scientists who were more familiar with the earlier failures, challenged Krimigis to brief the strategic planning committee on the ways Explorer succeeded where Planetary Observer failed—and to give a presentation the next morning. This was the pre-PowerPoint era of viewgraphs, a time when presentations took hours to create, with painstaking effort.

NASA schedules are demanding, and that week was no exception. Just a few days earlier, Krimigis had reported to NASA's Goddard Space Flight Center (GSFC) on the results of a Phase A study—that is, the study of a baseline mission concept—of a space physics project called the Advanced Composition Explorer (ACE), led by a single PI, Ed Stone of the California Institute of Technology. ACE was competing for a slot in the Explorer Program. The fate of the ACE proposal was then unknown, but because

---

9   Niebur, S. (2009, 10 September). Personal interview with J. Veverka. Located in the "CONTOUR" file, NASA Historical Reference Collection, History Division, NASA Headquarters, Washington, DC.

10   Niebur, S. (2009, 24 September). Personal interview with T. Krimigis. Located in the "Discovery Program" file, NASA Historical Reference Collection, History Division, NASA Headquarters, Washington, DC.

Krimigis had just given that GSFC briefing, he had something almost as valuable as an endorsement: viewgraphs explaining the Explorer concept.

Krimigis presented the viewgraphs at the plenary meeting, introducing the planetary community to the low-cost, rapid-turnaround program that the solar and space physics community had built with Explorer.[11] He demonstrated a new leadership model that put science at the top of the organization chart, with a single PI in charge of the mission and co-investigators in charge of each instrument carried by the spacecraft. This structure, a topsy-turvy way of mission development from an engineering perspective, had been shown to work on the Active Magnetospheric Particle Tracer Explorers (AMPTE), a recent Explorer mission on which Krimigis was PI. (AMPTE was a scientific success as well, operating with a small science team for five years.)[12]

The presentation intrigued committee members and representatives from NASA Headquarters. Veverka publicly challenged Krimigis on the cost for this self-contained mission when propulsion, nine instruments, and the full range of subsystems were included, saying that a project of that scope would likely cost $400 million. Krimigis responded, "Well, you know, you're close, except you have one zero too many."[13] The ACE spacecraft was estimated to cost $40–45 million, plus $30 million for its instruments—an estimate supported by the fact that the same team had just delivered AMPTE on cost and schedule.[14]

Geoffrey Briggs, director of the Solar System Exploration Division at NASA Headquarters, was intrigued. In true NASA fashion, he appointed a science working group to study the low-cost mission approach, asking Brown to chair the working group as he had the original panel. The working group met about six months later in late 1989, and again in May 1990, to study potential mission concepts. (They did not, however, define program parameters.)[15] The panel had one notable recommendation: the new program should be called Discovery.

Briggs also took a direct approach to the concept, asking Krimigis to lead a fast-paced, NASA-funded study at the Applied Physics Laboratory for a mission that would fit into this new type of planetary program.

As word spread, community support for the new initiative began building. It was not without difficulty, however. While the working group commissioned by Briggs

---

11   Krimigis, S. M., and Joseph Veverka. (1995, October–December). "Foreword: Genesis of Discovery." *The Journal of the Astronautical Sciences*, 43(4), 345–347.

12   Niebur, S. (2009, 24 September). Personal interview with T. Krimigis. Located in the "Discovery Program" file, NASA Historical Reference Collection, History Division, NASA Headquarters, Washington, DC.

13   Ibid.

14   Ibid.

15   Krimigis, S. M. and Joseph Veverka. (1995, October–December). "Foreword: Genesis of Discovery." *The Journal of the Astronautical Sciences*, 43(4), 345–347.

discussed possibilities, Lew Allen, director of JPL, spoke publicly about his lab's internal small spacecraft studies, remarking: "It's been a disappointment to me that I have not been able to generate much enthusiasm for small spacecraft."[16] Proud of JPL's contributions to NASA's planetary exploration efforts to date, he continued: "We have done a reconnaissance of the solar system that has done most of the simple measurements that can be made with small, inexpensive instruments."[17] The trouble, he explained, was that planetary scientists wanted to take difficult measurements that required new, more sophisticated instrumentation that would in turn demand additional money to develop, miniaturize, and harden for the extreme environments of space. It would be a challenge to bring the entire community to consensus that a novel programmatic approach—frequent, low-cost missions each designed to perform smaller experiments on specific phenomena, as opposed to larger, well-instrumented spacecraft designed to get big, holistic science—could ultimately return all the complex measurements and breakthrough science they desired.

A Little Garage with a Car

Meanwhile, back at NASA Headquarters, Briggs began other studies that would lay the groundwork for future Mars missions. What Briggs really wanted was a way to get back to the surface of Mars while simultaneously breaking the mindset of sending one giant mission once a decade, adding instrument after instrument, dollar after dollar, up to the maximum capacity of the spacecraft and its launch rocket. How could NASA return to the surface of Mars without falling into the same trap that had ensnared Mars Observer? Joe Boyce, then the Mars Program Scientist at NASA Headquarters, recalled that Briggs was convinced that you could get back to Mars on the cheap, but the science instrumentation that spacecraft carried would have to be limited to only the most essential and inexpensive experiments.

In 1990, Briggs commissioned NASA's Ames Research Center to develop a low-cost Mars mission concept. Previously, scientists had devised a latticework of Mars exploration initiatives and research built around a sample return concept, but NASA budgets had rendered sample return impossible. Ames Research Center began work on what would eventually be called the Mars Environmental SURvey (MESUR)—a mission concept that would see a network of small landers alight on the Martian surface, each focused on some specific science (e.g., atmospheric science, geology, geochemistry) and thus meet Briggs's request for a light science payload per mission.[18]

---

16   Allen, L. (1990, June). "Face to Face with Lew Allen." *Aerospace America*, 28(6), 10–11.

17   Ibid.

18   Conway, E. M. (2015). *Exploration and Engineering: The Jet Propulsion Laboratory and the Quest for Mars*. Baltimore: Johns Hopkins University Press, 41.

Briggs also called his good friend Gene Giberson, of the advanced planning office at JPL, and shared the challenge. Giberson, who was also the assistant lab director for flight projects, was captivated by the idea and offered to examine the capabilities of various types of small launch vehicles. He wanted to see if it would be possible to return to Mars without paying for a large, expensive rocket to carry a smaller spacecraft and its instruments and fuel. Giberson would have his team conduct this and other engineering studies.

There was a catch: at JPL, any mission to Mars was expected to meet certain standards and to be done in certain ways. A Mars landing was expected to follow the meticulous and successful engineering standards set by Viking, the lab's previous Mars surface mission. Viking was a mammoth pair of life-detection landers that each reached the Martian surface by continuously firing rockets to slow descent. If too many people knew about Giberson's "radical" study, word would likely reach unfriendly members of management, and the project would soon be killed—even though he was an assistant lab director. To avert this, Boyce recalled Giberson assigning only two employees to work on the problem. "We'll do this on the quiet," Boyce remembered Giberson saying, "not asking for any money to support the studies, because a line of funding would raise suspicion and the project would risk cancellation."[19]

Boyce recalled something else from his conversations with Briggs during this brainstorming phase: "I thought Geoff was crazy.... He said, 'I want this package to land on the surface, and I want it to have a little garage with a car.'"[20] Years later, when Mars Pathfinder landed softly on the surface of Mars, the first Discovery mission would commence with the gentle opening of the lander's petals and, later, a little rover called Sojourner rolling out of its garage. It was the first wheeled vehicle on Mars.

By the time Briggs left NASA Headquarters to work at Ames, he had conscripted JPL Advanced Planning to work on the Mars study as well. Meanwhile, APL was working on a small mission study, and the science working group was developing the concept of a new small mission line.

At NASA Headquarters, agency brass hired Wesley Huntress as the Division Director responsible for robotic exploration of the solar system. Huntress sought to establish a program for low-cost planetary missions that would return data from the solar system continuously, rather than in fits and starts, as had theretofore bedeviled the agency because it had only one or two projects per decade.

"The only way to do that," he said, "was to have a larger number of smaller, less expensive missions, so that you could launch more frequently and have spacecraft

---

19   Niebur, S. (2009, 22 March). Personal interview with J. Boyce. Located in "Discovery Program" file, NASA Historical Reference Collection, History Division, NASA Headquarters, Washington, DC.

20   Ibid.

operating at planets as continuously as possible."[21] Culturally—and despite Director Lew Allen's desire to build small missions at JPL—it was not a popular idea overall at JPL, said Huntress, who had spent much of his career there as an employee. Big, billion-dollar missions laden with instruments guaranteed consistent, long-term "business" for the lab. If JPL didn't win every small mission contract, business would see gaps. "The way that they fed their people was to have them all working on these big missions, and they had no concept how to break them up and work them on smaller missions."[22]

Outside of Huntress's new division, there were examples across the country of low-cost missions in various stages of development. One was Clementine, an effort by the Strategic Defense Initiative Organization (SDIO) to test space-based sensors useful for a national missile defense shield. They would do this by mapping the Moon. Huntress remembered: "I instantly ran over to the Pentagon and talked to this young guy, named Mike Griffin, and I said[,] 'How can we do this together?'"[23] The mission was soon jointly supported by SDIO (which sponsored the spacecraft design, manufacture, and integration), the Navy Research Laboratory (which handled mission execution), the Department of Energy's Lawrence Livermore National Laboratory (which did instrument design and manufacture), and NASA (in charge of the science team and navigation). The mission would become a success.[24]

Huntress's conceptual low-cost planetary mission program, meanwhile, was mired in bureaucracy. Huntress disbanded the committee led by Robert Brown and restructured it, putting experienced hands in space exploration in charge of the science and engineering aspects, saying, "I didn't want contemplation; I wanted action. So, I restructured that committee and gave it to Veverka [of Cornell University].... He would go right to the throat and so would Jim Martin [former program manager of the Viking program]."[25] The science team, led by Veverka, was challenged to think differently: to define a focused science mission in an environment where the community at the time treated every spacecraft as the last bus out of town. Huntress worked closely with the committee to keep them focused and reminded them to work with Martin's engineering group to see what could be done.

---

21 Wright, R. (2003, 9 January). Personal interview with W. Huntress. Located in "Wes Huntress" file, NASA Historical Reference Collection, History Division, NASA Headquarters, Washington, DC.

22 Ibid.

23 Niebur, S. (2009, 13 March). Personal interview with W. Huntress. Located in "Wes Huntress" file, NASA Historical Reference Collection, History Division, NASA Headquarters, Washington, DC.

24 Ibid.

25 Wright, R. (2003, 9 January). Personal interview with W. Huntress. Located in "Wes Huntress" file, NASA Historical Reference Collection, History Division, NASA Headquarters, Washington, DC.

Meanwhile, Martin led a team charged with defining Discovery cost and management; providing an independent assessment of the feasibility of the program; and figuring out, essentially, how to do low-cost NASA-led planetary missions. According to Huntress, he chose Martin, whom he described as "a fabulous person, gruff, tough and smart as hell," because Martin had been a program manager on Viking and had built one of the most challenging planetary missions in NASA's history. His experience would keep optimism in check.[26] Huntress wanted a diverse and highly experienced engineering team, calling upon project managers (PMs) and engineers from the APL, Goddard Space Flight Center, JPL, and Ames Research Center. This team visited government labs, aerospace contractors, and NASA centers, and the members were willing to talk with anyone who had experience on lower-cost projects or studies.

Then Huntress issued a challenge to APL and JPL: to develop simultaneous, competitive studies on a low-cost asteroid mission. Huntress chose the small-bodies target because of the relative ease and low general cost of such missions.[27]

"The Next Phase Is an Exploration Phase"

As the two laboratories vied for the first directed mission in a nascent Discovery Program, members of the planetary science community began to weigh in on potential science priorities. In April, the news of a new low-cost mission line had surfaced in the media, with a Planetary Science Division wish list of Lunar Observer, a Mars lander network, a Neptune orbiter, a Pluto flyby, a mission to an asteroid, a Mercury orbiter, and a Venus probe. Huntress told *SpaceNews*, "We've finished the reconnaissance phase of every planet in the solar system except Pluto.... The next phase is an exploration phase, conducting global surveys [of the planets] with orbiters and atmospheric probes and in-depth studies using landers and sample return spacecraft."[28] Meanwhile, scientists like Michael Belton of Belton Space Exploration Initiatives, LLC, and Alan Delamere of Delamere Space Sciences—both private firms that conducted planetary science research outside the auspices of academia—were taking the case for the Discovery Program to the larger community, presenting papers on specific low-cost missions

---

26   Niebur, S. (2009, 13 March). Personal interview with W. Huntress. Located in "Wes Huntress" file, NASA Historical Reference Collection, History Division, NASA Headquarters, Washington, DC.

27   Wright, R. (2003, 9 January). Personal interview with W. Huntress. Located in "Wes Huntress" file, NASA Historical Reference Collection, History Division, NASA Headquarters, Washington, DC.

28   David, L. (1991, 15–21 April). "Scientists Urge Unmanned Planetary Probes." *SpaceNews*. 6.

at the Asteroids, Comets, and Meteors meeting at the Lunar and Planetary Institute in Houston, as well as the workshop on Micro-Spacecraft for Planetary Exploration, hosted by the Planetary Society in Pasadena, California, on 23 September 1991.[29]

NEAR

The challenge set by Huntress for APL and JPL, specifically, was to fly a mission to an asteroid for $150 million or less (excluding the costs of the launch vehicle and mission operations). In May 1991, the JPL and APL teams met at a hotel in Pasadena, California, to present their concepts of a low-cost mission to a near-Earth asteroid. Scientists who were present remember it as "a shoot-out."[30]

At the meeting, scientist Ed Stone, who four months earlier had become the new director of JPL, welcomed both teams, as well as NASA Headquarters personnel, to the lab's hometown. Then the JPL team began their presentation.

"You People Think We Are Stupid, Don't You?"

According to Richard Vorder Bruegge, a planetary scientist formerly of Brown University and then a contractor at NASA Headquarters, "It couldn't have been more than 30 minutes after Ed Stone said we're going to do this for $150 million" that JPL team leadership said, essentially, "We don't believe that the first mission can be done for less than $300 million, but if you give us enough money, by the time we get to the third mission we'll get it to $150 million."

JPL's approach was to accept that flying a planetary mission for $150 million was not possible as a starting point. Instead, JPL opted for an incremental approach: start with a spacecraft bus with essentially no science instruments, fly it, and see if it survives. Then do it again, but this time put a camera on it and see if you could stabilize the spacecraft well enough to take pictures. Then do it a third time and add another science instrument, perhaps a spectrometer, and try to orbit an asteroid. While low-risk, this strategy would take 10 years and cost $450 million.

Huntress wasn't the only stunned audience member. "I remember Jim Martin getting red in the face," said Tom Krimigis of APL. He recalled Martin saying: "You people think we are stupid, don't you?"[31]

---

29   Belton, M., and Alan Delamere. (1991). "Low-Cost Missions to Explore the Diversity of Near-Earth Objects." *Asteroids, Comets, Meteors 1991*; ibid.

30   Niebur, S. (2009, 24 January). Personal interview with S. Keddie, M. Saunders, and R. Vorder Bruegge. Located in "Discovery Program" file, NASA Historical Reference Collection, History Division, NASA Headquarters, Washington, DC.

31   Niebur, S. (2009, 24 September). Personal interview with T. Krimigis. Located in the "Discovery Program" file, NASA Historical Reference Collection, History Division, NASA Headquarters, Washington, DC.

Then the APL team presented their strategy. Tom Coughlin, the study manager at APL, briefed NASA Headquarters on their competing mission concept, a single flight estimated to cost $112 million. The mission was similar to one that they had been briefing for a decade and was perfectly in line with Huntress's request. Bob Farquhar was in charge of mission design, and Krimigis had tapped Andy Cheng, an early-career scientist, for the position of project scientist, with Rob Gold as the instrument manager. The proposal had heritage with other recent APL projects such as AMPTE, which was done for $30 million.[32] APL had proposed a mission at half the price of JPL's first mission and accomplished the objectives without requiring additional flights.

"When I got the results, boy it was clear who knew how to build low-cost missions: APL. I mean, there was just no doubt," Huntress said.[33] APL would eventually be awarded the mission, which would be called the Near-Earth Asteroid Rendezvous.

Meanwhile, Huntress wished to make headway on the Mars lander network sought by the planetary science community, which was being studied internally at JPL and Ames Research Center (a competition that had become something of a friction point between the two labs). He favored JPL to lead the mission but knew that the lab needed competition if its culture were to change to meet the demands of Discovery. "I had decided to stop the rivalry between Ames and JPL. I gave MESUR to JPL," he said, explaining that he wanted a long-term program to explore Mars, and that "no other place is going to run that except JPL." MESUR, he said, "was going to be their entrée into low-cost missions, this Mars MESUR thing."

Huntress pressed Ed Stone, director of JPL, to place Tony Spear, a project manager at JPL, in charge of the newly minted JPL MESUR project. Describing Spear as "a maverick in the JPL system," Huntress said: "I trusted Tony was the guy to be able to upset the JPL apple cart, because I watched him on [Venus mapper] Magellan."[34]

Turf wars at NASA Headquarters jeopardized Huntress's plans, however. As part of an agency-wide reorganization to support NASA's human spaceflight ambitions, the lunar science program had been transferred from his Office of Space Science to a separate Office of Exploration. Huntress feared that Mars might be next.[35] "So I decided to marry MESUR into Discovery and have it be one of the first missions in Discovery." Huntress had secondary motivations to make MESUR part of Discovery:

---

32   Niebur, S. (2009, 27 August). Personal interview with T. Krimigis. Located in the "Discovery Program" file, NASA Historical Reference Collection, History Division, NASA Headquarters, Washington, DC.

33   Wright, R. (2003, 9 January). Personal interview with W. Huntress. Located in "Wes Huntress" file, NASA Historical Reference Collection, History Division, NASA Headquarters, Washington, DC.

34   Ibid.

35   Conway, E. M. (2015). *Exploration and Engineering: The Jet Propulsion Laboratory and the Quest for Mars*. Baltimore: Johns Hopkins University Press. 47.

the challenge. "Landing on Mars is pretty damn hard, and I don't know if anybody can do it like NASA JPL."[36]

"NASA Is Determined to Constrain Discovery Program Costs"

Now NASA had its first two Discovery missions, but it still lacked a program with which to manage them. The agency convened a Discovery Cost and Management Team of Advisers to develop a program structure; policies for organization, staffing, and meetings; and guiding principles to ensure that the program could effectively administer small science missions. It was hardly glamorous work—the stuff of a true bureaucracy—but it was necessary to ensure that there would be a third Discovery mission, and then a fourth, and so on.[37]

In July 1991, that team issued a report outlining the intended parameters for the implementation of the program. The report concluded that Discovery could be successful, given one important limitation: "NASA is determined to constrain Discovery Program costs, through the annual and project run-out, to predetermined funding levels."[38] Other key recommendations from the group included the following:

- All projects proposed for implementation as part of the Discovery Program shall be constrained to a total cost of $150 million in Fiscal Year 1992 dollars.
- All projects shall launch within three years of a project's start.
- Spacecraft instrument payloads must have demonstrated feasibility and maturity, or else they should not be selected, or the mission should be deferred.

GRAND VISIONS

To organize and represent the perspective of the scientific community, the Discovery Science Working Group discussed similar implementation issues but was unable to come to consensus. A letter from working group leader Veverka to Huntress on 11 September 1991, discussed options considered by the group. They observed that while an informal set of working groups might be the most efficient way forward, it might be better to establish rigid, structured procedures, which could open the field to more potential

---

36 Niebur, S. (2009, 13 March). Personal interview with W. Huntress. Located in "Wes Huntress" file, NASA Historical Reference Collection, History Division, NASA Headquarters, Washington, DC.

37 Logsdon, J. M. (1995, January). *Exploring the Unknown: Selected Documents in the History of the U.S. Civil Space Program* (Vol. 5). Washington, DC: NASA History Division. 467.

38 Martin, J. S. (1991, 10 July). *Report of the Discovery Program Cost and Management Team.*

investigators. No matter what, said Veverka, NASA Headquarters should continue to work the specifics of the program and not be distracted by any calls for re-proving the case, which had been made by the Brown Committee the previous year.[39]

The Woods Hole Space Science and Applications Advisory Committee (SSAAC) Workshop met in the summer of 1991. Established under the aegis of the NASA Advisory Council, its purpose was to help establish agency goals and priorities and resolve scientific and programmatic conflicts at the subdiscipline level for major NASA initiatives. In a 16 September letter, Huntress summarized the challenge of Discovery and its integration into space science by noting that the challenge was to devise a plan for the Nation's robotic space efforts for that decade, balancing different goals and financial constraints. Specifically, he wanted to develop small planetary missions that would enable better access to space. The SSAAC accepted Discovery as a level-of-effort program with those goals.

This Woods Hole meeting situated the Discovery program in a position corresponding to an FY 1996 New Start, a dedicated, long-term line of funding in the NASA budget. Congressional interest in the Mars Pathfinder and NEAR missions helped with this accelerated New Start for Discovery.

Meanwhile, the Commission on Physical Sciences, Mathematics, and Applications of the National Research Council's Committee on Planetary and Lunar Exploration (COMPLEX) endorsed the idea of the fledgling Discovery Program in a report released in 1991, with several caveats, including this: "the mission and program structure should be such that no single element absorbs the program resources for more than two years," and that a large investment in engineering design must not be required for missions. Moreover, data should be delivered "in a timely manner," with "adequate funding for data analysis and related theoretical modeling." The report explained that such rules encapsulated the best aspects of the Explorer mission line and NASA policies for Earth probes.[40]

"It's Not Just Your Program; It's the Public's Program"
Background work was also happening on the political level. Key personnel at the Applied Physics Laboratory briefed Senator Barbara Mikulski, who represented the Maryland-based organization in Congress, about this exciting new program of small, low-cost planetary spacecraft that could be built with significant participation from

---

39   Veverka, J. (1991, 11 September). Letter to Wes Huntress. Susan Niebur's personal collection.
40   National Research Council. (1991). *Assessment of Solar System Exploration Programs 1991.* Washington, DC: The National Academies Press. 30–31. *https://doi.org/10.17226/12323.*

the academic and research communities.[41] This work bore fruit for Discovery, though the broader space program was not so fortunate. On 11 July 1991, Senator Mikulski spurred the Senate Committee on Appropriations, of which she was a member, to send a bill called HR 2519 to the main floor of the chamber. This was the Fiscal Year 1992 appropriations bill written by members of the subcommittee through which NASA was then funded. Amendments were introduced as well, alongside Senate Report No. 102-107.

The Senate report contained a litany of committee recommendations, including specific additions and subtractions to particular missions—though mostly subtractions, in keeping with a new fiscal climate caused by spending caps in the federal government established in an earlier, 1990 budget agreement. The report recommended the removal of $112.3 million from the Comet Rendezvous Asteroid Flyby (CRAF)/ Cassini budget, effectively canceling CRAF, Cassini's twin intended to probe a comet. Moreover, the report recommended,

$1M from planetary research and analysis, taken as a general reduction. The Committee has been supportive of comprehensive planetary missions proposed by NASA in the past. However, with fiscal issues in mind, NASA is directed to consider science missions using small low-cost planetary spacecraft to complement its larger missions. In particular, the Committee directs NASA to prepare, with input from the scientific community, a plan to stimulate and develop small planetary or other space science projects, emphasizing those which could be accomplished by the academic or research communities. The plan should be submitted by February 1, 1992.[42]

The Discovery Program's legislative origin was thus tinged by and entwined with the unfortunate cancellation of the large CRAF mission, all in the context of a tight budget climate. According to Huntress, then director of the Solar System Exploration Division, this devastated the Office of Space Science and Applications (OSSA), which managed the NASA science portfolio. He explained, "[T]he plan we came up with…was no longer realistic…. We had to cancel CRAF." In addition, the office had to restructure the planned Advanced X-ray Astrophysics Facility (AXAF) into two missions (one of which, ultimately, was canceled). Huntress already had JPL Mars, APL asteroid,

---

41 Niebur, S. (2009, 10 September). Personal interview with J. Veverka. Located in the "CONTOUR" file, NASA Historical Reference Collection, History Division, NASA Headquarters, Washington, DC. See also Niebur, S. (2009, 13 March). Personal interview with W. Huntress. Located in "Wes Huntress" file, NASA Historical Reference Collection, History Division, NASA Headquarters, Washington, DC. See also Niebur, S. (2009, 24 September). Personal interview with T. Krimigis. Located in the "Discovery Program" file, NASA Historical Reference Collection, History Division, NASA Headquarters, Washington, DC.

42 Congressional Research Service. (1991, 11 July). Senate Appropriations Committee Report: S. 107, 102nd Congress. pp. 130–140.

and programmatic studies in progress, suggesting that NASA could do such missions and meeting this new congressional mandate for something that sounded exactly like Discovery.[43]

On 26 September 1991, Huntress requested that the National Research Council's COMPLEX review the 1991 Solar System Exploration Division Strategic Plan created by yet another NASA committee during this time. The review was completed that fall, with an endorsement of Discovery from Larry Esposito, COMPLEX chair, and the committee.

The Discovery Science Working Group, led by Veverka, issued a report in October 1991 endorsing the concept as well, capping missions at $150 million or less. The report recommended a rendezvous with asteroid 1943 Anteros as its first mission. This was the target for which APL had been planning.[44]

By the end of 1991, the groundwork had been established for the Discovery Program, built on three main principles: 1) frequent access to space; 2) best possible science; and, 3) as Huntress put it, an "element of public interest, because they're paying the bill." He understood that this might be at odds with what scientists wanted but sought to remind them that the program "has to be exciting to the people who are writing the checks. It's not just your program; it's the public's program."[45]

They Liked Mars, and They Liked Low-Cost

Federal agency budgets are not spur-of-the-moment inventions but are carefully planned and negotiated with the White House Office of Management and Budget (OMB) years in advance. In fact, part of the motivation for the establishment of the Discovery Program was to avoid the annual churn of congressional approval; a single line item for the program would be more stable and predictable and would not require the massive amounts of work required for a New Start.

But before that could happen and missions could be proposed, selected, and developed routinely without individual approval by Congress, Discovery itself was on the table as a New Start. The program was introduced as a concept in the Fiscal Year 1993 NASA budget request as one that would "examine the feasibility of using small (i.e., Delta [expendable rocket] class) spacecraft with high technological inheritance and

---

43   Niebur, S. (2009, 13 March). Personal interview with W. Huntress. Located in "Wes Huntress" file, NASA Historical Reference Collection, History Division, NASA Headquarters, Washington, DC.

44   Discovery Science Working Group. (1991, October). *Discovery: Near-Earth Asteroid Rendezvous (NEAR) Report*. 2. This is from the executive summary. Joseph Veverka chaired the group.

45   Wright, R. (2003, 9 January). Personal interview with W. Huntress. Located in "Wes Huntress" file, NASA Historical Reference Collection, History Division, NASA Headquarters, Washington, DC.

limited science payloads of two or three instruments in an effort to develop low-cost, scientifically viable missions with short development schedules."[46]

The following year, the NASA budget introduced Discovery by name, explaining that it "would be constrained by highly focused science (few instruments), strict cost caps, short development times and use of the smallest launch vehicles capable of escape trajectories." The Fiscal Year 1994 budget reflected the planned phasing of the Discovery missions: Mars Pathfinder first and NEAR second.[47]

THE CENTERPIECE OF NASA FOR THE 1990s

In April 1992, NASA presented the "Small Planetary Mission Plan: Report to Congress," as requested the previous July.[48] This document, drafted by Huntress, noted that "the current budgetary environment challenges NASA's ability to sustain a program of high science value and opportunity. As part of an overall approach to maintaining the vitality and progress of the science community, NASA is emphasizing the introduction of small projects in its near-term plans.... [T]wo years ago, small planetary missions were just beginning to be discussed by the scientific community. Today, they are the centerpiece of NASA's new programs for the 1990s."[49]

The plan—which also discussed a "staged program to ascertain the prevalence and character of other planetary systems and to construct a definitive picture of the formation of stars and their planets"[50] (dubbed TOPS, or Toward Other Planetary Systems)—emphasized general principles such as focused scientific objectives; mission designs requiring little or no new technology development; fixed cost ceilings and schedules, with reasonable contingencies; and the ability to sustain the scientific community by increasing the number of opportunities for direct investigator involvement.

The small missions would be completed in just three years from project start to launch. Each mission would be cost-capped at $150 million, with an annual total program cost cap of $85 million. Notably, these constraints would cause problems in the later years of the Discovery Program, as mission after mission exceeded its annual forecasted costs, suffered technical delays, and threatened the very future of the program. These

46   NASA. (1992). *NASA Budget Estimates, Fiscal Year 1993. https://planetary.s3.amazonaws.com/assets/pdfs/FY1993-Budget-Estimates-Volume-1.pdf.*

47   NASA. (1993). *NASA Budget Estimates, Fiscal Year 1994, https://planetary.s3.amazonaws.com/assets/pdfs/FY1994-Budget-Estimates-Volume-1.pdf.*

48   NASA. "Small Planetary Mission Plan: Report to Congress." April 1992. Reprinted in Logsdon volume V, pages 460–468.

49   Niebur, S. (2009, 13 March). Personal interview with W. Huntress. Located in "Wes Huntress" file, NASA Historical Reference Collection, History Division, NASA Headquarters, Washington, DC.

50   Solar System Exploration Division. "TOPS: Toward Other Planetary Systems," *https://web.archive.org/web/20210414164816/http://web.gps.caltech.edu/classes/ge133/reading/TOPS.pdf.*

problems would not manifest for a decade, but the seeds were planted in this report to Congress, which touted benefits of the Discovery Program, including "rapid response to emerging scientific opportunities, participation in cooperative ventures with other agencies, the timeline is more in line with graduate degree programs and academic resources, increased breadth of activity in the solar system exploration program, and enhanced timeliness for new information return on important scientific questions."[51]

The author of the "Small Planetary Mission Plan: Report to Congress" stated pointedly that Discovery-class missions would not have the robust safeguards found in previous NASA spacecraft, explaining that "lower costs may imply the acceptance of a modest increase in the level of risk." (This would change after the consecutive failures of the Mars Climate Orbiter and Mars Polar Lander in 1999.)

A commitment to cost containment was equally prominent.[52]

"His Eyes Got Real Big"

On 1 April 1992, Dan Goldin, who was formerly an engineer for NASA's Lewis Research Center and then the vice president and general manager of contractor TRW Space and Technology Group in Redondo Beach, California, was confirmed as the ninth Administrator of NASA. Goldin subsequently promoted Huntress to the position of Associate Administrator for Space Science the following year, and the Discovery Program was well on its way, awaiting only congressional action to give it a New Start.[53]

Sometime during the first four months of Goldin's tenure, he and Huntress were discussing planetary science missions, when, Huntress said, Goldin "started talking about Battlestar Galacticas and trading them in for low-cost planetary missions." The Administrator instructed Huntress to establish a line of low-cost planetary science missions.

"I said, 'well wait a minute[,] Dan, there is already one on the table. It's called Discovery. It is in your 1994 budget,'" Huntress recalls saying. "And his eyes got big. [Goldin] said, 'What? Really? Tell me more about it.' Something clicked in his mind, and his eyes got real big when he saw that it was already on the table."[54]

---

51 Logsdon, J. M. (1995, January). *Exploring the Unknown: Selected Documents in the History of the U.S. Civil Space Program* (Vol. 5). Washington, DC: NASA History Division. 460–468.

52 Ibid.

53 Wright, R. (2003, 9 January). Personal interview with W. Huntress. Located in "Wes Huntress" file, NASA Historical Reference Collection, History Division, NASA Headquarters, Washington, DC.

54 Niebur, S. (2009, 13 March). Personal interview with W. Huntress. Located in "Wes Huntress" file, NASA Historical Reference Collection, History Division, NASA Headquarters, Washington, DC.

On 15 August 1992, this informal introduction was made formal when Huntress presented the Discovery mission concept to Goldin.[55] Most items on the list of potential Discovery missions would actually launch over the next decade. These included MESUR Pathfinder (which became Mars Pathfinder); NEAR; multiple asteroid and comet flyby missions (realized as CONTOUR and Dawn); an Earth-orbiting telescope (which would fly as Kepler); a Mars aeronomy orbiter (later manifesting as MAVEN, or Mars Atmosphere and Volatile Evolution Mission, in the Mars Scout program); Lunar scout missions (the first of which was the Lunar Prospector orbiter); and comet reconnaissance missions to include a sample return (which would be Deep Impact and then Stardust).

Vested in a Single Individual: The PI

Huntress likewise formally introduced the new small mission program to the planetary science community through a Discovery Mission Workshop planned for 17–20 November 1992.[56] The Discovery Program constraints were outlined as focused scientific objectives; small payloads of only two or three instruments; the aforementioned $150 million cost cap with $85 million in program funding each year; a development time of three years or less; and launch vehicles in the small Delta class, or even smaller. Missions would be solicited by NASA Headquarters through "Announcements of Opportunity" (AOs)—formal requests for organizations to submit proposals that align with a set of scientific goals and technical and financial limitations.

The purpose of the workshop was to identify and evaluate promising mission concepts. At the time, the Solar System Exploration Division announced that it would fund three to six mission concept studies in 1993. (The number was later increased to 10, and after a request for reconsideration, 11 were finally selected.) Workshop participation would consist of all who submitted a one-page letter of intent by 2 July 1992; designated reviewers; and observers. Valid letters of intent would include the scientific objectives of a prospective mission and a brief description of the proposer's approach to technical implementation—a significant request for the time.

Carl Pilcher, advanced studies branch chief of the Solar System Exploration Division, believed strongly in the mandate to keep the missions focused, and he envisioned that if the program worked as intended, the scientific community would get a continuous flow of data from the multiple missions and students would also get to work on a mission from start to finish during their academic careers.[57]

---

55   Huntress, W. (1992, 15 August). "Discovery: A Program of Small Planetary Flight Missions." Unpublished slides, presented to Daniel Goldin. Susan Niebur's personal collection.

56   Huntress, W. (1992, 5 June). Dear colleague letter to mission concept proposers.

57   NASA Headquarters. (1992, 15 June). "Little Guys Make Big Science in Discovery Program." *NASA HQ Bulletin.*

By July, 89 letters of intent had been received from would-be Principal Investigators—so many more than expected that an extra day had to be added to the workshop. NASA Headquarters sent the 1992 Small Planetary Mission Plan to each proposer, along with additional information such as cost cap, development time, and launch vehicle limits.[58]

The accompanying letter included a clear vision for the role of a PI: "Overall responsibility for mission success must be vested in a single individual, in most cases the PI." This endorsement was a change from the "top-down" model of mission development, in which the NASA Science Mission Directorate directed exploration targets and science to agency centers, which in turn might solicit PI-led instruments from other organizations in government, industry, and academia. Principal Investigator mission models, rather, would be "bottom up," in which a single scientist (the PI) would take point in building mission teams and proposals in competition with others, for consideration by NASA Headquarters.[59] The agency released the names and concept titles of all proposers, encouraging teams to combine resources and ideas, as merging teams might strengthen the concepts for consideration and lessen the evaluating workload. Proposers were told to prepare ten-, then fifteen-page concept descriptions to discuss scientific, technical, and programmatic aspects of their missions and demonstrate that their missions could fit credibly within the program guidelines. Thirty-five copies of each report were due on 9 September 1992.

This Is What NASA Ought to Be

In September, NASA received 70 detailed, 15-page mission concepts. The list was distributed to all proposers on 29 September 1992, with instructions for attendees.[60] The meeting was open, except for panel deliberations at the end of the week, which were closed. In contrast to later practice, the workshop would offer "no provisions for protection of proprietary material. Participants must assume that all information sent to or presented at the workshop will be generally available."[61]

During September and October, the concepts were reviewed by scientists across the country for science merit. Reviewers sent reviews by mail; science members of Discovery workshop evaluation panels were charged with "integrating these written reviews with their own assessments."[62]

The draft evaluation criteria were widely distributed on 21 October 1992, in a letter from Geoffrey Briggs, then the Scientific Director of the Center for Mars Exploration at

---

58   Pilcher, C. (1992, 15 July). Dear Colleague letter to proposers. Susan Niebur's personal collection.

59   Bolles, D. (2022, 9 May). "Mission Models—Strategic and PI-Led." Retrieved 9 May 2022 from *https://science.nasa.gov/about-us/science-strategy/mission-models-strategic-and-pi-led.*

60   Nash, D. (1992, September 29). Letter from Discovery Program Workshop Organizer. Susan Niebur's personal collection.

61   Ibid.

62   Ibid.

Ames, along with the names of the evaluation panel members and their subpanel assignments. This practice of openly identifying the evaluation panel would be short-lived.

The Advanced Studies Branch of the NASA Solar System Exploration Division held the Discovery Program Mission Concept Workshop from 15 to 20 November 1992 at the San Juan Capistrano Research Institute in California. More than 200 scientists, engineers, and project managers attended.[63] Nearly 100 PIs were invited to present their mission concepts. Each presenter was allotted 10 minutes for presentation and 10 minutes to answer questions. The concepts were grouped into themes such as Atmospheres; Dust, Fields, and Plasma; Small Bodies; and Solid Bodies. Within each theme, the missions were grouped by target (e.g., Mercury, Venus, Mars, comets, and asteroids). After three days of oral presentations by the proposers, the panels began to discuss the merits of each proposal. At this first evaluation, co-investigators were not excluded from the evaluation of competing mission concepts, and the panel members were publicly identified. The organizing committee was identified in widely distributed letters as Carl Pilcher of NASA Headquarters; Doug Nash of the San Juan Capistrano Research Institute; Briggs of NASA's Ames Research Center; Jurgen Rahe of NASA Headquarters; Richard Vorder Bruegge of SAIC; and Pat Dasch, also of SAIC.[64]

NASA Administrator Goldin made a last-minute surprise visit to the workshop. He challenged the evaluation panel and those assembled to be ambitious.[65] The next day, he sang Discovery's praises as he addressed a regular meeting of the Space Studies Board.

You know, I just went to this Discovery meeting. It was the most wonderful experience I had. I think it's the world's best kept secret.... They have 78 presentations of programs under $150 million. Some programs are $50 to $60 million that take three years that do everything you ever dreamed about doing. I didn't know that this existed. I knew that there was a Discovery Program, but I didn't find out about this until last week. There were a couple of hundred people down here in San Juan Capistrano and they said the first mission may get funded by 1998.... This is what the civil space program ought to be: a diversity of opinion; people that are bold, not afraid to take risks; a launch a month instead of a launch a decade; graduate students and professors building things; organizations that have the best idea and power to do things instead of the bureaucracy coming in and suffocating new ideas.... This is the most wonderful thing that ever happened to the space program. Here we can have a launch a month and with a launch a month, you could go to the cutting

---

63   Vorder Bruegge, R. W. (1993, 21–23 September). "The Discovery Program: A New Approach to Planetary Exploration." *AIAA Space Programs and Technologies Conference and Exhibit 93-4090.* Huntsville: American Institute of Aeronautics and Astronautics.

64   NASA. (1992, 15–21 November). *Evaluation Panel Handbook: General Information.* San Juan Capistrano: San Juan Capistrano Research Institute.

65   Ibid., 39.

edge, and you could lose three or four spacecraft a year. It would be okay because you keep launching.[66]

The results of the San Juan Capistrano meeting were communicated to the scientific community via an open letter to the 246 attendees.[67] Twenty-two concepts were judged to have exceptional or high science merit and low or medium risk, including precursors for Deep Impact, CONTOUR, Dawn, Kepler, Genesis, and six missions to explore Venus.

Mission concepts included observatories, space station payloads, flyby spacecraft, orbiters, atmospheric probes, airplanes, rough landers, and sample return spacecraft, with targets throughout the solar system and even including extrasolar planets (the first of which had only just been discovered, with its announcement earlier that year, on 9 January 1992). The spacecraft would draw their power from combinations of radioisotope thermoelectric generators, solar panels, and batteries.

Management structures were not generally streamlined, mature, or well-defined with respect to the roles of the PI and project manager. The review panels noted the layers of management and observed: "The management guidelines for the program recommended in July 1991 by the Discovery Program Cost and Management Team do not appear to have received wide circulation among the community."[68]

There were other general problems with power supplies, including radioisotope thermoelectric generators, whose costs, at $15 million to $50 million each, exceeded that which was available in the Discovery Program; launch vehicles that could not reach outer solar system objects; reliance on international partners that increased implementation risk; and requirements for technology development resources. The Concept Study Review portion of the NASA Discovery Program Workshop Summary concluded, "NASA should not begin another brave new program unless and until it has the resources to provide each project with adequate definition."[69]

The decision to distribute the report, including assessment matrixes that reported science value and risk ratings, opened the doors for feedback beyond what proposers had seen before or since. That December alone, at least 15 participants, including PIs and others, sent letters to NASA Headquarters or to Doug Nash at San Juan Capistrano Research Institute disputing their evaluations.[70] Eleven asked specifically

---

66   Goldin, D. (1992, 18 November). Remarks at the 108th Space Studies Board Meeting, Irvine, CA. [transcript].

67   Nash, D. (1992, 18 December). *NASA Discovery Program Workshop Summary Report.* 3–12.

68   Briggs, G. (1992, 18 December). *Report on the Discovery Mission Concept Workshop Held at the San Juan Capistrano Research Institute, 16 to 20 November 1992.* Submitted to the Science Mission Directorate with a cover letter from Doug Nash.

69   Nash, D. (1992, 18 December). *NASA Discovery Program Workshop Summary Report.* 3–12.

70   Letters in Susan Niebur's personal collection.

for a response from the evaluation panel.[71] While highly complimentary of the program and its process, proposers also cited concerns such as the consequences of disagreements among technical panels, concerns over NASA's decision-making when choosing cheaper or more expensive missions within the cost cap, issues concerning the time allotted between announcement and review date, frustration with the limited number of pages allowed for concept proposal in light of the detail expected by the panel, and the concern that the large number and diversity of the concepts in a given panel made it difficult for a small number of scientists to be well-versed in all topics. In addition, at least one proposer noted the high ratings on his review and took the opportunity to ask for study money. Another letter, from a colleague of a PI who objected to the premise that high-risk concepts should not be first on the list to be funded for study, took his complaints up the chain to NASA Administrator Goldin, who responded, "I am assured that they [the Solar System Exploration Division] are not ruling out concepts simply because they were judged to be of high risk by the workshop panel. To the contrary, they recognize that high-risk concepts may, in some cases, be those that could most benefit from additional study."[72]

NASA originally planned to select three to six mission concepts for study. Overwhelmed by the response, the agency increased the number to ten. After the proposers received their evaluations, several objected to their scores and ratings. Don Burnett, proposer of the Solar Wind Sample Return mission, was among those asking for reconsideration of the review of his mission concept. The NASA Headquarters program official on the receiving end of that request agreed to stretch the promised funding to 11 rather than 10, funding Burnett's study.[73] After the initial announcement, 3 additional studies (led by Veverka, Bill Boynton of the University of Arizona, and David Paige of the University of California, Los Angeles) were also funded, bringing the total to 14.[74]

High-Quality Science for a Reasonable Cost

The 14 selections represented the participation of a large part of the planetary science community. The concepts were led by PIs from 11 institutions total, viz., six universities, two NASA centers, the National Optical Astronomy Observatory, the United

---

71   Nash, D. (1992, 22 December). Letter to Discovery Workshop Evaluation Panel. Susan Niebur's personal collection.

72   Goldin, D. (n.d.) Undated letter to Laureano Cangahuala at JPL. Cangahuala's letter was dated 31 December 1992.

73   Niebur, S. (2009, 24 March). Personal interview with D. Burnett. Located in "Genesis" file, NASA Historical Reference Collection, History Division, NASA Headquarters, Washington, DC; NASA, (1993, 11 February). "NASA Selects 11 Discovery Mission Concepts for Study." NASA Press Release 93-027.

74   Saunders, M., and M. Kicza. (1994). "Discovery Program Overview." AIAA Space Programs and Technologies Conference, 27–29 September 1994.

States Geological Survey, and the Lunar and Planetary Institute (LPI); with management proposed at four management centers, viz., APL, NASA's Goddard Space Flight Center, JPL, and NASA's Ames Research Center; and a variety of industrial partners, viz., Boeing, TRW, Hughes, Lockheed Martin, and Ball.[75]

Selected Mission Concept Studies

Mission Concept	PI	PI Institution	Management
Mercury Polar Flyby	Paul Spudis	LPI	JPL
Hermes Global Orbiter	Robert Nelson	JPL	JPL
Venus Multiprobe Mission	Richard Goody	Harvard	JPL
Venus Composition Probe	Larry Esposito	U Colorado, Boulder	ARC
Cometary Coma Chemical Composition	Glenn Carle	ARC	JPL
Mars Upper Atmosphere Dynamics, Energetics, and Evolution Mission	Timothy Killeen	U Michigan, Ann Arbor	GSFC
Comet Nucleus Tour	Joseph Veverka	Cornell University	APL
Small Missions to Asteroids and Comets	Michael Belton	National Optical Astronomy Observatories	JPL
Near Earth Asteroid Returned Sample	Eugene Shoemaker	USGS, Flagstaff	APL/GSFC
Earth Orbital Ultraviolet Jovian Observer	Paul Feldman	Johns Hopkins University	GSFC
Solar Wind Sample Return	Don Burnett	California Institute of Technology	JPL
Mainbelt Asteroid Rendezvous Explorer	Joseph Veverka	Cornell	JPL
Comet Nucleus Penetrator	William Boynton	U Arizona, Tucson	JPL
Mars Polar Pathfinder	David Paige	UCLA	JPL

The Jet Propulsion Laboratory refocused efforts on these "faster, better, cheaper" missions in part due to the new Discovery initiative and in part due to the 1993 budget

---

75   Ibid.

freeze and outlook for flat growth over the next few years. In the new budget climate, said JPL Director Ed Stone, the lab must ensure that "the projects and programs we develop are doable, they're affordable, they're supportable, and they're interesting."[76] Assistant Director Charles Elachi agreed, saying that upcoming missions would be "done on a short time frame and at a low cost." Elachi was known at the time for taking Discovery proposals under his wing. As Don Burnett, Genesis PI, later recalled, "He met with everyone."[77] On 24 March 1993, Elachi would even set up an office at JPL to support PIs for these new missions.[78]

Science management at Johns Hopkins University's APL, meanwhile, articulated eight principles essential for the management of small cost-capped missions shortly after the launch of NEAR.[79] All but one were compatible with the Discovery Program paradigm; the last, wherein a single agency manager interfaces with the development teams, was a simplification of the Discovery reporting structure: Program Manager, Program Executive, Program Scientist.

Realistic and Achievable

The Discovery Management Workshop, chartered by NASA Headquarters on 1 February 1993, met to "consider management aspects of the Discovery Program, particularly the roles and relationships of the PI and his or her institution, any industrial partner, any NASA center involved, and NASA Headquarters."[80] Held 13–16 April 1993, the workshop was charged by NASA with focusing on practical applications: what their charter called the "hows," rather than the philosophy, of management.

The workshop was asked to determine how Discovery might be realistically managed, how PIs would lead, how the periodic Announcements of Opportunity would be structured, how fast and how large a mission rate would be realistically achievable, and how contracts would be structured. NASA Headquarters invited two dozen experienced space program scientists, engineers, and managers to attend the three-day meeting.

Participants in the Discovery Management Workshop concluded in their final report: "It is unmistakably clear that everyone unanimously and enthusiastically supports the Discovery concept and its goals; the notion of accomplishing valuable solar

76   Boyer, W. (1993, 22–28 February). "JPL Plans Smaller, Cheaper Missions." *SpaceNews*. 16.

77   Niebur, S. (2009, 24 March). Personal interview with D. Burnett. Located in "Genesis" file, NASA Historical Reference Collection, History Division, NASA Headquarters, Washington, DC.

78   Elachi, C. (1993, 24 March). Letter to Glen Carle.

79   Krimigis, S. M., T. B. Coughlin, and G. E. Cameron. (2000). "Johns Hopkins APL Paradigm in SmallSat Management." *Acta Astronautica*, 46(6), 187–197.

80   Carr, F. (1993, 25 May). *Final Report on the Discovery Mission Concept Workshop Held at the San Juan Capistrano Research Institute, 16 to 20 November 1992.*

system exploration science in a faster, better, cheaper mode is seen by the Workshop participants as not only exciting, but realistic and achievable as well."[81]

Key findings included the following:

- The concept, goals and objectives of Discovery (NTE $150M, 3-year development) are terrific and achievable[.]
- Discovery should aim for one start and one launch per year, on-going[.]
- Headquarters should not attempt to manage the Program alone[.]
- A contract management and technical "oversight" office is needed.
- Most PI's will not wish to be "Project Manager" of their mission[.]
- A few PI's do not wish to team with a NASA Center[.]
- Most PI's will favor roles as mission architect and science leader.
- Most Universities have neither the will nor the means to accept sole responsibility for an entire mission.
- Use of "new technology" is supported—within the Discovery boundary conditions.
- The traditional AO process can be improved (quicker and cheaper, just as effective)[.]
- Each bi-annual AO should select 3 missions for short Phase A's, then downselect for Phase B, and go into development only after criteria are met and reviewed.
- Be prepared to cancel any non-performing mission, in any Phase, A to C/D.
- Performing Criteria: good probability of valid science within cost & schedule commitments[.]
- Every mission needs a credible: management plan, cost, schedule, & reserves[.]
- Should have a fall back science floor (minimum acceptable objectives & capabilities)[.]
- An approved Project Plan for each mission is a must.[82]

The final report also noted the success of the Strategic Defense Initiative Organization, now the Missile Defense Agency, saying the "SDIO found it is possible to achieve launch times of 12–18 months from go-ahead and still follow all procurement regulations, FAR's [Federal Acquisition Regulations]," and other restrictions.[83]

---

81   Ibid.
82   Ibid.
83   Ibid.

26

The Time for Workshops Is Now Over

Approximately one month later, the executive committee of the April 1993 workshop wrote a letter to Huntress, now the Associate Administrator of the Office of Space Science (OSS) at NASA Headquarters.[84] In that letter, Jim Martin, the former program manager of Viking and now spearheading a study of Discovery feasibility; Gene Giberson of JPL; and Frank Carr of NASA Headquarters—relying on "the 100 years of executive committee members' experience with space program development"—provided their Recommendations for Discovery Policy and Implementation Guidelines. This was a surprising coda to a successful workshop report. Typically, when an ad hoc federal committee reports, the chair submits the report and is thanked for his or her service, and the committee is then dissolved. But in this case, Martin, Giberson, and Carr felt that some issues were unresolved. They took it upon themselves not only to publicize or emphasize the issues decided by the full workshop, but to have additional discussion and present what amounted to an additional white paper on the program.[85]

The first Discovery Management Workshop recommendations were revised, enhanced, and supplemented with new recommendations from the three, who wrote strong language declaring that "the time for workshops is now over, and that it is essential for OSS to take the high ground now in order to effectively compete for the scarce resources that might be available for starting new programs." After the report, they noted, key issues remained, including the preferred modality for a PI leading this new kind of mission; the relative responsibilities of and for the project manager; funding approaches; and NASA Headquarters management mechanics and philosophy.[86] They discussed three options for the implementation of the role of Principal Investigator. The first would be for the Principal Investigator to serve in a combined role of project scientist and project manager, taking all the responsibility.

The second would be for the Principal Investigator to serve as project scientist, a well-defined NASA role, and team with a NASA center for project management. In this second option, the Principal Investigator would formally delegate responsibility for several engineering tasks such as spacecraft, mission design, and ground data system to the project manager, who would then be accountable directly to NASA. "Under this option, the PI shall be responsible for the scientific success of the mission, and the NASA project manager shall be responsible for the successful implementation of the overall mission, including acquisition of science data."

A third option would be the creation of the consortium model, where the PI would partner with a consortium of providers, including a project manager who "shall be

---

84   Susan Niebur's personal collection.

85   Martin, G., and F. Carr. (1993, 15 May). Letter to the community with a Dear Colleague letter from Bill Piotrowski. Susan Niebur's personal collection.

86   Ibid.

responsible for the implementation of the overall mission, including acquisition of the science data."[87]

Martin, Giberson, and Carr covered significant ground in this white paper, including the structure and function of the presumed Discovery Program Office and a detailed schedule for any potential Announcements of Opportunity. For the program itself to be agile as designed, the NASA Headquarters–driven Announcements of Opportunity and the surrounding process would have to be designed in a way consistent with the growing philosophies consistent with faster, better, cheaper. The overall process, from the start of preparations for the Announcement of Opportunity (AO) to the public announcement of mission selections, should take no more than 10 months, including a one-month reserve. The 10 months could be divided as follows:

1. The initial draft of the AO would take three months, after which a draft would be released for comment.
2. The comments would be adjudicated, and the final announcement would be released two months after the draft.
3. "Because of the draft release, one month should be sufficient for proposal preparation and submittal."
4. The "AO evaluation cycle should not require more than three months, including all NASA approvals and selection announcements."
5. The funding should start 60 days after announcement, with no funding gaps between phases.[88]

Later that year, NASA Headquarters management fleshed out requirements for the program, including an emphasis on technology transfer and education and public outreach efforts. At the request of Congress, NASA Headquarters management also added specific requirements for small and disadvantaged business subcontracting.[89] The 1993 Discovery Program Implementation Plan soon followed, with four program goals clearly articulated:[90]

1. Retain U.S. scientific leadership in planetary science by assuring continuity in U.S. solar system exploration program (increasing mission flight rate and "launch schedule certainty");

---

87   Ibid.

88   Ibid.

89   Saunders, M., and M. Kicza. (1994). Discovery Program Overview. AIAA Space Programs and Technologies Conference, 27–29 September 1994.

90   Solar System Exploration Division. (1993, 7 August). NASA Discovery Program Implementation Plan [viewgraphs]. Susan Niebur's personal collection.

2. Introduce new ways of doing business (industry, university involvement and responsibility, full and open team competition, mission life cycle duration consistent with undergraduate/graduate student involvement, streamline NASA management organization);

3. Emphasize use of new technologies in achieving mission objectives (identify and support development of technologies to enable/enhance Discovery, infuse new technologies into Discovery missions cost effectively with low risk, tech transfer); and

4. Keep the general public aware, involved, and excited about Discovery.

NASA Headquarters Discovery Program planners designed the goals to be achievable, quantifiable, and measurable, and they were intended to influence mission proposals.[91] The planners did not and could not have foreseen, however, the way outside forces and events would change the way Discovery operated. As the program grew less risk-tolerant in later years, the emphasis on new technology first diminished and then became a liability.

By the time the Discovery goals were codified, they had changed yet again, emphasizing the quality of the scientific investigations that were perhaps assumed in the 1993 version. Missions would now do the following:

- Perform high-quality scientific investigations that will maintain U.S. scientific leadership in planetary science and will assure continuity in the U.S. solar system exploration program.
- Pursue innovative ways of doing business, particularly as demanded by short development schedules, low costs, and competitively selected PI-led teams.
- Encourage the use of new technologies in achieving program objectives, particularly to achieve performance enhancements and cost reductions. The transfer of new technologies to broader communities is also encouraged.
- Enhance general public awareness of, and appreciation for, solar system exploration, and support the nation's educational initiatives.
- Increase the participation of small and small disadvantaged businesses in high technology areas of Discovery missions.[92]

The Discovery Program Implementation Plan also established that the program manager should be an experienced manager from a private-sector aerospace company. Duties included being responsible and accountable for strategic planning, programmatic

---

91   Ibid.
92   Saunders, M., and M. Kicza. (1994). Discovery Program Overview. AIAA Space Programs and Technologies Conference, 27–29 September 1994.

management and oversight, and achievement of Discovery Program goals and objectives. The program manager would prepare and issue the AO, perform the proposal review with the community, prepare a selection recommendation, and coordinate education and public outreach initiatives. Moreover, the program manager would oversee up to two NASA Headquarters civil servants and report directly to the Deputy Associate Administrator of the OSS.[93]

Acting Solar System Exploration Division Director Bill Piotrowski sent a "Dear Colleagues" letter to the community emphasizing the importance of community cohesion for the program to flourish. He wrote: "The ultimate success of the Discovery Program will depend to a substantial degree on the willingness of the individual members of the planetary community to unite behind each successive mission, even though one or the other of their two anchor missions may not be their personal favorite."[94]

NEW START

NASA Headquarters gave the Discovery Program a formal budget request, or New Start, in the Fiscal Year 1994 budget, which President Bill Clinton signed into law on 28 October 1993. Two candidate missions, Mars Pathfinder and NEAR, were thus slated officially for development.[95]

The goal of the Discovery Program would be to launch every year, with Announcements of Opportunity issued every 12 to 18 months, depending on the level of funding available. Huntress emphasized that in uncertain budget environments, proposers should not "propose to the cap" of $150 million, but rather, in order to maintain a mission cadence, hesitate to load spacecraft with science instruments whenever possible.[96] In accordance with this guidance, Discovery Program management at NASA Headquarters encouraged the submission of proposals both at and under the cap in order to allow the selection of a balanced program. The first formal Announcement of Opportunity was issued on or around 2 July 1994. Proposers would have 60 days to respond.[97]

On 26 July 1994, NASA Headquarters released a Draft Program Management Plan for Discovery. Throughout the history of the Discovery Program, officials would con-

---

93   Ibid.

94   Piotrowski, B. (1993, 26 August). Letter to the planetary science community. Susan Niebur's personal collection.

95   Congressional Research Service. (1993, 4 October). Congressional Record Bound Edition, vol. 139, Part 16. 23343-23360. *https://www.congress.gov/bound-congressional-record/1993/10/04/house-section?q=%7B%22search%22%3A%5B%22%5C%22discovery+program%5C%22+1994%22%2 2%5D%7D&s=1&r=3.*

96   Huntress, W. (1994, June 1). "Dear Colleagues" letter. Susan Niebur's personal collection.

97   Ibid.

tinue to work closely with the planetary science community at regular Lessons Learned Workshops, Preproposal Conferences (called "bidders' conferences"), and science meetings, as well as through the various incarnations of the Solar System Exploration Subcommittee of NASA's Office of Space Science during the 1990s and 2000s.

Selection: Mars Pathfinder

In 1993, NASA Headquarters selected Mars Pathfinder to become the first flight of the Discovery Program. Richard Cook of JPL served as mission manager, responsible for day-to-day operations of the lander and rover.[98] Matthew Golombek of JPL was the project scientist, responsible for all decisions affecting mission science. Tony Spear of JPL was the project manager. NASA scheduled the mission for a 1996 launch with a Fiscal Year 1995 funding request of $77.5 million. The agency projected that Pathfinder would "land on Mars for less than 10 percent of the cost of landing there with Viking in 1976."[99]

Joe Boyce, the Mars Program Scientist at NASA Headquarters, later credited Golombek with keeping the Jet Propulsion Laboratory from adding new science or engineering elements to the lander, overreaching and thus breaking the cost cap. Boyce and others at NASA Headquarters were never certain that JPL could pull off a Mars rover without going over budget and had initially been reticent to support it.

According to Boyce, Golombek took the initiative as project scientist to wheel and deal with colleagues and international partners to get as much as possible for as little as possible. Components of the Alpha Particle X-Ray Spectrometer were provided by the Max Planck Institute in Germany, for example, in return for access to the data sent to Earth from Mars.

Meanwhile, the project manager, Spear, was a famously hard driver of his team. "You can't burn people out, but he did expect one hundred percent of your effort, all the time, and there's a type of person that likes that," said Boyce.[100]

The Solar System Exploration Subcommittee endorsed Mars Pathfinder one year earlier, in December 1992. The planetary science community initially had issues with the mission. According to Huntress, "The scientists really had trouble with it because it was a tech demo. Why are we spending our money to do a tech demo? And that's

---

98   NASA. (1997, July). Mars Pathfinder Landing Press Kit.

99   NASA. (1995). "NASA's Discovery Program: Solar System Exploration for the Next Millennium" [foldout]. In folder 17070, NASA Historical Reference Collection, NASA Headquarters, Washington, DC.

100   Niebur, S. (2009, 22 March). Personal interview with J. Boyce. Located in "Discovery Program" file, NASA Historical Reference Collection, History Division, NASA Headquarters, Washington, DC.

always been the problem, in the agency: getting money to get technologies to the right TRL [technology readiness level]."[101]

NASA added experiments to the mission. "Originally it was just supposed to be a camera to show that it actually had succeeded in landing," said Huntress. Investigations built by university scientists would join the payload, as long as they could remain within cost and mass constraints.[102]

Mars Pathfinder investigations included studying the form and structure of the Martian surface and its geology; examining the elemental composition and mineralogy of surface materials, including the magnetic properties of airborne dust; conducting a variety of atmospheric science investigations, examining the structure of the atmosphere, meteorology at the surface, and aerosols; studying soil mechanics and properties of surface materials; and investigating the rotational and orbital dynamics of the planet from two-way ranging and Doppler tracking of the lander as Mars rotated.[103] Mars Pathfinder ultimately carried several useful scientific instruments that enabled nine experimental investigations.

The Imager for Mars Pathfinder (IMP) was a stereo imager with color filters in each of its two camera channels, providing panoramic images and multispectral images with as many as 13 spectral bands.[104] IMP was mounted such that it could look out at the rocks, determining their composition, and up at the sky, investigating the atmosphere as it blocked the view of the Sun during the day or the Martian moon Phobos at night.

Years later, after the mission's success, one such observation of the predawn sky showed thin, bluish clouds, which the scientists thought to represent water ice forming on micrometer particles in the local atmospheric haze.[105] IMP found a "complex surface of ridges and troughs covered by rocks that have been transported and modified by fluvial, aeolian, and impact processes. Analyses of the spectral signatures in the scene revealed three types of rock and four classes of soil."[106] IMP could also image windsocks that were spread out at various heights along a one-meter mast, to assess wind speed and direction: a clever way of measuring wind characteristics with a camera, and the first vertical wind profile measured on Mars. Other properties of the local area could be observed through equally wily tricks, such as a set of magnets with differing field

---

101 Niebur, S. (2009, 13 March). Personal interview with W. Huntress. Located in "Wes Huntress" file, NASA Historical Reference Collection, History Division, NASA Headquarters, Washington, DC.

102 Ibid.

103 Golombek, M. P., and A. J. Spear. (1997, July). Mars Pathfinder Science investigations and objectives. 45th Congress of the International Astronautical Federation, 9–14 October 1994. See also: NASA. (1997, July). Mars Pathfinder Landing Press Kit.

104 NASA. (1997, July). Mars Pathfinder Landing Press Kit.

105 Smith, P. H., et al. (1997, 5 December). Results from the Mars Pathfinder Camera. *Science*. 278. 1758–1764.

106 Ibid.

strengths attached to the lander. Periodic images would show the accumulation of dust on these magnets, indicating the composition of the dust blowing by; the imager determined that the dust did indeed include magnetic composite particles, with a mean size of one micron.[107] IMP was developed by a team led by IMP Principal Investigator Peter Smith of the University of Arizona. (Smith would later use this experience to successfully propose and deliver the Mars Phoenix mission.)

The second instrument was the mobile Alpha Proton X-ray Spectrometer (APXS), used to determine the elements that make up the rocks and soil both near the lander and farther away—a scientific investigation made possible by the "little car" technology of the rover. The APXS was designed to measure the amounts of all elements present at greater than 0.1 percent of the soil sample, excluding hydrogen.

When placed in position by a robotic arm on the back of the rover, the instrument would bombard a five-centimeter circular area of rock or soil with charged particles released by the small pieces of radioactive curium-244. The particles that bounced back, along with any generated x-rays or photons, were counted to give the abundance of the elements in the sample. Their energies revealed which elements were present.[108] Years later, among other things, APXS revealed that the soil samples were consistent with those examined by the Viking landers in the late 1970s, albeit with higher levels of aluminum and magnesium, and lower levels of iron, chlorine, and sulfur.[109]

Germany contributed the alpha and proton portions of the instrument. APXS was a heritage instrument derived from a type carried on the Russian Vega and Phobos missions and identical to the instrument that was to fly on the ill-fated Russian Mars '96 mission. The x-ray spectrometer portion of APXS was developed by a team at the University of Chicago. The Principal Investigator for the instrument was Dr. Rudolph Rieder of the Max Planck Institute for Chemistry in Mainz, Germany; co-investigators were Dr. Thanasis Economou of the University of Chicago and Dr. Henry Wanke of the Max Planck Institute for Chemistry.

The Atmospheric Structure Instrument/Meteorology Package (ASI/MET), officially an engineering subsystem, took advantage of the landing opportunity to acquire atmospheric data both during descent and on the surface of Mars. During the lander's entry and descent, the ASI/MET measured the vertical density, pressure, and temperature of the Martian atmosphere, enabling scientists to later reconstruct a profile of the atmosphere below 160 kilometers. On the surface, the ASI/MET monitored these variables, which together make up surface meteorology and climate.

---

107   NASA. (1997, 4 November). "Mars Pathfinder Winds Down After Phenomenal Mission." NASA News Release 97-255.

108   NASA. (1997, July). Mars Pathfinder Landing Press Kit.

109   Williams, D. (2004, 30 December). "Mars Pathfinder Preliminary Results." *https://nssdc.gsfc. nasa.gov/planetary/marspath_results.html.*

Scientists would eventually find that the "atmospheric structure and the weather record are similar to those observed by the Viking 1 lander at the same latitude, altitude, and season 21 years ago, but there are differences related to diurnal effects and the surface properties of the landing site."[110]

ASI/MET was based on Viking lander instruments. Ames Research Center's Alvin Seiff, still working in retirement under the auspices of the San Jose State University Foundation, led the instrument definition team, and Tim Schofield of JPL led the science team. This instrument package was built and implemented by JPL as a facility experiment.

Other investigations included a windsock investigation led by Robert Sullivan and Ron Greeley of Arizona State University; a materials adherence study led by Geoffrey Landis of NASA Lewis (now Glenn) Research Center; a magnetic properties investigation led by Jens Knudsen from the University of Copenhagen;[111] and smaller investigations: one prompted by wheel abrasion, and another involving radio science that was enabled by the X-band communications with Earth.[112]

The Sojourner rover on Pathfinder, not much heavier than a bowling ball, was packed gently with blocks of aerogel, a lightweight thermal insulator that conserved both mass and power. This change protected the electronics and reduced the rover's mass by more than 2.6 kilograms, 20 percent of the rover's weight.[113]

Mars Pathfinder operated on Mars for 83 sols (4 July to 27 September 1997), nearly three times the projected mission lifetime of 30 days. The Sojourner rover operated for 12 times its design lifetime of seven days. The mission returned more than 16,000 images from the lander, 550 images from the rover, and 15 chemical analyses of rocks.[114]

A Non–NASA Center Mission

Meanwhile, at the Applied Physics Laboratory in Laurel, Maryland, Andy Cheng was named the Project Scientist of the NEAR mission, which would be the first NASA

---

110   J. T. Schofield et al. (1997, 5 December). The Mars Pathfinder Atmospheric Structure Investigation/Meteorology (ASI/MET) Experiment. *Science*, 278(5344), 1752–1757.

111   S. F. Hviid et al. (1997, 5 December). "Magnetic Properties Experiments on the Mars Pathfinder Lander: Preliminary Results." *Science*, 278(5344), 1768–1770.

112   W. M. Folkner et al. (1997, 5 December). "Interior Structure and Seasonal Mass Redistribution of Mars from Radio Tracking of Mars Pathfinder." *Science*, 278(5344), 1749–1751.

113   Jet Propulsion Laboratory. (1995, 10 March). "See-Through, Smoky-Blue Aerogel Will Help Protect Mars Pathfinder Rover." *JPL Universe* vol. 25, no. 5.

114   NASA. (1997, 4 November). "Mars Pathfinder Winds Down After Phenomenal Mission." NASA News Release 97-255; NASA.

planetary mission not conducted by a NASA center.[115] Cheng later recalled first encountering the NEAR mission because of a science working group report that crossed his desk during his tenure on COMPLEX, a standing body founded in the early 1970s by the Space Studies Board of the National Academies. He recommended NEAR to NASA as a good example of a small, low-cost planetary mission, and something APL could certainly achieve. It would go on to become the second slated mission to launch under the nascent Discovery Program. When APL management asked Cheng to be project scientist, he was, at the time, a Galileo interdisciplinary scientist working on magnetospheres, and he had experience working with various disciplines and instruments on space missions.[116]

Tom Krimigis, head of the Space Physics and Instrumentation Group at APL, asked Bob Farquhar, an astrodynamicist and mission designer who had been named the NEAR flight director, to look at the range of possible launch dates for a mission to visit a near-Earth asteroid. Krimigis later recalled: "Initially, we had an asteroid that would have a launch, I think, in '98 or thereabouts.... So, he looks at it, comes to me, and says: 'You know, I got something. If we do an Earth flyby, we can go to Eros, and it would launch in February of '96.'" Eros, he said, was a much more interesting asteroid than the original target, Anteros.[117] APL went to NASA Headquarters with the finding, and NASA Headquarters approved Eros as the target.

Development of NEAR kicked off in December 1993. Its science payload included six scientific investigations. Joe Veverka was the PI of the Multispectral Imager (MSI), a camera with an eight-position filter wheel enabling images to be taken over the visible to near-infrared wavelengths (450 to 1,050 nanometers), and the Near-Infrared Spectrometer (NIS), measuring reflectance in the 800- to 2,700-nanometer range. These two instruments, along with the X-Ray/Gamma Ray Spectrometer (XRS-GRS) package built by Jack Trombka and his team at NASA Goddard Space Flight Center, were used to determine the mineralogy of the rocks and dust on the surface of the asteroid. The magnetometer was built by Mario Acuna of Goddard and Chris Russell of UCLA. The NEAR Laser Rangefinder, built by a team led by Maria Zuber at Goddard, was used primarily for spacecraft navigation, but also as a laser altimeter at asteroid encounters, yielding the shape of the object. Don Yeomans at NASA's Jet Propulsion Laboratory led the radio science and gravimetry investigations, with Alexander Konopoliv of JPL and Jean-Pierre Barriot of Centre National d'Études Spatiales. The mass and gravity

---

115   Niebur, S. (2009, 31 July). Personal interview with A. Cheng. Located in "Discovery Program" file, NASA Historical Reference Collection, History Division, NASA Headquarters, Washington, DC; Applied Physics Laboratory (1996, 9 April). "Applied Physics Laboratory Honors NEAR Team for Underbudget Development and Launch."

116   Niebur, S. (2009, 31 July). Personal interview with A. Cheng. Located in "Discovery Program" file, NASA Historical Reference Collection, History Division, NASA Headquarters, Washington, DC.

117   Ibid.

variations determined using radio science could be combined with results from the multispectral imager and the laser rangefinder to estimate the density and internal structure of the asteroids 253 Mathilde and 433 Eros.

NEAR, said Andy Cheng, was not a PI-led mission. NASA, he recalled, had no website at the time. "It was NEAR that put up the first mission website...and the AO for participating scientists—that was the first one, also, that the call went out over the web. We had to do it for them because there was nobody at NASA who knew how." NEAR also pioneered interfacing with the Planetary Data System, the online NASA archive of data collected by planetary missions. Every member of the NEAR science team, and all mission-associated scientists, would have access to all data from every instrument. Science team leaders from each of the investigations would coordinate and approve plans for data analysis and publication.[118] "There was a lot of resistance," explained Cheng. "This business of not allowing people to have proprietary data rights—see, that was an innovation.... A lot of people didn't like it."[119]

Data sharing was not the only new way of doing business on a planetary mission. As Mark Saunders, who was the program manager for the Discovery Program at NEAR's launch, recalled: "They said they could do it for $125 million, total, and [NASA] Headquarters even went: 'We don't believe this.' The science objectives didn't change."[120] (This was before the establishment of "baseline" and "floor" science requirements.)

APL did not plan for cost contingencies during the development of NEAR. "If you identify contingency, everybody thinks it's theirs, and then they go ahead and plan on spending it," Krimigis later said.[121] He explained: "In this place, we worked with agreements between the program office and the supervisors who did the technical work in their groups, and we kind of signed internal contracts where we would say, 'Okay, you are doing the C&DH [command and data handling] system. Here are the specifications. Tell me how much it would cost.' The group supervisor would sign a contract with the program manager that it was going to cost[,] say, $2 million—with

118   Cheng, A. F., et al. (1997, October). "Near-Earth Asteroid Rendezvous: Mission Overview." *Journal of Geophysical Research*. 102(E10). pp. 23695–23708.

119   Niebur, S. (2009, 31 July). Personal interview with A. Cheng. Located in "Discovery Program" file, NASA Historical Reference Collection, History Division, NASA Headquarters, Washington, DC.

120   Niebur, S. (2009, 24 January). Personal interview with S. Keddie, M. Saunders, and R. Vorder Bruegge. Located in "Discovery Program" file, NASA Historical Reference Collection, History Division, NASA Headquarters, Washington, DC.

121   Niebur, S. (2009, 27 August). Personal interview with T. Krimigis. Located in the "Discovery Program" file, NASA Historical Reference Collection, History Division, NASA Headquarters, Washington, DC.

details, mind you, and people and resources and everything, it was all there. We would sum things up."[122]

NASA Headquarters sent evaluators from SAIC, an independent systems engineering review firm, to check on the program's progress and cost several times throughout development. Six or eight months after the start of the program, SAIC estimated the total cost-to-complete to be "at least two and a half times" the Applied Physics Laboratory's estimate, said Krimigis. Several months later, SAIC returned and found that the overrun was going to be much less, but still 50 percent higher than APL's estimate. No changes were made to the contract, and no additional NASA Headquarters–level reviews were held, other than the standard gateway and launch readiness reviews. APL continued working to keep Betsy Beyer, the NEAR program manager at NASA Headquarters, informed and involved throughout the process.

By not identifying contingency within the program, APL kept to its budget without requesting additional resources. Krimigis possessed deep knowledge of his people and leveraged that to deliver the mission on time and on budget. (A year after NASA selected the NEAR mission, Krimigis was surprised to learn that NASA Headquarters had indeed held project reserve on NEAR and had not told the project about it.)

The mission went through a plethora of development reviews before launch. The technical and cost review was held 1–3 December 1993, whereupon technical experts reviewed the planned spacecraft hardware, performance, and reliability projections, as well as mission operations plans and its cost realism. The Preliminary Design Review occurred on 25–26 April 1994, to evaluate the completeness and consistency of the spacecraft's initial design before engineers might begin the detailed design of the hardware. The Critical Design Review of the integrated spacecraft, to verify whether its design was mature enough to enter final design and fabrication, happened on 29–30 November 1994. The investigation readiness reviews of science instruments fell on 1 December 1994. The mission entered integration and testing on 4 June 1995.[123]

"After That, We Couldn't Do Anything Wrong"

NEAR launched on 17 February 1996. It was the Platonic ideal of a faster, better, cheaper mission. The Discovery Program required a development time of less than 36 months; NEAR left Earth in 26 months. The cost-to-launch-plus-30-days requirement—that is, the total expenditures on the mission up to one month after liftoff—was $150 million

---

122   Niebur, S. (2009, 24 September). Personal interview with T. Krimigis. Located in the "Discovery Program" file, NASA Historical Reference Collection, History Division, NASA Headquarters, Washington, DC.

123   NASA. (2012, 14 August). "NASA Space Flight Program and Project Management Requirements." NPR 7120.5E.

or less. APL estimated that the mission would cost $112 million. Instead, it came in at approximately $108.4 million, meaning it cost less than one-third of the cost of the least expensive previous planetary mission.[124]

On 15 April 1996, two months after the launch of NEAR, from Cape Canaveral, Florida, the lab held a celebration. Representatives presented NASA Administrator Dan Goldin and Senator Barbara Mikulski, who represented the Maryland-based lab in Congress, with an oversized, ceremonial check for $3.6 million. It was the first mission in NASA history to give money back to NASA Headquarters. "After that, we couldn't do anything wrong," said Krimigis.[125]

"One of the Most Successful Flybys of All Time"

As an example of the rich science that can be done even by the small Discovery missions, consider NEAR's flyby of the asteroid Mathilde, which had been planned as a target of opportunity along its trajectory. On its way to Eros, NEAR passed Mathilde and took pictures, just as a tourist might do out the window of a train. Mathilde was unexplored territory: a black, carbon-rich rock, believed to be the most primitive material left in the asteroid belt.[126] To conserve power needed at Eros, the team turned on only one of the six instruments on the spacecraft, the multispectral imager. Even so, "the Mathilde encounter was one of the most successful flybys of all time," said Robert Farquhar, NEAR's flight director. "We got images that were far better than we thought possible, especially since the spacecraft was not designed for a fast flyby."[127]

Mission operations at Eros were not perfect. When Mark Holdridge was hired as NEAR mission operations manager at APL in 1997, he sought to expand the operations group to avert burnout and wanted greater testing—and more responsible testing methodologies—for what he felt were "sloppily performed" midcourse maneuvers.[128] APL had never flown a deep space mission; the team was literally making it up as they went along. Holdridge insisted on regular spacecraft performance assessments and wanted closer ties between the mission and Jet Propulsion Laboratory. Software

---

124   NASA. (1995). "NASA's Discovery Program: Solar System Exploration for the Next Millennium" [foldout]; Applied Physics Laboratory (1996, 9 April). "Applied Physics Laboratory Honors NEAR Team for Underbudget Development and Launch." *http://web.archive.org/web/20200713071051/ https://www.jhuapl.edu/PressRelease/960409*; Krimigis, T. (2020, 4 November). "Exploring Asteroid EROS: The Better, Faster, Cheaper Paradigm" [slides].

125   Niebur, S. (2009, 24 September). Personal interview with T. Krimigis. Located in the "Discovery Program" file, NASA Historical Reference Collection, History Division, NASA Headquarters, Washington, DC.

126   Applied Physics Laboratory. (1997, 19 June). "NEAR Fast Approaching Asteroid 253 Mathilde" [news release].

127   NASA. (1997, 30 June). "Asteroid Mathilde Reveals Her Dark Past" [news release].

128   McCurdy, H. (2005). *Low-Cost Innovation in Spaceflight: The NEAR Shoemaker mission.* 41. *https://history.nasa.gov/monograph36.pdf.*

limits on the spacecraft lateral acceleration, coupled with missing code necessary for burn-abort routines, caused NEAR to miss its encounter with Eros. The mission team would work tirelessly to stabilize the spacecraft and plan another attempt to encounter the asteroid.

"What saved the mission was our resilient mission design," said Farquhar. "We had worked out contingency plans ahead of time and had plenty of margin. If it wasn't for that we wouldn't have recovered."[129] The mission did recover, taking another orbit around the Sun before a second Eros encounter.[130]

Ultimately, NEAR did indeed end the mission with a victory, and the agile little Discovery mission proved itself, the concept of Discovery, and the faster, better, cheaper paradigm. NEAR did eventually acquire clear photos of Eros.[131]

CONCEPT THROUGH DATA ACQUISITION

Mark Saunders first joined NASA as a logistics manager for Space Station Freedom in 1989. After working at NASA Headquarters and in the Space Station Program Office in Reston, Virginia, he was experienced in both the technical acquisition process and the knowledge of what it really took to get programs moving forward in Congress. When the Reston office closed, a result of the reformulation and management restructuring of the space station program under the Clinton administration, Goddard and NASA Headquarters created jobs to retain top talent. The Science Mission Directorate hired Saunders to become the first Discovery Program Manager.

The AO strategy had been well-defined by 1994. A contractor, Richard Vorder Bruegge, wrote the first draft of the AO Evaluation Plan. He explained: "Wes [Huntress] was sort of the brains behind it, and Al [Diaz, the Deputy Associate Administrator] was sort of overseeing the mechanics, making sure that certain things happened."[132]

The scope of this AO would be significantly different from other federal requests for proposals. Instead of soliciting a spacecraft bus and instruments—a hardware acquisition, in other words—this AO solicited a full science mission from concept

---

129 Worth, H. (1999, 29 January). "NEAR Team Recovers Mission After Faulty Engine Burn" [news release].

130 Asker, J. R. (1999, 4 January). "Missed Asteroid Rendezvous Cues Probe of Low-Cost Missions." *Aviation Week & Space Technology*.

131 Niebur, S. (2009, 24 September). Personal interview with T. Krimigis. Located in the "Discovery Program" file, NASA Historical Reference Collection, History Division, NASA Headquarters, Washington, DC; McCurdy, H. (2005). *Low-Cost Innovation in Spaceflight: The NEAR Shoemaker Mission. https://history.nasa.gov/monograph36.pdf*; Russell, C. T. (1997). *The Near-Earth Asteroid Rendezvous Mission*. Dordrecht, The Netherlands: Kluwer Academic Publishers.

132 Niebur, S. (2009, 24 January). Personal interview with S. Keddie, M. Saunders, and R. Vorder Bruegge. Located in "Discovery Program" file, NASA Historical Reference Collection, History Division, NASA Headquarters, Washington, DC.

development through data acquisition. This strategy, the AO noted, would require "a careful tradeoff between science and cost incurred to produce missions with the highest possible science per unit cost."[133]

In March, a draft AO was released to the community for comment. The AO began its route to concurrence through the many offices at NASA Headquarters in May. After changes by officials up to and including the Administrator, NASA Headquarters released AO 94-OSS-03 on 4 August with proposals due on 21 October 1994.

Twenty days later, Discovery program officers held the first Discovery Preproposal Conference. They explained the parameters of the AO to more than 300 attendees present.[134] A technology fair was held concurrently, with 36 exhibitors, including many with experience in the planetary program as well as low-cost Explorer missions. Exhibitors spanned the range of potential partners, with seven NASA centers, the Jet Propulsion Laboratory, Ball Aerospace, the Southwest Research Institute, Boeing, Martin Marietta, Hughes, Orbital Sciences, McDonnell Douglas, TRW, Honeywell, Spectrum Astro, and others sending representatives and working the room to position themselves as trustworthy, knowledgeable, and reliable partners for the Principal Investigator's mission concepts.

The AO solicited proposals for focused scientific investigations that could be completed using small planetary missions. It required missions to adhere to proposed cost, schedule, and technical specifications, with no additional infusions of cash from NASA. It limited the development phase, Phase C/D, to $150 million and required completion in 36 months or less. Operations (Phase E) were limited to $35 million, but time was not capped. NASA would launch the selected mission on a Delta-class or smaller expendable launch vehicle before 31 August 2001. Small radioactive power sources (such as heaters) were acceptable in designs, but larger radioisotope thermoelectric generators were not.

Any samples returned would belong to the NASA Johnson Space Center Office of the Curator (now called the Astromaterials Acquisition and Curation Office), with the science team allocated up to 25 percent of the mass of materials brought back to Earth. Unlike the samples, though, NASA granted teams no proprietary data rights, and the teams would deliver said data to the Planetary Data System (PDS) in the shortest time possible. NASA reserved the right to add guest investigators to the team.

There was freedom in the management and technical requirements; the AO allowed each team to follow its own processes, procedures, and methods as consistent with overall NASA policies such as NPG 7120.5, the agency's "Program and Project Management

---

133   NASA. (1994, August). Announcement of Opportunity.
134   Saunders, M., and M. Kicza. (1994). Discovery Program Overview. AIAA Space Programs and Technologies Conference, 27–29 September 1994.

Processes and Requirements."[135] NASA encouraged innovation when improvements in cost, schedule, or technical performance could be demonstrated. Requirements in the management area included a detailed Work Breakdown Structure, a well-defined management approach, a named project manager, and sufficient attention to the approach for management of risk. The proposal would also have to include technology infusion, technology transfer, educational activities, public information programs, and a commitment to meeting NASA's goals for small businesses and small disadvantaged businesses. Though the AO teemed with requirements, it left big decisions, such as management structure, management approach, and contracting up to the proposing team. Over 30 teams submitted notices of intent to propose, with 28 submitting full proposals by the October deadline.

Huntress signed the AO Evaluation Plan on the same day. The plan recognized that

[t]he evaluation process and procedures used here are different from those used in the traditional evaluation of investigations proposed in response to AOs released by NASA's SSED. These differences stem from the fact that Discovery Program success will not only be measured in terms of scientific and technical achievements, but will also be measured by the accomplishment of those achievements within agreed-upon cost and schedule (i.e., management) constraints. Thus, in this Discovery Mission AO evaluation process, the overall merits of a proposal from a cost and management perspective will be considered on a par with the overall merits from a scientific and technical standpoint.[136]

The Discovery Program Manager, Mark Saunders, would be assisted by the Discovery Program Engineer, Mary Kaye Olsen, and the Discovery Program Scientist, Henry Brinton, together forming the first Discovery Program Office.

"We Were Trying to Do Things Differently"

With the proposal evaluation plan in hand, 72 reviewers (scientists and engineers from across industry and military aerospace, as well as eight NASA members) prepared for a week of reviews at the Lunar and Planetary Institute. "We were trying to do things differently," Saunders recalled. "If I get just NASA people doing these reviews, I'm going to get the same stuff. If they think this is a bit risky and we're trying something new, they'll trash it. None of the innovation will come."[137] According to Susan Keddie, a

---

135   NASA. (2012, August 14). "NASA Space Flight Program and Project Management Requirements." NPR 7120.5E.

136   Announcement of Opportunity Evaluation plan. Susan Niebur's personal collection.

137   Niebur, S. (2009, 24 January). Personal interview with S. Keddie, M. Saunders, and R. Vorder Bruegge. Located in "Discovery Program" file, NASA Historical Reference Collection, History Division, NASA Headquarters, Washington, DC.

reviewer and scientist at SAIC, "We would meet in the morning to review a proposal, and then the afternoon and night we would read the next one, which we would review it the next day."[138]

The first three days would include subpanel discussions, integrating individual comments and developing general consensuses. The subpanels would reach consensus on adjectival ratings and rank the mission proposals. The last two days would be spent in plenary to assure that all proposals were treated equally. Review criteria involved cost and science return (the two weighted approximately equally), as well as project management and technical approaches. The goal was to get the best science per dollar. The panels also scored tech transfer, education, public outreach, and small business participation, including by small businesses owned by socially and economically disadvantaged individuals.

A Space Science Steering Committee would review the evaluation, studying the processes used by the panel and their conclusions, and then discuss any programmatic issues that needed to be considered. After the Steering Committee concluded its work, the Source Selection official would review the results of the evaluation panel and the steering committee and make a selection.

The Discovery office received 28 proposals from a combination of 36 universities, 37 aerospace companies and small businesses, 12 national labs and federally funded research and development centers, 12 foreign institutions, and 10 nonprofit research institutes and observatories to study a wide range of solar system objects—comets, asteroids, Mercury, Venus, Mars, the Moon, Earth—and to look at Jupiter's Io torus, the solar wind, and planets around other stars.

Scientifically First-Rate Space Exploration Using Small, Advanced Spacecraft

NASA Headquarters revealed the Announcement of Opportunity results at a press conference on 28 February 1995.[139] One proposal, called Lunar Prospector, was selected for flight. Three other proposals were selected for a partially funded nine-month concept study:

- Stardust, which would collect dust from the coma of a comet
- Venus Multiprobe mission, which would drop 16 probes into the Venusian atmosphere
- Suess-Urey, a solar wind mission

---

138   Ibid.

139   Huntress, W. (1994, 21 October). Announcement of Opportunity Evaluation Plan; Niebur, S. (2009, 13 March). Personal interview with W. Huntress. Located in "Wes Huntress" file, NASA Historical Reference Collection, History Division, NASA Headquarters, Washington, DC.

Stardust, led by Don Brownlee of the University of Washington with contractor partner Martin Marietta, came in at a cost of $208 million. Venus Multiprobe, led by Richard Goody of Harvard University with contractor partner Hughes Communications and Space Company, would cost $202 million; Suess-Urey was estimated to cost $214 million, and its Principal Investigator was Don Burnett of the California Institute of Technology, with Martin Marietta Astronautics as its partner.

All three were between 61 and 66 percent of the allowed cost cap. All three were proposed by the Jet Propulsion Laboratory.[140] This was not surprising, as the lab had submitted over a dozen proposals.[141]

At a press conference, Dan Goldin, Administrator of NASA, said: "I am absolutely thrilled with the potential of these missions, and with the universally high quality of the 28 proposals submitted to us.... The university and aerospace industry communities should be proud of their efforts, which represent a model of how to pursue scientifically first-rate space exploration using small, advanced spacecraft."[142]

We've Turned the Old Way of Doing Business Upside Down

NEAR, the first Discovery mission, launched on 17 February 1996. Mars Pathfinder, the second Discovery mission, was launched on a clear night exactly as planned, at 1:58 a.m., 4 December 1996. The Pathfinder rover was named by 12-year-old Valerie Ambroise as part of a national grade-school essay contest. She suggested that it be called Sojourner, after Sojourner Truth, who made it her mission to "travel up and down the land."[143]

In the end, the Applied Physics Laboratory delivered NEAR for one-third of the cost of the previously least-expensive mission in the history of planetary exploration. Mars Pathfinder, meanwhile, placed a lander on the surface of Mars for a small fraction of the cost of the last time NASA so landed, in 1976—and included a rover, another first for Mars. The mission schedules were equally aggressive: each took less than three years from the start of development to launch. The Discovery Program was on track to launch, on average, one mission every 18 months or so, a much higher flight rate than planetary exploration had ever before achieved.[144]

The next Discovery mission was going to the Moon.

---

140   Ainsworth, D. (1995, February). "Three JPL Discovery Concepts Selected for Possible Development." *JPL Universe*, 25(5).

141   Niebur, S. (2009, 22 March). Personal interview with G. Vane. Located in "Discovery Program" file, NASA Historical Reference Collection, History Division, NASA Headquarters, Washington, DC.

142   "Three JPL Discovery Missions Selected for Possible Development," press release #9515, 28 February 1995, *https://www2.jpl.nasa.gov/releases/95/release_1995_9515.html*.

143   "Heroines and History Well Represented in Worldwide Competition to Name Rover." (1996, December 13). *JPL Universe*, 26(25).

144   NASA Office of Space Science. (1995, July). "NASA's Discovery Program: Solar System Exploration for the Next Millennium."

Figure 1-1: NEAR spacecraft

The Near Earth Asteroid Rendezvous (NEAR) spacecraft undergoing preflight preparation in the Spacecraft Assembly Encapsulation Facility-2 (SAEF-2) at Kennedy Space Center (KSC). (Image credit: NASA, image no. 9701593)

Figure 1-2: NEAR image of Eros

Mosaic of asteroid Eros's Northern Hemisphere, photographed by the Near Earth Asteroid Rendezvous mission. (Image credit: NASA/JPL/JHUAPL, image no. PIA02923)

Figure 1-3: Mars Pathfinder and Sojourner

The Sojourner rover and undeployed ramps aboard the Mars Pathfinder spacecraft, photographed by the Imager for Mars Pathfinder (IMP). (Image credit: NASA/JPL, image no. PIA00621)

CHAPTER 2
Big Dreams

LUNAR PROSPECTOR: LEVERAGING PRIOR INVESTMENT

The first Discovery Program Announcement Opportunity, released in 1994, outlined detailed expectations for candidate missions based on principles set forth in the earlier Discovery Program Handbook.[1] Selection of missions was to be through a two-step proposal process with two separate review panels to rate the missions on scientific merit, relevance, and cost effectiveness, as well as technical, management, cost, and outreach qualifications. The community responded with dozens of high-quality proposals.[2] After thorough review of the initial proposals, on 28 February 1995, NASA Headquarters selected the $59 million Lunar Prospector for implementation. It was the first time that such a decision was made through a competitive AO, and it was the third mission of the Discovery Program, after Mars Pathfinder and NEAR.

---

1   NASA. (1992). Discovery Program Handbook. Washington DC: NASA.

2   NASA. (N.d.). "NASA Discovery Program." Downloaded from *http://stardust.jpl.nasa.gov/mission/sd-dscvr.htm* on 30 May 2011.

Discovery Program missions would, and continue to, adhere to a general NASA project life cycle. During the "concept study" phase, called "Step 1," a prospective mission is said to be in "pre-Phase A." Upon a successful review, the study is "down selected"—chosen from competing mission concepts—and enters Phase A. Here, its overall approach and the technology to achieve it are enhanced and refined. The resultant "Step 2" study is again reviewed and, if selected, enters Phase B. At this point, its preliminary design and the necessary technology are completed. Further reviews and, ultimately, a nod from NASA bring the project to Phase C, during which time the final design of the spacecraft and instruments is settled upon and the fabrication of components and subsystems begins. Again, a successful review sends the project into the next stage of its life: Phase D, at which point the spacecraft is assembled, integrated with its science payload, tested, and launched into space. The operations phase of the mission is called Phase E, and once the mission is complete, it enters Phase F, when it is closed out.

Wes Huntress credited Lunar Prospector's success to concept studies of the project having been completed in advance of the competition. "They didn't need a Phase A," he said. "They were ready for flight."[3]

Although Lunar Prospector was the only Discovery mission to be selected based on its initial proposal alone, the mission was straightforward, with high-heritage instruments, clearly defined goals, a high probability of staying within its proposed low budget—and it appeared relatively straightforward to accomplish. The team had proposed a simple, challenging question: "Is there or is there not water at the South Pole?"[4]

Amazingly Fair and Amazingly Good

Alan Binder, the Principal Investigator of Lunar Prospector, has thoroughly documented all phases of the mission in his book, *Lunar Prospector: Against All Odds*.[5] For his mission, Binder selected a very small team of co-investigators.[6] The project manager was Tom Dougherty at Lockheed Martin Missiles & Space in Sunnyvale, California. Joe Boyce served as the Lunar Prospector Program Scientist at NASA Headquarters. The mission would be designed in 22 months, at a cost of $63 million.[7] Lunar Prospector would be launched on a Lockheed Martin Athena 2 expendable launch vehicle.

---

3   Niebur, S. (2009, 13 March). Personal interview with W. Huntress. Located in "Wes Huntress" file, NASA Historical Reference Collection, History Division, NASA Headquarters, Washington, DC.

4   "Lunar Prospector Poised for Monday Launch." (1998, 4 January). CNN.

5   Binder, A. (2005). *Against All Odds*. Tucson: Ken Press. 213.

6   Binder, A. (1998, 4 September). "Lunar Prospector: Overview." *Science* 281(5382). 1475–1476.

7   Ibid.

In his book, Binder wrote about his debrief with Mark Saunders, the Discovery Program Manager, after selection.[8] Binder encapsulated the science per dollar argument with a cogent anecdote about the briefing: "We received a good on science. I asked Mark how we could have done better, and he replied, 'The only way you could have done better on science was to have more of it, but that would have raised your cost.' We had received an excellent on cost, so to get an excellent on science by doing more of it would have meant that we would have only gotten a good or very good on the cost—so that would have been a wash."[9]

NASA Headquarters assigned mission management to Ames Research Center, with Scott Hubbard in the role of mission manager. All held out high hopes that this little mission would answer a very big question about the amount of water at the moon's South Pole.[10] Hubbard explained that he and Binder had a common goal: "We wanted to show that for the cost of a typical Hollywood movie, you can explore interplanetary space...."[11]

The goal of the Lunar Prospector mission was to map the abundance of certain elements on the Moon's surface and to search for water ice deposits at the poles. Water ice is important for human exploration initiatives. Its extraction has obvious applications for life support and rocket fuel, as hydrogen and oxygen are necessary elements for both.[12] Moreover, the mission would map the Moon's gravity and magnetic fields at a higher fidelity than any previous attempt.[13]

Not Another Clementine

There was concern in the planetary science community that data returned from Lunar Prospector would offer only an incremental increase in knowledge over another lunar mission, Clementine. The joint NASA–Defense Department spacecraft had launched almost exactly one year earlier, on 25 January 1994. A comparison of the two missions, however, demonstrated instead that Lunar Prospector would be complementary, not duplicative. Clementine had an imaging system, altimetry hardware, and gravity investigations. Lunar Prospector, on the other hand, employed six experiments:

- Gamma Ray Spectrometer (GRS)
- Alpha Particle Spectrometer (APS)

---

8   Binder, A. (2005). *Against All Odds.* Tucson: Ken Press. 213.

9   Ibid.

10   "Lunar Prospector Poised for Monday Launch." (1998, 4 January). CNN.

11   Ibid.

12   Binder, A. (1998, 4 September). "Lunar Prospector: Overview." *Science*, 281(5382). 1475–1476.

13   "Missions to the Moon, Sun, Venus, and a Comet Picked for Discovery." (1995, 28 February). NASA News Release 95-19.

- Neutron Spectrometer (NS)
- Doppler Gravity Experiment (DGE)
- Electron Reflectometer (ER)
- Magnetometer (MAG)

The gamma ray spectrometer would map the Moon in radioactive elements (uranium, thorium, potassium) and those that emit gamma rays when hit by cosmic rays or particles in the solar wind (iron, titanium, oxygen, silicon, aluminum, magnesium, calcium). A map of the latter set of elements would provide information about the composition of the Moon, which was known to be composed of 98 percent of these elements, by mass. Such maps would show not just the bulk elemental composition of the Moon, but also its mineralogy: information on the types of rocks present on the global surface that could then be compared with the rocks returned by the Apollo missions in the 1960s and '70s. Such measured elements were also key in determining the prevalence of "KREEP"—material rich in potassium (K), rare earth elements (REE), and phosphorus (P)—and, therefore, lunar evolution. KREEP may represent some of the last remaining melt after the lunar crust was formed. Together, these elements would help scientists understand how the Moon formed and the surface continued to change. The mission also emphasized the detection of resources needed for future construction on the Moon. Scott Hubbard was the Principal Investigator for this instrument.

The neutron spectrometer was built by Bill Feldman and his team at Los Alamos National Laboratory to map the global concentrations of hydrogen, iron, titanium, calcium, aluminum, and other elements on the surface. The team represented one of the premier gamma ray and neutron instrument providers for the United States, later providing instruments for, and serving as co-investigators on, the Discovery missions MESSENGER and Dawn.

Alan Binder was the PI for the alpha particle spectrometer, designed to detect the radioactive decay of radon and its daughter, polonium—possibly the result of low-level volcanic activity and the source of the tenuous lunar atmosphere. The mission's emphasis on resources for future human exploration was promoted again here, as radon gas is released with other gases essential for life support.

The Doppler gravity experiment, led by Alexander Konopoliv from the Jet Propulsion Laboratory, would use the Doppler shift observed in the S-band tracking signal of the spacecraft at Earth to estimate the lunar gravity field of the near side of the Moon and the corresponding location and size of any mass anomalies from the surface, lithosphere, or internal structure of the Moon. The variance of the gravity field over the surface of the Moon would indicate particularly dense areas of the crust.

The electron reflectometer investigation measured the energy spectrum and direction of electrons in order to determine the location and strength of the lunar remnant paleomagnetic fields. It was led by Robert Lin of University of California, Berkeley.

The magnetometer was mounted on a 0.8-meter boom extending from the electron reflectometer, away from internal spacecraft magnetic fields, to measure the locations and strengths of regional (low-intensity) magnetic fields in the crust. Such magnetic anomalies could show how the magnetic fields formed and could be used with the gravity data to infer the size of the Moon's core, thought to be composed of iron. Mario Acuna, from Goddard Space Flight Center, and Lon Hood, from the University of Arizona, were the co-principal investigators of the magnetometer.[14] Altogether, the instruments weighed just 21.4 kilograms; the spacecraft mass was 223 kilograms, with no onboard computer.

These instruments would fly on a small (296 kilograms) drum-shaped (1.37 meters in diameter, 1.28 meters in height) spacecraft bus built by Lockheed Martin.[15] Mission refinements, development, integration, and testing were all completed in just 22 months, and the spacecraft was delivered to Cape Canaveral at the end of 1997.

The Evidence of Water Ice Is Quite Strong

Lunar Prospector launched at 9:28 p.m. EST on 6 January 1998, from Launch Complex 46 at Cape Canaveral and reached the Moon just four days and nine hours later. The spacecraft began collecting data almost immediately. Binder was elated at the spacecraft's performance and scientific data yield about the Moon. The Lunar Prospector team announced the presence of water ice at both poles, but Bill Feldman cautioned that although the evidence was strong, there likely was a low concentration of water at the poles. While results were qualified, spacecraft performance was not. "This spacecraft has performed beyond all reasonable expectations," said Scott Hubbard at this initial press conference.[16]

Later analyses refined results and changed interpretations. "The data show clearly where the hydrogen is. It's localized in spots near the poles, and it has to be buried about half a meter or so," said Feldman a few months later. "In making our initial

---

14   Binder, A. (1998, 4 September). "Lunar Prospector: Overview." *Science*, 281(5382). 1475–1476.

15   Ibid.

16   National Aeronautics and Space Administration. (1998, 6 March). "Lunar Prospector Finds Evidence of Ice at Moon's Poles." *ScienceDaily*. Retrieved 5 August 2021 from *http://www. sciencedaily.com/releases/1998/03/980306043804.htm.*

estimates, we assumed the water was spread over the footprint [area scanned by] the instrument. As we've gathered more data, we've found that it's not spread out as we first assumed, but concentrated," he said.[17]

Throughout the mission, Lunar Prospector continued to provide firsts, such as the first operational gravity map of the entire lunar surface. David Lawrence, a physicist on the neutron spectrometer team at Los Alamos National Laboratory, said: "Before Lunar Prospector, we only saw 20 percent of the moon. Now we're mapping a whole other planet, and that's really exciting."[18]

After the completion of its one-year primary mission, Lunar Prospector executed a six-month extended mission.

End of Mission

At end of mission, with NASA's full approval, the team crashed the spacecraft into the Moon. Just before 6 a.m. the morning of 31 July 1999, the spacecraft impacted a dark crater near the South Pole. The ejecta of such an impact, observed by the Hubble Space Telescope in Earth orbit and the McDonald Observatory in Texas, would reveal the characteristics of water ice if a large amount was present.[19] David Goldstein of the University of Texas at Austin encouraged astronomers to request Director's Discretionary Time on their telescopes to watch the impact as well.[20] The probability of success before impact was estimated to be only 10 percent, but, as Guenter Riegler, then-director of the Research Program Management Division, Office of Space Science, at NASA Headquarters, said: "While the probability of success for such a bold undertaking is low, the potential science payoff is tremendous."[21] Unfortunately, no plume was observed.[22]

Papers continued to be published in myriad scientific journals, including *Geophysical Research Letters*, on the results from Lunar Prospector for several years. Exemplary of these were the results of the magnetometer investigation, which proved to be a small

---

17   Connor, S. (1998, 3 September). "Scientists Find Billions." *The Independent*. Downloaded from *http://www.independent.co.uk/news/scientists-find-billions-of-tons-of-ice-lying-under-the-moons-poles-1195839.html*.

18   Hoffman, I. (1999, 1 August). "Results of Moon-Probe Crash Examined." *Albuquerque Journal*.

19   Phillips, T. (1999, 21 July). "Bracing for Impact." NASA Science. Downloaded from *https://science.nasa.gov/science-news/science-at-nasa/1999/ast21jul99_1/*.

20   Goldstein, D. B., et al. (1999 15 June). "Impacting Lunar Prospector in a Cold Trap to Detect Water Ice." *Geophys. Res. Lett*, 26(12). 1653–1656.

21   NASA. (1999, June 2). "Lunar Prospector Set to Make Science Splash." Press release 99-36AR.

22   NASA Space Science Data Center. (N.d.). "Lunar Prospector." Downloaded from *https://nssdc.gsfc.nasa.gov/planetary/lunarprosp.html* on 3 May 2023.

instrument with big results. Scientists on the magnetometer team estimated a magnetic core roughly 680 kilometers ±180 kilometers in diameter—only 1 to 3 percent of the Moon's mass—making it an order of magnitude smaller than Earth's core-mass ratio.[23]

This unexpected result supported the "impact origin" of the Moon, a theory put forth by scientists William Hartmann and Donald Davis in 1975.[24] In this theory, during the early days of the solar system, a Mars-size planetesimal hit the early Earth, knocking a good bit of its outer material into space.[25]

STARDUST

The 1994 Discovery Announcement of Opportunity in which Lunar Prospector was selected also resulted in a Phase A competition of three other missions, of which one would be selected nine months later.[26] As the Discovery Program matured, the complexity of the selected missions increased. Leading these missions required PIs to manage ever-larger teams and find solutions to technical and scientific issues that fit within the strict cost cap of the Discovery class.

Esker K. "Ek" Davis, manager of the Jet Propulsion Laboratory's Planetary and Space Physics Missions Program Office, oversaw the submission of 15 JPL Discovery mission proposals in 1994 and was "the key person at JPL who established the foundation for our approach to the Discovery Program," according to Charles Elachi, then-director of the lab's Space and Earth Science Programs Directorate.[27] Under Davis, three missions developed by JPL were selected by NASA Headquarters for Phase A competition in 1995: Stardust, Suess-Urey, and Venus Multiprobe.[28]

The three mission teams performed ten-month concept studies to refine mission design, perform early trades, answer reviewer concerns about technology readiness, and demonstrate that each respective spacecraft was ready for flight. Despite the widely

23 "Moon Has Small Core, Say LP Scientists." (1999, 9 August). *Space Daily.* Downloaded from *http://www.spacedaily.com/news/water-99l.html.* See also Hood, L., et al. (1999, 1 August). "Initial Measurements of the Lunar Induced Magnetic Dipole Moment Using Lunar Prospector Magnetometer Data." *Geophysical Research Letters,* 26(15). 2327–2330.

24 Hartmann, W. K., and Davis, D. R. (1975). "Satellite-Sized Planetesimals and Lunar Origin." *Icarus,* 24(4), 504–515.

25 "Moon Has Small Core, Say LP Scientists. (1999, 9 August). *Space Daily.* Downloaded from *http://www.spacedaily.com/news/water-99l.html.*

26 NASA. (1995, 6 October). Discovery 4 Down Select Review Plan.

27 Whalen, M. (1995, 1 December). "Discovery Office Manager 'Ek' Davis Dies." *JPL Universe* 25(24).

28 Ainsworth, D. (1995, 10 March). "Three JPL Discovery Concepts Selected for Possible Development." *JPL Universe,* 25(5).

spread rumors of the imminent selection of Venus Multiprobe (due to its significantly lower cost and elegant design), when the results were announced on 11 November 1995, the winner was Stardust.[29]

Wes Huntress, newly promoted to Associate Administrator of Space Science, as well as being a selecting official, told the teams and the media: "Stardust was rated highest in terms of scientific content and, when combined with its low cost and high probability of success, this translates into the best return on investment for the nation." When asked how the decision between the missions was made, Huntress credited the "plan to communicate the purpose and results of this exciting mission to educators and the public" as a deciding factor.[30] The irresistible potential for public engagement acting as the wind in its sails, NASA selected Stardust as the fourth Discovery mission, the agency's first mission to a comet, and the first sample return mission since Apollo.

Keep It Simple

Selection of the Stardust mission concept broke new ground in the Discovery Program.[31] The mission would be small, focused, and achievable, despite scientists and engineers attempting the improbable: sample return in a cost-capped mission environment. This meant, in addition to encountering a target, taking measurements, and returning the data to Earth, that at least part of the spacecraft would have to be returned to Earth safely, with the samples collected intact.

Don Brownlee, Stardust Principal Investigator and a professor at the University of Washington, had spent years studying interplanetary dust particles collected on rooftops, high-altitude balloon flights, flights of U2 and ER-2 airplanes, sounding rocket flights, the Apollo program's precursor missions Gemini X and XII, Skylab, Russia's Mir space station, and the International Space Station, among others. He mined the dust for the secrets that they held about the beginning of our solar system.[32] These fluffy micron-sized particles, which came to be known as Brownlee particles, were amalgamates of minerals with extraterrestrial isotopic ratios, which suggested that they had existed at

---

29   Niebur, S. (2009, 25 March). Personal interview with D. Brownlee. Located in "Stardust" file, NASA Historical Reference Collection, History Division, NASA Headquarters, Washington, DC.

30   Ainsworth, D. (1995, 1 December). "Stardust Named Next Discovery Mission." *JPL Universe.* 25(24). See also NASA. (1995, 22 November). "Comet Sample Return Mission Picked as Next Discovery Flight." NASA press release. Niebur, S. (2009, 13 March). Personal interview with W. Huntress. Located in "Wes Huntress" file, NASA Historical Reference Collection, History Division, NASA Headquarters, Washington, DC.

31   Brownlee, D. E., et al. (2003), "Stardust: Comet and Interstellar Dust Sample Return Mission," *J. Geophys. Res.*, 108, 8111, doi:10.1029/2003JE002087, E10.

32   Doughton, S. (2006, 13 January). "Stardust Space Capsule to Touch Down Sunday." *The Seattle Times.* Niebur, S. (2009, 25 March). Personal interview with D. Brownlee. Located in "Stardust" file, NASA Historical Reference Collection, History Division, NASA Headquarters, Washington, DC.

the formation of the solar system. Brownlee recognized their significance and made a career of studying them with custom-built mass spectrometers and other specialized laboratory instrumentation. Although there had been no previous missions to study interplanetary dust, Brownlee was invited to join lunar investigations as early as Apollo 12 and continued as a lunar sample investigator after that. He was also a co-investigator on Giotto, the ESA mission to Comet Halley.

The Challenge of Sample Return

The Jet Propulsion Laboratory had studied comet missions as far back as 1959, but the concept became more pressing with the imminent return of an ancient visitor, Comet Halley, which would swing by Earth in 1986. Two of the key engineers working in the advanced projects division at JPL in 1981 were Ken Atkins, who led a development team whose spacecraft used ion rocket technology, and Lou Friedman, who led a team to use solar sail technology. The two had a good-natured rivalry, competing to demonstrate their engineering designs for a Halley's Comet intercept mission. After a "shootout" where the two teams presented their competing ideas to an impartial technical review panel, the ion rocket technology came out on top.

Atkins's team worked with the European Space Agency (ESA) on the mission, even improving the plan to include a probe that would be dropped at the comet before the spacecraft continued on to rendezvous with another comet, 10P/Tempel.[33] Meanwhile, Geoff Briggs, who then led the Solar System Exploration Division at NASA Headquarters, called Brownlee and co-investigator Peter Tsou of JPL, asking if it would be possible to analyze samples recovered from the comet. The projected encounter speed—70 kilometers per second—and the additional challenge of Earth microbial contamination on the spacecraft precluded such an operation. Still, the notion inspired Robert Farquhar of APL, Brownlee, Tsou, and others on the team, and the quest for sample return from a comet's coma thus began.[34]

The team was motivated by the premise that a simple sample return concept using minimal instrumentation could be contained in a cost box of $50 to $100 million—a very low price relative to pre-Discovery half-billion-dollar NASA missions that often invited radical descopes to cut costs. "We furiously started designing something called Halley–Earth Return (HER), which would go on the trajectory flying past Halley and

---

33   Niebur, S. (2009, 12 August). Personal interview with P. Tsou. Located in "Stardust" file, NASA Historical Reference Collection, History Division, NASA Headquarters, Washington, DC.

34   Niebur, S. (2009, 25 March). Personal interview with D. Brownlee. Located in "Stardust" file, NASA Historical Reference Collection, History Division, NASA Headquarters, Washington, DC. See also Milstein, M. (1999, February–March). "Bring Me the Tail of Wild-2." *Air & Space*. 55-61.

then come back to Earth," recalled Brownlee.[35] The spacecraft carried only a sample collector and a camera—a step in the right direction, but the technology was insufficiently advanced to capture the material in a readily usable state. A key element of the proposed mission involved "capture cell technology," which destroyed the captured particles, leaving only atoms behind for analysis. The resultant "atomized sample return," as it was called, was simply not useful to mineralogists, however. Maintaining the integrity of minuscule particles of dust and understanding the composition of adjacent materials would be essential to their analysis; numbers of elemental atoms in that context would have been useless.

"The bulk composition isn't that valuable to know," reflected Brownlee in a 2009 interview. "What may have sounded like a dramatic thing at the time was probably not a good thing to have done."[36] The interest in capturing cometary material and returning it to Earth intensified. The planetary community wanted sample return—something not achieved since the Apollo missions. Before development on a mission to Comet Halley could really begin, however, it was canceled on 30 September 1981, amid a weak economy; a smaller federal budget; and a consequent, broader culling of the planetary portfolio.[37] "When they finally shot us down," said Atkins, "the Europeans, nonplussed about that, started their own program called Giotto."[38]

Tsou and colleagues at JPL worked 15 years on potential designs for "intact capture," which would meet the objectives of mineralogists.[39] They experimented with many kinds of foam to strike a delicate balance: sturdy enough to stop the particles released from the comet but soft enough for the materials to survive intact.

Giotto's Comet Halley flyby was 70 kilometers per second, and "there are all kinds of reasons why you wouldn't expect to be able to collect any captured intact particles.[40] The work evolved over time. Tsou experimented with low-density targets, successfully

---

35   Niebur, S. (2009, 25 March). Personal interview with D. Brownlee. Located in "Stardust" file, NASA Historical Reference Collection, History Division, NASA Headquarters, Washington, DC.

36   Ibid.

37   Westwick, Peter J. (2006), "Planetary Exploration in Extremis." *Engineering and Science*, 69(4). pp. 32–43.

38   Niebur, S. (2009, 10 August). Personal interview with K. Atkins. Located in "Genesis" file, NASA Historical Reference Collection, History Division, NASA Headquarters, Washington, DC.

39   Doughton, S. (2006, 13 January). "Stardust Space Capsule to Touch Down Sunday." *The Seattle Times*.

40   Niebur, S. (2009, 12 August). Personal interview with P. Tsou. Located in "Stardust" file, NASA Historical Reference Collection, History Division, NASA Headquarters, Washington, DC; Niebur, S. (2009, 25 March). Personal interview with D. Brownlee. Located in "Stardust" file, NASA Historical Reference Collection, History Division, NASA Headquarters, Washington, DC.

demonstrating the first intact capture with a soft aluminum projectile and a piece of commercial Styrofoam in 1984.[41] "I was dogged by the idea," said Tsou, who continued to squeeze in experiments between funded JPL work. "You name the foam, I've used it."[42]

Meanwhile, an international flotilla of spacecraft was set to intersect the orbit of Halley's Comet, including the Russian Vega 1 and 2, the Japanese Sakigake and Suisei, and ESA's Giotto. JPL continued to struggle with comet concepts and proposals. The lab and Goddard Space Flight Center proposed to the Planetary Observer Program in 1985 a joint project called the Comet Intercept Sample Return Mission: a coma sample return mission with intact capture in a Discoverer Capsule.[43] JPL and ESA also proposed flying a spare Giotto spacecraft as Giotto II that same year. In 1988, JPL then targeted the small Explorer program, proposing an Earth-orbiting mission called the Cosmic Dust Intact Capture Explorer, which would capture interplanetary particles.[44]

In addition, Jet Propulsion Laboratory employees had joined with Japanese colleagues to study a low-cost flyby sample return. They proposed jointly to NASA and Japan's Institute of Space and Astronautical Science in 1992 a spacecraft called the Sample of Comet Coma Earth Return (SOCCER). There was also the Comet Nucleus Sample Return, yet another mission to emerge from the lab—this one a lander—and priced at $2 to $4 billion.[45] It was not selected for flight. Nor was a coma flyby mission projected to come in at $800 million.[46]

A flagship-class mission called Comet Rendezvous and Asteroid Flyby Return—a twin to Cassini, the spacecraft set for the Saturnian system, and well into development—was canceled by Congress in 1992. (Congress, notably, withheld the large program's money at the exact same time the Senate gave NASA direction to plan a small planetary science program which would become Discovery.) In Europe, the sample return element of the Rosetta comet mission was dropped, and Japan's SOCCER mission evolved into a spacecraft called Muses-C, then later Hayabusa, which was now an asteroid mission. In total, Peter Tsou recounts 12 comet-encounter mission concepts at JPL alone that had been rejected by the time of the first competitive Discovery AO in 1994.[47]

41   Tsou, P., D. E. Brownlee, and A. L. Albee, "Experiments on Intact Capture of Hypervelocity Particles," *JGR* 89 supl. C866–C867, 1984.

42   Milstein, M. (1999, February–March). "Bring Me the Tail of Wild-2." *Air & Space*. 55–61.

43   Tsou, P., et al. (1983, March). "Sample Collection on Comet Flybys." *Lunar and Planetary Science XIV.* 794–795.

44   Niebur, S. (2009, 25 March). Personal interview with D. Brownlee. Located in "Stardust" file, NASA Historical Reference Collection, History Division, NASA Headquarters, Washington, DC.

45   Niebur, S. (2009, 12 August). Personal interview with P. Tsou. Located in "Stardust" file, NASA Historical Reference Collection, History Division, NASA Headquarters, Washington, DC.

46   Vellinga, J. (2007, 6 February). "Bringing a Comet Home." Project Management Challenge 2007.

47   Milstein, Michael, "Bring Me the Tail of Wild-2," *Air & Space*, February/March 1999, 55–61; Peter Tsou interview; and Tsou, Peter, "Origins of the Stardust Mission," Stardust newsletter, vol. 1, no. 4, December 2003, p. 1.

No U.S. team had ever been successful in launching a mission to a comet. The opportunity to propose missions for this new program enticed, but the mission would have to be low-cost, quickly developed, and adhere to a tightly focused science investigation. It would be a challenge, but new technology and advances in development methodology and cometary understanding made this audacious goal possible for the first time. In the years following the earlier, rejected proposals, four major new technological advances had been made across industry and academia that would enable a realistic mission that included both interstellar and cometary sample return paradigms: namely, the development of an intact particle capture technology called aerogel; a low-energy sample return trajectory that could match a comet's velocity to just over 6 kilometers per second using minimal fuel for velocity changes (thereby enabling the use of a smaller spacecraft that could be launched by a Discovery-friendly Boeing Delta II rocket); the identification of micron-sized interstellar grains currently entering the solar system with the neutral interstellar helium gas (as seen by dust detectors on Ulysses and Galileo); and dramatic improvements in analytical instrumentation for determining the isotopic, mineralogical, elemental, and chemical compositions of micron-sized grains or their components.[48]

While development on the nascent mission concept called Stardust had been targeted to return fresh interstellar grains, the plan was modified in 1994 to study and return both "fresh" interstellar grains recently injected into the interstellar medium and ancient interstellar grains and nebular condensates frozen in comets. The highly experienced Stardust team had flown instruments on other U.S. and international missions, and their plans employed flight spares from JPL's stores wherever possible. The team drew on the rich heritage of cometary encounter and sample return mission concepts as they attempted a straightforward mission concept—"bring the comet home"—for a bargain-basement price. The team agreed on a singular primary science objective: collect 1,000 cometary particles greater than or equal to 15 microns in diameter and return them to Earth for laboratory analysis, with image collection and the capture of interstellar grains as secondary objectives. With these modifications and with so many years and so many studies of mission concepts, Stardust was selected by the Discovery Program on its first try.

---

48 Grün, E., Zook, H., Baguhl, M., et al. (1993). "Discovery of Jovian Dust Streams and Interstellar Grains by the Ulysses Spacecraft." *Nature*, 362. 428–430. *https://doi.org/10.1038/362428a0*; Grün, E., et al. (1994). "Interstellar Dust in the Heliosphere." *Astron. Astrophys.* 286. 915–924; Brownlee, D., et al. (1994, 21 October). "Stardust: Comet Coma Sample Return Plus Interstellar Dust Science and Technical Approach." Downloaded from *http://stardust.jpl.nasa.gov/science/ sci.html* on 11 September 2010.

Proposal and Concept Study

In fact, the Stardust Step 1 proposal had been submitted late.[49] It was a testament to its merits that Stardust was still selected for concept study, alongside Venus Multiprobe and Suess-Urey. However, the review panel challenged the team to address weaknesses in project management, mission operations, and science.[50] Regarding management issues, to name one example, there were personnel disagreements between JPL and aerospace contractor Martin Marietta Associates—a problem that could prove disastrous for that project and others.

Ek Davis was the Discovery Program Manager at JPL who made the decision. Davis had previously managed the flagship planetary exploration missions Galileo and Voyager and overseen the development of all of JPL's Step 1 proposals. He identified one of the proposal managers at JPL—Ken Atkins, who had been assigned to an asteroid sample return proposal called ASTER—as having performed particularly well, and he asked Atkins to step in as manager for the Stardust Step 2 proposal. His work on ASTER reflected his earlier work on Halley mission concepts HIM—the Halley Intercept Mission—and HER—the Halley–Earth Return.[51]

Atkins had extensive hardware delivery experience, which he credited as a major factor in his successful guidance of the Stardust proposal, but he was lacking one significant skill: "I didn't know how to get a proposal ready to do this." He later recounted, "I called Tony Spear up and I said, 'I need help in proposal, in just getting this proposal together from a JPL standpoint.' And he said, 'Come see me.' He had the proposal that he'd done for Pathfinder. He'd been through the gauntlet and been beaten around and it was a thing that [NASA] Headquarters liked."[52] Spear also offered Atkins the loan of a deputy who had successfully written the Pathfinder proposal, along with the technical writer and the mission planner. Overwhelmed with gratitude, Atkins asked Spear why he would offer to do all this for the Stardust project. "Well," said Spear, "you're the only one who asked."[53]

---

49   Niebur, S. (2009, 10 August). Personal interview with K. Atkins. Located in "Genesis" file, NASA Historical Reference Collection, History Division, NASA Headquarters, Washington, DC. Stardust was selected for concept study, along with Venus MultiProbe and Suess-Urey. The team was challenged to address the identified weaknesses in project management, mission operations, and science.

50   Niebur, S. (2009, 4 September). Personal interview with T. Duxbury. Located in "Stardust" file, NASA Historical Reference Collection, History Division, NASA Headquarters, Washington, DC.

51   Niebur, S. (2009, 10 August). Personal interview with K. Atkins. Located in "Genesis" file, NASA Historical Reference Collection, History Division, NASA Headquarters, Washington, DC.

52   Ainsworth, D. (1995, 1 December). "Stardust Named Next Discovery Mission." *JPL Universe*, 25(24).

53   Niebur, S. (2009, 10 August). Personal interview with K. Atkins. Located in "Genesis" file, NASA Historical Reference Collection, History Division, NASA Headquarters, Washington, DC.

Because they had worked so well together on the ASTER proposal, Atkins recruited Tom Duxbury, also of JPL, who had experience in optical onboard navigation, to handle mission operations and interactions with the science. Martin Marietta Aerospace, which would soon merge with the Lockheed Aircraft Company to form a division called Lockheed Martin Astronautics (LMA), had a strong program manager in Joe Vellinga, who led Stardust, Suess-Urey, and five other proposed concepts on the spacecraft side. "He is amazing," Don Brownlee, PI of Stardust, recalled of Vellinga. "He always gets everything done."[54]

While the Stardust team worked hard on the Concept Study Report, Atkins sought an edge that would put his proposal above the three JPL candidates. One rainy day, he attended a lunchtime seminar at the lab given by Bob Ballard, who had just discovered the Titanic on the bottom of the ocean floor using remote undersea robots. Ballard described his educational outreach program, JASON, named for the Greek figure and concerned with connecting students and satellite information about the ships' search. Atkins was intrigued and pitched Brownlee the idea to partner with the JASON team for student outreach. Katherine Collins, Stardust's outreach coordinator, put together a partnership with JASON as well as the Omniplex (now called the Science Museum of Oklahoma), a museum in Oklahoma City recommended by co-investigator Benton Clark.[55]

The Stardust team did make another smart decision about their education and public outreach plan. When the team looked at existing JPL missions for guidance, they realized quickly that they could not afford to be as comprehensive as the wide-ranging student outreach plans of flagships like Galileo and Cassini. The team focused on middle school children in grades five through eight. They followed a template established by Pathfinder, bringing in experts to help develop the outreach plan with 10 educators per year. After the first 10 developed the education material and beta-tested it, they assisted in selecting a subsequent 10, whom they would also mentor.

They "had the greatest reach of any program that I know," said Aimee Meyer, Stardust education and public outreach lead during flight. Atkins and the project team were very supportive of those outreach efforts. Meyer sat down separately with the science team and asked them to be open, to talk about their science with her so that the educational materials could reflect new discoveries. The science team responded with more information and requests of their own, such as web links back to their own

---

54   Niebur, S. (2009, 25 March). Personal interview with D. Brownlee. Located in "Stardust" file, NASA Historical Reference Collection, History Division, NASA Headquarters, Washington, DC.

55   Niebur, S. (2009, 10 August). Personal interview with K. Atkins. Located in "Genesis" file, NASA Historical Reference Collection, History Division, NASA Headquarters, Washington, DC.

university sites. In the first year alone, 25 educators reached over 1 million people, adding formal and informal talks at schools, Rotary Clubs, malls, libraries—anywhere they could, because they had become so excited about "their" mission.[56]

Management Approach

To stay within the Discovery cost cap, Stardust management worked diligently to keep the science focused and to forestall any temptations to let it grow. They kept the mission design and operations simple and reused as much as possible. As the team later reported: "Inheriting parts, hardware, software, and designs is required to leverage dollars and get efficient in doing missions faster and better, while staying inside a constrained budget."[57] Like Mars Pathfinder and NEAR before them, this team also used several innovative management techniques during the mission's design and implementation that can be summarized as follows:

- Adhering to a single, inspiring goal
- Designing to cost, employing only a strategic release of reserves
- Creating a flat management structure with communication between partners
- Resisting scope creep and strategically managing reserves

Joe Vellinga, the Stardust project manager, later explained that during development, he was often asked how to do "faster, better, cheaper," and what was necessary to leave out of the program. Nothing, he said, was left out, but much was done in less depth than previous methods would have required. Testing and planning were often done to a "good enough"—rather than a fail-safe—standard. The mission revolved around a single primary objective: to collect 1,000 cometary particles of a size greater than 15 micrometers and return them to Earth in satisfactory condition for analysis.

Discovery Program manager Mark Saunders had convinced the team that any overrun—or any projected increase identified by the Earned Value Management system—would lead to termination. There would be no 15 percent overrun allowance as seen on other projects and codified in the NASA Procedures and Guidelines document 7120.5A. A mission would have to manage its reserves and adjust in order to stay within the cost. Nevertheless, the team believed that it could be done and designed the mission to cost, prepared to make any compromises necessary to deliver the primary objective within the financial limits. They prioritized project science into primary, secondary, and tertiary science, and the engineering was planned accordingly. Primary science was

---

56   Niebur, S. (2009, 2 September). Personal interview with A. Meyer. Located in "Stardust" file, NASA Historical Reference Collection, History Division, NASA Headquarters, Washington, DC.

57   Atkins, K. et al. (2000, 2–5 May)." Stardust: Implementing a New Manage-to-Budget Paradigm." *Proceedings of the Fourth IAA Conference on Low Cost Spacecraft.*

nonnegotiable; other science was in the baseline but would be the first to be descoped if development threats made it necessary. Moreover, they would design the mission using as many existing capabilities as possible. For instance, they would buy existing components from other projects or industry rather than design them from scratch.[58]

In fact, Stardust was able to reuse quite a lot of systems, hardware, and experience from other missions. Where most JPL projects developed their own ground data systems, Stardust would reuse Mars Surveyor Operations Project (MSOP), the Mars Ground Data System from the late '90s. This was a real change from the old JPL paradigm of "having many teams with chiefs, having a lot of levels," Tom Duxbury, who handled Stardust mission operations, recalled, adding, "and they were not happy initially."

Duxbury fought resistance to change by implementing an open-door policy, welcoming discussion from anyone on the project without going through supervisors. "By eliminating a level or two in the organization, there were so few people working on the project at JPL that it was very easy for me to work with each of them one-on-one if needed."[59] The camera was also a re-flown technology. The lens, filter, wheel, and shutter were Voyager spares, and the charge-coupled device was a spare from Cassini. Other components inherited their designs from Cassini and Mars Pathfinder but were built new.[60] Lockheed Martin would operate the spacecraft. Even the Lockheed Martin Product Development Office was shared with Mars Surveyor '98. The team soon initiated project-to-project communication, shared parts stores and procurements, shared staffing where possible, and shared JPL and Lockheed Martin facilities. The team designed the mission to be done within the resource envelope and emphasized this approach at the System Requirements Review, which they also treated as a Capability and Requirements Review (CRR)—the culmination of design-to-cost. Preparation for the CRR included an examination of possible existing capabilities for meeting the requirements, what modifications were required and what gaps remained, and what components needed to be developed for Stardust alone. This was essentially an

---

58   Vellinga, J. (2007, 6 February). "Bringing a Comet Home." Project Management Challenge 2007. See also K. L. Atkins (2004). "How to Plan and Manage Reserves Effectively." *2004 IEEE Aerospace Conference Proceedings* (IEEE Cat. No.04TH8720), vol. 6. 3942–3955 doi:10.1109/AERO.2004.1368212.

59   Niebur, S. (2009, 4 September). Personal interview with T. Duxbury. Located in "Stardust" file, NASA Historical Reference Collection, History Division, NASA Headquarters, Washington, DC.

60   Newburn, Ray, and Ken Williams, "Pictures from Space," Stardust Newsletter, vol. 1. no. 4, December 2003.

inheritance review of each item, complete with risk assessment and detailed justification for reserve requirements on new or modified hardware; a reserve of 100 percent for new hardware required for the primary objective was not unusual for this project.[61]

An integrated schedule (and the budget change log) helped managers see when the major challenges to the mission were likely to occur and quantify their possible effects, driving the reserve required for that component and thus the overall level of reserves required at any given time in the mission. As major milestones were met, a percentage of the reserves could be released, as the soft lien that had been held against it was no longer necessary. Stardust in many ways redefined design-to-cost for a science-driven mission in a cost- and schedule-capped environment like the Discovery Program.

Tom Duxbury looked to Clementine's "faster, better, cheaper" techniques for mission operations and science. He eliminated organizational boundaries where possible and slashed management positions to flatten the organization. "The Discovery philosophy was that we were a 'team' and not a group of contractors and subcontractors," he later said. "I did not have a group of JPL system engineers on project staff looking over Lockheed Martin and MSOP shoulders. We had a simple mission and did not need to complicate the operations by having layer upon layer of organization." The Stardust project office consisted of a part-time manager, a secretary, and a part-time accountant; the rest of the JPL team members remained in their respective Technical Divisions. This was a radical departure from the structure of most projects at JPL. "It was easy to determine the key positions that needed to be filled and those that could be reduced or eliminated," said Duxbury.[62]

The mission plan was treated as a partnership in all ways, formalized with the Mission Definition and Requirements Agreement, a four-party agreement signed by NASA, Principal Investigator Brownlee, JPL, and Lockheed Martin.[63] JPL provided only very limited oversight with Lockheed Martin. In return, Lockheed Martin opened all its activities to JPL and Brownlee, and the group made communication a priority. The team took full advantage of new telecommunication options, issuing team members pagers to be used for urgent questions; the person paged would simply dial in to a standing "meet me" telephone number and answer the question without the need to

---

61   K. L. Atkins (2004). "How to Plan and Manage Reserves Effectively." *2004 IEEE Aerospace Conference Proceedings* (IEEE Cat. No.04TH8720), vol. 6. 3942–3955 doi:10.1109/AERO.2004.1368212. Niebur, S. (2009, 10 August). Personal interview with K. Atkins. Located in "Genesis" file, NASA Historical Reference Collection, History Division, NASA Headquarters, Washington, DC.

62   Niebur, S. (2009, 4 September). Personal interview with T. Duxbury. Located in "Stardust" file, NASA Historical Reference Collection, History Division, NASA Headquarters, Washington, DC.

63   "Stardust Mission Definition and Requirements Agreement, Rev 3." (2000, June). Located in Stardust Project Library, Jet Propulsion Laboratory, Pasadena, CA.

get on a plane and view the work in person. The system allowed over 30 calls to be held concurrently. Moreover, regular telecons helped the partners get to know each other, which facilitated trust.

JPL agreed to use commercial off-the-shelf software to which Lockheed Martin was accustomed, including Microsoft Project, Microframe Program Manager, and FastTrack for top-level schedules, so that both could see various levels of detail of cost, schedule, and the like. E-mail became commonly used, and servers were replicated, mirroring each other every 30 minutes through the existing firewalls—a significant technical advance for the time. Teams worked together on a project-to-project level to identify parts stores and common procurements to save the project—rather than their institution—money. Management worked to integrate the team beyond the standard capabilities and provide an overarching sense of camaraderie. The team went so far as to note later: "The [communication] structure promotes team cohesiveness and open communications—there are no secrets across institution boundaries." They added that this "new openness and partnership" enabled the electronic exchange of timely internal earned-value information heretofore unobtainable.[64]

The Stardust team became advocates of "virtual co-location" by arranging Monthly Management Reviews by web and telephone and urging other project managers to do the same.[65] These frequent virtual meetings helped to reinforce the team dynamic, even as it was spread out between Pasadena (JPL), Denver (Lockheed Martin), Seattle (University of Washington, where the Principal Investigator was based), Chicago (University of Chicago, which was building the Dust Flux Monitor Instrument), Germany (Max Planck Institute, which was building the Cometary and Interstellar Dust Analyzer), and co-investigator institutions, with launch preparation in Florida and preliminary examination and sample distribution in Texas.

Earned Value Management was one of the last project areas to be filled. Bredt Martin joined the project as Manager of Business Operations and Information Systems in January 1996 after 10 years at JPL as an engineer working on spacecraft thermal environments, managing Hubble Space Telescope planning, and managing program control for the SeaWinds scatterometer project, among other things. When Martin asked to join the Stardust project, not only was he welcomed, but, as he had experience with

---

64   Atkins K. L., et al. (2000, 2–5 May). "Stardust: Implementing a New Manage-to-Budget Paradigm." *Proceedings of the Fourth IAA Conference on Low Cost Spacecraft.* Laurel: Johns Hopkins University.

65   Atkins, K. L., et al. (2000, 2–5 May). "Stardust: Implementing a New Manage-to-Budget Paradigm." *Proceedings of the Fourth IAA Conference on Low Cost Spacecraft.* Laurel: Johns Hopkins University. See also Vellinga, J. (2007, 6 February). "Bringing a Comet Home." Project Management Challenge 2007. See also Atkins, K. L. (2004). "How to Plan and Manage Reserves Effectively." *2004 IEEE Aerospace Conference Proceedings* (IEEE Cat. No.04TH8720), vol. 6. 3942–3955 doi:10.1109/AERO.2004.1368212.

Earned Value Management using the same software as was used at Lockheed Martin, he was asked to lead business operations and implement an Earned Value Management system on Stardust. (JPL was not a regular user of Earned Value Management software, as it had not previously been required by NASA or other sponsors.)

Since NASA told the project team that financial, technical, and schedule performance were of equal weight, the team took an optimistic approach to scheduling, planning for the best case and managing additional work as needed within the constraints of Earned Value Management. Earned Value was determined each month at the subsystem level, using both definitive milestones and honest assessments of its status to provide an early-warning system of lagging progress so that action could be taken by the project long before the problem worsened. The Earned Value Management system was shown to be effective within a few months of the start of Phase C/D, when the personnel ramp-up and work performed at Lockheed failed to keep up with the aggressive baseline schedule. Because Earned Value Management alerted the team of Lockheed's impending bottleneck, they were able to do a recovery replan early in the program. In another example, the team incorporated into the resource baseline a month of funded schedule margin before Assembly, Test, and Launch Operations; two months during Assembly, Test, and Launch Operations in Denver; and one month at the Cape. This funded schedule margin was viewed as a planned early release of schedule reserves—a resource that could be tapped as required. The team focused on early identification of problems, with workarounds; early release of reserves (this plan was identified by the team as a form of self-insurance); and risk reduction actions that could be developed quickly as necessary.[66] Stardust credited the use of Earned Value Management, Total Quality Management, and Reengineering principles for keeping costs under control.[67]

Requirements Creep Camel

There was both an individual and a collective resistance to scope creep on Stardust. The mission's unofficial mantra became: "Do not allow the 'requirements creep camel' to get his nose under the tent." There were certainly opportunities for scope creep, such as the science team's midcourse introduction of a mechanism to capture volatiles as well as particles. Because the process added unknown risks to the mission, the project rejected its inclusion. Other "nice to have" technologies included additional instrumentation for the new heatshield design, this time pushed by another NASA center, Ames, through

66   Atkins, K. L., et al. (2000, 2–5 May). "Stardust: Implementing a New Manage-to-Budget Paradigm." *Proceedings of the Fourth IAA Conference on Low Cost Spacecraft.* Laurel: Johns Hopkins University.

67   Atkins, K. L., et al. (2000, 2–5 May). "Stardust: Implementing a New Manage-to-Budget Paradigm." *Proceedings of the Fourth IAA Conference on Low Cost Spacecraft.* Laurel: Johns Hopkins University; Vellinga, J. (2007, 6 February). "Bringing a Comet Home." Project Management Challenge 2007.

NASA Headquarters, but the project held the line and did not incorporate the changes (even though it would have benefited heatshield analyses for future missions). Only one major improvement was accepted: the addition of variable-density aerogel, at no additional cost. To keep the cost fixed, the team quickly learned that the set mission requirements could under no circumstances change. "When cost is committed," said Joe Vellinga of Lockheed Martin, "requirements are frozen."[68] The project committed to the Mission Definition and Requirements Agreement (MDRA) and pushed back on new mandates without appropriate levels of reserves attached, later emphasizing: "The use of original MDRA reserve to cover added scope not in the MDRA is never justifiable."[69] The mission's commitment to not allowing requirements creep was challenged a number of times, but Ken Atkins of JPL held the line so diligently that at his retirement, Brownlee gifted him with a toy camel of his own.[70]

Stardust developed and followed a reserves management plan based on its design-to-cost approach.[71] The plan included reserves scheduled to be released at key points in the mission or to buy down risk. As the design matured, new capabilities were found and new requirements suggested, but the mission stood firm; new requirements were not allowed to find their way into the baseline mission.[72] At Monthly Management Reviews, Atkins would present risk, reserves, and the price of "full-time equivalent" workers to combat a particular issue. Over the lifetime of the project, said Atkins, "I was able to release reserves to preemptively counter threats and risk. Looking for ways to attack risk before it attacked us, we spent about a million dollars on risk reduction before launch."[73] The mission would have no project-level overruns, with over a million dollars remaining in the budget at launch.

68   Vellinga, J. (2007, 6 February). "Bringing a Comet Home." Project Management Challenge 2007. See also Atkins, K. L. (2004). "How to Plan and Manage Reserves Effectively." *2004 IEEE Aerospace Conference Proceedings* (IEEE Cat. No.04TH8720), vol. 6. 3942–3955 doi:10.1109/AERO.2004.1368212.

69   Atkins, K. L. (2004). "How to Plan and Manage Reserves Effectively." *2004 IEEE Aerospace Conference Proceedings* (IEEE Cat. No.04TH8720), vol. 6. 3942–3955 doi:10.1109/AERO.2004.1368212.

70   Vellinga, J. (2007, 6 February). "Bringing a Comet Home." Project Management Challenge 2007.

71   Atkins, K. L. (2004). "How to Plan and Manage Reserves Effectively." *2004 IEEE Aerospace Conference Proceedings* (IEEE Cat. No.04TH8720), vol. 6. 3942–3955 doi:10.1109/AERO.2004.1368212.

72   Vellinga, J. (2007, 6 February). "Bringing a Comet Home." Project Management Challenge 2007. See also Atkins, K. L. (2004). "How to Plan and Manage Reserves Effectively." *2004 IEEE Aerospace Conference Proceedings* (IEEE Cat. No.04TH8720), vol. 6. 3942–3955 doi:10.1109/AERO.2004.1368212.

73   Atkins, K. L. (2006, 1 April). "Stardust: The Rewards of Commitment, Care, and Communication." *ASK Magazine*, 23. 14–17.

Stardust was selected by NASA in November 1995 to be the agency's next Discovery mission. Don Brownlee and co-investigator Ben Clark called Atkins with the news.[74] "At first I couldn't believe it," Atkins said. "I thought we had been the dark horse in this competition for a long time, so when I heard, it was like winning the lottery."[75] Atkins was thrilled to join the Discovery Program as a project manager. That afternoon, he went to share the news with Ek Davis, the Discovery Program Manager, who was at home, cancer-stricken. Davis was very pleased to hear of Stardust's selection, and the two sat and talked about the achievement. A local radio station called for comment, and Atkins did the interview from Davis's house, with Davis there in his wheelchair. "I think I was about the last JPLer to talk to him because the next day, he was gone," said Atkins.[76] Davis died of cancer on 24 November 1995.[77]

The Mission

When Mark Saunders, the Discovery Program Manager, debriefed the proposing teams, Atkins recalled, "[I]t was totally equal in terms of the number of points except in one spot. The deciding factor in this was outreach and you won."[78] The outreach plan had been developed in line with everything else on the mission—simple, straightforward, and leveraging work previously developed on other projects. "It was kind of amazing to me that somehow all of a sudden we came out on top. We had never gotten very far before," said Brownlee, the mission PI, recalling the many comet mission proposals in previous years.[79]

The fundamental breakthrough for this mission as a scientific investigation was its design. By bringing the samples home, the in situ analysis at the comet could be reduced to virtually zero. This eliminated instrument miniaturization costs and flight testing for an instrument payload, to include radiation, vibration, and environmental assessments to ensure its survival on top of a rocket. "The point of sample return is to flip the paradigm," said Atkins. "If I can bring back a sample and hand it to you, there's no limit to the science you can do."[80]

74   Atkins, K. L. (2003, 1 October). "Mr. Stardust's Wild Ride." *ASK Magazine*, 14. 16–19.

75   Ainsworth, D. (1995, 1 December). "Stardust Named Next Discovery Mission." *JPL Universe*, 25(24).

76   Niebur, S. (2009, 10 August). Personal interview with K. Atkins. Located in "Genesis" file, NASA Historical Reference Collection, History Division, NASA Headquarters, Washington, DC.

77   Whalen, M. 1995, 1 December. "Discovery Office Manager 'Ek' Davis Dies." *JPL Universe*, 25(24).

78   Niebur, S. (2009, 10 August). Personal interview with K. Atkins. Located in "Genesis" file, NASA Historical Reference Collection, History Division, NASA Headquarters, Washington, DC.

79   Niebur, S. (2009, 25 March). Personal interview with D. Brownlee. Located in "Stardust" file, NASA Historical Reference Collection, History Division, NASA Headquarters, Washington, DC.

80   Milstein, M. (1999, February–March). "Bring Me the Tail of Wild-2." *Air & Space*. 55–61.

The primary objective of the mission was to collect 1,000 cometary particles greater than 15 microns and return them to Earth in a condition satisfactory for analysis. The particles were expected to consist of a mixture of the ancient, pre-solar interstellar grains and nebular condensates that were frozen into comets at the far edges of the solar nebula during the formation of the solar system. Mission success hinged on that objective.

Secondary science objectives were to take 65 images of the comet's nucleus within 2,000 kilometers; to image the coma; to analyze particles in situ within the coma; and to collect and return 100 small, high-velocity, "new" interstellar particles from a stream of "fresh" interstellar grains discovered entering the solar system from the same direction as interstellar gas.[81]

Tertiary objectives—not critical but considered important by the team—were to measure certain aspects of the comet as the spacecraft flew through its coma. These aspects included the coma dust flux, particle size distribution, integrated dust fluence, large particle momentum, and dust flux profiles over the spacecraft's path. Another tertiary objective was to collect coma volatiles and perform in situ compositional analyses of interplanetary dust particles, interstellar particles, and any other particle types encountered during the cometary flyby. To accomplish all this, the Stardust mission was outfitted with a sample collector, a mass spectrometer, a dust detector, and a shared engineering optical navigation camera.[82]

The choice of comet, like all comet missions, was limited by those traveling through the inner solar system at the projected time of encounter. This mission, however, also required the selection of a comet traveling slowly enough to allow Stardust to approach and eventually pass the comet, collecting samples as the speeds converged, limiting particle fragmentation. Comet 81P/Wild (also called Wild 2) was identified as an accessible target by JPL flight engineer Chen-Wan Yen.[83] Discovered by Swiss astronomer Paul Wild in 1978, Wild 2 is a relatively fresh, four-kilometer-wide comet whose outer layers have been subjected to limited heating by the Sun.[84] For centuries, it had been in a stable orbit with a perihelion of 4.9 astronomical units (AU) and an aphelion of 25 AU. Then, in 1974, the comet passed near the giant planet Jupiter, which caused a reverse Jupiter gravity assist, knocking the comet into an orbit much closer to the

81   Grün, E., et al. (1993). "Discovery of Jovian Dust Streams and Interstellar Grains by the Ulysses Spacecraft." *Nature* 362(28–430).

82   Brownlee, D. E., et al. (2003), "Stardust: Comet and Interstellar Dust Sample Return Mission," *J. Geophys. Res.*, 108, 8111, doi:10.1029/2003JE002087, E10.

83   Milstein, M. (1999, February–March). "Bring Me the Tail of Wild-2." *Air & Space*. 55–61.

84   Platt, J. (1997, 18 April). "Stardust Team Studies Wild 2, Hale-Bopp's Cometary Cousin." Downloaded from *https://www.jpl.nasa.gov/news/nasas-stardust-team-studies-hale-bopps-cometary-cousin*.

Sun, with a perihelion of 1.58 AU and an aphelion of 5.2 AU.[85] This interaction put a comet made of materials from the faraway Kuiper belt region of the solar nebula within reach of Earth's scientists—without the decades-long journey that would ordinarily be required. It was the ultimate shortcut to sampling the outer solar system.

"Stardust could provide a new window into the distant past," said Simon Green of the Open University's Planetary and Space Science Research Institute.[86] The conditions in the early solar nebula were both unknown and vital to understanding the formation conditions and subsequent evolution of planets such as Earth. Since the icy cometary particles would be unchanged by heating or other evolutionary processes over the 4.5-billion-year interval, they would reflect an accurate measurement of the outer solar system at formation. A major fraction of the dust particles incorporated in the comet, in fact, would be interstellar grains that predated even the solar nebula. "There's nothing left on Earth's surface that's nearly as old as these bits of crystals and minerals," said Carlton Allen, who worked with the mission as astromaterials curator at NASA's Johnson Space Center in Houston, Texas.[87]

Staffing Up

Staffing the new mission was an unexpected challenge. In 1995, NASA Administrator Dan Goldin prepared to implement a Reduction in Force at NASA Headquarters. Many management positions were eliminated, and, separately, JPL employees working on various mission proposals had gone back to their day jobs. There was a renewed focus at the lab on employees working on projects instead of employees managing others, and lab leadership told Atkins, the Stardust project manager, that his mission could not have a Deputy Project Manager. This made traditional project management activities difficult, but Atkins agreed. He divided mission responsibilities into as few areas as possible: science, led by Brownlee, the Principal Investigator; flight system, led by Lockheed Martin; and mission design, operations, and navigation, led by Tom Duxbury.

Once that was complete, all that remained was to create the organization chart to justify the decision and to obtain the right people to lead these areas and the next level down. Among the personnel brought on board was Rick Grammier, who had been Atkins's deputy in the electronics area. Management appointed Grammier as project engineer. For adjudicating issues where the Principal Investigator and project manager disagreed, Atkins created an oversight board chaired by the PI and reporting to the project manager; with Charles Elachi, director of the JPL Space and Earth

---

85   Brownlee, D. E., et al. (2003), "Stardust: Comet and Interstellar Dust Sample Return Mission," *J. Geophys. Res.*, 108, 8111, doi:10.1029/2003JE002087, E10.

86   Briggs, H. (2006, 15 January). "Stardust Capsule Returns to Earth." *BBC News.*

87   Irion, R. (2009, 25 November). "The Secrets Within Cosmic Dust: Dust Captured by a Spacecraft from a Comet's Tail Holds Clues to the Origin of the Solar System." *Smithsonian.*

Science Programs Directorate; Noel Hinners, the vice president of flight systems at Lockheed Martin Space Systems; and the NASA Discovery Project Manager. Atkins also set up an advisory board for real-time mentoring with experts like Tony Spear of Mars Pathfinder; Tom Gavin, the Cassini flight systems manager; Mike Sander, deputy director of JPL's Space and Earth Science Programs Directorate; and Joe Savino, an electronics expert.[88] Staffing up had to be accomplished quickly, since Phase A and B together were limited to 18 months.[89]

Mission Design

The most challenging aspects of the Stardust mission were expected to be the development of the aerogel collectors and the spacecraft's survival in a challenging environment. For the first few months after launch, several instruments on the spacecraft would operate, but the sample collectors would remain closed. En route to Wild 2 and on the return, a sample collector would open to collect interstellar grains. An optional flyby of the asteroid Annefrank would allow testing of the in situ instrument payload and the encounter software. Shortly before the spacecraft flew past Wild 2, the aerogel collectors would open to collect particles of ancient cometary dust at a crawling relative speed of just 6.1 kilometers per second. The collectors would then close, and the spacecraft would continue its two-year journey back to Earth.

Aerogel—Stardust's "secret weapon"—is extremely low-density silicon glass that is 99 percent empty space, with a density of less than 1 percent of that of typical glass. Some members of the team called it "frozen smoke." According to Brownlee, the PI, "Aerogel is only a little bit denser than air. Sometimes we lay it on the lab table, and we can't find it."[90]

The astonishing substance was not invented for Stardust. The first scientific papers announcing the substance were published in 1931 and 1932 by Samuel Kistler, an instructor at the College of the Pacific. Having just begun his doctoral work in the summer of 1927, Kistler spent the academic year teaching undergraduate courses. He learned to work with wet gels from a professor there, J. W. McBain, and, with assistance from undergraduate Charles H. Learned, employed supercritical fluid drying to create the first aerogel.[91] This new material was a silica aerogel: a substance that captured imaginations with its wispy appearance, extremely low density, and incredible strength.

88   Niebur, S. (2009, 10 August). Personal interview with K. Atkins. Located in "Genesis" file, NASA Historical Reference Collection, History Division, NASA Headquarters, Washington, DC.

89   Ainsworth, D. (1996, 12 January). "JPL Adds New Discovery Mission to Its Agenda." *JPL Universe*. 3.

90   David, L. (1996, July–August). "Dr. Brownlee's Comet Catching Machine." *Final Frontier*. 8–9.

91   Kistler, S. (1931). "Coherent Expanded Aerogels and Jellies." *Nature*, 127(741). *https://doi. org/10.1038/127741a0*. See also Kistler, S. S. (1932). "Coherent Expanded-Aerogels." *The Journal of Physical Chemistry*, 36(1), 52–64. *https://doi.org/10.1021/j150331a003*.

Kistler licensed aerogel to Monsanto Corp. in the early 1940s. The company described it as a "light, friable, slightly opalescent solid containing as much as 95 percent air volume," created by replacing the water in a special silica gel with alcohol and heating the material to 550 degrees F under a constant pressure, and then dropping the pressure to 20 inches of mercury for 10 minutes. The process is called supercritical fluid drying.[92]

Aerogel was used for different coating and detector experiments in the years before Stardust. "There were several physics departments around the world that were actually making aerogel for these Cherenkov counters," said Brownlee, "so the word of aerogel and its properties was sort of floating around the physics community at some level."[93] Tsou first encountered the material on a visit to Los Alamos, where he saw a small piece on a windowsill and was intrigued with its properties. In the mid- to late 1990s, Brownlee and Tsou came up with ways to fly aerogel in space on the Shuttle. Larger tests, using space station–attached payloads and European missions, soon "indicated you could collect particles at this kind of speed and have them survive intact. And that's really the technology that made Stardust possible, finding low-density capsule materials," said Brownlee.[94]

Aerogel proved the enabling technology for cometary sample return on this mission; over 1,000 particles larger than 15 microns were expected in the 1,000 square centimeters of ultra-fine mesostructure silica aerogel. Laboratory tests led the scientists to expect, among other things, hydrated silicates, noble gases, and organic material to be retained during the material's approximate 6-kilometer-per-second encounter with the comet.[95]

The spacecraft was based on the Lockheed Martin SpaceProbe deep space bus, built with flat panels made of thin sheets of graphite over a lightweight aluminum "honeycomb" core. The spacecraft had a minimum of moving parts: one to deploy the sample tray assembly out of the sample return capsule and the NavCam scanning mirror for tracking the comet's nucleus.[96] Duxbury described the sample tray assem-

---

92   Kistler, S. (1943, February). *Chemical and Metallurgical Engineering*, February. 144.

93   Niebur, S. (2009, 25 March). Personal interview with D. Brownlee. Located in "Stardust" file, NASA Historical Reference Collection, History Division, NASA Headquarters, Washington, DC.

94   Ibid.

95   Tsou, P., Brownlee, D., Sandford, S., Hörz, F., & Zolensky, M. (2003). "Wild 2 and Interstellar Sample Collection and Earth Return." *Journal of Geophysical Research*, 108. *https://doi.org/10.1029/2003JE002109.*

96   Brownlee, D. E., et al. (2003), "Stardust: Comet and Interstellar Dust Sample Return Mission," *J. Geophys. Res.*, 108, 8111, doi:10.1029/2003JE002087, E10.

bly as having "shoulder and wrist joints," both of which could bend for deployment with the appropriate surface aligned with the direction of incoming dust particles.[97] Subsystems were fully redundant, except for the spacecraft battery.[98]

The spacecraft was protected by multilayer "Whipple shields" that functioned like the front bumpers on cars, stopping incoming particles from impacting the solar arrays and other sensitive elements of the main spacecraft. Cometary dust—the mission's raison d'être—was also its greatest nemesis. Mission designers had to collect sufficient dust on the sample collectors for future analysis but also protect the spacecraft from the dust encountered. Because the cometary environment was not well known at all, the mission faced a tough challenge indeed.[99]

The science team was small, consisting only of the most critical personnel needed to design a sample return mission. They were cometary scientists who could design the collectors and set requirements for the sample return, but the bulk of actual analyzing scientists were added later.

The mission would be in development for three years and in flight for seven. "For a low-cost mission, you can't really support a big science team," said Brownlee. "We were focused on getting the sample back.... If we had a little more money, it would have been nice to have a bigger science team, because the encounter images we got were fantastic," and the team could definitely have used more people to do image processing.[100]

Communication

In the early phases of spacecraft design, scientists and engineers of a new team must learn to communicate effectively with each other. This is especially important in cost-capped missions like those in the Discovery Program, as misunderstandings may lead to problems that cost time and money to fix. For instance, as Mike Zolensky, then-curator of stratospheric dust at Johnson Space Center, explained, "There was a meeting where we'd talk about the design of the sample return capsule—the SRC. The guy who designed that, he'd be in there showing us the design for the SRC, and someone would make some offhand comment, saying, 'Gee, what if we did this,' and then we'd forget about it. The next meeting, when we came back, he'd have totally redesigned the SRC,

---

97   "Stardust Reaches for Cosmic Dust." (2002, 16 August). *JPL Universe*, 32(17).

98   Brownlee, D. E., et al. (2003), Stardust: Comet and interstellar dust sample return mission, *J. Geophys. Res.*, 108, 8111, doi:10.1029/2003JE002087, E10.

99   Niebur, S. (2009, 10 August). Personal interview with E. Hirst. Located in "Genesis" file, NASA Historical Reference Collection, History Division, NASA Headquarters, Washington, DC.

100   Niebur, S. (2009, 25 March). Personal interview with D. Brownlee. Located in "Stardust" file, NASA Historical Reference Collection, History Division, NASA Headquarters, Washington, DC.

just because of this little comment that was just tossed out, this little discussion point, and he worked very hard to do that. That happened several times."[101] As soon as the spacecraft launched, the sample return capsule designer retired.[102]

The sample return capsule was derived from a prospective Mars sample return capsule designed by Martin Marietta Aerospace (which eventually became Lockheed Martin) in Littleton, Colorado.[103] The capsule design had some unresolved stability issues, but engineers added tungsten weights to its front, changing the center of gravity and the spin rate to partially address the problem. Another modification made was the addition of a drag chute to forestall the capsule turning upside down on reentry.[104]

Because of the planetary science community's extensive study of interstellar dust particles, as well as the history of cometary impacts on Earth, John Rummel, planetary protection officer, confidently declared that "comets are extremely unlikely places for life. Stardust will come back to us with a clean bill of health. Containment is not warranted."[105] The problem was the exact opposite: While a few grains of interstellar dust and a dash of cometary material posed no threat to Earth, Earth posed a threat to the sample. To mitigate this, the science team created a Contamination Control Plan prescribing the handling of the sample return capsule down to the sample grains themselves.[106] The canister had to be decontaminated before launch so as to minimize the introduction of Earth particles to cometary material. The team was dedicated to returning a clean sample for scientific analysis—a goal that had not been attempted since Apollo. The team planned carefully for sample return, starting with a thorough examination of the Apollo records still at Johnson Space Center.[107]

---

101   Niebur, S. (2009, 24 March). Personal interview with M. Zolensky. Located in "Stardust" file, NASA Historical Reference Collection, History Division, NASA Headquarters, Washington, DC.

102   Miscommunications between scientists and engineers can result in suboptimal teaming, personal frustrations, and lost time. In a cost-capped program, lost time always incurs a concurrent financial cost—even if no actual changes are made. The story of the redesigned canister also reinforces another principle that would come to define good Discovery mission development: The resistance to scope creep. Every change costs money and time and should thus be resisted unless absolutely necessary.

103   Brownlee, D. E., et al. (2003), "Stardust: Comet and Interstellar Dust Sample Return Mission," *J. Geophys. Res.*, 108, 8111, doi:10.1029/2003JE002087, E10.

104   Niebur, S. (2009, 25 March). Personal interview with D. Brownlee. Located in "Stardust" file, NASA Historical Reference Collection, History Division, NASA Headquarters, Washington, DC.

105   Ballingrud, D. (1999, 14 January). "Next, NASA to Send Craft to Chase Comet." *St. Petersburg Times*, 1A.

106   Zolensky M.E. and Girard T. (1997). "Stardust Spacecraft Program Contamination Control Plan." *JSC Publication 27954*. 26.

107   Niebur, S. (2009, 24 March). Personal interview with M. Zolensky. Located in "Stardust" file, NASA Historical Reference Collection, History Division, NASA Headquarters, Washington, DC.

Instruments

The primary goal of the Stardust mission was to safely return collected cometary material. In-flight science was limited largely to images collected by the Optical Navigation Camera (NavCam); dust flux and size measurements taken by the Dust Flux Monitor Instrument; and in situ analyses of particle composition using the Cometary and Interstellar Dust Analyzer (CIDA) instrument.

NavCam was a modified version of a Voyager Wide Field and Planetary Camera and featured a 1024 × 1024 charge-coupled device detector built originally for the Cassini Imaging Science Subsystem with digital electronics modified from the Clementine spacecraft. The camera optics used a Voyager Wide Angle Optical Assembly with a 200-millimeter focal length lens. The filter wheel and shutter were also Voyager spares. Stardust added a scan mirror mechanism to vary its available viewing angles (this design had heritage from Mars Pathfinder) and a new periscope to protect the scanning mirror in the coma's dust particle storm. The images would have a resolution of 59.4 microradians (mrad) per pixel—an order of magnitude better than Giotto's images of Comet Halley. Co-investigator Ray Newburn of the Jet Propulsion Laboratory was responsible for the imaging science from this camera.[108]

Any spacecraft flying so close to a comet would necessarily encounter a great deal of dust. To study this phenomenon, the spacecraft's Dust Flux Monitor Subsystem included two quartz piezoelectric acoustic sensors, which were called, collectively, the Dual Acoustic Sensor System; as well as the dedicated Dust Flux Monitor Instrument, itself a copy of the High Rate Detector element of the Cosmic Dust Analyzer instrument used on Cassini. The sensor unit of the 1.7-kilogram Dust Flux Monitor Instrument—a highly sensitive instrument designed to detect particles as small as a few microns—was based on a special polarized plastic dust sensor developed in the laboratory of John Simpson in Chicago, and it was mounted on Stardust's Whipple shield to measure oncoming particles. Because the instrument could measure the flux of interplanetary dust encountered throughout the mission, its data could be employed for multiple purposes: to protect the spacecraft from the high flux of particles in the coma, to understand spacecraft anomalies, to measure the impact rate and mass distribution of particles during the spacecraft's encounter with the comet, and to provide context for the collected dust samples.[109]

Anthony Tuzzolino of the University of Chicago, the instrument lead, was no stranger to spaceflight, having contributed his expertise to 35 space missions, including the dust

---

108   Newburn, R. L., Bhaskaran, S., Duxbury, T. C., Fraschetti, G., Radey, T., and Schwochert, M. (2003), "Stardust Imaging Camera." *J. Geophys. Res.*, 108, 8116, doi:10.1029/2003JE002081.

109   Tuzzolino, A. J., Economou, T. E., McKibben, R. B., Simpson, J. A., McDonnell, J. A. M., Burchell, M. J., Vaughan, B. A. M., Tsou, P., Hanner, M. S., Clark, B. C., & Brownlee, D. E. (2003). "Dust Flux Monitor Instrument for the Stardust mission to comet Wild 2." *Journal of Geophysical Research: Planets*, 108(E10). *https://doi.org/10.1029/2003JE002086.*

detectors on the two spacecraft Vega 1 and Vega 2, both bound for Halley's Comet, and the High Rate Detector on Cassini. Despite this wealth of experience, Tuzzolino was frank in interviews, saying that he couldn't predict the exact particle size distribution with precision. "I just don't know. Every comet is different."[110]

The second dust detector, CIDA, had strong heritage from the instruments that flew on Giotto, as well as PUMA 1 and 2 that flew on Vega 1 and 2 to Halley's Comet. The CIDA instrument was a 100-square-centimeter silver target hooked up to a mass spectrometer capable of measuring particle mass. When a dust particle impacts the silver target, charged ions are produced that then travel down an instrument tube and bounce off a reflector for counting. Since heavier ions take longer to travel through the tube, the time of flight of each ion from the target to the detector can be used to calculate its mass and determine the elemental and chemical compositions of cometary or interstellar particles. CIDA measurements of in-flight impacts could be compared with the returned interstellar samples for context; in return, the returned samples would provide ground truth data for the instrument's measurements. The instrument co-investigator was Jochen Kissel of the Max Planck Institut für Aeronomie.[111]

The team expected the dust detectors to return plenty of data, just as the sample return capsule would return plenty of particles. "We'll have more than enough," said Thanasis Economou, Stardust and Mars Pathfinder co-investigator from the University of Chicago.[112] While the large number of particles would be a boon for scientists, it was a challenge for the engineers who had to design the spacecraft and its protective systems. The spacecraft would have to survive not only the thundering launch and coldness of space, but also the cometary hailstorm pelting the spacecraft at relative speeds many times that of rifle bullets. Later, the spacecraft would have to survive a faster reentry than any previous spacecraft. At 2.7 AU, the spacecraft solar cells would also have to operate farther from the Sun than any previous mission. At that distance, sunlight would be less, and thus available power diminished.[113]

The last Stardust investigation would involve no dedicated hardware but rather used existing engineering systems for scientific observations. The X-band transponder, originally developed for Cassini and used in the spacecraft telecommunications system, would also estimate the upper limits of the overall mass of the comet. The spacecraft gyro and accelerometer necessary for its attitude control subsystem could

---

110   Knoppes, S. (2003, 31 December). "University of Chicago instruments to reach comet, Mars in same busy week." University of Chicago news release.

111   Kissel, J., Glasmachers, A., Hoerner, H., & Henkel, H. (2001). "Cida-A Cometary and Interstellar Dust Analyzer for The Stardust Mission." *COSPAR Colloquia Series*, 11, 370. *https://doi. org/10.1016/S0964-2749(01)80087-1.*

112   Bridges, A. (2004, 6 January). "NASA spacecraft on way home to Earth with comet sample." *USA Today.*

113   Vellinga, J. (2007, 6 February). "Bringing a Comet Home." Project Management Challenge 2007.

be used to estimate the magnitude of large particle impacts and the overall dust flux. John Anderson at JPL led these dynamic science investigations.[114] All the in-flight science would be considered supporting measurements for the primary goal of sample collection and would give context to the returned cometary and interstellar particles.

Phase B

Shortly after selection, Ken Atkins, the Stardust project manager, realized that the $9.6 million available in his first budget would be insufficient to kick-start the project, and he was soon proved correct. After selection, the team discovered that transponders—necessary for spacecraft telemetry, command, and control—were needed earlier than planned. Atkins asked for additional funds to procure them as "long-lead items": components that, though not required for assembly until Phase C, would need to be developed much earlier, in Phase B. This would provide time for production and integration into the telecom system. Atkins approached Don Brownlee, the Principal Investigator, but Brownlee held the line, knowing the tight constraints of the Discovery Program. Here, an overrun of one dollar could trigger cancellation. Thankfully, NEAR had recently reported an under-run, and that money was available for use by Stardust to prevent a later overrun in cost, schedule, or both.

In October 1996, all flight instruments and spacecraft subsystems passed the Preliminary Design Review held for Jet Propulsion Laboratory management, NASA Headquarters representatives, and an independent review board.[115]

As the spacecraft moved into its final design phase, the science team and other astronomers continued to make observations of Comet Wild 2 to better understand its brightness, as well as the size and quantity of the gas and dust particles, in order to prepare for data collection and spacecraft protection. Observations were done at Lowell Observatory, the Lunar and Planetary Laboratory (University of Arizona), the W. M. Keck Observatory, and Palomar Observatory.[116]

The spacecraft design, including all flight instruments and spacecraft subsystems, passed the Critical Design Review in August 1997. "We've tried to use as much inherited, proven, and low-cost subsystem elements as possible. However, we needed to design some unique elements, such as the means for capturing comet dust and interstellar

---

114 Brownlee, D. E., et al. (2003), "Stardust: Comet and interstellar dust sample return mission," *J. Geophys. Res.*, 108, 8111, doi:10.1029/2003JE002087, E10.

115 Platt, J. (1996, 1 November). "Stardust passes preliminary design review." *JPL Universe.*

116 Platt, J. (1997, 18 April). "Stardust team studies Wild 2, Hale-Bopp's cometary cousin." *JPL Universe.* Downloaded from *https://www.jpl.nasa.gov/news/nasas-stardust-team-studies-hale-bopps-cometary-cousin.*

particles," said Atkins. Sixty million dollars had been spent by this time, with another $68 million planned for spending before launch. Thirty-seven million dollars would be needed for operations and the return to Earth.[117]

Stardust was approved to begin assembly and testing in early January 1998. In February, project engineers performed a successful drop test of the sample return capsule at the U.S. Army's Dugway Proving Grounds at the Utah Test and Training Range near Salt Lake City. The sample return capsule was lifted 3,960 meters using a balloon, and then dropped, swinging gently beneath its parachute to make a soft landing.[118]

Delivery and Launch

Aerogel development was an unexpected challenge. It terrified the team to learn just how friable it was during shipping from the Jet Propulsion Laboratory in California to Lockheed Martin in Colorado. "Oh my God," thought Brownlee, "if it did that just going from Pasadena to Denver, what's it going to do on the mission?"[119] Thankfully, it proved hardier when shipped to Cape Canaveral, which occurred on 11 November 1998.

Stardust launched on the second day of its twenty-day launch window, on 7 February 1999. The spacecraft, mounted atop a Delta II rocket, carried with it the hopes and dreams of not only the mission team and NASA, but also the names of over a million individuals, etched onto two microchips. Most of the names had been collected online by way of the mission website, The Planetary Society, the National Space Society, and a website for the movie Deep Impact, a comet disaster flick. The launch carried the spacecraft to a holding orbit 115 miles above Earth. Thirty minutes later, the upper-stage rocket ignited, freeing Stardust from its planet of origin. The launch was so accurate that the mission's intended first course correction maneuver was judged to be unnecessary.[120]

From a hill as close as one could safely get to Pad 17A, Brownlee watched the launch with Aimee Meyer, the mission's education and public outreach lead, and with a group of Stardust Educator Fellows. After a celebratory press conference, both he and project manager Atkins again drove to the launch site, Atkins recalled, "just to be sure that it's gone, and be glad."[121]

Several months after the successful launch, Atkins retired. Mission manager Tom Duxbury was promoted to project manager in August 2000. Duxbury had not intended to stay on the project after launch but was inspired by the loss in 1999 of two spacecraft

117   Platt, J. (1997, 22 August). "Stardust spacecraft passes critical design review." *JPL Universe.*

118   Murrill, M. B. (1999, July–August). "Stardust readies for Feb. launch." *JPL Universe.* 4.

119   Niebur, S. (2009, 25 March). Personal interview with D. Brownlee. Located in "Stardust" file, NASA Historical Reference Collection, History Division, NASA Headquarters, Washington, DC.

120   Stardust status report, 8 May. (1999, 5 March). NASA/JPL news release.

121   Niebur, S. (2009, 10 August). Personal interview with K. Atkins. Located in "Genesis" file, NASA Historical Reference Collection, History Division, NASA Headquarters, Washington, DC.

at Mars, which brought home the importance of development personnel remaining with their missions during the operations phase. (Duxbury agreed to stay with the stipulation that he would serve as project manager only half-time. He would spend the other half working on Mars science, an agreement that he promoted as perfectly in line with Discovery's "faster, better, cheaper" philosophy.)[122]

Cruise Phase

It wasn't smooth sailing for the spacecraft en route to Wild 2. Stardust went into safe mode 10 times during flight. Most notable, perhaps, was when a solar flare hit the spacecraft on 8 November 2000, confusing its star cameras and causing its onboard computer to reboot five times in six minutes, leaving the spacecraft in terminal safe mode.[123] Each safe mode event required controllers to wait for the next opportunity to communicate with the spacecraft and restart normal operations.[124]

Later testing revealed that the launch had not been incident-free. Test images taken by the navigation camera (and necessary to image Comet Wild 2) appeared blurry, as if the pictures were taken through a dirty lens. The team theorized that spacecraft degassing—that is, the diffusion and desorbing of compounds from the spacecraft surface—could have caused contaminants to be deposited on the lens surface, creating a thin film. In an attempt to remedy this, the operations team heated the optical path of the camera several times to burn off the contamination. Subsequent pictures taken just before Earth flyby in January 2001 showed that the resolution had been restored to nearly normal; the camera was now able to detect dimmer stars than before the fix.[125]

Interstellar Dust Collection

The CIDA instrument had been powered on shortly after launch. As the spacecraft traveled outbound, particles would splatter on its target with increased relative velocity, maximizing measurements of the stream of interstellar particles and enabling the study of smaller and rarer varieties.[126]

---

122   Ibid.

123   Atkins, K. L. (2006, 1 April). "Stardust: The rewards of commitment, care, and communication." *ASK Magazine*, 23. 14–17.

124   Atkins, K. L. (2006, 1 April). "Stardust: The rewards of commitment, care, and communication." *ASK Magazine*, 23. 14–17. See also "Stardust spacecraft enters 'safe' mode; transmits first image from space." (1999, 23 March). *CNN*; Niebur, S. (2009, 14 May). Personal interview with D. Jarrett and Kate Wolf. Located in "Discovery Program" file, NASA Historical Reference Collection, History Division, NASA Headquarters, Washington, DC.

125   NASA. (2001, 11 January). "NASA can see clearly now—just before Earth flyby." NASA News Release.

126   Brownlee, D. E., et al. (2003), "Stardust: Comet and interstellar dust sample return mission," *J. Geophys. Res.*, 108, 8111, doi:10.1029/2003JE002087, E10.

On 18 January 2000, and again on the 20th and 22nd, the spacecraft fired its propulsion system in a three-part maneuver to put it on target for an Earth gravity assist.[127] Several weeks later, with the spacecraft well on the inbound portion of its trajectory, scientists deemed the spacecraft as being parallel to a stream of interstellar particles passing through the solar system. Parallel vectors meant the impacts would be lessened, and on 22 February the team deployed the Stardust collector for its first interstellar dust collection period. Shortly after the collector's petals were closed on 1 May, several Co-Is working on data from CIDA announced they had detected complex carbon molecules one hundred times the size of a water molecule. Their size led Jochen Kissel, a co-investigator on Stardust, to tell the press: "Only organic molecules can reach those sizes." Don Brownlee, the Principal Investigator, urged caution when interpreting the in situ measurements but acknowledged that "if that is the composition of the interstellar particles, it's very exciting."

Organic molecules were intriguing to the mission scientists because contact with liquid water on the young Earth could have triggered the type of chemical reactions that are a prerequisite for the origin of life.[128] Scientists external to the team took it a step further, theorizing that the molecules might not only be carbon molecules, but rather, fragments of bacteria. Professor Chandra Wickramasinghe of Cardiff University, studying the data with his brother Professor Dayal Wickramasinghe of Australian National University, told a Scottish newspaper, "The results show oxygen and nitrogen at roughly the 10 percent level. That is just about the fraction we find in the molecules of life."[129] Years before sample return, the Stardust samples were already intriguing researchers.

Stardust's Earth flyby occurred on 15 January 2001. It passed early that morning approximately 5,950 kilometers above Earth, just southeast of the southern tip of Africa. This gave the spacecraft the energy boost necessary to speed its orbit from a two-year trip around the Sun to a one-and-a-half-year journey, taking it to Wild 2.[130]

As it flew, Stardust collected additional particles between 5 August and 9 December 2002. This interstellar dust was produced by the current generation of stars, opening new lines of research, including the possible comparison of ancient and newer dust compositions, yielding new clues to galactic evolution.[131] By the end of the year, Stardust had met and exceeded its goal of collecting interstellar particles for 150 days.[132] "We

127 "Stardust completes velocity maneuver." (2000, 4 February). *JPL Universe*, 30(3). 1.

128 Whitehouse, D. (2000, 3 May). "Organic molecules found in 'stardust.'" *BBC News Online.* Downloaded from *http://news.bbc.co.uk/1/hi/sci/tech/734780.stm* on May 15, 2009.

129 Euan, M. (2000, 4 May). "We're all aliens; Scientists find evidence that life began in space." *Daily Record.* 11.

130 "Stardust Earth flyby successful." (2001, January). *JPL Universe.* 2.

131 "Stardust reaches for cosmic dust." (2002, 16 August). *JPL Universe*, 32(17). 1.

132 Vellinga, J. (2007, 6 February). "Stardust: Bringing a Comet Home." Project Management Challenge 2007.

are getting the very best primitive samples that there are in the solar system. In my view, it's even better than we would have had if we had landed on the comet," said Brownlee about the interstellar particles.[133] "We believe that some of the particles in the comet will, in fact, be older than the Sun."[134]

Annefrank Flyby

Just before midnight on 1 November 2002, the Stardust spacecraft flew within 3,000 kilometers of asteroid Annefrank. The team used this incidental flyby as an engineering test for the spacecraft subsystems, performing a "full dress rehearsal, with the cometary dust detector deployed, the spacecraft poised in its flyby attitude, and with all science instruments on," described Brownlee.[135] Though the navigation camera had trouble distinguishing faint objects from Annefrank due to similar levels of brightness, it ultimately succeeded, with 71 of the 106 images taken featuring the asteroid.[136] The Dust Flux Monitor Instrument took data for 27 minutes, and Kissel was encouraged by the test of the interstellar dust analyzer. The spacecraft performed extremely well under these demanding circumstances. So the team was greatly encouraged in their planning for the Wild 2 encounter that would occur 14 months from then.

"We learned a lot that will improve our operations at Wild 2 based upon the lessons learned at Annefrank, but the bottom line is that if Annefrank had been Wild 2, we would have succeeded," said Tom Duxbury, the mission manager. As a bonus, the Stardust team was surprised to discover that Annefrank was about twice the size (8 kilometers instead of 4 kilometers) estimated by remote observations, due to its dimmer surface.[137]

SRLIDAP and Progress Back at the Lab

At launch, there had been only four sample analysts on the science team and the plan for science analysis was still in development. Moreover, the team was divided as to the best way to proceed with sample analysis after Earth return and preliminary examination at the curation facility. More scientists were needed, but there was not widespread agreement as to the best use of their time. "There were huge fights for years in meetings," said Mike Zolensky of Johnson Space Center, but at last they came up with a plan. "We invited the augmented science team at the last minute before recovery with a few people to enlarge it, then we also invited on anyone from the community who

---

133   Groshong, K. (2005, 22 December). "Stardust ready for landing." *Pasadena Star News*.

134   Potter, N. (2005, 22 December). "Comet mission set for return to Earth." *ABC News*.

135   Webster, G. (2002, 8 November). "Stardust's Annefrank flyby successful." *JPL Universe*, 32(23). 1.

136   David, L. (2002, 4 November). "Scientist surprised: Stardust sees details of asteroid Annefrank." Space.com.

137   Webster, G. (2002, 8 November). "Stardust's Annefrank flyby successful." *JPL Universe*, 32(23). 1.

wanted to do analysis of the samples." This approach worked. Scientists worldwide were eager to get their hands on the samples, and few required funding. With very little additional investment, "it grew from having a few people on the science team analyzing the samples to over 200 people analyzing the samples," added Zolensky. "Having the whole community involved in the examination smoothed over the process of handling [the samples]."[138]

Preparing the clean room at Johnson Space Center also required quite a bit of work and planning, and the team did not initially allocate enough time or money to do so. The team thought they "could plan the lab, build it, and test it out, all in a couple of years. It's more like five years…. We were rushing like crazy," Zolensky recalled. The particles to be returned were submicron in size (less than 1/25,000 of an inch), and they would be overwhelmed easily by the grime in even a normal clean room. To put the amount of dust returned into perspective, Brownlee said, "There's more comet dust collected in your backyard than we're bringing home." This is because of the regular influx of cometary material in the atmosphere falling to Earth. The problem is that it is mixed with tons of soil and nearly impossible to isolate. The advantage of sending a spacecraft to the comet is that the material would be pristine, unaltered, and kept frozen in the ices from the beginning of the solar system.[139]

Zolensky explained: "You might wonder what you can do with particles that are microscopic…." With the proper equipment, technique, and patience, "you can take a grain and slice it like you were slicing a loaf of bread into hundreds of slices."[140] Analysis would require new techniques. Scientists would have to determine which *portions* of a single grain were desired for various research purposes.[141] Study of these tiny particles required new instruments, and NASA provided them, with millions of dollars spent through the Sample Return Laboratory Instruments and Data Analysis program (SRLIDAP) and the Planetary Major Equipment (PME) program. To ensure congruence with mission goals, SRLIDAP was run by Dave Lindstrom, Program Scientist of the sample return capsule, called Genesis, and PME was run by Susan Niebur, the Discovery Program Scientist.

Comet Wild 2

As Stardust approached the comet, no one knew exactly what to expect. The only previous close encounter of a comet was ESA's mission Giotto, but Stardust would get

---

138   Niebur, S. (2009, 24 March). Personal interview with M. Zolensky. Located in "Stardust" file, NASA Historical Reference Collection, History Division, NASA Headquarters, Washington, DC.

139   Williams, D. (2006, 13 January). "Stardust of yesterday." CNN.com; Kridler, C. (2005, 22 December). "Capsule to bring back dust for examination." *Florida Today.*

140   Carreau, M. (2006, 7 January). "NASA craft's payload may offer a big payoff." *Houston Chronicle.*

141   "Dr. George Flynn Takes the Lead on NASA Stardust Project." (2009, 18 August). SUNY Plattsburgh website.

even closer. This level of uncertainty required dynamic decision-making, with dust models updated frequently as new data were collected. The models, in turn, were used to determine the optimum parameters for closest approach, and the spacecraft team would update spacecraft commands accordingly. Successful real-time changes required a joint effort between the navigation team, the scientists responsible for the camera, and the spacecraft team implementing decisions as new commands for the spacecraft. The team added staff for the encounter phase, trained them, and defended the flyby plans in a series of peer reviews and reviews with upper management. These sessions included presentations and careful discussion of identified risks and contingency plans.

On 13 November 2003—49 days before encounter—team members arrived at work to find that the optical navigation camera had successfully taken close-up images of Comet Wild 2 and delivered the images to Earth. "When I first looked at the picture, I didn't believe it," said Shyam Bhaskaran, the mission navigator. "We were not expecting to observe the comet for at least another two weeks. But there it was."[142] The team was exhilarated and relieved. "We weren't sure how close we would have to get to actually resolve the nucleus of the comet," said Ed Hirst, the mission system manager. Team members had to balance their excitement with responsibilities. "You kind of find snippets of time to steal away to look at the excitement without forgetting that you have to keep flying the spacecraft."[143]

On 2 January 2004, Stardust flew 236 kilometers ahead of Comet Wild 2 and held course. As the faster-moving comet passed close beneath it, the spacecraft trapped cometary dust particles smaller than one-hundredth the diameter of a human hair.[144] The images were better than the science team expected. Instead of being simply a dirty snowball, Comet Wild 2 turned out to feature a diverse landscape.

Pinnacles 100 meters tall and kilometer-wide craters 150 meters deep made up a substantial portion of the 5-kilometer-wide comet. The comet was practically living and breathing.

"Stardust was absolutely pummeled. It flew through three huge jets that bombarded the spacecraft with about a million particles per second," including some that pierced the top layer of the Whipple shields around the spacecraft, said mission manager Tom

---

142   Agle, D. C. (2003, 12 December). "Stardust's big day also approaches." *JPL Universe*, 33(24). 1.

143   Niebur, S. (2009, 10 August). Personal interview with E. Hirst. Located in "Genesis" file, NASA Historical Reference Collection, History Division, NASA Headquarters, Washington, DC.

144   "NASA probe set for launch to collect and return comet dust." (1999, 14 January). *Aerospace Daily*.

Duxbury.[145] The event received sizable press coverage despite being the *second* NASA press conference of the day. President George Bush had called in to congratulate the Mars Exploration Rover team on its successful landing earlier that day.[146]

Brownlee called the images captured "fantastic," and the comet "incredible," noting that it achieved its flyby science objectives with a camera that wasn't technically a science instrument but rather was intended primarily to be used as a navigation tool.[147] Such was the nature of a Discovery project: By keeping the mission concept focused on the successful return of samples, in situ observations were sacrificed. Though scientists sometimes lamented the lack of in situ capability, previous decades demonstrated that a larger, instrument-laden mission might never have gotten off the ground.

Discovery 5

Concurrently, the Discovery Program at NASA Headquarters entered a period of review. Months after Stardust launched, two spacecraft were destroyed. On 23 September 1999, Mars Climate Orbiter—a faster, better, cheaper spacecraft designed to study the long-term weather, surface, and atmospheric conditions at Mars—vanished. It was later determined to have either burned up in the Martian atmosphere, or to have skipped off it and bounded back into deep space.[148] Investigators blamed the failure on a software error: NASA engineers used metric units in a spacecraft subsystem, and Lockheed Martin, which manufactured the spacecraft, used imperial units. On 3 December 1999, Mars Polar Lander crashed into Planum Australe, near that planet's South Pole. This was likely due to a propulsion system switching off 40 meters above the Martian surface.[149]

A flurry of investigation boards and reports ensued. NASA's Office of Inspector General studied the faster, better, cheaper concept and its implementation.[150] NASA

---

145   Platt, J. (2004, 17 June). "NASA Spacecraft Reveals Surprising Anatomy of a Comet." NASA news release.

146   Niebur, S. (2009, 4 September). Personal interview with T. Duxbury. Located in "Stardust" file, NASA Historical Reference Collection, History Division, NASA Headquarters, Washington, DC.

147   Brownlee, D. E., Horz, F., Newburn, R. L., Zolensky, M., Duxbury, T. C., Sandford, S., Sekanina, Z., Tsou, P., Hanner, M. S., Clark, B. C., Green, S. F., & Kissel, J. (2004). "Surface of young Jupiter family comet 81P/Wild 2: view from the Stardust Spacecraft." *Science* (New York, NY), 304(5678), 1764–1769; Niebur, S. (2009, 25 March). Personal interview with D. Brownlee. Located in "Stardust" file, NASA Historical Reference Collection, History Division, NASA Headquarters, Washington, DC.

148   Azka Naheem. (2020). "NASA Mars Climate Orbiter Project Failure (1999) Report." *https://doi. org/10.13140/RG.2.2.15107.94243.*

149   Albee, A., Battel, S., Brace, R., Burdick, G., Casani, J., Lavell, J., Leising, C., MacPherson, D., Burr, P., & Dipprey, D. (2000). "Report on the Loss of the Mars Polar Lander and Deep Space 2 Missions." NASA STI/Recon Technical Report N, 00, 61967.

150   NASA Office of Inspector General. (2001, 13 March). "Faster, better, cheaper: policy, strategic planning, and human resource alignment." IG-01-009.

convened a special board called the NASA Integrated Action Team to study the results and make recommendations that would be applied to all of NASA's small missions.[151] The list of reforms included a reinvestment in the NASA workforce, with a focus on hands-on experience, mentoring, and training; invigorating the agency's technology portfolio to better balance existing, new, and emerging technologies; and reemphasizing risk mitigation policies, including project and program reviews, refined success criteria, and closer contractor communication.

Though neither lost spacecraft was part of Discovery, the fact that the program itself was a manifestation of the faster, better, cheaper philosophy meant extensive, expensive new mandates that NASA would have to cover for missions going forward. Arguably, no single act would have further-reaching and more devastating budgetary and cultural implications for the Discovery Program. For NASA, risk aversion would become paramount in a program where risk was intrinsic.

The Integrated Action Team recommendations came following years of internal reassessments of best practices of Discovery at a programmatic level. It wasn't the first time a group made such recommendations. Five years earlier, NASA had held a "lessons learned" workshop, whose steering committee recommended, among other things:[152]

- Discovery mission selection should be conducted using a two-step process;
- Step 1 proposals should be selected on cost and detailed science evaluation, adjusted for risk;
- Step 2 proposals should further include public awareness, educational opportunities, and cost risk;
- A proposal's science should be evaluated based on its number of objectives, the importance of those objectives, and its thoroughness, to be assessed using strategies and guidelines by the National Academies Committee on Planetary and Lunar Exploration, and NASA;
- Science risk should reflect the probability that the science generated is equal to the science proposed, in terms of instrumentation, measurement assessments, the quality of data management archiving, and science team composition.

The recommendations overall reflected a desire by the planetary science community to enhance the analytical approach used to select missions. The list would most prominently be reflected in the Discovery 5 AO and mission selection the following year. The announcement came on 20 September 1996. NASA wanted concepts for a

---

151 NASA Integrated Action Team. (2000, 21 December). "Enhancing Mission Success—A Framework for the Future." Downloaded from *https://history.nasa.gov/niat.pdf*.

152 Saunders, M. (1995, 14–15 June). Report of Workshop on Discovery Lessons Learned.

Discovery mission that could be developed and prepared for launch within six years—on or before 30 September 2002—at a cost of less than $183 million plus $43 million for the operations phase (both in Fiscal Year 1997 dollars). Ken Ledbetter, director of the Mission and Payload Development Division in the OSS, stated in the press release that accompanied the Announcement of Opportunity: "If more than one mission can be accommodated within the stated budget, NASA will consider selecting more than one."[153]

Language in the cover letter emphasized that the solicitation imposed strict cost caps; shortened the procurement cycle; and gave the Principal Investigator responsibility for all aspects of the investigation's design, development, implementation, launch, and operations. Two years later, all three emphases would become huge problems for the selected missions. In 1996, however, this was not obvious, and NASA received 34 proposals, including at least seven that would later be selected in some form, becoming CONTOUR, Genesis, MESSENGER, Deep Impact, Dawn, Kepler, and Juno. The Jet Propulsion Laboratory alone submitted 20—a number that Gregg Vane, then–deputy division manager of JPL's Observational Systems Division, would later recall as "way too many. At the time, the Discovery Program was new to all of us. People didn't appreciate just how much work it takes to create a credible Step 1 proposal."[154]

It would become even more work yet. The 1996 AO was the first to use the two-step selection process endorsed by the Discovery Lessons Learned Workshop.

Seven months later, NASA Headquarters selected five missions for concept study:

- Aladdin, a mission to the Martian moons Phobos and Deimos, which would gather samples by firing four projectiles into the moons' surfaces and gathering the ejecta during slow flybys before returning the samples to Earth for detailed study
- Genesis—a re-proposal of the now-renamed Suess–Urey mission—which would collect a sample of the solar wind and return it to Earth for detailed analysis
- CONTOUR—the Comet Nucleus Tour—a mission to take images and comparative spectral maps of at least three comet nuclei and analyze the dust flowing from them
- MESSENGER—the MErcury Surface, Space ENvironment, GEochemistry and Ranging mission—an orbiter carrying seven instruments to image and study the nearest planet to the Sun

---

153   NASA. (1996, 20 September). "NASA seeks proposals for fifth Discovery mission." News release 96-161.

154   Niebur, S. (2009, 22 March). Personal interview with G. Vane. Located in the "Discovery Program" file, NASA Historical Reference Collection, History Division, NASA Headquarters, Washington, DC.

- VESAT—the Venus Environmental Satellite—an orbiter spacecraft to study the atmospheric chemistry and meteorology of Earth's cloud-covered neighbor using an imager, a near-infrared spectrograph, a temperature mapper, and an X-band radar

Each of the implementation feasibility studies would take four months and be funded at $350,000, with reports due on 15 August 1997, for a projected October selection.

"This excellent and innovative set of proposals really demonstrates the maturing nature of the Discovery Program," said Wes Huntress, Associate Administrator of the Office of Space Science, in announcing the missions chosen for Step 2.[155]

As hinted at by Ken Ledbetter, on 20 October NASA Headquarters announced the selection of Genesis and CONTOUR for implementation, at total costs to NASA of $216 million and $154 million, respectively. (Although the AO allowed the mission costs to grow by up to 20 percent in the four-month feasibility study, JPL-designed Genesis did not grow at all, while the APL-designed CONTOUR grew almost 15 percent.)

Genesis was to launch in January 2001 and return to Earth in August 2003. CONTOUR was to launch in July 2002, flying by Comet Encke in November 2003, Comet Schwassmann–Wachmann 3 in June 2006, and Comet d'Arrest in August 2008.

"This was a very difficult selection," said Huntress. "We picked two based on our distribution of resources and the excellent fit of the timetables for these missions with other robotic space science explorers."[156] The Discovery Program had set high standards, with each of its first three missions to fly accomplishing great science quickly and at low cost. Now it would push boundaries by launching two missions—Stardust and Genesis—that would achieve the holy grail of planetary science missions: sample return.

This presented the new, untested challenges of sample collection, handling, storage, and Earth re-entry, to say nothing of the required upgrades to laboratories nationwide on a scale not seen since the meteoroid debris return from the Long Duration Exposure Facility in 1990, as well as lunar samples from both the Soviet Luna missions from 1970 to 1976 and the Apollo program.

---

155   NASA. (1997, 23 April). "Five Discovery mission proposals selected for feasibility studies." News release 97-78. Downloaded from *http://nssdc.gsfc.nasa.gov/planetary/text/nasapr_970423.txt*.

156   NASA. (1997, 20 October). "Missions to gather solar wind samples and tour three comets selected as next Discovery Program flights." News release 97-240. Downloaded from *http://nssdc.gsfc.nasa.gov/planetary/text/Discovery_pr_971020.txt*.

Figure 2-1: Lunar Prospector spacecraft
The fully assembled Lunar Prospector spacecraft sits atop the Star 37 Trans Lunar Injection module. Lunar Prospector mapped the Moon's elemental composition, gravity fields, magnetic fields, and resources. (Image credit: NASA, image no. ACD97-0047-6)

Figure 2-2: Stardust Sample Return Capsule

The Stardust Sample Return Capsule (SRC) shortly after landing in the Utah desert. Stardust was the first spacecraft to return a cometary sample and extraterrestrial material from outside the orbit of the Moon to Earth. (Image credit: NASA, image no. PIA03669)

Figure 2-3: Aerogel in the Payload Hazardous Servicing Facility

The aerogel grid from the Stardust Sample Return Capsule, fully deployed in the Payload Hazardous Servicing Facility for final closeout. The aerogel captured the interstellar dust and cometary particles from comet Wild 2 that were returned to Earth. (Image credit: NASA, image no. KSC-98pc1872)

CHAPTER 3

Harsh Landings

The Genesis mission had an advantage over Stardust: without travel to a faraway comet, its mission lifetime could be much shorter, and the samples could be returned to Earth even before the previously selected Stardust. Born of the challenge to collect a sample of the solar wind for laboratory analysis, Genesis would employ five ultrapure collectors, new solar array deployment mechanisms, autonomous on-board decision-making, and a daring Earth return complete with Hollywood stunt pilots, all to return tiny particles of the solar wind totaling the mass of just a few grains of salt (all that was necessary for analysis to better understand solar wind).[1]

To successfully return the samples, the scientists and engineering team would have to plan for many different situations and develop contingency plans against numerous possible failures. In the end, it would be those contingency plans—printed in binders

---

1   "A Little Glitz Goes a Long Way for NASA's Genesis." (2004, 3 September). Jet Propulsion Laboratory. Downloaded from *https://www.jpl.nasa.gov/news/a-little-glitz-goes-a-long-way-for-nasas-genesis*.

and clutched in arms as the team waited for capsule return at the Utah Test and Training Range—that would allow Genesis scientists to save the samples when the spacecraft crashed in the desert.

GENESIS

The Genesis mission as flown evolved from an idea that PI Don Burnett had shortly after Apollo. He and Marcia Neugebauer, a solar physicist at JPL, had been talking about understanding elemental abundances in the solar wind. The astronauts of Apollos 11, 12, 14, 15, and 16 emplaced aluminum and platinum foil experiments on the lunar surface, where their exposure to space, free of Earth's magnetosphere, would trap solar wind particles for a return to Earth. The quantities sent back were inadequate to the needs of some scientists.[2]

Over the next few years, they continued to discuss what might be done, but there were no opportunities to propose a mission for flight. They talked to colleagues about the concept through the years, recruiting Mark Thiemens, an isotope geochemist at the University of California, San Diego.[3] When NASA announced the Discovery Program, Burnett, Neugebauer, Thiemens, and the other co-investigators recognized an opportunity to revolutionize their science.

They called their initial concept the Solar Wind Sample Return mission. Like the other proposals submitted for consideration at the 1992 Discovery Program Mission Concept Workshop at San Juan Capistrano Research Institute, it was very conceptual (and at that point promoted as part of a larger asteroid sample return mission), but it was enough to capture the notice of the reviewers and program officials. The concept was not originally selected as one of the ten mission concepts, but after Burnett requested reconsideration, NASA Headquarters selected it for funding, and the Solar Wind Sample Return mission concept soon evolved into a more detailed mission plan with each passing year. The team was able to parlay their successful NASA funding effort into additional support from JPL, with both engineering support and direct support from three leaders at JPL: Ed Stone, Director of the lab; Assistant Director Charles Elachi; and Firouz Naderi, who was assigned to the Genesis team as proposal manager.[4] Burnett and Naderi led the team through the next proposal competition in 1994. The mission was renamed Suess–Urey, honoring Harold Urey and Hans Suess, who

---

2   Niebur, S. (2009, 24 March). Personal interview with D. Burnett. Located in "Genesis" file, NASA Historical Reference Collection, History Division, NASA Headquarters, Washington, DC.

3   Behne, J. (N.d.). Personal interview with M. Thiemens. Located in "Genesis" file, NASA Historical Reference Collection, History Division, NASA Headquarters, Washington, DC.

4   Niebur, S. (2009, 24 March). Personal interview with D. Burnett. Located in "Genesis" file, NASA Historical Reference Collection, History Division, NASA Headquarters, Washington, DC.

wrote an early paper on the origin of the elements; the paper posited that the observed abundance of the elements comes directly from their abundance in the stars in which they were created.[5] Naderi introduced Burnett to key members of the engineering team and set up a management plan that got rave reviews from a 1994 review panel, according to Burnett.[6] It was essentially the same mission as before, minus the asteroid sample return, and it was selected for additional funding through a concept study.

In 1996, the team again proposed Suess-Urey to the Discovery Program, this time with a new proposal manager, Chet Sasaki, and under a new name: Genesis. Naderi had moved to a different management position at JPL by then, and Sasaki was appointed on his recommendation. In 1997, after a fiercely fought Phase A competition, Genesis and the Comet Nucleus Tour mission, CONTOUR, were selected for implementation.[7] Don Burnett was the Genesis PI, with Chet Sasaki as project manager and, not long after, Amy Jurewicz as the JPL project scientist.

Pre-proposal, Naderi had recommended Don Sweetnam for mission operations and Don Savilla in mechanical design, a move which Burnett called a stroke of genius. "Genesis was very mechanism-intensive," he said. "Mechanisms always scare review panels. But Savilla was so good, he could stand up and defend all these little things about why this would work without any problem, and it did, by the way. His part worked 100 percent perfect."[8] (The same could not be said for every element of the mission, as we shall see.) Don Sweetnam was project manager. Lloyd Oldham served as Deputy Project Manager at Lockheed Martin.

The team faced an immediate challenge, however: overcoming concerns about the recent disaster of the JPL-led, Lockheed Martin–built Mars Climate Orbiter—one of the two lost spacecraft that impugned the faster, better, cheaper model and, by extension, cast a shadow over the Discovery Program, which flew neither mission. The mishap had, by the time of Genesis, been scrutinized stem to stern, with investigative committee recommendations implemented on current projects, but Genesis would be an early reteaming of JPL and Lockheed Martin on a new project.

---

5   Suess, H., and Harold C. Urey. (1956, January). "Abundances of the Elements." *Reviews of Modern Physics*, 28(1).

6   Niebur, S. (2009, 24 March). Personal interview with D. Burnett. Located in "Genesis" file, NASA Historical Reference Collection, History Division, NASA Headquarters, Washington, DC.

7   Burnett, D. S., Barraclough, B. L., Bennett, R., Neugebauer, M., Oldham, L. P., Sasaki, C. N., Sevilla, D., Smith, N., Stansbery, E., Sweetnam, D., & Wiens, R. C. (2003). "The Genesis Discovery Mission: Return of Solar Matter to Earth." *Space Science Reviews*, 105(3), 509–534. *https:// doi.org/10.1023/A:1024425810605*; Cochran, A., Veverka, J., Bell, J., Belton, M., Benkhoff, J., Benkhoff, A., Clark, B., Feldman, P., Kissel, J., Mahaffy, P., Malin, M., Murchie, S., Neimann, H., Owen, T., Robinson, M., Schwehm, G., Squyres, S., Thomas, P., Whipple, F., & Yeomans, D. (2000). "The Comet Nucleus TOUR (CONTOUR): A NASA Discovery Mission." *Earth, Moon, and Planets*, 89(1/4), 289–300. *https://doi.org/10.1023/A:1021567007750.*

8   Niebur, S. (2009, 24 March). Personal interview with D. Burnett. Located in "Genesis" file, NASA Historical Reference Collection, History Division, NASA Headquarters, Washington, DC.

The Genesis collector arrays were to be built by JPL; the solar wind concentrator and solar wind monitors would be built by Los Alamos National Laboratory. Of the whole project, mission contamination control lead Eileen Stansbery said, "Everyone worked very, very well together."[9]

Science

The mission's first and foremost science requirement: to bring back samples of the solar wind.[10] Solar wind is the collection of particles and gas ejected from the Sun that streams through the solar system and eventually dissipates into interstellar space. The particles are tiny—atoms, not molecules—and are invisible to the naked eye. Although most people on Earth are unaware of this continuous stream of particles bombarding our atmosphere, in sufficient quantities they have caused widespread blackouts of cell phones, televisions, and other electronic communications equipment across wide areas. Individual particles in the solar wind hold secrets from the dawn of the solar system, when they were swept up from the diffuse solar nebula by a spinning protostar that grew quickly into the Sun we know today. The elemental composition of the nebula is preserved in the solar photosphere, and, by measuring the particles traveling in the solar wind, scientists can gain insights into the composition of that pre-solar nebula now retained in the photosphere of the Sun.[11]

The mission had four basic science objectives:

- Provide data on the isotopic composition of solar matter sufficiently precise for planetary science studies
- Significantly improve our knowledge of the elemental composition of solar matter
- Provide a reservoir of solar matter sufficient to meet the needs of 21st-century planetary science
- Provide independent measurements of the different kinds of solar wind[12]

The elemental and isotopic composition of the protosolar nebula could also be used in models of the formation and evolution of the solar system, constraining both processes over the billions of intervening years, and answering what had until then been unknowable. "Most of our models and how we understand the formation and

---

9   Niebur, S. (2009, 25 March). Personal interview with D. Sweetnam and Eileen Stansbery. Located in "Genesis" file, NASA Historical Reference Collection, History Division, NASA Headquarters, Washington, DC.

10   Niebur, S. (2009, 24 March). Personal interview with D. Burnett. Located in "Genesis" file, NASA Historical Reference Collection, History Division, NASA Headquarters, Washington, DC.

11   NASA. (2001, July). "Genesis set to catch a piece of the sun." Genesis Launch Press Kit.

12   Ibid.

evolution of the solar system, processes that formed our planets, asteroids, comets, and... planetary atmospheres, all of that requires an assumption of an initial starting composition of our solar system," said Meenakshi "Mini" Wadhwa, Genesis co-investigator and cosmochemist at the Field Museum in Chicago. This solar wind composition and the composition of the initial solar nebula must be equivalent, she explained, since the Sun makes up over 99 percent of the mass of the solar system.[13]

Genesis would capture the solar wind in a way that was both sensible and innovative. Not all solar wind is the same. Physicists had identified three main types of solar wind, but before the Genesis mission, no one knew whether or how the elemental and isotopic compositions of different types of solar wind would differ.

The three main types of solar wind are fast, slow, and from coronal mass ejections (CMEs). Fast solar wind is high-speed and uniform streams emanating from holes in the Sun's corona. Slow solar wind is, as its name suggests, low-speed, and with variable streams originating in the Sun's streamer belt. CMEs are particles blown in chunks from the solar atmosphere.

Measurements by the Ulysses spacecraft had shown that the very act of ejecting matter from the Sun's photosphere affected the solar wind's mass composition in a predictable way, dependent on properties of each ion such as the "first ionization time," as well as the ion's mass and the charge. Since the three types (called regimes) of solar wind differ in source and ejection, perhaps their composition would differ as well.[14] Accordingly, Neugebauer insisted that the new mission concept be designed to capture each of the known solar wind regimes in separate collectors.

Out of that requirement came the portion of the spacecraft design that included three separate collector arrays—one for each kind of material implanted from the solar wind. The team now had to determine the material to place in each collector tray, figure out how to deploy each tray individually, and decide when to change trays to collect different incoming particles. This would be a challenge; although the three solar wind regimes were distinct, there would not be time to download each day's data and analyze it before deciding whether change was warranted.

The three types of solar wind could be distinguished by a combination of solar wind proton speed (fast vs. slow), temperature and density, abundance of alpha particles (also known as helium nuclei), and whether the electron streams were arriving from two directions (fast/slow vs. coronal mass ejection). This information, and the need to develop the mission within the cost-capped culture of Discovery, drove the design

---

13   Harwood, W. (2001, 30 July). "NASA to seek clues to solar system's origin." *The Washington Post*. A7–A8.

14   Neugebauer, M. (1991, 19 April). "The Quasi-Stationary and Transient States of the Solar Wind. *Science*, 252(404–409). See also Fisk, L. A., Schwadron, N. A., & Zurbuchen, T. H. (1998). "On the Slow Solar Wind." *Space Science Reviews*, 86(1/4), 51–60. *https://doi.org/10.1023/A:1005015527146.*

of the mission. The scientists would have to develop an algorithm for determining which tray should be deployed for the current solar wind regime, and the engineers would have to link the algorithm to a series of mechanisms—moving parts—that would deploy and stow each.

Instrument Hardware and Sampling

The Genesis spacecraft was made of aluminum, composite materials, and titanium, the goal being to conserve mass without sacrificing strength. Command and data handling (C&DH) was performed by a RAD6000 computer: a radiation-hard version of the Power PC chip used in Macintosh computers of the time. The system carried 128 megabytes of random-access memory and three megabytes of nonvolatile memory. Two standard silicon solar array panels generated a total of 254 watts at Earth and a nickel-hydrogen battery provided power storage.

In terms of layout, the center of the spacecraft held the collector trays—one for each solar wind regime—as well as two bulk solar wind collectors in the lid and cover of the stacked trays. There was an ion concentrator underneath. The concentrator and five collector trays were encased in an aluminum science canister tucked into a sample return capsule that was based on the same one under development for Stardust. The sample return capsule was encased in its backshell and heatshield on a set of support struts and attached to the main body of the spacecraft, which was equipped with the avionics and solar panels, as well as thrusters, antennas, and other subsystems. The Genesis Ion Monitor instrument (GIM) and Genesis Electron Monitor (GEM) composed the mission's science instrument payload and were used to monitor impacts from the solar wind.

Sample collection would work like this. Data from GEM and GIM fed into the onboard computer, and an algorithm in the C&DH spacecraft subsystem translated the impacts to real parameters of the solar wind. In addition to physical quantity measurements, GEM electron data could determine the presence of bi-directional electron streams. When the electrons seem to be coming from two opposing directions simultaneously, they were likely part of a coronal mass ejection lifted from the Sun's outer layer. If no such bi-directional electron stream was present, the solar wind was either in the "fast" or "slow" regime.

Once the data were taken and analyzed on board for regime identification, the collector trays would move autonomously into position, collecting additional samples and protecting that which had already been collected. The correct voltage was applied on the solar electrostatic concentrator. The team wrote software and selected mechanisms to carry out the commands so that the whole process could be done onboard without waiting for the impossibly slow human intervention from Earth.

"There was no ground decision-making in deciding what got deployed and for how long," said Ed Hirst, the Genesis mission manager who was also part of the Stardust mission. "It was pretty innovative."[15] Although some automation on Mars missions was by then standard, the level of automation found on Genesis was a departure for JPL, which was accustomed to ground-based commands and the ability to make changes during mission operations. As such, engineers tested spacecraft mechanisms extensively, including the sample return capsule.

But major challenges remained. First, determining the perfect, pure material or materials to collect these micron-size grains of solar wind, and second, to manufacture and integrate them into the spacecraft such that there were no single-point failures in the overall sample collection system—the collector surfaces had to be strong enough to withstand the pressures of launch and reentry.

The purity was vital: their composition had to be well known such that their signals could be subtracted from the measurements of any collected microscopic grains.

The highest-priority measurements were the relative amounts of

- O isotopes, because they provide the basis for understanding observed meteorite variations;
- N isotopes, because they are a key reference point in the eventual understanding of large but totally unexplained N isotopic variations in planetary materials; and
- Noble gas isotopes and elements, because they provide the basis for interpreting the compositions of terrestrial planet atmospheres.[16]

Each of the bicycle-tire-size aluminum collector trays was designed to hold 55 palm-size hexagonal tiles about 10 centimeters across. Ultimately, the team settled on tiles made of diamond, silicon carbide, and diamondlike carbon.[17]

---

15   Niebur, S. (2009, 10 August). Personal interview with E. Hirst. Located in the "Discovery Program" file, NASA Historical Reference Collection, History Division, NASA Headquarters, Washington, DC.

16   Burnett, D. S., Barraclough, B. L., Bennett, R., Neugebauer, M., Oldham, L. P., Sasaki, C. N., Sevilla, D., Smith, N., Stansbery, E., Sweetnam, D., & Wiens, R. C. (2003). "The Genesis Discovery Mission: Return of Solar Matter to Earth." *Space Science Reviews*, 105(3), 509–534. *https://doi. org/10.1023/A:1024425810605.*

17   Meyer, A. (2009, November). "Collecting Solar Wind." JPL Website. Downloaded from *https:// solarsystem.nasa.gov/genesismission/gm2/mission/collecting.htm.*

The spacecraft instrument payload was kept to the minimum necessary to support sample collection. There would be no magnetometer, no energetic particle investigation, no radio wave experiment, or the like; the mission remained focused on sample return and the supporting GIM and GEM.[18]

To measure the bulk concentration of solar wind, a team led by Roger Weins and Beth Nordholt, both of Los Alamos National Laboratory, developed an ion concentrator assembly intended to filter out light protons and alpha particles, concentrating heavier ions onto a special collector tile under the stack of collector trays. By repelling hydrogen, which composes 99 percent of the solar system, the signal of nitrogen and oxygen would be improved significantly, with concentrations designed to be increased by a factor of 20 while filtering out elements that could obscure later measurements. Using the solar wind flow speed and temperature measurements from GIM and GEM, the internal ion optics of the concentrator could be optimized for varying conditions of the solar wind.[19]

Mission Design

After launch, the spacecraft would travel 1.5 million kilometers (930,000 miles) from Earth to Lagrange Point 1, a stable point between Earth and the Sun where gravity is balanced between them. Because of this gravity balance, the Genesis spacecraft, like the Advanced Composition Explorer (ACE) and other missions, could be kept relatively stationary, in a small halo orbit around that point in space, with only the occasional need for small station-keeping adjustments from onboard thrusters. After several years of collection, the spacecraft would fire its thrusters and return to Earth, deploying the sample return capsule for midair capture by one of two helicopters standing by at the U.S. Air Force's Utah Testing and Training Range. The helicopter midair grab was to save the samples from even the slight bump of a parachute landing.

The sample return capsule was only 162 centimeters in diameter but weighed 210 kilograms. Hinged like a clamshell, the capsule opened to reveal the science canister with its collectors and the ion concentrator stowed inside. After completion of the collection phase, the capsule would close and seal tightly, shielded with a graphite-epoxy composite heat shield covered with a thermal protection system of carbon-carbon to

---

18   Barraclough, B., Dors, E., Abeyta, R., Alexander, J., Ameduri, F., Baldonado, J. R., Bame, S. J., Casey, P., Dirks, G., Everett, D., Gosling, J., Grace, K. M., Guerrero, D., Kolar, J., Kroesche, J., Lockhart, W., McComas, D., Mietz, D., Roese, J., & Wiens, R. (2003). "The Plasma Ion and Electron Instruments for the Genesis Mission." *Space Science Reviews*, 105, 627–660. *https://doi. org/10.1023/A:1024426112422.*

19   Nordholt, J. E., Wiens, R. C., Abeyta, R. A., Baldonado, J. R., Burnett, D. S., Casey, P., Everett, D. T., Kroesche, J., Lockhart, W. L., MacNeal, P., McComas, D. J., Mietz, D. E., Moses, R. W., Neugebauer, M., Poths, J., Reisenfeld, D. B., Storms, S. A., & Urdiales, C. (2003). The Genesis Solar Wind Concentrator. *Space Science Reviews*, 105(3), 561–599. *https://doi.org/10.1023/A:1024422011514.*

protect the capsule as it re-entered Earth's atmosphere. The backshell was also made of graphite-epoxy composite covered with a silicon-based material first developed by Lockheed Martin for the Viking missions to Mars in the 1970s. When the capsule descended to about 30 kilometers above sea level, a gas cartridge would pressurize a mortar tube, firing to deploy a 1.6-meter drogue chute to provide stability to the falling capsule. At an altitude of about six kilometers, the capsule's main 10-meter by 4-meter chute would deploy. This would slow the capsule's fall to about 5 meters per second for the midair helicopter capture.

The helicopter would be crewed in part by pilots with Hollywood stunt experience. Even Burnett, the mission PI, admitted that the capsule capture plan "raised a lot of eyebrows in the beginning."[20] The pilots were agile and eager to participate, however.[21] The helicopter teams practiced repeatedly, hoping to eliminate the possibility of mistakes. Peter Doukas, Lockheed Martin's lead mechanical engineer on Genesis, said of the helicopter pilots, subcontracted through Vertigo, Inc.: "They've done 35 to 40 missions to practice hooking the parachute and never missed one."[22] This was before Genesis had even launched.[23]

Planetary protection was also not a concern, confirmed John Rummel, the planetary protection officer for NASA. Ions from the Sun "have no biological potential or concern associated with them."[24] Burnett said he worried about Earth contaminating the samples—not the other way around.[25]

Management

Risk management was led by mission system engineer Richard Bennett, who had formerly led the Advanced Projects Design Team (Team X) at Jet Propulsion Laboratory. The twin top risks identified during the design phase were the need to return the samples undamaged and contamination-free, and the possibility of cost overages. The second requirement implied schedule pressure to make the target launch window. Risks were quantified and triaged by likelihood and consequence, with additional analyses that produced a list of the 20 percent of the risks that would cause 80 percent of the impact to activities—a step that focused management attention. The risk management system adapted by Genesis prompted the "buying down" of risk throughout the project, in large part by reducing the likelihood of occurrences of risks identified early. For example, the

---

20   Dunn, M. (2001, 13 July). "NASA aims to catch a bit of Sun." *The Express.*
21   Agle, D. C. (2004, 27 August). "Genesis prepares for copter catch." *JPL Universe,* 34(17). 1.
22   Schrader, A. (2001, 29 May). "Genesis craft to go sunbathing." *Denver Post.* B3.
23   Dunn, M. (2001, 13 July). "NASA aims to catch a bit of Sun." *The Express.*
24   David, L. (2004, 31 August). "Genesis Maneuver Aims Spacecraft Toward Utah." Space.com.
25   Chien, P. (2004, 5 September). "Spacecraft visible returning from outer space." *The North Lake Tahoe Bonanza.*

lack of recent "spin-stabilized" spacecraft experience by team members was shown to ripple through the project as potential design errors. To compensate, the project hired additional staff with greater experience. This was a small cost when compared with the potential expense later in the project. The first risk assessment, completed during the project's Preliminary Design Review, led to half of the high risks being reduced to "mediums" and "lows" within a few months. The Critical Design Review (CDR) and its preparation identified additional risks, but the number of high risks decreased again shortly afterward. Later, when the project approached its launch date, it became much more difficult to reduce the likelihood of risk, as engineering decisions would be locked down, so the team shifted its approach to mitigating consequence, often developing operational workarounds.[26]

Meanwhile, because the sample return capsule was very similar to the one used on Stardust—also developed by Lockheed Martin—the team expedited its testing. This seemed reasonable. When engineers made a few small changes to the capsule to accommodate a larger sample return, however, they forgot to adjust the gravity switch, used for drogue chute timing, and did not catch the change before launch. This would have terrible consequences later.[27]

In contrast to Stardust, having a team spread out across the country was a challenge for Genesis. "One of the most difficult problems to overcome is the lack of co-location," said Bennett. "I find many engineers are visual people. We sketch things to make points." In this respect, telephone and e-mail communication could not wholly take the place of in-person meetings. "When you get to know people, you understand what motivates them and that builds trust," said Bennett. "When you are working difficult contractual issues that means spending more resources, you need to understand and know the people you are dealing with in order to maximize the benefits for the whole project."[28]

Sample Analysis Preparations

Genesis was the first NASA mission to require a class 10 clean room, allowing only 10 particles of contaminant per cubic meter. "At class 10, this is the cleanest cleanroom complex in NASA. The lab is located in building 31, one floor below the complex of

26   Roberts, B. B., and Richard B. Bennett. (2000, 20 July). "Risk management for the NASA/ JPL Genesis mission: A case study." Downloaded from *https://trs.jpl.nasa.gov/bitstream/ handle/2014/14256/00-0668.pdf?sequence=1.*

27   Niebur, S. (2009, 24 March). Personal interview with M. Zolensky. Located in "Stardust" file, NASA Historical Reference Collection, History Division, NASA Headquarters, Washington, DC.

28   Krueger, A. (1999, 2 September). Personal interview with R. Bennett. Downloaded from *https:// web.archive.org/web/20090412093314/http://genesismission.jpl.nasa.gov/gm2/team/people/bennett/ interview1.htm.*

labs that houses the Apollo lunar samples," noted Carlton Allen, the then-astromaterials curator at Johnson Space Center.[29] Such stringent measures were to ensure that the analyzed samples were of material from space, not material on Earth.

The first draft of the Contamination Control Plan was based on Stardust's plan, which had history tracing back to the Apollo program.[30] The eventual Genesis samples would also be able to leverage the work done for the meteorite and cosmic dust collections curated at Johnson Space Center by fine-tuning sample handling procedures, clean room requirements, shipping and tracking procedures, and regular collection maintenance.

"I believe we were able to do it better and easier than anyone else because what we could do is take the expertise learned from Apollo," said Eileen Stansbery, the mission contamination control lead. She worked alongside Jack Warren, a Johnson Space Center contractor who had opened the first lunar rock box and taught generations of meteoriticists how to handle fine dust in the collections (including the author of this text). Also on the team was Judy Alton, a geochemist at Johnson who did the first lunar core, and Carol Schwartz, also of Johnson and who managed multiple collections, with experience analyzing every material type ever introduced to NASA's system of astromaterials.

"Since our responsibility is maintaining the scientific integrity of the return samples, providing a good understanding of the provenance of those samples and the materials that were going to be in the collector boxes was very important," said Stansbery. "I did take advantage of the depth of experience that exists within the organization to develop plans that took advantage of all the things that we had learned for the last 30 years."[31]

The Sample Return Laboratory Instruments and Data Analysis program (SRLIDAP) was created at NASA Headquarters to fund instrument development at labs nationwide in preparation for the Stardust and Genesis samples. Even the mission would be longer than usual, allowing time for funded analysis of the samples before the official end of mission. This was a new way of thinking, and one that would be useful in planning future missions such as Mars sample return.[32] At Open University in the United

---

29   David, L. (2004, 31 August). "The Genesis payload: Just how dangerous are its contents?" Space.com.

30   Niebur, S. (2009, 24 March). Personal interview with M. Zolensky. Located in "Stardust" file, NASA Historical Reference Collection, History Division, NASA Headquarters, Washington, DC.

31   Niebur, S. (2009, 25 March). Personal interview with D. Sweetnam and Eileen Stansbery. Located in "Genesis" file, NASA Historical Reference Collection, History Division, NASA Headquarters, Washington, DC.

32   Harwood, W. (2001, 30 July). "NASA to seek clues to solar system's origin." *The Washington Post.* A7–A8.

Kingdom, where co-investigators Colin Pillinger and Ian Franchi were to analyze the solar wind particles, a new building with a brand-new clean room facility awaited the delivery of the samples.[33]

Launch

Genesis's original launch date was January 2001. The team proposed a launch slip of several months to have more time in ATLO, or "assembly, test, and launch operations," which would give them more time to build and test its systems both individually and integrated. Chet Sasaki, the mission project manager, went to NASA Headquarters with the request, and, according to Burnett, "He was very, very effective."[34]

The proposed delay conflicted with the launch of the Mars Odyssey spacecraft, a water-finding orbiter. Burnett later recalled that Jet Propulsion Laboratory management feared that if Genesis had problems, it would deflect attention from the Mars spacecraft. The launch was delayed by half a year, but the decision was made after ATLO had already been completed.[35]

Genesis was shipped to the Cape aboard a U.S. Air Force C-17 aircraft and arrived at Kennedy Space Center for preflight processing at 3:30 a.m. on 31 May 2001. Over the next month and a half, engineers in Florida conducted a battery of tests to ensure that nothing had become jarred during transport and that, once spaceborne, everything would work as intended. The sequence of testing was as follows: a functional test; an electrical systems test; deployment of the solar arrays; verification of the radio links to the Deep Space Network, a global array of communications dishes that talked to all NASA spacecraft beyond cislunar space; and, finally, the operations of science instruments. After the spacecraft passed all the tests, the solar arrays were cleaned and stowed for launch in preparation for flight.

Meanwhile, on 12 June, the Delta 7326 launch vehicle was stacked for launch at Pad 17-A. Five days later, the spacecraft was mated to a Star 37 upper-stage booster. On 18 July, the spacecraft and booster were mounted on the Delta II, and engineers performed a spacecraft functional test to again ensure all was well. On 25 July, the payload fairing was installed. Launch was scheduled for 30 July 2001 at 9:36 a.m.[36]

---

33   Arthur, C., and Steve Connor. (2004, 9 September). "A blur of speeding metal, then a cloud of dust as space mission plummets to Earth." *The [UK] Independent.*

34   Niebur, S. (2009, 24 March). Personal interview with D. Burnett. Located in the "Discovery Program" file, NASA Historical Reference Collection, History Division, NASA Headquarters, Washington, DC.

35   Ibid.

36   Heil, M. (2001, 8 June). "Genesis arrives at KSC." *JPL Universe*, 31(12). 1.

"We Couldn't Have Killed Anybody If We Tried"

Genesis had two possible launch openings in 2001: a two-week window ending on 14 August and then another in December. Launch was delayed five times that first week. Weather was not accommodating, and then there were concerns about a power supply component in the spacecraft's star tracker. A duplicate model had failed environmental testing on the ground in France. No one was sure whether the part on Genesis was defective as well, and JPL and Lockheed Martin performed accelerated testing to determine whether a launch was worth the risk. "That turned out to be a last—very last—minute call," recalled David Jarrett, the program manager of the Discovery Program.[37]

Genesis departed Earth at last on 8 August at 12:13 p.m. EDT, embarking on a million-mile path taking it to Lagrange Point 1. It arrived there on 16 November and prepared to begin its science mission. Despite Stardust's head start—it had launched two years earlier, on 7 February 1999—Genesis was set to collect its samples and return them to Earth long before the comet mission. From the start, the team recognized that their plan for a midair capture was a new one to NASA. "We were aware very early that this was kind of horrifying to review boards," said Sweetnam. A daring helicopter catch wasn't the only thing that worried NASA, however. This would be the first sample return to Earth since Apollo.[38] As such, in the event of a problem, there were few applicable contingency plans on which the mission could rely.

The Genesis team worked out ways that the science might be recovered even in case of mishap. Very early in pre-Phase A, they decided to make the material in each collector tray a different thickness so that information on the collecting regime would not be lost in case of breakage. In terms of science return, said Stansbery, "We thought of contingency more in terms of the condition of the samples than the events that can go wrong." The team identified possible end states, such as a slightly leaky sample return capsule that would allow reentry gases onto the samples, or even the "shards across the desert scenario," and listed the personnel, roles and responsibilities, equipment, and procedures that would follow nearly any disaster.[39]

The loss of Space Shuttle Columbia in 2003 had a significant effect on Genesis, as it did for the entire American space program. At a review in February 2004, Gentry Lee, a famed JPL engineer who chaired the review committee, challenged the Genesis

---

37   Niebur, S. (2009, 14 May). Personal interview with D. Jarrett and Kate Wolf. Located in "Discovery Program" file, NASA Historical Reference Collection, History Division, NASA Headquarters, Washington, DC.

38   Niebur, S. (2009, 25 March). Personal interview with D. Sweetnam and Eileen Stansbery. Located in "Genesis" file, NASA Historical Reference Collection, History Division, NASA Headquarters, Washington, DC.

39   Ibid.

team to prove that nothing could go wrong on the spacecraft that would cause loss of life on the ground. The sample return capsule was about the size of one tire on the Columbia Shuttle.

"We were, in the eyes of the review boards, just woefully unprepared," said Ed Hirst, the Genesis mission manager. "There were so many things that we hadn't considered. And our team was small. We were focused on getting the capsule to the ground, and so we had the core engineering done, but there was a lot of other things that we had forgotten to think about." NASA's risk tolerance had changed, and Discovery missions were now being held to a higher standard than they were when proposed. Discovery Program leaders worked with the Genesis team on risk assessment and risk communication until the review boards were satisfied—and then insisted on *additional* contingency planning in a way that hadn't been done before.

"The thing about both the Genesis and Stardust capsules is that entry, descent, and landing sequence. The things that would happen, [from] the deployment of the back shells to deployment of the parachutes, all of that was hardwired into the hardware. We couldn't do anything to change any of it," said Hirst. Instead, the team spent considerable time and money assessing where the reentry risk lay. Since the assessment would only identify the risks, but not change the outcome, not everyone on the team was convinced that this was the best way to spend resources, but the team followed the recommendations of the review boards all the same, spending millions of dollars on extra analyses, reviews, and contingency planning.[40]

Range safety and the probability of hitting a civilian with a returning object became a concern. Range safety has its own language, and several members of the team needed to learn it, and fast. The team had to determine and minimize the probabilities of a person being hit, of property being damaged, of aircraft being damaged, of boats in the sea being damaged—everything. The Utah Test and Training Range is a 2,675-square-mile bombing range west of Salt Lake City, controlled by the Air Force in the air and the Army on the ground. The landing ellipse was secure, but the team also had to consider the effects should something go wrong along the reentry track. "I led much of this work under the guidance of people like Gentry Lee, who was kind of instrumental in opening our eyes and saying, 'Look, you really need to set the precedent for future sample return missions...what are the things that we should do to make sure that future sample return missions do them properly,'" said Hirst.[41]

---

40   Niebur, S. (2009, 10 August). Personal interview with E. Hirst. Located in "Genesis" file, NASA Historical Reference Collection, History Division, NASA Headquarters, Washington, DC.

41   Ibid.

After all the analysis, documentation, population maps, and distribution probabili-ties, said Don Burnett, the mission PI, "we couldn't have killed anybody if we tried… if we lost all control over the spacecraft, it would crash in northeast Nevada, where there was one person per square mile."[42]

Battery Scare

Not long after launch, telemetry from Genesis revealed that the battery inside the sample return capsule was heating up noticeably, reaching 23 degrees Celsius by early November 2001. This caused concern because the temperatures were projected to further rise to 42 degrees—well above a 25-degree requirement that engineers had planned for. After comparing the performance of similar batteries, mission managers judged the projected 42 degrees to be within acceptable limits. Researchers could not understand why the temperature was rising rapidly. One theory blamed a potentially deteriorating thermal blanket above the battery, so the team sent commands to crack the sample return capsule lid open to vent trapped gas and cool itself off. Regardless, the team wanted to solve—or at least understand—the problem during cruise to forestall any potential problems that would be compounded on re-entry.[43]

The engineering team advocated closing the spacecraft early, bringing it home with-out the planned exposure time on the collectors, fearing that the overheated batteries would jeopardize the entire mission. But Burnett wanted the full exposure time: the solar wind measurements required it—and as PI, he had the final say. The project had spent a lot of time and money on the spacecraft's thermal design, and it didn't work. But after extensive testing of hundreds of batteries on the ground once the anomaly was detected, mission engineers determined that even if the sample return capsule battery reached 60 degrees, there would be no apparent repercussions to the hardware or samples within.[44]

A Piece of the Sun, Down to Earth

Sample and data analysis—sometimes an afterthought on planetary science missions to be addressed at mythical "later dates"—was always integral to the Genesis plan. As Eileen Stansbery, who led the mission contamination control team, explained,

> *That was one of the things that I think was most important and unique about Genesis. Don Burnett was adamant that he fund the analysis of the samples; that just getting something*

---

42   Niebur, S. (2009, March 24). Personal interview with D. Burnett. Located in "Genesis" file, NASA Historical Reference Collection, History Division, NASA Headquarters, Washington, DC.

43   Ibid.; Young, K. (2001, November 10). "NASA doesn't think hot battery will curtail probe's mission: Genesis to collect solar wind particles." *Florida Today.*

44   Niebur, S. (2009, 24 March). Personal interview with D. Burnett. Located in "Genesis" file, NASA Historical Reference Collection, History Division, NASA Headquarters, Washington, DC.

back on earth wasn't what the mission was about.... The baseline mission funded two years of scientific analysis after recovery just as part of the project.... In addition, not all of the instruments that were part of the mission flew. There were two very important instrument developments that were analytical facilities on the ground as part of the project. And that was all built into this tiny Genesis mission budget.... And I think that was not just a unique, but a very important mental leap for NASA missions.[45]

Unnerving battery readings from the collection capsule aside, sample capture went off without a hitch. The team activated GEM and GIM, the electron and the ion sensors, on 23 and 24 August 2001. They functioned normally, and as they ran for the next year, there were no anomalies to report.

The collectors opened on 3 December 2001 to catch the solar wind. It was exhilarating for team members because the space weather, as described by Wiens, was "stormy"—troublesome for some space missions, but ideal for Genesis.[46] Just over two years after the collectors opened, the work was done. The team deactivated and stowed the sample collectors on 1 April 2004. As the month drew to a close, Genesis fired its thrusters to begin the long journey home.[47]

CONTOUR

Selected alongside Genesis was the Comet Nucleus Tour, or CONTOUR. When it was chosen as the sixth Discovery mission, Joseph Veverka, the mission PI, was well suited to the role, having over three decades of spacecraft experience.[48] His graduate adviser at Harvard was Fred Whipple, the celebrated astronomer and comet expert (and he of the "Whipple shield"). Also on Whipple's staff was a lecturer and researcher named Carl Sagan, who was just 10 years out of graduate school. Sagan would later hire Veverka to do data analysis on Mariner 9, NASA's first Mars orbiter.

After that first taste of mission life, Veverka never looked back. He continued his planetary mission involvement with Viking, the life-detection missions to Mars; Voyager, the twin spacecraft that revealed the moons of fire and ice beyond the asteroid belt, visiting each of the outer planets but Pluto; Galileo, the Jupiter system mission; Mars Observer, the mission that vanished at Mars; and CRAF—the Comet Rendezvous

---

45   Niebur, S. (2009, 25 March). Personal interview with D. Sweetnam and Eileen Stansbery. Located in "Genesis" file, NASA Historical Reference Collection, History Division, NASA Headquarters, Washington, DC.

46   Heil, M. (2001, 3 December). "Genesis spacecraft begins mission to collect samples of the sun." NASA Press Release.

47   Pountney, M. (2004, 7 September). "Stunt pilots to catch space capsule." *The Melbourne Herald Sun*; Erickson J. (2004, 20 August). "Fliers seek to lasso Sun." *The Rocky Mountain News*.

48   Matthews, R. (2002, 23 June). "NASA launches probe to see what lies at the heart of a comet: Asteroid's near miss highlights need for mission to prevent impacts on Earth." *The Sunday Telegraph*. 14.

Asteroid Flyby—Cassini's twin that was to study "surface properties of comets and asteroids, eolian processes on Mars, and the connection between geologic processes and photometric properties on icy satellites."[49] (Budget cuts in the 1980s killed CRAF.)

During this time, Veverka met a mission planner named Bob Farquhar, who joined the Applied Physics Laboratory after serving at NASA Headquarters during the Discovery Program's infancy. (It was Farquhar who processed the funding for Tom Krimigis's study of the NEAR mission.) Farquhar had also worked previously with JAXA, the Japanese space agency, "trying to convince them to do sort of a multiple asteroid-comet flyby mission" years earlier.[50] Farquhar and Veverka got to talking about celestial mechanics and the possibilities of sending missions to comets and asteroids within the context of the Discovery cost box, and Farquhar came up with "this very clever idea which would not only allow you to visit several comets but, in the original incarnation, you could actually get to Comet Encke," recalled Veverka.

Because Encke has a close perihelion to the Sun, it is a hard target to approach energetically. But by having a spacecraft in Encke's orbit, it would re-encounter Earth every six to 12 months, depending on celestial mechanics, which would allow engineers to change the spacecraft's trajectory. "It would allow you to redirect the spacecraft to an Oort cloud comet if it came by," said Veverka, "so it did something that most mission concepts couldn't do. You could visit multiple comets."[51]

Farquhar put together the trajectory. Veverka put together the science team, relying in large part on people who had worked with him on the CRAF imaging team.

"On a Discovery mission, what you were trying to do is to find people who have good instruments, who will deliver them on time, on cost," said Veverka.[52] He selected Hasso Nieman, the PI on CRAF's Neutral Gas and Ion Mass Spectrometer instrument, and his team, including Paul Mahaffey of Goddard Space Flight Center, who later succeeded Hasso as PI.[53] Also from CRAF were Jochen Kissel, who led its Cometary Matter Analyzer, and his group in Germany, who had just built an instrument for Giotto, the European Space Agency's first deep space mission; and Don Yeomans, who had been in charge of radio science investigation on CRAF.[54]

---

49   Friedlander, B. (2001, 27 September). "Honoring Veverka, a man who chases snowballs and discovers continents." *Cornell Chronicle.*

50   Niebur, S. (2009, 10 September). Personal interview with J. Veverka. Located in the "CONTOUR" file, NASA Historical Reference Collection, History Division, NASA Headquarters, Washington, DC.

51   Ibid.

52   Ibid.

53   Weissman, P., & Neugebauer, M. (1991). "The Comet Rendezvous Asteroid Flyby Mission: A Status Report." *Asteroids, Comets, Meteors 1991,* vol. 765, 235.

54   Niebur, S. (2009, 10 September). Personal interview with J. Veverka. Located in the "CONTOUR" file, NASA Historical Reference Collection, History Division, NASA Headquarters, Washington, DC.

Several scientists at APL joined the team, including Andy Cheng, the NEAR Project Scientist, and Scott Murchie, a geologist at the Jet Propulsion Laboratory. Steve Squyres, who had previously led a competing proposal called RECON—Rendezvous with a Comet Nucleus—in the 1994 competition, was added to the team in 1996. Andy Cheng coined the name CONTOUR.[55] Regarding the inventive trajectories from Bob Farquhar, Cheng recalled: "To this day, I don't know when those trajectories were actually discovered, whether it was, you know, decades earlier. He just came in and had boxes and boxes of folders and things like that.... I've never known a time when Bob wasn't talking about something like the CONTOUR mission because that's always been his first love: multiple flyby, and comets."[56]

Veverka avoided naming a project scientist. "On a project as small as a Discovery mission," he said, "I don't think you need a project scientist because what it implies is that the project scientist is a conduit for some information from the science team to the engineering project team.... I think that's a bad idea on a Discovery mission. I think everybody is one team."[57]

CONTOUR was one of the initial "$100,000 studies" that emerged from San Juan Capistrano, but it was not selected, mostly for reasons of cost.[58] It had been conceived as a big, traditional spacecraft launching on a big rocket. That would have to change. The team brought Mary Chiu on as project manager. She was, at the time, the spacecraft manager of the ACE, a space weather probe at Lagrange Point 1.

Veverka and Chiu forged a close working relationship as PI and project manager, respectively, which included a weekly tag-up about "anything and everything," said Chiu. They also talked throughout the week when issues arose. "He was also in contact with a lot of the instrument developers at APL."[59]

This took a light hand on Veverka's part. "On the one extreme, you have a PI who gets involved in everything and makes life miserable," said Veverka, "And then, on the other extreme, you have people who basically just disappear after the mission has been selected. And, when the data start coming on, they reappear again." He called

55   Niebur, S. (2009, 31 July). Personal interview with A. Cheng. Located in "Discovery Program" file, NASA Historical Reference Collection, History Division, NASA Headquarters, Washington, DC.

56   Ibid.

57   Niebur, S. (2009, 10 September). Personal interview with J. Veverka. Located in the "CONTOUR" file, NASA Historical Reference Collection, History Division, NASA Headquarters, Washington, DC.

58   Ibid.

59   Niebur, S. (2009, 16 September). Personal interview with M. Chiu. Located in the "Discovery Program" file, NASA Historical Reference Collection, History Division, NASA Headquarters, Washington, DC.

both extremes unhelpful, explaining, "I tried very hard not to get in the way of people who knew what they were doing…. But, I think, to be honest, it's nothing that I did. It's the fact that we had a first-rate group of people."[60]

The people set the mission up for success, but what put it over the top was its mission design. Yet again, Bob Farquhar came up with a trajectory that proved to be the mission's breakthrough feature. "This very, very creative mission design," said Chiu, "allowed us to have a relatively small low-cost spacecraft to fly by three comets. I mean, that's an absolutely incredible feat."[61]

Rather than launch on a large, expensive rocket to get the power and precision necessary to visit multiple comets, which was CONTOUR's aim, Farquhar calculated that it was much easier to launch into Earth's orbit, and from there, fire a payload assist rocket stage. You could avoid all the variables of Earth's atmosphere, with the bonus of precise tracking and extreme accuracy in how you employ velocity changes. In other words, by buying a million-dollar payload stage rocket, you could save ten million dollars.[62] CONTOUR would come in at half the cost cap of a Discovery mission: $153 million, which included the launch vehicle, mission operations, and reserves.[63] NASA selected the mission for flight in August 1997.

More Ideas Than Facts

Comets are not studied simply because they are strange and beautiful. Rather, they may possess the answers to the most fundamental questions vexing humankind. "Comets are the building blocks of the early solar system," explained Don Yeomans, a co-investigator on CONTOUR and one of the Jet Propulsion Laboratory's comet experts.[64] One of the ways planetary scientists study the nature of comets as they relate to Earth is by measuring their compositions. "What is the deuterium-to-hydrogen ratio in the atmosphere of the comet and is that ratio the same as the ratio of the earth's oceans? If it is, comets are likely the source of much of the earth's oceans."[65] Among the other

---

60   Niebur, S. (2009, 10 September). Personal interview with J. Veverka. Located in the "CONTOUR" file, NASA Historical Reference Collection, History Division, NASA Headquarters, Washington, DC.

61   Niebur, S. (2009, 16 September). Personal interview with M. Chiu. Located in "Discovery Program" file, NASA Historical Reference Collection, History Division, NASA Headquarters, Washington, DC.

62   Morring, F. (2002, 24 June). "Hardened probe targets two comets." *Aviation Week & Space Technology.* 94.

63   Niebur, S. (2009, 31 July). Personal interview with E. Reynolds. Located in the "CONTOUR" file, NASA Historical Reference Collection, History Division, NASA Headquarters, Washington, DC; Farquhar, R. (2011). *Fifty Years on the Space Frontier: Halo Orbits, Comets, Asteroids, and More.* Denver: Outskirts Press. 215.

64   Lane, E. (2002, 25 June). "NASA to launch a flyby of comets." *Newsday.*

65   Morring, F. (2002, 24 June). "Hardened probe targets two comets." *Aviation Week & Space Technology.* 94–95.

questions asked: Is it plausible that the air we breathe in the atmosphere was once comet stuff? Is it likely that the original input of molecules that led to the origin of life on Earth came from comets?[66]

To help answer these questions, and assess the diversity of comets in the inner solar system, the CONTOUR mission carried four instruments: the CONTOUR Remote Imaging SPectrograph (CRISP); the CONTOUR Forward Imager (CFI); a Neutral Gas and Ion Mass Spectrometer (NGIMS), provided by Goddard Space Flight Center; and the Comet Impact Dust Analyzer (CIDA).[67] CRISP and CFI were expected to return images an order of magnitude more resolved than Deep Space 1's pictures of Comet 19P/Borrelly and 25 times better than Giotto's images of Comet 1P/Halley, itself the first flyby close enough to image a comet's core.[68] NGIMS would measure noble gases like xenon and krypton in the atmosphere of the comets. If the isotopic ratios of xenon and krypton isotopes matched those in Earth's atmosphere, it would be an indication that Earth's atmosphere indeed came from comets.[69] CIDA, meanwhile, would do gas chemistry in the coma.

"We really have more ideas than facts," said Michael Belton, CONTOUR's Deputy Principal Investigator.[70] The mission had 18 co-investigators, including Fred Whipple, the "grand old man of comets," as Carolyn Shoemaker later wrote in his obituary.[71] It was he who, in the 1950s, argued that comets are icy conglomerates, or "dirty snowballs" of ice, ammonia, methane, and carbon dioxide at the core, with a disperse particle tail. He was correct, and he joined the CONTOUR mission in 1999 at age 92.[72] "Hopefully, if I live to be 100," Whipple said at launch, "I'll get to see the samples of a comet that CONTOUR brings back."[73]

---

66   David, L. (2002, 12 June). "CONTOUR's tale of two comets." Space.com.

67   Cochran, A., Veverka, J., Bell, J., Belton, M., Benkhoff, J., Benkhoff, A., Clark, B., Feldman, P., Kissel, J., Mahaffy, P., Malin, M., Murchie, S., Neimann, H., Owen, T., Robinson, M., Schwehm, G., Squyres, S., Thomas, P., Whipple, F., & Yeomans, D. (2000). "The Comet Nucleus TOUR (CONTOUR): A NASA Discovery Mission." *Earth, Moon, and Planets*, 89(1/4), 289–300. *https://doi.org/10.1023/A:1021567007750.*

68   Ibid.; Singer, E. (2002, 1 July). "Tailing comets for clues to life: NASA plans this month to launch CONTOUR, its latest probe to explore these celestial balls of dust and ice, which hold secrets older than Earth." *Los Angeles Times.* A-10.

69   Lane, E. (2002, 25 June). "NASA to launch a flyby of comets." *Newsday.*

70   Ballingrud, D. (2002, 1 July). "On the trail of comets." *St. Petersburg Times.*

71   Obituary of "Fred L. Whipple (1907–2004)." (2004, 31 August). *Boston Globe.*

72   Ballingrud, D. (2002, 1 July). "On the trail of comets." *St. Petersburg Times*; "Fred Whipple, World-Renowned Astronomer, Dies." (2004, 7 September). *Space Daily.* Downloaded from *http://www.spacedaily.com/news/comet-04j.html* on 11 August 2021, and available in the NASA Archives, "CONTOUR" folder.

73   Szaniszlo, M. (2002, 6 July). "Dr. Comet's pioneering ideas take off." *Boston Herald.* 5.

Despite his age and prominence, Whipple was no figurehead. He was a full member of the science team, and worked as such, attending meetings when they were held in the Northeast. As Veverka recalled: "He occasionally would give a talk. He took this very, very seriously."[74]

CONTOUR was scheduled for launch into a highly elliptical initial orbit at 2:56 a.m. on 1 July 2002. It would leave Earth on a 7425 Delta II with four solid-fuel tanks. Seven weeks later, the spacecraft would fire its payload assist stage—a Star 30 solid rocket motor—to push it into its initial trajectory. Over a projected four-year mission lifetime, the spacecraft would use four Earth gravity assists to reach the comets, which then were in a difficult-to-encounter position in the inner solar system. "It's like having two launches," explained Bobby Williams, leader of the team that landed NEAR on Eros in 2001 and member of the CONTOUR navigation team. "We have to fire a rocket to go into orbit around earth and then about six weeks later fire another rocket to push the spacecraft out of earth orbit."[75] Unbeknownst to Williams, that "second launch" would prove catastrophic.

Found to Be Good, or So We Thought

Costs were climbing for CONTOUR. Between the mission's selection by NASA Headquarters and its actual implementation at APL, prices grew due to factors no one could have foreseen. "It was right after the Mars problems," explained Mary Chiu, the project manager. "For some reason, it was also a time when salaries shot up." (That reason was a rise in base government pay, signed into law by President Bill Clinton, which rippled across government vendors as well.)[76] This significantly inflated staff and contractor costs. "The biggest cost that we had was people. If you got a fairly hefty increase in just that, you've blown your reserve. And that's what hit. We blew our reserve almost before we started out."[77]

Moreover, in the aftermath of the failed Mars Climate Orbiter and Mars Polar Lander, NASA Headquarters implemented project "red team reviews" to find flaws in missions before launch. "What was coming through was a lot more scrutiny, a lot more paperwork, a lot more reviews," said Chiu, and they weren't cheap. "We had not

---

74   Niebur, S. (2009, 10 September). Personal interview with J. Veverka. Located in the "CONTOUR" file, NASA Historical Reference Collection, History Division, NASA Headquarters, Washington, DC.

75   "JPL Navigators Drive Two-for-one Comet Mission." (2002, 1 July). Press release.

76   Folkenflik, D. (1999, 9 September). "4.8% pay increase for federal employees OK'd; Congressional negotiators lift past Clinton request; full Congress to vote." *Baltimore Sun*. Retrieved 28 July 2022 from *https://www.baltimoresun.com/news/bs-xpm-1999-09-10-9909100269-story.html*.

77   Niebur, S. (2009, 16 September). Personal interview with M. Chiu. Located in the "Discovery Program" file, NASA Historical Reference Collection, History Division, NASA Headquarters, Washington, DC.

anticipated that at all. So, we got hit by a double whammy."[78] Use of the Deep Space Network (DSN) proved more expensive than APL management had anticipated, through no fault of CONTOUR. None of this was helping the lab's stellar record with respect to handing in projects within cost. In the end, it was CONTOUR's undoing. To save $300,000, the project purchased a Star 30 solid rocket motor that was two years older than its shelf-life.

"CONTOUR was, you might say, a victim of being exceptionally cost-conscious," recalled Krimigis, who was by then head of the Space Department at APL. The Star 30 was bought secondhand from Hughes Aerospace Corporation and recertified for flight by Alliant Techsystems. The project did not test fire the rocket before launch.[79]

"Everybody was very reassuring," said Krimigis. "And the NASA review teams, you know, the excellent review teams, nobody raised a flag on that. Ultimately, it was my fault because we were running tight."[80] When CONTOUR was selected for flight by Ed Weiler, the Associate Administrator of NASA's Space Science Enterprise, it was approved without a mass spectrometer. The project was not confident that the instrument would fit at the proposed cost of the mission.

To get the critical science instrument on board, Krimigis cut a deal. "I said, 'Look, you know that we are not likely to go much into the contingency,' so I said, 'If you increase the program cost, if you put in five million, I'll guarantee you that we'll never use five million of the contingency.' He said, 'Okay.' That's how the mass spectrometer got on board the spacecraft."[81] It was a smart move, but the project had to remain mindful of the cost cap at all times, because the moment it was in danger of exceeding its proposed price tag, the mass spectrometer would have been descoped.

"I always viewed myself as the guardian of the science, and that's why I was insisting, for example, that the mass spectrometer on CONTOUR stay on the payload—I mean, I understood the science," said Krimigis. "I really felt that the whole philosophy of the department was that we're here to maximize the science."[82]

Saving money on a kick stage was one way to ensure that the mission would achieve a maximal amount of science return. The STAR30-BP Thiokol motor was a known quantity at selection, having been used routinely in space missions since its introduction

---

78   Ibid.

79   Niebur, S. (2009, 27 September). Personal interview with T. Krimigis. Located in the "Discovery Program" file, NASA Historical Reference Collection, History Division, NASA Headquarters, Washington, DC.

80   Niebur, S. (2009, 27 August). Personal interview with T. Krimigis. Located in the "Discovery Program" file, NASA Historical Reference Collection, History Division, NASA Headquarters, Washington, DC.

81   Ibid.

82   Niebur, S. (2009, 27 September). Personal interview with T. Krimigis. Located in the "Discovery Program" file, NASA Historical Reference Collection, History Division, NASA Headquarters, Washington, DC.

in 1984, with only two failures in 86 missions. NASA had used solid rocket motors in other missions, including Magellan, where one worked perfectly even after 15 months of transit time to Venus.[83]

Originally, there were three comets in CONTOUR's planned trajectory: Encke, 73P/Schwassmann–Wachmann 3, and 6P/d'Arrest. The kick stage was essential to the plan.

Comet 2P/Encke, first discovered in 1786 by astronomer Johann Franz Encke, is an older, quieter comet. "Although it does have gases and dust coming out forming an atmospheric coma, Encke really does not have the kind of classical tail that you associate with a very bright comet," explained Veverka.[84] There is evidence that Encke, 4.8 kilometers in size, broke apart from a giant 80-kilometer comet about 20,000 years ago, creating a disperse trail of dust and debris that Earth encounters every June and November.[85] This dust stream is popularly known as the Taurids. It was Fred Whipple in 1940 who figured out that the meteor shower was connected to Encke.[86]

Schwassmann–Wachmann 3, in contrast, is much younger, with dust clouds, and was described by Don Yeomans, a CONTOUR co-investigator, as a "young, fragile object," in contrast to "tough, blackened, old Comet" Encke.[87] The spacecraft would quickly fly near Comet Encke so Tony Taylor, the chief of the Jet Propulsion Laboratory's navigation team, viewed his team's job as protecting the ten minutes of time available to obtain science data. The spacecraft would have to be more careful around Schwassmann–Wachmann 3, which had split into at least three pieces only a few years earlier, in 1995. Loose particles from the cometary cataclysm made the encounter more dangerous, but it also made it undeniably attractive. Young comet surfaces are rare, and this one would likely be exposing pristine material from its creation. Still, CONTOUR would pass so close to Encke—anywhere from 100 to 160 kilometers—that any comet dust impacting the spacecraft would hit much harder than a speeding

---

83 Moomaw, B. (2002, 26 August). "Full impact of CONTOUR mission destruction remains to be seen." *Space Daily*. Downloaded from *http://www.spacedaily.com/news/contour-02i.html* on 11 August 2021, available in the NASA archives, "CONTOUR" folder.

84 Ray, J. (2002, 3 July). "Probe launched to see fossils from formation of planets." *Spaceflight Now*.

85 Matthews, R. (2002, 23 June). "NASA launches probe to see what lies at the heart of a comet: Asteroid's near miss highlights need for mission to prevent impacts on Earth." *The Sunday Telegraph*. 14.

86 Whipple, F. L. (1940). "Photographic Meteor Studies. III. The Taurid Shower." *Proceedings of the American Philosophical Society*, 83, 711–745.

87 Singer, E. (2002, 1 July). "Tailing comets for clues to life: NASA plans this month to launch CONTOUR, its latest probe to explore these celestial balls of dust and ice, which hold secrets older than Earth." *Los Angeles Times*. A-10.

bullet. Engineers performed simulations on Earth using 10 inches of Nextel ceramic covering and Kevlar, which would shield the spacecraft, hitting the barrier with nylon pellets flying 15,000 miles per hour.[88]

Such a hazardous environment made camera design difficult as well. "Dust particles at 28 kilometers per second are not very good for precision optics," said Jeff Warren, CONTOUR's camera systems engineer. The high-resolution camera would be kept under the dust shield until the last possible moment.[89]

Testing

Leading up to launch, set for 1 July 2002, the CONTOUR spacecraft was submitted to rigorous testing to ensure that there would be no surprises in deep space. Vibration, spin balance, and acoustic tests were conducted with an inert Thiokol Star 30 solid rocket motor attached. (It weighed 70 pounds more than the one used for flight.) To simulate the motor for thermal vacuum testing, the inert motor was replaced with heaters. The only time the spacecraft and actual flight motor were tested together during the final, pre-launch checkout at the Cape was limited to spin balance testing.[90]

CONTOUR engineers, meanwhile, conducted all the recommended tests of the Star 30 solid rocket motor. To verify the integrity of its welds, for example, they even brought the spacecraft to a medical facility and placed it in an x-ray machine. Fuel samples were tested constantly.

In late June, launch preparations were delayed by some of the very types of particles that scientists had hoped to collect: dust. This was after spiders had been found near the spacecraft.[91] (The would-be arachnid astronaut worried mission managers but did not delay the launch—not even the one crawling on the rocket's third stage was deemed consequential enough to delay things.) Then, however, after the eight-sided spacecraft had been loaded atop a Delta II rocket at Cape Canaveral, and as technicians were installing the payload fairing to seal in CONTOUR, they noticed a fine layer of dust on the spacecraft's top solar panel.[92]

That was a showstopper. It was soon determined that a HEPA filter had not been changed recently in the clean room at the top of the launch pad, which meant the

---

88   Young, K. (2002, 8 July). "Experts set to check comet chaser: CONTOUR to undergo tests as spacecraft orbits Earth." *Florida Today*.

89   Kridler, C. (2002, 22 July). "Images of universe not easy to capture: Space photography much more complex than point and shoot." *Florida Today*.

90   Morring, F. (2002, 2 September). "CONTOUR team wants to build a new probe." *Aviation Week & Space Technology*. 40.

91   Young, K. (2002, 1 July). "Dusty coating delays launch of comet-bound probe." *Florida Today*.

92   Berger, B. (2002, 28 June). "Fine layer of dust halts CONTOUR launch preparations." *SpaceNews*.

spacecraft would need to be cleaned before liftoff.[93] Siad Ali, the project's contamination and quality assurance representative at the Cape, called the situation totally unacceptable. Launch was postponed by two days.[94]

Already, the project was planning an extended mission for CONTOUR. After it encountered Encke and Schwassmann–Wachmann 3, Farquhar's trajectory allowed a 2008 encounter with Comet d'Arrest, Comet Boethin, Comet Wilson–Harrington, or another "target of opportunity" that might arise after launch.[95] "If you want to look at the diversity of cometary nuclei, this is the way to do it," said Farquhar.[96]

To that end, the CONTOUR team and the team from Rosetta, a European Space Agency mission set originally to launch in 2003 and visit Comet 46P/Wirtanen, were already working together to improve each other's science. The project scientist of Rosetta, Gerhard Schwehm, even served on both missions, along with Jochen Kissel of the Max Planck Institut for Extraterrestrische Physik in Germany. "We're all after the same knowledge," said Schwehm. "What we learn from the NASA missions will help us to be even better prepared for our big task at Comet Wirtanen."[97]

In a news briefing before launch, Colleen Hartman, Director of the Solar System Exploration Division, highlighted the constellation of missions being launched by NASA and ESA that would begin observations in the next few years, saying, "We're about to enter into a golden era of comet investigation."[98] And indeed it was poised to be. If all had gone well, CONTOUR would have reached Encke right before the launch of Deep Impact (a NASA spacecraft designed to study the interior of Comet 9P/Tempel) and just before Stardust's flyby of Wild 2, with Rosetta reaching far-off Comet Wirtanen in 2011.

Launch

Liftoff promised an astonishing journey ahead. "It was a great launch," Veverka said. "What was amazing was that within hours of the launch, the spacecraft was working

---

93 Ibid.; Niebur, S. (2009, 14 May). Personal interview with D. Jarrett and Kate Wolf. Located in "Discovery Program" file, NASA Historical Reference Collection, History Division, NASA Headquarters, Washington, DC.

94 Behne, J. (2009, 16 September). Personal interview with M. Chiu. Located in "CONTOUR" file, NASA Historical Reference Collection, History Division, NASA Headquarters, Washington, DC.

95 Young, K. (2002, 9 June). "CONTOUR spacecraft explores comet's center." *Florida Today*; Ray, J. (2002, 3 July). "Probe launched to see fossils from formation of planets." *Spaceflight Now*.

96 Ruane, M. E. (2000, 13 July). "Up close and personal with comets; Hopkins scientists hope new satellite will provide rare glimpse of history." *The Washington Post*. M10.

97 (2002, 1 July). "Rosetta wishes CONTOUR luck chasing comets." ESA news release.

98 David, L. (2002, 12 June). "CONTOUR's tale of two comets." Space.com.

amazingly." They were able to test all spacecraft subsystems but the camera, the latter set to be turned on after the spacecraft had left Earth's orbit so as to protect it from debris or distortion from the firing of the solid rocket motor.[99]

As planned, Mary Chiu retired, taking a post-retirement vacation with her family, and Ed Reynolds became project manager at launch. CONTOUR was to fire its Thiokol Star 30 solid rocket motor 42 days after launch, at 4:49 a.m. EDT, 15 August, putting it on a path toward Encke. It was a routine maneuver; when a spacecraft is scheduled for an engine burn and course correction, there is typically tension—years and sometimes entire careers are atop those boosters—but NASA has been doing this a long time.

"I was in the control room," recalled Reynolds. "The burn has to happen at perigee. It just so happened that perigee occurred, like, 100 miles over the middle of the Indian Ocean. There's no ground stations. We got the spacecraft spinning.... [I]t was pointed perfect. The ops team pretty much watched it go over the horizon," Reynolds continued, saying everything was nominal. [100] "So, you let it go at, like, 4:30. And then, 40 minutes later, you kind of say, 'Okay, it's burning now....' And I forget what the time duration was, but it was like an hour after the burn to get a contact."[101]

The DSN antennas on Earth, located in California, Australia, and Spain, should have picked up a signal at 5:35 a.m., just as the East Coast was waking up. But the signal never came. The spacecraft, built to be bulletproof in a five-layer dust shield of Kevlar and Nextel, was no longer there.

"It was nothing, nothing, nothing, nothing," described Reynolds of the interminable wait for a signal from the spacecraft. An hour or two elapsed. "They were calling in our best RF [radio frequency] people to interact with the DSN and JPL people. Then, at one point they kind of were like, 'We're seeing a signal.' And you get real hopeful. 'Okay. All right, it's there. It's still broadcasting.' And then, you find out that that was noise.... I think it was a day and half of just looking, looking, looking, looking."[102]

On that first day, mission controllers at APL searched for the spacecraft along its predicted trajectories. There was plenty of hope for a successful recovery. Mission managers first assumed that the problem was with the DSN stations in California, Australia, or Spain, which were to first receive the signal.[103] After it became clear that the global antenna array was not the problem, they faulted the spacecraft telemetry, holding out hope that a planned resend of the signal might be received. As a safeguard, the mission

---

99   Niebur, S. (2009, 10 September). Personal interview with J. Veverka. Located in the "CONTOUR" file, NASA Historical Reference Collection, History Division, NASA Headquarters, Washington, DC.

100   Niebur, S. (N.d.). Personal interview with T. Carro. Susan Niebur's personal collection.

101   Niebur, S. (2009, 31 July). Personal interview with E. Reynolds. Located in the "Discovery Program" file, NASA Historical Reference Collection, History Division, NASA Headquarters, Washington, DC.

102   Ibid.

103   Young, K. (2002, 17 August). "Comet-chasing probe feared lost." Florida Today.

had an automatic backup computer program—set to run 24 hours after any loss of contact after the engine burn—that would fire small thrusters, turning the spacecraft so that it would use another of its four antennas to send signals back to Earth.[104]

NASA called the North American Aerospace Defense Command to request help locating the spacecraft. Several military assets, such as ground radars used by the Air Force and Defense Support Program infrared early-warning satellites, could have observed the 50-second burn on 15 August.[105] The press criticized the agency for performing the rocket burn, a critical maneuver, "in the blind," as had been done a few years earlier, during Mars Polar Lander's failed descent to the planet's surface.[106]

Astronomers joined in the search for the lost comet hunter. Researchers at Kitt Peak, Arecibo, and Goldstone, as well as amateurs around the world, pointed their telescopes at CONTOUR's last known location, the point where it was expected to be if the engine had fired normally, and many points in between, as well as other likely locations.

By the next morning, the news had broken that the spacecraft had been observed in two pieces. Jim Scotti, planetary scientist at the Lunar and Planetary Laboratory at the University of Arizona, and colleague Jeff Larsen, using the 70-inch telescope at Kitt Peak, had captured a picture of two objects, just 155 miles apart, moving past the Moon's orbit and away from Earth, approximately where the spacecraft was expected to be.[107] The spacecraft had broken into several pieces, just as Comet Schwassmann–Wachmann 3, its intended target, had broken seven years earlier.

"We called everyone into the meeting room," recalled Reynolds. "We had to just say, 'There's three pieces. It looks bad. And we'll keep looking, but it really does look bad.' …[A]t that point it was not really recoverable, and everybody kind of accepted it."[108]

The mission was not immediately declared a failure; there was still hope that the two pieces were an intact spacecraft and a piece of insulation, or the dust shield.[109] In addition to the 16 August planned rotation of CONTOUR to use a different antenna to send its signal, the spacecraft would also send a distress signal—using both transmitters and all four antennas simultaneously—96 hours after the burn.[110] This set of

---

104   Carreau, M. (2002, 17 August). "Images show NASA craft in two pieces." *Houston Chronicle.* 1; Zabarenko, D. (2002, August 16). "NASA loses contact with comet-chasing spacecraft." *Reuters.*

105   Morring, F. (2002, 19 August). "Comet probe feared lost after maneuver." *Aviation Week & Space Technology.* 27.

106   "Comet tour: learn and try again." (2002, 26 August). *Aviation Week & Space Technology.* 74.

107   Antczak, J. (2002, 17 August). "Telescope image suggests catastrophe for lost NASA spacecraft." *AP Newswire.*

108   Niebur, S. (2009, 31 July). Personal interview with E. Reynolds. Located in the "Discovery Program" file, NASA Historical Reference Collection, History Division, NASA Headquarters, Washington, DC.

109   Morring, F. (2002, 26 August). "Hopes are fading fast for lost comet probe." *Aviation Week & Space Technology.* 68.

110   Leary, W. (2002, 17 August). "Missing spacecraft may have broken apart." *The New York Times.*

signals would continue for 60 hours, from 19 to 22 August.[111] Farquhar optimistically said that the two-object image meant that the mission controllers "know where to look now."[112] The CONTOUR team was given continuous use of the DSN antennas around the world on both 16 August and 19 August, but to no avail. DSN access was reduced to once a week after 25 August.[113]

The science team reacted strongly to the loss. Peter Thomas, a co-investigator and astronomer at Cornell, told a local newspaper, "At this point, it is in the hands of the folks who know how to track the spacecraft down."[114] Thomas had been through a burn anomaly before, with NEAR, which had been out of contact for 27 hours before it was recovered. Jim Bell, a co-investigator and assistant professor of astronomy at Cornell, also hoped for a NEAR repeat.[115] Anita Cochran, a co-investigator and astronomer at the University of Texas, said, "If indeed the picture is what it appears to be, we can only hope to learn why it happened."[116] Instead of hearing the signal they hoped for, however, on 22 August, the team learned that new telescopic observations confirmed three objects in the field where CONTOUR went missing.[117]

The mission controllers tried repeatedly to contact the spacecraft during the window between solid rocket burn and the point of no return: the time when the spacecraft's hydrazine tanks would no longer be sufficient to return it on a trajectory back to Earth. Farquhar admitted that the chance of contact was, by then, "one chance in 10,000."[118] They continued to search for the spacecraft, listening over the DSN for nine days straight, and then for eight hours once a week until December.[119]

By this time, the CONTOUR team and NASA were beginning to understand what had happened. The solid rocket motor shut down early, 48 seconds into the 50 second burn, just 3 percent shy of its optimum performance. What was not well understood was why, or what might have been observed by possible "dark assets" believed to have been deployed to watch CONTOUR's burn over South Asia.[120] Shortly thereafter, a

111   Boyd, R. (2002, 22 August). "What's in the core? Comets." *The Lexington Herald Leader*. B8.
112   "Astronomers not giving up on missing US space probe." (2002, 18 August). *Agence France-Presse*.
113   Morring, F. (2002, 26 August). "Hopes are fading fast for lost comet probe." *Aviation Week & Space Technology*. 68.
114   James, R. (2002, 20 August). "Cornell's comet mission goes to pieces." *The Post-Standard*. A2.
115   "Cornell scientists holding out hope for comet mission." (2002, August 20). *AP Newswire*.
116   James, R. (2002, 20 August). "Cornell's comet mission goes to pieces." *The Post-Standard*. A2.
117   "More evidence shows breakup of cometary probe." (2002, August 22). *Los Angeles Times*. A17.
118   Morring, F. (2002, 26 August). "Hopes are fading fast for lost comet probe." *Aviation Week & Space Technology*. 68.
119   Bridges, A. (2002, 26 August). "Scientists consider replacing comet probe." *Contra Costa Times*. 12.
120   Morring, F. (2002, 26 August). "Hopes are fading fast for lost comet probe." *Aviation Week & Space Technology*. 68.

U.S. Space Command spokesman confirmed that they were watching, saying that the data would be made available to the CONTOUR Mishap Investigation Board on a "need to know" basis, and with appropriate security clearances.[121]

Farquhar characterized the members of his team as "heartsick" and "pretty depressed" over the loss.[122] But the team regrouped.

On Monday, 25 August—10 days after the ill-fated rocket burn—CONTOUR mission leadership conceded that there was little hope of salvaging the mission. They immediately announced their plans to launch a replacement, CONTOUR 2, as early as April 2006. A 2006 launch would enable them to reach Encke and Schwassmann–Wachmann 3 as planned. An immediate start to the sequel project would keep the 100 APL team members and 60 scientists and engineers at other institutions from facing job losses or career changes.[123]

A rebuild of the CONTOUR spacecraft—sans solid rocket motor—would save $10 to $20 million over the first spacecraft's $159 million cost, according to mission planners. There is no doubt that technical, management, and cost reviews would have scrutinized this proposal and cost estimate carefully, delving into the details of whatever would replace the Star 30 solid rocket motor—if, indeed, the Star 30 would be replaced. As Veverka admitted, "I have been trying to talk Bob [Farquhar] into not using a solid rocket motor on this particular mission."[124]

Farquhar, in a separate interview, was on the same page, observing that a 2006 launch would not require a two-phase launch strategy and solid rocket motor.[125] Instead, the spacecraft could utilize a Delta II Heavy launch vehicle with nine strap-on boosters and a greater hydrazine fuel load to use for larger course corrections that would be necessary during flight.[126]

The team was planning to "proceed aggressively with CONTOUR 2," as Veverka, who would again be Principal Investigator, explained at the time.[127] NASA Headquarters expressed less enthusiasm and did not solicit plans for CONTOUR 2; it would have to wait until the next Discovery competition four years away, in 2006.

---

121   David, L. (2002, 9 September). "CONTOUR loss viewed by U.S. military sensors." Space.com.

122   Roylance, F. (2002, 24 August). "Hopes of recovering spacecraft are slim, NASA official says: CONTOUR, sent to study comets, fell silent Aug. 15." *The Baltimore Sun.*

123   Roylance, F. (2002, 27 August). "Another CONTOUR could be launched: After loss of spacecraft, scientists quickly plan new comet-probe mission." *The Baltimore Sun.* 3A.

124   Young, K. (2002, 26 August). "Comet craft likely lost; replacement postponed." *Florida Today.*

125   Lane, E. (2002, 27 August). "2nd Comet craft envisioned." *Newsday.* A16.

126   Morring, F. (2002, 9 September). "CONTOUR team wants to build a new probe." *Aviation Week & Space Technology.* 40.

127   Roylance, F. (2002, 27 August). "Another CONTOUR could be launched: After loss of spacecraft, scientists quickly plan new comet-probe mission." *The Baltimore Sun.* 3A.

As an act of due diligence, mission controllers on 17 December 2002, sent commands to the largest piece of the tracked spacecraft, using 34-meter and 70-meter antennas in the DSN, and listened for a response. The session lasted 12 hours, ending just past midnight. The team tried again to contact the spacecraft during a 4-hour window on Friday, 20 December, when the spacecraft antenna, if it still existed and was attached to a functional spacecraft, would again be pointed at Earth. When no signal was received that week, NASA and the Applied Physics Laboratory declared CONTOUR lost.[128]

APL received support for the ensuing investigation, but the science team did not receive sufficient funds for an orderly closeout and archiving of the project, according to Veverka.[129]

CONTOUR Mishap Investigation Board

Almost immediately, NASA convened a CONTOUR Mishap Investigation Board (MIB) to investigate the loss.[130] APL had its own mishap investigation board, as did Alliant Techsystems. Each had its own motivations, and each wanted to know what had gone wrong.[131]

Ed Weiler, the Associate Administrator for space science at NASA Headquarters, appointed Theron M. Bradley, Jr., the agency's chief engineer, to lead the investigation. The board would have an estimated work time of six to eight weeks.[132] To help ameliorate "information overload," the MIB used new NASA Investigation Organizer software to map the 145 CONTOUR mission review documents and 50 photos onto a representation of the main spacecraft system. Beyond that, little is known publicly because of U.S. intelligence assets involved in the investigation, and only those with an appropriate security clearance could attend every briefing.[133]

The NASA MIB rarely commented on its work. In February 2003, Bradley broke the board's silence, telling the Associated Press that, while other causes for the loss of CONTOUR, such as collision with space debris, had not been ruled out, "the leading cause in our report" will be a faulty design of the spacecraft, with the motor positioned so that hot gases from the engine exhaust unexpectedly heated the probe.[134]

---

128 Leary, W. E. (2002, 21 December). "NASA gives up on CONTOUR." *New York Times.* 17; and CONTOUR MIB report.

129 Niebur, S. (2009, 10 September). Personal interview with J. Veverka. Located in the "CONTOUR" file, NASA Historical Reference Collection, History Division, NASA Headquarters, Washington, DC.

130 NASA. (2003, 31 May). Contour mishap investigation board report.

131 Niebur, S. (2009, 31 July). Personal interview with E. Reynolds. Located in the "CONTOUR" file, NASA Historical Reference Collection, History Division, NASA Headquarters, Washington, DC.

132 Carreau, M. (2002, 27 August). "NASA begins investigation into lost craft." *Houston Chronicle.*

133 David, L. (2002, 27 August). "CONTOUR investigation using new software to probe mishap." Space.com.

134 Bridges, A. (2003, 13 February). "Design defects may have doomed CONTOUR spacecraft." *The Associated Press.*

The final report bore this out, calling the hot exhaust plume from the solid rocket motor the "probable proximate cause" without ruling out three other possible causes: orbital debris, failure of the control systems, or catastrophic failure of the kick motor.[135] The report of the CONTOUR MIB included a fault tree with details on each of these possible proximate causes and their potential relevance, as well as the identification of three root causes; seven significant observations; and additional recommendations addressing the effectiveness of communicating NASA's lessons learned, engineering and documentation rigor, and the level of detail in technical reviews. The root causes include the CONTOUR project's reliance on "analyses by similarity," inadequate systems engineering processes, and inadequate reviews. Significant observations included the lack of telemetry during a critical event; significant reliance on subcontractors without adequate oversight, insight, and review; inadequate communication between APL and subcontractor Alliant Techsystems; use of Alliant Techsystems analytic models that were not specific to CONTOUR; limited understanding of plume heating environments for the solid rocket motor in space; no plan for encounters with orbital debris; and a limited understanding of CONTOUR and solid rocket motor operating conditions.[136]

Veverka recalled of the investigation: "I was not even invited into some of the reviews of the mishap. I had to get the information through Ed Reynolds. It was very bad.... It kind of illustrated this thing that—we pretend that the PI is in charge of a Discovery mission, but not really."[137] Interestingly, Project Manager Mary Chiu was never contacted by the MIB, despite being in overall charge of spacecraft success.[138]

Looking back, memories would differ about the fundamental issues of the solid rocket motor. Recalled Chiu, "Bob keeps saying that it was over its lifetime. I don't remember that. I thought it was within lifetime.... I knew it was near the end of its lifetime, but I don't think it was over, because I think we'd have run into some problems on that one. But the details kind of blur a little bit."[139]

Farquhar, now deceased, described in his memoir the CONTOUR disaster data captured by military assets, along with his disdain of the MIB's findings:

The 50-second burn appeared to go as expected for 48 seconds, but with only two seconds remaining, there was a dramatic increase in brightness. Although I am not an expert at interpreting the satellite data, it was fairly obvious that something catastrophic had occurred. This conclusion was later confirmed by telescopic observations that showed three

135   NASA. (2003, 31 May). Contour mishap investigation board report.

136   Ibid.

137   Niebur, S. (2009, 10 September). Personal interview with J. Veverka. Located in the "CONTOUR" file, NASA Historical Reference Collection, History Division, NASA Headquarters, Washington, DC.

138   Niebur, S. (2009, 16 September). Personal interview with M. Chiu. Located in "CONTOUR" file, NASA Historical Reference Collection, History Division, NASA Headquarters, Washington, DC.

139   Ibid.

separate objects following CONTOUR's targeted heliocentric trajectory. The telescopic data was consistent with an incomplete solid-rocket burn.[140]

He blamed residual solid rocket fuel that failed to remain bonded to the rocket wall breaking away, plugging the nozzle, and exploding. "NASA's Mishap Investigation Board admitted that this failure scenario was a possibility, but they preferred to believe that the failure was caused by an improbable sequence of events that only someone like Rube Goldberg could envision."[141]

Ultimately, though, was it all a waste? Ed Reynolds said not entirely. "People will say, 'Oh, you blew $150 million….' The money got distributed across the country really nicely. But we missed out on doing the science that we said we were going to do."[142]

GENESIS AND STARDUST REVISITED

On 8 September 2004, just as the Discovery Program was regaining equanimity after the loss of CONTOUR, the Genesis sample return capsule crashed into Earth.

"Between an Eight and Nine"

On 8 September 2004, Hollywood stunt pilots planned to capture a capsule containing bits of the Sun. It would be the first NASA craft to re-enter Earth's atmosphere since the Shuttle Columbia's destruction in February the previous year.[143] The Genesis team was ready. The helicopter pilots were ready, though one of them, interviewed at a NASA pre-return briefing, said of the challenge of a midair snag: "Out of a scale of one to ten, this is between an eight and nine."[144]

NASA had never retrieved a sample in midair before. For that matter, the last NASA sample return had been done manually by the Apollo astronauts, who literally picked up rocks and carried them home. Still, midair capture had been around for a while. Nearly 50 years earlier, the Air Force had used a similar technique, and for decades it retrieved hundreds of film canisters from photoreconnaissance satellites.[145]

The reentry of a human-made object at a precise date and time provided opportunities for other types of research to be done as well. NASA's Near Earth Object Observations program treated the incoming spacecraft as a tracking test, "to see if

---

140   Farquhar, R. (2011). *Fifty Years on the Space Frontier: Halo Orbits, Comets, Asteroids, and More.* Denver: Outskirts Press. 220.

141   Ibid.

142   Niebur, S. (2009, 31 July). Personal interview with E. Reynolds. Located in the "CONTOUR" file, NASA Historical Reference Collection, History Division, NASA Headquarters, Washington, DC.

143   David, L. (2004, 31 August). "The Genesis payload: Just how dangerous are its contents?" Space.com.

144   Klotz, I. (2004, 21 August). "Probe set to return with sun sample." *The Discovery News.*

145   Day, D. (1998). *Eye in the Sky: The Story of the Corona Spy Satellites.* Washington, DC: Smithsonian Institution Press.

our software can predict a real impactor, instead of a near miss," said Don Yeomans, previously of the CONTOUR team, and the Near Earth Object Observations project manager at JPL.[146] Other astronomers prepared to watch the hot shock wave expected in front of the capsule during reentry, in hopes of learning more about entry conditions for incoming meteors.[147] An Air Force plane, the Flying Infrared Signature Technologies Aircraft (FISTA), planned to observe the spectrum of the radiation associated with the spacecraft's reentry as the air molecules around it became hot. Several groups of engineers were interested in the condition of the return capsule itself: data on its condition would help future mission designers determine the necessary parameters for future Earth return payloads of dust, rocks, and even astronauts.[148]

Engineers at Lockheed Martin were so confident of hitting the target ellipse that they actually set up a betting pool, complete with a map of the Utah Test and Training Range, to guess where in the ellipse the capsule would land. They expected the spacecraft to hit the 20.5-mile by 6.2-mile target (known as "the keyhole") in the atmosphere over Oregon and the sample return capsule to return to Earth at just the right angle for the safe delivery of its contents. "The angle has to be controlled to better than a tenth of a degree," said Joseph Vellinga, the Genesis project manager at Lockheed Martin. "It has to be hit very accurately."[149]

The preceding 6 September critical trajectory maneuver was "right on the money," according to Kenny Starnes, Genesis Team Chief at Lockheed Martin.[150] Everything was lined up for a thrilling day.

A Thrilling Day

After 884 days collecting solar wind, on 8 September 2004, at 9:52 a.m. MDT, the 1.5-meter, 210-kilogram sample return capsule entered Earth's atmosphere "with pinpoint accuracy," according to Chris Jones, Director of Solar System Exploration at JPL.[151] It streaked across the sky over Oregon at 24,861 miles per hour, with energy "like a 4.5 million pound freight train traveling at 80 miles per hour," according to Bob Corwin, the Lockheed Martin capsule recovery chief.[152] As hoped, it entered the entry ellipse at the Utah Test and Training Range. Two helicopters were in the air, ready to catch the spacecraft after its two parachutes deployed, first a small drogue chute and then a larger, rectangular one. Crowds in Utah and across the country watched events

---

146 McKee, M. (2004, 5 September). "Capsule to bring the sun down to Earth." *New Scientist.*

147 Pountney, M. (2004, 7 September). "Stunt pilots to catch space capsule." *The Melbourne Herald Sun.*

148 McKee, M. (2004, 5 September). "Capsule to bring the sun down to Earth." *New Scientist.*

149 Erickson, J. (2004, 6 September). "Rocket scientists take their best guesses on Genesis." Scripps Howard News Service.

150 David, L. (2004, 7 September). "Genesis hits the mark for Utah reentry Wednesday." Space.com.

151 McKee, M. (2004, 9 September). "Solar wind space capsule crashes." *The New Scientist.*

152 Gugliotta, G. (2004, 9 September). "Spacecraft crashes with solar data." *The Washington Post.* A3.

unfold live on television. The helicopters were in the air at 9:25 a.m. The first images of the returning capsule appeared visible at 9:53 a.m. The spacecraft grew larger and larger as it approached. The pilots waited. The crowds waited. The parachutes waited. The helicopters waited. The capsule wasn't slowing down. The drogue chute, expected to open two minutes and seven seconds after atmospheric entry, at an altitude of 33 kilometers, did not deploy. The larger parafoil, intended to open six minutes later, at 6.1 kilometers, did not either.

"We do not see a drogue," said a voice on television.[153] Rather than drift gently for Hollywood stunt teams to snatch and set down, the spacecraft began to tumble wildly, falling far faster than anyone expected to see that day. Mission scientists, gathered for the moment of triumph, watched stone-faced.[154]

Chris Jones, the Director of Solar System Exploration at JPL, was on the air at the time. "Clearly something has gone wrong," he said.[155] The next words that television viewers around the world heard were those of the mission controller: "Ground impact."[156]

The precious samples of the Sun that NASA had spent over $350 million to obtain and prepare for analysis hit the ground at 190 miles per hour. Half of the canister jutted pitifully from the earth; it and its inner sample container plates were breached and contaminated with mud. The soft floor of the Great Salt Lake Desert was the capsule's salvation—it acted as a cushion for the human-made impactor. As Eileen Stansbery, the mission contamination control team lead, explained: "We actually landed sort of in a mud puddle. So, we had damp Utah soil interacting with the collector materials, although the energy associated with the impact sort of flash dried it...and therefore turned into concrete."[157]

Genesis Project Scientist Amy Jurewicz later admitted that her first thought was, "Oh, my God. It's a pancake."[158] Don Burnett, the mission PI, later recalled: "We were too busy to be traumatized. We had work to do. This was a contingency we had planned for."[159]

Burnett pulled out the binder of landing contingencies the team had written years earlier. "We didn't think we'd ever have to use it, but we were ready for it," he later said. "The problem was the rest of NASA management didn't know how ready we were." The team had rehearsed an impact scenario a week earlier. They knew who would go

153   Chong, J. (2004, 9 September). "In the end, Genesis finds mud on Earth." *The Los Angeles Times*.

154   "Movie magicians fail to catch star dust." (2004, 9 September). ABC News.

155   Chang, K., and Maria Newman. (2004, 9 September). "Space capsule crashes in Utah." *The New York Times*.

156   Ibid.

157   Niebur, S. (2009, 25 March). Personal interview with D. Sweetnam and Eileen Stansbery. Located in "Genesis" file, NASA Historical Reference Collection, History Division, NASA Headquarters, Washington, DC.

158   Erickson, J. (2006, 15 March). "Genesis findings emerge." *Rocky Mountain News*.

159   Rincon, P. (2006, 16 March). "Solar riches survive probe crash." BBC News.

to the site and what they would do there. "We knew the plan was to go out and pick up the pieces. It was worse than what we thought.... Everything was bent and broken, and there was a lot of stuff spilled out. Most of the material was contained inside, all broken. Karen [McNamara, the Genesis curation recovery lead] went out for two days and picked up stuff out of the dirt. She just shoveled the dirt in at some point."[160]

Dave Lindstrom, the Program Scientist for the mission at NASA Headquarters, explained just how bad the situation was, saying, "The canister has been ripped open, and there is a six-inch gap between the top and bottom...the spacecraft is on one edge so that one major part of the cylindrical sample container was severely crushed. The other side was undamaged."[161]

The sample recovery team secured the capsule and moved it to a temporary clean room at the Dugway Proving Ground, a U.S. Army facility south of the Utah Test and Training Range. The press had questions.[162]

Colin Pillinger, a co-investigator and professor at the Open University in the United Kingdom, told the BBC, "There could be fragments inside there that still contained some kind of scientific information. But the contamination from the desert is going to be a killer at the end of the day for the scientists."[163] Kevin McKeegan, a co-investigator and professor at UCLA, reminded reporters, "The solar wind ions cannot fall out from being hit hard."[164]

Before shipping the samples to Houston, the team spent weeks in Utah painstakingly documenting the state of the samples and collector material. Everything was photographed, hand-drawn, and measured for its size and shape with notation on its configuration (e.g., this is highly scratched; that has mud splotches; that endured salt spray from the vaporizing of the dirt on impact). Everything was then extracted and packaged to minimize further damage and mitigate any further contamination during shipping.

According to Eileen Stansbery of the sample recovery team, the original plan called for the samples to be shipped to Houston by truck. She convinced the Director of Johnson Space Center to send an airplane for the sample team and the recovered

---

160 Niebur, S. (2009, 24 March). Personal interview with D. Burnett. Located in "Genesis" file, NASA Historical Reference Collection, History Division, NASA Headquarters, Washington, DC.

161 Gugliotta, G. (2004, 10 September). "NASA hopes data can be salvaged from crashed craft." *The Washington Post*. A3.

162 "Solar capsule crashes into Earth." (2004, 9 September). BBC News.

163 Ibid.; Radford, T. (2004, 9 September). "Scientists left to pick up the pieces over the $250M can that fell to Earth." *The [U.K.] Guardian.*

164 "Movie magicians fail to catch star dust." (2004, 9 September). ABC Online.

material. "We basically rode the samples home on the aircraft, on the NASA jet," she recalled. "It was a much smoother ride. It took less time...."[165] The rest of the capsule was shipped to Lockheed Martin for use in their investigation of what had gone wrong.

In a rare bit of good news, the spacecraft's ion concentrator, which filtered out light protons and alpha particles, concentrating heavier ions onto a special collector tile, survived the crash. "Finding these concentrator targets in excellent condition after the Genesis crash was a real miracle," said Roger Wiens, a mission co-investigator and the lead for the instruments provided by Los Alamos National Laboratory. "It raised our spirits a huge amount the day after the impact."[166] Andy Dantzler, the Director of the Solar System Exploration Division, credited the robustness of the spacecraft design with saving the samples despite the catastrophic landing.

The materials safely in Houston, the sample team got to work. "In addition to what was done in Utah, we would take a couple more images to sort of give you a gross characterization of how dirty it is before we start," said Stansbery. "We have an imaging system that we were developing techniques on to count up the size and number of particles on a surface. So, you basically get an average dirt load off of it. We also needed to identify which regime that particular wafer was. That was something we could not do in Utah."[167]

Because each of the five collector trays was designed with a different thickness, the team was able to use a measurement device to determine with certainty which tray the samples came from.

Physics made cleaning the sample trays difficult. "The energy of the impact pulverized a lot of stuff to extremely small particle sizes—small enough particle sizes to where those particles, although sitting on the surface, they were attached by van der Waals forces," Stansbery recalled. Ultrasonic cleaning with pure water was inadequate to the task. "Because the particle sizes were sufficiently small, we had to go to megasonic frequencies on the ultra-pure water." Before the spacecraft had launched, the team had developed the megasonic technique to clean the collector array body.[168]

165   Niebur, S. (2009, 25 March). Personal interview with D. Sweetnam and Eileen Stansbery. Located in "Genesis" file, NASA Historical Reference Collection, History Division, NASA Headquarters, Washington, DC.

166   "NASA Announces Key Genesis Science Collectors In Excellent Shape." (2005, 20 April). NASA Press Release. Downloaded from *https://www.nasa.gov/home/hqnews/2005/apr/HQ_05102_genesis_collectors.html*; Genesis Mission Status Report. (2004, 10 September). NASA Press Release. Downloaded from *https://solarsystem.nasa.gov/genesismission/mission/status_report5.html*.

167   Niebur, S. (2009, 7 July). Personal interview with E. Stansbery. Located in the "Discovery Program" file, NASA Historical Reference Collection, History Division, NASA Headquarters, Washington, DC.

168   Niebur, S. (2009, 7 July). Personal interview with E. Stansbery. Located in "Genesis" file, NASA Historical Reference Collection, History Division, NASA Headquarters, Washington, DC.

They started with the worst, most compromised samples—tiny fragments with little conceivable scientific utility—and sought to determine whether the cleaning technique would work. NASA Headquarters signed off on the experiment. In addition, the team sent out several samples to different labs to develop new cleaning techniques. Though the samples were consigned by the project to oblivion, in the end, those materials yielded science as well.

Mishap Investigation Board

NASA Headquarters appointed the Genesis Mishap Investigation Board (MIB) within three days of the crash landing, per agency protocol. They announced on 10 September 2004 that the MIB would be led by Dr. Michael Ryschkewitsch, the director of the Applied Engineering and Technology Directorate at Goddard Space Flight Center. One week after the crash, the MIB held its first meeting. Their task was to determine the proximate cause of the crash, the root cause, and contributing factors, and to make recommendations for preventing similar problems with missions such as Stardust, which was next to return and used some similar design elements.

Ed Hirst, the mission manager of Genesis, recalled well the moment he found out. "Monday, as I'm driving into work, I got a phone call that says, 'You need to make arrangements to go to Utah.' And I'm on a plane by, like, two o'clock that afternoon," he explained. "My job at that point was to be able to answer questions—as many questions as I could—from the Mishap Board." He brought all the procedures, materials, and information he had available to the Utah Test and Training Range, where he met investigators and other members of the team.[169] Ryschkewitsch, for his part, was careful not to hinder the science recovery underway.[170]

The first observed problem was that the drogue chute did not deploy. The drogue chute did not deploy because the pyrotechnics did not fire. The immediate question raised by the MIB was *why* the explosives didn't go off. Was it the overheating battery that vexed the spacecraft early on? The explosives, Bob Corwin, the Lockheed Martin capsule recovery chief, pointed out, are part of a chain reaction. If the battery had failed, the pyrotechnics would not have ignited and the drogue chute and parafoil would not have deployed midair.[171]

---

169 Niebur, S. (2009, 10 August). Personal interview with E. Hirst. Located in "Genesis" file, NASA Historical Reference Collection, History Division, NASA Headquarters, Washington, DC.

170 Niebur, S. (2009, 25 March). Personal interview with D. Sweetnam and Eileen Stansbery. Located in "Genesis" file, NASA Historical Reference Collection, History Division, NASA Headquarters, Washington, DC.

171 Harwood, W. (2004, 9 September). "Genesis capsule slams back to Earth." *Spaceflight Now.*

Other possible culprits included issues with the onboard gravity sensor, intended to indicate Earth arrival, or some sort of electronic glitch in the capsule.[172] Navigation had been precise, the spacecraft landing within the intended eight kilometers of target area. The navigation team felt certain whatever went wrong was not their work.

Initial analysis soon indicated that the likely cause of the crash was a flawed gravity switch design. It was installed properly, but a flaw prevented it from sensing the slowdown caused by the spacecraft's atmospheric entry, and thus it did not start the timing sequence leading to the drogue and parafoil deployments.

The problem, at least in theory, could have been caught by pre-launch testing and initial reviews. Sweetnam explained, "I believe that there was a point early in the design phase where you're essentially at a peer review level. Your avionics engineers, who really know about this, I think that's the point where we had the best shot of catching this error." As for prelaunch testing, he explained, it wasn't simply a lapse in procedure. Rather it was the nature of the Discovery Program. "We were constrained. And so, we, the project, convinced itself that it didn't need to do a system level test of the capsule. So, this was a money and time integration issue. They did some limited testing of the avionics boxes. They dropped them and the [gravity] switches worked. Well, okay, but had they put the capsule on a spin table and spun it up to simulate the deceleration forces, and *actually gone through the process* to simulate the entry deceleration curve, it would have caught it."[173]

Though Stardust and Genesis shared similar hardware, the latter spacecraft's avionics were sufficiently different that, regardless of the tests that Stardust ran, they would not have applied to Genesis. On 7 January 2006, the *Salt Lake Tribune* quoted Ryschkewitsch as saying Lockheed Martin had skipped a critical pre-launch test. "Clearly there was an error made, and there were some shortfalls in processes that you would hope would catch it.... [T]he safety nets were not there."[174] The MIB report released on 13 June 2006 in part faulted the faster, better, cheaper philosophy for the disaster.[175]

A Good Planet to Crash Into

Eileen Stansbery, who led the sample recovery team, later recalled a quote by Don Burnett: "If you have to crash into a planet, Earth's a good one to crash into because

---

172   David, L. (2004, 9 September). "Bad battery may have doomed Genesis." Space.com.

173   Niebur, S. (2009, March 25). Personal interview with D. Sweetnam and Eileen Stansbery. Located in "Genesis" file, NASA Historical Reference Collection, History Division, NASA Headquarters, Washington, DC.

174   *Salt Lake City Tribune*. (2006, 7 January). "Testing oversight may have doomed NASA's $264M Genesis capsule."

175   NASA. (2005, 30 November). Genesis Mishap Investigation Board Report.

you can go get it."[176] The team had great success in recovering samples. Just 18 months after the crash landing, mission co-investigators presented their first science results at the annual Lunar and Planetary Science Conference in Houston, TX.[177] Stansbery explained, "Even though the recovery was not the nominal plan, it all worked because the team was a good team, had good relationships, and everyone knew what to do in a wide variety of circumstances."[178]

Amy Jurewicz credited the mission PI for the good relationships and strong communication among the missions' scientists. "Don has been very innovative about making sure that everybody he could possibly get involved is involved…. He's gone out to select not only people who are good at what they do, but also people who get along well together."[179]

In late 2009 Ansgar Grimberg and colleagues published a striking analysis of the Genesis metallic glass exposed to the solar wind, their findings reverberating back to Apollo's "aluminum foil experiments." The Moon-based science project saw pieces of aluminum foil left on the ground for up to 45 hours at each of the five Apollo landing sites and then brought back to Earth for study. The idea was to collect atomic particles hailing from the Sun. Analyses showed that there was inconsistent enrichment of the captured heavier isotopes. Scientists attributed the variable enrichment to discrete high-energy events.[180] The measurements of the Genesis metallic glass samples, on the other hand, revealed no need for such events.

Researchers using the Genesis samples were able to solve this long-debated quandary due to two aspects of good experiment design: the exposure environment was well-defined, and the selection of materials was an improvement over the foils used in the past. The metallic glass sample was exposed for three years, during which the state of the solar wind was consistently measured by other heliospheric spacecraft, including the Advanced Composition Explorer. ACE data showed that although there were significant high-energy solar flares during the time of flight, the fluence of the particles was far too small to reproduce the neon ratios seen in the lunar samples. Further, the time of flight was so short that very little neon would have been added to

---

176   Niebur, S. (2009, 25 March). Personal interview with D. Sweetnam and Eileen Stansbery. Located in "Genesis" file, NASA Historical Reference Collection, History Division, NASA Headquarters, Washington, DC.

177   Rincon, P. (2006, 16 March). "Solar riches survive probe crash." BBC News.

178   Niebur, S. (2009, 25 March). Personal interview with D. Sweetnam and Eileen Stansbery. Located in "Genesis" file, NASA Historical Reference Collection, History Division, NASA Headquarters, Washington, DC.

179   Niebur, S. (2009, 24 March). Personal interview with A. Jurewicz. Located in "Genesis" file, NASA Historical Reference Collection, History Division, NASA Headquarters, Washington, DC.

180   Geiss, J., Bühler, F., Cerutti, H., Eberhardt, P., Filleux, Ch., Meister, J., & Signer, P. (2004). "The Apollo SWC Experiment: Results, Conclusions, Consequences." *Space Science Reviews*, 110(3/4), 307–335. *https://doi.org/10.1023/B:SPAC.0000023409.54469.40*.

the sample by the spallation of cosmic rays. These additional components could thus be ignored, and the investigators could determine whether the observed neon was consistent with a single source: the quiescent solar wind. [181]

Unlike the aluminum foil, when the bulk metallic glass was cleaned (etching in vacuo), the material allowed researchers to create high-resolution depth profiling of the implanted noble gases. Researchers were ultimately able to eliminate the need for an additional flux of high-energy solar particles that had long been theorized for the lunar foils.[182]

The Care and Feeding of a Discovery AO

In 1998, the Discovery Program held a "lessons learned" workshop—something it had done consistently so as to keep the program "of the community." Attendees were candid in their responses. Ultimately, NASA Headquarters accepted several recommendations to emerge from the community: First, the Discovery Program would increase the number of proposal reviewers. It would also constrain the proposal summary issued with the post–Step 1 press release, to protect proprietary information. The program would shorten the evaluation process. Moreover, NASA would establish a steering committee to investigate the possibility of funding future mission studies and to provide recommendations for implementation.

On 31 March 1998, NASA's Office of Space Science Applications released the 1998 Discovery Announcement of Opportunity. This AO was the first with Technical, Management, Cost, and Outreach (TMCO, later called TMC) to be run by the program support office at NASA's Langley Research Center. This process would remain in effect for the next decade. Wayne Ritchie was the first Discovery Acquisition Manager at Langley; Brad Perry succeeded him in this role and was then named director of the Science Support Office (later called the Science Office for Mission Assessments). Gloria Hernandez, and later, Carlos Liceaga, filled the acquisition manager role for Discovery.

The process by which the AO had been drafted was by then well established, having been hashed out previously over several AO cycles led by the Discovery Program Office at NASA Headquarters and implemented by the Lunar and Planetary Institute in Houston. The Langley office further formalized the process, crystallizing it into standard operating procedures. When an AO was to be released, the program scientist at NASA Headquarters took the previous AO and made modifications in accordance with policy changes prompted by reviews, management, and lessons learned.

---

181   Wimmer-Schweingruber, R. F., *SOHO (Artificial satellite), & Advanced Composition Explorer (Artificial satellite)* (Eds.). (2001). "Solar and galactic composition: A joint SOHO/ACE workshop": Bern, Switzerland, 6–9 March 2001. American Institute of Physics.

182   Grimberg, A., Baur, H., Bochsler, P., Bühler, F., Burnett, D. S., Hays, C. C., Heber, V. S., Jurewicz, A. J. G., & Wieler, R. (2006). "Solar Wind Neon from Genesis: Implications for the Lunar Noble Gas Record." *Science*, 314(5802), 1133–1135. *https://doi.org/10.1126/science.1133568*.

Approximately six months before the release date, the program scientist would share the plans and revisions with a corresponding acquisition manager at Langley. Together, they would review the AO for clarity and to ensure that the necessary details—and only the necessary details—were requested as requirements or guidelines. In other programs, this work was often done in concert with the program executives as well, but "in planetary, it traditionally has always been a very strong interface role with the program scientist," said Brad Perry in a 2009 interview.[183]

The acquisition manager would then populate a program library with supporting documentation. This program library was originally released with each AO but now lived on a static website (updated before the release of each AO) that could be used by the community in planning future missions even before the AO was released.

Langley would support and implement a "pre-proposal bidders' conference" for PIs, project managers, and, increasingly, new business representatives from the management institutions and industry partners wishing to bid. At this conference, extensive question-and-answer sessions were encouraged, and a transcript would be posted online afterward so that the discussion could be done "fairly, uniformly, inclusively," in Perry's words.[184] In later days, the bidders' conferences would be opened to participation by telephone and/or streamed live over the web to ensure that prospective bidders' questions would be answered in full view of competing teams.

Even before proposals were submitted, TMCO review teams had been selected from experts in the community and leaders in their subfields. They were the proposers' peers: people who had substantially contributed to previous missions in the space science community. Staffing such panels could be difficult, as in the search for well-qualified reviewers, the majority of people still working on space science missions were either still involved in proposing space science missions, collaborating with scientists or managers listed on current proposals, or employed by an institution proposing to the particular opportunity they would be reviewing. People in any of those situations would be "conflicted" and thus not eligible to serve on review panels. To streamline the forming of review panels, many reviewers were pre-selected during the proposal period from people not involved in any form or fashion with the proposing teams. The standard areas of cost, schedule, and management could be filled this way, with specific technology experts added as the need for them became apparent based on the proposals received by the due date.

After a compliance screening by the program scientist and other program support specialists at NASA Headquarters and their contractor staff, the Discovery

---

183   Niebur, S. (2009, April 27). Personal interview with B. Perry. Located in the "Discovery Program" file, NASA Historical Reference Collection, History Division, NASA Headquarters, Washington, DC.

184   Ibid.

Program Acquisition Manager at Langley would then lead an independent Technical, Management, Cost review of all proposals and attend the categorization, steering, and selection meetings at NASA Headquarters.

Separately, the program scientist would lead a review of the proposals' scientific merit with planetary scientists and exoplanet scientists from the community, and education and outreach professionals would evaluate the completeness of the education and outreach plans. Some years, the latter part was done by education and public outreach professionals serving on the Technical, Management, Cost panels; some years, the education and outreach plans would be reviewed separately under the direction of the Science Mission Directorate education and public outreach lead or his or her designee. In all, the proposals would be evaluated using the five criteria from the 1998 AO:

- Scientific merit of the investigation
- Total cost of the mission to NASA
- Technical merit and feasibility of the science investigation
- Feasibility of the mission implementation scheme
- Education, outreach, technology, and small disadvantaged business activities[185]

The "scientific merit" criterion was given the greatest weight, with the "cost of the mission to NASA" item given a slightly lower weight. The remaining three criteria were given still lower and approximately equal weighting.[186] The results of these reviews could be summed up in a matrix consisting of scientific merit adjectival ratings (Excellent, Very Good, Good, Fair, Poor) and TMC/TMCO risk ratings (Low Risk, Medium Risk, High Risk). These ratings were presented at a NASA Headquarters Categorization Committee, which, *based on the ratings alone*, would divide the mission concepts into four categories.

A mission rated "Excellent" and "Low Risk" was typically Category I or II. A mission rated "Fair" or "Good" and "High Risk" would be Category IV. A mission that would be Category I except for a single risky technology could be called Category III if funds were available to help the proposing institution or institutions develop that technology to a satisfactory technology readiness level in the near term, but this was not a requirement on NASA Headquarters; such missions could easily be assigned Category IV in years where insufficient money was available to assist.

After categorization came the steering committee, an ad hoc NASA Headquarters committee that evaluated how the review panels were run and the categorization decided.

---

185 Bergstralh, J. (1998, January 28). "AO Overview, Proposal Review Process, Categorization, & Evaluation." Presentation to the Discovery Missions Program Lessons Learned Workshop.

186 Ibid.

Once the steering committee determined that the review had been held appropriately and the categorizations were upheld, the program scientist and acquisition manager could take the Category I mission concepts to the Associate Administrator for selection. The selection meeting was a formal affair, attended by the Associate Administrator, one or more of his or her deputies, all the division directors, including resource management, as well as many top-level managers in the office, including the chief scientist, chief engineer, and chief technologist. The discussion would be pre-decisional and confidential. After the discussion, the program scientist and division director, among others, would prepare a press release, signed and released by the Associate Administrator, with three to five mission concepts formally selected for further study.

After the proposing teams were debriefed, those funded for mission concept studies—often called Phase A—were invited to a kickoff meeting, typically at or near NASA Headquarters. Since the competing concept studies were being reviewed almost entirely for their respective technical, management, cost, small business, and outreach plans, the Concept Study Review kickoff meetings and presentations were led in large part by the acquisition manager at Langley, who defined the rules of engagement for the proposing teams as they performed the next stage of work, prepared their Concept Study Report, and hosted the TMC reviewers for a site visit.

The proposing teams would have several months to perform a concept study and refine their mission concept while reducing perceived risks to the mission. After each concept study was completed, 30 to 50 copies of the report would be delivered to NASA Headquarters. The reports would then be thoroughly dissected by TMC reviewers, who would provide each team with questions of clarification to be answered at the site visit, rather than impetuses for new work. Typically, the questions were provided only a few days to a couple of weeks before the site visit. The TMC reviewers contracted by Langley were heavily engaged in both review processes and site visits. The site visits were a chance for a two-way exchange between select reviewers, representing all the major areas of review, and the mission teams. This "Step 2 review" was in sharp contrast to the parameters observed in the Step 1 review, where the reviewers gave reasonable benefit of the doubt to each proposal team.

"If they have an inconsistency in their proposal between one section and another, we try to read what their intent was," said Brad Perry, then–Discovery acquisition manager at Langley. "If it is within reason to give benefit of the doubt, we do that. We try to not have interaction with the proposal teams during this first step review process. All of that is changed when we do the site visit process on Step 2 or Phase A

Concept Study Report review. There we get to drill down and get absolute detail at the lowest available information level so that we can completely understand the situation and eliminate any doubt."[187]

Select reviewers would visit the proposing team's location of preference, hear the answers to the submitted questions, and interact fully with the team, producing a supplemental set of information complementing the Concept Study Report. Activities were in large part up to the proposing team, who often arranged a site tour, a technology demonstration, science exhibits, and anything else that might be convincing to the reviewers that the team was up to the challenge.

Phase A by 1998 was very competitive, as both the stakes and the odds of selection were higher when just a handful of teams were competing for the chance to build a $300 million mission.[188] AO parameters that year allowed the proposal of investigations addressing elements of solar system exploration, or the search for extrasolar planetary systems. Missions were cost-capped at $190 million in Fiscal Year 1999 dollars over 36 months, with a total mission cost of $299 million. Any mission was required to launch by 30 September 2004.

Missions of opportunity, as well as proposals for scientific investigations and instrumentation as part of a foreign mission, were encouraged to be submitted at the same time; the number of opportunities for U.S. scientists to fly instruments on non-NASA missions had increased without a corresponding funding avenue for instrument design and construction, or subsequent data analysis. Previously, instrument PIs on non-NASA missions could propose for support using an unsolicited proposal to NASA Headquarters, but there was no infrastructure, published guidelines, or peer review for this process. By allowing this opportunity in the Discovery Program, such smaller, $35 million–capped investigations could undergo scientific merit, technical, management, and cost reviews with rigor approximating the rigor with which full missions were reviewed and selected.[189]

Once the AO went out, "notice of intents" from proposers were due in one month: on 30 April 1998. Full proposals were then due two months after, on 29 June. While the proposals were in review, Wes Huntress, who had spearheaded the Discovery Program and was a selecting official for the AO, retired from NASA. On 28 September 1998, Ed Weiler—who had served as the science director of the Astronomical Search for Origins and Planetary Systems theme of the OSS since March 1996—was appointed

---

187 Niebur, S. (2009, 11 April). Personal interview with B. Perry. Located in the "Discovery Program" file, NASA Historical Reference Collection, History Division, NASA Headquarters, Washington, DC.

188 Ibid.

189 Niebur, S. (2008, October). Personal interview with J. Bergstralh. Located in "Discovery Program" file, NASA Historical Reference Collection, History Division, NASA Headquarters, Washington, DC.

acting Associate Administrator. The same week that the Discovery selections were announced, Weiler assumed the role permanently. He lavished praise on the concepts under study, saying: "The degree of innovation in these proposals climbs higher each time we solicit ideas."[190]

On 12 November 1998, NASA Headquarters selected five missions for concept study out of 30 proposals: Aladdin, Deep Impact, INSIDE Jupiter, MESSENGER, and VESPER. (Of the 30, seven were to explore comets and asteroids; seven would explore elements of the Mars system; four each were proposed for Mercury and Venus; two were set for the Moon; one would observe Jupiter; four were telescope-type investigations; and one was a mission of opportunity to contribute to an instrument on the European Space Agency's Mars Express.)

Aladdin would send small impactors to the surface of the two Martian moons, Phobos and Deimos; fly through the plumes of excavated material; and deploy a "flying carpet" to collect the samples before returning them to Earth.[191] The mission would be led by Dr. Carle Pieters of Brown University and developed by APL at a total mission cost to NASA, including launch vehicle and operations, of $247.7 million.

Deep Impact would be a flyby mission designed to fire a 1,100-pound (500-kilogram) copper projectile into the Comet 9P/Tempel 1, excavating a large crater more than 65 feet (20 meters) deep to expose its pristine interior of ice and rock. Deep Impact would be led by Dr. Michael A'Hearn of the University of Maryland. The proposal manager was Dr. Cliff Anderson at the Jet Propulsion Laboratory. The planned trajectory included launch in January 2004, an Earth gravity assist flyby in January 2005, and arrival at Tempel 1 in July 2005, just five months earlier than the planned DS-4/Champollion landing on a comet. Measurements would include camera; white-light and medium-band images of the impact and resulting crater; and near-infrared spectral images of the outflowing hot debris, surface, and outgassing to the coma before, during, and after the event. The total proposed cost was $203.8 million.[192]

The Interior Structure and Internal Dynamical Evolution of Jupiter, or INSIDE Jupiter, would orbit Jupiter in a high-inclination orbit passing within 1,000 kilometers of the surface of the planet. The mission would be led by Dr. Edward Smith, Ulysses project scientist, with Tom Spilker as proposal manager and a co-investigator. INSIDE Jupiter would launch on a Delta II rocket in February 2004, fly by Earth in January 2006, and arrive at Jupiter in April 2008. It would observe and study the gas giant's interior and its relationship to the atmosphere for 15 months before mission's end in August 2009. The high-inclination orbit would be ideal for mapping the planet's gravity and

---

190   "JPL-teamed Discovery proposals selected for study." (1998, 25 November). *JPL Universe*, 28(24). 1.

191   Taverna, Michael A., "Mercury and Venus sample returns eyed," *Aviation Week & Space Technology*, 15 February 1999, p. 23.

192   "JPL-teamed Discovery proposals selected for study." (1998, 25 November). *JPL Universe*, 28(24). 1.

magnetic fields. Co-investigator John Anderson led the gravitational fields investigation. Other investigations would include radio occultation experiments to study the atmospheric structure and an energetic particle spectrometer (led by co-investigator Neil Murphy) to study magnetic fields and characterize the environment. Other co-investigators included Andrew Ingersoll of Caltech, David Hinson of Stanford, William Hubbard of the University of Arizona, Barry Mauk of Johns Hopkins University, David Stevenson of Caltech, and G. Leonard Tyler of Stanford. The spacecraft would be designed and built by Ball, with program management by the PI's institution, JPL. It would cost $227.3 million.[193]

The MErcury Surface, Space Environment, Geochemistry and Ranging mission, or MESSENGER, would carry seven instruments to image the entire planet Mercury for the first time. MESSENGER would be led by Dr. Sean Solomon of the Carnegie Institution, Washington, DC, and developed at APL, for a total cost of $279.3 million.

The Venus Sounder for Planetary Exploration, Vesper, was an orbiter concept carrying four instruments to measure the composition and dynamic circulation of the middle atmosphere of Venus and its similarities to processes in Earth's atmosphere. Vesper would be led by Dr. Gordon Chin of NASA's Goddard Space Flight Center, Greenbelt, MD, at a total cost of $195.8 million. Aladdin and MESSENGER had also been finalists in the previous round of Discovery Program mission selections in 1997.

NASA's Office of Space Science also announced the selection of a mission of opportunity without the need for concept study. The funded investigation would supply portions of an instrument—the Analyzer of Space Plasmas and Energetic Atoms, or ASPERA-3—to study the interaction between the solar wind and Martian atmosphere. It would fly on ESA's Mars Express in 2003. ASPERA-3's PI was Dr. Rickard Lundin of the Swedish Institute of Space Physics in Kiruna, Sweden. The co-investigator funded by NASA was Dr. David Winningham of the Southwest Research Institute, San Antonio, TX. NASA would provide approximately $5.3 million for the electron and ion spectrometer to be prepared for launch in 2003 aboard the Mars Express mission. In the same announcement, NASA confirmed that Missions of Opportunity would be welcome in all future Discovery and Explorer Program Announcements of Opportunity.[194]

Each team received $375,000 to conduct a four-month implementation feasibility study focused on technical, management, and cost plans, including small business and

---

193 Ibid.

194 NASA. (1998, 12 November). "Five Discovery Mission proposals selected for feasibility studies." NASA press release 98-203.

educational outreach. Cost was allowed to grow 20 percent. Concept study reports would be due 31 March 1999. APL submitted only two proposals to this round; both were selected for concept study.[195]

Discovery Program Office

While the teams were performing concept studies and writing their Phase A reports, NASA and the Discovery Program were not standing still. Dan Goldin was executing yet another massive Reduction in Force at NASA Headquarters and sending program management to agency centers across the country. Program management of Discovery had been transferred to the NASA Management Office (NMO) at JPL, who filled the position of Discovery Program Manager with Dave Jarrett in February 1999. Jarrett, already program manager of Discovery at NASA Headquarters, thus became a NASA Headquarters civil servant stationed at the NMO overseeing projects that were managed by JPL and its competitors. He was to be supported by Bob Metzger, who was to run the Discovery Program Support Office, and JPL personnel. Metzger had just finished working with New Millennium, a NASA project to improve the engineering validation of new technologies for space applications. Both men reported to Bob Parker, who led the NMO.

Jarrett met with Jim Barrowman of the Explorers Program Office at Goddard Space Flight Center and worked with Metzger to define the office needs. Several of the first hires, such as Sherry Asplund, a strong advocate for education and public outreach, and Kate Wolf, NMO contracting officer and procurement specialist, continued to support the program for years. Wolf's civil servant position was critical, as the Discovery Program budget required distribution of funds to APL, the Southwest Research Institute, and universities across the country—a task that JPL contractors, many of whom were Caltech employees, could not tackle. Wolf received the budget and contracting information from Craig Tupper at NASA Headquarters and was immediately set to work keeping the money flowing, particularly at critical junctures such as phase transitions—colloquially called "bridge funding"—which would be a contracting challenge for several AO competition cycles.

Bridge funding was to help proposal teams move from phase to phase financially seamlessly, even though proper contracts took many months to fully execute. Bridge funding and the need to set up multiphase contract vehicles (which JPL practices did not support at the time) had been an issue since the 1992 San Juan Capistrano Workshop. The trouble was exacerbated by the fact that JPL itself was run under contract

---

195   Roylance, F. (1998, 27 November). "Maryland would play major role in 4 missions considered to planets; Universities, Goddard make space big industry. "*The Baltimore Sun.* 2B.

to Caltech; JPL was not allowed to issue contracts beyond the period of performance of their own contract, presenting difficulties for every mission that overlapped two JPL periods of performance.[196]

Jarrett and Wolf eventually met with numerous offices, including Goddard's legal department and JPL's legal department, to enable multiphase contracts that ran from the selection of the investigation to the end of the mission, with huge benefit to the Discovery Program and its missions.

Jarrett and Wolf would go on to streamline other contracting changes, including changing the Genesis and Stardust PI funding vehicles from grants issued by the project (which then reported to the PI) to contracts developed by the NMO and issued by NASA Headquarters. The contract structure allowed monthly reports from the PI to NMO and NASA Headquarters, where the previous grant-from-the-project structure would have had the PI reporting to the project, which reported to the PI, which was effectively circular. The change increased accountability from the PI directly to NASA, in keeping with the goals of NASA Headquarters at the time. It also reduced overhead necessary when JPL, for example, administered a PI's grant, as no JPL overhead funds would be necessary if the funding vehicle was issued directly from procurement at NASA Headquarters.

Wolf and Jarrett also made an effort to start the contracts at concept study, to avoid later procurement-based delays, but this effort was thwarted by the NASA Headquarters procurement office, which preferred to issue a single contract for the concept study to the lead institution, rather than separately to APL, JPL, Goddard, and the PIs as would be required.

Jarrett would hold annual project retreats to increase communication between the project office, the project managers, and the PIs in the different projects. At first, he said, he was asked point-blank why a program office was necessary, as the projects didn't really need to communicate. Over time, that changed, and the retreats became once or twice a year, depending on whether an AO was out in the wild. Jarrett recalls interactions with Joe Veverka, the experienced CONTOUR PI, when he arrived, who argued that the APL funding should flow through his institution, Cornell, instead of through JPL or directly from NASA Headquarters. If one is to consider issues of accountability, Veverka was right on target with this request. The person who holds the contract is, de facto, in charge. Jarrett and Wolf were convinced...to an extent. To avoid the overhead imposed by Cornell on pass-through funds to APL or JPL, Wolf created a form that required the PI's signature before any funds would be transferred

---

196   Niebur, S. (2009, 14 May). Personal interview with D. Jarrett and Kate Wolf. Located in "Discovery Program" file, NASA Historical Reference Collection, History Division, NASA Headquarters, Washington, DC.

for the project. Once the PI signed, she would request that NASA Headquarters send the funds directly to APL or JPL, avoiding the overhead on the pass-through yet giving the PI full control of the distribution of funds.[197]

Just as the project office was getting into the swing of things with the CONTOUR, Genesis, and Stardust missions, NASA selected two new missions on 7 July 1999: the comet impact mission Deep Impact, and MESSENGER, the "flagship-quality" mission to Mercury.[198]

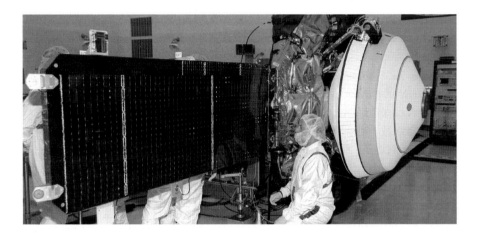

Figure 3-1: Genesis spacecraft
Workers in the Payload Hazardous Servicing Facility check the solar arrays on the Genesis spacecraft. The white object on the end, in front of the arrays, is the Sample Return Canister backshell, inside of which are the collector arrays. (Image credit: NASA, image no. KSC-01pp1073)

---

197   Ibid.

198   "NASA Selects Missions to Mercury and a Comet's Interior as Next Discovery Flights." (1999, 7 July). NASA Press Release. Downloaded from *http://nssdc.gsfc.nasa.gov/planetary/news/ discovery_pr_19990707.html*.

Figure 3-2: Genesis Sample Return Capsule

The Genesis Sample Return Capsule on the ground in Utah. The impact occurred near Granite Peak on a remote portion of the Utah Test and Training Range. (Image credit: USAF 388th Range Sqd./NASA)

Figure 3-3: Genesis sample returns to Johnson Space Center

Containers of solar wind samples from the Genesis Sample Return Capsule are unloaded upon arrival at Johnson Space Center (JSC). Samples are en route to the JSC Astromaterials Curation Facility. (Image credit: NASA, image no. jsc2004e43847)

CHAPTER 4

Applying Lessons Learned

STARDUST SAMPLE RETURN AND STARDUST NEXT

The Genesis crash landing set off a cascade effect across NASA's planetary science program, beginning with Stardust, which shared spacecraft design elements. "It affected us because Genesis had done everything right," said Don Brownlee, the PI of Stardust. The project endured a dozen reviews in the Genesis aftermath. "A lot of money and a lot of time. A tremendous amount of strain on people when they should have been really worried about making sure everything worked right. They had to do all these studies."[1]

Even Mars was dragged into the fray. Lockheed Martin, which had built the ill-fated Genesis and, before that, the doomed Mars Climate Orbiter, endured additional agency oversight as it continued building a new spacecraft, the Mars Reconnaissance

---

1   Niebur, S. (2009, 25 March). Personal interview with D. Brownlee. Located in the "Discovery Program" file, NASA Historical Reference Collection, History Division, NASA Headquarters, Washington, DC.

Orbiter.[2] Even missions still on the drawing board were given additional scrutiny. In the distant future, the Mars Program was set to culminate with a sample return mission. What if a capsule of pristine soil from Mars crashed on Earth? Mars microbes could conceivably spill onto the surface of Earth.[3]

NASA required the Stardust project to conduct additional ground tests to ensure that the robot in space would work as planned. Engineers pulled blueprints for analysis and studied pre-launch photos of the Stardust hardware for any possible oversights. They even looked at previous spacecraft for insight on what they might expect. Another rigorous investigation lasted more than three months and was intended to determine whether the gravity switches on the Stardust capsule were installed in the correct orientation.

"In the end," Brownlee said, "we felt very confident that if there was some screw up it was not for some entirely stupid thing."[4] According to Tom Duxbury, the Stardust project manager, "Because of the Genesis mishap, we had full JPL management attention. Shortly after that, we had mission assurance, system engineering, navigation chief, safety, etc. positions filled and review boards beyond our imagination." Testing had to account for return conditions very different for Stardust versus Genesis. "Significantly more effort was required for reporting and review. Genesis operated in broad daylight at three o'clock in the afternoon at 70-degree temperatures. We came in at 3:00 in the morning at minus 20 degrees where it could be snowed in, fogged in, or rainstorms."[5] At a pre-return news conference in December 2005, Ed Hirst, Stardust mission manager, stated that his team was very confident that the Genesis problem would not be repeated on Stardust.

The team started working through the worst-case scenarios one by one. "If we do hit hard, what do we expect to happen, and what should we be prepared to do? If we land in a puddle—there was a list of, half a dozen things that we needed to be ready to address," Hirst recalled. "That was the second part of the lesson learned: Don't assume everything's going to happen nominally."[6]

---

2   "NASA putting extra scrutiny on other missions in wake of Genesis." (2004, 19 October). *Aviation Week's Aerospace Daily*, 21(13).

3   David, L. (2004, 20 September). "Genesis mishap renews debate about Mars sample return." *SpaceNews*. 8.

4   Niebur, S. (2009, 25 March). Personal interview with D. Brownlee. Located in the "Discovery Program" file, NASA Historical Reference Collection, History Division, NASA Headquarters, Washington, DC.

5   Niebur, S. (2009, 4 September). Personal interview with T. Duxbury. Located in the "Discovery Program" file, NASA Historical Reference Collection, History Division, NASA Headquarters, Washington, DC.

6   Niebur, S. (2009, August 10). Personal interview with E. Hirst. Located in the "Discovery Program" file, NASA Historical Reference Collection, History Division, NASA Headquarters, Washington, DC.

Duxbury recalled the hours before Stardust's arrival at Earth. "We had clear skies and nearly a full moon with the temperature near freezing, much better than what we trained and were prepared for," he said. In addition to the recovery team of 15 members of the Stardust project, "mission control" at the Utah Test and Training Range hosted officials from the Army, the Air Force, NASA, and JPL. He said the team modeled its recovery effort on that used by the Federal Emergency Management Agency.[7]

Just after midnight on Sunday, 15 January, the Stardust spacecraft released its 46-kilogram sample return capsule. Four hours later, it entered Earth's atmosphere over California near the Oregon border.[8] The Stardust capsule blazed through the atmosphere at 46,440 kilometers per hour.[9] Duxbury said, "When we saw that drogue chute open, we knew we were home safe."[10]

People in California, Nevada, and Utah who were up at this early hour had a spectacular view of the capsule's arrival. When it reached ten thousand feet at 5:05 a.m., Duxbury said over the radio: "All stations, the main chute is open, and we're coming down slow." Shortly thereafter, he added: "Okay, we're on the ground." Unlike Genesis, which also arrived on the ground, the Stardust capsule did so gracefully. The space-craft return capsule bounded five times through soft mud due to wind at the landing site, settling on its rim before rolling, wobbling, and spiraling to a rest at 5:12 a.m. EST.[11] Three helicopter crews raced to find the capsule in the pre-dawn darkness, a task made more difficult by winds that morning. A storm had preceded the landing, and another followed.[12]

The team had intended to have a television camera set up onsite to send back live coverage of the recovery, but at the last minute, the Blackhawk helicopter and crew were dispatched to Iraq. (The United States had invaded the country three years earlier.) A smaller Bell helicopter, assigned now to the recovery, did not have enough room for both the recovery team and TV equipment.

The first helicopter sighted the main parachute on the ground at 5:43 a.m., and the capsule itself six minutes before 6 a.m. on Sunday, 15 January 2006. "The

---

7   Niebur, S. (2009, September 4). Personal interview with T. Duxbury. Located in "Stardust" file, NASA Historical Reference Collection, History Division, NASA Headquarters, Washington, DC.

8   Gugliotta, G. (2006, January 16). "Stardust capsule brings first comet sample to Earth." *The Washington Post.*

9   Potter, N. (2005, December 22). "Comet mission set for return to Earth." ABC News; Niebur, S. (2009, September 4). Personal interview with T. Duxbury. Located in "Stardust" file, NASA Historical Reference Collection, History Division, NASA Headquarters, Washington, DC.

10   Hunt, K. (2006, January 18). "Galaxy's secrets land safely in desert." *Tooele (UT) Transcript Bulletin.*

11   Gugliotta, G. (2006, 16 January). "Stardust capsule brings first comet sample to Earth." *The Washington Post*; Bauman, J. (2006, 18 January). "Stardust cargo is flown to Houston." *Deseret Morning News (UT).*

12   Niebur, S. (2009, 4 September). Personal interview with T. Duxbury. Located in "Stardust" file, NASA Historical Reference Collection, History Division, NASA Headquarters, Washington, DC.

canister is closed tight," reported Scott Sandford, a co-investigator and member of the recovery team.[13] The capsule was pristine. No water penetrated it upon landing in the muddy ground.

The recovery teams collected the capsule and flew it to the clean room at Dugway Proving Grounds. Duxbury recalled: "Everyone wanted to jump in a helicopter and go see the capsule while it was being prepared to be brought back.... We all wanted to be there."[14] A support team remained ready at the command center in case the recovery team encountered problems.

Inside the cleanroom, the capsule was opened by unscrewing the backshell, removing it and the heat shield, and then extracting the science canister. The sample team purged the canister with nitrogen and packed it carefully for its flight to Johnson Space Center.

Thin slices of the already microscopic grains of dust collected by the Stardust aerogel collectors were distributed to 180 scientists worldwide. Early results included the identification of complex carbon molecules, along with organics—the kinds necessary for the evolution of life, giving credence to the concept that the precursor ingredients for life on Earth may have originated in space.[15] These organics were unusual enough, oxygen- and nitrogen-rich, with large amounts of alcohols and other volatiles, to lead Sandford to conclude, months later, "A portion of the organic material in the samples is unlike anything seen before in extraterrestrial materials."[16]

By March 2006, researchers had announced that the cometary particles contained minerals that formed under extremely high temperatures, indicating their formation around a star, either our own or one elsewhere in the galaxy. "In the coldest part of the solar system we've found samples that formed at extremely high temperatures," Brownlee explained. "When these minerals were formed, they were either red-hot or white-hot grains, and yet they were collected in a comet, the Siberia of the solar system."[17] This was an unexpected result for grains contained in a comet formed in the icy-cold outer edges of the solar system. By December, researchers had found a very unusual particle indeed—one that contained 150 percent more heavy oxygen (^{17}O or ^{18}O) than typical for the Sun, Earth—indeed, the whole solar system.[18]

---

13   "Pinch of comet dust lands safely on Earth." (2006, 18 January). *New Scientist*.

14   Niebur, S. (2009, 4 September). Personal interview with T. Duxbury. Located in the "Discovery Program" file, NASA Historical Reference Collection, History Division, NASA Headquarters, Washington, DC.

15   Leake, J. (2006, 5 March). "Comet dust holds building blocks of life." *Times of London*.

16   Bluck, J. (2006, December). "NASA study finds new kind of organics in Stardust mission." *Astrogram*. 3.

17   "Comet samples add to 'Mystery Story'." (2006, 20 March). *SpaceNews*. 15.

18   Bryner, J. (2006, 14 December). "Space probe brought real stardust down to Earth." Space.com.

Grain by Grain

The analysis of the Stardust material was grain by grain, and three years after analysis began, pieces of nearly every particle remained. In the end, although NASA rules (from the AO) allowed the Stardust team to consume up to 25 percent of the sample during the funded period, the measurements were so painstaking and so precise that the team consumed less than 1 percent of the returned sample initially and only a few percent of the samples in the first three years.[19]

Meanwhile, one-third of the aerogel cells were removed and sent to White Sands for safekeeping. These were contingency samples that could be analyzed for generations using whatever techniques might be state-of-the-art a century from now.

Already, though, the samples were a science bonanza. In addition to the 2006 discovery of glassy particles that required high temperatures to form, in 2009, researchers at Goddard Space Flight Center announced the discovery of glycine, an amino acid, in the Stardust samples.[20] Jamie Elsila, first author of the paper published in the journal *Meteoritics & Planetary Science*, commented, "Our discovery supports the theory that some of life's ingredients formed in space and were delivered to Earth long ago by meteorite and comet impacts."[21] Interestingly enough, this important discovery was made not by studying the particles in aerogel, but by examining the bonus surfaces—the aluminum foil that the team used to line the chambers. Elsila believed that some gaseous molecules adhered to the foil when going through the aerogel.

In nearly every conceivable way, the daring, low-cost sample return mission encapsulated what could be done in the Discovery Program and set the stage for planetary missions that otherwise would have been impossible. NASA had brought home the stuff of comets. For their next trick, the agency was going to pulverize one.

DEEP IMPACT AND EPOXI

Mike Belton, a planetary scientist at the National Optical Observatory, and Alan Delamere, an engineer at Ball Aerospace, wanted to smash a comet with an impactor, and they knew immediately that the Discovery Program would help them do it. They first proposed the mission concept at the San Juan Capistrano meeting of Discovery in 1992 and did so again in 1994. Neither proposal was selected. Michael A'Hearn of the University of Maryland College of Computer, Mathematical, and Natural

19   Niebur, S. (2009, 24 March). Personal interview with M. Zolensky. Located in "Stardust" file, NASA Historical Reference Collection, History Division, NASA Headquarters, Washington, DC.

20   Williams, C. (2006, 16 March). "Stardust finds comets are born of fire and ice." *(UK) Register.*

21   Elsila, J. E., Glavin, D. P., & Dworkin, J. P. (2009). "Cometary glycine detected in samples returned by Stardust." *Meteoritics & Planetary Science*, 44(9), 1323–1330. *https://doi.org/10.1111/j.1945-5100.2009.tb01224.x.*

Sciences later joined the team, and they modified the concept this time to hit an asteroid, 3200 Phaethon, with a dumb impactor. They submitted it under the name "Deep Impact" to the 1996 AO. Again, they were passed over—such was the nature of Discovery—but comments by reviewers encouraged them to keep going, and the trio again submitted the mission in 1998. This time, they would again target a comet—9P/Tempel 1—but do so using a "smart impactor" with guidance capabilities.

NASA selected the mission for flight, with A'Hearn as its Principal Investigator, Belton as his deputy, and Delamere as a co-investigator. Their team of co-investigators was made up of five veterans of CONTOUR: Belton; Joe Veverka of Cornell; Joachen Kissel of the Max Planck Institut for Extraterrestrische Physik in Germany (who had also been on Stardust); Peter Thomas of Cornell; and Don Yeomans of the Jet Propulsion Laboratory (who had also been on NEAR). Other co-investigators included Karen Meech, who would lead ground-based observations from the University of Hawai'i; Jay Melosh of the University of Arizona; Peter Schulz from Brown University; and Jessica Sunshine of Science Applications International Corporation.

Studying comets was nothing new. The innovation of Deep Impact was the concept of destroying part of one in the name of science. "The whole science community has been studying comets for a long time," said Orlando Figueroa, the Deputy Associate Administrator of the Science Mission Directorate at NASA Headquarters. "We have flown by them, we have observed them from afar, and this year we go for the home run."[22]

Selection

Ed Weiler, the Science Mission Directorate Associate Administrator, described Deep Impact as a complement to the other two small bodies missions already in the Discovery Program, Stardust and Genesis.[23] Deep Impact's science goal was to determine the composition of a comet both at the surface of its nucleus and in its interior so as to understand the differences between both. Moreover, the mission would help scientists understand the evolutionary processes at work in those outer layers.[24] In addition to composition, the mission would answer longstanding questions about the structures of comets: were they tightly packed or porous?

At its heart, the mission was an excavation intended to reveal primordial material that yielded our world and the solar system all around us. "We're doing celestial archae-

---

22   Malik, T. (2005, 12 January). "NASA's comet smashing mission ready to fly." Space.com.
23   "Lab wins Discovery mission." (1999, 9 July). *JPL Universe*, 29(14).
24   A'Hearn, M. F., Belton, M. J. S., Delamere, A., & Blume, W. H. (2005). "Deep Impact: A Large-Scale Active Experiment on a Cometary Nucleus." *Space Science Reviews*, 117(1–2), 1–21. *https://doi.org/10.1007/s11214-005-3387-3*.

ology, digging up the past to see what the solar system was made of 4.5 billion years ago," said Lucy McFadden, the mission's education and public outreach coordinator.[25]

Comet Tempel 1, the mission's target, was discovered in 1867 by Ernst Wilhelm Tempel, a German astronomer. Tempel 1 is a dark-colored comet, 7.6 miles long and 4.9 miles wide, with an orbital period of 5.56 years. The comet was nothing special, all things considered, and the team chose it for convenience.[26] And yet, this ordinary pickle-shaped icy dirt ball held secrets. Jessica Sunshine said of it: "We may finally learn whether these comets…are dirty snowballs, as many astronomers have thought, or snowy dirtballs instead."[27]

Because the nucleus of a comet is hidden beneath its surface and coma, the design of Deep Impact was necessarily different from previous such missions. This mission would be less an expedition and more an experiment, and the first of its kind in that its impact and observations were both done on flight. (Lunar Prospector, the third Discovery mission selected for flight, collided with the Moon at the end of its science phase, but the study and data collection of the collision's aftermath were conducted from Earth-based observatories and the Hubble Space Telescope.) The daring Deep Impact design relied on a two-part spacecraft consisting of the flyby spacecraft and a copper smart impactor.

"With most missions, you send a spacecraft out to fly by something and you look at it from a distance," said co-investigator Peter Thomas at the time. "The fun thing about this mission is we're doing an active experiment—trying to make a crater in this comet, thereby seeing what's on the inside.... We don't have a good idea as to what's going to happen."[28]

To see beneath the surface of the comet, Deep Impact approach would Tempel 1 at speeds greater than 37,014 kilometers per hour—ten times faster than a bullet fired from a rifle—and release the impactor. The 372-kilogram projectile would smash a hole in the comet's surface, exposing the nucleus beneath. Instrumentation on the flyby spacecraft would concurrently observe the impact at different wavelengths, including optical, to help scientists understand what actually happened during impact and immediately afterward. The task—to hit a comet accurately and observe the results during a single flyby—was daunting, and there would be no second chances. Deep Impact could not reload.

---

25   "Md. Spacecraft to fly collision mission." (2004, 19 December). *The (Hagerstown, MD) Herald-Mail.*

26   Maugh, T. (2005, 3 July). "NASA's spacecraft closes in on comet." *Los Angeles Times.*

27   Perlman, D. (2005, 2 July). "Scientists on edge of seats: ship zooms toward comet." *San Francisco Chronicle.*

28   "Smashing Idea: Craft set to blast comet tonight." (2005, 3 July). *NY Daily News.*

Scientists and engineers were not sure what to expect from the impact. Since this mission would be the first such interception of a comet, the exact nature of the crust—and its reaction to a solid impactor—were unknown. A hard, icy crust would react quite differently than a thin, fragile crust held together by gases or liquid.

Predictions ranged from a small hole to a football stadium–size crater 14 stories deep.[29] A light, fluffy comet, like packed snow, for example, could absorb the impactor deep into the nucleus while creating only a small surface crater. A very porous comet, packed as loosely as a bowl of corn flakes, could fail to stop the impactor entirely. It would simply punch clean through the celestial object.[30]

SETI Institute astronomer Peter Jenniskens and his colleague Esko Lyytinen stated: "If Comet 9P/Tempel 1 breaks during NASA's Deep Impact mission, a meteoroid stream will be created in much the same manner as what causes most of our meteor showers.... Depending on how the kinetic energy of the impact will be distributed, there is a real possibility that sufficient internal gas pressure builds up to break the comet apart."[31]

Don Yeomans, however, reduced this possibility to a "way outside chance," saying, "The bottom line is that we have an object the size of a washing machine colliding with a comet the size of Manhattan Island. No contest."[32]

Due to its impact speed—greater than 10 kilometers per second—there was no need to add explosives to the impactor. Any heavy material would have sufficed to blow a hole in Tempel 1, given sufficient mass. The best match, however, would be something similar to the comet's expected density.[33] Since the impactor was expected to vaporize upon impact, mixing in with any ejecta, the prudent choice was an element not expected in comets and one that wouldn't combine with water ejecta that would confuse the spectrometers observing the impact. Since noble metals like gold, silver, and platinum were far outside a Discovery-class budget, engineers decided to make the material out of copper. Of the 372 kilograms that composed the entire projectile, 112 kilograms were simply copper ballast to magnify the impact. It carried also a medium-resolution telescope instrument called the Impactor Targeting Sensor—essentially the same one the spacecraft deploying the impactor would carry, though without a filter wheel. Whereas the impactor was simple, the flyby spacecraft carried four additional instruments for observation of the impact event.

---

29   David, L. (2004, 9 October). "Comet crashing mission prepped for launch." Space.com.

30   Leary, W. E. (2005, 11 January). "Blasting into the core of a comet to learn its secrets." *The New York Times.* 11.

31   Jenniskens, P., & Lyytinen, E. (2005). "Meteor Showers from the Debris of Broken Comets: D/1819 W 1 (Blanpain), 2003 WY 25, and the Phoenicids." *The Astronomical Journal,* 130(3), 1286–1290. *https://doi.org/10.1086/432469.*

32   David, L. (2005, 28 June). "Cosmic crash won't destroy comet or Earth." Space.com.

33   Reichardt, T. (2005, April–May). "Comet cracker: A summer mission has a simple plan: launch. Crash. Watch." *Air & Space.* 36–39.

The Deep Impact flyby spacecraft's High Resolution Instrument (HRI) was "the most powerful camera to fly in deep space," said Michael A'Hearn, the Principal Investigator. "We know so little about the structure of cometary nuclei that we need exceptional equipment to ensure that we capture the event, whatever the details of the impact turn out to be."[34] The instrument incorporated a 30-centimeter (11.8-inch) telescope that fed light to the multispectral camera and infrared spectrometer, with a resolution of four to six feet on the comet's surface at closest approach. The Medium Resolution Instrument, meanwhile, contained a 12-centimeter (4.7-inch) telescope and imager.

Mission formulation began on 3 January 2000, with implementation scheduled to start in April 2001. It would launch on 3 January 2004. Originally, Deep Impact was intended to have an 18-month cruise phase—time enough for checkout, software development, revisions, and plenty of practice runs—hitting the comet on 4 July 2005. Budget shortfalls in 2002 and 2003 required significant revisions to the mission, however. As altered, the flight would take just six months—practically instant gratification in space exploration. Budget cuts also affected the mission's launch vehicles, requiring a change from a Delta II Heavy to a Delta II with fewer strap-on boosters.

Mission development, meanwhile, was complicated by the building of additional, fully functional "smart" hardware. "In a sense, this program is building two 100-percent capable spacecraft. And that has been a big challenge," said Monte Henderson, the Deputy Project Manager at Ball Aerospace. "The impactor has become a very smart, fully-autonomous spacecraft. It's capable of maneuvering and taking care of its own positioning and targeting completely independent of what's going on with the flyby spacecraft."[35]

Missions designed and implemented by the Jet Propulsion Laboratory are required to follow the JPL Design Principles, a set of rules and guidelines proven to yield successful spacecraft and minimize risk. In 1998, those principles required that every mission retain mass, power, and schedule margins at major reviews. New technology and one-off missions required margins above and beyond the standard: it was not uncommon for some untested technology to retain a one hundred percent mass margin until it reached a mature benchmark. (All three kinds of margin are necessary for most missions, as it is not always predictable which will be strained the most during development.)

Deep Impact experienced a number of changes in design, which strained the schedule margin to its limits. One such alteration was due to the rocket's fairing size: Early in development, Brian Muirhead, then–project manager of the mission, discovered

---

34   "Comet probe prepares for lift-off." (2005, 12 January). BBC News.

35   David, L. (2003, 25 November). "Deep Impact: Probing a comet's inner secrets." Space.com.

that the spacecraft as designed wouldn't quite fit inside its intended payload fairing, necessitating a redesign of the flyby spacecraft.

Another design issue and necessary change highlighted differences between the JPL approach and the Ball way of doing things. The problem involved how the mission would manage heat generated by the impactor. "The impactor started out with the front end being a thermal radiator. As we went along, Ball decided to change it—so they covered it with blankets," said A'Hearn, the Principal Investigator. "I didn't catch this early on," he continued. He realized that thermal blankets would be penetrated by dust and potentially send chaff in front of the camera. "So, then we had a fight between Ball and JPL about how to deal with that issue."[36]

The conflict was not quickly resolved and proved eventually to be a useful lesson for the Discovery Program overall in how Principal Investigators manage—and, when necessary, mandate—changes.[37] The culture clash would become even more evident during spacecraft testing processes, which play a much larger role on planetary missions than on orbital Earth missions. "Ball has a philosophy from their Earth orbital heritage of putting as little money as possible into testbeds, but once you're in orbit around the Earth you can fix things in software. You can't do that on planetary missions," A'Hearn explained. "There are so many one-shot events where you don't know the problem until you get there if you don't have really good testbeds."[38] He explained that from his desk, it seemed that Ball thought of testing more as conceptual sequences rather than detailed command-by-command sequences that are reviewed very thoroughly and run through testbeds again and again.

"This was just a lack of communication between JPL and Ball," the PI continued. "It is a culture difference. They would use the same terms thinking they meant same thing. Testbed didn't mean the same thing on the one side of the Rockies and the other."[39] A'Hearn learned quickly that when dealing with engineers from different aerospace companies and institutions, it is not enough to use the same words. One must understand whether the words mean the same thing. This, too, was a valuable lesson learned for future Principal Investigators about the consequences of failing to ask probing questions.

Clashes over budgets did not help the relationship. Each institution brought its best approaches and skillsets to fiscal issues, but, as A'Hearn recalled: "There were prudent

---

36   Niebur, S. (2009, 11 March). Personal interview with M. A'Hearn. Located in the "Discovery Program" file, NASA Historical Reference Collection, History Division, NASA Headquarters, Washington, DC.

37   Ibid.

38   Ibid.

39   Ibid.

decisions on where to cut costs. Part of the driving thing was JPL's focus on getting it right and Ball's focus on trying to stay in cost. That drove part of the conflict."[40]

In May 2000, the project held its first gateway review; a year later, its preliminary design and confirmation reviews. Mission costs had grown with spacecraft redesigns and a mandated mass reduction of the impactor. The effort ate $11 million in reserves in order to remain under the cost cap.

Depending on one's perspective, Deep Impact had the misfortune (or fortune) of holding its Preliminary Design Review just two years after the twin failures of Mars Polar Lander and Mars Climate Orbiter. It was thus subjected to a level of scrutiny more intense than that of any previous Discovery mission. Steve Wissler, Deep Impact's mission operations systems engineer, was a team member on both Stardust and Deep Impact. The subsystem Preliminary Design Review for Stardust's mission operations systems was essentially a couple of viewgraphs at the wider project review, he remembered. The same subsystem review for Deep Impact was "a multi-day [mission operations systems] [Preliminary Design Review] with a stack of documentation about that thick [gestures] that we had to produce. So, part of that is the changing environment between when the project is originally costed and the risk you're allowed to *actually* have at the time you launch."[41]

In a first for the Discovery Program, Deep Impact was not confirmed immediately after its original confirmation review—another consequence of the Mars failures, the ensuing NASA Integrated Action Team report, a change in the agency's risk posture, and increased attention to the evaluations of reviewers. The program went into an extended Phase B. NASA issued stronger guidelines for the project, with open issues that needed to be addressed—everything from the mass and cost margin definition to mission/system complexity. Moreover, to pass its "delta" confirmation review, the project had to demonstrate 20 percent cost reserves.[42]

Additional funding of $8.7 million—which could not be applied to the new reserve requirement—was provided by NASA Headquarters to cover costs for "mission success enhancements" and to address unforeseen post-Mars recommendations by the NASA Integrated Action Team. The new cost cap was $279.2 million. The Deep Impact team could do no long-lead procurements or development work until after the delta

---

40   Ibid.

41   Niebur, S. (2009, 10 August). Personal interview with B. Blume, Tim Larson, Al Nakata, and Steve Wissler. Located in "Deep Impact" file, NASA Historical Reference Collection, History Division, NASA Headquarters, Washington, DC.

42   Weiler, E. (2001, 30 March). Letter to Mike A'Hearn, cc'd to 16 additional people.

review.[43] They passed on 23 May 2001, and NASA issued a press release the next day confirming the confirmation.[44]

At a Critical Design Review held from 29 January to 2 February 2002, the review team concluded that Ball Aerospace was overstaffed due to instrument problems. A few months later, the project discovered what it believed to be a cost phasing problem. That issue intensified over the summer, and, in August, the project admitted to NASA Headquarters that the problem was more than accounting issues: Deep Impact was going to exceed the projected estimate to completion by $1 million.

Headquarters called for a cost review. Jet Propulsion Laboratory management, meanwhile, added Tom Gavin, deputy director of the Space and Earth Science Programs Directorate and a longtime lab engineer with deep experience in launching successful spacecraft, to the project. The cost review, completed in September, revealed that Deep Impact required an additional infusion of $15 million in order to complete its mission and restore its reserves.

NASA Headquarters thus initiated a mission termination review, held on 10 October 2002. Every aspect of the mission—including cost, schedule, technical, risk, and future performance goals—was subjected to inquiry. The agency was taking a hard line on mission cost overruns. Joe Boyce, the program scientist, recalled of the meetings: "I'd hear associate administrators, as they'd come along, division directors, administrators, saying that what we need to do is cancel one of these damn things—that'll teach them. I kept thinking: Which *them* are you talking about? *Them* is you too!"[45]

In the end, NASA Headquarters allotted Deep Impact an additional $7.4 million for costs outside of project's control but required follow-up meetings and changes. The project reported significant changes on 13 November 2002, including replacing its project manager, replanning its schedule, initiating weekly review boards, conducting staffing level analysis, renegotiating the award fee for Ball Aerospace, and meanwhile continuing its progress toward all science objectives and committing to delivering the spacecraft within the cost cap. The shakeup required a new letter of intent, which was signed by the University of Maryland, Jet Propulsion Laboratory, and Ball.[46]

Ed Weiler, the Associate Administrator of the Science Mission Directorate at NASA Headquarters, wasn't satisfied. The following week, he sent a letter to the team stating

---

43 Ibid.

44 Tune, L. (2001, 24 May). "NASA Gives Go Ahead for Building of 'Deep Impact' Spacecraft." NASA press release.

45 Niebur, S. (2009, 22 March). Personal interview with J. Boyce. Located in "Discovery Program" file, NASA Historical Reference Collection, History Division, NASA Headquarters, Washington, DC.

46 NASA. (2005). Program Assessment Rating Tool. Downloaded from *https://web.archive.org/web/20051005023614/http://www.ombwatch.org/regs/2005/PART/2005budget/PARTs/nasa.pdf* on 16 August 2021.

that several conditions for the project's continuation were not fully met. Technical, schedule, and cost were fully integrated; personnel changes were not complete; and negotiations with Ball were not the same thing as a new award fee agreement. He declared that there would be a delta termination review in two months, mid-January 2003. He also wanted ongoing weekly status reports.

NASA held the second termination review on 21 February 2003. It was clear to everyone involved that the original launch date was no longer viable and that the mission would be delayed a year. Still, the mission survived. Despite the much later launch, the spacecraft would still arrive at the comet on time, as the original proposal had included an extra one-year loop around the Sun on the mission's outset so as to comply with launch date constraints mandated in the 1998 Announcement of Opportunity.

"At that time, I was still not coming to grips with how badly things had been underestimated in cost.... I don't know how much of that was changes driven by design and how much was just actual bad bid," said Michael A'Hearn, the mission PI.[47]

In March, Colleen Hartman, the director of the Planetary Science Division at NASA Headquarters, told the project that an additional $14.4 million had been approved so that it might launch on time, with its required reserves of 20 percent. In all, this brought the mission cost to $298.2 million, excluding Deep Space Network costs. She noted that the mission's overruns were coming at a price to the broader scientific community: because of Deep Impact, NASA would delay the next Discovery AO.

When Lindley Johnson, a civil servant with years of Defense Department experience, moved to NASA Headquarters as a program executive in October 2003, the Deep Impact team—a year from launch—was enduring yet another problem: an unexpected delay in the delivery of the flight computers.[48]

NASA again held a continuation review on 23 January 2004. Though it was specifically not called a "termination review," an experienced termination review board might have thought it was. "There was serious talk about terminating Deep Impact because it was going to be a serious overrun on the program, something like $30 million," said Johnson. "In fact, I have the draft of the termination letter on my computer. I was asked to go ahead and draft it up and have it ready to go if that decision was made."[49]

Ed Weiler, the Associate Administrator, levied a new requirement that all Science Mission Directorate missions henceforth have 25 percent unencumbered reserves through the end of Phase D, minus launch vehicle, at confirmation. (The requirement

---

47 Niebur, S. (2009, 11 March). Personal interview with M. A'Hearn. Located in "Deep Impact" file, NASA Historical Reference Collection, History Division, NASA Headquarters, Washington, DC.

48 Niebur, S. (2009, 4 September). Personal interview with L. Johnson. Located in "Deep Impact" file, NASA Historical Reference Collection, History Division, NASA Headquarters, Washington, DC.

49 Ibid.

was not retroactive but did apply to missions such as Dawn and Kepler, then in the study phase.)[50]

In retrospect, said Steve Wissler, the mission operations systems engineer, Deep Impact "should have never been a Discovery class mission. This was horribly underfunded for what we had to do."[51] He explained that "the last 18 months of the mission, people were working 60-to-80-hour weeks for 18 months straight. There were some 100-hour weeks leading up to launch."[52]

It didn't help that the mission had no permanent project manager. Lindley Johnson recalled:

When I first came on, John McNamee was the project manager, but it was only a few months later that Rick Grammier took that position. And so, there was some turmoil still through that period at the management level on the project. But, when Rick came on, I think some of the things that they did was focus teams a little bit more on various aspects, various problems, as opposed to what I think was before was kind of a blanket approach, as everybody was trying to work everything. I think Rick also spent quite a bit of time helping to rebuild the relationship with the prime contractor, because I know previous to my being on there, that relationship was pretty adversarial.... You've got to be as efficient as you can. So, you've got to have everybody feel that they're part of the same team as opposed to, oh, they're the contractor and we're the implementing agency. I think Rick did a lot to try to improve that relationship.[53]

Tim Larson and Keyur Patel subsequently joined the team as project manager and deputy project manager, respectively.

"It was an interesting project. Never had we seen so many people so demoralized about a mission," said Patel. "They didn't believe they could actually make it happen."[54] The technical issues alone were overwhelming. It was not until nine months from launch that the spacecraft got its flight computer. The delay was a direct result of manufacturing problems with field programmable gate arrays at the Southwest Research Institute in Boulder.

---

50   NASA. (2005). "Program Assessment Rating Tool." Downloaded from *https://web.archive.org/web/20051005023614/http://www.ombwatch.org/regs/2005/PART/2005budget/PARTs/nasa.pdf* on 16 August 2021.

51   Niebur, S. (2009, 10 August). Personal interview with B. Blume, Tim Larson, Al Nakata, and Steve Wissler. Located in "Discovery Program" file, NASA Historical Reference Collection, History Division, NASA Headquarters, Washington, DC.

52   Ibid.

53   Niebur, S. (2009, 4 September). Personal interview with L. Johnson. Located in "Discovery" file, NASA Historical Reference Collection, History Division, NASA Headquarters, Washington, DC.

54   Niebur, S. (2009, 10 August). Personal interview with K. Patel. Located in the "Discovery Program" file, NASA Historical Reference Collection, History Division, NASA Headquarters, Washington, DC.

Steve Wissler explained of the project manager roulette: "We had several turnovers in senior project management that was, I think, very hard on the rest of the team." Each manager, he said, had his own method for running Deep Impact, which amounted to complete project reorganizations multiple times. "Since people were doing multiple tasks, it took a while to settle down after a project management change to really understand what your new role is and where you fit in."[55]

One Year Before Launch

From a project management perspective, when Patel and Larson joined the project, things looked grim. "The fault protection was still open, flight software—a host of issues," said Patel. "That's always a problem, but a year before launch, you're fixing bugs, not working out basic functionality-type stuff.... The gyros had an issue with cracked wells and all of that type of stuff. And then, the whole 800-pound gorilla in the room: 'How do you hit a comet?'"[56]

That question is what made the flight computer problems so vexing. "If you're just checking off level three requirement boxes and you're not executing the system as a mission and finding those bugs, you don't discover those bugs," Patel explained.[57]

The Deep Impact team, overexerted and demoralized, risked falling into abject despair. To introduce a new vitality to the group, Patel brought in several new managers and key engineers: people, he said, "with experience on other projects, can-do attitude, and a lot more doing than talking or whining."[58] Management was confident and committed up front to instilling that same sense of confidence in the team: to remain positive about finishing this star-crossed spacecraft on time and with precision.[59]

Before launch, Patel recalled that the spacecraft only managed to hit the comet once or twice in simulation. "One of the issues we had was everybody had assumed a different reference frame." This was the coordinate system to which a spacecraft's attitude is referenced. "Simulation had assumed a different reference frame. The nav guys had a different reference frame. The attitude guys had a different reference frame. The system that displayed telemetry had a different reference frame."[60]

Engineers determined that what was needed was a "Rosetta stone" of reference frames: how to get you from one reference frame to another. "We were fighting this

---

55   Niebur, S. (2009, 10 August). Personal interview with B. Blume, Tim Larson, Al Nakata, and Steve Wissler. Located in "Deep Impact" file, NASA Historical Reference Collection, History Division, NASA Headquarters, Washington, DC.

56   Niebur, S. (2009, 10 August). Personal interview with K. Patel. Located in "Dawn" file, NASA Historical Reference Collection, History Division, NASA Headquarters, Washington, DC.

57   Ibid.

58   Ibid.

59   Ibid.

60   Ibid.

six months before launch," Patel explained. His dual roles on the project helped move some decisions along. "I was the chief engineer and the Deputy Project Manager, so in a way it was nice, because I could recommend something on one side and hammer it home on the other side." By the end of March, Patel was confident that the mission would be a success.[61]

To solidify the ever-frayed relationship between the Deep Impact team and its contractor workforce, the project put boots on the ground. The idea, said Lindley Johnson, the mission's program executive, was to build bonds. "They're not just somebody at the other end of the phone or the other end of the video-con. They're somebody real, somebody that's another individual, too, just trying to do the best damn job they can on the project," he said.[62]

Communication opened a lot of doors. "The way Ball was used to doing business with their other partners, they would be given a very detailed list of requirements and it'd probably match something that they'd already built before, and so they would get those requirements, go off and build a spacecraft, and then turn it over to the customer," said Steve Wissler, the mission operations systems engineer. "JPL doesn't really work in that environment, especially with these one-of-a-kind. There was just this constant back and forth on the requirements and the validation and the amount of work that Ball had to do I think was far more than they had really considered. They ended up building a great spacecraft, but there was, again, a lot of tension back and forth on how much oversight JPL had, and what it was doing in terms of the profit Ball was going to make on this big op, at the end."[63]

The 976-kilogram Deep Impact spacecraft launched from Pad 17B on a Delta II rocket on 12 January 2005. Its next stop was Comet Tempel 1, a comet 83 million miles away (though because of celestial dynamics, had to travel 268 million miles to get there). The mission originally was to have an 18-month cruise phase, during which the operations team could become intimately familiar with their spacecraft and how it responded in space. Because the mission lost a full year on the ground due to developmental woes, the team would have to learn how to fly their spaceship in six months.

Al Nakata, who worked mission operations, recalled: "Both teams are pretty busy. The cruise team was just busy every day during the six-month cruise mission phase operating the spacecraft and conducting instrument calibrations and trajectory correction maneuvers. And of course, the encounter team is conducting encounter develop-

61   Ibid.

62   Niebur, S. (2009, 4 September). Personal interview with L. Johnson. Located in the "Discovery Program" file, NASA Historical Reference Collection, History Division, NASA Headquarters, Washington, DC.

63   Niebur, S. (2009, 10 August). Personal interview with B. Blume, T. Larson, A. Nakata, and S. Wissler. Located in the "Discovery Program" file, NASA Historical Reference Collection, History Division, NASA Headquarters, Washington, DC.

ment plus testing, and Steve [Wissler, the mission operation systems engineer] had the most work to do."[64] That was yet another consequence of the mission's budgetary issues. It wouldn't be the last.

Extreme Optimism

Over the course of the project, costs had increased for reasons beyond the technical. As Bill Blume, the mission design lead, put it: "Deep Impact was proposed in the Faster, Better, Cheaper environment, and the first proposal went out—the Step 1 proposal in 98 and the Step Two in 99—and Deep Impact was accepted just months before the Mars '98 failures…. People were making cost estimates with just extreme optimism, and there's a competitive nature in the proposal process that just makes you optimistic."[65]

Moreover, public failures unrelated to Deep Impact suddenly became Deep Impact's problem. As Wissler explained, "The rules kept changing out from under us. Every time there would be a mission failure or something, we would be held to a higher standard than what had been costed originally."[66]

This manifested at the Jet Propulsion Laboratory in the form of new sets of stringent, conservative, structured approaches to spacecraft development called Flight Project Practices and Design Principles. After the twin embarrassments of two consecutive Mars failures, the lab was tightening screws, and no one was exempt.

The lab's new guidelines meant a stringent, independent verification and validation review process on the hardware, software, processes, and subsystems to certify the spacecraft as ready for launch. It felt invasive to Deep Impact's leadership. No previous project had faced such scrutiny, and budget increases did not accompany the new expensive reviews and processes.

Already overworked in the runup to launch, with the added stressors of verification and validation processes, the handoff from the integration and testing team to the mission operations team "was really a shaky process," recalled Wissler.[67] Losing that year meant losing precious time in space to do spacecraft and instrument calibrations.

Having only six months from launch to encounter made the cruise phase a crucible. The team had to work out bugs in everything from "fault protection" mechanisms in the spacecraft to navigation. The High-Resolution Instrument, for example—one of the largest experiments ever built for a planetary science mission, and essential to mission success—failed to yield "perfect focus." Initial images were blurry, but a routine "bake out" of residual moisture accumulated during launch should have sharpened

---

64   Ibid.
65   Ibid.
66   Ibid.
67   Ibid.

things. It did not.[68] The quality was adequate for the spacecraft's auto-navigation but had the potential to diminish the optical navigation campaign during the approach to the comet. The science team developed new image processing and calibration techniques to improve the situation.[69] (Ultimately, investigators determined that it was a manufacturing flaw.)

If Deep Impact was still getting its space legs and giving its team a lot of sleepless nights, Tempel 1 was doing all it could to help make the mission a success. Data from the Hubble Space Telescope and the Spitzer Telescope revealed that the comet had a 41-hour period of rotation—very slow, and perfect for a thorough imaging of the post-impact crater.[70]

And upon impact, *everyone,* it seemed, would be watching. NASA coordinated with the leadership of several space telescopes, including Hubble, Spitzer, the Chandra X-ray Observatory, and the Submillimeter Wave Astronomy Satellite (which was awakened from an eleven-month hibernation) to observe the comet before and after impact. Observation conditions were ideal: the crater would be lit by the Sun because of the comet's angle. The telescopes would be observing everything from geology to possible water molecules vaporized during or after impact.[71]

On Earth, meanwhile, ground-based observatories and telescopes everywhere from Hawai'i to Boulder would be trained on the comet before, during, and after the impact. These included every telescope on Mauna Kea and two on Haleakalā, both in Hawai'i; Palomar Observatory, Lick Observatory, and Mount Laguna Observatory in California; and telescopes in Spain and Australia.[72] In addition, the project's public outreach campaign encouraged private astronomers to try observing the impact. If the impactor hit the comet in a bright spot, even binoculars should have been able to view the event.

While "practicing" on 14 June 2005 for the 4 July impact event, the Hubble Space Telescope captured a plume erupting from Tempel 1, blasting 1,400 miles toward the Sun. This was unexpected and raised hopes by some scientists that the NASA mission's

68   NASA. (2019, 24 July). "Deep Impact/EPOXI In Depth." Downloaded from *https://solarsystem.nasa.gov/missions/deep-impact-epoxi/in-depth/*; NASA. (2005, 25 March). "NASA Releases Deep Impact Mission Status Report." Downloaded from *https://www.nasa.gov/home/hqnews/2005/mar/HQ_05086_deep_impact.html.*

69   Niebur, S. (2009, 10 August). Personal interview with B. Blume, Tim Larson, Al Nakata, and Steve Wissler. Located in "Deep Impact" file, NASA Historical Reference Collection, History Division, NASA Headquarters, Washington, DC.

70   Roylance, F. D. (2005, 5 July). "Spacecraft races to rendezvous with a comet." *The Baltimore Sun*; Bakich, M. E. (2005, June 22). "Getting set for Deep Impact." *Astronomy Magazine.*

71   Ferster, W. (2005, 11 July). "Satellite awakened to study probe's collision with comet." *SpaceNews.* 9.

72   TenBruggencate, J. (2005, 28 June). "Island eyes on heavens for Deep Impact." *Honolulu Advertiser*; Lieberman, B. (2005, 5 July). "Collision of spacecraft, comet may be visible." *The San Diego Union-Tribune*; Rincon, P. (2005, 5 July). "Comet crash clues for Europe." BBC News.

impactor might cause quite a spectacular event. Paul Feldman, an astronomy professor at Johns Hopkins University and a co-investigator on the CONTOUR mission, attributed the plume creation to a ray of Sun heating a pocket of subsurface volatile gas such as carbon dioxide or carbon monoxide ice.[73]

The Planetary Society, a nonprofit space advocacy outfit, started a betting pool for people to predict what would happen on impact. The Deep Impact science team even joined in.[74] The Pasadena, California–based group sponsored an online contest for space enthusiasts to guess the size of the crater.[75] But first the impactor had to actually hit the comet.

Rick Grammier, one of the mission's many former PMs, explained the difficulty of the far-off maneuvers by saying, "It's a bullet trying to hit a second bullet with a third bullet, in the right place at the right time."[76] It was more than a collision, though: the impactor would be released ahead of time and sent into the comet's path.[77]

Sixty-nine days before impact and 39.7 miles away, the spacecraft was close enough to the comet to begin tracking it visually.[78] Those cometary plumes and outbursts were proving much larger than expected and erupting much more often than predicted. Events occurred in as short a span as two days apart. This was more than a bit unnerving to some at NASA, who feared the spacecraft might be destroyed.[79]

Before Encounter

As Deep Impact closed in on the comet, the Deep Impact team continued closing out computer issues and anomaly reports. The issues were not always minor. Going into the encounter phase of the mission, the star tracker component built by Ball and used for navigation began reporting peculiar data. It was not tracking stars properly (a nontrivial issue for *a star tracker*), reporting inaccurate quaternions. Keyur Patel, the Deputy Project Manager, was incensed. "Now, it's amazing in the sense that there were people at Ball who knew about this, but the Ball guys from Deep Impact were

---

73 Dominguez, A. (2005, 28 June). "Hubble comet image preview of July 4 collision." Associated Press; Graham, S. (2005, 28 June). "Comet puts on show while waiting for its close-up." *Scientific American.*

74 Dayton, L. (2005, 28 June). "Betting on a Big Bang." *Australian.*

75 "Smashing Idea: Craft set to blast comet tonight." (2005, 3 July). *NY Daily News.*

76 Leary, W. E. (2005, 28 June). "Spacecraft is on a collision course with a comet, intentionally." *The New York Times.*

77 Chwallek, G. (2005, 12 January). "Deep Impact on Independence Day." *The [SA] Star & Independent.*

78 "NASA'S Deep Impact Spacecraft Spots Its Quarry, Stalking Begins." (2005, 27 April). NASA News Release 05-108.

79 Dornheim, M. (2004, 4 July). "Crash Course." *Aviation Week.*

never told about this."[80] The problem, it turned out, could be corrected in software. They loaded it on the impactor spacecraft but decided against installing it on the flyby spacecraft.

That was nothing next to another issue plaguing the impactor. "In all the simulations we did," said Patel, "the impactor, as it was going in, would do the zigzag maneuver."[81] The impactor, on final approach, would perform three targeting maneuvers. The first put the spacecraft on course with the comet. The second veered way off course, sure to miss it. And then the third maneuver put the impactor back on course. It was a strange interaction between the auto-navigation system, the attitude determination and control system, the gyros, and other spacecraft subsystems. Even after correcting ancillary issues discovered by the team, every time they ran the simulation, the zigzag behavior remained unchanged.

"So, now it comes," said Patel. "We know how to fix this thing. We've got a couple of months to go, or three months to go.... And my position is: we're not fixing it."[82] He explained that there was no need to compensate for the weird behavior. Despite the zigzag, it still worked every time.... The decision by the project manager, Rick Grammier, was we're going to fly as-is, based on all the test history and everything else."

Then, a few days before the encounter, the comet itself threw the team a curveball. A plume, to be specific.

"Everybody starts freaking out," recalled Patel. "What if that happens as you're going in? How's the auto-nav going to behave?" He wasn't worried—they had accounted for "anything and everything" in the navigation algorithms.[83] "That last 24 hours," said Tim Larson, "those were kind of like this Zen-like calm. Because there wasn't a whole lot that could be done at that point."[84]

Indeed, the final full day before the encounter, the team made as few decisions as possible. Nobody yet knew exactly what the comet would look like and how they would handle it. As images arrived, it looked first like a banana, and then like a boat. Neither mattered. The team had laid out a detailed decision tree a priori. "We did not want to decide anything going in or put anything up for debate," said Patel. "If it was less than this, greater than this, do this, this, this thing. It was a flow chart, right. And everybody wanted to know what the decision was that it gave." Nominal decisions were locked in,

---

80   Niebur, S. (2009, 10 August). Personal interview with K. Patel. Located in the "Discovery Program" file, NASA Historical Reference Collection, History Division, NASA Headquarters, Washington, DC.

81   Ibid.

82   Ibid.

83   Ibid.

84   Niebur, S. (2009, 10 August). Personal interview with B. Blume, T. Larson, A. Nakata, and S. Wissler. Located in the "Discovery Program" file, NASA Historical Reference Collection, History Division, NASA Headquarters, Washington, DC.

and for off-nominal decisions, information could be plugged into the decision matrix. Said Patel, "We never had a single off-nominal moment.… We released and watched it for two hours. I went home, slept like a baby, because my issues were over."[85]

The impactor behaved exactly as the team knew it would. "One thing most people don't know about on Deep Impact is there was no communication between the flyby spacecraft and the impactor," said Patel. "The flyby was just a bent pipe, but the flyby had to independently figure out where the impactor was going to hit, because it never knew where the impactor was going."[86] The impactor zigzagged just as the simulations predicted. And just as the simulations predicted, it corrected itself perfectly for the third maneuver.

No Threat to Earth

PI Michael A'Hearn believed the final 24 hours of the impactor's life would yield truly landmark cometary science data. He realized that so little was known about cometary nuclei that this mission would be revolutionary.

Don Yeomans, a mission co-investigator, had to correct the record on a sensational rumor seeping into news stories: that the comet might be bumped into a collision course with Earth. "In the world of science, this is the astronomical equivalent of a 767-airliner running into a mosquito," he said. "The impact simply will not appreciably modify the comet's orbital path."[87]

Impact occurred at 1:52 a.m. Eastern Time on 4 July 2005. The copper impactor collided with the comet and vaporized, creating a hole and releasing debris. The flyby spacecraft was a scant 5,300 miles away at the time.

According to Steve Wissler, just days before the encounter, there didn't seem to be high confidence that they were actually going to pull this thing off. But the team had images coming down in real time at the mission support area. "That first impact image was so spectacular that everybody just erupted, jumped up and down and erupted." They had hit a bullet with a bullet fired from another bullet. "That was one of the probably most exciting moments in my life, seeing that first image come down."[88]

There was such pandemonium in the mission support area, with cheering and celebration, that Wissler had to get on the radio network and remind everyone that their work wasn't finished: they still had a spacecraft with a job to do for another

---

85   Niebur, S. (2009, 10 August). Personal interview with K. Patel. Located in the "Discovery Program" file, NASA Historical Reference Collection, History Division, NASA Headquarters, Washington, DC.

86   Ibid.

87   "NASA Announces Spectacular Day of the Comet." (2005, 9 June). NASA news release.

88   Niebur, S. (2009, 10 August). Personal interview with K. Patel. Located in "Discovery Program" file, NASA Historical Reference Collection, History Division, NASA Headquarters, Washington, DC.

13 minutes, until closest approach. During that time, the spacecraft took pictures of the impact site before turning to shield itself from particles during its closest shave with the comet—310 miles—which occurred at 2:06 a.m. After it cleared the coma, the spacecraft swiveled around to take more images of the receding Tempel 1.

On impact, the plume expanded rapidly at 3.1 miles per second.[89] In fact, the impact released two plumes of cometary dust and gas—one likely softer, layered material on the surface and the other, thick, hard crust, each stretching for thousands of kilometers into space.

On 14 October 2005, the journal *Science* published a special issue for Deep Impact's early results. These included the first detection, with imaging, of water ice on the surface of any comet, and a delayed flash and asymmetrical plume indicating a highly porous, fine-grained, compressible surface like fluffy snow, which created a fog that blocked the spacecraft's view of the crater.[90]

Sixteen days after impact, NASA Headquarters agreed to retarget the flyby spacecraft and its high-powered, if slightly out-of-focus, planetary telescope for a new, future mission to a nearby comet or asteroid. After downloading the captured data and performing a post-encounter calibration, Jet Propulsion Laboratory engineers issued commands to the spacecraft to fire its thrusters and change its course. It would orbit the Sun and swing back near Earth by 2008. Deep Impact went into hibernation while NASA decided what to do with it next.

STARDUST NEXT

Comet 9P/Tempel 1, however, was still awake...and so was the Stardust spacecraft. Indeed, the Discovery Program had three capable small-body spacecraft in orbit around the Sun now—Stardust, Genesis, and Deep Impact—and scientists were not short on ideas for how to use them. Though its sample collection mission had been completed successfully, with planetary scientists on Earth gleefully studying fragments of Wild 2, the Stardust spacecraft and its payload of science instruments—a camera, a dust analyzer, and a dust flux monitor—were as functional as the day they launched from Earth.

Joe Veverka of Cornell, formerly Principal Investigator of the ill-fated CONTOUR and co-investigator on Deep Impact, had an idea for a new mission for Stardust after its sample return was complete. He called it Stardust NExT (New Exploration of Tempel 1), saying it was "the tale of two missions: Deep Impact and the Stardust mission."[91]

---

89   Gugliotta, G. (2005, 5 July). "NASA succeeds in crashing craft into comet." *The Washington Post.*

90   Roylance, F. D. (2006, 13 January). "Mission to comet finds complexity." *The Baltimore Sun.*

91   Veverka, J. (2010, 10 September). "25 Years: First Comet Encounter." From NASA event presentation.

When NASA Headquarters released the 2006 Discovery Announcement of Opportunity, it decided to try an experiment of its own. Large strategic science missions—the multi-billion-dollar "flagships" such as Galileo and Cassini—had defined procedures involving senior reviews to extend their purpose each time a science mission was completed. The Solar System Exploration Division had no such process for the small Discovery-class missions. The 2006 AO would solve that. The agency would competitively select mission extensions—proposals to do new science—with an existing spacecraft. This was the first time that NASA's planetary missions had to compete for an extended mission. Any proposal would have to undergo both a Step 1 and a Step 2 review process.

Veverka's proposal, originally called Scar Quest, was led by a team of scientists from previous missions. Indeed, of the dozens of co-investigators, only five were first-timers to Discovery.[92] To call it an experienced team was an understatement, and Veverka himself was a veteran of NASA's Mariner 9, Viking, Voyager, Galileo, Mars Global Surveyor, NEAR, Deep Impact, CONTOUR, and Cassini missions.

The science objectives of Stardust NExT were to return to Tempel 1, whence Deep Impact had just returned, and

- document the surface changes on the comet's nucleus between successive perihelion passages;
- measure the comet's dust properties and compare them with data taken from Wild 2;
- provide additional information on enigmatic layering and flow features discovered by the Deep Impact mission; and
- use on-board instruments to image the comet's nucleus surface and jets, count the size and distribution of its dust particles during closest approach, and study the dust composition for further ground analysis.

Moreover, Stardust NExT would determine how the Deep Impact experiment modified the surface of Tempel 1, including studying the crater the impactor had created.[93] This latter objective was important because Deep Impact's view of the crater was obscured by fine dust and ice ejected upon impact. The mission would "get the glimpse we never got with Deep Impact," said co-investigator Jay Melosh, who was also part of the Deep Impact mission.[94]

---

92   Erickson, J. (2006, 16 March). "Colorado craft could return to the stars." *Rocky Mountain News.*

93   "Stardust NExT." (N.d.) Downloaded from *https://www.jpl.nasa.gov/missions/stardust-next* on 16 August 2021.

94   Erickson, J. (2006, 16 March). "Colorado craft could return to the stars." *Rocky Mountain News.*

The Stardust NExT proposal received $250,000 for the team to conduct concept studies. It was selected by NASA Headquarters for implementation. Compared to Deep Impact, the Stardust spacecraft, packing a smaller instrument payload, was a breeze to operate.

Michael A'Hearn, PI of Deep Impact and co-investigator of Stardust NExT, compared the two spacecraft, explaining: "Stardust NExT has PI owned instruments. Deep Impact did not: they are all facility instruments, so the whole team owns all the data. That's not true on Stardust NExT." The division of responsibilities would lead to an easier flow of information. Moreover, he said, "Stardust NExT was much easier to fly, for two reasons: First, it is built and flown by Lockheed. It is not flown by JPL. Lockheed flies a low budget operation. Second, the spacecraft is far less capable and therefore designing observance sequences is trivial. There is one camera that you can use at encounter in parallel with the dust counter that takes data. The [Cometary Secondary Ion Mass Analyzer] analyzes its particles, and that's it. You don't have enough memory storage to do very many images. So, the observing sequence is trivial."[95]

NASA approved the mission on 3 July 2007. It would encounter Tempel 1 on Valentine's Day, 2011. When it arrived, it would zip by the comet in just 20 minutes—more than enough time to achieve its goals.

Education and public outreach would also be easy, compared to most missions. Aimee Meyer, who had previously led EPO for Magellan, Mars Pathfinder, and Stardust, still had her army of Education Fellows engaged with the mission and interested in seeing it continue. "I honestly believe that we got extended because of the fact that there were so many teachers who probably wrote letters to continue the mission," she said.[96]

EPOXI

A'Hearn had an idea for how best to repurpose the dormant Deep Impact, and he called it DIXI: the Deep Impact Extended Investigation. They could send the probe to another comet, collect data, and perform comparative science. "Half the discoveries at Tempel 1 were from the flyby data taken before impact," he said. "DIXI can

---

95   Niebur, S. (2009, 11 March). Personal interview with M. A'Hearn. Located in "Deep Impact" file, NASA Historical Reference Collection, History Division, NASA Headquarters, Washington, DC.

96   Niebur, S. (2009, 2 September). Personal interview with A. Meyer. Located in "Stardust" file, NASA Historical Reference Collection, History Division, NASA Headquarters, Washington, DC.

return half the science of Deep Impact for much less than 10 percent of the cost of Deep Impact."[97]

They would visit the Comet 85D/Boethin in December 2008, image its nucleus, and increase the scientific understanding of comet diversity. The small, short-period comet had never before been visited. Doing so would allow the Discovery Program to recover some of the science lost with the 2002 failure of the CONTOUR mission—itself intended to do comparative studies of multiple comets.

That wasn't the only idea for what to do with Deep Impact, however. L. Drake Deming of Goddard Space Flight Center, in Greenbelt, Maryland, wanted to look outward from our solar system and find Earth-size planets circling other stars. The Deep Impact spacecraft and its powerful planetary telescope was the perfect tool for the job. He called it EPOCh—the Extrasolar Planet Observation and Characterization mission— and it could take special advantage of Deep Impact's flawed high-resolution camera.

To find planets circling other stars, rather than image them directly, as the Hubble Space Telescope might look at Jupiter or Mars, the project would infer the existence and characteristics of a planet or planets, should any be discovered, using transit detection. The camera would measure variations in a star's brightness. A planet passing in front of a star would dim the star; accordingly, brightness levels, the rate of the transit, and known information about the star, among other data points, could reveal information about the planet found. Moreover, the camera would observe previously discovered planets and use changes in known measurements to determine variations in cloud structures and measure the planets' temperatures. Indeed, much more than that might be detected.[98]

"We have bright stars that we know have transiting planets, at least one transiting. But, if you stare at them for a long time, they may have another planet in the system whose transit is too infrequent and too shallow to have been noticed before." Even planetary systems were possible to detect. "The giant transiting planets themselves may have moons or rings or other subtle signatures in their transit light curves that can be extracted from high-precision photometry."[99]

Because the Deep Impact camera was out of focus, the light from measured stars would be seen not as a single point, but as a gradient across multiple pixels. This would actually lessen the noise in the data—perfect for EPOCh's purposes. As Deming

---

97   University of Maryland. (2006, 16 May). "Two Deep Impact daughter comet missions proposed." News release. Downloaded from *http://www.spaceflightnow.com/news/n0605/16deepimpact/* on 16 August 2021.

98   Niebur, S. (2009, 10 July). Personal interview with D. Deming. Located in the "Discovery Program" file, NASA Historical Reference Collection, History Division, NASA Headquarters, Washington, DC.

99   Ibid.

explained, "We convert that focus flaw into an asset."[100] It would make its observations during the spring and summer of 2008.

The team proposed initially to move spacecraft operations from the Jet Propulsion Laboratory to Goddard, though NASA killed that idea pretty quickly. "It's probably a good thing," said Deming. "Goddard is wonderful, but it's a very complicated spacecraft. It would have been a really steep learning curve and it probably would have cost a lot more."[101]

Both missions stood independently, but A'Hearn anticipated that NASA Headquarters, rather than approving one or the other, might mandate that the mission concepts get merged into a single super mission. "We coordinated writing the proposals so that they would be easy to combine, but kept them separate in case NASA wanted to pick one but not the other." They knew that NASA could not approve both as independent Missions of Opportunity; the budget would not allow it. Ultimately, the agency did as expected and had the principal investigators fuse the missions into a single concept study.[102]

One of Deming's colleagues at Harvard, Dave Charbonneau, came up with the idea of taking EPOCH and DIXI and gluing the two acronyms together, with EPOXI.[103] When A'Hearn presented the merged project to Alan Stern, the Associate Administrator of the Science Mission Directorate, the first thing Stern said was, "Oh, nice acronym."[104] On 3 July 2007, NASA selected EPOXI, the extended mission of Deep Impact, for implementation, with A'Hearn as its Principal Investigator.

COMET BOETHIN

Stardust NExT soon experienced a first for planetary science: its target of exploration disappeared.[105] Before Stardust NExT, Comet Boethin, its intended quarry, had been spotted only twice: when it was discovered in 1975, and again in 1986. Though it had

---

100   Shiga, D. (2006, 1 November). "Deep Impact's blurry camera may study exoplanets." *New Scientist.*

101   Niebur, S. (2009, 10 July). Personal interview with D. Deming. Located in "Discovery Program" file, NASA Historical Reference Collection, History Division, NASA Headquarters, Washington, DC.

102   Niebur, S. (2009, 11 March). Personal interview with M. A'Hearn. Located in "Discovery Program" file, NASA Historical Reference Collection, History Division, NASA Headquarters, Washington, DC.

103   Niebur, S. (2009, 10 July). Personal interview with D. Deming. Located in "Deep Impact" file, NASA Historical Reference Collection, History Division, NASA Headquarters, Washington, DC.

104   Ibid.

105   Niebur, S. (2009, 11 March). Personal interview with M. A'Hearn. Located in "Deep Impact" file, NASA Historical Reference Collection, History Division, NASA Headquarters, Washington, DC; Chang, A. (2007, 5 July). "New tasks given to old NASA spacecraft." NASA press release.

not been spotted in 1997, astronomers were unsurprised at the time, as the Sun's glare would have concealed it due to the relative positions of the comet, the star, and Earth.

It is possible that during that solar approach, the comet disintegrated, though it was an unlikely scenario. Only one comet had theretofore done such a thing: Comet C/1999 S4 (LINEAR), which vanished in 2000. More likely, telescopes just weren't looking in the right place; due to the paucity of previous observations, astronomers never calculated its orbit with extreme precision. The main reason the Deep Impact team had chosen it as a target is because it was quick and easy to reach. With it vanished from the cosmos, clearly that was no longer the case.

Thankfully, the team had a secondary target: Comet 103P/Hartley (Hartley 2), a small, Jupiter-family comet with a 6.47-year orbit. "When Comet Boethin could not be located, we went to our backup, which is every bit as interesting but about two years farther down the road," said Tom Duxbury, the EPOXI project manager.[106] That two-year cruise phase extension would cost NASA another $40 million. The spacecraft would fly within 620 miles of Hartley 2, with its rendezvous scheduled for 11 October 2010.[107]

EPOCH, meanwhile, had problems of its own. The camera's charge-coupled device, or CCD—its image sensor—had a resolution of 1,024 × 1,024 pixels, though because of memory constraints for long star transit observations, the team planned to use only 64 × 64 pixels. A star in focus would occupy only about 10 pixels. In practice, that didn't work because of pointing jitter and absolute pointing accuracy. The team ended up using a 128 × 128 mode for most of its work, with which, even then, it proved difficult to keep the star centered.

"If you were off center slightly," said Drake Deming, the PI of the EPOCH portion of EPOXI, "then with the pointing jitter, sometimes it would actually leave the array, and we would lose data. Now, it's not a complete disaster to lose data because we're looking for the star for weeks at a time, and we lose data anyway because we turn the spacecraft to downlink, and we're not observing. So, it wasn't that big of a disaster, but, of course, when we don't want to lose data is when there's an actual transit or a secondary eclipse of the planet."

JPL engineers created a mode that used a 256 × 256 subarray during periods of transit and eclipse, and a 128 × 128 subarray at other times. "This kind of mode meant that during a critical part, we would always have the star," said Deming. "The reason that we didn't propose anything like that was because, in the initial proposal, I wasn't

---

106   Borland, J. (2007, 14 December). "Aging spacecraft set on new comet hunt." *Wired.*

107   O'Brien, D. (2008, 16 February). "Spacecraft to look for Earth-like planets; Second life for comet chaser." *The Baltimore Sun.* 1A.

sure how much DSN time we would get. It turns out that we were able to get DSN downloads every couple days. So that meant that we could store more data."[108]

Over the course of the mission, the CCD changed as pixels died due to space radiation—no problem when imaging a comet up close, but brutal for something as delicate as searching for planets transiting stars.

EPOCH also made observations of Earth, reducing it to a single pixel and studying its rotational light curves. The idea would be to figure out what such data looked like for a known planet so that it could be applied to unknown planets circling distant stars. The team found that when the Pacific Ocean rotated into view, the blue light curve peaked.

"So, you can mathematically invert that to say that the planet must have an ocean blob at that location," said Deming. The maps had no latitudinal resolution, but "nevertheless, you could see, there are two oceans and two land masses. The two land masses are Europe, Asia, Africa as one big blob, and then the Americas. So, to be able to infer the existence of continents and oceans on another world would be, of course, astounding. And so, we demonstrated that that's possible with signal-to-noise ratios that would be reasonable for extrasolar earthlike planets."[109]

---

108   Niebur, S. (2009, 10 July). Personal interview with D. Deming. Located in the "Discovery Program" file, NASA Historical Reference Collection, History Division, NASA Headquarters, Washington, DC.

109   Ibid.

Figure 4-1: Deep Impact—Comet Tempel 1 just after impact

Comet Tempel 1, imaged by Deep Impact's flyby spacecraft after impact on 4 July 2005. The burst of light on the right side of the comet is sunlight reflected from the ejecta thrown up by the impact. (Image credit: NASA/JPL-Caltech/University of Maryland, image no. PIA02137)

Figure 4-2: Deep Impact spacecraft

The Deep Impact spacecraft inside the mobile service tower on Launch Pad 17-B at Cape Canaveral Air Force Station, awaiting fairing installation. (Image credit: NASA, image no. KSC-05pd-0074)

CHAPTER 5

Breaking the Bank

MESSENGER: AN AMAZING CONCEPT

The MErcury Surface, Space ENvironment, GEochemistry, and Ranging spacecraft, or MESSENGER, was, without a doubt, the most ambitious mission ever selected in the Discovery Program.

It was the second effort to get such a Mercury mission going. An earlier, $257 million (in Fiscal Year 1996 dollars) proposal was selected for a concept study but was not selected for flight. When it was proposed again in 1998, the price had increased to $286 million (Fiscal Year 1998 dollars) with a few significant upgrades to the instruments, namely: the gamma ray spectrometer became the Gamma Ray and Neutron Spectrometer (GRNS), and the energetic particle spectrometer became an energetic particle and plasma spectrometer.

MESSENGER was thus selected, first for study on 7 July 1999, and then, after being chosen for flight, it entered the implementation phase on 7 June 2001. At the time of selection, NASA Headquarters scientists and managers heralded the team's plan to go back to Mercury for the first time in over 20 years, and with a large suite of instruments and ambitious goals.[1]

The Team

Sean Solomon, a planetary geologist and geophysicist at the Carnegie Institution of Washington, led the science team as its Principal Investigator. The project manager was Max Peterson at APL. The MESSENGER team was an all-star one: Ralph L. McNutt, also at APL, was the project scientist; Brian J. Anderson and Deborah L. Domingue were deputy project scientists at APL. Bob Farquhar was mission manager (as he had been on NEAR and CONTOUR). Robert Gold was the payload manager on both MESSENGER and NEAR. In fact, nine of the 20 original co-investigators, including McNutt, had been co-investigators on NEAR, APL's previous Discovery mission.

Solomon had been participating in space science missions since graduate school, when his graduate adviser, Navi Toxos, led the seismic experiments on Apollo 11 and 12. Eleven years later, he joined his first mission as a co-investigator on Magellan, which explored Venus. He also worked on the altimetry teams for Mars Observer and Mars Global Surveyor with Dave Smith at Goddard Space Flight Center and served on the Committee on Planetary and Lunar Exploration (COMPLEX) and other such advisory groups. Solomon was the rarity among Discovery PIs in that he had not originally proposed at the 1992 Discovery Workshop at San Juan Capistrano.

MESSENGER, in fact, while PI-led, was not even conceived by the PI. APL began working on a Mercury orbiter concept in March 1996, soon after word came down from NASA Headquarters of the upcoming Discovery 1996 Announcement of Opportunity.[2]

Solomon said, "APL was a very lean organization with not a lot of hierarchical structure and fit very well into developing low-cost but technically ambitious missions and were always looking for good ideas."[3]

Lab scientists and management at APL recruited a science team to work out the key unsolved science questions of Mercury and how best to answer them. The first people they approached worked on the NEAR spacecraft to the asteroid Eros. John Applebee,

---

1   NASA. (2001, 8 June). "NASA gives official nod to robotic mission to Mercury." NASA News release.

2   McNutt, R. L., Solomon, S. C., Gold, R. E., & Leary, J. C. (2006). "The MESSENGER mission to Mercury: Development history and early mission status." *Mercury, Mars and Saturn*, 38(4), 564–571. *https://doi.org/10.1016/j.asr.2005.05.044*.

3   Niebur, S. (2009, 22 March). Personal interview with S. Solomon. Located in "MESSENGER" file, NASA Historical Reference Collection, History Division, NASA Headquarters, Washington, DC.

who was the head of development for the Space Department at APL, approached Solomon, saying: "We are looking to put together a team of scientists for a Discovery proposal, a Mercury orbiter. Would you be interested?"[4]

Solomon had written papers previously on Mercury and was one of the two authors of the Mercury chapter in the 1978 COMPLEX report on exploration of the inner planets. The organizing question was: "What are the strategic goals for the exploration of Mercury after Mariner 10?" Nobody at APL knew the answer.

Solomon thought it sounded like fun. "I hadn't given a great deal of thought to Mercury for almost 20 years.... But it was something I had wanted to do for 20 years. It was a chance." He didn't know that much about APL or the team that would compose MESSENGER, though. Later, Tom Krimigis, the head of the Space Department at APL, called and asked Solomon to visit APL. Solomon agreed to do so. "I had never been to APL," Solomon recalled. "And I come into this room with 10 people waiting for me. And the gist of it was… 'You already said you would be on the science team for the mission, how about being PI?'"[5] Part of the motivation for recruiting a scientist outside of APL was feedback from the previous Discovery round. Headquarters had told Krimigis that an external PI would broaden the menu of expertise that could be called upon to lead a science team.[6] Though much of the science team had already been built—most from NEAR—Solomon agreed to be PI on the condition that he could add to the team.[7] APL management acceded.

APL had great success in the 1996 Discovery round, winning not one but three concept studies for CONTOUR, MESSENGER, and Aladdin. It was almost a catastrophic victory. As Ralph McNutt, the project scientist for MESSENGER, remembers: "One of the guys here came to me and had this look of horror on his face. I said, 'We didn't get any of them?' And he said, 'No, we got all three of them.' And so, it was like, 'Oh, my God,' because now we had to field three teams."[8]

Solomon said his inexperience and naivete worked against the Mercury proposal after the first-round selection, however. "I put a lot of effort into the science rationale, which was the first 25 pages of the proposal," he said, adding that he lacked the technical experience to critically evaluate engineering solutions to technical challenges. "I didn't know that much then about risk management…. Nor did I know how to evalu-

---

4   Niebur, S. (2009, 22 March). Personal interview with S. Solomon. Located in the "Discovery Program" file, NASA Historical Reference Collection, History Division, NASA Headquarters, Washington, DC.

5   Ibid.

6   Ibid.

7   Ibid.

8   Niebur, S. (2009, 31 July). Personal interview with R. McNutt. Located in the "MESSENGER" file, NASA Historical Reference Collection, History Division, NASA Headquarters, Washington, DC.

ate project managers, the first time around."[9] The science component of the proposal was strong, particularly because there had never been a spacecraft in Mercury's orbit before. But the second selection round was driven by a review of the proposal's technical, management, cost, and other factors.

"At the time of our site visit, we had a development path for the solar arrays, which was worked out. But in the questions and answers, it was clear we didn't have a sufficient contingency plan. If any of the testing proved that our assumptions were not appropriate," he said, "we didn't have a deep plan to what to do next."[10] Specifically, NASA had concerns about the solar arrays so close to the Sun and how the adhesives connecting solar cell to solar panel might endure. Moreover, the budget did not come together by the site visit. The numbers had only been compiled the night before the presentation, and some of the information that had gone out to the site review team didn't add up. The project manager, recalls Solomon, was in front of the room and getting questioned on budgets and couldn't answer the questions. And there was nobody there who could help him because nobody had seen it.[11]

Reproposal

The team was determined to propose MESSENGER again, this time to the 1998 Announcement of Opportunity. Solomon's condition for again being Principal Investigator was to choose the next project manager. "I knew what skills I wanted, including communication," said Solomon. "That we had to have a rapport, someone who could work well with his own engineers. Somebody whose budgets I believed. Somebody who knew about risk."[12]

APL had just the person: Max Peterson, a long-time lab engineer with multiple missions under his belt. Peterson and Solomon hit it off from the start. With that problem solved, they got to work on the solar array issue. The lab used its own money to develop a testing protocol and to do the actual testing at NASA's Glenn Research Center. "By the time we wrote our second proposal," said Solomon, "and particularly by the time of the second site study we could say, 'Not only do we have a solution for the solar arrays; here are all the tests that validate our models.' Yes, they loved it. So, the first time we proposed we were Low Risk in round one and High Risk after the site visit. High risk being the solar arrays and not having a good project manager. But we were Low Risk both times the second time through."[13]

---

9   Niebur, S. (2009, 22 March). Personal interview with S. Solomon. Located in "Discovery Program" file, NASA Historical Reference Collection, History Division, NASA Headquarters, Washington, DC.

10   Ibid.

11   Ibid.

12   Ibid.

13   Ibid.

The 2001 selection of MESSENGER for flight promised to advance Mercury science immeasurably. NASA had not sent a spacecraft to Mercury since Mariner 10 in 1974.[14] Robert Strom, a professor emeritus at the University of Arizona Lunar and Planetary Laboratory, had been lobbying for a return to Mercury since NASA's last foray there.[15] He became a co-investigator on MESSENGER. Much earlier, he in fact served on Mariner 10 as deputy team leader for the imaging experiment. "Mariner 10 was a mission that was designed as a reconnaissance of Mercury in order to characterize it to plan a Mercury orbiter," he said. "That orbiter was supposed to be planned and launched by about 1980. Well, it's been 30 years."[16]

As Sean Solomon, the MESSENGER PI, said, "For nearly 30 years, we've had questions that couldn't be answered until technology and mission designs caught up with our desire to go back to Mercury.... Now we are ready."[17] A mission to Mercury had been studied by both the Jet Propulsion Laboratory and Goddard Space Flight Center, but the costs in every case precluded its execution. The Mercury Dual Orbiter, a Goddard concept and the last studied by the planetary program, came in at around $700 million. (MESSENGER was less than half that price.) The price tag, coupled with the relatively low priority of Mercury exploration at NASA, meant it would never get the traction necessary for flight. Discovery was a paradigm shift, though. The New Frontier program did not yet exist; Discovery was the only way such a mission would ever fly.

Scientific Questions

MESSENGER sought to answer six fundamental questions, which trace their heritage back to the 1978 COMPLEX report coauthored by Solomon.

1. What planetary formational processes led to Mercury's high ratio of metal to silicate?
2. What is the geological history of Mercury?
3. What are the nature and origin of Mercury's magnetic field?
4. What are the structure and state of Mercury's core?
5. What are the radar-reflective materials at Mercury's poles?
6. What are the important volatile species and their sources and sinks near Mercury?[18]

---

14   Ibid.
15   Stauffer, T. (2004, 31 July). "His 30-year wait to end with launch to Mercury." *Arizona Daily Star.* B2.
16   Harwood, W. (2004, 3 August). "Probe roars away from Earth on voyage to orbit Mercury." *Spaceflight Now.*
17   Perlman, D. (2004, 1 August). "MESSENGER ready to deliver." *San Francisco Chronicle.*
18   Solomon, S. C., McNutt, R. L., Gold, R. E., & Domingue, D. L. (2007). "MESSENGER Mission Overview." *Space Science Reviews,* 131(1–4), 3–39. *https://doi.org/10.1007/s11214-007-9247-6.*

Each of these questions drove a science objective for the mission, and each of the science objectives was addressed by a well-defined set of measurement objectives that could be reached by two or more instruments in the suite of seven that made up the payload.[19] The answers to those questions had great generality for understanding each of the inner planets—not just Mercury.

The direct tracing of objectives to measurements to instruments, and ultimately to spacecraft and mission design, contributed significantly to the ability of the mission to be "ambitious in its scientific scope for a Discovery mission, a tribute to the fact that scientific requirements guided the development of spacecraft and mission design at every stage in the project, from initial concept through all design trades and testing," and mission operations.[20]

The seven instruments were designed to measure a wealth of data about the surface, atmosphere, and magnetosphere of this largely unknown planet. Not only would the mission bring back global maps of Mercury, but also a wealth of information about its geochemistry, geology, geophysics, thin atmosphere, and active magnetosphere. The team wanted to cover as many bases as an orbiter would permit.[21]

Solomon explained that, at the time, the most fundamental question the team was most interested in answering is how Mercury got put together and what the processes were that contributed to the inner planets turning out so differently from the outer planets. "They formed by common processes," he said. "The inner planets are all litter mates, if you will, products of a single early stage in the evolution of a star and a planetary system." To understand what processes most affected the outcomes, it was useful to study Mercury, the most extreme of those outcomes.[22]

"Mercury is an unusual planet even by the standards of the inner solar system," elaborated Solomon, with "an unusual rotation rate such that the solar day on Mercury

---

19   Ibid.

20   McAdams, J., Farquhar, R., Taylor, A., & Williams, B. (2007). "MESSENGER mission design and navigation." *Space Sci Rev*, 131, 219–246. *https://doi.org/10.1007/s11214-007-9162-x*; Leary, J. C., Conde, R. F., Dakermanji, G., Engelbrecht, C. S., Ercol, C. J., Fielhauer, K. B., Grant, D. G., Hartka, T. J., Hill, T. A., Jaskulek, S. E., Mirantes, M. A., Mosher, L. E., Paul, M. V., Persons, D. F., Rodberg, E. H., Srinivasan, D. K., Vaughan, R. M., & Wiley, S. R. (2007). "The MESSENGER Spacecraft." *Space Science Reviews*, 131(1–4), 187–217. *https://doi.org/10.1007/s11214-007-9269-0*; Solomon, S. C., McNutt, R. L., Gold, R. E., & Domingue, D. L. (2007). "MESSENGER Mission Overview." *Space Science Reviews*, 131(1–4), 3–39. *https://doi.org/10.1007/s11214-007-9247-6*; Holdridge, M. E., & Calloway, A. B. (2007). "Launch and Early Operation of the MESSENGER Mission." In D. L. Domingue & C. T. Russell (Eds.), *The Messenger Mission to Mercury* (pp. 573–600). Springer: New York. *https://doi.org/10.1007/978-0-387-77214-1_17*.

21   Harwood, W. (2004, 30 July). "MESSENGER awaits launch on marathon trek to Mercury." *Spaceflight Now*.

22   Ibid.

lasts two Mercury years. It has the highest intrinsic density of any planet; the density is so high that two-thirds of the planet must be iron metal."[23] A mission to Mercury, ultimately, is a mission to the innermost part of the nebula out of which the planets formed.[24]

Before MESSENGER, not much was known about Mercury. Its density and magnetic field were comparable to Earth's, but the planet is much smaller and made mostly of metal. All this was so, perhaps, because the interior region of the solar nebula was enriched in metals. Or maybe the planet was originally covered with a rocky surface that baked off in the intense heat caused by its proximity to the Sun. Or it could be that the crust broke off in an early impact. MESSENGER's instruments, by measuring the composition of the crust, would likely be able to distinguish between the three hypotheses and determine the planet's original composition and its evolution. Moreover, there was evidence that an unexpected material might be found in Mercury's craters at the poles that are never exposed to sunlight. This material might have been frozen water ice, comet-delivered sulfur, or silicates, hidden in the dark crevices that stay very cold, hundreds of degrees below zero.

Its oddly strong magnetic field and unknown core size and composition were also unexplained. Did it possess a spinning liquid outer core?[25] Its geology was curious as well, including its giant escarpments sometimes a mile high and hundreds of miles across, formed most likely when the planet cooled.[26]

To answer those and other questions, MESSENGER's instrument payload consisted of the Mercury Dual Imaging System, a Gamma Ray and Neutron Spectrometer, an X-Ray Spectrometer (XRS), a magnetometer, the Mercury Laser Altimeter, the Mercury Atmospheric and Surface Composition Spectrometer (MASCS), and an Energetic Particle and Plasma Spectrometer (EPPS), as well as a radio science investigation.[27]

---

23   Ibid.

24   Spotts, P. N. (2004, 29 July). "The long and winding road to a hot planet." *The Christian Science Monitor.*

25   Coledan, S. (2004, 3 August). "NASA's MESSENGER probe departs for Mercury." *The New York Times.*

26   Hill, R. L. (2004, 28 July). "Earth sends MESSENGER to Mercury." *The Portland Oregonian.*

27   Hawkins, S., Boldt, J., Darlington, E., Espiritu, R., Gold, R., Gotwols, B., Grey, M., Hash, C., Hayes, J., Jaskulek, S., Kardian, C., Keller, M., Malaret, E., Murchie, S., Murphy, P., Peacock, K., Prockter, L., Reiter, R., Robinson, M., & Williams, B. (2007). "The mercury dual imaging system on the MESSENGER spacecraft." *Space Science Reviews*, 131, 247–338. *https://doi.org/10.1007/s11214-007-9266-3*; Goldsten, J. O., Rhodes, E. A., Boynton, W. V., Feldman, W. C., Lawrence, D. J., Trombka, J. I., Smith, D. M., Evans, L. G., White, J., Madden, N. W., Berg, P. C., Murphy, G. A., Gurnee, R. S., Strohbehn, K., Williams, B. D., Schaefer, E. D., Monaco, C. A., Cork, C. P., Del Eckels, J., Miller, W. O., Burks, M. T., Hagler, L. B., DeTeresa, S. J., & Witte, M. C. (2007). "The MESSENGER Gamma-Ray and Neutron Spectrometer." *Space Science Reviews*, 131(1–4), 339–391. *https://doi.org/10.1007/s11214-007-9262-7*; Schlemm, C. E., Starr, R. D., Ho, G. C., Bechtold, K. E., Hamilton, S. A., Boldt, J. D., Boynton, W. V., Bradley, W., Fraeman, M. E., Gold, R. E., Goldsten, J. O., Hayes, J. R., Jaskulek, S. E., Rossano, E., Rumpf, R. A., Schaefer, E. D., Strohbehn, K., Shelton, R. G., Thompson, R. E., Trombka, J. I., & Williams, B. D. (2007). "The X-Ray Spectrometer on

---

"To go to a planet that had never had an orbiter and to study the core and the geology and the topography and the composition of the surface materials and the exosphere, the magnetosphere, and the charged particle distribution...you need a pretty broad science team," said Sean Solomon, who led the mission science as its Principal Investigator. "Early on, because it had to be fairly big to have the scientific breadth, we imposed a structure to the team to give it a better ability to internally manage. So, from the beginning we divided the team into four discipline groups and put people in charge of the discipline groups."[28]

The spacecraft had several spatial constraints that might otherwise have impeded the collection of science data, including a giant, 2.5-meter by 2-meter sunshade protecting the instruments. Because the spacecraft would be so close to Mercury, it would have to endure a Sun whose rays are 11 times as concentrated as they are on Earth. To compensate for the protective ceramic-fabric sunshade, and because of the highly elliptical orbit of the spacecraft, the camera was mounted on a pivot.

According to Louise Prockter, the deputy project scientist of MESSENGER and Instrument Scientist for the Mercury Dual Imaging System, "Our pivot goes 40 degrees toward the Sun shield and 50 degrees away from the Sun shield. It covers 90 degrees. Doesn't sound like much, but believe me, it makes a difference. And when we're in orbit or doing a flyby, we're moving it in tiny increments all the time back and forth as we're tracking across the surface."[29]

---

the MESSENGER Spacecraft." *Space Science Reviews*, 131(1–4), 393–415. *https://doi.org/10.1007/s11214-007-9248-5*; Anderson, B. J., Acuña, M. H., Lohr, D. A., Scheifele, J., Raval, A., Korth, H., & Slavin, J. A. (2007). "The Magnetometer Instrument on MESSENGER." *Space Science Reviews*, 131(1–4), 417–450. *https://doi.org/10.1007/s11214-007-9246-7*; Cavanaugh, J. F., Smith, J. C., Sun, X., Bartels, A. E., Ramos-Izquierdo, L., Krebs, D. J., McGarry, J. F., Trunzo, R., Novo-Gradac, A. M., Britt, J. L., Karsh, J., Katz, R. B., Lukemire, A. T., Szymkiewicz, R., Berry, D. L., Swinski, J. P., Neumann, G. A., Zuber, M. T., & Smith, D. E. (2007). "The Mercury Laser Altimeter Instrument for the MESSENGER Mission." *Space Science Reviews*, 131(1–4), 451–479. *https://doi.org/10.1007/s11214-007-9273-4*; McClintock, W. E., & Lankton, M. R. (2007). "The Mercury Atmospheric and Surface Composition Spectrometer for the MESSENGER Mission." *Space Science Reviews*, 131(1–4), 481–521. *https://doi.org/10.1007/s11214-007-9264-5*; Andrews, G. B., Zurbuchen, T. H., Mauk, B. H., Malcom, H., Fisk, L. A., Gloeckler, G., Ho, G. C., Kelley, J. S., Koehn, P. L., LeFevere, T. W., Livi, S. S., Lundgren, R. A., & Raines, J. M. (2007). "The Energetic Particle and Plasma Spectrometer Instrument on the MESSENGER Spacecraft." *Space Science Reviews*, 131(1–4), 523–556. *https://doi.org/10.1007/s11214-007-9272-5*; Srinivasan, D. K., Perry, M. E., Fielhauer, K. B., Smith, D. E., & Zuber, M. T. (2007). "The Radio Frequency Subsystem and Radio Science on the MESSENGER Mission." *Space Science Reviews*, 131(1–4), 557–571. *https://doi.org/10.1007/s11214-007-9270-7*.

28   Niebur, S. (2009, 22 March). Personal interview with S. Solomon. Located in "MESSENGER" file, NASA Historical Reference Collection, History Division, NASA Headquarters, Washington, DC.

29   Niebur, S. (2009, 10 December). Personal interview with L. Prockter. Located in the "MESSENGER" file, NASA Historical Reference Collection, History Division, NASA Headquarters, Washington, DC.

As far back as 2002, the camera team had put thought into their orbital strategy, data collection, polar data acquisition, how they were going to fill in the base map, what colors were needed, and the minimum number of filters necessary to answer their science questions about composition.[30]

The role of an Instrument Scientist, according to Prockter, is "to take the science goals from the proposal, the high-level science traceability matrix, and make sure that that instrument can do that science." That's not just making sure, on a camera, for instance, that you've got the right focal length on the instrument, she explains. It's much more nuanced than that, involving things like the correct planes and filters to do color imaging. "It's also making sure that once you're in orbit around Mercury, you're in the right orbit that your camera's going to work, you've got the right amounts of time to do that." She explains that calibrations done in flight validated the camera's functionality and ironed out many of the quirks in the system and bugs in the software.[31]

Most instrument scientists on MESSENGER worked for the Applied Physics Laboratory, and most of the spacecraft's instruments were built there as well. The laser altimeter and atmospheric and surface composition spectrometer were built at Goddard Space Flight Center and the University of Colorado, respectively. By the time the mission launched, the set of people who had put in at least two months of work on the mission numbered nearly a thousand, over half at the Applied Physics Laboratory.[32]

The instruments carried, spacecraft design, and overall mission were driven by several factors, including mass. MESSENGER was limited by the heaviest Delta II rocket, the 7925H, which had a lift mass of a little over 1,100 kilograms. Propellant took 54 percent of the launch mass, leaving only 508 kilograms of dry mass for its payload. To retain the dry mass needed for launch, MESSENGER engineers thoroughly integrated the structure and the propulsion system.[33]

Ralph McNutt, the MESSENGER project scientist, explained that mass issues came in unexpected places, including the wiring harness. Early on, engineers decided to use a smaller wire gauge for the harness, which meant smaller connectors. That led to issues because those connectors were not as sturdy and would break.[34]

There were delays in the delivery of key subsystems by subcontractors. A small company called Composite Optics, which was responsible for the spacecraft structure, ran late on the project in line before MESSENGER: the Mars Exploration Rovers. That delay set back the Mercury mission from the start. Another company, responsible for

30   Ibid.

31   Ibid.

32   Niebur, S. (2009, 31 July). Personal interview with R. McNutt. Located in the "MESSENGER" file, NASA Historical Reference Collection, History Division, NASA Headquarters, Washington, DC.

33   Solomon, S. (2007, 19 September). Presentation at the Discovery@15 workshop, Huntsville, AL.

34   Niebur, S. (2009, 31 July). Personal interview with R. McNutt. Located in the "MESSENGER" file, NASA Historical Reference Collection, History Division, NASA Headquarters, Washington, DC.

the inertial measurement unit, was acquired by Northrop Grumman, which proceeded to close the Santa Barbara–based factory. Because an insufficient number of engineers at the closed plant wished to move to Los Angeles, where the new owners were located, Northrop Grumman had to reproduce the expertise necessary to build very complicated gyroscopes.[35] As if those problems weren't enough, the electromagnetic interference filters on most of the payload instruments had manufacturing flaws that could lead to critical failures, necessitating the remanufacture of electronics boards.[36] Every delay compounded. Moreover, MESSENGER would be a very long mission with a six-and-a-half-year cruise phase. Combined with the hazardous thermal environment, this necessitated fully redundant systems.

During development, instruments saw redesigns that enabled the spacecraft to stay in mass and on budget. The camera was altered to handle optical navigation. The gamma ray spectrometer, meanwhile, was, initially, very similar to the one used on NEAR. As the team would learn, the instrument only worked best when the spacecraft landed on the asteroid. In flight, it had high background noise and low signals. To compensate, the instrument team had to change from using scintillator crystals in the spectrometer to using high-purity germanium crystal—a great engineering challenge.[37]

The failure of the Mars probes in 1999 and the subsequent NASA Integrated Action Team report, and the recommendations therein, grossly complicated spacecraft development. Like all other Discovery missions, MESSENGER had to pass through numerous institutional and agency-level reviews before confirmation and the beginning of Phase C/D. The team endured 33 formal, external independent reviews with around 100 reviewers at the subsystem and system level.[38] Preliminary and critical design reviews for instruments added an additional 29 formal reviews and 226 reviewers.[39]

The excessive reviews were overly burdensome for the project team. "I complained [to NASA Headquarters] at one time that we had a third of the staff acting on the recommendations from the previous review; another third preparing for the next review; and the final third was actually doing work," said Krimigis.[40]

---

35   Niebur, S. (2009, 10 August). Personal interview with S. Solomon. Located in "MESSENGER" file, NASA Historical Reference Collection, History Division, NASA Headquarters, Washington, DC.

36   McNutt, R. L., Solomon, S. C., Gold, R. E., & Leary, J. C. (2006). "The MESSENGER mission to Mercury: Development history and early mission status." *Mercury, Mars and Saturn*, 38(4), 564–571. *https://doi.org/10.1016/j.asr.2005.05.044.*

37   Niebur, S. (2009, 31 July). Personal interview with R. McNutt. Located in the "MESSENGER" file, NASA Historical Reference Collection, History Division, NASA Headquarters, Washington, DC.

38   McNutt, R. L., Solomon, S. C., Gold, R. E., & Leary, J. C. (2006). "The MESSENGER mission to Mercury: Development history and early mission status." *Mercury, Mars and Saturn*, 38(4), 564–571. *https://doi.org/10.1016/j.asr.2005.05.044.*

39   Ibid.

40   Niebur, S. (2009, 27 August). Personal interview with T. Krimigis. Located in the "Discovery Program" file, NASA Historical Reference Collection, History Division, NASA Headquarters, Washington, DC.

Such obstacles raised the cost of the mission by about $40 million and ultimately delayed its launch. As McNutt added: "You can't test for everything. Now, I'm not supposed to say that, because you're supposed to test for everything, but it's not going to happen." During testing, McNutt was confident in the engineering. "Some of the other people in the process"—NASA Headquarters among them—"didn't think we were okay. And we actually slipped the launch window twice."[41]

Even the definition of "NASA Headquarters" for the team was a moving target. From Phases B to D, NASA's Solar System Exploration Division had four directors. The Discovery Program had three program managers and added a new position—program director—in 2004. Consequently, there were five successive Discovery management organizations.

In any event, NASA's newfound conservatism felt punitive. "They were imposed on the system, and at the same time not paid for, and also not relaxing the schedule in any way, because we had a specific deadline to launch and so on," said Krimigis.[42]

The twin losses of the Mars spacecraft were not the only failed missions to give MESSENGER fiscal heartburn and burdensome oversight. One cost savings maneuver employed by MESSENGER was to time-share with CONTOUR's mission operations staff. Both were APL missions. Once CONTOUR encountered one comet and was en route to another, it would enter hibernation mode. Its people and ground systems, already paid for from the CONTOUR budget, would have nothing to do. MESSENGER would thus use them for *its* mission, free of charge. It was a brilliant bit of accounting, unless CONTOUR was destroyed, which it was in 2002. Though MESSENGER would not launch until 2004, it still had to account for the team it would eventually have to hire.[43] Moreover, reviews subsequent to the CONTOUR fiasco gave MESSENGER a closer look. Again, both were APL missions. Did they share the same spacecraft faults? (They did not, but review boards were going to review things all the same.)[44]

41   Niebur, S. (2009, 31 July). Personal interview with R. McNutt. Located in the "MESSENGER" file, NASA Historical Reference Collection, History Division, NASA Headquarters, Washington, DC.

42   Niebur, S. (2009, 27 August). Personal interview with T. Krimigis. Located in the "Discovery Program" file, NASA Historical Reference Collection, History Division, NASA Headquarters, Washington, DC.

43   Niebur, S. (2009, 14 May). Personal interview with D. Jarrett and Kate Wolf. Located in "Discovery Program" file, NASA Historical Reference Collection, History Division, NASA Headquarters, Washington, DC.

44   Niebur, S. (2009, 10 August). Personal interview with S. Solomon. Located in "MESSENGER" file, NASA Historical Reference Collection, History Division, NASA Headquarters, Washington, DC.

Sean Solomon, the mission PI, said: "To be honest, many of the reviews are a blur." The most valuable reviews by far, he said, were informal tabletop subsystem-level reviews, where the project brought in subject matter experts who really understood such issues as thermal design.[45]

"Surge capability"—that is, finding people within the Applied Physics Laboratory who could solve problems that emerged (or were created by NASA Headquarters mandates)—was an institutional strength. The Space Department, responsible for MESSENGER, was but one division of APL. When problems emerged, Krimigis might go through the head of the lab's Technical Services Department, or another department, and ask for someone they might spare. For budgets, the issue was largely uncomplicated; everyone's paycheck came from the same place; it was just a matter of charging certain time to certain budgets. Negotiations for time would ensue and were trickier. Because of the urgency and national profile of MESSENGER, it sometimes involved asking for priority when conflicting projects tied up necessary engineers.

One such surge was required when the mission's project manager, Max Peterson, retired in 2002 for health reasons. Just before his retirement, his deputy—who had been groomed to take the project manager position—disappeared, figuratively, never showing up for work at the Applied Physics Laboratory again, as Solomon remembers. "Max, who treated this guy like a son, drove out to his house. He would barely talk to him."[46]

APL management persuaded Dave Grant, the project manager on a NASA project called the Thermosphere Ionosphere Mesosphere Energetics and Dynamics mission (TIMED) to take over the project manager position for MESSENGER as well.[47] When Grant arrived, he quickly identified MESSENGER as a mission in trouble.

"Everywhere I looked there were cost and schedule problems," he said. "Now you have to understand: MESSENGER is a very tough mission. You have to keep your eye on the spacecraft weight, on the propulsion, and on the thermal.... It was clear to me, very clear, that we had blown the cost cap."[48]

Grant served as MESSENGER's project manager for just under five years, getting the spacecraft through the launch phase. He was then replaced by his deputy, Peter Bedini.

45   Ibid.

46   Ibid.

47   Niebur, S. (2009, 24 September). Personal interview with T. Krimigis. Located in the "Discovery Program" file, NASA Historical Reference Collection, History Division, NASA Headquarters, Washington, DC.

48   Niebur, S. (2009, 27 July). Personal interview with D. Grant. Located in the "MESSENGER" file, NASA Historical Reference Collection, History Division, NASA Headquarters, Washington, DC.

ORBITING HELL

Developmental headaches were perhaps a good preview of the hellish environment that the spacecraft was headed to. Getting MESSENGER into Mercury's orbit was no small task. NASA could launch directly there, as Mariner 10 did, but that would not get it into orbit. (Robert Farquhar, the mission manager and orbital dynamicist, explained that a direct orbital insertion would require a braking rocket as big and expensive as the Delta II that launched MESSENGER from Earth). In fact, when Mariner 10 launched, engineers at the time thought a Mercury orbit was physically impossible to achieve—that any spacecraft would fall prey to the Sun's pull. In the 1980s, a flight engineer at the Jet Propulsion Laboratory named Chen-Wan Yen discovered several complex flight paths that would slow a spacecraft down sufficiently to enter Mercury's orbit.[49] (She had previously discovered a way for the Stardust mission to get to Comet Wild 2.) Her plan used the gravity from three planets to slow the spacecraft down, passing by Earth once, Venus twice, and Mercury three times.[50] MESSENGER ultimately flew five billion miles to reach a planet an average of 125 million miles from Earth.[51]

Once there, Mercury was no pleasant place to visit. The spacecraft would have to endure an 840°F environment that posed great challenges to onboard instrumentation. Not only did it have to survive the Sun's heat, but Mercury's as well, which was hot enough to melt lead.[52] "We are orbiting hell, but in this case, hell is very interesting," said Robert G. Strom, a co-investigator and planetary geologist at the University of Arizona.[53]

Mercury is a planet of extremes. At its equator, the temperature rises to 1,100°F. In its shaded polar craters, it is 270°F below zero. MESSENGER's components were tested to 800°F.[54] The spacecraft's body was made of a lightweight heat-tolerant graphite composite, covered with layers of insulation, radiators, and pipes to move away the heat. The large, reflective, heat-resistant sunshade carried by MESSENGER was 8 feet (2.4 meters) tall and 6 feet (1.8 meters) across, with quarter-inch layers of Nextel ceramic cloth, front and back, surrounding Kapton plastic insulation. Because of all this, the spacecraft would operate at a comfortable 68°F, surprisingly.[55] Temperatures on the shielding, meanwhile, would reach 600°F.

---

49   Ibid.; Yen, C.-W. L. (1989). "Ballistic Mercury orbiter mission via Venus and Mercury gravity assists." *Journal of the Astronautical Sciences*, 37, 417–432.

50   Tytell, E. (2004, 31 July). "For Mercury probe, the future looks very, very bright." *Los Angeles Times.*

51   Asaravala, A. (2004, 27 July). "Mercury mission set to launch." *Wired News.*

52   Perlman, D. (2004, 1 August). "MESSENGER ready to deliver." *San Francisco Chronicle.*

53   Gugliotta, G. (2004, 2 August). "Mission to Mercury is the stuff of mystery." *The Washington Post.* A10.

54   Sine, R. (2004, 29 July). "2004: A Mercury Odyssey." *The Washington Post.* Prince George's Extra, 12.

55   Leary, W. E. (2004, 27 July). "Mercury will become the next planet to get its close-up." *The New York Times.*

Cleverly, the solar panels were made of alternating solar cells and mirrors to reflect a good bit of sunlight so that the arrays wouldn't overheat. Two-thirds of the panels were mirrors, and one-third were solar cells.

Science operations in such an environment would be a challenge. The Applied Physics Laboratory provided the hardware and infrastructure for science team members to access their data. Data arrived at the Science Operations Center (SOC) from mission operations. Before launch, Deborah Domingue, who was responsible for science operations within both the science team and mission operations, said she and a handful of others had to figure out the requirements for the SOC: What it was supposed to do, and how it would do it? "Each instrument needs somebody who's dedicated to doing the sequencing, putting together the command load," she said. "Then, each instrument needs an Instrument Scientist to make sure that that command load meets the science goals, what we're trying to accomplish."[56] Instruments would also need an Instrument Engineer to make sure the commands didn't blow up the experiment or fry its optics. All instruments were coordinated under a payload operations manager.

The spectrometer and the imager were perhaps the most complex instruments on the mission. The former, because it had to map the surface, and coverage was always an issue. The latter had independent pointing capabilities. Made up of two cameras—a narrow-angle and a wide-angle (the latter having color capability)—operations were time-consuming, with a very complex command load.[57]

Before the MESSENGER science operations team could get to work, however, the MESSENGER spacecraft had to launch. In 2003, the launch was delayed until August 2003. The cost of the mission would break the $299 million Discovery cost cap by $12 million—the first mission ever to do so.

That it even got the reprieve of a delay was a stroke of fortune. When it became clear that it would break its budget, Ed Weiler, the Associate Administrator of the Science Mission Directorate, went to the scientific community to ask whether this was a road they wanted to go down. "I did not want to make the decision on my own to allow the first mission ever to break the Discovery cost cap," he said.[58]

After receiving community input, NASA delayed the next Announcement of Opportunity for a new Discovery mission. It also implemented a new rule requiring the eventually selected mission to hold a full quarter of its budget in reserve to deal with technical, management, and schedule challenges that might be encountered.[59]

---

56   Niebur, S. (2010, 11 January). Personal interview with D. Domingue. Located in "MESSENGER" file, NASA Historical Reference Collection, History Division, NASA Headquarters, Washington, DC.

57   Ibid.

58   Berger, B. (2003, 22 September). "Messenger Busts Cost Cap, Prompting Changes to NASA's Discovery Program." SpaceNews. 1–3.

59   Ibid.

The MESSENGER team was going to miss its first launch window of March 2004. On 24 October, Orlando Figueroa at NASA Headquarters formally accepted the slip.

The team really started solving outstanding issues at that point. Rumors circulated that the team at the Applied Physics Laboratory was cutting corners on testing—a rumor that Grant found outrageous. "This was totally unfounded.... I was especially angry over this since the source of the rumors was a couple of malcontents who eventually left the program. I let APL management know it and NASA management as well."[60]

After shipping the completed spacecraft to Cape Canaveral for a May launch, Grant got a call from the Administrator of NASA, Mike Griffin. "There's concern that we haven't done enough testing of the autonomy system," he recalled Griffin saying. "They want you to do more testing in several areas." Grant replied that if NASA wanted the team to do extra testing, they would do extra testing. "They have to understand the consequences," he said. The next possible launch date was in August. "If we go from May to August there's a development cost.... We have an Earth flyby, two Venus flybys and three Mercury flybys before we get into orbit. Also, five major propulsive burns." It was a much higher-risk trajectory, with tighter power and thermal margins, and the cost impact could have been as much as $30 million. "NASA's got to decide if the additional testing is worth it," said Grant.[61] He recalled Griffin's response: "It's nonnegotiable."

The MESSENGER team had to do all of the testing at the Cape remotely from APL, where the testing apparatuses were located. After the extended testing phase was complete, NASA held a Launch Readiness Review on 31 July 2004. The $429 million spacecraft was ready for launch.[62] It left Earth on 3 August 2004, on a Delta II 7925H-9.5 rocket at 2:16 a.m.—just dodging Hurricane Alex in the Atlantic Ocean.

The mission operations team quickly had to find its space legs. Because of the twice-delayed liftoff—the second so late in the process—the team had to start over, essentially, on mission planning. The analyses, science planning, and mission design done before launch needed to be rebuilt. Meanwhile, the team had to learn how to fly the spacecraft, which involved a level of trial and error.

"Initially, the spacecraft was difficult to operate," said Grant. "When we did little thruster burns, for trajectory correction, there were errors, and they were significant enough that they had to be corrected.... We had plume impingement—that wasn't anticipated prior to launch.... In the meantime, there are literally thousands of different parameters onboard. There were a few that needed adjustment.... The first time

---

60   Niebur, S. (2009, 27 July). Personal interview with D. Grant. Located in the "MESSENGER" file, NASA Historical Reference Collection, History Division, NASA Headquarters, Washington, DC.

61   Ibid.

62   Harwood, W. (2004, 3 August). "Probe roars away from Earth on voyage to orbit Mercury." *Spaceflight Now.*

we tried something, it didn't work exactly the way we had hoped it would, so we had to go back and correct it…. The shakedown cruise for MESSENGER was much more difficult than I thought it was going to be."[63]

Such was the fate of complex new technology being flown for the first time. Grant explained, "The engineering team stayed with it. They ran every problem to ground…. And finally, one day, we all realized all the problems were pretty much fixed and that MESSENGER was an excellent spacecraft."[64]

On 2 August 2005, MESSENGER executed its Earth gravity assist—a flyby of Earth whereby it used our planet's gravity to adjust its velocity and course. The spacecraft's closest approach was 1,458 miles over central Mongolia, and it experienced a significant trajectory change as it was sent hurtling toward Venus. Science instruments, including the camera, were powered on and tested as if Earth were an alien planet.[65] The camera team later released a video using the images collected during the encounter.

"That movie is so beautiful," said Louise Prockter, the Instrument Scientist on the camera and later deputy Principal Investigator of the mission. "You can just watch the Earth going around. You can see the specular reflection on the oceans. You know there's water down there just from our movie of the Earth as we flew by it."[66]

Later, during the first Venus flyby on 24 October 2006, the spacecraft was out of radio contact; its position on the opposite side of the Sun made radio contact impossible for two weeks. The science team decided against turning on the instruments and flew at a high altitude of 3,000 kilometers above the Venusian surface.[67]

In January 2007, Peter Bedini was promoted from deputy project manager to project manager, assuming the role from Dave Grant. Five months later—on 5 June 2007—MESSENGER flew by Venus again at just 209 miles above the surface. The team coordinated with the team running the European Space Agency's Venus Express, which began orbiting the planet in April 2006.[68] It was a rare opportunity to do synergistic science.

"This is the first time that we are able to take observations [at Venus] from two different vantage points," said Sean Solomon, the MESSENGER Principal Investigator.

---

63   Niebur, S. (2009, 27 July). Personal interview with D. Grant. Located in the "MESSENGER" file, NASA Historical Reference Collection, History Division, NASA Headquarters, Washington, DC.

64   Ibid.

65   Buckley, M. (2005, 9 August). "MESSENGER spacecraft completes Earth swingby en route to Mercury." *JHU Gazette*; Solomon, S. C., McNutt, R. L., Gold, R. E., & Domingue, D. L. (2007). "MESSENGER Mission Overview." *Space Science Reviews*, 131(1–4), 3–39. *https://doi.org/10.1007/s11214-007-9247-6*.

66   Niebur, S. (2009, 10 December). Personal interview with L. Prockter. Located in the "MESSENGER" file, NASA Historical Reference Collection, History Division, NASA Headquarters, Washington, DC.

67   Niebur, S. (2009, 10 August). Personal interview with S. Solomon. Located in "MESSENGER" file, NASA Historical Reference Collection, History Division, NASA Headquarters, Washington, DC.

68   "Venus probe makes science orbit." (2006, 10 May). BBC News.

Although many space missions include planetary encounters in order to boost the velocity of the spacecraft, the Venus encounter was planned to slow the spacecraft down—from 22.7 to 17.3 miles per second—so that an orbital insertion around Mercury would later be possible upon arrival.[69] It was the largest velocity change of the mission, and it was risky in the sense that instrument exposure to the Sun for any appreciable length of time would be hazardous to the instruments.[70]

"Typically, spacecraft have used planetary flybys to speed toward the outer solar system," said Andy Calloway, MESSENGER mission operations manager. "MESSENGER, headed in the opposite direction, needs to slow down enough to slip into orbit around Mercury."[71]

In addition to changing the spacecraft's speed, it would also change its orbit. "The second Venus flyby was June of 2007, and that was a much closer approach," recalled Solomon. "We needed that close approach because we not only slowed the spacecraft down but we changed the plane of the orbit. Venus is almost in the same orbital plane as the Earth. Mercury's orbital plane is inclined a little more than 7 degrees to the ecliptic. So it was that Venus flyby that put us in Mercury's orbital plane instead of Earth/Venus plane." The team turned on every science instrument on the spacecraft. "All of them," said Solomon. "We wanted to practice the Mercury flybys."[72]

It turned out "beautifully," Solomon remembered. "Virtually everything that we had programmed in, worked. We learned a few things about some of the sequencing on the imaging system that we put to good use on Mercury. But all the instruments worked well. We actually got some science out of the flyby because we worked with the Venus Express guys who of course were in orbit around Venus at the time we flew by." The combination of measurements the two spacecraft made would later appear in papers that the two teams collaborated on.[73]

The First Mercury Flyby

MESSENGER finally reached Mercury on 14 January 2008, passing just 125 miles above the surface of the nearest planet to the Sun at 2:04 p.m. Eastern time.[74] The encounter

---

69   Dominguez, A. (2007, 5 June). "Probe passing Venus on way to Mercury." Associated Press.

70   Stauffer, T. (2004, 31 July). "His 30-year wait to end with launch to Mercury." *Arizona Daily Star.* B2.

71   "NASA Spacecraft Ready for Science-Rich Encounter With Venus." (2007, 4 June). NASA News Release 07-129.

72   Niebur, S. (2009, 10 August). Personal interview with S. Solomon. Located in "MESSENGER" file, NASA Historical Reference Collection, History Division, NASA Headquarters, Washington, DC.

73   Ibid.

74   Solomon, S. C., McNutt, R. L., Watters, T. R., Lawrence, D. J., Feldman, W. C., Head, J. W., Krimigis, S. M., Murchie, S. L., Phillips, R. J., Slavin, J. A., & Zuber, M. T. (2008). "Return to Mercury: A Global Perspective on MESSENGER's First Mercury Flyby." *Science,* 321(5885), 59–62. *https:// doi.org/10.1126/science.1159706.*

would be close enough for the instruments to take their initial data measurements and collect 1,200 images, filling the flight recorder with more than 700 megabytes of data during the 55 hours of flyby operations.[75]

All seven instruments worked perfectly, and among the images collected by the spacecraft were many of parts of Mercury never before seen.[76] Where Mariner 10 mapped 45 percent of the surface of Mercury, MESSENGER in its very first flyby uncovered an additional 21 percent.[77] Scott Murchie, a co-investigator on MESSENGER, noted that being inundated with data was terrific.

Robert Strom, who was a co-investigator on both Mariner 10 and MESSENGER, said: "I couldn't sleep on the eve of the encounter.... I've waited 30 years for this. Every part of the planet seen or unseen is new. This is a whole new planet."[78]

He was not exaggerating. MESSENGER had not even entered orbit and was already set to fundamentally transform the scientific understanding of Mercury. Its next flyby of the planet, on 6 October 2008, would uncover an additional 30 percent of its surface, leaving just 4 percent unknown.[79] Among those initial surprises captured was a very unusual spider feature, never before observed on Mercury or the Moon. It was an impact crater, the name derived from its appearance: a big black circle with long legs extending from it—a central depression with over a hundred narrow flat-footed troughs called grabens radiating out from it. The feature would later be named Apollodorus. Other initial surprises included evidence of ancient volcanoes on many parts of the planet's surface, huge cliffs, and formations snaking hundreds of miles, indicating patterns of fault activity from Mercury's formation more than four billion years ago.[80]

The initial results from the first Mercury flyby were published on 3 July 2008 in 11 articles in the journal *Science*. Among the findings were the following:

- Water, whether from ice in permanently shaded regions, impacts from comet and meteorite strikes, or from the interaction of the soil with the solar wind.[81]

---

75   Kaufman, M. (2008, 14 January). "Today's Mercury flyby to be the first since 1974." *The Washington Post*.

76   "Surprises stream back from Mercury's MESSENGER." (2008, January 30). APL News Release.

77   Solomon, S. C., McNutt, R. L., Watters, T. R., Lawrence, D. J., Feldman, W. C., Head, J. W., Krimigis, S. M., Murchie, S. L., Phillips, R. J., Slavin, J. A., & Zuber, M. T. (2008). "Return to Mercury: A Global Perspective on MESSENGER's First Mercury Flyby." *Science*, 321(5885), 59–62. *https:// doi.org/10.1126/science.1159706*.

78   Spotts, P. N. (2008, 31 January). "MESSENGER images show hidden face of Mercury." *The Christian Science Monitor*.

79   "Message from Mercury safely down to Earth." (2008, 19 January). *Space Daily*.

80   Minard, A. (2008, 31 January). "Weird Spider Volcanism Discovered on Mercury." *National Geographic*.

81   Carreau, M. (2008, 3 July). "MESSENGER's flight reveals water source on Mercury." *Houston Chronicle*.

- An active magnetic field, suggesting a solid iron core and an enormous outer core of molten iron. Motion in the outer core would likely generate an active magnetic field around the planet. This was similar to Earth, though dissimilar to Venus or Mars.[82]
- Volcanic vents, previously unseen by Mariner, that showed ancient lava flows that contributed to surfacing. Bright smooth plains on the planet's surface, it was hypothesized, might be lava flows instead of material ejected from meteor impact craters as previously thought.[83]
- Surface contraction, a result of the cooling core and the condensing of molten iron. The planet, in other words, is shrinking like a dried apple—the reason for its titanic cliffs called "lobate scarps."[84] The magnitude of the contraction is about one mile of the planet's 1,400-mile radius.

MESSENGER had yet to enter orbit around Mercury. On the third and final flyby of Mercury, at about 5:55 p.m. EDT on 29 September 2009, it sped by at about 12,000 miles per hour, imaging some of the same terrain as it did in its second flyby, but this time with slightly different lighting conditions. New angles of sunlight helped better show the planet's topography. The probe briefly lost contact with Earth, losing some science data.[85] Still, the encounter not only completed the planet's surface map to 98 percent but also revealed high amounts of heavy metals like titanium and iron, calling into question the prevailing hypotheses about how Mercury evolved. It also revealed more about how seasons on Mercury manifest, in the form of chemical compositions in its wispy atmosphere.[86]

The primary purpose of the flyby was always to use Mercury's gravity to adjust its trajectory and velocity until it could enter into formation with the planet. "The spacecraft after being lapped by Mercury many times in its race around the Sun will eventually match the 88-day orbital period of the innermost planet," explained Eric Finnegan, MESSENGER's mission system engineer, at the time.[87]

Once in orbit, scientists would get the equivalent of two Mercury flybys every single day.[88] Before entering orbit, Bedini explained, the team worked to plan all observations,

82   Roylance, F. D. (2008, 4 July). "Water traces on Mercury." *Baltimore Sun*; Scanlon, B. (2008, 7 July). "Sun's role in Mercury's tail surprises scientists." *Rocky Mountain News*.

83   "Volcanic eruptions helped shape planet Mercury." (2008, 7 July). AFP.

84   "MESSENGER spacecraft reveals Mercury secrets." (2008, 7 July). InTheNews.co.uk.

85   Thompson, A. (2009, 2 October). "Mercury's mysterious bright spot photographed up close." Space.com.

86   Hsu, J. (2009, 29 December). "Astronomy Milestones in 2009." Space.com.

87   Amos, J. (2008, 14 January). "MESSENGER primed for Mercury pass." BBC News.

88   Niebur, S. (2009, 9 July). Personal interview with P. Bedini. Located in "MESSENGER" file, NASA Historical Reference Collection, History Division, NASA Headquarters, Washington, DC.

by all elements of the science payload, for an entire year. The team planned also for command errors or missed observations with ongoing, week-long command loads. Every month, the team would validate that the data on the ground was what they wanted to achieve their science goals. If not, they would run the baseline plan from that point to the end of the mission to fill in the missing observations—things that they knew they would want to observe again but weren't yet sure what those things were. To do such planning, they used a tool called SciBox developed at the Applied Physics Laboratory and used on the Cassini orbiter at Saturn, the Mars Reconnaissance Orbiter, and other missions. It was the first time the software was ever used to coordinate the measurements of a full payload of seven instruments.[89] (They did not use SciBox for any of the flybys because there was still ample time to do it by hand and because SciBox was still in development.)

MESSENGER entered Mercury's orbit on 18 March 2011, kicking off its first year of observations.[90] During orbital insertion, four hundred members of the MESSENGER team, and friends, met at the Kossiakoff Auditorium at APL for the milestone event in space exploration. Addressing the crowd, Ed Weiler said: "I remember the day we selected this mission…. That was 12 years ago…. It's 12 years from PowerPoint to Mercury."[91]

At 9:10 p.m., the Mission Operations Control Center received word from the spacecraft that the maneuver was a success.[92] Sean Solomon, the mission Principal Investigator, rejoiced at the time: "This is when the real mission begins."[93]

———————

THE 2000 AO: BE BOLD, TAKE RISKS

On 19 May 2000, NASA released the fourth Discovery Announcement of Opportunity with a cost cap of $299 million. The AO expanded the program and added new requirements. Mission concepts intended to achieve science goals of missions already in the NASA strategic plan were no longer excluded. Participating scientist programs and data analysis programs were strongly encouraged, and costs related to said programs would not count against the mission cap. Missions of opportunity proposals could be part of missions sponsored by other NASA organizations outside of the Office of Space Science, extensions of current missions, or data buys. Moreover, the cost cap was increased. Proposed education and public outreach programs were now mandatory in

———————

89   Ibid.

90   Solomon, S. C., McNutt, R. L., Gold, R. E., & Domingue, D. L. (2007). "MESSENGER Mission Overview." *Space Science Reviews*, 131(1–4), 3–39. *https://doi.org/10.1007/s11214-007-9247-6.*

91   Weiler, E. (2011, 18 March). Public comments at Mercury orbit insertion event at APL.

92   "NASA spacecraft now circling Mercury—a first." (2011, 18 March). *USA Today.*

93   Ibid.

the electronic proposal. Moreover, co-investigators were required have well-defined roles on the mission. Concepts with international participation would be under additional requirements, as would those that were affected by U.S. export laws and regulations. A risk management plan would be required. Funding for the Phase A concept study was increased from $375,000 to $450,000, but the number of investigations to be selected was reduced from four-to-six to three-to-five.[94] At a preproposal conference by the Langley Science Support Office, proposers were shown clear and unambiguous definitions of the technical-management-cost risk envelope definitions.[95]

When the window closed three months later, on 18 August 2000, NASA had received 26 proposals. This was the first Discovery Announcement of Opportunity review after the Mars failures of 1999, and the ensuing reports and changes. As Gregg Vane, who managed Discovery proposals at Jet Propulsion Laboratory, remembered: "Dan Goldin had told everyone: be bold, take risks. An occasional failure is okay. The Mars failures occurred. He got up on the stage of Von Kármán [auditorium, at JPL] and said, 'I take the blame for this. I pushed you guys too far. Now let's back off and see what's the right approach.' We started doing that immediately, of course, through all of our programs at JPL, including Discovery."[96]

While the lab was already independently starting to tighten the stringency of its mission proposals and requirements, there were still several projects in the pipeline that had been formulated and were being implemented in the now-moribund faster, better, cheaper era. "So," said Vane, "the failures, or the cost overruns, or whatever, kept coming." This led to a sort of accordion effect, where management at the lab and across the agency, not realizing that new protections were already being implemented to forestall future Mars-like disasters, added even more onerous requirements yet. "By the time things finally caught up," Vane explained, "we had a very, very complex, burdensome system, in terms of the level of the proposal that had to be prepared, the level of scrutiny that it was being given."[97]

Many of the questions and comments coming back from the technical-management-cost reviews were, in the eyes of some, verging on the more advanced Preliminary Design Review level. "The nature of expectations from NASA changed quite a lot from the beginning," said Vane. "It took a while really for the science community to really internalize that. I can't tell you how many painful conversations I had over those years with my scientific colleagues who wanted to propose something that was just totally

94   NASA. (2008). Discovery Announcement of Opportunity.

95   Niebur, S. (2009, 27 April). Personal interview with B. Perry. Located in "Discovery Program" file, NASA Historical Reference Collection, History Division, NASA Headquarters, Washington, DC.

96   Niebur, S. (2009, 10 August). Personal interview with S. Solomon. Located in "MESSENGER" file, NASA Historical Reference Collection, History Division, NASA Headquarters, Washington, DC.

97   Niebur, S. (2009, 22 March). Personal interview with G. Vane. Located in "Discovery Program" file, NASA Historical Reference Collection, History Division, NASA Headquarters, Washington, DC.

off in the blue. Being out of scope, impossible to do. The technologies didn't even exist, let alone being mature. For innovative new management roles and models that no one in their right mind who knows project management would have ever done. They were insistent that we had to try it this way because it was Faster, Better, Cheaper—that's what Dan Goldin said—and they were still living in an old paradigm."[98]

The Jet Propulsion Laboratory submitted 13 proposals in 2000, down from 16 in 1998 and 20 in 1996. On 4 January 2001, three missions were selected for concept study.

The Dawn mission was designed to look back at the conditions and processes active at the dawn of the solar system by orbiting the asteroids Vesta and Ceres and measuring their geophysical and geochemical properties. These two large asteroids were expected to be very different due to their locations in the asteroid belt; by sending the same instruments to each unevolved body, scientists could discover the conditions at these two distances from the Sun during planetary formation, which would unlock not just secrets of the asteroids but how the planets themselves formed at different distances from the Sun. Dawn, led by Principal Investigator Chris Russell of UCLA and managed by Sarah Gavit at the Jet Propulsion Laboratory, would launch in July 2005 and arrive at Vesta in June 2008 and Ceres in May 2013. The spacecraft would be built at Orbital Sciences; the overall cost of the mission was proposed at $271 million.[99]

Kepler was a space telescope designed to detect Earth-size exoplanets—that is, planets orbiting other stars in the galaxy. It would monitor 100,000 stars over a four-year mission for a total cost of $286 million. Kepler had received funding previously, in 1999, to perform a technology demonstration.

Edward Smith, former project scientist of the Ulysses solar mission, would lead the concept study for a Jupiter orbiter, a daring mission under the Discovery cap. It was called the Interior Structure and Internal Dynamical Evolution of Jupiter (INSIDE Jupiter). The mission would determine the internal structure of the largest planet in the solar system, observing and measuring processes within the Jovian magnetosphere and atmosphere, and obtaining high-resolution maps of magnetic and gravity fields, determining "if Jupiter's dynamic atmosphere is a visible response to flows in the deep interior of the planet." The mission would cost $296 million and be managed by Smith's institution, the Jet Propulsion Laboratory. Ball would build the spacecraft, to launch in November 2005 and arrive at Jupiter in September 2011.[100]

Meanwhile, NASA Headquarters also selected for concept study a suite of instruments to be built by the Jet Propulsion Laboratory and incorporated into the larger instrument suites on the French-led NetLander mission to Mars. Bruce Banerdt of JPL would lead American participation in seismology, meteorology, and geodesy (i.e.,

---

98   Ibid.

99   Whalen, M. (2001, 19 January). "JPL-led Discovery proposals move forward." *JPL Universe*. 31(2).

100   Ibid.

using radio tracking to measure rotational irregularities) experiments, for a total cost of $35 million. As there was ample time before the NetLander spacecraft launch in 2007, the team was given $250,000 to demonstrate the project readiness through a feasibility study.[101]

NetLander aside, each of the mission concepts received $450,000 to conduct a four-month implementation feasibility study, which would be due 24 July 2001.

Selection

After review of the concept study reports and, later, site visits in early to mid-September 2001, the Dawn and Kepler mission concepts were selected for formulation that year on 21 December.

"Kepler and Dawn are exactly the kind of missions NASA should be launching, missions that tackle some of the most important questions in science yet do it for a very modest cost," said Associate Administrator Ed Weiler.[102] PI Bill Borucki believed that the Kepler mission could help answer the age-old question, are we alone in the universe?

Meanwhile, on 20 December 2000, NASA released an unprecedented Announcement of Opportunity to replace the canceled Pluto/Kuiper Express mission to the farthest planet in the solar system. This was highly unusual, as large outer planet missions were typically directed without competition to various NASA centers. Large cost increases for Pluto/Kuiper Express, deemed unacceptable by NASA Headquarters, had led to a stop-work order three months earlier, on 12 September 2000. In issuing the AO, NASA cited the great success of competitively selected Discovery missions and other PI-led mission lines.

The competition would be structured similarly to Discovery, with a three-month proposal opportunity for complete mission investigations to the Pluto-Charon system and the Kuiper belt, peer review, two-phase selection, and a down-select set for August 2001. Weiler was searching for innovation, new partners, and competitive mission designs.[103]

The next year would bring more praise yet with the establishment of the New Frontiers mission line, which was described as "Discovery Plus."[104] In May, Weiler introduced the program in congressional testimony on NASA's science priorities by

---

101   Ibid.

102   "NASA selects missions to explore two large asteroids and search for Earth-like planets." (2001, 21 December). NASA news release 01-254. See also "Dawn of a new mission begins '02." (2002, 4 January). *JPL Universe.* 32(1). 1.

103   "NASA seeks proposals for Pluto mission; plans to restructure outer planet program." (2000, 20 December). NASA news release 00-201.

104   Niebur, S. quoted in slides presented by Colleen Hartman in various venues. Unable to locate this citation.

saying, "The New Frontiers Planetary Program will be structured and managed along with the lines of a highly successful Discovery Program.... All New Frontiers missions will be selected through a fully open, competitive, and peer-reviewed process."[105]

Brad Perry, who was later the Director of the Science Office for Mission Assessments at the Science Mission Directorate, later explained what had happened. He said: "New Frontiers grew out of the success of Discovery. Discovery was the beginning: the opportunity to do significant science on a relatively modest budget."[106]

Discovery Program Office Dissolved

In late 2003, NASA Headquarters dissolved the Discovery Program Office at the NASA Management Office in Washington, DC. It had been led for years by Dave Jarrett and staffed by Kate Wolf, who was badged by NASA Headquarters, with education and public outreach leadership by Shari Asplund, who was badged by JPL. NASA asked JPL to undertake management of a new office that would report up through the JPL management chain, hoping that it would give the lab more ownership of, and cooperation between, the projects and the project office. JPL had experience with such an arrangement through its Mars Program Office, headed by Firouz Naderi since 2000.[107]

On 7 January 2004, Charles Elachi, Director of the Jet Propulsion Laboratory, announced the formation of the Discovery and New Frontiers Program Office at JPL.

Meanwhile, cost overruns from two Discovery missions—MESSENGER and Deep Impact—severely delayed the release of what would have been the 2002, and then 2003, but what was finally the 2004 Announcement of Opportunity for a new Discovery mission. In October 2002, Deep Impact needed $7.4 million, so the AO was pushed to January 2003. But then MESSENGER needed $3.2 million. This pushed the AO until April. But Deep Impact needed an additional $14.4 million, which pushed the release to August. Then MESSENGER needed $9.5 million for its Phase E, which delayed the AO until October. Lastly, the Mercury mission needed another $11.9 million, pushing the AO to 2004, when it was finally released.[108]

105 Weiler, E. (2002, 9 May). "NASA's Science Priorities": Hearing before the Subcommittee on Space and Aeronautics, Committee on Science, House of Representatives. S. 2, 107th Congress. Serial number 107-64.

106 Niebur, S. (2009, 27 April). Personal interview with B. Perry. Located in "Discovery Program" file, NASA Historical Reference Collection, History Division, NASA Headquarters, Washington, DC.

107 "JPL names Naderi as new head of Mars Program Office." (2000, 7 April). Press release. Downloaded from *http://marsprogram.jpl.nasa.gov/msp98/news/news73.html* on 18 August 2009.

108 Niebur, S. (2003, 23 October). "Discovery Program Update." Presentation for the Solar System Exploration Subcommittee.

Figure 5-1: MESSENGER spacecraft

The MESSENGER spacecraft is lowered onto a test stand using an overhead crane. Members of the Johns Hopkins University Applied Physics Laboratory then began final processing for launch, including checkouts of the power systems, communications systems, and control systems. (Image credit: NASA, image no. KSC-04pd0595)

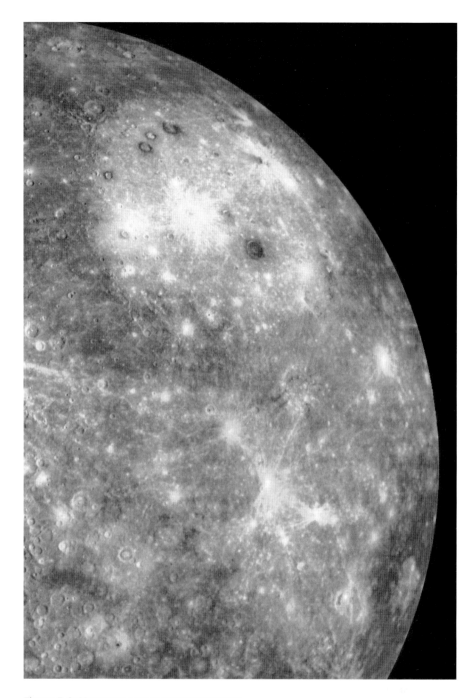

Figure 5-2: Mercury as seen by MESSENGER

This color mosaic shows the eastern limb of Mercury as seen by the MESSENGER spacecraft following its first flyby of the planet in January 2008. (Image credit: NASA/JHUAPL/Carnegie Institution of Washington, image no. PIA12842)

CHAPTER 6

Renewed Commitment: Dawn

Dawn and Kepler, selected on 21 December 2001 (in response to the 2000 Announcement of Opportunity) had to pay, in some respects, for the mistakes and overruns committed by previous missions. Dawn, a high-heritage mission to study the asteroids Ceres and Vesta; and Kepler, a planet-finding mission to be launched into Earth's orbit, were initially seen as more achievable missions than the previous two.[1] Although NASA management professed to judge each mission on its own merits, it was impossible for the various mission and review teams to conduct business as usual without regard for the problems that had come before. There was increased vigilance, along with additional reviews at earlier and earlier times, but with that came a team determination to not make the same mistakes as earlier mission leaders had and to

---

[1]   Russell, C. T., Coradini, A., Christensen, U., De Sanctis, M. C., Feldman, W. C., Jaumann, R., Keller, H. U., Konopliv, A. S., McCord, T. B., McFadden, L. A., McSween, H. Y., Mottola, S., Neukum, G., Pieters, C. M., Prettyman, T. H., Raymond, C. A., Smith, D. E., Sykes, M. V., Williams, B. G., Wise, J., & Zuber, M. T. (2004). "Dawn: A journey in space and time." *Planetary and Space Science*, 52(5–6), 465–489. *https://doi.org/10.1016/j.pss.2003.06.013*; Basri, G., Borucki, W. J., & Koch, D. (2005). "The Kepler Mission: A wide-field transit search for terrestrial planets." *New Astronomy Reviews*, 49(7–9), 478–485. *https://doi.org/10.1016/j.newar.2005.08.026.*

prove that their missions would be delivered successfully, on time, and on budget, unlike Deep Impact and MESSENGER, and technically perfect, unlike CONTOUR and Genesis. This was easier said than done.

DAWN AND KEPLER

The two missions faced challenges early on. Dawn suffered financial threats and challenges, identified in pre-confirmation reviews and by the mission team. Kepler fought scope creep by the scientists on the mission. Technical problems abounded. Dawn responded responsibly, by descoping two of their five instruments and presenting a shortened mission at their confirmation review. Shockingly (to mission leadership), this was not enough to convince NASA management that the problems had been solved. After a bit of deal-making behind the scenes, the team was allowed to continue. Dawn's problems, however, had only just begun, and technical problems proliferated.

The Dawn mission would be the first mission to orbit multiple asteroids and perform comparative planetology: studying each with the same suite of instruments to determine differences in their origin and evolution. As the first asteroid, Vesta, was dry and the second, Ceres, was likely to be partially composed of water, this investigation would help determine differences in the initial composition of the inner and outer planets, composed of similar building blocks at the origin of the solar system. The mission was boldly, if simply, scoped, with sequential orbital distances and significant travel time between the asteroids. The trouble was that the mission's designers did not adequately define the mission's science requirements at proposal. When funding for both Phases A and B was delayed, the Jet Propulsion Laboratory changed its internal commitments, and the mission had trouble adapting to the changing environment.

Without a narrowly focused set of requirements, it was impossible for Dawn's team to clearly prioritize measurements, instruments, and orbital stay times in the face of declining available budgets. The mission thus failed its confirmation review. Its major industry partner, Orbital Sciences, was a new player in the planetary missions game, and the mission management structure at proposal did not include adequate insight into their progress. Without "boots on the ground" oversight by NASA and JPL, contractors struggled to deliver subsystems on time and within budget. The mission continued to be beset by a string of technical challenges, the visibility of which did not inspire confidence in the continuation of the mission. Without a clear plan to address and minimize the effect of technical failures, the mission stumbled toward a standdown and eventually project termination.

Ultimately, the mission was both threatened and saved by its use of ion engines, which could swap mass margin for power and make up transit time in flight. The mission's troubled development required different project managers to lead each phase: formulation, development, integration and test, and mission operations.

The First Real Interplanetary Spaceship

Like nearly every Discovery mission so far selected, Dawn traced its origins to the 1992 Discovery Workshop at San Juan Capistrano, where Chris Russell outlined the potential of a different mission: the Venus CLOUD concept. NASA Headquarters did not select that concept for study, but a chance meeting at that workshop led directly to the development of Dawn, which would see selection nine years later. It was there that Russell, a space physicist at the University of California, Los Angeles, met J. Mark Hickman from the Lewis Research Center (now Glenn Research Center) in Cleveland. Hickman was proposing a concept that used solar-electric propulsion to power a spacecraft designed to measure Earth's magnetosphere. The mission concept, inelegantly called the Magnetospheric Mapping and Current Collection in the Region from LEO to GEO, was inappropriate for the new solar system program, and Russell told Hickman so.[2] However, he said, the concept's ion propulsion engines were an idea that could do wonders for planetary exploration.

Hickman and his management were as intrigued by the propulsion's potential as Russell, and they asked Russell to gather a group of scientists who might advise them on planetary mission concepts. As these ideas grew into a real proposal, the Jet Propulsion Laboratory asked to join, creating an unusual collaboration for the time. Lewis Research Center agreed, and this partnership led to Russell's 1994 proposal of Diana, a six-thruster solar-electric propulsion mission to the Moon that would then spiral away from the Moon and encounter a near-Earth asteroid: the dormant Comet Wilson–Harrington. The mission even included a subsatellite to measure the backside gravity of the Moon. The proposal did not review well in the faster, better, cheaper environment of the new Discovery Program, however. As Russell put it, "It was a little bit too ambitious for the time."[3]

The well-studied, low-cost Lunar Prospector mission was selected instead. Since the solar system exploration community and its management were charged with exploring a broad swath of the solar system through the Discovery Program, missions to the Moon were less likely to be selected in the next round. Savvy scientists knew this,

---

2   Russell, C. T., Capaccioni, F., Coradini, A., De Sanctis, M. C., Feldman, W. C., Jaumann, R., Keller, H. U., McCord, T. B., McFadden, L. A., Mottola, S., Pieters, C. M., Prettyman, T. H., Raymond, C. A., Sykes, M. V., Smith, D. E., & Zuber, M. T. (2007). "Dawn Mission to Vesta and Ceres: Symbiosis Between Terrestrial Observations and Robotic Exploration." *Earth, Moon, and Planets*, 101(1–2), 65–91. *https://doi.org/10.1007/s11038-007-9151-9.*

3   Niebur, S. (2009, March 24). Personal interview with C. Russell. Located in "Dawn" file, NASA Historical Reference Collection, History Division, NASA Headquarters, Washington, DC.

and the Moon was discarded as a viable target for the 1996 proposal opportunity. JPL abandoned plans for Diana.

After receiving feedback from science and technical reviewers via a NASA Headquarters debriefing, the no-longer-Diana team took their list of weaknesses and began to solve the perceived risks while meanwhile considering their next target. Russell turned to planetary science colleague Tom McCord of the University of Hawai'i and asked his opinion on the next-most-important body after the Moon. As it happened, McCord had observed Vesta as a young scientist and had concluded in 1970 that the reflected spectra of Vesta were very similar to certain basaltic achondrites (those with pigeonite predominant).[4] The Howardite–Eucrite–Diogenite meteorites, as they were later known, could be used as "ground truth" for their presumed parent body, Vesta. Later, McCord used characteristics of the asteroid's reflectivity and laboratory measurements of the Howardite–Eucrite–Diogenite meteorites to develop a thermal evolution model for Vesta that showed that the asteroid had melted and differentiated, with a basaltic surface like the Moon or Hawai'ian volcanoes and (probably) an iron core, with remnant magnetism. The asteroid, in other words, had experienced volcanism. This was a very interesting target indeed!

This mission that emerged from their discussions was the Main Belt Asteroid Rendezvous (MBAR), which would orbit Vesta, 857 Glasenappia, and 21 Lutetia, the latter two asteroids conveniently located at the time MBAR would depart from Vesta.

The team also submitted a proposal for the Comet Nucleus Rendezvous that would match orbits with Comet Tempel 2. Both proposals were led by Russell, managed by the Jet Propulsion Laboratory, and designed around NASA Lewis's ion engines. Proposing competing missions was a gutsy move on Russell's part, but one that did not bring success, possibly in part because they were reviewed by the same peer review panel. Neither was selected, but, as Russell put it, "We got twice as many good comments from NASA that time."[5]

Two years later, the team proposed MBAR again. During that interval, however, the asteroids had moved farther apart, making MBAR a two-asteroid mission instead of three. Vesta and 21 Lutetia were still within reach, but 857 Glasenappia, a small asteroid 2.24 AU from the Sun, had moved away in its trajectory and was no longer reachable within the mission parameters. In the meantime, Rosetta had been selected by ESA, so Russell's team assumed, incorrectly, that a comet mission would not be among NASA's top priorities. The team put all their energies behind the asteroid pro-

---

4   McCord, T. B., Adams, J. B., & Johnson, T. V. (1970). "Asteroid Vesta: Spectral Reflectivity and Compositional Implications." *Science*, 168(3938), 1445–1447. *https://doi.org/10.1126/science.168.3938.1445.*

5   Niebur, S. (2009, 24 March). Personal interview with C. Russell. Located in "Dawn" file, NASA Historical Reference Collection, History Division, NASA Headquarters, Washington, DC.

posal. Not coincidentally, the first deep space solar-electric propulsion mission (and the first technology demonstration mission in the New Millennium line), Deep Space 1, was also near launch. "Just when the proposals went to the selection committees," Russell recalled, "Deep Space 1 was launched and its engines didn't start right away. So I figured that what happened was, let's wait and see how Deep Space 1 really goes before we commit to this. So I didn't pass the 1998 review, either."[6]

As the team reviewed the possible asteroid targets for a mission proposal in 2000, they noticed that large asteroid Ceres would be closer to Vesta by the time their would-be spacecraft reached the asteroid belt. Instead of a small main-belt asteroid such as Lutetia (not visited until Rosetta's approach on 13 July 2010), the mission could now visit the largest and most-well-known asteroid of them all.[7] The proposal clearly demonstrated that the mission to orbit Vesta and then Ceres could be accomplished only once every 17 years because of the synodic period between the two bodies; this time-critical element may have added to the desirability of the mission. By the time the proposal was reviewed following the 2000 Announcement of Opportunity, the ion engines had been space-qualified on Deep Space 1. That, plus an extended life test of the NASA Solar Technology Application Readiness (NSTAR) ion propulsion system technology, which took place during Dawn's Phase A and B, provided additional confidence in the engine lifetime. Engineers on the team were enthusiastic about the use of ion engines.[8] The mission, now named Dawn, was selected by NASA Headquarters for a Phase A study and then implementation.

The Dawn science team went "right back to 1992 when I put together the team for developing ion propulsion missions for Lewis," said Russell, the Principal Investigator of Dawn. The team was compact by design, as Jay Bergstralh, then–program scientist of Discovery, was insistent on the point. Further, the team was assembled with an eye toward succession planning since the mission would have extended cruise phases before and between the asteroid encounters. "I made sure that with each of the teams there was a younger person to take over," said Russell.[9]

Russell's words were backed up by his actions. The Dawn Deputy PI was Carol Raymond, 18 years his junior, to whom he gave great responsibility. Explained Raymond: "We had an understanding, which still holds to this day, that this wasn't going to be a project scientist role." Instead, Russell described her role as the equivalent of a PI. "He basically gave me authority of the PI's voice in my interactions."[10]

---

6   Ibid.

7   Ibid.

8   "Dawn of a new mission begins '02." (2002, 4 January). *JPL Universe*. 32(1). 1.

9   Niebur, S. (2009, 24 March). Personal interview with C. Russell. Located in "Dawn" file, NASA Historical Reference Collection, History Division, NASA Headquarters, Washington, DC.

10   Niebur, S. (2009, 11 August). Personal interview with C. Raymond. Located in "Dawn" file, NASA Historical Reference Collection, History Division, NASA Headquarters, Washington, DC.

The Dawn mission was designed to fit within the acknowledged constraints of the Discovery Program. All missions professed this goal, but Dawn was overt about it, being designed by scientists who already bore battle scars from previous missions and continued to keep their lessons in mind. As he frequently reminded the team at milestone reviews, Russell had served on the Independent Assessment Team for Deep Impact, and he had seen just how important proper planning could be. He incorporated lessons learned into the planning of his own mission. These lessons drove decisions as late as the Preliminary Mission & Systems Review, where Russell was determined not to repeat the mistakes of Deep Impact.

Foreign partners would be key to the successful implementation of the Dawn mission. In addition to providing members of the science team, two-thirds of the instrument payload were developed by international partners. The Deutsches Zentrum für Luft- und Raumfahrt in Germany sponsored work on the framing camera. The Agenzia Spaziale Italiana (ASI, the Italian Space Agency) funded work on the mapping spectrometer. The third instrument was developed by Los Alamos National Laboratory and paid for by NASA out of the funded proposal for Dawn.

The only major change for Dawn during the concept study was that the plan for a combined framing camera/spectrometer was discarded. Instead of the Italians providing just the focal plane for the spectrometer, they would now provide the mass spectrometer as a complete and separate instrument. The science team also added detail to the project implementation plan, the initial level one requirements, and the mission roles and responsibilities.[11]

Asteroid 4 Vesta is about 578 kilometers by 560 kilometers by 458 kilometers, dry and with an iron core. It was discovered by Heinrich Wilhelm Olbers on 29 March 1807 during a search for additional objects in the area between Mars and Jupiter. Mathematician Carl Friedrich Gauss calculated the first orbit for the asteroid in only 10 hours, and Olbers allowed Gauss to name it after the Roman goddess.[12] Vesta has been shown to be the origin of 20 percent of the meteorites that strike Earth. Its shape is nearly spheroid, with a massive chunk—a crater 460 kilometers across and 13 kilometers deep—missing from the South Pole. This crater provides an intriguing peek into the mantle of this differentiated asteroid. It rotates once every 5 hours, 20 minutes, and orbits the Sun at 2.34 AU.

Ceres, the largest and first-discovered asteroid, is 975 kilometers by 909 kilometers and nearly spherical. This low-density planetoid rotates once every 9 hours, 5 minutes, and orbits the Sun at 2.77 AU. For many years, including the early years of Dawn mission development, planetary scientists presumed that Ceres was homogenous, in

---

11   Ibid.

12   Schmadel, Lutz D. (2003). *Dictionary of Minor Planet Names: Prepared on Behalf of Commission 20 Under the Auspices of the International Astronomical Union*. New York City: Springer. 15.

part because its measured reflectance spectrum was relatively featureless, similar to carbonaceous meteorites that do not show evidence of significant thermal processing. However, new observations by the Dawn team using the Hubble Space Telescope indicated that Ceres might have either a frozen water interior and a mantle of ice, a rock and ice core covered by a global ocean, a layer of convecting ice and a very hard crust of ice supporting surface dust, or a rocky core with 400 kilometers of silicate and then 90 to 100 kilometers of surface ice.[13]

"We think that Ceres might be the best place to go to tank up with water when you're cruising through that part of space—a lot easier to get to than Europa," said Chris Russell, the mission PI, shortly before launch. When the water observations reached NASA Headquarters near the time of the mission's confirmation, this caused slight panic, because where there is water, there might be life. Although the NASA Planetary Protection Officer, John Rummel, declined to make it an issue at confirmation, the mission was later directed to conserve sufficient propellant in order to pull the spacecraft back up to a high enough orbit that would not quickly decay onto the asteroid's surface. Landing at the eventual end of mission was thus prohibited.[14]

Ceres's rise to prominence during mission formulation was enhanced by the Great Planet Debate during the first decade of the 21st century. Called a planet at its discovery in 1801, Ceres was then redefined as an asteroid as more and more asteroids were discovered. Two hundred years later, the International Astronomical Union (IAU) promoted Ceres to "dwarf planet" status, which raised its profile as scientists and the public debated the status of Pluto. Mark Sykes, a Dawn co-investigator and head of the Planetary Science Institute, engaged publicly in the debate, talking frequently about Dawn's mission to the largest asteroid—and the smallest planet—over the next few years.

"I think [the IAU's definition] is going to collapse by 2015 when the Dawn mission gets to Ceres and the New Horizons mission gets to Pluto because we're not going to see irregular-shaped, impact crater-filled, boring surfaces. We're going to see dynamic worlds," Sykes said.[15]

To further understand the significance of the Dawn mission, consider the protosolar nebula. As the dust and gas that would become our solar system swirled around the young protostar that would become our Sun, particles of dust and rock in similar orbits began to join, or accrete, into rocks and then planets, sweeping large areas of the solar system clear with their own gravity. In the area that is now the asteroid belt,

13   Thomas, P. C., Parker, J. Wm., McFadden, L. A., Russell, C. T., Stern, S. A., Sykes, M. V., & Young, E. F. (2005). "Differentiation of the asteroid Ceres as revealed by its shape." *Nature*, 437(7056), 224–226. *https://doi.org/10.1038/nature03938*; Russell, C. (2007, 19 September). Presentation at the Discovery@15 workshop in Huntsville, Alabama.

14   Ibid.

15   Pawlowski, A. (2009, 25 August). "What's a Planet? Debate over Pluto Rages On." CNN.

Jupiter's gravity prevented large accretions of rock from forming an even larger body, called a planet. The assemblages never gained enough mass to sweep the area clear. As a result, the asteroid belt is a collection of large numbers of planetoids at every size that preserve a record of the conditions at their orbital distance in the early solar system.

The planetoids are not all the same. Only the rocks closer to the Sun were affected by its warmth; any liquid water on these rocks quickly boiled off. Rocks further away retained water and became icy. (Before Dawn reached Ceres, hypotheses about the dwarf planet suggested that any retained water ice might be hiding under a thin residual layer of clay and dark carbonaceous material; the water ice at the surface would be unstable in the relative warmth of the Sun's light, as compared to the darker, colder outer solar system.)[16]

The solar system continued to evolve over the next 4.5 billion years. The planets and some of the larger protoplanets (asteroids) between Mars and Jupiter began to differentiate. Only the larger protoplanets had accumulated sufficient amounts of radioactive material, such as [26]Aluminum, to power thermal evolution; the decay of this radioactive material heated the interior of the planetoids to the melting point. Heavy metals like iron fell into the core of the rocky asteroids, and lighter elements like magnesium moved to the surface. Vesta showed direct evidence of differentiation into a crust, mantle, and core, with likely resurfacing as liquid lava oozed out of the planet's interior, forming the basaltic rock surface suspected by reflectance spectra that match the laboratory measurements of the Howardite–Eucrite–Diogenite meteorites, while concentrating the heavy elements in the core.[17] These layers are exposed in the crater created at Vesta's South Pole. Debris from that impact crater spiraled inward toward Earth, survived the tumultuous entry through the atmosphere, and were discovered and called meteorites. The ones that match Vesta's reflectance spectrum "provide us with detailed information on geochemical processes that have occurred within specific sites on Vesta from the time of its formation at the beginning of the solar system," said Dawn co-investigator Sykes.[18]

Ceres also differentiated, with heavy elements in the core and lighter minerals near the surface. Astronomers found that the surface dust included water-bearing minerals, indicating the possible presence of water ice underneath the crust. The Dawn

16   Thomas, P. C., Parker, J. Wm., McFadden, L. A., Russell, C. T., Stern, S. A., Sykes, M. V., & Young, E. F. (2005). "Differentiation of the asteroid Ceres as revealed by its shape." *Nature*, 437(7056), 224–226. *https://doi.org/10.1038/nature03938*.

17   McCord, T. B., Adams, J. B., & Johnson, T. V. (1970). "Asteroid Vesta: Spectral Reflectivity and Compositional Implications." *Science*, 168(3938), 1445–1447. *https://doi.org/10.1126/science.168.3938.1445*.

18   Stiles, L. (2001, 19 January). "UA Astronomer Is Scientist for Proposed 'Dawn' Discovery Mission." *UA News. https://news.arizona.edu/story/ua-astronomer-scientist-proposed-dawn-discovery-mission*, accessed 10 May 2023.

spacecraft would be able to answer this question. Ceres, as the largest of the asteroids (accounting for about one-third of the total mass of the asteroid belt), may even have retained a weak atmosphere.

Because it is much farther away from the Sun than Vesta, Ceres is much more like the icy moons of the outer solar system. "The differences between Ceres and Vesta are a real puzzle," said Tom McCord, a co-investigator on Dawn, before arrival. "It's fair to speculate," he said, "that if you have liquid water over a warm core, you might have hydrothermal vents."[19]

By comparing rocky Vesta with icy Ceres, the Dawn scientists could study two very different primordial bodies using the same spacecraft and the same instruments. The chance to do comparative planetology at or near the place in the solar system that divided the inner rocky planets from the outer icy planets was unprecedented in the Discovery Program, and the mission was eagerly anticipated.

"I think of Dawn as two journeys," Russell said. "One is a journey into space.... We're going to explore a region for the first time to find out what the conditions are today. Dawn is also a journey back in time. Ceres and Vesta have been altered much less than other bodies. The Earth is changing all the time; the Earth hides its history, but we believe that Ceres and Vesta, formed more than 4.6 billion years ago, have preserved their early record."[20] The Dawn mission would also be compared, in the span of a few hours around launch, to an archaeological expedition, a time machine, a commuter tour bus, the Prius of space, and "the first real interplanetary spaceship," in Marc Rayman's words.[21]

Assume That It May Not Work

Dawn would carry three instruments. A pair of framing cameras to be used for imaging and navigation were designed, built, and contributed by the Max Planck Institut für Sonnensystemforschung in Germany, with assistance from the Institut für Planetenforschung of the DLR in Berlin and with a data-processing unit built by the Institut für Datentechnik und Kommunikationsnetze of the Technische Universität Braunschweig. The cameras were identical and redundant. Each had a frame transfer CCD with 1024 × 1024 sensitive pixels, sampling the surface of a body 200 kilometers below with a resolution of 18.6 meters per pixel. Each had a filter wheel with one clear

19   Spotts, P. N. (2007, 26 September). "NASA spacecraft set to probe two planet wannabes." *The Christian Science Monitor*.

20   Ray, J. (2007, 7 July). "Dawn Asteroid Probe Won't Launch Until September." *Spaceflight Now*.

21   Ibid.; Perlman, D. (2007, 7 July). "Craft to seek Dawn of solar system." *San Francisco Chronicle*; Johnson, J. (2007, 28 September). "NASA's 'time machine' lifts off." *The Los Angeles Times*; Mclean, D. (2007, 28 September). "NASA probe launches to asteroids in hunt for clues." *Bloomberg*; Dunn, M. (2007, 28 September). "NASA launches mission to asteroid." AP.

filter and seven color filters, which could be used to get stereo imagery for topography on the order of tens of meters. The camera had heritage from the cameras on Venus Express and Rosetta. The team was led by co-investigator Holger Sierks.[22]

A Mapping Spectrometer to measure the asteroids' surface composition was a modification of the VIRTIS mapping spectrometer on Rosetta, which had significant heritage from Cassini's VIMS.[23] The instrument combined a visible channel from 0.25 to 1.0 micron and an infrared channel from 1 to 5 microns to cover the spectral range from the near ultraviolet (UV; 0.25 micron) through the near IR (5 microns). Spectral resolution at 200 kilometers was 500 meters per pixel, a moderate to high spectral resolution. The spectrometer was designed, built, and tested at Galileo Avionica and provided to Dawn by ASI under the direction of Angioletta Coradini of the Instituto Nazionale Di Astrofisica.[24]

The Gamma Ray and Neutron Detector (GRaND) would map the abundances of major elements in rock-forming minerals (oxygen, silicon, iron, titanium, magnesium, aluminum, and calcium), major elements found in ices (hydrogen, carbon, and nitrogen), as well as trace element (uranium, thorium, potassium, galodinium, and samarium) composition. In addition, it would detect neutrons on surface, an indicator of near-surface water. GRaND was built by Bill Feldman, Tom Prettyman, and colleagues at the Los Alamos National Laboratory (LANL), who brought strong technical heritage from the Gamma Ray and Neutron Spectrometer on Lunar Prospector and the neutron spectrometer on Mars Odyssey. GRaND began as a copy of the Lunar Prospector sensor head, two bismuth germanate scintillator detectors for gamma rays, surrounded by boron-loaded plastic as an anti-coincidence shield, bolted to the Dawn spacecraft. Designing a magnetometer without a boom made some things simpler but made some measurements, such as determining the gamma ray and neutron background counts created by the attached spacecraft and its xenon tanks, more complicated. A segmented design and a variety of coincidence signatures enabled separate detection of background radiation. A new detector of layers of boron-loaded plastic and

22   Russell, C. T. (2005). "Dawn Discovery Mission: Status Report." *Proceedings of 6th IAA International Conference on Low-Cost Planetary Missions*, 6, 283–289. Retrieved from *https://escholarship.org/uc/item/2xr140qr*.

23   Russell, C. T., Coradini, A., Christensen, U., De Sanctis, M. C., Feldman, W. C., Jaumann, R., Keller, H. U., Konopliv, A. S., McCord, T. B., McFadden, L. A., McSween, H. Y., Mottola, S., Neukum, G., Pieters, C. M., Prettyman, T. H., Raymond, C. A., Smith, D. E., Sykes, M. V., Williams, B. G., Wise, J., & Zuber, M. T. (2004). "Dawn: A journey in space and time." *Planetary and Space Science*, 52(5–6), 465–489. *https://doi.org/10.1016/j.pss.2003.06.013*.

24   Russell, C. T., Coradini, A., Christensen, U., De Sanctis, M. C., Feldman, W. C., Jaumann, R., Keller, H. U., Konopliv, A. S., McCord, T. B., McFadden, L. A., McSween, H. Y., Mottola, S., Neukum, G., Pieters, C. M., Prettyman, T. H., Raymond, C. A., Smith, D. E., Sykes, M. V., Williams, B. G., Wise, J., & Zuber, M. T. (2004). "Dawn: A journey in space and time." *Planetary and Space Science*, 52(5–6), 465–489. *https://doi.org/10.1016/j.pss.2003.06.013*.

lithium-loaded glass, termed a "phosphor sandwich," added the capability to detect both thermal and epithermal neutrons.

The modified Lunar Prospector detector still could not detect gamma rays below about three megaelectronvolts (MeV). The cutting-edge technology was high-purity germanium, which would add resolution, but at significant cost, and an additional requirement for cryocooling, which would add mass and complexity. Instead, as early as the concept study review, the team began to investigate adding a promising new type of detector, cadmium-zinc telluride (CZT). CZT was not ideal, as the sensors are damaged by radiation and the high-energy particles from the space environment, but the engineers built into GRaND the capability to remove the damage by annealing the sensors at high temperature, a change that eventually required an increase in photo-multiplier tubes for readout from two to 21. The CZT did not have the high degree of heritage that the main unit did, so primary operations planning was performed using the other detectors alone, with the CZT as bonus. Since the technology was so new, Prettyman said, "You have to assume that it may not work."[25]

The tight budget meant that the team could only afford to build a flight unit, for-going a flight spare, in sharp contrast to NASA's earlier, larger missions. For instance, engineers built so many flight spares for Voyager that a modified tenth and final spare flew on Stardust, over 21 years later.[26]

As proposed, Dawn also had two additional instruments: the magnetometer and a laser altimeter. The magnetometer was to be built by Russell at UCLA. The mag-netometer had heritage from "a long line of missions including OGO5 (launched in 1968), ISEE 1 and 2 (1977), Pioneer Venus (1978), Galileo (1989), Polar (1996), and ST5 (in fabrication)."[27] The Laser Altimeter, led by David Smith and Maria Zuber, was designed as a follow-on to the MESSENGER laser altimeter, built by Smith and Andy

25   Russell, C. T. (2005). "Dawn Discovery Mission: Status Report." Proceedings of 6th IAA International Conference on Low-Cost Planetary Missions, 6, 283–289. Retrieved from *https:// escholarship.org/uc/item/2xr140qr*. See also Prettyman, T. H., Feldman, W. C., Ameduri, F. P., Barraclough, B. L., Cascio, E. W., Fuller, K. R., Funsten, H. O., Lawrence, D. J., McKinney, G. W., Russell, C. T., Soldner, S. A., Storms, S. A., Szeles, C., & Tokar, R. L. (2003). "Gamma-ray and neutron spectrometer for the Dawn mission to 1 Ceres and 4 Vesta." *IEEE Transactions on Nuclear Science*, 50(4), 1190–1197. *https://doi.org/10.1109/TNS.2003.815156*.

26   Niebur, S. (2009, 12 August). Personal interview with P. Tsou. Located in "Stardust" file, NASA Historical Reference Collection, History Division, NASA Headquarters, Washington, DC. See also Whalen, A. (2003, 26 November). "Stardust Navigation Camera." Downloaded from *http:// stardust.jpl.nasa.gov/mission/camera.html*.

27   Russell, C. T., Coradini, A., Christensen, U., De Sanctis, M. C., Feldman, W. C., Jaumann, R., Keller, H. U., Konopliv, A. S., McCord, T. B., McFadden, L. A., McSween, H. Y., Mottola, S., Neukum, G., Pieters, C. M., Prettyman, T. H., Raymond, C. A., Smith, D. E., Sykes, M. V., Williams, B. G., Wise, J., & Zuber, M. T. (2004). "Dawn: A journey in space and time." *Planetary and Space Science*, 52(5–6), 465–489.

Cheng, the project scientist on NEAR. Cost and schedule issues eventually pushed the design to a build-to-print copy of the earlier instrument.

Dawn scientists would also perform a radio science investigation to determine the gravity fields, mass, principal axes, rotational axes, and moments of inertia of each asteroid. A mass and the shape model could be used to determine the bulk density of the asteroid. The shape model and gravity model could be used to characterize density variations in the crust and mantle. If a rotational wobble was detected, that, combined with shape and gravity models, could show the possible differentiation and formation of a metallic core.[28]

THE SPACECRAFT

The Dawn spacecraft itself would be 1.64 meters long, 1.27 meters wide, and 1.77 meters high, with a 1.52-meter high-gain antenna, dwarfed by the two 63-kilogram, 8.3- × 2.3-meter solar panels, together capable providing more than 10 kilowatts that could be stored in the onboard 35-amp-hour rechargeable nickel-hydrogen battery. When the solar panels were deployed, the spacecraft measured 19.7 meters tip to tip. The spacecraft bus, like many others built by Orbital at the time, was a graphite composite cylinder, surrounded by aluminum panels. Inside the central tube were two large tanks: one for the hydrazine needed for the reaction control system, and a much larger xenon tank that would hold nearly 500 kilograms of propellant. Onboard temperatures would be controlled by blankets, surface radiators, finishes, and heaters. The spacecraft weighed 1,217.7 kilograms at launch: 747.1 kilograms spacecraft, 425 kilograms xenon propellant, and 45.6 kilograms hydrazine propellant.[29]

To reach the asteroids in a reasonable amount of time at low cost, the team chose to incorporate three ion engines into the design. The mission would incorporate chemical propulsion at launch and then be powered entirely by solar-electric propulsion. The ion engines used electricity generated by the solar panels to accelerate ions from the xenon fuel to a speed of up to 10 times that of chemical engines. They used only 3.25 milligrams of xenon per second at maximum thrust, enabling two thousand days of operation over the mission's lifetime using only 425 kilograms of xenon propellant. Although 3.25 milligrams of xenon per second produced only 91 millinewtons of force, the near-constant operation of the engines over the duration of cruise between Earth and Vesta added up to a total change in velocity from ion propulsion similar to

---

28   Ibid.

29   NASA. (2007, September). "Dawn Launch: Mission to Vesta and Ceres" [press kit].

that produced by Dawn's Delta II rocket launch, including its first, second, and third stages, and the nine solid-fuel boosters.[30]

Marc Rayman, Dawn project systems engineer and project manager of DS-1, recalled that, like many of his generation, his first encounter with ion propulsion was while viewing a 1968 *Star Trek* episode, and, he quipped, with its three ion engines instead of two, "Dawn does the Star Wars TIE fighters one better."[31] The science fiction analogies were apt and helped explain the complicated process of solar-electric propulsion to the generations that grew up pretending to fly *Star Wars* spaceships.[32] Rayman had a gift for explaining the complicated ion propulsion system, saying that it "works by ionizing, or giving an electric charge to, atoms of xenon gas and then it uses a high voltage to shoot these ions through this metal grid at very high speed, up to almost 90,000 miles per hour. The action of the ions leaving the thruster causes a reaction that pushes the spacecraft in the other direction.... It really does emit this cool, blue glow like in the science fiction movies." Holding up a piece of paper, he said "the thruster pushes on the spacecraft about as hard as this single piece of paper pushes on my hand (91 millinewtons, to be precise). But in space, the effect of this gentle, almost whisper-like thrust gradually builds up over time until we can achieve very high speeds." Rayman concluded, "It's what I like to call 'acceleration with patience.'" It would take Dawn four days to accelerate from zero to 60 mph, but it would only use two pounds of fuel in the process.[33]

Of course, the ion propulsion units depended on adequate output of the large solar panels. The electricity generated from the solar panels charged a stream of xenon gas particles, firing the xenon ions of the onboard propellant out a nozzle to generate thrust, slowly building up speed. The Dawn engineering team tested the solar panels extensively because of issues related to the low intensity of sunlight to be expected at the spacecraft's targets and the low temperatures found there.[34]

Ion propulsion missions have several distinct advantages over missions that rely on chemical propulsion alone, including the ability to restart propulsion after a period orbiting a solar system body. The propulsion system also makes trades much easier—or much more complicated. "Margin management on an ion propulsion mission is much

---

30   "DS1's ion propulsion engine keeps on firing." (2001, 8 April). Jet Propulsion Laboratory Press Release. Downloaded from *http://spaceflightnow.com/news/n0104/08ds1/*.

31   Shiga, D. (2007, 28 September). "Dawn spacecraft launches to study giant asteroids." *New Scientist*; Dunn, M. (2007, 28 September). "NASA launches mission to asteroid." AP.

32   Shiga, D. (2007, 28 September). "Dawn spacecraft launches to study giant asteroids." *New Scientist*.

33   Harwood, W. (2007, 26 September). "Dawn Set For Exploration Of Largest Asteroids." *Spaceflight Now*.

34   Niebur, S. (2009, 11 August). Personal interview with C. Raymond. Located in "Dawn" file, NASA Historical Reference Collection, History Division, NASA Headquarters, Washington, DC; Russell, C. (2007, 19 September). Presentation at the Discovery@15 workshop in Huntsville, Alabama.

different than on other missions because a lot of things are linked that you may not think are linked," said Russell. "Power and mass, money and time and all those things are all linked through how you thrust."[35]

Russell explained that without ion propulsion, its Delta II launch vehicle would have been insufficient to launch the spacecraft into the correct orbit to reach Vesta. Using chemical propulsion alone, the mission would have required a more powerful Atlas V, or even a Delta IV rocket, for a mission just to Vesta, or just to Ceres. Orbiting both asteroids "would require two launches, at a total cost perhaps $1.5 billion. I look at this and say we saved NASA $1 billion. NASA looks at that and says, 'No, this mission costs us $0.5 billion.'"[36]

Unfunded Mandates and External Threats

In January 2001, NASA Headquarters selected Dawn, Kepler, and INSIDE Jupiter to perform competitive Phase A concept studies. However, funding from the agency was not immediately available, so the projects began work several months late. Although NASA Headquarters released the AO with the intent to possibly select two missions, with the text on page one clearly stating, "This AO invites proposals for investigations for the ninth Discovery mission (and possibly the tenth)," there was insufficient funding for two missions to start Phase B.[37] To accommodate the dual selection, NASA delayed the start of Phase B for Dawn by almost a year, to late 2002.[38] The teams understood the rationale, but that it didn't make it easy.

Dawn could accommodate a two-year launch window because of the inherent flexibility of ion propulsion. The funding delays affected the science, as a delayed launch meant delayed arrival at Vesta and then Ceres. Since the asteroids continued in motion, a different surface would be illuminated by the Sun at the spacecraft's arrival. Vesta's new lit area would include the South Pole, an area of intense interest to planetary scientists. Russell reflected, "I don't think the delay between selection and Phase A was a problem; I think we were able to get around that. When you go into a Phase A study, it is a staffing-up problem because there are more people

35   Niebur, S. (2009, 24 March). Personal interview with C. Russell. Located in "Dawn" file, NASA Historical Reference Collection, History Division, NASA Headquarters, Washington, DC.

36   Russell, C. (2007, 19 September). Presentation at the Discovery@15 workshop in Huntsville, Alabama.

37   NASA. (2000, 19 May). Announcement of Opportunity: Discovery 2000.

38   Russell, C. T., Capaccioni, F., Coradini, A., Christensen, U., De Sanctis, M. C., Feldman, W. C., Jaumann, R., Keller, H. U., Konopliv, A., McCord, T. B., McFadden, L. A., McSween, H. Y., Mottola, S., Neukum, G., Pieters, C. M., Prettyman, T. H., Raymond, C. A., Smith, D. E., Sykes, M. V., Williams, B., & Zuber, M. T. (2006). "Dawn Discovery mission to Vesta and Ceres: Present status." *Advances in Space Research*, 38(9), 2043–2048. *https://doi.org/10.1016/j.asr.2004.12.041.*

needed for Phase A than for writing the proposal, the initial proposal. Those people were available when we needed them."[39]

While the Dawn team was in the study phase, the NASA Integrated Action Team (NIAT) issued reports on the Mars mission failures. The Dawn team was encouraged by NASA Headquarters to identify NIAT-type risks and to ask for additional funding where necessary. This additional funding would also include costs for additional reviews and the additional oversight that were sure to come. Whereas earlier missions such as MESSENGER complained about the additional oversight, the Dawn team was affected so early on that they simply responded.[40]

The day before the mission's site visit, as the team gathered at Orbital Sciences in the Washington, DC, suburbs for a dry run, news broke that terrorists had attacked the Pentagon, just across the river from NASA Headquarters, and the World Trade Center in New York City, as part of a coordinated airplane hijacking plot. The date was 11 September 2001. The site visit was canceled that day, the evaluation materials taken to a secure area at Langley Research Center, and the review was postponed until normalcy could be restored later in the year.[41] The nation adjusted to a new normal, and NASA selected Dawn for flight on 21 December 2001, with a launch date of 27 May 2006—nearly a year later than the proposed launch date.

Once the Phase A work had been delayed, the postponement of the launches of both Dawn and Kepler were inevitable. Costs (including overhead rates) went up, commitments weakened, and management changed.[42] Internal burden rates had increased during the delays, causing an unexpected financial hit to the project as it prepared to start work again in August 2002. Russell appealed this increase to the Jet Propulsion Laboratory Center Director, but Charles Elachi was also being squeezed by the changing times. As the lab suffered the loss of the anticipated Europa mission, all projects had to bear the collective burden of the cost of management and facilities. Dawn's share was nearly $5 million, a number that challenged this small mission before the work of development even began.

---

39   Niebur, S. (2009, 24 March). Personal interview with C. Russell. Located in "Dawn" file, NASA Historical Reference Collection, History Division, NASA Headquarters, Washington, DC.

40   Ibid.

41   Russell, C. T., Capaccioni, F., Coradini, A., De Sanctis, M. C., Feldman, W. C., Jaumann, R., Keller, H. U., McCord, T. B., McFadden, L. A., Mottola, S., Pieters, C. M., Prettyman, T. H., Raymond, C. A., Sykes, M. V., Smith, D. E., & Zuber, M. T. (2007). "Dawn Mission to Vesta and Ceres: Symbiosis Between Terrestrial Observations and Robotic Exploration." *Earth, Moon, and Planets*, 101(1–2), 65–91. *https://doi.org/10.1007/s11038-007-9151-9.*

42   Russell, C. T., Capaccioni, F., Coradini, A., De Sanctis, M. C., Feldman, W. C., Jaumann, R., Keller, H. U., McCord, T. B., McFadden, L. A., Mottola, S., Pieters, C. M., Prettyman, T. H., Raymond, C. A., Sykes, M. V., Smith, D. E., & Zuber, M. T. (2007). "Dawn Mission to Vesta and Ceres: Symbiosis Between Terrestrial Observations and Robotic Exploration." *Earth, Moon, and Planets*, 101(1–2), 65–91. *https://doi.org/10.1007/s11038-007-9151-9.*

Other changes were afoot, with the addition of an official business manager to the project in August. Elachi also mandated that a deputy project manager with experience in large contracts be added to the project to assist Sarah Gavit, the project manager. Gavit pushed back and, with the assistance of others at JPL, was successful in stopping this $1 million addition to the project, as Dawn had committed in the concept study report to having Mark Rayman, the payload manager, act in the deputy role. As time passed, the laws of celestial mechanics added to the difficulty, as a properly illuminated Vesta became even more difficult to reach.

As the Discovery Program restored its reserves and NASA moved into the 2003 fiscal year, Dawn's mission development started to spin up. Work began in earnest in September 2002, with science and engineering teams largely on contract by January 2003. The first review milestones were set for April and August. By March, however, the team had already encountered their first technical failure, and they abandoned their plan to use a lightweight composite xenon propellant tank in favor of a heavier titanium tank with composite overwrap.[43]

Meanwhile, the massive overruns of the Deep Impact and MESSENGER projects necessitated increased attention to the financial reserve posture of subsequent missions. Amid a particularly contentious monthly review with the relevant NASA Center Directors and Division Directors at NASA Headquarters, Ed Weiler upped the mandatory reserve posture to 25 percent for all missions in development as well as those selected through future Announcements of Opportunity. Missions would have to meet this requirement at major mission milestones. Unsure of the applicability to Dawn and Kepler, missions already selected but not confirmed, Dawn's program scientist immediately asked for clarification. Weiler confirmed that both Dawn and Kepler would have to meet the 25 percent reserve requirement in order to be confirmed. Later negotiations clarified that the 25 percent would be on Phases B/C/D, excluding launch costs, but the new mandate could not be waived.

This put Dawn in a difficult situation, as Dawn's reserve posture at selection was 17 percent.[44] In addition, Dawn's reserves had dropped sharply as they entered Phase B due to Jet Propulsion Laboratory rate changes, which had increased during the delay, and a failure in the xenon propellant tank design.

"It was an ambitious mission, very low cost. We had very little place to try to reengineer the mission and get back funds. So, I'd say the project just started off in a crisis," said Raymond. "The project was starting to staff up and starting to get a hold of what had to be done.... There was the PMSR [Preliminary Mission and Systems Review], the project mission System Requirements Review." While focusing on that,

---

43   Raymond, C. (2003, March). "Dawn news." *Dawn's Early Light*, 2(1). 1.
44   Niebur, S. (2009, 11 August). Personal interview with C. Raymond. Located in "Dawn" file, NASA Historical Reference Collection, History Division, NASA Headquarters, Washington, DC.

"we realized that we've got to start finding ways to lower the cost." Early descopes included removing the solid-state data recorder and, with it, all capability for significant nonvolatile data storage.[45]

Although the new reserve posture was designed to increase the possibility of recovery from implementation failures, the increase in reserves did not increase confidence in the mission's cost containment from the team's perspective. In fact, the mission management team would later claim the opposite as a "lessons learned," explaining: "Ultimately, increasing reserves simply leads to increased costs."[46] In 2009, Russell remained focused on reserves, stating that project reserves were clearly important, but other reserves were also necessary: "hidden reserves" from everyone, including staff; "items you can get rid of without affecting the program," perhaps "30 percent, maybe 50 percent"; "robust reserves that nobody can raid, whether it's your people or some other project"; the ability to refuse to lend other projects money; and the ability to continue to function when NASA Headquarters hits a "dry period" and "they just don't give you the money."[47]

The Meeting Did Not Go Well

Four months later, the project held its PMSR at the Jet Propulsion Laboratory. The team had continued to push back on JPL's rate changes and increased management requirements. They increased reserves where they could and presented what they believed to be a credible plan to get to the Preliminary Design Review.

The meeting did not go well. There was widespread agreement among the reviewers that the mission's requirements were not adequately defined—particularly for a review that would evaluate them. There were also concerns that the project was immature for its expected stage.

"It was clear that the project wasn't together at that point. They hadn't done the work that was necessary to successfully complete the [System Requirements Review] and there were several iterations of that. It wasn't clear that the initial project manager really understood what needed to get done," recalled Kurt Lindstrom, Dawn Program Executive.[48]

Russell also blamed Sarah Gavit, the project manager. "Experience is important," he said. "That is a lesson I've had, and I beat into people. I said my problem with Sarah

---

45   Ibid.

46   Fraschetti, T. C., M. D. Rayman, C. T. Russell, and C. A. Raymond. (2005). "Dawn Discovery mission: Lessons learned." *Proceedings of 6th IAA International Conference on Low-Cost Planetary Missions, Kyoto, Japan.*

47   Niebur, S. (2009, 24 March). Personal interview with C. Russell. Located in "Dawn" file, NASA Historical Reference Collection, History Division, NASA Headquarters, Washington, DC.

48   Niebur, S. (2009, 31 July). Personal interview with K. Lindstrom. Located in "Dawn" file, NASA Historical Reference Collection, History Division, NASA Headquarters, Washington, DC.

[Gavit] was she really was not experienced."[49] Russell asked that Gavit be replaced as project manager. JPL agreed to consider the request but asked him to wait for a replacement project manager until after the launch of the Mars Exploration Rovers in June and July 2003.

Meanwhile, the laser altimeter was having cost troubles independently of the mission cost issues. The instrument employed 47 people on the project, many of them civil servants. Every lead engineer was a civil servant. NASA was undergoing a transition to full-cost accounting, whereby each civil servant's salary must now "cost" the project its full amount, plus burden, which can often double the salary. This caused the cost for the laser altimeter, previously estimated using the cost from the MESSENGER laser altimeter (not under full-cost accounting), to increase dramatically. Gavit pushed to descope the instrument, but Goddard Space Flight Center Director Al Diaz acted to protect his center's role in the mission, agreeing to cover the cost and burden of more than 32 full-time employees over the four years of development at no cost whatsoever to the project. In addition, Diaz agreed to cover any overrun of the instrument, and he provided a letter of commitment to that effect, with a clear bottom line: "GSFC will commit to building the Dawn Laser Altimeter within your budget of $8.06M."[50]

This was an excellent deal for Dawn, which would be protected from future overruns and personnel cost increases, and yet the instrument's presence was still not assured. The instrument would have to be delivered not only on budget, but on time—and this was now in question due to delays of the delivery of the MESSENGER laser altimeter, built by the same team in the same labs. The instrument was on the critical path for Dawn and needed to be delivered with the other instruments by 29 April 2005. Russell was adamant that the laser altimeter not be thrown off, saying in the 6 May meeting that he would rather the mission not be confirmed than lose the laser altimeter.[51] The team then proceeded with other reviews, including a Project Cost Review in June, the first major reporting of the implementation of Earned Value Management.

Russell made it clear to NASA Headquarters that he would not descope the laser altimeter, taking his chances at Preliminary Design Review and confirmation against the advice of Dawn's program scientist at NASA Headquarters, who reminded him that doing so without making other significant descopes would not comply with the JPL or NASA Headquarters policy requiring 25 percent reserves.[52] Russell and Raymond appealed directly to Division Director Colleen Hartman for relief from the requirement in a closed meeting in July 2003. Said Raymond, "I think we expected to get some

---

49   Niebur, S. (2009, 24 March). Personal interview with C. Russell. Located in "Dawn" file, NASA Historical Reference Collection, History Division, NASA Headquarters, Washington, DC.

50   Niebur, S. (2003, 6 May). Program scientist's notes. Susan Niebur's personal collection.

51   Ibid.

52   Ibid.

sympathy or some relief because, for instance, Kepler had just completely been allowed to re-plan their budget to accommodate JPL management.... We were asking for a much smaller amount to comply with a rule that hadn't been part of the deal initially."[53]

Hartman was not reassuring, Raymond remembers. "I could not have predicted the hostility on the part of Colleen that we received in bringing this up. And it was basically, this: You were given a directive. This is the rule, and your job is to go off and figure out how you're going to do it.... I was pretty surprised. So, off we went. This put this huge stress on the project, and so, as I said, Sarah didn't have a lot of places to go to fix this problem...and then we ended up getting a new project manager... after the review board came back and said things like you've got to start throwing stuff overboard.... Chris is nothing if not confident and unswayable when he believes something very strongly.... He said, 'No way.'"[54]

The team needed a fresh direction from a project manager who could lead them successfully to the launch pad. Russell was "looking for somebody who was experienced, who really knew how space systems worked," he said.[55] The Jet Propulsion Laboratory tapped Tom Fraschetti, who had spent 15 years in the aerospace industry working on defense projects before coming to JPL and filling a series of progressively more responsible roles, from small tasks for the Defense Department to writing proposals and building spaceflight instruments including the Cassini imager, when he was promoted into management as division manager. After 20 years at JPL, Fraschetti was working as Deputy Director for the Engineering and Science Directorate when he was tapped to be Dawn's second project manager.

Fraschetti brought more than experience to the project; he brought a fresh look at the engineering and at the relationship between scientists and engineers. "I worked a lot with scientists and I appreciated science, which made me a little different than a lot of other project managers, at least at JPL. They tended to come up through the spacecraft ranks, and their concern was getting a spacecraft someplace, and a secondary concern was the science. My concern was let's do some great science, and, by the way, we got to have a spacecraft that gets us there," he explained.[56]

---

53   Niebur, S. (2009, 11 August). Personal interview with C. Raymond. Located in "Dawn" file, NASA Historical Reference Collection, History Division, NASA Headquarters, Washington, DC.

54   Ibid.

55   Niebur, S. (2009, 24 March). Personal interview with C. Russell. Located in "Dawn" file, NASA Historical Reference Collection, History Division, NASA Headquarters, Washington, DC.

56   Niebur, S. (2009, 12 August). Personal interview with T. Fraschetti. Located in "Dawn" file, NASA Historical Reference Collection, History Division, NASA Headquarters, Washington, DC.

Russell saw Fraschetti as "a real leader in that the engineers who were working with him respected him and listened to him and went to him for guidance."[57] Russell was reassured by this and began to trust Fraschetti to deliver the spacecraft.[58]

Concurrently, the PI agreed to spend more days away from the JPL campus, in response to Sarah Gavit's complaints of interference. Russell later explained: "I try not to micromanage. It may sound like I was micromanaging.... All I was doing is to try to take a top-level look and make sure that mission risk was minimized."[59]

As things stood after Dawn's Preliminary Mission and Systems Review, the team had insufficient power, mass, and cost margins to send the spacecraft to Vesta and Ceres. Although the team had new management, the technical and cost challenges remained, as the next few months brought more challenges and more changes. "When I came onboard," said Fraschetti, "they had looked at everything where they could cut. And basically, it was spending a lot of money and we weren't making any forward progress." A decision had to be made, or the mission may as well have folded before confirmation.[60] The team added a fifth solar panel to the spacecraft design, increasing available power margin at Ceres, but the cost issues remained.

In August, the team announced that they had decided to launch on a lighter launch vehicle, a standard Delta 2925, adding a Mars gravity assist to the trajectory, and to delete the laser altimeter from the mission in order to save reserves and avoid cost overruns.[61] Potential solutions to noted problems with power margin and cost reserves were iterated, with a replan requested by 15 August and delivered on 22 August.[62]

Throughout the summer and fall, the team moved forward with a plan to descope their greatest strength: the visit to icy Ceres, which provided a contrast to dry, rocky Vesta. NASA Headquarters warned the team that this descope did not preserve the proposed science of the mission and would not be accepted, but they moved forward anyway, fighting to preserve science in other ways. This included resistance to any further descoping of instruments. Dawn was built to be a lean mission, with only five instruments and flight-tested technology. All the instruments were essentially rebuilds or slight modifications of instruments previously flown on other missions. Therefore,

57   Niebur, S. (2009, 24 March). Personal interview with C. Russell. Located in "Dawn" file, NASA Historical Reference Collection, History Division, NASA Headquarters, Washington, DC.

58   Niebur, S. (2009, 12 August). Personal interview with T. Fraschetti. Located in "Dawn" file, NASA Historical Reference Collection, History Division, NASA Headquarters, Washington, DC.

59   Niebur, S. (2009, 24 March). Personal interview with C. Russell. Located in "Dawn" file, NASA Historical Reference Collection, History Division, NASA Headquarters, Washington, DC.

60   Niebur, S. (2009, 12 August). Personal interview with T. Fraschetti. Located in "Dawn" file, NASA Historical Reference Collection, History Division, NASA Headquarters, Washington, DC.

61   Russell, C. (2003, August). "Dawn status." Dawn's Early Light, 2(2). 1–2.

62   Niebur, S. (2003). Presentation to the American Astronomical Society Division of Planetary Science Fall Conference.

there was not a lot of margin built into the proposed costs for any of the instruments or subsystems that could be used to cut the costs directly.[63]

Saving money on the launch vehicle did come at a cost to science, however. The lighter launch vehicle did not have as much delta-v to offer, so the addition of a Mars gravity assist, necessary to boost the spacecraft into a trajectory that would reach the asteroid belt, reduced the possible stay time at Vesta from 11 down to 8 months, and the stay time at Ceres from 11 down to 7 months. The team was disappointed by this reduction but hoped that this decision could be reversed when the final margins became clear, noting that the gravity assist could be skipped and the stay times increased at the last minute because of the flexibility granted by the ion engines.[64]

Meanwhile, as on every mission, opportunities to improve the science return arose, the scientists lobbied for additions, and the PI was faced with decisions. Augmenting the science return would be tempting for any scientist, but Russell held the line. Fraschetti and the engineers appreciated this resistance to scope creep. "I had a great PI," said Fraschetti. "He did not let requirements creep." Russell did allow that there was potential for an improved mission if margins allowed, but he did not change the system requirements, such as to enable longer stay times. Once the requirements were finally set at PDR, they stayed set. JPL and NASA Headquarters were watching the mission's margins closely, and the team continued to make trade after trade to meet the requirements as proposed.[65]

The Dawn mission team had been praised early on for bringing in Orbital Sciences, a new player in deep space missions. Orbital had extensive experience in building Earth-orbiting spacecraft and integrating the instruments with the bus; they proposed similar roles for their work with the Dawn mission. This was widely seen as a smart move on Dawn's part and an asset for the community, as even the more experienced industry partners were beginning to overrun their costs on other missions in the early days of Dawn. Orbital's experience in Earth-orbiting missions made them look like a new player, but a reliable new player, which appealed to NASA management. Orbital introduced both a new East Coast location and company culture into the planetary mission community. The assumptions that the Jet Propulsion Laboratory held because of their experience with Lockheed Martin, TRW, and Ball did not necessarily hold with Orbital. Orbital's expectations of NASA due to their work with GSFC did not neces-

---

63   Niebur, S. (2009, 24 March). Personal interview with C. Russell. Located in "Dawn" file, NASA Historical Reference Collection, History Division, NASA Headquarters, Washington, DC.

64   Russell, C. T. (2005). "Dawn Discovery Mission: Status Report." *Proceedings of 6th IAA International Conference on Low-Cost Planetary Missions*, 6, 283–289. Retrieved from *https:// escholarship.org/uc/item/2xr140qr*.

65   Niebur, S. (2009, 12 August). Personal interview with T. Fraschetti. Located in "Dawn" file, NASA Historical Reference Collection, History Division, NASA Headquarters, Washington, DC.

sarily hold as they began to work with JPL. The agreements signed between the two companies began to collapse as the two began discussing details of mission operations.

Orbital had based their proposal on their experience launching spacecraft for NASA. JPL assumed a certain level of familiarity with deep space operations that Orbital did not have. As the details were hammered out over conference calls and in-person meetings, the discrepancies began to show. Orbital's experience operating Earth-orbiting systems had led them to believe that they needed one, or very few, operators for Dawn. JPL, however, knew that this deep space mission with several instruments would take more work. Orbital was accustomed to launching a spacecraft and then turning it over to its customer to operate. JPL typically operated its own missions, over years or decades. Orbital would need to create a long-term mission operations center. JPL already had a multi-mission operations center that could be used for encounters and routine housekeeping during cruise. Orbital would need to create, purchase, borrow, and install new software to control missions over time. JPL already had the expertise and the trained personnel—not a minor cost. Orbital did not budget for extensive operations, as JPL had assumed. As JPL began to teach Orbital the depth of effort that was required, Orbital's cost and possible risk went up, negating any original savings recognized by the proposal to do mission operations at the new facility at Orbital. To save money on training, software, facilities, personnel, and the additional oversight required, JPL brought the mission operations center back to JPL before confirmation. Even with the costs of change, this effort would result in significant savings and decrease in risk in operations by a new partner. The project began to replan the operations phase. Since JPL had decades of experience operating deep space mission operations, its cost increase would be much less than the startup plus operations cost at Orbital, a new player. JPL could fold it into the mission with a smaller delta cost, use existing tools and its own multi-mission systems, make any necessary modifications, and pull the appropriate people from other projects on lab. The project benefited from flexibility not just in the mission parameters related to ion propulsion, but also in the resources available at JPL. Training would not be an issue at JPL, the premier place in the United States for planetary science missions and operations. "We value people that can fly missions," said Fraschetti.[66]

The mission passed the 14–16 October Preliminary Design Review of technical merit, entering confirmation with a mission plan that, in the view of several at NASA Headquarters, did not meet the minimum science mission outlined in the 2000 proposal.[67] The team had chosen to delete the Ceres encounter from the mission, reducing a mission whose greatest asset was that of comparative planetology to a mission that

---

66   Ibid.

67   Niebur, S. (2003, 23 October). "Discovery Program Update." Presentation for the Solar System Exploration Subcommittee.

would only orbit one asteroid. Although the spacecraft would now fly by an additional asteroid on the way to Vesta, the GRaND spectrometer, one of only two remaining American instruments, would be useless in a flyby. The engineering specs had not been changed (and no money had been thereby saved in development), in accordance with the team's proposal to add the Ceres encounter to an extended mission, a clear attempt to solve the present financial crisis by postponing the need for those funds to a future request. This plan passed the technical merit Preliminary Design Review held by the managing institution, but the Program Scientist warned—as she had since May—that such a gambit would not pass NASA Headquarters scrutiny, which would include a value judgment of the science investigation that remained.

You're Not Confirmed

In December, it was NASA Headquarters' turn. The Dawn team arrived at the confirmation review with a mission in which the most compelling science investigation, comparative planetology using Vesta and Ceres as endmembers of the evolutionary process, had been removed. No option was presented that preserved the comparative planetology—which sold the mission itself in 2000—in the baseline mission, leaving NASA Headquarters with the single decision of whether to continue buying a very expensive mission to a single asteroid with a single U.S. instrument, a German camera, and an Italian mass spectrometer, or to reject the replan and "non-confirm" the mission. There was precedent for the latter case, and, after a difficult session behind closed doors, NASA Headquarters rejected the proposed descope of the Ceres orbit. This left the mission over budget and with insufficient mass margin: an unacceptable situation for a mission that had not yet been confirmed.

Just days after the Letter of Agreement between Agenzia Spaziale Italiana and NASA was finally signed, the mission failed confirmation.[68] The mission was canceled, and the team notified, on Christmas Eve 2003.[69] Russell called it "a surprise," noting that the team did not understand the decision, and "don't understand to this day."[70] Carol Raymond, the deputy Principal Investigator, however, said the opposite. "Ed [Weiler] said that he didn't select the mission to go only to Vesta. He could have selected another mission to go to Vesta. I can absolutely understand why he would say that. What I

68   Agenzia Spaziale Italiana. (N.d.). "Minor Bodies of the Solar System." Downloaded from *http://www.asi.it/en/activity/solar_system/dawn*.

69   Niebur, S. (2009, 12 August). Personal interview with T. Fraschetti. Located in "Dawn" file, NASA Historical Reference Collection, History Division, NASA Headquarters, Washington, DC.

70   Niebur, S. (2009, 24 March). Personal interview with C. Russell. Located in "Dawn" file, NASA Historical Reference Collection, History Division, NASA Headquarters, Washington, DC.

don't understand is why it wasn't recognized when we went in there [a year earlier] and said, this is an impossible job, why are you changing the rules?"[71]

Dawn was an ambitious, lean, low-cost mission placed in the context of more mature missions suffering serious overruns, in an environment of rapidly decreasing risk tolerance. This situation was not unique to Dawn, but this team did not acknowledge the need for the mission to compensate for others' mistakes, continuing to pursue their original mission design despite increasingly conservative rules for allowable margins of all kinds by both JPL and NASA Headquarters.

This point was illustrated very clearly when Dawn came to its confirmation review with a proposal to preserve the technical capabilities (power, mass, propellant) required to do the orbits at Vesta and Ceres but not the technical margins required to include Ceres in the baseline mission.[72] This calculated approach put mission, project, and NASA Headquarters management in a difficult position. No matter how much the players wanted to preserve the science mission and execute the spacecraft, the Jet Propulsion Laboratory could not approve a mission that violated their Design Principles, which included sufficient margins on spacecraft and dry mass, power, and budget for the mission design. So the team reacted to those requirements by moving the Ceres encounter to a possible "extended mission," a move that would allow JPL to pass Dawn at its Preliminary Design Review, where science is not considered. Following standard practice, however, the NASA Headquarters review *did* consider the science. Since the mission science without Ceres was not consistent with the originally proposed and accepted comparative planetology goals, Headquarters could not approve it, and the mission failed confirmation.

Ultimately, without sufficient mission reserves, Dawn could not be approved for its mission as conceived. Without available program reserves (which existed for a few years but had been more than spent by Deep Impact and MESSENGER), the Discovery Program could not confirm a mission that stood a high risk of needing additional cash infusions. Without generous NASA-wide reserves, an impossibility due to the congressional budget cycle, even NASA could not bail out a mission at its margins and sure to grow. The whole program was in a tight situation, just as the project was, with no solution apparent within NASA.

The team had pulled out all the stops, too. The Principal Investigator and science team had given up the laser altimeter. The engineering team had eliminated all but one test bench. The team had cut the dwell time at Vesta and Ceres to the bare minimum. The project was nonconfirmed, with no hope of restart or reconsideration. Then, the

71   Niebur, S. (2009, 11 August). Personal interview with C. Raymond. Located in "Dawn" file, NASA Historical Reference Collection, History Division, NASA Headquarters, Washington, DC.

72   Ibid.

day after Christmas, "This big bag of money fell out of the sky," said Raymond, "in the form of Orbital's fee."[73]

Dave Thompson, Orbital CEO, called Orlando Figueroa at NASA Headquarters and reminded him that Orbital was very interested in continuing with the mission and breaking into the planetary mission field. He then did the unthinkable and told Figueroa that Orbital would commit to doing the job for cost only, returning the for-profit company's $15 million fee to NASA. Figueroa was impressed by Orbital's dedication to getting the job done, and he agreed. The program scientist was skeptical, wondering what the motivation of Orbital would then be to complete the job on time and for the originally proposed cost, but the program executive and division director, who had more experience, were incredibly impressed. The team agreed to move forward and give the Dawn team another chance. The Dawn team would have two weeks to look at the budget, mass, and power problems with this additional $15 million to work with and see if a mission could be done within the design principle margins and the science expectations.[74]

What happened next was unexpected in the context of the Discovery Program, which had put cost caps on the missions to control growth during formulation and development but had become accustomed to the cost caps also controlling the habitual raiding of the mission operations period where the science measurements were actually taken at faraway planets, comets, and asteroids. Having scrubbed the spacecraft costs repeatedly, the team did the unthinkable: they scrubbed Phase E.

"We scrubbed the operations phase because this was a mission cost cap, not a spacecraft cost cap," reasoned Raymond, "we chopped the length of time we were at each asteroid down to the bone." They shortened the mission substantially and accepted impacts to the science. "We shortened the low altitude mapping orbit and accepted that we were going to do topography with imaging with very little analysis of what that entailed, either in terms of the observing strategy, in terms of the analysis of the lighting conditions, of what methods would be expected to yield what accuracy," said Raymond. The team was throwing a Hail Mary pass in an attempt to save the mission, cutting anything that looked promising—and it worked.[75]

After a few days of frantic phone calls, replanning meetings, and pleas to reconsider, the mission was once again on its way to confirmation, having reduced costs to

---

73   Ibid.
74   Ibid.
75   Ibid.

a level comparable to that at the submission of the Concept Study Report in 2001.[76] Orbital continued to perform on the mission, with Fraschetti, the project manager, emphasizing, "Orbital gave us their very best team." It wouldn't be an easy path to launch, particularly as Dawn would be Orbital's first deep space mission, but "they made a commitment and they stood by that commitment." They wanted to expand their business to deep space missions in addition to the Earth-orbiting ones they had launched in the past, and that commitment was clear from the top down. Orbital worked hard to make Dawn a success.[77]

Chris Russell, the Dawn Principal Investigator, also credited the successful landing of the Mars rovers in January 2004, which "relieved a lot of pressure from the system as far as we're concerned. JPL felt better, maybe even NASA Headquarters felt better. So we were resurrected."[78]

However, the drastic cuts to the mapping orbits and the spacecraft instrumentation would affect the science return of the mission. Russell said when you cut instruments, you have to have a very solid plan, or you're going to end up paying for it, and more, in operations.[79]

The replan was not easy. In addition to the financial replan to reconstitute the reserves, the mission needed more power margin, and the purchase of an additional solar panel would add another million dollars to the project's deficit. Recalled Raymond, "Ed Miller, who was one of the key people on the project, came into a meeting one day in his typical laid back way and said, 'Rosetta's flying a solar array that's very similar to Dawn's. Has anybody checked what they paid?'" Orbital asked Dutch Space for a quote, and the project immediately changed suppliers.

"The clouds opened, the Sun came out," said Raymond. "That broke the logjam."[80] The Dutch Space solar array was obtainable at a lower cost, lower mass, and with promises of a power output that was much higher than the original arrays. This new solar array was a game-changer. The extra power helped solve the power problem and the mass problem as well, since on an ion propulsion mission, extra power margin

---

76 Russell, C. T., Capaccioni, F., Coradini, A., De Sanctis, M. C., Feldman, W. C., Jaumann, R., Keller, H. U., McCord, T. B., McFadden, L. A., Mottola, S., Pieters, C. M., Prettyman, T. H., Raymond, C. A., Sykes, M. V., Smith, D. E., & Zuber, M. T. (2007). "Dawn Mission to Vesta and Ceres: Symbiosis Between Terrestrial Observations and Robotic Exploration." *Earth, Moon, and Planets*, 101(1–2), 65–91. *https://doi.org/10.1007/s11038-007-9151-9.*

77 Niebur, S. (2009, 12 August). Personal interview with T. Fraschetti. Located in "Dawn" file, NASA Historical Reference Collection, History Division, NASA Headquarters, Washington, DC.

78 Niebur, S. (2009, 24 March). Personal interview with C. Russell. Located in "Dawn" file, NASA Historical Reference Collection, History Division, NASA Headquarters, Washington, DC.

79 Niebur, S. (2009, 24 March). Personal interview with C. Russell. Located in "Dawn" file, NASA Historical Reference Collection, History Division, NASA Headquarters, Washington, DC.

80 Niebur, S. (2009, 11 August). Personal interview with C. Raymond. Located in "Dawn" file, NASA Historical Reference Collection, History Division, NASA Headquarters, Washington, DC.

could compensate for some of the lost mass margin. The problems of mass and power were fixable, and the team proceeded to rework the mission timeline.

Raymond explained, "The day before we were leaving to go to NASA Headquarters we have a briefing with Charles [Elachi] to go over the final package, and we get a message from Orbital saying: We have a problem. Something fundamental about the spacecraft wasn't adequate, and they needed more money to fix it.... Charles challenged us to show him why he should be confident that we could proceed. On the spot, Marc Rayman and I said, we still have margin. We'll cut a few months out of the plan, and that's what we did."[81] The team changed the mission plan and brought a new set of charts to the Delta Confirmation Review, surprising even their Program Scientist and program executive.

The team went into the Delta Confirmation Review with a new plan and came out with renewed approval for the mission—with one significant stipulation. "As we were getting back on track after that, Weiler took the magnetometer off," said Russell. "Before we were allowed to go forward, I had to sacrifice my first born [the magnetometer] for the mission. That was a really big scientific mistake."[82] Raymond was terribly disappointed, revealing, "That was absolutely the lowest point for me, since my career had started by looking at the Earth's magnetic field and then going on to Mars' magnetic field, and here I was poised to expand the portfolio to protoplanets, but that chance had evaporated."[83] Even years later, the senior leadership of the mission continued to maintain "the magnetometer was demanifested by NASA's selecting official for reasons that still are unclear but plainly invalid."[84]

The mission was confirmed, with a modified instrument payload, trajectory, and operations plan, on 6 February 2004. The mission would continue with less science return and more reserves.[85] The need for increased reserves was also driven by JPL's insistence that the mission follow the institution's well-known Design Principles. Changes were made so that Dawn would have 15 percent power margin at all mission stages, 20 percent mass margin in Phase C, and 25 percent cost reserves at confirmation. The mission would spend less time observing both Vesta and Ceres as a result. The reductions were significant. Vesta's time was now set for seven months and Ceres at five months rather than the 11 months at each body as originally planned. This change primarily

81   Ibid.

82   Niebur, S. (2009, 24 March). Personal interview with C. Russell. Located in "Dawn" file, NASA Historical Reference Collection, History Division, NASA Headquarters, Washington, DC.

83   Niebur, S. (2009, 11 August). Personal interview with C. Raymond. Located in "Dawn" file, NASA Historical Reference Collection, History Division, NASA Headquarters, Washington, DC.

84   Russell, C. T. (2005). "Dawn Discovery Mission: Status Report." *Proceedings of 6th IAA International Conference on Low-Cost Planetary Missions*, 6, 283–289. Retrieved from *https://escholarship.org/uc/item/2xrl40qr*.

85   Russell, C. T. (2004, February). "Dawn mission status." *Dawn's Early Light*, 3(1). 1.

affected data return from the GRaND instrument, which required long stay times for integration of the data at multiple distances from the surface. The engineering specs were not changed, still allowing the mission to add time observing each body if time, power, and cost profile would allow.[86]

The mission's science objectives were now finalized:

1. Determine the bulk density of Vesta and Ceres to ≤1 percent.

2. Determine the spin axis orientation of Vesta and Ceres to ≤0.5°.

3a. Determine the gravity field of Vesta with a half-wavelength resolution ≤90 kilometers.

3b. Determine the gravity field of Ceres with a half-wavelength resolution ≤300 kilometers.

4a. Obtain images of ≥80 percent of the surface of Vesta with a sampling ≤100 meters per pixel and a signal-to-noise ratio ≥50 in the clear filter and in ≥3 color filters.

4b. Obtain images of ≥80 percent of the surface of Ceres with a sampling ≤200 meters per pixel and a signal-to-noise ratio ≥50 in the clear filter and in ≥3 color filters.

5a. Obtain a topographic map of ≥80 percent of the surface of Vesta, with a horizontal resolution ≤100 meters and a vertical resolution ≤10 meters.

5b. Obtain a topographic map of ≥80 percent of the surface of Ceres, with a horizontal resolution ≤200 meters and a vertical resolution ≤20 meters.

6a. Measure and map the abundances of major rock-forming elements to a precision ≤20 percent with a resolution ~1.5 times the mapping altitude over the upper ~1m of the entire surface of Vesta and Ceres.

6b. Measure and map the abundance of H over the upper ~1m of the entire surface of Vesta and Ceres.

6c. Measure and map the abundances of K, Th, and U over the upper ~1m of the entire surface of Vesta and Ceres.

7a. Obtain ≥10,000 spectral frames [a two-dimensional data structure with one axis representing space and the other representing spectral wavelength] of Vesta's surface at wavelengths of 0.25–5 micrometers with a spectral resolution ≤10 nanometers. At least half of these spectral frames will be at a spatial resolution ≤200 meters per pixel, with the rest at a spatial resolution ≤800 meters per pixel.

---

86   Ibid.

7b. Obtain ≥8,000 spectral frames of Ceres's surface at wavelengths of
0.25–5 micrometers with a spectral resolution ≤10 nanometers. At least half
of these spectral frames will be at a spatial resolution ≤400 meters per pixel,
with the rest at spatial resolution ≤1,600 meters per pixel.[87]

The lack of solid requirements had been a problem since proposal. Two project
managers struggled to manage a project without clear science drivers and definitions of success. The project necessarily had to execute replans several times without
the road map that a clear set of requirements could provide. It was being managed
by NASA Headquarters to its proposal—but with conflicting statements in the very
purpose of the mission that caused disagreement for years. A mission that proposed
comparative planetology but called the descope of the second planetoid acceptable
was self-contradictory, and nobody at the time was happy with the result.

———

A STRING OF TECHNICAL FAILURES

That spring, Dawn again requested restoration of the magnetometer to the mission, but
NASA said no.[88] Jim Robinson became Dawn Program Executive at NASA Headquarters,
replacing Kurt Lindstrom, who needed additional time to shepherd the larger New
Horizons mission through the National Environmental Policy Act process. Dawn
continued to pass reviews throughout the year and passed its CDR in June of 2004.[89]
The ATLO Readiness Review followed on 14–15 December 2004. The project passed,
officially entering Assembly, Test, and Launch Operations (ATLO), the assembly phase
led by Orbital, on 19 January 2005.[90]

Xenon Tank

The spacecraft's propellant was to be stored in a large tank, sized to carry nearly 500
kilograms of xenon, with a titanium liner welded from two pieces around the belly of

———

87   Rayman, M. D., Fraschetti, T. C., Raymond, C. A., & Russell, C. T. (2006). "Dawn: A mission in
development for exploration of main belt asteroids Vesta and Ceres." *Acta Astronautica*, 58(11),
605–616. *https://doi.org/10.1016/j.actaastro.2006.01.014.*

88   Russell, C. T., Capaccioni, F., Coradini, A., De Sanctis, M. C., Feldman, W. C., Jaumann, R.,
Keller, H. U., McCord, T. B., McFadden, L. A., Mottola, S., Pieters, C. M., Prettyman, T. H.,
Raymond, C. A., Sykes, M. V., Smith, D. E., & Zuber, M. T. (2007). "Dawn Mission to Vesta and
Ceres: Symbiosis Between Terrestrial Observations and Robotic Exploration." *Earth, Moon,
and Planets*, 101(1–2), 65–91. *https://doi.org/10.1007/s11038-007-9151-9.*

89   Russell, C. T. (2004, August). "Dawn Successfully Passes Critical Design Review." *Dawn's Early
Light*, 3(3). 1.

90   Russell, C. T. (2005, March). "Dawn Mission Status." *Dawn's Early Light*, 4(3). 1; Morris, J.
(2005, June 13). "Discovery program to release revamped AO." *Aviation Week's Aerospace Daily
& Defense Report*, 214(51).

the tank and covered with a composite overwrap. Construction of this xenon tank and a spare was complete. After a few tests were run on the flight tank, it was inserted into the cylindrical core of the spacecraft structure and screwed into place so that ATLO could proceed, taking the remaining xenon tank qualification tests off the critical path to regain much-needed schedule margin. Since the flight tank had passed its initial tests, this was considered a low-risk move. However, the tank failed a test after confirmation, bursting at a pressure lower than the nominal operating pressure and just below that at which the tank would qualify.[91] Stunned, the team rallied quickly to determine what could be done and whether the flight tank already installed in the spacecraft could be trusted.[92] Meanwhile, spacecraft integration continued. The team was stuck with the tank already installed inside the spacecraft, but the spacecraft could not proceed to launch without certainty that it would work.

The team was running out of options and out of time. One solution that remained viable throughout the six months of analysis and review, however, was one of the simplest. The team could simply lower the amount of fuel in the tank to a level that ensured that pressures would not rise to the critical level. Once the team had a better estimate of the amount of fuel required to reach and orbit Vesta and then Ceres, they would be able to load the tank more precisely and see if that changed the analysis. The calculations were done, reserve propellant was added, and the analysis was repeated. The mission did not require that the tank be filled to the tested level; at a reduced load—say, 425 kilograms rather than the planned 450 kilograms—the xenon had more room to expand, even in situations like a hot summer day on the launch pad in Florida, should the air conditioning cooling the spacecraft break down. The team's own analysis supported this, but NASA required outside review.

The new Discovery and New Frontiers Program Office (D&NFPO) got involved. The office, explained program manager Todd May, knew that the team at JPL knew how to build and operate a planetary mission, but "the program office could make real contributions to problem solving and decision-making, and we could bring technical expertise to bear when needed. We would not impose [Marshall Space Flight Center's] specific set of 'how-to' rules on them. Instead, we wanted to focus our energies almost entirely on enabling and supporting the success of these project teams. We strove for trust and mutual respect, not control." This approach was put to the test on the xenon tank. Earlier, the program office had been able to help JPL engineers working on Dawn understand the behavior of the 454 kilograms of xenon because of their direct experience with superfluid helium slosh dynamics on another mission, Gravity Probe B. When the xenon tank failed just below the qualifying pressure, pro-

91   May, T. (2008, December). "Cooperation, Not Control." *Ask Magazine.*
92   Niebur, S. (2009, 12 August). Personal interview with T. Fraschetti. Located in "Dawn" file, NASA Historical Reference Collection, History Division, NASA Headquarters, Washington, DC.

gram managers got involved again. "Focusing on the goal of mission success rather than the letter of the law of requirements," reported May, "the Discovery Program Office grabbed pressure vessel experts and worked alongside the project to develop the recommendations and rationale to lower the operating pressure while maintaining mission performance requirements. This avoided the significant delay and expense that redesigning, rebuilding, and requalifying the tank—which was already installed on the vehicle—would have caused."[93]

Initially worried, Tom Fraschetti was reassured by the interventions. To be sure that the somewhat inelegant solution of filling the tank only partway would provide acceptable margin, the team had to truly understand the failure—and prove that to outside review teams from the Discovery Program Office and elsewhere. Since the flight tank was tucked away inside the spacecraft at Orbital and not available for pressure testing, the team took the qualification tanks apart, examined the splits, and tested the materials in many ways to be sure that the failure was understood and that the flight tank at the 425-kilogram fill and predicted pressures would not burst. "That was very costly," said Fraschetti. "I was paying for an army of experts doing this, and experts with varied opinions."[94]

It didn't happen quickly. "The solution was, now that we know where the break point is, to put in less xenon and that's what we did. We could make that decision immediately. But people involved in this process had to investigate it to death," said Chris Russell, the Principal Investigator, "and we had difficulty in getting the review committee to release the report so we could go forward."[95]

The team was finally able to satisfy the review panels, reporting the results at a conference in 2005: "The root causes for the reduced pressure at rupture are now known and how to build stronger tanks understood."[96] The change in tank fill did not require other engineering trades for the mission lifetime or science return within the level-one requirements.[97]

93   May, T. (2008, December). "Cooperation, Not Control." *Ask Magazine.*

94   Niebur, S. (2009, 12 August). Personal interview with T. Fraschetti. Located in "Dawn" file, NASA Historical Reference Collection, History Division, NASA Headquarters, Washington, DC.

95   Niebur, S. (2009, 24 March). Personal interview with C. Russell. Located in "Dawn" file, NASA Historical Reference Collection, History Division, NASA Headquarters, Washington, DC.

96   Russell, C. T. (2005). "Dawn Discovery Mission: Status Report." *Proceedings of 6th IAA International Conference on Low-Cost Planetary Missions*, 6, 283–289. Retrieved from *https:// escholarship.org/uc/item/2xr140qr.*

97   Niebur, S. (2009, 12 August). Personal interview with T. Fraschetti. Located in "Dawn" file, NASA Historical Reference Collection, History Division, NASA Headquarters, Washington, DC.

Ion Propulsion Development

It was not the only hardware issue to emerge. In January 2000, Hughes Space & Communications Company, which built the Deep Space-1 ion engine and which was going to rebuild it for Dawn, sold itself to The Boeing Company, which had less interest in the technology. Managers rotated rapidly through the ion engine unit, their top priority rarely the ion engine itself. Word was that Boeing intended to sell off the unit, which meant its managers were more determined to prove their worth *outside* of the division in order to preserve their position in the company. Meanwhile, technicians also rotated through the unit. The union shop meant that technicians who had greater seniority could replace more junior technicians, even if their specialties were not an exact match. Many technicians coming into the project had to be trained to work on the ion engines. In other words, the mission lost the heritage that they had thought they bought by contracting with the same company that had built Deep Space-1.

Management churn, with five general managers in three years, made it difficult to work with the company at the management level. Fraschetti talked to managers and even the president of the unit. They made agreements, but nothing seemed to stick. Eventually, even Charles Elachi, Director of Jet Propulsion Laboratory, intervened, making a trip to the company in person to secure new commitments to the completion of the project on time and on budget. Even that didn't stick. "If you got a commitment from somebody, three months later he would be gone and you have to go get the commitment again," remembered Fraschetti. "And then, ultimately in the middle of the project, they did sell it and another company took them over."[98]

New management arrived. Some engineers stayed after the acquisition. Some left. The Dawn team had a terrible time during this churn. "It was bad," said Fraschetti. "But, on the good side, once they were all in place, we did get a real management commitment out of them. They really were committed, which was the first time. Of course, we were already six or eight months late in delivering."[99] Worse, as Orbital lagged behind, they faulted the late delivery of the ion engines, pointing to that as a reason that they, too, could not live up to their contract. Orbital now had a good excuse for not meeting milestones, as the ion propulsion system delivery became later and later.

Although the ion propulsion power unit was designed to be exactly the same as the one flown on Deep Space-1, the actual implementation of the design surprised even the Dawn managers. Fraschetti said, "The problem was that while the actual electronic design was good, in fact, it was an excellent design, the packaging was a disaster." Assembly and test of the units showed problem after problem, as parts failed, unsuit-

---

98   Niebur, S. (2009, 12 August). Personal interview with T. Fraschetti. Located in "MESSENGER" file, NASA Historical Reference Collection, History Division, NASA Headquarters, Washington, DC.

99   Ibid.

able parts were purchased, and incorrect parts were installed. "They were buying the wrong parts, or they'd buy the right parts and still put the wrong ones in."[100] When a simple bump of the soldering iron weakened a stack capacitor and caused it to explode, the project, JPL management, and NASA Headquarters considered that the last straw. "If you'd looked at the picture of the hardware incident, you would think the whole box was blown up," said Keyur Patel, who was later the mission project manager. He explained that a blown capacitor created a cloud of black dust. "It looks like there is a lot of collateral damage when, in reality, it's localized collateral damage with a lot of soot thrown all over the place."[101] The capacitor was replaced and the box put back together in three days, but the effects of this explosion would last much longer.

The project decided that the ion engine team needed JPL direction. Chuck Garner, the ion propulsion system engineer, began to work onsite at the company every day, directing the contractor team and enforcing proven procedures.[102] But even this direction was not enough to rescue the unit. "We just had failure after failure after failure after failure with that thing until we finally actually, at some point, just brought it in-house," said Tom Fraschetti.[103]

The Jet Propulsion Laboratory required the company to relinquish the unit, the spare parts, the boxes, the paperwork—everything—and brought it all back to the lab to finish. They looked for help and found the original designer of the unit, who was no longer working at the El Segundo plant. JPL hired him on as a consultant, and that helped the team move past their problems to complete the unit. Fraschetti also credited JPL's expertise: "We got our best techs in there. They were careful. The inspection was so much more thorough here," and reassembly went smoothly, without causing additional problems.[104]

ATLO Delays

While work on the West Coast was getting back on schedule, on the East Coast, all was not proceeding smoothly. At first, the JPL team was not aware of the delays because the Orbital manager was protective of his people and their work. As time went on, the project became worried, and the flight system manager began to spend more time onsite at the contractor. "What we needed at Orbital was the same thing we needed at

---

100   Ibid.

101   Niebur, S. (2009, 10 August). Personal interview with K. Patel. Located in "Discovery Program" file, NASA Historical Reference Collection, History Division, NASA Headquarters, Washington, DC.

102   Niebur, S. (2009, 11 August). Personal interview with C. Raymond. Located in "Dawn" file, NASA Historical Reference Collection, History Division, NASA Headquarters, Washington, DC.

103   Niebur, S. (2009, 12 August). Personal interview with T. Fraschetti. Located in "Dawn" file, NASA Historical Reference Collection, History Division, NASA Headquarters, Washington, DC.

104   Ibid.

Boeing," said Carol Raymond. The spacecraft harness was a difficult build for Orbital and took significantly longer than expected. The flight harness was not ready at the start of ATLO, and the workarounds increased the cost. The project struggled with these three problems, but the team felt that they had solutions. The solutions, however, would require additional financial resources, as the team had used all their reserves. Fraschetti returned to NASA Headquarters to request additional funds for the project. It did not go easy.[105]

STANDDOWN

On 11 October 2005, NASA Headquarters, frustrated at the string of technical and cost problems on the mission, abruptly told the Dawn mission team to stand down pending the outcome of a review. At this point, the projected cost was as much as 11 percent to 20 percent over the approved $373 million budget, and the schedule was delayed by up to 14 months.[106] All work except "that which was critical to maintaining the viability of the Dawn mission to launch on a delayed schedule, still achieving all of its scientific objectives" was halted.

Russell characterized the standdown as "in response to concerns about the availability of funding in [Fiscal Year 2006] to cover any problems that might arise during environmental and performance testing," but agency officials remembered it as more than a Fiscal Year 2006 issue.[107] Colleen Hartman, then–Deputy Associate Administrator for science, was quoted in the media as saying: "We had concerns about scientific issues and about cost containment," citing a 20 percent increase in cost.[108] "There was too much risk left on the table to go forward."[109]

Although two-thirds of the JPL engineers and other project personnel were taken off the project during this phase, not all Dawn team members and contractors stood down in late 2005.[110] A core set of the mission team continued to work on test procedures, doing dry runs on the testbed and identifying the problems that remained.[111]

105   Niebur, S. (2009, 11 August). Personal interview with C. Raymond. Located in "Dawn" file, NASA Historical Reference Collection, History Division, NASA Headquarters, Washington, DC.

106   Berger, B. (2005, 21 November). "Technical, Management Problems Prompted Delay of Dawn Mission." *SpaceNews.* 11; David, L. (2005, 7 November). "NASA Dawn asteroid mission told to 'stand down.'" Space.com.

107   Russell, C. T. (2005, November). "Dawn Mission Status." *Dawn's Early Light*, 4(2).

108   Cooper, C. (2005, 18 November). "Future of JPL's Dawn mission is in doubt." *La Cañada Valley Sun.*

109   Clark, S. (2006, 27 March). "NASA Restarts Once-dead Dawn Asteroid Mission." *Spaceflight Now.*

110   Cooper, C. (2005, 18 November). "Future of JPL's Dawn mission is in doubt." *La Cañada Valley Sun.*

111   Raymond, C. (2006, April). "Dawn Spacecraft Nearing Final Integration." *Dawn's Early Light*, 5(1). 2.

Solvable problems were addressed during the standdown; more difficult ones were put into the replan. "We had open issues," said Patel. "The standdown period actually helped in getting some of those resolved."[112] Project spending decreased drastically during the three-month standdown, and the pace of mission readiness slowed to a crawl. Through it all, the team believed that they would be allowed to restart; education and public outreach activities continued, with Jacinta Behne of McRel, a knowledge and educational outreach company, still working to engage the public, inviting them to submit their names for the "Send Your Name to the Asteroid Belt" campaign, where eventually 365,000 names were etched on an 8- by 8-millimeter microchip and bolted to the spacecraft.[113]

That the mission was having failures during ATLO was not debatable. But among the team members, the need for a standdown was. The project team viewed the technical failures as simply part of the design process—typical for any project of this size.[114] NASA Headquarters, meanwhile, already vigilant because of Dawn's recurring problems with the xenon tanks and the ion propulsion units, was watching the project closely. Dawn was the first project in development after the very costly 2003 overruns by Deep Impact and MESSENGER, and the agency could not afford another mission with the same kinds of overruns. There was no reserve line in the Discovery Program capable of handling those issues again, and the operational environment was charged with caution. If NASA management missed signs of trouble on a mission now, it could make the whole program vulnerable.

There was a new dedication to catching technical problems early and intervening before a mission ran tens of millions of dollars over budget. Couple that vigilance with a program executive overseeing his first NASA project; a Discovery program manager and a division director, both of whom had arrived well after the overruns (and Dawn's cancellation) in 2003; and the third Associate Administrator in as many years, and the system was not inclined to forgive failures. Subsystem after subsystem on Dawn had failures, and the program executive duly reported them to his management. With each failure, NASA Headquarters lost confidence in the ability of the Dawn team to execute the mission. Dawn failures became the talk of the halls, and there was a widespread perception that the team was not progressing as they should. When the ion propulsion power unit built by Boeing failed, the project told the program executive.

---

112   Niebur, S. (2009, 10 August). Personal interview with K. Patel. Located in "Discovery Program" file, NASA Historical Reference Collection, History Division, NASA Headquarters, Washington, DC.

113   Jones, K. C. (2005, 12 December). "More than 29,000 people signed up this week to have their names put on a microchip that will travel aboard a spaceship for the Dawn mission." TechWeb.com.

114   Niebur, S. (2009, 12 August). Personal interview with T. Fraschetti. Located in "Dawn" file, NASA Historical Reference Collection, History Division, NASA Headquarters, Washington, DC.

The program executive reported the failure to the division director. The Dawn project was told to stand down.

The shutdown came before the reviews, not after—a move that frustrated the Dawn leadership. NASA assembled no Integrated Action Team to review the project before shutdown. The Discovery and New Frontiers Program Office at Marshall Space Flight Center did not conduct a review. The NASA Engineering and Safety Center was not called on. Instead, NASA Headquarters told the team to stand down and *then* sent an Integrated Action Team to gauge progress on all the major subsystems, so that agency leadership could make an informed decision. The team showed the review board the spacecraft at Orbital and the status of the subsystems. Tom Fraschetti, the project manager, remembered that members of the review board were surprised to see the progress that had been made, saying, "I don't know what kind of information was being passed by our program exec, but the board came onboard thinking that we only had a few subsystems done. When they came onboard, all the instruments were delivered, and 90 percent of the spacecraft was together and working."[115]

NASA, however, had seen subsystem after subsystem and part after part fail during ATLO, to the point that it was almost an expected result, and the perception was that the existing team was not capable of making it to the launch pad unassisted. So, the team changed. During the nearly six-month standdown, NASA cut Dawn's funding drastically. There was no longer any money to pay the salaries of all of the existing team members. For instance, the funding for the operations team was cut entirely. "So, they all went and got other jobs, which you would expect. And so, when we started up again, it was all new people," said Fraschetti.[116]

NASA was cautious to keep funding critical positions at Orbital and some at the Jet Propulsion Laboratory, not including the project manager. "There is no way that standing down was going to save any money," said Chris Russell. "All of that period of time was just an added cost to Dawn from the management side of the house."[117]

Fraschetti also later expressed frustration about the standdown, saying, "If they would have come in there and said, 'You know, Tom, you ain't cutting it. I'm going to put Keyur in your place,' and let him just take over, they would have finished that job for no more than $35 million, launched it earlier than they did because we lost months of time in the standoff. It dragged on for months and months. It would have saved them a lot of time and a lot of money. It would have been a lot better. But they did it in a really odd way. And I have to blame the program exec, because I think he

---

115   Ibid.
116   Ibid.
117   Niebur, S. (2009, 24 March). Personal interview with C. Russell. Located in "Dawn" file, NASA Historical Reference Collection, History Division, NASA Headquarters, Washington, DC.

just kept running up there. Of course, you know what happened to him."[118] (Shortly after reinstatement, Dawn's program executive was arrested and imprisoned on an unrelated matter.)[119]

In a January 2006 interview, Russell explained that the team's Earned Value Management system, recently implemented by many JPL projects in response to the Mars mission failures, had indicated a potential $7 million overrun. A subsequent grass roots estimate yielded an even higher cost, $17 million. Funded cost and schedule reserve brought the potential overrun to $40 million, which was enough to alarm NASA officials.[120]

Russell characterized the standdown as frustrating, saying, "We were going full bore toward launch, running as fast as we could. We saw the finish line in sight." But Andy Dantzler, the division director, reported a picture not nearly as rosy, saying that Dawn was running behind schedule and the launch had already been expected to slip at least two months before the standdown.[121]

An independent review team, assembled by the D&NFPO, visited subcontractors, including L3, the manufacturer of troubled power processing units; the Dawn team at Orbital; and the Dawn team at the Jet Propulsion Laboratory.[122] After this work, they recommended the program's continuation but found a large number of outstanding major issues, cost growth of 20 percent, and a 14-month launch delay.[123] In all, the review found 29 unresolved technical issues, worrying NASA managers, who were not convinced that the mission's technical problems were close to resolution.[124]

The Principal Investigator complained about the large number of reviews to which his project was subjected. Russell later said, "Reviewers are most sensitive to the issues of the previous mission in the queue and trying to make sure your mission does not make the same mistake as the last one." He added: "Perceived risk is almost as dangerous—or perhaps even more at times—than real risk."[125]

---

118   Niebur, S. (2009, 12 August). Personal interview with T. Fraschetti. Located in "Dawn" file, NASA Historical Reference Collection, History Division, NASA Headquarters, Washington, DC.

119   "NASA office searched in child-porn probe." (2006, 31 March). *NBC News.* Downloaded from *https://www.nbcnews.com/id/wbna12102570* on 20 August 2021.

120   Clark, S. (2006, 3 March). "Probe built to visit asteroids killed in budget snarl." *Spaceflight Now.*

121   Groshong, K. (2006, 3 March). "Dawn asteroid mission killed, says report." *New Scientist.*

122   Russell, C. T. (2005, November). "Dawn Mission Status." *Dawn's Early Light,* 4(2).

123   David, L. (2006, 3 March). "NASA's Dawn asteroid mission cancelled." Space.com.

124   Chang, A. (2006, 6 March). "Scientists lament cancelled NASA mission." AP; Groshong, K. (2005, 14 November). "NASA stall puzzles techies." *Pasadena Star News.*

125   Russell, C. (2007, 19 September). Presentation at the Discovery@15 workshop in Huntsville, Alabama.

NO BUCKS, NO BUCK ROGERS: DAWN CANCELED

It was a difficult time to need money at NASA. The Fiscal Year 2007 budget request in February proposed cutting the Science Mission Directorate research and analysis budget by an additional 15 percent across the board (following unexpected cuts in 2006, with cuts as high as 50 percent for astrobiology), and NASA was beginning to take heat for this decision on Capitol Hill. Although Dantzler had announced in January that Dawn's summer launch had been indefinitely postponed, the community was concerned most about the research and analysis cuts, and, following an Appropriations Committee hearing, planetary scientists were asked to appear before the House Science Committee and testify as to the impacts of the proposed budget.[126] On 2 March 2006, a Nobel laureate, a Cassini co-investigator, and a former Associate Administrator testified as to the deleterious effects on current research, smaller missions, and future students. Fran Bagenal, professor at the University of Colorado at Boulder and a co-investigator on Cassini, noted the planned decrease in NASA science mission launches and highlighted data "that basically says NASA is going out of business."[127] Shortly after the hearing, Mary Cleave announced that the Dawn mission was canceled.[128]

NASA announced few details publicly. Dantzler characterized it as "the fiscally responsible thing to do," saying, "I believe it's the right one for the good of the Discovery Program" and indicating that the costs-to-go must have greatly exceeded the funds available, since the "sunk costs" already totaled $257 million.[129] "When we looked at the standdown information at that time, we felt in the [Science Mission Directorate] that there was too much risk still left on the table to go forward." Colleen Hartman, now Deputy Associate Administrator for the Science Mission Directorate, later characterized the increase in cost as "approximately 20 percent."[130]

Scientists were disappointed, and vocal. Bruce Barraclaugh, a co-investigator and researcher at Los Alamos National Laboratory, called the decision "heart wrenching."[131] Lucy McFadden, a co-investigator from the University of Maryland, said, "There are hundreds of people in this country and in Europe who have worked on the project for four years and had committed another decade to it…. What can I say? It makes me cry."[132] Bill Feldman, a co-investigator and lead of the GRaND instrument built

---

126   Cheng, A. (2006, 24 January). "NASA postpones mission to visit asteroids." Associated Press.

127   Morris, J. (2006, 3 March). "Scientists on Capitol Hill decry NASA's science budget request." *Aviation Daily & Defense Report.*

128   Groshong, K. (2006, 3 March). "Dawn asteroid mission killed, says report." *New Scientist.*

129   David, L. (2006, 3 March). "NASA's Dawn asteroid mission cancelled." Space.com; *The New York Times.* (2006, 28 March).

130   Clark, S. (2006, 27 March). "NASA Restarts Once-dead Dawn Asteroid Mission." *Spaceflight Now.*

131   Chang, A. (2006, 6 March). "Scientists lament cancelled NASA mission." AP.

132   David, Leonard, "NASA's Dawn asteroid mission cancelled," Space.com, 3 March 2006.

for Dawn at Los Alamos, admitted that he was stunned, but regrouped, saying, "We need to suck in our guts and rehabilitate this mission and fly it one way or another."[133]

A few days later, Cleave addressed the topic with the National Research Council Space Studies Board, saying that the cost was high and unresolved technical and management issues threatened to push it even higher; project managers couldn't get the project estimate back in the box, despite the mission's maturity, having already spent $284 million of the $446 million estimate to complete.[134] Rumors abounded, and articles were published stating that NASA was "cannibalizing its science missions to pay for the space shuttle and the space station and future plans to send astronauts back to the moon."[135]

On 6 March 2006, the Jet Propulsion Laboratory officially appealed to the Office of the Administrator using a new institutional procedure, informally called the reclama process, widely seen as the first time in recent memory that a NASA center challenged a NASA Headquarters decision on a mission.[136] Three days later, NASA announced that it would consider reinstating the mission. A team that included a newly promoted Associate Administrator Rex Geveden and NASA Chief Engineer Chris Scolese was assembled for a review that included presentations from JPL and the Dawn Integrated Action Team, including, reportedly, additional information from JPL not provided to the Science Mission Directorate earlier in the year.

The review proceeded quietly while, at the annual meeting of the Lunar and Planetary Science Conference the following week, co-investigators and other researchers harshly criticized the cancellation.[137] Gerhard Neukum, a co-investigator and professor of planetary sciences at Germany's Freie Universität Berlin, said, "It's totally unacceptable what's happening now. NASA has responsibility to their cooperation partners first and foremost before they go to the last resort of canceling a mission." The community was alternately suspicious that the money had been repurposed and confused about procedure, a fact not improved when Dantzler would not address the specifics of the cancellation publicly, saying, "It would not be wise to go into technical detail."[138]

Geveden's team reviewed the information and agreed that partially filling the xenon tanks would likely prevent tank failure. After significant work to identify the root

133   Chang, A. (2006, 6 March). "Scientists lament cancelled NASA mission." AP.

134   Leonard, D. (2006, 24 April). "Additional Information Prompts NASA To Reconsider Decision to Cancel Dawn." *SpaceNews.*

135   Chang, K., and W. Leary. (2006, 28 March). "Weeks After Killing It, NASA Resurrects Mission to Visit Asteroids." *The New York Times.* A13.

136   Alexander, A. (2006, 27 March). "A new day for Dawn." *Planetary Society*; Chang, A. (2006, 20 March). "NASA scrutinizes cancelled mission." Associated Press.

137   Malik, T. (2006, 3 April). "Researchers applaud NASA decision to revive asteroid mission." *SpaceNews.*

138   David, L. (2006, 17 March). "NASA's Dawn mission cancellation under review." Space.com.

cause, the power processing unit failures were deemed "understood" and blamed on transient thermal conditions in the test configuration. The project had a new process in place for replacing damaged capacitors and a plan forward that satisfied all the players. Later questions would be dealt with in the same way; when the project reached a pivotal point on which the experts from the Jet Propulsion Laboratory, the Discovery and New Frontiers Program Office, and the chief engineer's office had not been able to agree, Keyur Patel, the incoming project manager, called the parties together for an additional review of the requirements versus the risks. Their advice proved valuable in stopping an environmental test early. Patel had not only earned their trust but repaid it by asking advice again as needed.

"We believe, fundamentally, that there is not a flight hardware issue with those units, but rather a test configuration issue," said Geveden. "The technical resolution path seems pretty clear…. I think the risk posture on this mission is not atypical for this kind of mission. When you are doing deep planetary missions and dealing with the environments and the temperature regimes and the complication of integrating a suite of instruments, there are always pretty tall challenges."[139]

On 27 March 2006, NASA announced that the Dawn mission would be reinstated.[140] The originally approved mission, projected to launch in June 2006 at a cost of $373 million, was reinstated with a 13-month delay and an increase in the cost cap by $73 million, pushing the cost to $446 million. The reinstatement of the mission at this point was striking, leading reporters to ask whether the reversal was politically motivated, possibly by a NASA budget hearing before the House Appropriations panel, chaired by Rep. Frank Wolf, whose district included Orbital Space Sciences.[141] Colleen Hartman, now Deputy Associate Administrator for the Science Mission Directorate, told reporters, "The information on the table at the time was insufficient for us to feel comfortable going forward. Since that time there was additional information provided."[142] Rex Geveden simply said, "This is an example of how our system works now."[143]

Scientists, however, were relieved. "I'm astonished," said Lucy McFadden, a co-investigator, when the news dropped. "I'm excited. I'm ready to go."[144] Co-investigator Tom Prettyman of the GRaND instrument said, "Of course, we're in shock. We were in

---

139   Clark, S. (2006, 27 March). "NASA restarts once-dead asteroid mission." *Spaceflight Now*.

140   "NASA Reinstates the Dawn Mission." NASA Press Release 06-108.

141   Editorial. (2006, 10 April). *SpaceNews*. 18.

142   Clark, S. (2006, 27 March). "NASA restarts once-dead asteroid mission." *Spaceflight Now*.

143   Kridler, C. (2006, 28 March). "NASA: Mission to Asteroid Back On." *Florida Today*. See also David, L. (2005, 7 November). "NASA Dawn asteroid mission told to 'stand down.'" Space.com.

144   Chang, K., and Warren Leary. (2006, 28 March). "Weeks after killing it, NASA resurrects mission to visit asteroids." *The New York Times*.

shock when it was canceled, and we were pleasantly surprised when it was reinstated."[145] The Planetary Society issued a statement supporting the decision.[146] Geveden cave-ated the reinstatement, stating, "There is no sense in which it's okay to overrun on budget.... But you do have to recognize that for...missions of this nature, cost over-runs are pretty typical."[147]

Discovery mission leadership in the early days would have disagreed, as there were minimal overruns in the Discovery Program prior to Deep Impact and MESSENGER in 2003. Deputy Associate Administrator Hartman, a key player in the earlier reviews, indicated the difficulty of determining Dawn's fate, saying: "What we had here was a very gut-wrenching decision and significant management and technical hurdles to overcome, and we're happy to be going forward."[148] This time, it did not go unnoticed that the unexpected increase to the program would affect future mission selection options.[149]

Chris Russell was unapologetic in his criticism of NASA Headquarters, saying at the time: "The stand down spent money but did not progress us meaningfully toward launch. Also, we now have to rehire folks and retrain to get to launch. So, this whole process has wasted money. It defies logic what they did."[150] Years later, he maintained this attitude, saying, "There was never any reason to cancel the mission technically," and repeating his previous claim, "as far as we could tell the decisions were made totally on a desire to move money around."[151]

The next issue of the project newsletter indicated the extent of the mission changes: an outstanding need for almost $54 million more and new project managers at both the Jet Propulsion Laboratory and Orbital.[152] Keyur Patel, former Deputy Project Manager on Deep Impact, replaced Tom Fraschetti at the Jet Propulsion Laboratory; Ann Grandfield, former Deputy Project Manager under John McCarthy, became Project Manager at Orbital.[153] Coincidentally, the project management team at NASA Headquarters also changed at about this time, with Dave Lindstrom taking over the position of Program Scientist after Susan Niebur left NASA Headquarters in January, and with Kurt Lindstrom returning as program executive.

---

145   Arnold, J. (2006, 3 April). "NASA sends Dawn to space; asteroid program cancelled, reinstated." *Albuquerque Journal.*

146   Alexander, A. (2006, 27 March). "A new day for Dawn." *The Planetary Society.*

147   Carreau, M. (2006, 28 March). "NASA back on track with asteroids." *Houston Chronicle.*

148   Kridler, C. (2006, 28 March). "NASA: Mission to Asteroid Back On." *Florida Today.*

149   Malik, T. (2006, 27 March). "NASA reinstates cancelled asteroid mission." Space.com.

150   Clark, S. (2006, 27 March). "NASA restarts once-dead asteroid mission." *Spaceflight Now.*

151   Niebur, S. (2009, 24 March). Personal interview with C. Russell. Located in "Dawn" file, NASA Historical Reference Collection, History Division, NASA Headquarters, Washington, DC.

152   Russell, C. T. (2006, April). "Dawn Mission Status." *Dawn's Early Light*, 5(1). 1.

153   Raymond, C. (2006, April). "Dawn Status Report." *Dawn's Early Light*, 5(1). 1.

Despite these project management changes, which had proved so detrimental in the case of MESSENGER, the mission team continued its work, successfully passing the Environmental Test Readiness Review on 6–7 September 2006 and proceeding to acoustics, dynamics, and thermo-vac testing—the last at the Naval Research Lab, where the ion thrusters would be tested.[154] Work continued to progress in advance of the Post-Environmental Test Review (19 March 2007) and Pre-Ship Review (20–21 March), the last official hurdles before the spacecraft could be shipped to Cape Canaveral.[155]

Leading from Fear

During the standdown in late 2005, John McNamee, the Deputy Director for Solar System Exploration at JPL, served as interim project manager. Keyur Patel and Mike Sierchio, both veterans of Deep Impact, were part of the Integrated Action Team reviewing Dawn.[156] Their assessment was harsh toward project leadership, and as a result of the reviews, JPL dismissed the project manager and the mission flight system manager. Russell reportedly stood up and argued against the dismissal of the flight system manager, as he had great confidence in her work, but it wasn't enough. The culture demanded her replacement with someone perceived as tougher—more "in-your-face"—who would "insist" that Orbital deliver parts on time. The payload manager was also blamed for his calm management style as management and the Integrated Action Team argued for a sterner, more aggressive replacement.[157]

Lab leadership naming Keyur Patel as project manager guaranteed a more aggressive style. Even Tom Fraschetti, his predecessor, recognized in an interview years later that Patel's style worked. "When it came time to turn the project over to Keyur and his team, Keyur and his deputy just kind of cut right through…. And in fact, Dawn's a success because of it. That's not my style. I couldn't work in that environment, so it was actually best for me to move on and for him to take over."[158] Russell sounded similar notes, saying, "Keyur was really a tough manager. He wasn't trying to be liked. He was

---

154   Raymond, C. (2006, 2 October). "Environmental Testing of Dawn Spacecraft Begins." *Dawn's Early Light*, 5(2). 6.

155   Raymond, C. (2007, April). "Dawn ready to ship to launch site." *Dawn's Early Light*. 6(1).

156   Niebur, S. (2009, 10 August). Personal interview with K. Patel. Located in "Discovery Program" file, NASA Historical Reference Collection, History Division, NASA Headquarters, Washington, DC.

157   Niebur, S. (2009, 11 August). Personal interview with C. Raymond. Located in "Dawn" file, NASA Historical Reference Collection, History Division, NASA Headquarters, Washington, DC.

158   Niebur, S. (2009, 12 August). Personal interview with T. Fraschetti. Located in "Dawn" file, NASA Historical Reference Collection, History Division, NASA Headquarters, Washington, DC.

trying to get the job done."[159] The management style difference was stark. Patel was known to push the team hard and make clear when he was unhappy with their progress.

Patel explained to Orbital that their working relationship would change after the restart. Orbital's inexperience in launch-window-limited, long-lifetime deep space missions had been blamed in part for the ATLO delays, particularly in the delivery of the harness that partially prompted the standdown.

Patel learned from his experience on Deep Impact that having senior management present onsite at Ball every week helped speed deliveries. So, too, he believed, would it work for Dawn. From restart to the end of ATLO, either Patel, his deputy, the project system engineer, the chief engineer, or the mission assurance manager was at Orbital every week, in addition to visiting technical personnel.

"We always wanted to have boots on the ground," said Patel. "We're going to be there. If we're there, we're going to be in every meeting you have, and we're going to work with you to get this thing delivered on time as scheduled."[160] Dawn leadership at Orbital initially resisted.

"Orbital thought that they were way overboard, and maybe they were," said Kurt Lindstrom, the program executive, but the new approach identified issues with the spacecraft software and planned testing program. "Orbital's thought of testing was more commercial. You know, they test one to qual[ify], and then the rest of them are off an assembly line. But this spacecraft was not an assembly line. It had been modified" to operate well in deep space and over a long lifetime. Orbital's assumptions were not valid for this application, and the course correction was difficult. Orbital management brought in Dave Shiderly as ATLO manager; Patel would call him "one of the best guys I've ever worked with."[161] Patel also had warm words for the flight system engineer, Joe Makowski, and credited key Orbital personnel with working to understand the different requirements of a deep space mission and leading the team there to success.

Patel's aggressive style had served him well as he led Deep Impact to the launch pad, and he employed many of the same techniques for Dawn. He became known as a "closer" at JPL, capable of delivering troubled projects to space. Lab management praised his results, but key members of the Dawn team were not universally happy with the experience. "We had an Orbital manager quit because of him," said Russell.

---

159   Niebur, S. (2009, 24 March). Personal interview with C. Russell. Located in "Discovery Program" file, NASA Historical Reference Collection, History Division, NASA Headquarters, Washington, DC.

160   Niebur, S. (2009, 10 August). Personal interview with K. Patel. Located in "Discovery Program" file, NASA Historical Reference Collection, History Division, NASA Headquarters, Washington, DC.

161   Niebur, S. (2009, 31 July). Personal interview with K. Lindstrom. Located in the "Discovery Program" file, NASA Historical Reference Collection, History Division, NASA Headquarters, Washington, DC.

"I don't know if Orbital will ever work with JPL again." [162] Some employees wondered whether JPL chose hostile project management to seem tough on subcontractors or overruns, or whether JPL considered it the only way to manage a troubled project.[163]

Kurt Lindstrom, Dawn's program executive, favored a strong project manager—one that was "willing to push back on both their customer and their people,"[164] rather than being accommodating to everyone and taking action on each recommendation.

During the standdown, Tom Gavin, deputy director of the Space and Earth Science Programs Directorate at the Jet Propulsion Laboratory, offered Patel the position of project manager, and Patel led the re-plan. "I did not inherit somebody else's plan," said Patel. "The plan that was put forth is a plan that I had fully vested interest and commitment to." The largest constraint on the plan was schedule, as the project aimed for a June launch. A launch later than the fall would require unacceptable levels of change, as the ion propulsion system would have been insufficient to get the spacecraft to Vesta. When the project restarted, work moved into high gear. Just a year from launch, there was a lot of "open paper" on the project: waivers, requirements, and problem failure reports.[165]

The team completed the replan and included a punch list, a technique for finishing the work and moving personnel off the project. As they had on Deep Impact, Patel and Rick Grammier, director of Solar System Exploration at JPL, surveyed the status of all subsystems. As each subsystem neared completion, Patel checked again, just as a general contractor would on a home improvement project. The punch list created a common understanding of expectations, and as the items on the list were completed, people moved on to other work. The technique worked well and was repeated on other projects at JPL.[166]

The standdown review, and the others that followed, put additional pressure on the project. From the start, at the Preliminary Mission and Systems Review, the project was sensitive to being compared to previous projects. As members of the review board asked pointed questions about plans for development—digging in to understand where Dawn stood in relation to mistakes made on previous projects—the reviewers

---

162   Niebur, S. (2009, 24 March). Personal interview with C. Russell. Located in the "Discovery Program" file, NASA Historical Reference Collection, History Division, NASA Headquarters, Washington, DC.

163   Niebur, S. (2009, 11 August). Personal interview with C. Raymond. Located in "Dawn" file, NASA Historical Reference Collection, History Division, NASA Headquarters, Washington, DC.

164   Niebur, S. (2009, 31 July). Personal interview with K. Lindstrom. Located in the "Discovery Program" file, NASA Historical Reference Collection, History Division, NASA Headquarters, Washington, DC.

165   Niebur, S. (2009, 10 August). Personal interview with K. Patel. Located in "Discovery Program" file, NASA Historical Reference Collection, History Division, NASA Headquarters, Washington, DC.

166   Ibid.

would often slip, calling Dawn "Deep Impact." There was laughter in the room the first few times. After that, slips provoked more intense emotions for members of the project—particularly those who had indeed studied issues and lessons learned on previous projects. Dawn had more reviews than they expected at proposal, as did all the missions at that time, and project leadership lamented this fact at workshops.[167]

Technical Issues

As the only U.S. instrument, issues with GRaND were of correspondingly high priority. Development went smoothly, with only "one near-catastrophic problem," according to Tom Prettyman, a co-investigator. The instrument was put carefully into a vacuum chamber for a thermal test. After the first two cycles of extreme temperatures, several of the sensors did not work. Disassembly showed that the photomultiplier tube mechanical design itself was flawed, resulting in cracked tubes after thermal expansion and contraction. Prettyman convened a peer-review group to address the issue. When the Dawn team at large was told of the problem, Holger Sierks, the framing camera Principal Investigator, immediately offered to send the GRaND team additional photomultiplier tubes—the same ones used by his German high-energy physics colleagues. Mechanical engineer Steve Storms did an analysis to identify the root cause and redesigned the support brackets, getting quick feedback on the design from the committee. Prettyman gave credit to preflight testing, ample schedule, and budget built into the project for the project's ability to recover quickly from the failure.

"It was a very quick turnaround," he said. "You have to have the engineers right there working with you to do that. It was just amazing how they were able to come up with a new design and then implement it." Sierk's offer of help was also memorable. "We ended up not using the tubes, but it's just a very gracious thing." As for management, Chris Russell encouraged the team to keep working toward launch. Payload management Ed Miller and Betina Pavri, both of the Jet Propulsion Laboratory, were worried as ever, but Prettyman added, "They trusted us, but they were there to help us if we needed it…. We had the A team for the project interface. It just worked out very well."[168]

Meanwhile, the team ran into problems when it was time for thermal vacuum testing. Orbital fully supported the mission and would have supported a delay in using their facility, but the thermal chamber at Orbital was simply too small. The team had planned to use the thermal vacuum chamber at Goddard Space Flight Center, but the delay meant that the chamber was occupied with Space Shuttle materials, which

167   Russell, C., et al. (2007, 19 September). "Dawn Discovery Mission to Vesta and Ceres." Slides presented at Discovery@15 Conference. Susan Niebur's personal collection.

168   Niebur, S. (2010, 1 March). Personal interview with T. Prettyman. Located in "Dawn" file, NASA Historical Reference Collection, History Division, NASA Headquarters, Washington, DC.

could not be bumped. No other East Coast thermal vac chamber was large enough, available, and with sufficient specifications for use at that time. The team found one that might work at the nearby Naval Research Laboratory. However, the Dawn project had to modify the chamber to add additional pumping capacity and cold fingers to extract the xenon from the beam, augmenting the chamber out of their own funds. The spacecraft passed its full baseline test at Orbital and was thus shipped to the Naval Research Laboratory.

Then, the unthinkable happened. As Patel recalled:

We had a test readiness review before we closed the key vac door. And at that point, every subsystem swears up and down that they've reviewed all the data, and everything is go, or these are the issues, and this is why it's okay to proceed…. [We] closed the door, and the next day we discovered that one of the [power processing units] has a failure…. There was a set of senior people at Orbital who wanted to break chamber that day. And I said, "No, we're not going to break chamber that day. We're going to plow through." The way I brought everybody around to that realization was the following: Thermal vac test is not a performance test. It is a test you do to validate the thermal model. So, if you have failure in one box, you can go to the other box, do the test, but you have to be, now, really diligent should another failure happen, how you control the stuff in there…. And in a way, I'm glad we discovered this inside the chamber, because, if we had discovered this outside the chamber, the June launch would have been jeopardized. In fact, it would not have happened.[169]

The project was now, once again, in a bad situation. Politically and financially, they really needed to make the June launch. They did not have enough reserves to make it to September, and either way, after September the planned trajectory would need modifications. The team worked the issues in parallel and ran the tests.

Dave Shiderly, the Assembly, Test, and Launch Operations manager, began to rework the ATLO schedule to make it happen. Once the thermal vac test was complete, the team broke chamber, dropped several panels, pulled the power processing unit box off, and sent it to the Jet Propulsion Laboratory in a special suitcase. After the fix, the team shipped it back, reinserted it into the spacecraft, and prepared to do the penalty tests before it was time to deliver it to the Cape. JPL and Orbital disagreed on the extent of penalty test required. Patel pushed for skipping any penalty tests, since the whole spacecraft had already completed the whole series of environmental tests, but Orbital leadership wanted to rerun the full suite. The team discussed options, and then Patel proposed a compromise: rerun just the acoustic test to validate the reassembly of the

---

169   Niebur, S. (2009, 10 August). Personal interview with K. Patel. Located in "Discovery Program" file, NASA Historical Reference Collection, History Division, NASA Headquarters, Washington, DC.

large panels on the spacecraft. They did so, at the Naval Research Lab, and it passed. Dawn went directly from there to the Cape.

Orbital's expertise in launching Earth-orbiting spacecraft had prepared them to work to a launch date. Working to an immovable launch date, such as those defined by planetary windows, presented greater difficulty. For his work leading up to an on-time delivery of the spacecraft to the launch pad, Patel called Shiderly "one of the heroes" of the Dawn mission.[170]

Even at the Cape, JPL management kept "boots on the ground" so that they were both aware of schedule and available for any concerns from the launch team. Several were in residence at KSC, and Patel flew in every week until launch.

As with many missions, the actual launch date slipped several times, from 20 June to 30 June because of launch vehicle readiness; from 30 June to 7 July after a crane pulley seized as they were loading the solids on the booster rocket as it sat on the launch pad; and after multiple difficulties with telemetry relay support.[171] NASA's requirement for telemetry during the ascent would not be waived as had been permitted on the lost CONTOUR spacecraft. The launch trajectory required support in the middle of the Atlantic, where there are no islands. The team booked a boat and an airplane. The U.S. Navy boat left its port on time, but as it traveled down the coast, it had engine trouble and missed its berth in the Panama Canal. A quick engine fix in Puerto Rico and the boat looked okay, but large waves slowed its arrival in the Atlantic.[172] As for the airplane, the original plans for a P-3 Orion surveillance aircraft were scrapped as it wasn't available during the new launch dates, and a second telemetry aircraft, Big Crow, lost pressurization in its cabin just before it was needed; it was grounded for repairs in Puerto Rico, unusable during the planned launch windows.[173] Finally, summer thunderstorms delayed the launch a few days in early July, leading Marc Rayman, the payload manager, to quip, "Weather isn't quite as predictable as many things in rocket science are."[174]

On 9 July, Jim Green, Planetary Science Division Director in the Science Mission Directorate, announced an additional delay to 15 July, as high seas were keeping the tracking ship, OTTER (Ocean-going Transportable Test and Evaluation Resource),

---

170   Ibid.

171   Raymond, C. (2007, April). "Dawn ready to ship to launch site." *Dawn's Early Light*, 6(1); Berger, B. (2007, 9 June). "NASA Confident of July Launch for Dawn Despite Issues." *SpaceNews*.

172   Niebur, S. (2009, 24 March). Personal interview with C. Russell. Located in "Dawn" file, NASA Historical Reference Collection, History Division, NASA Headquarters, Washington, DC.

173   May, T. (2008). "Cooperation Not Control." *ASK Magazine*. 12–15.

174   Kleeman, E. (2007, 3 July). "Decision on Dawn spacecraft launch is postponed." *Los Angeles Daily News*.

from moving into position off the coast of Africa.[175] Dawn's launch window would last only until 19 July. With only a few days left, the team faced a dilemma: fuel the second stage and commit to launching (once the second stage is fueled, it cannot be unfueled), or scrap the plans for a July launch and try again in September. For seven days, the thunderstorms continued, with small windows of opportunity presenting themselves in the Florida late afternoons.

Dawn had another problem: competition. The Mars Phoenix launch window, soon to open, would be the only Mars opportunity for two years. The Discovery Program was up against the Mars Program, and, as Todd May, who ran the Discovery and New Frontiers Program out of Marshall, recounted, "the odds were increasingly against successfully launching both Dawn and Phoenix within their windows. Discussions were elevated to the highest levels in the agency, and our governance model was once again tested when there was disagreement" about whether the requirements for telemetry, which were so vital for understanding failures, could be waived.[176]

All this put Alan Stern, the Associate Administrator of the Science Mission Directorate, in a difficult position. If NASA fueled the rocket and pushed for Dawn's launch, a delay would mean missing the Mars Phoenix window, effectively canceling the 2007 launch opportunity in a program that had launched a Mars mission every two years since Pathfinder.

On the other hand, the cost of missing the Dawn launch window was estimated at $25 million. [177] To complicate matters, Space Shuttle Endeavour was preparing for a launch to the International Space Station as well, further limiting launch opportunities after the end of the original window.

On 10 July, he decided to delay the Dawn launch to the next opportunity, which opened 7 September. Engineers destacked the spacecraft, and the rocket was removed from the launch pad. The team now had to determine a new trajectory necessitated by a later launch.[178]

Ultimately, the delay worked in the mission's favor, however. "September presented a much better opportunity," said Russell, as Mars was in the proper position to offer a greater gravity assist.[179]

---

175   ASI. (N.d.). "Dawn: Minor Bodies of the Solar System." Downloaded from *http://www.asi.it/ en/activity/solar_system/dawn*; Berger, B. (2007, 23 July). "Despite delay, Dawn still on track to rendezvous with asteroids." *SpaceNews*.

176   May, T. (2008). "Cooperation Not Control." *ASK Magazine*. 12–15.

177   Berger, B. (2007, 23 July). "Despite delay, Dawn still on track to rendezvous with asteroids." *SpaceNews*. See also Niebur, S. (2009, 24 March). Personal interview with C. Russell. Located in "Dawn" file, NASA Historical Reference Collection, History Division, NASA Headquarters, Washington, DC.

178   Niebur, S. (2009, 24 March). Personal interview with C. Russell. Located in "Dawn" file, NASA Historical Reference Collection, History Division, NASA Headquarters, Washington, DC.

179   Ibid.

It looked like Dawn would at last leave Earth on 26 September. But, no, the launch was then scrubbed due to lightning within five miles of Dawn's pad, 17B. The next day, the planned 7:20 a.m. launch was delayed because a ship was downrange in the area where the rocket solid motors would fall. Then, the International Space Station passed overhead, delaying things further.[180] Once the ISS passed out of range, however, halfway through the 29-minute launch window, the countdown could conclude. "We had a perfect day for a launch," said Russell. "I was in the control center. I didn't even run outside. I have seen lots of launches."[181] Dawn launched at 7:34 a.m. EDT on 27 September 2007.

On 17 December 2007, after a successful checkout of all three ion engines, Dawn began the interplanetary cruise phase of its three-billion-mile journey to Vesta and Ceres.[182] The thrusters burned just 0.26 kilogram of xenon each day. To get to Vesta on time, the spacecraft passed just 549 kilometers from Mars on 18 February 2009. The Red Planet accelerated Dawn's speed by more than 9,330 kilometers per hour—a power boost equivalent to expending 104 kilograms of xenon fuel. "Without the gravity assist, our mission would not have been affordable, even with the extraordinary capability of the ion propulsion system," said Rayman.[183] The Mars flyby also provided an opportunity to calibrate the instruments in deep space, well before the spacecraft reached Vesta in 2011. The team coordinated with Mars Express, just as MESSENGER had coordinated with Venus Express, to provide additional science return during flight.[184]

After launch, and twice a year during cruise, the team checked out the instruments. The U.S.-built GRaND instrument performed very well.[185] During the cruise phase, Russell supported the addition of a Participating Scientist Program in 2010, saying, "During such a long mission, people age.... I have counted on that program all along to bring in new blood to the system."[186]

There was just one outstanding issue after the successful launch and instrument checkout: the effect of the development delays on the intended science. Since the aster-

---

180   Sorenson, D. (2007, 28 September). "Dawn leaves Earth on mission to asteroids." *Arizona Daily Star.*

181   Niebur, S. (2009, 24 March). Personal interview with C. Russell. Located in the "Discovery Program" file, NASA Historical Reference Collection, History Division, NASA Headquarters, Washington, DC.

182   Peterson, P. (2008, 2 January). "Dawn slowly picks up the pace." *Florida Today.*

183   Malik, T. (2009, 18 February). "Asteroid-bound probe zooms past Mars." Space.com.

184   DLR. (200913 February). "Asteroid spacecraft Dawn: A change in course near our neighbor, Mars." Press release. *http://www.dlr.de/en/desktopdefault.aspx/tabid-1/86_read-15853// usetemplate-print/,* accessed 15 May 2009.

185   Niebur, S. (2010, 1 March). Personal interview with T. Prettyman. Located in "Dawn" file, NASA Historical Reference Collection, History Division, NASA Headquarters, Washington, DC.

186   Niebur, S. (2009, 24 March). Personal interview with C. Russell. Located in "Dawn" file, NASA Historical Reference Collection, History Division, NASA Headquarters, Washington, DC.

oids had continued in motion while the spacecraft had remained delayed on Earth, when the spacecraft arrived, a different surface would be illuminated by the Sun. This was not necessarily bad news. Vesta's new lit area would include the South Pole, an area of intense interest to planetary scientists.[187] "The higher the Sun goes, the more spectra we can get, the more topographic information we can get," said Russell.[188]

Dawn entered the asteroid belt on 13 November 2009. After traveling 2.8 billion kilometers from Earth, the spacecraft arrived at Vesta, with orbital insertion on 16 July 2011. The plan at the time called for Dawn to enter orbit around Ceres on 6 March 2015. At each body, the spacecraft would spend time at three distinct distances from the planetoid. According to the plan, during the first orbit of Vesta, 2,700 kilometers planetocentric, data would be taken so that the team could generate a preliminary shape model. During the second set of orbits, much closer at 950 kilometers, the instruments would perform high-spatial-resolution imaging topography and spectrometry. In the closest orbit, 460 kilometers planetocentric, about 200 kilometers from the surface, GRaND would take its measurements of surface neutrons and any associated signs of water. The team planned for those sets of measurements to be repeated at Ceres, at 6,400 kilometers, 1,800 kilometers, and 1,180 kilometers planetocentric. The GRaND measurements would be taken in the lowest orbit, about 700 kilometers above the surface.[189] After years of work, if all went well, the Dawn mission would reveal just how different the asteroids are and what that says about the earliest building blocks of our solar system. Meanwhile, the Discovery Program moved forward.

---

187   Russell, C. (2007, 19 September). Presentation at the Discovery@15 workshop in Huntsville, Alabama.

188   Niebur, S. (2009, 24 March). Personal interview with C. Russell. Located in "Dawn" file, NASA Historical Reference Collection, History Division, NASA Headquarters, Washington, DC.

189   Russell, C. T., Capaccioni, F., Coradini, A., Christensen, U., De Sanctis, M. C., Feldman, W. C., Jaumann, R., Keller, H. U., Konopliv, A., McCord, T. B., McFadden, L. A., McSween, H. Y., Mottola, S., Neukum, G., Pieters, C. M., Prettyman, T. H., Raymond, C. A., Smith, D. E., Sykes, M. V., Williams, B., & Zuber, M. T. (2006). "Dawn Discovery mission to Vesta and Ceres: Present status." *Advances in Space Research*, 38(9), 2043–2048. *https://doi.org/10.1016/j.asr.2004.12.041.*

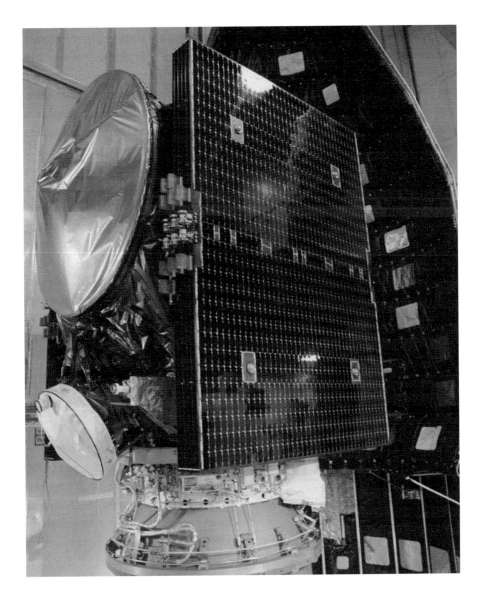

Figure 6-1: Dawn spacecraft

The Dawn spacecraft solar array wings are folded up in preparation for payload fairing installation. (Image credit: NASA/JPL, image no. PIA12018)

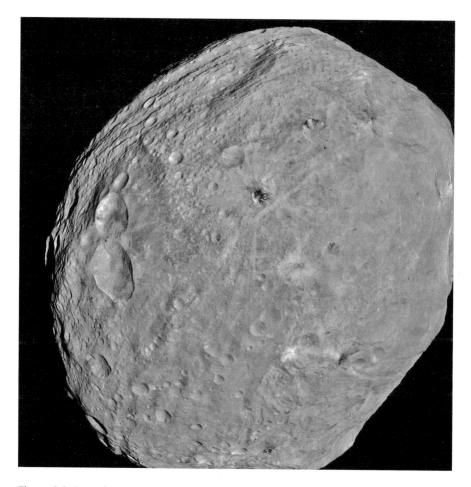

Figure 6-2: Dawn image of Vesta

Dawn obtained this image of the giant asteroid Vesta with its framing camera on 24 July 2011. Dawn entered orbit around Vesta on 15 July and spent a year orbiting the body. (Image credit: NASA/JPL-Caltech/UCLA/MPS/DLR/IDA, image no. PIA14317)

CHAPTER 7

Renewed Commitment: Kepler

William Borucki worked for 14 years to fly a photometer—a detector that returns a light curve as a function of time—in order to search for extrasolar planets. He persevered and ultimately submitted proposals for five Discovery opportunities, and he gave supporting talks regularly to the American Astronomical Society and other international meetings to gain support from the astrophysical and planetary science communities.[1] His interest in other planets that might harbor life extended back to his teenage years in the 1950s. He was a small-town kid in Wisconsin; read science fiction; launched homemade rockets; and, as president of his high school science club, worked with friends to build a magnetometer coupled with ultraviolet and infrared transmitters.[2]

---

1   Lawler, A. (2003, 1 May). "Bill Borucki's Planet Search." *Air and Space Magazine.*
2   Ward, L. (2009, 1 December). "10 most brilliant innovators of 2009: Kepler Space Telescope." *Popular Mechanics.* See also Perlman, D. (2009, 13 July). "Scientist scans galaxy seeking other earths." *San Francisco Chronicle.*

After obtaining his B.S. and M.S. degrees in physics at the University of Wisconsin, Madison, Borucki went to Ames Research Center in 1962 to work on the heat shield for the Apollo capsule.[3]

While Borucki was still in high school, Otto Struve published a paper positing the possibility of detecting extrasolar planets by observing very small oscillations in radial velocity with the most powerful ground-based Coude spectrographs in existence.[4] Two decades later, Frank Rosenblatt suggested that high-precision wide-field photometers be employed at three geographically separated sites to search for unusual transients. This transient detection method, Rosenblatt asserted, could yield a planet's size and orbital period.[5] Borucki became intensely interested in the problem of detection in the summer of 1982, after dropping by an Ames conference on extrasolar planets.[6] Borucki and Audrey Summers of Ames did calculations to correct Rosenblatt's earlier detection probability, suggesting in the journal *Icarus* an idea eerily like the mission that would become Kepler:

> *Although the precision required to detect major planets is already available with state-of-the-art photometers, the detection of terrestrial-size planets would require a precision substantially greater than the state-of-the-art and a spaceborne platform to avoid the effects of variations in sky transparency and scintillation…. Because the probability is so small of observing a planetary transit during a single observation of a randomly chosen star, the search program must be designed to continuously monitor hundreds or thousands of stars.[7]*

Despite this early start, significant work remained. At Borucki's urging, Ames Research Center sponsored technology workshops on high-precision photometry. The 20 astronomers at the 1984 workshops agreed that it would be theoretically possible to build suitable detectors, and colleagues at the National Bureau of Standards suggested the use of very precise—in fact, quantum-perfect—silicone diodes.[8] The Ames Research Center Director continued to fund Borucki's silicon diode detector development for several years, despite senior managers' skepticism. Later, NASA Headquarters funded the development and testing of proof-of-concept multichannel photometers.

---

3   Swift, M. (2009. 2 March). "Mountain View scientists giddy over NASA's Search for Faraway Planets." *San Jose Mercury News.*

4   Struve, O. (1952). "Proposal for a project of high-precision stellar radial velocity work." *The Observatory*, vol. 72. 199–200.

5   Rosenblatt, F. (1971). "A Two-Color Photometric Method for Detection of Extra Solar Planetary Systems." *Icarus*, vol. 14. 71–93.

6   Lawler, A. (2003, 1 May). "Bill Borucki's Planet Search." *Air and Space Magazine.*

7   Borucki, W. J., and A. L. Summers. (1984, April). "The photometric method of detecting other planetary systems." *Icarus,* vol. 58. 121–134.

8   Lawler, A. (2003, 1 May). "Bill Borucki's Planet Search." *Air and Space Magazine.*

By the time NASA selected the Kepler proposal, a decade and a half later, engineers had been able to design a photometer with a very wide field of view, 105 square degrees. It would be the sole instrument in a 0.95-meter-aperture Schmidt telescope, enabling astronomers to observe 100,000 target stars continuously. These changes led Borucki to expect to observe perhaps 400 Earth-size planets per year. In fact, by the time Kepler launched nearly 20 years after the original papers on the subject, the term "extrasolar planet" had entered the vernacular, and new discoveries were announced routinely on the evening news.

Around the time of the first Discovery Program Workshop in San Juan Capistrano, Borucki began gathering colleagues together to discuss the concept of using a photometric approach for planet-finding. David Koch, who would one day be Kepler's deputy Principal Investigator, remembered: "In 1992, Bill Borucki came to my office and asked if I'd help him with a concept of doing a transit search for planets. I said, 'Sure, Bill. I like building things.'"[9]

Koch soon encouraged Borucki to submit a proposal to Discovery, and he offered to collaborate. As Borucki recalled, "I thought, well, if I've got at least one person who's willing to work with me, I will give it a try."[10]

Borucki had photometer experience, but Koch had built telescopes too, including a gas-Cherenkov telescope to image gamma rays as a graduate student in the late 1960s. This early balloon experiment, under PI Ken Greisen, with 4.5 m[2] collecting area, was the first to detect pulse gamma rays from the Crab nebula, 100 MeV-1 GeV.[11] Koch went on to become the project scientist at American Science and Engineering on Uhuru, the first x-ray astronomy satellite, and HEAO-B (the Einstein Observatory), the first fully imaging, space-based x-ray telescope. Koch later served as project scientist at the Smithsonian on the Spacelab 2 infrared telescope (at the time, Ed Weiler was the program scientist at NASA Headquarters for Spacelab 2's flight on STS-51F in August 1985) and mission operations manager for what would be the Spitzer Space Telescope at Ames. He also put together a teacher education program on the Kuiper Airborne Observatory, hiring Edna DeVore as possibly the first project teacher for NASA. Moreover, Koch convinced NASA Headquarters to allow NASA centers to issue education grants for the first time. He was, in other words, both technically and politically savvy.[12]

---

9   "NASA's Kepler Telescope Set to Launch in Search of Other Earths." (2009, 26 February). *Satnews Daily.* Downloaded from *http://www.satnews.com/cgi-bin/story.cgi?number=549171030.*

10   Niebur, S. (2009, 16 December). Personal interview with W. Borucki. Located in "Kepler" file, NASA Historical Reference Collection, History Division, NASA Headquarters, Washington, DC.

11   Niebur, S. (2010, 6 January). Personal interview with D. Koch. Located in "Kepler" file, NASA Historical Reference Collection, History Division, NASA Headquarters, Washington, DC.

12   Ibid.

Koch had a good relationship with Harold Reitsema at Ball Aerospace, with whom he had worked to build the Submillimeter Wave Astronomy Satellite. Ball and American Science and Engineering, which was no longer in the business by this point, were known as good, solid, smaller companies that built "damn good instruments" for university PIs. The mission Koch and Borucki were proposing would be a way for Ball to establish itself as a capable contractor for an entire mission as well. The company would essentially be a "sole contractor" if the mission were selected, responsible end-to-end for building the spacecraft and instruments, and ultimately delivering the data that the scientists craved. This would put Ball in the same league as Martin Marietta as a NASA deep space mission provider. (The contracting paperwork would reflect this; a portion of the fee would be based on on-orbit performance.) This work was seen as an opportunity, and Ball was enthusiastic.[13]

Borucki invited other prominent scientists at Ames and at the SETI Institute to join the proposal team, including Kent Cullers, the first astronomer blind from birth, who would later be immortalized in the movie *Contact*. Carl Sagan was a member of the team for the first and all subsequent proposals until his death in late 1996. Experts in high-precision photometry and astrometry (stellar distances) were added. Astronomers with expertise in high-precision measurements, stellar variability, theoretical modeling, and other missions joined the team. Other co-investigators were added or promoted from the science working group one by one, to fill out the wide range of required expertise necessary for such a mission.

BASICALLY, IT WAS A MATTER OF PERSISTENCE

The first proposal for a mission of this sort, in 1992, was called FRESIP—the FRequency of Earth-Sized Inner Planets—and would fly an instrument with 42 charge-coupled device (CCD) detectors to convert the observed light into signals. Each star would be monitored simultaneously as a function of time. "This is a really simple experiment," described Gibor Basri, co-investigator and professor of astronomy at the University of California, Berkeley. "You're watching an eclipse, measuring the brightness of the star to two parts in 100,000 and noting every time it takes a dip."[14]

Borucki, who would later be the Principal Investigator of Kepler, recalled that the idea was warmly received but that the scientific and engineering communities believed that no suitable detectors existed. "Nobody had ever built detectors like that."[15] Despite the scientific merit, the review team was unconvinced that the described techniques

---

13   Ibid.

14   Watson, J. G. (2001, 23 January). "Other Earths: Are they out there." Space.com.

15   Niebur, S. (2009, 16 December). Personal interview with W. Borucki. Located in "Kepler" file, NASA Historical Reference Collection, History Division, NASA Headquarters, Washington, DC.

would work.[16] "The review panel," said Borucki, "found that the science value was very high and would have supported it had there been proof that detectors existed with sufficient precision and the requisite low noise to find Earth-size planets."[17]

The idea would eventually capture the attention of additional members of the science community, however, and in 1994, Borucki held a workshop called Astrophysical Science with a Space Borne Photometric Telescope at the SETI Institute in Mountain View, CA. The goal was to determine the most promising astrophysical investigations for a telescope that measured the individual brightness of 5,000 stars for four years.[18]

Later that year, the FRESIP proposal was fleshed out and submitted to the first Discovery Announcement of Opportunity.[19] Ames Research Center and Ball Aerospace led the proposal, with Borucki, Koch, and astronomers Ted Dunham and William "Bill" Cochran composing the core of the science team.[20] The 1994 proposal would use a 0.95-meter-aperture Schmidt telescope to continuously and simultaneously monitor 5,000 solar-like stars in a 12-degree field of view, using a halo orbit around the Lagrange L2 Point, where it would have a clear view without the risk of an eclipse by the Sun, Earth, or the Moon.[21] The FRESIP photometer would use charge-coupled devices (CCDs) instead of the originally considered silicon detectors. (CCDs may have sounded exotic then, but they would become a household technology, used in many digital cameras, camcorders, and smartphones.) Borucki had heard the skepticism of his own managers on the unknown performance of silicon diode detectors in space, and, at the behest of Ball, he agreed to change to CCDs. "I hate CCDs," he said in a 2003 interview, but he agreed to use them to reassure the community of reviewers, more accustomed to CCDs than silicon diodes.[22] (Eventually he used this familiarity to explain the concept to the general public, saying, "Kepler is your camcorder with a really big lens.")[23]

16   Niebur, S. (2010, 6 January). Personal interview with D. Koch. Located in "Kepler" file, NASA Historical Reference Collection, History Division, NASA Headquarters, Washington, DC.

17   Borucki, W. J. (2010, 22 May). "Brief History of the Kepler Mission." NASA History. Downloaded 10 May 2023 from *https://www.nasa.gov/kepler/overview/historybyborucki*. See also Borucki, W., et al. (2008). "Kepler: Search for Earth-size planets in the habitable zone." *Proceedings IAU Symposium No. IAUS253.*

18   Borucki, W. (2010, 22 May). "Brief History of the Kepler Mission." Downloaded 5 June 2010 from *http://kepler.nasa.gov/Mission/history/*.

19   Borucki, W., et al. (1994, June). "FRESIP: A Discovery Mission Concept to Find Earth-Sized Planets Around Solar Like Stars." American Astronomical Society, DPS Meeting 26, 08.01. See also *Bulletin of the American Astronomical Society*. (1994, June). Vol. 26. 1091.

20   Niebur, S. (2010, 6 January). Personal interview with D. Koch. Located in "Kepler" file, NASA Historical Reference Collection, History Division, NASA Headquarters, Washington, DC.

21   Borucki, W. J., et al. (1996). "FRESIP: A mission to determine the character and frequency of extra-solar planets around solar-like stars." *Astrophys. & Space Science*, 241. 111–134.

22   Lawler, A. (2003, 1 May). "Bill Borucki's Planet Search." *Air and Space Magazine*.

23   Watson, J. (2001, 23 January). "Other Earths: Are they out there." Space.com.

As part of the review of science, technical, management, and cost for the mission, a NASA review panel compared the photometer to space telescopes such as Hubble, determining that the cost would be similar (i.e., far beyond the budget limit). The proposal was thus rejected. The Hubble Space Telescope was built as one of the Great Observatories, a strategic mission with several sophisticated instruments. Kepler would be a single photometer—not a true telescope in the traditional sense of the word—although that would prove to be a difficult message to communicate. In addition, the project's mass had less margin than expected by the review panels, as so much propellant was necessary to take the telescope 1.5 million kilometers beyond Earth to the Lagrange L2 Point. The team believed that mass margin needs should not be applied to propellant, but the review panel did not agree. They deemed the cost high and the mass margin low. NASA thus did not select the proposal for study.[24]

The FRESIP team was not discouraged. They used small grants from NASA Headquarters and Ames Research Center to perform laboratory tests of the CCD detectors and demonstrated that they had sufficient precision and signal-to-noise ratios to detect the patterns of Earth-size transits.[25] The mathematical identification and removal of systematic noise was the breakthrough step that helped NASA recognize the intrinsic precision of the detectors.[26]

In 1996, a 1-meter-aperture, 12-degree-field-of-view photometer was proposed again, this time under the name Kepler, in honor of Johannes Kepler, who discovered the laws of planetary motion so essential in the theory and practice of planet-finding.[27] The photometer would be placed in a heliocentric, Earth-trailing orbit instead of a Lagrange point orbit, eliminating an upper-stage rocket and the station-keeping necessary to hold the spacecraft in orbit around the Lagrange point, which would reduce both mass and mission costs, while increasing margin. After that, mass margin was no longer an issue, as the telescope fit nicely on a launch vehicle.[28] The team predicted the detection of 480 Earth-class planets (including 60 cases of two or more planets in the same system), 160 detections of inner-orbit giant planets, 24 detections of outer-orbit

24   Niebur, S. (2010, 6 January). Personal interview with D. Koch. Located in "Kepler" file, NASA Historical Reference Collection, History Division, NASA Headquarters, Washington, DC.

25   Robinson, L., et al. (1995). "Test of CCD limits for differential photometry." *PASP*, 107. 1094–1098.

26   Borucki, W. (2010, 22 May). "Brief History of the Kepler Mission." Downloaded 5 June 2010 from *http://kepler.nasa.gov/Mission/history/*.

27   Borucki, W., et al. (1997, January). "The Kepler Mission: A Mission To Determine the Frequency of Inner Planets Near the Habitable Zone for a Wide Range of Stars." *Planets Beyond the Solar System and the Next Generation of Space Missions*. Proceedings of a workshop held at Space Telescope Science Institute, Baltimore, MD, 16–18 October 1996. ASP Conference Series, vol. 119. 153–173.

28   Niebur, S. (2010, 6 January). Personal interview with D. Koch. Located in "Kepler" file, NASA Historical Reference Collection, History Division, NASA Headquarters, Washington, DC.

giant planets, and 1,400 detections of planets with periods of less than one week.[29] To deliver this data to Earth, the team switched to the Ka-band with a high-gain antenna, allowing the observation of not just 5,000 stars, but 80,000. The new proposal manager was Larry Webster.

The new 1996 proposal used three different methods to show that mission costs were inside the Discovery cost envelope. This time, however, a review panel responded with specific weaknesses on the proposed CCD array, an ambitious undertaking that had not been proven in the laboratory.

Borucki and his team persisted, addressing the identified weaknesses, and making continuous improvements to the system. They tested CCDs and performed proof-of-concept studies. They built small prototype photometers with the financial support of both NASA Ames and NASA Headquarters.[30] They continued to meet, to write papers, and to present their concept at regular astronomy and planetary science meetings. The concept was so out-of-the-box, however, that Borucki vividly remembered being confronted at meetings after his presentations, with colleagues insisting that the methodology was folly.

"Everybody said my idea would never work," said Borucki, "You'd never have detectors with enough sensitivity and precision."[31] The team continued to work, resolving technical issues, and to promote the concept at every opportunity. "The strategy was to convince the community," said David Koch, Kepler's deputy Principal Investigator.[32]

As the years went by, the team composition evolved as some astrophysicists returned to work on other projects and others joined the team to help address some particular weakness, or because they added science or technical capability.

Team membership was not a direct ticket to fame and fortune, however. In the early years, team members paid their own way to meetings and to do supporting research. There was no project fund to support people. In Borucki's words, "We would write a proposal at every opportunity, and it would get rejected every time."[33] The steady stream of rejections was discouraging, but they pushed on, addressing weaknesses

---

29   Borucki, W., et al. (1997, January). "The Kepler Mission: A Mission To Determine the Frequency of Inner Planets Near the Habitable Zone for a Wide Range of Stars. *Planets Beyond the Solar System and the Next Generation of Space Missions.* Proceedings of a workshop held at Space Telescope Science Institute, Baltimore, MD, 16–18 October 1996. ASP Conference Series, vol. 119. 153–173.

30   Niebur, S. (2009, 16 December). Personal interview with B. Borucki. Located in "Kepler" file, NASA Historical Reference Collection, History Division, NASA Headquarters, Washington, DC.

31   Perlman, D. (2009, 13 July). "Scientist scans galaxy seeking other Earths." *San Francisco Chronicle.*

32   Niebur, S. (2010, 6 January). Personal interview with D. Koch. Located in "Kepler" file, NASA Historical Reference Collection, History Division, NASA Headquarters, Washington, DC.

33   Niebur, S. (2009, 16 December). Personal interview with W. Borucki. Located in "Kepler" file, NASA Historical Reference Collection, History Division, NASA Headquarters, Washington, DC.

and publicizing their efforts. As time went on, after three mission concept proposals, colleagues and astrophysicists Michel Mayor and Didier Queloz, followed by Geoff Marcy and Paul Butler, announced the discovery of the first extrasolar planets.[34]

That discovery fueled interest in Borucki's quest to discover Earth-size extrasolar planets, but as his methodology was still unproven, the burden of proof was on Borucki and the other scientists. The team installed a test photometer, nicknamed Vulcan, at Lick Observatory's Crocker Dome, and a receiving station at NASA Ames. By the time of the 1998 Discovery Announcement of Opportunity release, the Kepler team was successfully receiving simultaneous observations of 6,000 stars in a single field of view.[35] In the 1998 proposal, the Kepler team managed to successfully demonstrate the performance of their proposed CCDs, but the reviewers were *still* not yet convinced of adequate overall system performance—particularly regarding signal-to-noise on orbit.[36]

NASA Headquarters provided a half-million dollars (an amount matched by Ames Research Center) to Borucki and Koch to set up a numerical model and laboratory testbed to perform an end-to-end test of the approach and prove that the proposed CCD photometer could perform at the stated precision, reliably detect transits, and perform under various conditions required of the proposed spacecraft instrument. The testbed—including simulated star field; fast optics; a proven CCD detector; a computer to simulate onboard data processing; and a second computer to simulate ground data processing, construct light curves, and search for transits—was constructed in-house at NASA Ames in 88 days in 1998. Koch devised an elegant simulation of a 10^{-4} transit by placing a tiny wire in front of one of the 10^{-4}-meter holes in the star plate and running a very small current through the wire, heating it so that it expanded by 10^{-8} meters (10 nanometers, measured with a very small weight on the wire), resulting in a 10^{-4} change in signal. Using 40 small wires and 40 small holes, Koch simulated the star density of the galactic plane, even distributing the brightness of the stars from the fourth to nineteenth magnitudes. Koch and Fred Witteborn simulated spacecraft jitter with piezoelectric transducers underneath the dewar.

The project team then measured the resulting signal—with noise—using the CCDs built with Koch's previous instrument development grant, successfully demonstrating that the technique could be used to detect Earth-size planets, even in the presence of

---

34   Mayor, M., and D. Queloz. (1995). "A Jupiter-mass companion to a solar-type star." *Nature*, 378. 355; Marcy, G. W., & Butler, R. P. (1996). "A planetary companion to 70 Virginis." *The Astrophysical Journal*, 464(2). *https://doi.org/10.1086/310096.*

35   Borucki, W., et al. (1999, June). "Photometric observations of 6000 stars in the Cygnus field." *Proceedings of the NStars Workshop.* See also: Borucki, W., et al. (2001). "The Vulcan Photometer: A dedicated photometer for extrasolar planet searches." *PASP* . 113. 439–451.

36   Niebur, S. (2009, 16 December). Personal interview with W. Borucki. Located in "Kepler" file, NASA Historical Reference Collection, History Division, NASA Headquarters, Washington, DC. See also Borucki, W., et al. (2008). "Kepler: Search for Earth-size planets in the habitable zone." Proceedings IAU Symposium No. IAUS253.

the expected pointing jitter, sky noise, instrument noise, and other noise unavoidable in such an end-to-end system. This proof of concept was employed in the 2000 proposal, where the team once again made the case that this photometer could be successfully deployed to detect Earth-size planets orbiting other Sun-like stars.

With each proposal, the Kepler team put together a detailed case for selection, with an updated science plan based on what was learned in the rapidly changing field of extrasolar planet detection. They slowly developed an ever-strengthening case for their mission's relevance, interest, and achievability. Meanwhile, Ball Aerospace provided intricate designs and supporting tests, as well as the personnel and finances necessary to support the proposals. When asked whether that indicated that they believed in the proposal, Borucki conceded, "Either that or they're interesting gamblers." He added, "It cost several hundred thousand dollars to put a proposal in like this. To do it time and time again takes a lot of guts." Kepler would prove to be the most often proposed—and most often rejected—mission to fly in the first two decades of Discovery. But every time they were rejected, the team went back to work and returned with a more comprehensive proposal, and eventually, on the fifth try, NASA selected the Kepler photometer concept for flight.[37]

Selection

Selection came after a competitive Phase A study. Ball hosted the site review. At Koch's direction, the team prepared displays of the existing Kepler technologies and set up demonstrations of the mirror and detectors. They also exhibited education and public outreach plans, as well as other key points. Team members stood by the exhibits during session breaks, and the reviewers were able not only to hear about the team's achievements but see them as well. This maximized the usable time during the day of the site visit and encouraged reviewers to seek out technologies about which they were still uncertain, rather than holding their questions until a time that the Kepler team determined. It was a complete success (even though someone broke one of the lightweight honeycomb mirrors that day and sent it back to Ball in an envelope).

In late December 2001, Borucki got the phone call he had been waiting for since 1992. The Kepler mission had been selected for implementation. "I was just overjoyed that we finally got to the point where we were going to build it instead of talk about it," he said.[38]

---

37   Niebur, S. (2009, 16 December). Personal interview with W. Borucki. Located in "Kepler" file, NASA Historical Reference Collection, History Division, NASA Headquarters, Washington, DC.

38   Niebur, S. (2009, 16 December). Personal interview with W. Borucki. Located in "Kepler" file, NASA Historical Reference Collection, History Division, NASA Headquarters, Washington, DC; Erickson, J. (2001, 24 December). "Ball lands NASA space telescope project." *Rocky Mountain News*. 4A.

NASA Headquarters selected both the Dawn and Kepler missions, knowing that the budget was not robust enough to support two missions in formulation, and, later, implementation, at the same time. Since Dawn was constrained by a 2006 planetary launch window and the alignment of Vesta and Ceres, the solution was to implement a delayed start for the Kepler mission. Although the Kepler team had proposed to launch in 2005 into an Earth-trailing heliocentric orbit, the delayed start and other changes meant that Kepler would not be scheduled for launch until 2007.[39] Unlike other Discovery missions launched thus far, Kepler could be launched at just about any time of year, and in any year. This made it a great choice for such a double selection—but flexibility in start date and launch date did not make the mission immune to cost increases. Far from it, in fact, as a mission with no planetary launch window had no correspondingly urgent need to complete construction and testing, a factor that is often blamed for cost overruns.[40]

Much of this, however, was out of Kepler's control. Between proposal and selection, a new Office of Space Science policy had been established that gave management of all planetary science missions to the Jet Propulsion Laboratory and Goddard Space Flight Center. Kepler had proposed management by Ames Research Center, in accordance with the policies in place for the 2000 Announcement of Opportunity, but the change in policies necessitated a change in management—and management structure—for this mission. As a condition of selection, Principal Investigator William Borucki and his team were thus forced to agree to the addition of a layer of management in which JPL or Goddard would oversee the work done by Ames. While Phase B work commenced in March 2002, Borucki's team had to choose between the two NASA centers.[41] They decided ultimately that JPL and Goddard should pitch the PI and his team at NASA Ames.

In the summer of 2002, Borucki selected JPL and project manager Chet Sasaki.[42] Larry Webster, the Ames project manager, became the Deputy Project Manager. Sasaki would now oversee the JPL portion of the contract with Ball, managed onsite by Ball project manager Len Andreozzi.

---

39   Lawler, A. (2003, 1 May). "Bill Borucki's Planet Search." *Air and Space Magazine.*

40   Croft, J. (2008, 16 December). "NASA investigates effects of falsely certified titanium." *Flight International.*

41   Borucki, W., et al. (2004, January). "The Kepler mission: A technical overview." In "Second Eddington Workshop: Stellar structure and habitable planet finding," 9–11 April 2003, Palermo, Italy.

42   Niebur, S. (2009, 16 December). Personal interview with M. Moore. Located in "Kepler" file, NASA Historical Reference Collection, History Division, NASA Headquarters, Washington, DC; Borucki et al. (2004, January). "The Kepler mission: a technical overview." In "Second Eddington Workshop: Stellar structure and habitable planet finding," 9–11 April 2003, Palermo, Italy. 177–182.

The selection of the Jet Propulsion Laboratory as a management institution necessitated further changes to the management structure of the project. According to Michael Moore, Kepler Program Executive at NASA Headquarters, JPL "felt that they needed to have a serious piece of contracting activity in order to…make it real for their people." The management style of JPL "brought Ball around to a different mode of operation." Moore said: "I thought that this was a real learning opportunity for Ames as a center to have their people engaged with [JPL]…. There seemed to be a lot of what I call institutional resistance…. Toward the end, I think that they were working well together, but I didn't see the [Ames Research] Center perceiving this as a good opportunity to educate the workforce in the ways to execute these programs and projects."[43]

The contract was thus split. Ball would still build the photometer, including the optics, detectors, detector-unique avionics, Sun shield, and the supporting structure, under contract to Ames. JPL became responsible for the build of the spacecraft and the integration of the photometer and said spacecraft. Since the photometer would have to be delivered for the integration of the spacecraft, Moore explained, "you can almost imagine that Ames became a subcontractor to some point to the JPL side of the contract."[44]

Koch, the deputy Principal Investigator, credited Charlie Sobeck, engineer manager and Ames civil servant, with managing the contracting smoothly. "He is the fairest person that I know of, both in terms of handling the vendor and working within the federal system," said Koch.[45]

Details of this revised management structure were negotiated, and the budgets redone, for full-cost accounting was now required—another major policy change since Kepler's proposal. Delta II launch costs also increased, and Kepler's approved budget increased accordingly, to $457 million.

The one-year start delay was "really devastating, in that we had contracts that we were ready to execute because we knew, if we were going to be successful, we had to order the detectors early," said Borucki. In addition, he said, "We needed more detectors than any other mission had ever asked for, and they had to be excellent," in order to find the small changes in signal amid the noise.[46] As with other missions, the needs of the people involved became a factor as well. Borucki worried that key members of the team, particularly Jon Jenkins, a "soft money" researcher at SETI with a PhD

---

43   Niebur, S. (2009, 16 December). Personal interview with M. Moore. Located in the "Discovery Program" file, NASA Historical Reference Collection, History Division, NASA Headquarters, Washington, DC.

44   Ibid.

45   Niebur, S. (2010, 6 January). Personal interview with D. Koch. Located in "Kepler" file, NASA Historical Reference Collection, History Division, NASA Headquarters, Washington, DC.

46   Niebur, S. (2009, 16 December). Personal interview with W. Borucki. Located in "Kepler" file, NASA Historical Reference Collection, History Division, NASA Headquarters, Washington, DC.

in signal processing, who was building the algorithms to pull the statistics out of the noise, would accept other job offers if unpaid for a year or more. The new constraints made the mission implementation more difficult, but Borucki set about making the new schedule work, saying quietly to an interviewer a year later, "All I care about is the science."[47]

The project made the case to NASA Headquarters that beginning long-lead procurements on the CCDs and the optics would reduce mission risk. NASA responded by giving permission for Kepler to begin said procurements, a technique that had proven useful in previous missions.[48] NASA Headquarters provided $2 million and Ames provided $1 million in bridge funding to tide the mission team over until the official start of Phase B. Kepler put the money to good use, developing requirements for critical items and preparing to issue contracts.[49] In fall 2002, Kepler selected e2v and STA for parallel contracts for 30 flight CCDs. Borucki explained publicly that the team was hedging their bets. "This 'twin buy' approach ensures that the large number of detectors required for the Kepler focal plane will be available even if one of the vendors runs into difficulties."[50]

In parallel, Ball's negotiations with Kodak and other suppliers resulted in a move to an in-house build for the optical system. "That really, in my mind, brought the optics up as a key issue," said Moore.[51]

The science team, first furious at the delay and the many NASA-required changes, began working to develop algorithms and perform supporting observations essential to the future operation of the photometer. This included classifying the stars that would be in the photometer's field of view.[52] The Kepler team was the largest ever proposed for a Discovery mission, consisting of co-investigators and science working group members, instrument builders, and theorists.[53] Co-investigators, funded to do tasks essential to mission success, bore the brunt of the day-to-day work, while science working group members assembled at regular meetings, advising the team on implementation and the

47   Lawler, A. (2003, 1 May). "Bill Borucki's Planet Search." *Air and Space Magazine*.

48   Borucki, W. (2007, 19 September). Presentation at the Discovery@15 workshop in Huntsville, Alabama.

49   Niebur, S. (2009, 16 December). Personal interview with W. Borucki. Located in "Kepler" file, NASA Historical Reference Collection, History Division, NASA Headquarters, Washington, DC.

50   Borucki et al. (2004, January). "The Kepler mission: A technical overview." In "Second Eddington Workshop: Stellar structure and habitable planet finding," 9–11 April 2003, Palermo, Italy. 177–182.

51   Niebur, S. (2009, 16 December). Personal interview with M. Moore. Located in "Kepler" file, NASA Historical Reference Collection, History Division, NASA Headquarters, Washington, DC.

52   Lawler, A. (2003, 1 May). "Bill Borucki's Planet Search." *Air and Space Magazine*.

53   Niebur, S. (2009, August). "Principal Investigators and Mission Leadership." *Space Policy*.

balancing of the scientific objectives detailed in the selected proposal. Such a working group structure was new to Discovery, but traditional in Astrophysics missions that many on the Kepler team had worked on before.

Tim Brown and Ron Gilliland, team members and experts in solar seismology, became co-investigators as their involvement became more essential to key work on the mission. Ron Gilliland had been the first to detect the atmosphere on another planet. John Geary, once a panel reviewer, impressed the science team with his questions so much that after the evaluation was complete, he was invited to join the science team. Geary's experience building telescopes at the Smithsonian Astrophysical Observatory at Harvard (SAO) proved very useful as he collaborated with Ball. The project also invited astronomer Andrea Dupree, the first director who was a woman (and youngest director) at SAO's Center for Astrophysics, where Koch worked for a time, to join the science team.[54]

The team resolved from the start to include additional members of the community as Guest Observers: funded researchers interested in pursuing science not already included in the Kepler mission.[55]

Unlike some early Discovery missions, Kepler also employed theorists. "The standard theorist line is never [to] believe in an observation unless it has been confirmed theoretically," explained Jack Lissauer, a co-investigator from NASA Ames. "You have to be able to understand your observations theoretically and confirm your theories through observation."[56]

Science

The Kepler mission had well-defined science objectives. Even after the first observation of large Jupiters in 1997 and smaller planets of all kinds in the 2000s, the mission objectives remained constant and focused on counting, in a fixed field of view, the number of Earth-size planets in the habitable zone of stars like the Sun. This never changed.

As written by William Borucki, the Kepler Principal Investigator:

The general scientific goal of the Kepler mission is to explore the structure and diversity of planetary systems with special emphasis on determining the frequency of Earth-size planets in the HZ of solarlike stars. This is achieved by surveying a large sample of stars to:

- *Determine the frequency of terrestrial-size and larger planets in or near the habitable zone of a wide variety of spectral types of stars;*

---

54   Niebur, S. (2010, 6 January). Personal interview with A. Dupree. Located in "Kepler" file, NASA Historical Reference Collection, History Division, NASA Headquarters, Washington, DC.

55   Basri, G., et al. (2005). "The Kepler mission: A wide-field transit search for terrestrial planets." *New Astronomy Reviews*, 49. 478–485.

56   David, L. (2006, 5 February). "Finding New Worlds: Theoretical Conjecture Versus Hands-on Astronomy." Space.com.

- *Determine the distributions of sizes and orbital semi-major axes of these planets;*
- *Estimate the frequency of planets orbiting multiple-star systems;*
- *Determine the distributions of semi-major axis, eccentricity, albedo, size, mass, and density of short period giant planets;*
- *Identify additional members of each photometrically-discovered planetary system using complementary techniques; and*
- *Determine the properties of those stars that harbor planetary systems.*[57]

The habitable zone "is the area where things are just right," explained Borucki. "The planets are not too hot, they're not too cold, they're just right."[58] For life as we know it to exist, the planet must be able to have liquid water at the surface. Too hot, and any surface water would boil off. Too cold, and surface water would freeze into ice. The planet must be at just the right distance from a star of just the right temperature. The mission would search for the planets in the habitable zone and determine just how many might be out there.[59]

While the Kepler mission goals remained constant throughout the decade between first proposal and selection for implementation, NASA's plans for future astrophysical missions changed. Priorities shifted with budget availability, the development of new strategic planning roadmaps, and community pressure. The search for extrasolar planets from space, however, became more relevant rather than less, and by the time NASA selected Kepler, plans were in place for the flagship space telescope, Terrestrial Planet Finder, and precursors such as the Space Interferometry Mission. Kepler would provide the data needed for the capstone Terrestrial Planet Finder by performing a pathfinder exploration of a well-defined volume of space in the Summer Triangle, studying what kinds of stars were most likely to have planets around them, and identifying systems with terrestrial planets for further study by more advanced, and significantly more expensive, telescopes.

Mission Design

While Kepler was a very simple space telescope relative to those in NASA's Astrophysics Division, it also was a new kind of mission for the Discovery Program. Instead of sending a spacecraft to a distant planet, comet, or asteroid, Kepler would be launched into orbit around the Sun, in an Earth-trailing orbit with a period of just over a year (372.5 days). Over the course of the mission, this larger period would mean that the

---

57   Borucki, W. J. (2016). "Kepler Mission: Development and Overview." *Rep. Prog. Phys.* 79, 036901. Downloaded from *https://iopscience.iop.org/article/10.1088/0034-4885/79/3/036901* on 23 May 2023.

58   Malik, T. (2009, 6 March). "Pressure On for NASA's Friday Launch of Planet-Hunting Kepler." Space.com.

59   Erickson, J. (2007, 1 February). "Man sees dream coming into focus." *The Casper Star Tribune.*

spacecraft would slowly drift away from Earth, finally ending up 0.5 AU behind our planet after four years. The mission instrument suite, unlike the large science payloads for missions like MESSENGER, was in this case a single instrument: a wide-field photometer with a Schmidt-type telescope and an array of charge-coupled devices.[60] The instrument design was driven by requirements of photometric precision (to detect individual Earth-size transits of 6.5 hours), mission lifetime (sufficient to observe at least three transits), and number of stars to be observed to produce a statistically meaningful result (100,000 bright dwarf stars).[61]

The telescope itself was designed to continuously measure the relative brightness of all the stars in its field of view. This field of view was much larger than that of standard telescopes, which typically have approximately one square degree, and was necessary to enable it to simultaneously observe the brightness of the target stars of size comparable to our Sun's. To permit the detection of small changes in stellar brightness, the modified Schmidt telescope was built with a 1.4-meter-diameter F/1 primary mirror and a corrector plate with an aperture of 0.95 meter. The focal plane was built using a square foot of charge-coupled devices, each a separate 1- by 2-inch silicon chip, with a combined array of over 95 million pixels. Each CCD had two readouts, for a total of 84 output channels and thousands of wires to the processing electronics. Complicating matters, the focal plane had to be kept a cool 90 K (about 300°F below zero), separated from the 300 K electronics nearby.

After construction of the photometer, the instrument would be mounted to a spacecraft bus, launched, checked out, and set to observe the stars in a single area of the sky in Cygnus, the Summer Triangle, denoted by the first-magnitude stars Deneb, Vega, and Altair. These stars are familiar to many amateur astronomers, as they are bright (first magnitude) and visible in the northern hemisphere from spring into fall. The telescope would be set to view a star field slightly beyond the Milky Way and its high density of stars, and out of the plane of the solar system, away from our system's asteroids and their dust. Millions of stars are visible in this patch of sky.[62]

The telescope had no moving parts. Instead, the photometer recorded the intensity of each star's light at regular intervals, waiting for a minuscule dip in the brightness that would indicate that something nearby had passed directly in front of it, blocking part

---

60   Basri, G., et al. (2005). "The Kepler mission: A wide-field transit search for terrestrial planets." *New Astronomy Reviews*, 49. 478–485.

61   Borucki, W. J. (2016). "Kepler Mission: Development and Overview." *Rep. Prog. Phys.* 79, 036901. Downloaded from *https://iopscience.iop.org/article/10.1088/0034-4885/79/3/036901* on 23 May 2023.

62   DeVore, E. (2008, 15 August). "The Summer Triangle: Target of Kepler mission." Space.com. See also DeVore et al., (2010) "Science Education and Outreach: Forging a Path to the Future." ASP Conference Series, vol. 431, Jonathan Barnes, Denise A. Smith, Michael G. Gibbs, and James G. Manning, eds. Astronomical Society of the Pacific. A wide-ranging educational program and a program for planetariums were important parts of the mission.

of the star's light as seen by the photometer. If Kepler were to observe a planet the size of Earth, crossing directly in front of its Sun-size star, the dip in brightness would be less than one part in 10,000 (84 ppm). This tiny change would go undetected by most telescopes, but Kepler was built for high-precision photometry. The change would be noted as a potential planetary transit.[63] The photometer was so sensitive that if Kepler "were to look down at a small town on Earth at night from space, it would be able to detect the dimming of a porch light as somebody passed in front," according to Kepler project manager James Fanson.[64]

Planets in the habitable zone orbiting stars like the Sun complete their orbits in periods of a year to a few years, according to the laws of planetary motion. The time that each planet spends crossing the star (its transit) is comparably very short, lasting for 2 to 16 hours, depending on the exact sizes of the stars they orbit.[65] After this transit time (known as transit duration), the brightness will return to its initial value. Several months or years later (the orbital period), the brightness will dip again and remain low for the same transit duration as the planet travels again across the star. If the pattern repeats three or more times, with the same change in brightness and transit duration, the change in brightness is likely caused by a planet. This is called the transit method of detecting extrasolar planets.

Because of the large number of stars that are monitored, dozens of transits occur every day. Since each transit lasts only a few hours, it would be nearly impossible to move the telescope to study individual stars. Kepler was designed to monitor a fixed field of view so that it would not miss more than a small number of transits. The charge-coupled devices had to be of high precision to detect such tiny changes in brightness. About four transits of a given planet across a star would be sufficient to conclude that the effect was real.

The transit method of detection, while having significant advantages over other methods of planet detection, does have a significant drawback that will depress the statistics. In essence, as the planet orbits its star, it must pass directly in front of it, not angled appreciably, as seen from our solar system. Otherwise, if the orbit is askew from our perspective, the planet will simply circle the star, never causing a dip in brightness, and therefore be undetectable using this method. Kepler scientists calculated that the probability for the orbit to be properly aligned was equal to the diameter of the star divided by the diameter of the orbit; approximately 0.5 percent for an Earth-like orbit around a Sun-like star.[66]

---

63 Koch, D., and A. Gould. (2006, 7 August). "Overview of the Kepler Mission." NASA website.
64 Kluger, J. (2009, 6 March). "The Kepler Telescope: Taking a Census of the Galaxy." *Time*.
65 Koch, D. ,and A. Gould. (2006, 7 August). "Overview of the Kepler Mission." NASA website.
66 Ibid.; Jaffe, M. (2009, 9 March). "CU, Ball Space Mission Blasts Off." *Denver Post*.

The team used statistical analyses to deduce the actual number of planets by adding the number of missed planets to the observed number of planets. This allowed the frequency of occurrence of planets in our galaxy to be estimated. For every 100,000 good targets selected, the team predicted observation of 500 planets—more than the entire catalog of known extrasolar planets at launch and 500 more than had ever been observed when the mission was originally proposed in 1992, as well as in 1994, 1996, and 1998.

Based on the observed data from both the Kepler photometer and other telescopes, the use of the laws of physics provides information on the size of the planet, its distance from its star, and whether the planet is in the habitable zone. For example, Kepler's third law of motion allows astronomers to calculate the orbital size of the planet, given the period of the planet and the mass of the star deduced from its spectral classification. The size of the planet is found by considering the transit depth, the amount of light that the planet blocks as it crosses the star, and the size of the star. The planet's characteristic temperature can also be calculated given the planet's orbital size and the temperature and size of the star from its spectral classification and age. Questions of habitability could thus be considered.[67]

Finding the first rocky planets with liquid water on the surface and temperature conducive to life "will be the real breakthrough, when you find things that you'd actually like to own real estate on," said David Latham, a co-investigator from the Harvard-Smithsonian Center for Astrophysics, when the spacecraft was under development.[68]

As in all good experiments, the Kepler mission was designed such that a null result would be critically important to the determination of the rarity of such planets.[69] "One of the most interesting things we could find is zero," said Borucki. "That could mean we are alone in the universe."[70]

Masquerading as Transiting Planets

There was also a need for ground-based observations to verify potential transits. "There are several astrophysical phenomena that will masquerade as transiting planets and we have to sort those out from the ground," said project scientist Thomas "Nick" Gautier.[71] For instance, an eclipsing binary star or a triple system could also produce dips in the signal that could be mistaken for a transit. (Other space-based telescopes like Hubble and Spitzer have worked well for confirmation of especially important planetary can-

67   Koch, D., and A. Gould. (2006, 7 August). "Overview of the Kepler Mission." NASA website; Cowen, R. (2007, 14 July). "Passages: Revealing the nature of exoplanets." *Science News.*

68   Britt, R. (2002, 24 June). "Astronomers on brink of watershed in planet discoveries." Space.com.

69   Basri, G., et al. (2005). "The Kepler mission: A wide-field transit search for terrestrial planets." *New Astronomy Reviews,* 49. 478–485.

70   Modine, A. (2007, 13 April). "Kepler telescope primed to search for earth-like planets." *Register.*

71   Klotz, I. (2009, 17 February). "UK 'eyes' to hunt for other earths." *BBC News.*

didates, but observing time on these telescopes is too precious to be allotted only to confirmation of Kepler mission results. The thousands of planetary system candidates made assigning observing time by Hubble and Spitzer for all of them impossible.) The observers would use active optics imaging such as Guide Star Adaptive Optics at the Multi-Mirror Telescope Observatory, yielding pixel sizes of 0.02 to 0.04 arcseconds on the sky. "It's really powerful in the infrared, J, and K bands," said Dupree, who also observed the stars and star clusters for her astronomical research, cross-calibrating Kepler's photometry with the various spectroscopy from adaptive optics to try to calibrate the cluster ages, measure rotation, and image some of the clusters at high resolution.[72] Such work was complementary to the extrasolar planet research of Kepler but of high interest to astronomers who had made it their life's work.

Extrasolar Planets

The field of extrasolar planets—so new when William Borucki and colleagues prepared their initial proposal in 1992—had grown from a sample of zero to 300 giant planets by the time Kepler launched. The transit technique also had been demonstrated by several ground-based groups, including that of David Charbonneau, who would later become a Kepler participating scientist.[73]

Despite the field's fast growth, Kepler remained relevant due to its characterization as a pathfinder, its attention to detail, and its instrument sensitivity, able to detect even an Earth-size planet—something generally elusive to ground-based astronomy even with large telescopes and advances in adaptive optics. "This is exactly why you need to go to space," explained Dimitar Sasselov, co-investigator and astronomer at the Harvard-Smithsonian Center for Astrophysics, at an annual meeting of the American Astronomical Society.[74] Ground-based telescopes simply could not yet overcome the limitations of the atmosphere. In addition, the duty cycle of a space-based telescope was much greater than that of ground-based ones: observations could be done 24 hours a day instead of a few hours each night (weather permitting), eliminating the need for dark, clear skies during observations.[75]

72   Niebur, S. (2010, 6 January). Personal interview with A. Dupree. Located in "Kepler" file, NASA Historical Reference Collection, History Division, NASA Headquarters, Washington, DC.

73   Charbonneau, D., Brown, T. M., Latham, D. W., Mayor, M. (2000). "Detection of planetary transits across a sun-like star." *The Astrophysical Journal*, 529(1). *https://doi.org/10.1086/312457*; Cowen, R. (2007, 14 July). "Passages: revealing the nature of exoplanets." *Science News*.

74   Boyle, A. (2003, 6 January). "New technique finds farthest known planet." MSNBC.

75   Basri, G., et al. (2005). "The Kepler mission: A wide-field transit search for terrestrial planets." *New Astronomy Reviews*, 49. 478–485.

A Very Difficult Structure to Produce

The team knew from the start that one of the greatest technical challenges would be obtaining and installing the high-performance CCDs necessary for the implementation of this ambitious design. Kepler's large focal plane, requiring 42 high-resolution CCDs, each measuring 1 by 2 inches, for a total area of about a foot square, would have to function accurately and efficiently in the harsh environment of space. The CCDs would have to integrate seamlessly with the readout mechanism, withstand various temperature extremes without warping, and be several orders of magnitude more sensitive than the human eye. The temperature gradient endured by the instrument would be challenging, as the front of the telescope reached –85°C, while the electronics just behind it raised the temperature to a warm 30°C. Kepler was "a very difficult structure to produce because you don't want to warp it with temperature changes," said John Troelzch, program manager at Ball.[76]

CCD procurement began early, as a long-lead item, and with a twist. The proposal had included a preliminary buy of 30 detectors from each of two separate suppliers, each with a contract ready to execute upon selection of the mission, and an option to procure a total of 60 CCDs from the contractor who provided top-quality CCDs on time.[77] In May 2003, STA and e2v delivered evaluation-grade CCDs to the Kepler project.[78] In late October, the project executed the contract option to obtain all 60 from e2v.[79] "These devices were especially challenging, given what was wanted for the telescope and the time in which they wanted them," David Morris, e2v's lead engineer on the project, told BBC News.[80] (CCDs were finally delivered in August 2007.) In October 2003, the project passed its Systems Requirements Review, a major programmatic hurdle, and proceeded to award contracts to Ball to develop the optics and detectors, to Eastman Kodak for the optical subsystem, and to Corning for the primary mirror glass (they also manufactured materials for the Hubble Space Telescope).[81] Ball contracted Brashear to design and build the 1.4-meter lightweight primary mirror and the 0.95-meter fused-silica Schmidt corrector, with delivery expected two years later in 2005.[82]

---

76   Klotz, I. (2009, 17 February). "UK 'eyes' to hunt for other earths." *BBC News.*

77   Niebur, S. (2009, 16 December). Personal interview with B. Borucki. Located in "Kepler" file, NASA Historical Reference Collection, History Division, NASA Headquarters, Washington, DC.

78   Borucki et al. (2004, January). "The Kepler mission: a technical overview." In *Second Eddington Workshop: Stellar structure and habitable planet finding,* 9–11 April 2003, Palermo, Italy. 177–182.

79   Borucki, B. (2007, 19 September). Presentation at the Discovery@15 workshop in Huntsville, Alabama.

80   Klotz, I. (2009, 17 February). "UK 'eyes' to hunt for other earths." *BBC News.*

81   "NASA awards contracts for Kepler planet-finder search." (2002, October 29). *Aerospace Daily.* 4; "Corning joins NASA mission." (2003, 23 October). *Rochester Business Journal.*

82   Borucki et al. (2004, January). "The Kepler mission: a technical overview." In *Second Eddington Workshop: Stellar structure and habitable planet finding,* 9–11 April 2003, Palermo, Italy. 177–182.

The summer of 2004 was filled with 31 incremental preliminary design reviews of components and subsystems, culminating in the successful mission Preliminary Design Review on 12–15 October 2004. The project was on schedule for an October 2007 launch.[83]

While NASA Headquarters had expected there to be transient effects in the overlay of Jet Propulsion Laboratory management over Ames's management of Ball Aerospace, grossly insufficient attention was given to the conflict created by having JPL manage a mission that was designed to meet standards (test requirements, margins, etc.) that were not their own. Ball had experience working with Goddard Space Flight Center and, in order to ease the design, implementation, and review processes, had adopted Goddard's set of standards for flight missions. This straightforward decision—made undoubtedly in part to be a better partner to NASA—caused difficulty with their new NASA partner, JPL. The latter lab was now in the position of having to manage the project to, essentially, a competitor's specifications.

Whether this would cause an intractable problem was not immediately certain.[84] The team was relieved that the prior work was kept, and the mission continued as planned—not a certainty for those who had been in the business and seen this happen on other missions.[85]

Several coincidences eased this path for the initial stages of development. The Independent Review Team, for instance, had a number of members who had built hardware at Goddard and were able to help "translate" the standards and requirements to ensure that the planned tests met the needs of both project and management. Other review team members came from JPL's community and helped explain the needs of the project to its JPL management in its own terms.

Said Koch, "This is different than a planetary mission. It doesn't have to have quadruple redundancy and be a class A mission…. That was very counterculture to [JPL], and we worked real, real hard at JPL to not let them turn us into another JPL engineering extravaganza" that was not allowed to fail.[86] This was a difference in culture with far-reaching implications into such mundane areas as fault protection.

Whereas many Jet Propulsion Laboratory missions sling a spacecraft rapidly by a planet with a single opportunity or a small, discrete number of opportunities to collect data, the Kepler imager would have nearly four years to collect data. A fault shutting

83   Borucki et al. (2004, January). "The Kepler mission: a technical overview." In *Second Eddington Workshop: Stellar structure and habitable planet finding*, 9–11 April 2003, Palermo, Italy. 177–182.

84   Niebur, S. (2009, 16 December). Personal interview with M. Moore. Located in "Kepler" file, NASA Historical Reference Collection, History Division, NASA Headquarters, Washington, DC.

85   Niebur, S. (2010, 6 January). Personal interview with D. Koch. Located in "Kepler" file, NASA Historical Reference Collection, History Division, NASA Headquarters, Washington, DC.

86   Niebur, S. (2010, 6 January). Personal interview with D. Koch. Located in "Kepler" file, NASA Historical Reference Collection, History Division, NASA Headquarters, Washington, DC.

the system down wouldn't be an emergency requiring multiple redundancies (and many layers of depth) to reduce data loss. A fault, instead, could be treated more like a fault on a telescope, where a software patch could be sent on the next daily, or even weekly, upload with no loss in fidelity.

The initial tendency of the JPL managers and the Ball engineers was to protect the spacecraft with a Deep Impact–like multi-layer, multi-option fault protection system that had multiple levels of getting back up and running. The project began to spend significant time and financial resources on fault protection, testing, integration, and all the consequences of this design. And then, according to Michael Moore, the program executive, the question was asked: "Do we really need this?" He said, "Convincing everybody that what you really needed [instead] was a very robust but fairly simple fault protection safe mode approach was really fairly tough to do with the JPL guys."[87]

Although Ames, Ball, and JPL resolved most of the initial discrepancies, discussions about the roles and standards used for the final test and integration continued. Five degrees might not matter much in the build of an airplane, for instance, but for spacecraft components in stressful environments, it might determine whether the mission could achieve the four-year mission lifetime required to confirm the existence of an extrasolar planet.

Despite the inherent difficulties, JPL's expertise benefited the Kepler mission by bringing a broader experience base, additional resources, and the governmental oversight experience that had not been developed at the vast majority of potential industry partners—even those with prior NASA mission contractual experience. JPL also served as a greater "management counterweight," in Moore's words, sufficient to impress Ball.[88]

Refining the Field of View and Defining the Stellar Catalog

As a graduate student, Natalie Batalha read a report about FRESIP, the first iteration of the Kepler proposal, in the office of her collaborator and undergraduate adviser, Gabor Basri. On a National Research Council fellowship the next year, she worked on stellar variability—a relevant issue because 30 percent of the stars (she found) were so young and magnetically active that detection of their planets would be difficult or impossible. Meanwhile, Jon Jenkins, a researcher at SETI, did a study on solar variability based on recent Solar and Heliospheric Observatory data. Taken together, these two pieces helped demonstrate that "Earths" around Sun-like stars would be detectable and that enough stars are expected to be as quiet as the Sun. This was an important contribution in convincing planetary scientists and stellar astrophysicists alike of the virtues of detection endeavors.

---

87   Niebur, S. (2009, 16 December). Personal interview with M. Moore. Located in "Kepler" file, NASA Historical Reference Collection, History Division, NASA Headquarters, Washington, DC.

88   Ibid.

After selection, Batalha ran the robotic Vulcan telescope, a ground-based prototype for Kepler at Lick Observatory, before doing a study to optimize Kepler's field of view. "We discovered that the science yield would be higher if we pointed a little bit off the galactic plane just to get out of the glare of the giants that contaminate the field," said Batalha.[89] She would be named the project scientist of Kepler later in the mission.

Jenkins and collaborator Hema Chandrasekaran, then also of the SETI Institute, performed tradeoff studies, and they and Batalha talked about the results of the stellar population model simulations at the Kepler science working group meetings for about a year before proving in 2006 to the group that the shift in field of view was worthwhile. After that, the team had to identify the top 170,000 targets of the 4.5 million stars in the field of view, a "huge effort" that took nearly four years. Observing 170,000 stars would allow the observation of every star that was brighter than the 15th magnitude in the field of view.

The creation of the stellar catalog required a massive ground-based observation program to characterize all the stars in Kepler's field of view, identifying the surface temperature, surface gravity, metallicity, and size for each of the possible candidates. Initially, the science team had planned to classify the stars spectroscopically, but the task of quantifying enough of the millions of stars in the field of view in this way would stretch on much longer than the mission would allow. Even restricting the search to stars brighter than the 19th magnitude, 10^7 stars remained. The team had to completely rethink their strategy for an effort of this size. Kepler co-investigator Dave Latham settled on the necessary parameters, which would help define the size and nature of each star, and convinced the team. These characteristics would allow observers to exclude giants and early spectral types of stars from the target list. They built a photometer specifically for the purpose of creating the stellar catalog, dubbed Kepler Cam, on Whipple at Mt. Hopkins. Over the next several years, Latham took 1,600 pointings with multiple observations in every one of the broad and intermediate band filters to observe the stars at various colors. The observations took $2.5 million and over four years to complete.[90]

Co-investigator Tim Brown then used the results of the photometry to derive the stellar parameters for each star. This work resulted in the Kepler input catalog, with 1.5 million stars classified of the 13 million sources. Thus they completed a task that

89 Niebur, S. (2010, 6 January). Personal interview with N. Batalha. Located in the "Discovery Program" file, NASA Historical Reference Collection, History Division, NASA Headquarters, Washington, DC.

90 Brown, T., Latham, D., et al. (2011). "Kepler input catalog: photometric calibration and stellar classification." *Astron. J.* 142, 112.

a co-investigator would later recall as "an amazing, Herculean effort," and one that Borucki would proudly announce to the American Astronomical Society in 2007 as "the most comprehensive study of stars in this portion of our galaxy."[91]

Ground-based observatories, in fact, were an additional limitation on Kepler's mission design. Suitable exoplanet candidates would have to be within observing limits of terrestrial hardware. For example, if Kepler spotted a possible Earth-size planet at a sixteenth magnitude M dwarf star, but the ground-based observers couldn't follow it up because of their technical limits, Kepler's observation would not be nearly as useful, as it couldn't be confirmed from the ground. Out of all of this and other efforts (such as the Guest Observer Program, which added 3,000 targets of cluster stars, eclipsing binaries, and other stars) came a master list of 170,000 stars for observation during the four-year mission.

Development

Kepler passed its System Requirements Review on 2 September 2003, its Preliminary Design Review in October 2004, and its Confirmation Review on 2 December 2004.[92] The early management changes seemed to have settled into equilibrium, leading Borucki and team to state publicly: "The JPL team members have been smoothly integrated with those at Ames and [Ball Aerospace and Technologies Corporation]."[93] Further, the D&NFPO provided added value when small technical problems arose during development, finding experts to help the team solve problems in real time—both small ones in wiring and more significant ones, such as when the coating on the sapphire lenses began to peel. The strong optical department at Marshall Space Flight Center was able to step in and help the team understand the issues.[94]

Ames continued to support the mission as it ran into troubles as well, as Borucki relates: "We had difficulty when we purchased the glass for the Schmidt corrector and when we needed to grind and polish the corrector and the primary mirror. DX (i.e., military) programs had overlapping needs for optical glass, the grinding machines,

---

91   Niebur, S. (2010, 6 January). Personal interview with N. Batalha. Located in "Discovery Program" file, NASA Historical Reference Collection, History Division, NASA Headquarters, Washington, DC; Borucki et al. (2006, December). "Kepler mission development, update at the 2007 AAS/AAPT Joint Meeting, American Astronomical Society Meeting 209, #124.06." *Bulletin of the American Astronomical Society*, Vol. 38. 1071.

92   Koch, D. (2004, 27 October). "Kepler Mission: A Search for Habitable Planets." PowerPoint presentation to the Ames Internship Program. Downloaded from *http://kepler.nasa.gov/ppt/Ames_Internship_2004_10.ppt*; Borucki et al. (2006, December). "Kepler mission development, update at the 2007 AAS/AAPT Joint Meeting, American Astronomical Society Meeting 209, #124.06." *Bulletin of the American Astronomical Society*, Vol. 38. 1071.

93   Borucki et al. (2004, January). "The Kepler mission: A technical overview." In *Second Eddington Workshop: Stellar structure and habitable planet finding*, 9–11 April 2003, Palermo, Italy. 177–182.

94   Niebur, S. (2009, 16 December). Personal interview with W. Borucki. Located in "Kepler" file, NASA Historical Reference Collection, History Division, NASA Headquarters, Washington, DC.

the polishing machines, and for the facility for coating the glass. Both the Discovery Program Office and [Ames Center Director] Pete Worden were a huge help" in moving the optics development forward.[95] Kepler acquired a science director in Janice Voss, an astronaut assigned to Ames, from October 2004 to November 2007.[96]

On 25 January 2005, the Kepler mission entered Phase C/D and NASA simultaneously approved an eight-month launch slip, to 2008.[97] The contract for building the photometer, the instrument on the mission, was awarded to Ball in early February 2005.[98] The mirror was already being manufactured by L-3 Communications Brashear as a subcontract to Ball. L-3 had quickly fallen behind in the optics fabrication, however, "running a little late and being more expensive than we expected," said Michael Moore. He noted that personnel staffing loads at Ball were likewise running over what had been estimated during that time. The reason: the avionics system needed additional work. Ball responded by replacing the project's program manager, Len Andreozzi, with Monte Henderson, who had just managed the development phase of Deep Impact.[99] By October 2005, the Schmidt corrector and the 1.4 m aperture primary mirror were complete and were being polished. All 46 CCDs had been delivered and tested. The team was building and testing the CCD driver, data acquisition, and science data accumulator boards, as well as the first build of the flight software.[100] Meanwhile, the co-investigators continued to prepare the stellar catalog of targets.[101]

Over Budget and Behind Schedule

Kepler's initial cost of less than $300 million had been raised to $457 million shortly after selection for several reasons unrelated to the project team. First, the mission had to accommodate the slow start mandated by NASA Headquarters. There was the mandated change to full-cost accounting (which affected Kepler more than most, due

---

95   Ibid.

96   Whitney, P. (2008, 25 June). "Astronaut brings space adventures to Hanover Audience." *Madison Courier.*

97   Morris, J. (2005, 13 June). "Discovery program to release AO." *Aviation Week's Aerospace Daily & Defense Report.* 214(51).

98   Mewhinney, M. (2005, 14 February). "NASA awards contract for Kepler mission photometer." NASA Ames news release.

99   Berger, B. (2006, 23 January). "Despite problems, Kepler on track for June 2008 launch." *SpaceNews.*

100   Borucki, W. (2005, December). "Kepler Mission: Current Status, presented at the American Astronomical Society Meeting 207, #153.01." *Bulletin of the American Astronomical Society,* Vol. 37. 1412.

101   Latham, D., et al. and T. Brown. (2005, December) "Presentation at the American Astronomical Society Meeting 207." *Bulletin of the American Astronomical Society,* Vol. 37.

to the large number of NASA civil servants at Ames on the project). The cost for the Delta II rocket booster had increased. Finally, the project had to bear the extra layer of management added to the team by NASA.

Although a first look at the 2006 NASA budget held no surprises for Kepler and much of the Science Mission Directorate at NASA Headquarters, trouble was soon to come.[102] Kepler would face yet another delay—this time of undetermined length, and not of its own making. Rick Howard, deputy director of the Universe Division at NASA Headquarters, went on record as saying that the mission was coming along well, but due to overruns and problems on other missions within the Science Mission Directorate, the planet-finding telescope was hit with a $35 million reduction in the $136 million budget that year.[103] To accommodate that reduction, the launch date was again slipped to June 2008, and the total cost continued to increase toward $515 million.[104]

Years later, when asked about cost caps after the spacecraft had launched, Borucki said: "Although the AO said that you must cost the mission in 1998 dollars, the moment that we got accepted, cost estimates were changed to be in real-year dollars. That jumped the price up $20 million above what we had proposed. Further, as required, we had priced the proposal with government employees at no cost to the mission. [The new NASA requirement to employ full-cost accounting] also increased our cost estimate.... We were at $400 million from the $300 million estimate within a year although we [had] not yet started mission development. So, the thing to learn is that a lot of this—the rules and requirements change continuously."[105]

The move to full-cost accounting was a NASA-wide initiative intended to improve competitiveness for mission proposals from non-NASA centers. For years, aerospace contractors and other institutions had complained about the inherent advantage of NASA centers, since NASA civil service personnel were paid out of NASA general funds and projects were not charged for their use. Full-cost accounting would correct this. Meanwhile, projects affected during the transition were compensated for the apparent increase in funds needed so that their management and implementation would not be affected. It did have the effect, though, of increasing the *perceived* cost of missions caught in transition, and the Kepler mission more than most due to its management and implementation by NASA Ames civil servants, in cooperation with Ball engineers and technicians.

---

102 Zimmerman, R. (2005, 9 February). "Commentary: Analysis: A Promising NASA Budget." United Press International.

103 Berger, B. (2005, 7 June). "Big Universe: tightening budget: NASA looks for ways to pay for Hubble, cost overruns." *SpaceNews.*

104 Berger, B. (2009, 16 December). "Despite problems, Kepler on track for June 2008 launch." *SpaceNews.*

105 Niebur, S. (2009, 16 December). Personal interview with W. Borucki. Located in "Kepler" file, NASA Historical Reference Collection, History Division, NASA Headquarters, Washington, DC.

The upshot of all this is that Kepler was over budget and behind schedule, and there was no instrument easily descoped without affecting the core science of the mission. Indeed, cutting aspects of the science was not even an option—the only thing that could be cut was the quantity and certainty of the extrasolar planet candidates. The team found it a real challenge to cut science or make trades that affected the science, and they recognized this early on.[106]

In March 2006, a 21 percent cost overrun caused a corresponding slip in launch date to 1 November 2008, and raised the total cost of the mission to $550 million. In addition, the spacecraft design was modified to reduce risk, cost, and complexity by replacing its gimbaled high-gain antenna in the design with a fixed antenna. This change required the spacecraft body to change its attitude in order to downlink the scientific data; the team noted that the change in pointing would result in a loss of about one observing day per month. But there was more to it than that: although the team was still able to double the size of the data recorder, in order to downlink once a month instead of every fourth day, there was an additional loss in precision. The original requirement of 20 parts per million in four hours to see an Earth-size transit was relaxed to 20 parts per million integrated over five hours. After further changes, the final build specification was 20 parts per million integrated over six and a half hours. This was the upper limit, as that was the exact value for a grazing transit. (A central transit was 13 hours.)[107] With these changes, the Kepler mission proceeded into subsystem critical design reviews beginning in April 2006.

After years of delays and budget overruns, however, the Discovery Program had had enough. There simply was no money to provide to Kepler as needed. It was a cost-capped mission, and there was no extra discretionary money at the division level to cover expenses. To cover Kepler's price increases, the next Discovery Announcement of Opportunity would have to be pushed out uncomfortably far—and still, that would not be enough to fund the program fully in certain fiscal years. Andy Dantzler, director of the Planetary Science Division, went to talk to the Astrophysics Division director, Anne Kinney, and laid out his concerns. The program could no longer afford to pay for the increased costs of Kepler, yet the Astrophysics Division had adopted it as a key part of its exoplanet program. Thus, the mission could not be canceled. Despite being a strategic investment, however, the project was too small for its own project office.

---

106   Borucki, W. (2007, 19 September). Presentation at the Discovery@15 workshop in Huntsville, Alabama.

107   Niebur, S. (2010, 6 January). Personal interview with D. Koch. Located in "Kepler" file, NASA Historical Reference Collection, History Division, NASA Headquarters, Washington, DC.

Out of these meetings came an agreement: the mission would not be canceled, but the Astrophysics Division would pay for its overruns. The mission would continue to be managed out of the Discovery and New Frontiers Program Office.[108]

William Borucki made the issue crystal clear: "Kepler was in the middle of the two programs and thus an orphan. To succeed, there must be somebody at [NASA] Headquarters to look after it…. Everybody wants each of them to succeed because they will do great science. But [NASA] Headquarters always has a shortage of funds."[109] By moving the project and its overruns to Astrophysics, it got more attention from management, and problems were identified earlier and in the context of what they would cost the Astrophysics Division. Astrophysics now had fiscal responsibility and could weigh the value of funding increases against its plans for future exoplanet missions, flagship missions, and other needs.

On the Discovery side, this removed a huge potential lien from the program and enabled Discovery to begin planning for the next Announcement of Opportunity. On 8 August, the Kepler mirror—the largest optical mirror ever built for a mission beyond Earth's orbit—arrived at Ball for environmental testing and integration with the spacecraft.[110] In October, both the mission's Integrated Action Team and a center management review team participated in the intensive, five-day Critical Design Review, which was successfully concluded without any additional slips in launch date. In December, Borucki announced that plans for the 2007 Participating Scientist and 2008 Guest Observer Programs were on track.[111] But Kepler's financial troubles were far from over.

When a new Associate Administrator, S. Alan Stern, arrived to lead the Science Mission Directorate in April 2007, he had a very low tolerance for cost overruns. A Principal Investigator himself—of New Horizons, the first New Frontiers mission, bound for Pluto—he quickly appointed a new "front office" management team and set about making policy changes across the board.[112]

---

108   Niebur, S. (2009, 10 December). Personal interview with M. New. Located in "Discovery Program" file, NASA Historical Reference Collection, History Division, NASA Headquarters, Washington, DC; Niebur, S. (2009, 16 December). Personal interview with M. Moore. Located in "Kepler" file, NASA Historical Reference Collection, History Division, NASA Headquarters, Washington, DC.

109   Niebur, S. (2009, 16 December). Personal interview with W. Borucki. Located in "Kepler" file, NASA Historical Reference Collection, History Division, NASA Headquarters, Washington, DC.

110   Ball Aerospace. (2006, 8 August). Press release. Downloaded from *http://www.prnewswire.com/cgi-bin/stories.pl?ACCT=104&STORY=/www/story/08-08-2006/0004412377&EDATE=*. See also *https://spaceref.com/press-release/kepler-mirror-arrives-at-ball-aerospace-for-test-and-integration/*.

111   Borucki et al. (2006, December). "Kepler mission development, update at the 2007 AAS/AAPT Joint Meeting, American Astronomical Society Meeting 209, #124.06." *Bulletin of the American Astronomical Society*, Vol. 38. 1071.

112   Leary, W. (2008, 1 January). "Wielding a Cost-Cutting Ax, and Often, at NASA." *The New York Times*.

One of the first challenges for this new team was a request for an additional $42 million and a four-month launch slip for Kepler, due to difficulties building the focal plane. At $550 million, the mission already greatly exceeded the Discovery box for which it was selected, but because of the myriad NASA Headquarters fiscal, schedule, and management mandates, the overruns were largely outside the control of the mission itself. Despite this, Stern's immediate response was to reject the request and tell the project to come back with a replan in June, with no additional funds.

On 1 June, Kepler came back to NASA Headquarters with a revised request, this time asking for $54 million. Stern countered, "If you don't think I'm serious, just come back to me with numbers like these again and that will be the end of the project."[113]

And yet Stern gave the team another month to cut costs and present a replan within the current budget. He threatened to open the project to new bids for others to finish using the completed hardware as no-cost, government-furnished equipment. He held fast to this decision, later telling *The New York Times*, "Four times they came for more money and four times we told them 'No.'"[114]

Faced with a $54 million deficit, the team was directed to take a closer look at the overruns and replan both mission development and future operations. The replan was presented at a project management meeting in Boulder, Colorado, on 6 July 2007. The replan included everything from restructuring project management to eliminating tests from the project plan. The replan was regressive in some sense, as science operations were once again cut in Phase E to pay for development issues in Phase C. Six months of observations would be cut, purely to save the cost of monitoring the spacecraft and staffing the mission operations center. The 25 percent reserve rules had not, in the end, put an end to the robbing of the science return to pay for overruns in engineering; 12 percent fewer planets would be observed under the now-shortened three-and-a-half-year mission.

When the changes were announced to the public, Stern observed: "No tests that affect the safety or ultimate performance of the system have been dropped...no significant science will be lost." To restore project reserves to 24 percent without impinging on other current or future missions in the Astrophysics Division, Ball followed Orbital's lead from several years before and gave up some of its earned fee.[115]

Stern changed many things at NASA Headquarters, but he had reinforced former Associate Administrator Ed Weiler's earlier management strategy, stating publicly to

113   Berger, B. (2007, 17 July). "Kepler team cuts costs, avoids cancellation." Space.com.

114   Leary, W. (2008, 1 January). "Wielding a Cost-Cutting Ax, and Often, at NASA." *The New York Times*.

115   Stern, A. (2008, 13 March). Statement of S. Alan Stern, Associate Administrator for the SMD National Aeronautics and Space Administration, 13 March 2008, before the Subcommittee on Space and Aeronautics Committee on Science and Technology of the U.S. House of Representatives.

the Subcommittee on Space and Aeronautics Committee on Science and Technology of the U.S. House of Representatives: "NASA's approach to both the [Solar Dynamics Observatory] and Kepler issues conform[s] to the general principle that resources to solve project problems should come first from the mission lines or programs that include that project. Problems in programs and missions should be addressed within the Division (science area) in which they occur whenever possible."[116] Stern was willing to take those steps, and he approved the replan and the continuation of the project.[117]

The extent of Kepler's replan was unprecedented in the Principal Investigator–led mission line programs. To convince a reluctant Associate Administrator to continue their program, Kepler had to sacrifice engineering tests, part of the spacecraft provider fee, and even the position of the Principal Investigator. Everyone had to pay for the overruns. Like Dawn's first overrun, Stern predicated success in part on the agreement of the spacecraft provider to give up millions of dollars of their corporate bonus ("earned fee"). Wholesale management changes were also in order. A respected senior manager at the Jet Propulsion Laboratory, Leslie Livesay, was put in charge of the entire mission, outranking Ames project managers and even the ex–Principal Investigator. This change emphasized the role of the project manager. The mission had grown so large that it would now be managed as a larger mission, with increased attention to management and a decreased role for the Principal Investigator, as NASA Headquarters engaged in significant discussion over the appropriate role of the PI in a $600 million mission such as Kepler and future New Frontiers missions.

William Borucki, Principal Investigator of the whole mission, was reduced to science PI for the duration of the mission's development and operation, and his deputy was reduced to deputy science PI. This was a major change in how NASA executed small missions, reflecting its transition from the Discovery Program to a pathfinder role in the Terrestrial Planet Finder program in the Astrophysics Division.[118] The project organization and management of 2007 looked very little like it had even a few years earlier.

Throughout Kepler's development, extrasolar planets were discovered by ground-based telescopes, using the transit technique that Kepler would later employ. By late 2006, over 200 extrasolar planets had been discovered—eight of them using the transit

---

116   Ibid.

117   Leary, W. (2008, 1 January). "Wielding a Cost-Cutting Ax, and Often, at NASA." *The New York Times.*

118   David, L. (2009, 15 January). "Kepler spacecraft to hunt Earth-like worlds." Space.com.

technique.[119] These discoveries, and those of 16 more candidates discovered in a single Hubble image, led Kepler science working group team member Alan Boss to conclude, "Planets are everywhere."[120]

COROT, a French satellite designed to use the transit technique, launched in December 2006 and announced its first detection of a planet just five times the mass of Earth in May 2007. Early estimates showed COROT to be outperforming its sensitivity in design specification by 10 to 30 times.[121] While COROT was seeing the first signs of extrasolar planets, the Kepler team was still planning on a late 2007 launch— although with less certainty.[122]

Kepler would have an advantage in orbit, if not in time: Kepler's detector would be more sensitive, and its heliocentric, Earth-trailing orbit would be much better suited to extrasolar planet detection than the low orbit of COROT. Moreover, COROT had a much lower duty cycle for observations, as Earth, the Moon, and the Sun periodically blocked its view. Indeed, Kepler had every advantage over COROT—except launch date. COROT's effective aperture was 588 square centimeters; Kepler's was 5,800 square centimeters. COROT had a 9-square-degree field of view; Kepler's was over 100 square degrees. COROT was able to spend less than half a year on its target; Kepler planned to spend over four years.[123]

The first images of extrasolar planets were reported later that year in the journal *Science*, by two teams who independently reported seeing planets in images taken during observing opportunities. Christian Mario, of the Herzberg Institute of Astrophysics in Victoria, British Columbia, used adaptive optics on ground-based telescopes on Mauna Kea and software that acted like a coronagraph to block the light from the star, known as HR8799.[124] Paul Kalas of the University of California, Berkeley, used Hubble to observe nearby Formalhaut, one of the brightest and coolest stars with a massive dust disk. Such direct observation of extrasolar planets was one of the most speculative goals of the Hubble Space Telescope; even Ed Weiler, who spent most of his career nurturing Hubble through development and launch, was pleasantly surprised, saying, "I actually never thought it would happen."[125]

---

119   Than, K. (2006, 8 September). "Modified backyard telescopes find extrasolar planet." Space.com.

120   Spotts, P. (2006, 6 October). "Deep in the galaxy, signs of Jupiter-like planets." *The Christian Science Monitor*.

121   Clark, S. (2007, 4 May). "European planet hunters on brink of earth-sized prize." *New Scientist*.

122   Modine, A. (2007, 13 April). "Kepler telescope primed to search for earth-like planets." *Register*.

123   Koch, D. (2004, 27 October). "Kepler Mission: A Search for Habitable Planets." Presentation to the Ames Internship Program. Downloaded from *http://kepler.nasa.gov/ppt/Ames_Internship_2004_10.ppt*.

124   Overbye, D. (2008, 14 November). "Now in sight: Far-off planets." *The New York Times*.

125   Achenbach, J. (2008, 14 November). "In a first, astronomers report viewing planets of other suns." *Washington Post*.

By September 2007, the precision coating process of Kepler's primary mirror and the integration of the detector array assembly had been completed.[126] The spacecraft assembly had started, including work with the reaction control system, reaction wheels, attitude determination and control, and power. All subsystems had passed their environmental and performance tests. It was set for launch in February 2009. After much discussion at NASA Headquarters, the project initiated a Guest Observer program, in which scientists could propose that Kepler view objects within its field of view but not already in the Kepler Target Catalog. In Paris, meanwhile, the Kepler Asteroseismic Science Consortium, comprising over 100 astrophysicists led by Jørgen Christensen-Dalsgaard, held its first meeting in 2007 to organize an international data analysis team to determine the sizes and ages of a portion of the stars monitored by Kepler.[127]

In late 2008, however, an unexpected technical problem arose when engineers discovered that the titanium used to build the spider ring of the spacecraft was falsely qualified and made from "substandard and non-conforming titanium," according to the U.S. Attorney's Office.[128] The discovery of counterfeit parts led to a search warrant in April 2008 and a federal indictment against Western Titanium Incorporated and four company executives, including CEO Daniel Schroeder, in December 2009.[129] The indictment accused the company of "knowingly and intentionally" misrepresenting the quality of 7,900 parts made of nonconforming titanium to the Defense Department, in addition to the parts delivered to Ball Aerospace and its subcontractors for the Kepler mission. The titanium was bought at about the same time as titanium bought by the U.S. Air Force under military specification MIL-T-9046, reportedly requiring a rolled plate process in manufacturing, but the parts were alleged to be forged instead. "Titanium made with a forging process results in different properties and the strength of the metal is diffused through the finished product," explained Keith Meyer, Boeing materials specialist.[130] (The charges against the four executives were dismissed in 2011.)[131]

126 Ball Aerospace. (2007, 27 September). "Ball Aerospace Completes Primary Mirror and Detector Array Assembly Milestones for Kepler Mission." News release.

127 Borucki, W., et al. (2007, December). "Kepler mission: current status. Presented at the American Astronomical Society, AAS Meeting #211, #36.03." *Bulletin of the American Astronomical Society*, Vol. 39. 788.

128 Croft, J. (2008, 16 December). "NASA investigates effects of falsely certified titanium." *Flight International*.

129 Iannotta, B. (2009, 14 March). "Engineering society helps NASA combat counterfeit parts problem." Space.com.

130 Rector, G. (2009, 23 January). "Company denies allegations of falsely certifying parts." *Macon Telegraph*.

131 Western Titanium, Inc. (2011, 13 January). "Western Titanium Resolves Pending Charges." Retrieved September 21, 2022, from *https://www.prnewswire.com/news-releases/western-titanium-resolves-pending-charges-113487664.html*.

The parts were used on U.S. Air Force F-15s, F-22s, and C-17s, according to the U.S. Attorney's Office in San Diego.[132] Ball Aerospace, who apparently bought the titanium in good faith, and NASA were concerned. Internal e-mails cited by the media indicate that "it was concluded by the program personnel that the substituted titanium was a mission catastrophic risk should it fail," according to NASA lead counsel Richard McCarthy.[133] NASA inquired into the actual material properties of the titanium and indicated that testing would be done to determine whether the incorporated titanium would be appropriate for the spacecraft, saying, "We cannot, I imagine, get a 're-do' accomplished in time if it turns out that the Kepler mission has a defective critical part."[134] In March 2009, acting NASA Administrator Chris Scolese testified to the House Science and Technology subcommittee on cost implications: "If you don't find out about them at receipt, you find out about them when you are in test or you find out about [them] when you're sitting on the top of the rocket, or worse, you find out about it when you're in space. And all of those have cost implications."[135]

Miraculously, given Kepler's track record and despite concerns, the spacecraft passed its pre-ship review and was shipped to the Cape, arriving on 6 January 2009.[136]

"An Image of a Blue Ball"

Kepler was fitted with a DVD containing the names of millions of people wanting to participate in some small way in a mission to space.[137] Along with the names, participants were given the chance to express their thoughts about the importance of the planet-finding mission as part of the celebration of the International Year of Astronomy 2009, four hundred years after the astronomer Johannes Kepler published the first two laws of planetary motion. A copy of the names and messages would be stored at the Smithsonian's National Air and Space Museum.

National and global outreach was essential to Kepler, which was itself a mission immediately understood by a swath of the public: the search for another Earth. As San

---

132   Iannotta, B. (2009, 14 March). "Engineering society helps NASA combat counterfeit parts problem." Space.com.

133   Croft, J. (2008, 12 December). "Suspect Titanium could ground NASA planet-finding satellite." *Flight Global.*

134   Croft, J. (2008, 16 December). "NASA investigates effects of falsely certified titanium." *Flight International.*

135   Iannotta, B. (2009, 14 March). "Engineering society helps NASA combat counterfeit parts problem." Space.com.

136   NASA. (2008, August). News release. Downloaded from *http://www.nasa.gov/centers/ames/news/releases/2008/08-111AR.html*; Dean, J. (2008, 22 December). "Kepler ready for delivery to space coast." *Florida Today.*

137   Jones, K.C. (2008, 7 May). "NASA to launch names into space in search for planets." *Information Week.*

Francisco State University astronomer Debra Fischer said at the time, "The ultimate goal of NASA, in 15 years or so, [is] to take an image of a blue ball. Kepler will tell us how to get (to that goal)."[138]

In 2009, Ed Weiler called Kepler a pathfinder for more sophisticated missions that may one day study the atmospheres of Earth-like planets to look for signs of biological—or even industrial—activity. Before the astronomy community could take that next step, however, "we've got to be sure there are at least a few earthlike planets out there. That's why Kepler is so important."[139]

Expectations rose, and quickly.[140] Author and planetary scientist Alan Boss spoke enthusiastically about Kepler and COROT at the annual meeting of the American Association for the Advancement of Science, promoting their potential for finding Earth like planets. The media took his words and ran with them, reporting that the potential for habitable worlds had risen to "billions," "trillions," and "one hundred billion trillion"—as many Earths as there are stars in the universe. The media was enchanted with this idea and the inevitability of which Boss spoke when he said, "If you have a habitable world and let it evolve for a few billion years then inevitably some sort of life will form on it."[141] Many of those associated closely with the mission, however, were careful to be cautious in their optimism.[142]

In the early-morning hours of 19 February, the Kepler spacecraft arrived at Launch Complex 17 at Cape Canaveral Air Station, ahead of its March 2009 launch. Several days later, the spacecraft and its third stage booster were mated to the United Launch Alliance Delta II 7245 rocket, and the work at the launch pad began.[143]

Because of concern over the recent launch failure of the $270 million Orbiting Carbon Observatory, an Earth System Science Pathfinder mission, which launched on 24 February 2009, on the Orbital Sciences–made Taurus XL and failed to reach orbit, Kepler's launch was delayed a day to allow additional analysis of the commonalities between launch vehicles.[144]

138   Robert Sanders, "With March 6 Kepler launch, work begins for Berkeley astronomers," 3 March 2009. *https://www.berkeley.edu/news/media/releases/2009/03/03_kepler.shtml.*

139   Harwood, W. (2009, 9 March). "Kepler Spacecraft Leaves Earth To Discover New Worlds." *Spaceflight Now.*

140   Niebur, S. (2010, 6 January). Personal interview with D. Koch. Located in "Kepler" file, NASA Historical Reference Collection, History Division, NASA Headquarters, Washington, DC.

141   Alleyne, R. (2009, 16 February). "AAAS: 'One hundred billion trillion' planets where alien life could flourish." *Daily Telegraph*; AFP. (2009, 20 February). "NASA readies mission to find Earth-like planets."

142   Klotz, I. (2009, 17 February). "UK 'eyes' to hunt for other Earths." BBC News.

143   Dean, J. (2009, 19 February). "Kepler reaches Cape launch pad." *Florida Today.*

144   Swift, M. (2009, 1 March). "Mountain View scientists giddy over NASA's search for faraway planets." *Silicon Valley Mercury News.*

Finally, at age 70, surrounded by his wife, daughters, grandchildren, and team, William Borucki saw his photometer mission launched on 6 March 2009 at 10:49 p.m. EST.[145] The rocket soared into the air and out of it, sending the spacecraft away from Earth and boosting it into an Earth-trailing solar orbit as planned. By trailing Earth, the spacecraft could avoid observing it; there would be no light interference or occultation of the stars in Kepler's field of view by our own planet.

Shortly before 11:30 p.m. EST, the spacecraft attained orbit, and control of the spacecraft was transferred to the mission operations center at the University of Colorado's Laboratory for Atmospheric and Space Physics. The center was staffed by a mix of students and professionals from the university and technicians from Ball Aerospace, who oversaw their contract. It was a way to train students while providing mission operations at a lower cost. Bill Possel, director of mission operations, characterized Kepler operations as "maybe a notch above" that of ICESat.[146]

Two students who were quoted on the first night of operations noted that the two-month checkout would be demanding. Expectations included "No life for the next two months," said Laura Bush, an aerospace graduate student. Matt Lenda, another student, agreed, saying "this is definitely the coolest thing." Twenty students had been trained and would be overseen by 16 professionals. As Lenda said, "In space operations, boring is good. You want boring."[147]

Even before the photometer took its first images of the star field, important data collection was taking place. "We have thoroughly measured the background noise so that our photometer can detect minute changes in a star's brightness caused by planets," said Borucki three weeks after launch. After those measurements were completed, the 1.7- by 1.3-meter oval protective dust cover—key for protecting the photometer from particle contamination and stray light during launch—was jettisoned into space. Engineers at the Laboratory for Atmospheric and Space Physics mission operations center heated up the "burn wire" remotely. As the thin wire heated with an electrical current, it weakened and broke, releasing a latch on the photometer's cover. The spring-loaded cover swung open, the fly-away hinge released, and then it was gone.[148] As the photometer continued moving away from Earth at about a kilometer per second, the engineers and scientists prepared to take the mission's first stellar measurements—its "first light."

"I came in early that morning—I was holding my breath in anticipation," said Jon Jenkins, a researcher at SETI, of the day the first data came down. Once he opened the software with the Kepler data and the light curve for HAT-P-7, an early target,

145   Dunn, M. (2009, 9 March). "Telescope Blasts into Space To Find Other Earths." AP.
146   David, L. (2009, 15 January). "Kepler Spacecraft to hunt Earth-like worlds." Space.com.
147   Jaffe, M. (2009, 9 March). "CU, Ball Space Mission Blasts Off." *Denver Post.*
148   "Cover taken off planet-hunting telescope." (2009, 9 April). Space.com.

Jenkins saw distinctive dips in the light curve. Excitedly, he showed them to the team, saying, "I think we are looking at our first science paper."[149] The transit signal was so strong that both the transit and the eclipse of the planet as it passed behind the star were clearly detected.

A "hot Jupiter" had thus been spotted in the first ten days of the mission. The planet had been detected previously by ground-based telescopes, demonstrating Kepler's detection capabilities. The paper would be published in the journal *Science* the first week of August 2009, but the team could not wait to release the first images to the press and the American people, who funded the mission.

The release policy for Kepler data was strict, requiring that planet detections be validated by ground-based observations that met rigorous requirements.[150] Since it takes time to schedule telescope operations and to make the observations on a clear night and from observatories that can see the Summer Triangle clearly, no data of new planets would be released until several months after the first transits were detected.[151]

The first new science discoveries were announced in January 2010, at the American Astronomical Society meeting and in a special issue of *Astrophysical Journal Letters*. Twenty-eight papers were published on the first 10 days of data, including that (rare) special issue of the journal. On 15 June 2010, the Kepler data release contained 165,000 stars monitored for planetary transits, 750 of which had candidates for transiting planets.[152]

The Kepler data also revealed stellar oscillations, or "starquakes." Such data allowed astroseismologists to study the interior of stars in much the same way that seismologists study earthquakes to understand the interior of Earth. Daniel Huber, lead author on a Kepler Asteroseismic Science Consortium study, said, "Kepler data ultimately will give us a better understanding of the future of our Sun and the evolution of our galaxy as a whole." The first results released included detailed studies of the six-billion-year-old stars KIC 11026764 and RR Lyrae, shown to oscillate with not only the well-known period of 13.5 hours, but also an additional oscillation period twice as long.[153]

On 10 January 2011, the Kepler science team announced the discovery of the first rocky planet outside the solar system, orbiting a star now named Kepler 10. Scientists confirmed the observations with the W. M. Keck Observatory 10-meter telescope in

---

149   Swift, M. (2009, 7 August). "Kepler Spacecraft Discovers Atmosphere of 'Exoplanet.'" *San Jose Mercury News.*

150   Bryson, S., et al. (2020). "The occurrence of rocky habitable zone planets around solar-like stars from Kepler data." *Astron. J.* 161, 36. See also Kepler Data Processing Handbook, KSCI-19081-003, (2020) edited by Jon M. Jenkins.

151   Borucki et al. (2004, January). "The Kepler mission: A technical overview." In *Second Eddington Workshop: Stellar structure and habitable planet finding,* 9–11 April 2003, Palermo, Italy. 177–182.

152   NASA. (2010, 26 October). "NASA's Kepler Mission Wins 2010 Software of the Year Award." NASA news release 10-245.

153   NASA. (2010, 26 October). "NASA's Kepler Spacecraft Takes Pulse of Distant Stars." NASA news release 10-276.

Hawai'i and measured the planet's properties. Kepler 10b, its second planet, is 1.4 times Earth's size, 4.6 times Earth's mass, and has an average density of 8.8 grams/cubic centimeter. Measurements of the variation in Kepler 10's light showed that Kepler 10b has an orbital period of 0.84 days; Kepler 10b is therefore over 400 times closer to its star than Earth is to the Sun, and the planet is not in the habitable zone.[154] Just over a year earlier, after a meeting at NASA Headquarters held on 16 December 2009 that included a presentation by William Borucki providing a peek at the mission's first results, NASA announced the transfer of management of all operations for the Kepler mission from JPL back to NASA Ames. James Fanson was succeeded as project manager by Roger Hunter, who had joined the project earlier in 2009 as Kepler project manager at Ames. Borucki and Koch retained their roles as science Principal Investigator and Deputy PI. "The transition of the mission leadership from JPL to Ames is the culmination of a transition plan agreed to some time ago by the two centers," Hunter said. "Ames had a large role in the development of the mission and plays an even larger role in its operation. The transfer of the project management role is the final milestone of this mission transition."[155]

During its eight years of operation, the Kepler/K2 mission detected over 2,600 confirmed planets with several thousand more candidates. These range from rocky planets like Earth to giant planets that have densities as low as that of plastic foam.[156] Many of these planets are similar in size to Earth, and a fraction are in the habitable zone of their stars where life might be possible. The results show that there are more planets than stars in our galaxy and imply that there are billions of Earth-size planets in the habitable zone. The Kepler mission provided the data needed to develop more advanced (and much more expensive) space missions that will be able to determine which planets have an atmosphere, liquid water, and signs of life.

THE MOON MINERALOGY MAPPER (M³)

While Dawn and Kepler were moving toward launch, NASA selected a mission of opportunity to be implemented through the Discovery Program: the Moon Mineralogy Mapper (M³). The instrument, led by Carle Pieters of Brown University, would map the mineral composition of the entire lunar surface at high resolution, flying on the Indian Space Research Organisation's (ISRO's) Chandrayaan-1 spacecraft, which was

---

154   NASA. (2011, 10 January). "NASA's Kepler Mission Discovers its First Rocky Planet." NASA news release 11-007.

155   NASA. (2009, 16 December). "NASA Transfers Kepler Mission Management to Ames Research Center." NASA news release 09-156AR.

156   Borucki, W. (2016). "Kepler Mission: Development and Overview." *Rep. Prog. Phys.* 79, 036901.

scheduled to launch in late 2008. Pieters was also a team member on the Dawn mission. The selection by the Discovery Program was only a first step toward approval for M³. It still needed to be selected by ISRO for flight.

To hedge its bets, NASA gave M³ a six-month Phase A, at $250,000 in real-year dollars in April 2005, that would occur concurrently with the ISRO selection time frame. If selected by the space agency, NASA and ISRO would work together to draft an international agreement before confirming the Moon instrument for full development.[157] The investigation complemented other experiments selected by NASA in response to the Announcement of Opportunity for the Lunar Reconnaissance Orbiter (LRO), a spacecraft set to launch in 2009 to study the Moon for future human missions.

Driving the science of M³ was the search for direct evidence of water ice pockets inside craters near the lunar poles. The instrument was an 8.3-kilogram visible–to–near-infrared grating spectrometer (0.43 to 3.0 microns), with a 24-degree field of view and two imaging modes: global (140 meters spatial, 20–40 nanometers spectral) and targeted (70 meters spatial, 10 nanometers spectral), all at higher resolutions than any previous, similar lunar science instrument. The spectrometer would acquire long, narrow, 40-kilometer images of the lunar surface in a 260-color spectrum. A full map of the lunar surface would be created by combining over 274 image strips after the data were received back on Earth.

The lunar mission Chandrayaan-1 ("moon craft" in Sanskrit) would carry 11 instruments in its payload, with six provided by consortia outside India. In addition to orbiting the Moon, it would carry a 64-pound smart impactor with camera, altimeter, and spectrometer, which would be released from the spacecraft to plow into the lunar surface.

The notion of a joint U.S.–India mission emerged from the Next Steps in Strategic Partnership, announced by President George W. Bush and Prime Minister Atal Bihari Vajpayee in January 2004.[158] Four years later—long after M³ was approved by ISRO—NASA Administrator Mike Griffin and ISRO Chairman G. Madhavan Nair announced the renewal and expansion of an older international agreement for cooperation between the two space programs in the areas of Earth and space science, exploration, and human spaceflight. (The previous agreement, signed on 16 December 1997, had addressed only the areas of Earth and atmospheric sciences.)[159]

There were, initially, concerns among observers about International Traffic in Arms Regulations (ITAR) requirements, particularly since nuclear weapons development and ISRO's space program are closely tied. In fact, "initially, ISRO refused to sign the ITAR

---

157   NASA. (2005, 2 February). "NASA Selects Moon Mapper for Mission of Opportunity." NASA news release 05-037.

158   "Chandrayaan marks new beginning in Indo-U.S. relation." (2008, 4 February). *Times of India.*

159   "India, U.S. to cooperate in space exploration." (2008, 4 February). *Press Trust of India.*

agreements," said project manager Thomas Glavich of M³, because the ITAR agreements characterized India's role as "technical assistance." The agency repeatedly pointed out that it was *their spacecraft*, and *they were helping us*, not the other way around.

M³ was required to have a "Technical Assistance Agreement" prior to its confirmation review, scheduled for February 2006. To make progress on instrument development despite legal formalities, the M³ team developed a document they called "Assumed Requirements" based on ISRO information, for internal use only. Work on the Technical Assistance Agreement continued at NASA Headquarters, the State Department, and the U.S. Embassy in New Delhi. It was finally signed the day before its immovable deadline.[160]

There was an international learning curve. Bonnie Buratti, a planetary scientist at the Jet Propulsion Laboratory, who was part of the M³ team, said: "I think the big thing was coming to terms with the fact that the Indians do things a lot different than we do…." That didn't mean the mission was beset with problems. Just the opposite. "The thing that really amazed me is that this is the only project I've ever been on where the schedule was speeded up."[161]

The team noted that "the technical sophistication of the ISRO is every bit the equal of NASA's." The processes, however, were not the same. There was no integrated control document as part of the ISRO process, for example, so the M³ team and the Chandrayaan-1 team had to work together to create one. Management, system engineers, and subsystem leads from each team spent four days in a conference room in Bangalore with M³'s export compliance officer, Discovery and New Frontiers Program management, and two engineers from Marshall Space Flight Center. Since Marshall already had a Memorandum of Understanding in place with ISRO, their engineers could communicate more freely with the ISRO team. On the fifth day, they signed the integrated control document, and all returned home, communicating frequently by teleconference, e-mail, and WebEx.[162]

Another difference was apparent in scheduling. The project director maintained the schedule and schedule control; the project did not use schedule tracking software or Earned Value Management. Late schedule problems were solved by reducing the number of tests. The day-to-day integration and testing schedule, however, was really in

160   Glavich, T., and M. White. (2010). "The Moon Mineralogy Mapper on Chandrayaan-1." Presentation at the 2010 Project Management Challenge. Downloaded from *http://pmchallenge. gsfc.nasa.gov/docs/2010/Presentations/Glavich.pdf*.

161   Niebur, S. (2009, 11 August). Personal interview with B. Buratti. Located in the "Moon Mineralogy Mapper" file, NASA Historical Reference Collection, History Division, NASA Headquarters, Washington, DC.

162   Glavich, T., and M. White. (2010). "The Moon Mineralogy Mapper on Chandrayaan-1." Presentation at the 2010 Project Management Challenge. Downloaded from *http://pmchallenge. gsfc.nasa.gov/docs/2010/Presentations/Glavich.pdf*.

the hands of experienced personnel who had worked together for many missions and were familiar with the software. As with many new partnerships, vernacular became an issue, as M³ and Chandrayaan-1 engineers with the same job titles often had different responsibilities. Daylight between ISRO and NASA requirements was most visible during project reviews and in the test verification and validation processes.[163]

The pre-ship review from M³ was held just a year after the Critical Design Review, in May 2007. The instrument—the first of the eleven instruments to fly on Chandrayaan-1—was delivered in August.[164] Thermal and vacuum testing took place the following summer, and the spacecraft survived a 20-day test at temperature extremes between −100° and 120°.[165] Final integration and checkout occurred in August 2008.

Then the M³ team waited. And waited.

Because lunar mission launch windows open every two weeks, Chandrayaan-1 was not under the extreme time pressure that constrains many planetary missions. The original launch date of 9 April 2008 slipped when two ESA instruments were delayed.[166] As late as the end of May, the launch date was still unknown, with news organizations reporting the launch scheduled sometime between July and September.[167] Finally, a launch date of 19 October materialized, with a window extending to 28 October.[168]

After four days of heavy rain over and around the spaceport, the 575-kilogram Chandrayaan-1 spacecraft launched to cloudy skies at 6:20 a.m. on 22 October 2008, atop a 4-stage core Polar Satellite Launch Vehicle—India's 44.4-meter, 316-ton rocket with six strap-on boosters—from the Satish Dhawan Space Centre, in the Sriharikota range in Andhra Pradesh in southern India.[169]

Eighteen minutes later, the rocket had placed Chandrayaan-1 into an elliptical geostationary transfer orbit, just as planned. After a series of firings by its liquid rocket engine, the spacecraft eventually rose from an orbit of 14,200 miles to 235,000 miles from Earth. It entered lunar orbit two and a half weeks after launch, on Saturday, 8 November 2008.[170] Its orbit over the lunar surface was lowered eventually to a circular path about 62 miles up. On Friday, 15 November, at 8:06 p.m. Indian Standard Time (9:36 a.m. EST), an impactor named "Aditya" was released from Chandrayaan-1.

A video camera transmitted images as it descended, and the impactor also had an onboard radar altimeter and mass spectrometer. At 8:31 p.m. Indian Standard Time

---

163   Ibid.

164   Clark, S. (2008, 29 May). "India's moon probe being fitted with instrument suite." *Spaceflight Now.*

165   "Spacecraft for moon mission unveiled." (2009, 19 September). PTI.

166   Srikanth, B. (2008, 19 September). "Mission Moon." *Hindustan Times.*

167   Clark, S. (2008, 29 May). "India's moon probe being fitted with instrument suite." *Spaceflight Now.*

168   Srikanth, B. (2008, 19 September). "Mission Moon." *Hindustan Times.*

169   "Rocket completes mission, India's first moon spacecraft now in orbit." (2008, 22 October). Thaindian.com

170   Clark, S. (2008, 10 November). "First Indian 'moon craft' goes into lunar orbit." *Spaceflight Now.*

(10:01 a.m. EST), the 29-kilogram, 375- by 375- by 470-millimeter honeycombed Moon impact probe crashed successfully into a crater at the Moon's South Pole. It impacted at 1.6 kilometers per minute. The probe was the first time India had touched the lunar surface, and painted on four sides of the impactor were miniature Indian national flags, to commemorate the birth of the country's first prime minister, Jawaharlal Nehru (a holiday known as Children's Day), on that day 119 years earlier. (Nehru was prime minister when the modern Indian space program was initiated in 1962.)[171]

Finding Water

Before launch, the strategy was to use the spacecraft's first optical period to acquire global mode data, and the three remaining periods to target prioritized regions "likely to exhibit mineral diversity (fresh craters, large central peak craters, basin massifs, mare basalt boundaries, etc.)." The project also sought "recommended priority targets from the science community."[172] On 24 September 2009, Carle Pieters, the M^3 Principal Investigator, and the M^3 team published a paper in the journal *Science* titled "Character and Spatial Distribution of OH/H_2O on the Surface of the Moon Seen by M^3 on Chandrayaan-1."[173] Detailed findings from the Moon Mineralogy Mapper revealed absorption features near 2.8 to 3.0 micrometers on the lunar surface. This is characteristic of hydroxyls or water-bearing minerals. The signature was widely distributed across the Moon and strongest at the poles, suggesting that water processes are feeding cold traps that astronauts might one day use for long-duration lunar missions.

As Pieters explained, "When we say, 'water on the moon,' we are not talking about lakes, oceans or even puddles. Water on the moon means molecules of water and hydroxyl that interact with molecules of rock and dust specifically in the top millimeters of the moon's surface."[174]

Jessica Sunshine of the University of Maryland, a scientist on M^3, said, "With our extended spectral range and views over the North Pole, we were able to explore the distribution of both water and hydroxyl as a function of temperature, latitude, composition, and time of day…. Our analysis unequivocally confirms the presence of these molecules on the Moon's surface and reveals that the entire surface appears to be hydrated during at least some portion of the lunar day."[175]

---

171   "India slams probe into the moon." (2008, 15 November). Space.com.

172   Pieters, C., et al. (2007, March). "M^3 on Chandrayaan-1: Strategy for mineral assessment of the moon." LPSC XXXVIII.

173   Pieters, C., et al. (2009, 24 September). "Character and Spatial Distribution of OH/H_2O on the Surface of the Moon Seen by M^3 on Chandrayaan-1." *Science.*

174   Asplund, S. (2009, November). "M^3 Reveals Water Molecules on Lunar Surface." *Discovery and New Frontiers News.* 1.

175   Ibid.

It was consistent with data captured by the Visual and Infrared Mapping Spectrometer on the Cassini spacecraft, which a decade earlier had made observations on the Moon that suggested water and hydroxyls at all latitudes of the Moon, including in daylight.[176] The Deep Impact mission, in its extended phase called EPOXI, made observations of the Moon during a flyby and likewise observed water signatures in June 2009.[177] On 19 May 2009, ISRO announced the "successful completion of all major mission objectives" and raised Chandrayaan-1 from a 100-kilometer lunar orbit to 200 kilometers, ostensibly to enable imaging of a wider swath of the lunar surface. A broken star sensor caused the spacecraft to lose pointing accuracy—an early sign of trouble to come. On 29 August 2009, ISRO lost contact with the Chandrayaan-1 mission. In addition to the spacecraft's star sensor, its thermal and power supply systems likewise had been uncooperative. The spacecraft in total operated for 312 days and circled the Moon more than 3,400 times. Despite the premature ending, the large volume of data from Chandrayaan-1's instrument payload included mapping more than 90 percent of the lunar surface and met most of the scientific objectives initially laid out.[178] The mission was a great success for India, and the presence of M³ proved the responsiveness of the Discovery Program to inexpensive Missions of Opportunity.

---

176   NASA. (2009, 24 September). "Cassini's Look at Water on the Moon." Downloaded from *https:// www.nasa.gov/topics/moonmars/features/clark1.html.*

177   NASA. (2009. 24 September). "Deep Impact Identifies Water on the Lunar Surface." Downloaded from *https://www.nasa.gov/topics/moonmars/features/sunshine1.html.*

178   Asplund, S. (2009, November). "M³ Reveals Water Molecules on Lunar Surface." *Discovery and New Frontiers News.* 1.

Figure 7-1: Kepler spacecraft

The Kepler spacecraft at Ball Aerospace & Technologies Corp. in Boulder, Colorado. The Kepler mission surveyed a region of the Milky Way galaxy, discovering the first Earth-size exoplanets and determining that there are more planets than stars in our galaxy. (Image credit: NASA/JPL-Caltech/Ball, image no. PIA11733)

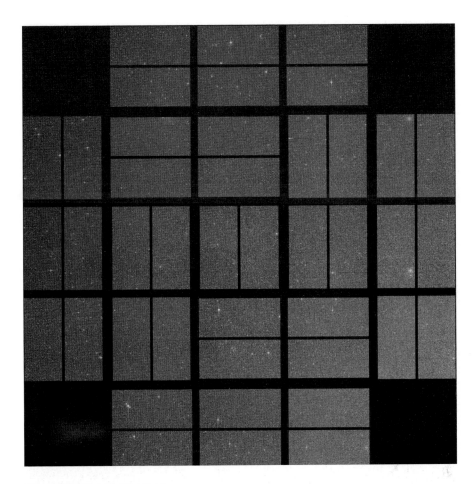

Figure 7-2: Kepler's first light

This image from the Kepler mission shows the telescope's "first light": a full field of view of an expansive star-rich patch of sky in the constellations Cygnus and Lyra stretching across 100 square degrees. (Image credit: NASA/Ames/J. Jenkins)

CHAPTER 8
Lessons Learned from the Evolution of the Program

In the first two decades after its founding, the Discovery Program continued to evolve in response to external pressures of budget, risk tolerance, and competing priorities, in addition to internal pressures like overruns and technical challenges on individual missions. The first five years of the program, 1992–1997, encouraged a significant amount of experimentation in many aspects of mission planning. After the failures of the adjacent Mars Program, the level of risk tolerance contracted, and the second five years of the program brought additional requirements from the NASA Integrated Action Team, increased agency scrutiny of the planetary program, additional project-level review, and the belief that more reviews meant fewer possible errors. For the first time, meanwhile, the Discovery Program had a Program Plan and a Program Commitment Agreement required by the agency.

But by the end of the first decade, a sharp dissonance manifested between the projects selected in the era of experimentation and management scrutiny intended to identify possible signals of future failure. CONTOUR failed shortly after launch. MESSENGER's deputy project manager disappeared, potentially overwhelmed at the late delivery of parts and potential overruns. Deep Impact suffered cost threats, requiring a delayed Preliminary Design Review and additional oversight of industry partners. Dawn suffered after its own management institution changed the burden rates and reserve requirement, requiring descopes even before the project really began. Kepler was selected at a time when the management of most NASA space science and planetary missions was a privilege reserved for Goddard Space Flight Center and the Jet Propulsion Laboratory; as such, Ames management had an extra layer of management foisted on their project. All these missions, except CONTOUR, would require additional resources to compensate for project delays, funding delays, and new program requirements. The CONTOUR failure was, ironically, the only thing that kept the program in the black from 2001 to 2003, as much of the funding intended for mission operations was redirected to cover overruns in later missions. Nevertheless, the failure and later overruns put the Discovery Program in a difficult situation, and program management at NASA Headquarters worried about congressional scrutiny should the overruns continue.

This chapter will discuss lessons learned in the decade that followed, as identified formally from studies by the National Research Council; the NASA Planetary Science Subcommittee; the Discovery and New Frontiers Program Office; and, informally, by mission management, the proposing community, and program management. This chapter will also demonstrate how the program evolved as lessons learned were implemented into the program's guidelines and assessment, represented by each of the planned Announcements of Opportunity—snapshots in time of current policies. It will also examine aspects and challenges of the program in 2011, where this narrative ends.

The decade began with National Research Council and Independent Review Team reports, and the postponement of the 2002 Announcement of Opportunity due to financial pressures. The 2003 Decadal Survey of planetary science that created the New Frontiers program line praised and prioritized the Discovery pipeline. A Discovery Lessons Learned Retreat was held. As funding became available in the outyears, the 2004 Announcement of Opportunity became a reality. Non-selections and a protest postponed the traditional Lessons Learned Workshop following that AO. The 2005 Announcement of Opportunity was announced with the selection of M^3, but it also had to be postponed, eventually becoming the 2006 AO as a flurry of cost studies were commissioned by NASA Headquarters.

The findings and recommendations of these studies by the Space Studies Board, NASA, the Science Support Office, and the Discovery and New Frontiers Program Office in the second half of the decade will be discussed, tabulated, compared, and traced to changes that resulted in the 2010 AO. It is important to keep in mind, however, that while these studies excelled at capturing the zeitgeist of the times, recording lessons learned and discussion by mission leadership, and in codifying recommendations proposed and advocated by both the proposing community and management, there is rarely a one-to-one correspondence between recorded lessons learned and changes in program policy. Recommendations may be rejected or ignored, particularly where they correctly identify the problem but propose a solution that is impractical in the current environment, is inappropriate for reasons of directorate policy, or has already been rejected by upper management. No response from NASA is required to these studies, and so the results are rarely tracked, as report after report is issued and ultimately sits on someone's shelf. This chapter is one attempt to look at the recommendations and corresponding changes in policy over the second decade of the Discovery Program.

COMPLEX AND THE NRC REPORT: ASSESSMENT OF MISSION SIZE TRADEOFFS

Periodically, NASA asks the National Research Council's Space Studies Board to study a particular question relevant to space and Earth sciences. As part of the Fiscal Year 1999 budget process, the Senate conference report directed NASA to contract with the National Research Council "for a study across all space science and Earth science disciplines to identify missions that cannot be accomplished within the parameters imposed by the smaller faster, better, cheaper regime. The [study] report should focus on the next 15 years, and attempt to quantify the level of funding per project that would be required to meet the specified scientific goals."[1]

NASA commissioned the study with a letter on 22 April 1999 to the Space Studies Board, noting that although future mission planning was currently underway at NASA and "a complete allocation of science objectives to particular missions cannot be made at this time," NASA would like the study to identify "the general criteria for assessing strengths and limitations of small, medium, and large missions in terms of scientific productivity, including quality and amount of science value returned, responsiveness to evolving opportunities, ability to take advantage of technological progress, and other factors" and to identify which of NASA's planned science goals would require the use of medium and large missions, where medium-class missions would cost between $150 million and $350 million.[2] Since Discovery fell squarely in the medium category, the most relevant results would be a) input and b) output from the discussion on criteria for discussing strengths and limitations of medium-size missions.

---

1   Congressional Research Service. (1998). Department of Veterans Affairs, Housing and Urban Development, and Independent Agencies Appropriations Bill, 1999: S. 2, 105th Congress. pp. 105–216.

2   Asrar, G., and E. Weiler. (1999, 22 April). Letter to C. Canizares. See also: Space Studies Board. (2000). *Assessment of Mission Size Trade-Offs for NASA's Earth and Space Science Missions.* National Academies Press: Washington, DC. 91.

The National Research Council's Committee on Planetary and Lunar Exploration proposed the following criteria for evaluating the mission mix:

- Addresses high-priority scientific goals
- Optimizes science return for the money spent
- Exhibits compatibility between mission goals and scale
- Demonstrates a balanced-risk strategy
- Considers future application of new technologies
- Shows balance between technology and science
- Involves community in mission/instrument/technology selection
- Promotes stable funding and continuous planetary exploration
- Is consonant with Deep Space Network and Mission Operations and Data Analysis support
- Uses diverse modes of mission implementation (principal investigator–led, university-industry-NASA, NASA-led)
- Incorporates education and public outreach[3]

Several of these criteria were then folded into Recommendation 2 of the Ad Hoc Committee on the Assessment of Mission Size Trade-offs for Earth and Space Science Missions: "Ensure that science objectives—and their relative importance in a given discipline—are the primary determinants of what missions are carried out and their sizes, and ensure that mission planning responds to 1) the link between science priorities and science payload, 2) timeliness in meeting science objectives, and 3) risks associated with the mission." How Recommendation 2 would be implemented, however, was not as clear.

Selection of Discovery missions required that three major criteria be met: the science is of high merit and relevance, the instruments are appropriate for the investigation and of sufficient technology readiness level, and the mission is of low or medium risk. No one factor counted significantly more than the others; a proposal that scored "Excellent" or "Very Good" on science merit would still be un-selectable if it was high-risk. A "Good" science proposal would not likely be selected even if it was low-risk. This overall philosophy had not changed since the 1996 AO.

The second phrase in the recommendation urged the Science Mission Directorate to consider the relative importance of the proposed science objectives in a given discipline when making selection or planning decisions. On the face of it, this was a plausible recommendation, but when one looked at it from a Discovery perspective, this was impossible. Missions proposed to Discovery were *required* to show their relevance to

---

3   Space Studies Board. (2000). *Assessment of Mission Size Trade-Offs for NASA's Earth and Space Science Missions.* National Academies Press: Washington, DC. 91.

the NASA strategic plan, but the strategic plans can be quite broad. Even the strictest interpretation of requirements allowed Discovery missions to focus their investigations on nearly any aspect of the origin or evolution of planetary bodies, as well as the search for exoplanets (in some Announcements of Opportunity). Selection was always based on the presentation of high-quality science tempered with an acceptable level of risk within the constraints of cost and schedule.

The second half of Recommendation 2 urged the correspondence of science priorities and science payload, which was the mechanism for fellow scientists and instrument builders to determine whether the proposing team had chosen appropriate instrumentation for the mission so that the major questions in the investigation could be answered. (The remainder of the recommendation was satisfied by the tenets of the Discovery Program: development time constraints and acceptable risk were always criteria of selection.)

Returning to the COMPLEX criteria, the question of whether the missions optimized science return for money spent was a hot debate in the early years of the first decade of the twenty-first century in both Discovery and Explorer mission lines, particularly under the leadership of Paul Hertz, chief scientist in the Science Mission Directorate and, later, head of the Astrophysics Division. Hertz and others determined that Discovery missions were explicitly not looking at "science per dollar," but instead looking to maximize science return within the Discovery cost cap. This was a subtle but important distinction that drove proposal strategy. If Discovery was looking for "science per dollar," proposers would likely underbid as a strategy, coming in with plenty of "room to the cap." Since room to the cost cap was ignored in most competitions in the first twenty years of the Discovery Program, this strategy, and the recommendation, could be set aside. The program continued to approach the process with the strategy of optimizing science return within the program cost cap instead.

The criterion that each mission should exhibit "compatibility between mission goals and scale" is interesting in the context of the time; MESSENGER had, at the time, been recently selected by the Discovery Program, and it was touted as "a flagship-quality mission" in a Discovery box.[4] The study was correct in foreseeing that an incompatibility would cause the program all kinds of problems, including the delay of future Announcements of Opportunity, as will be shown later in this chapter. However, that did not stop the program from selecting the Kepler photometer the next year.

The "balanced-risk strategy" became meaningless at about the time that the report was issued, as the pendulum of NASA's risk tolerance swung far to the cautious side with the 1999 Mars mission failures and the subsequent NASA Integrated Action Team

---

4   "Lab wins Discovery mission." (1999, 9 July). *JPL Universe*, 29(14). 6.

recommendations. No longer was the occasional failure an acceptable outcome of the faster, better, cheaper missions. Instead, the projects would have additional requirements, reviews, and deliverables, in many cases far more than they were bound to at selection.

The technology metrics, and the subsequent committee Recommendation 3—"Maintain a vigorous technology program for the development of advanced space-craft hardware that will enable a portfolio of missions of varying sizes and complexi-ties"—and 4—"Develop scientific instrumentation enabling a portfolio of mission sizes, ensuring that funding for such development efforts is augmented and appropriately balanced with space mission line budgets"—were largely ignored, as NASA's new risk posture required the adoption of more mature technologies developed through other programs, minimizing development during the Discovery formulation phases. The early Announcements of Opportunity encouraged new technologies and significant technology transfer, but this disappeared with the changes in the 2004 AO. Additionally, the metric that the mission mix should show "balance between technology and sci-ence," in fact, conflicted with the first recommendation, that science objectives be the primary determinant of mission selection.

The metrics that the community be involved in mission, instrument, and technology selection; that the division approach promote stable funding and continuous planetary exploration; and that the missions incorporate education and public outreach were core values of the Discovery Program that did not change in the following decade. The missions were supported with Mission Operations and Data Analysis as proposed and also in external data analysis programs as necessary. From the NEAR data analysis program (2001–2003) to the Discovery data analysis (2003–2006) to the planetary missions data analysis program, the Planetary Science Division made sure that there were opportunities and funding for data analysis from the Discovery missions.

One proposed metric was seemingly forgotten: using diverse modes of mission implementation (e.g., PI-led, university-industry-NASA team, NASA-led) is no longer a priority in the PI-led era. NASA-led missions are reserved for large flagship missions; small or medium Discovery missions are always PI-led, with teaming arrangements at the discretion of the PI and his or her team.

After receiving these metrics and other input from the four standing committees of the Space Studies Board, the ad hoc committee met 8–10 September 1999 and released its report, "Assessment of Mission Size Trade-Offs for NASA's Earth and Space Science Missions," on 15 January.[5] In addition to the recommendations discussed above, the committee had Recommendation 5, "Develop more affordable launch options for gaining access to space, including—possibly—foreign launch vehicles, so that a mixed portfolio of mission sizes becomes a viable approach," which was out of scope for the

---

5   Space Studies Board. (2000). *Assessment of Mission Size Trade-Offs for NASA's Earth and Space Science Missions*. National Academies Press: Washington, DC. 91.

OSS in terms of both policy and budget; and Recommendation 6, "Encourage international collaboration in all sizes and classes of missions, so that international missions will be able to fill key niches in NASA's space and Earth science programs. Specifically, restore separate, peer-reviewed Announcements of Opportunity for enhancements to foreign-led space research missions.[6] The former was a policy for a few years, until an overdependence on international collaborations caused the Associate Administrator to resist selecting proposals with heavy dependence on foreign instruments, and the latter finally became a policy with the initiation of the first Stand-ALone Missions of Opportunity Notice (SALMON) in 2008.

The committee report noted several findings on the effectiveness of the faster, better, cheaper approach, with an important caveat: "Policy makers looking for guidance on these programs in terms of cost and size trade-offs should be made aware that the variables are more numerous and much more complex than might at first be supposed."[7] While this is certainly true, the 1999 National Research Council findings are included here as external evaluations of the Discovery and Explorer programs run in the faster, better, cheaper mode.

The committee supports several principles being implemented in the FBC methodology. Specifically, it found a number of positive aspects of the FBC approach, including the following:

- *A mixed portfolio of mission sizes is crucial in virtually all Earth and space science disciplines to accomplish the various research objectives. The FBC approach has produced useful improvements across the spectrum of programs regardless of absolute mission size or cost.*
- *Shorter development cycles have enhanced scientific responsiveness, lowered costs, involved a larger community, and enabled the use of the best available technologies.*
- *The increased frequency of missions has broadened research opportunities for the Earth and space sciences.*
- *Scientific objectives can be met with greater flexibility by spreading a program over several missions.*

Nonetheless, some problems exist in the practical application of the FBC approach, including the following:

- *The heavy emphasis on cost and schedule has too often compromised scientific outcomes (scope of mission, data return, and analysis of results).*
- *Technology development is a cornerstone of the FBC approach for science missions but is often not aligned with science-based mission objectives.*
- *The cost and schedule constraints for some missions may lead to choosing designs, management practices, and technologies that introduce additional risks.*

---

6   Ibid., p. 5.
7   Ibid., p. 2.

- *The nation's launch infrastructure is limited in its ability to accommodate smaller spacecraft in a timely, reliable, and cost-effective way.*[8]

The first criticism was a reaction to NASA's approach to overruns in development in the previous decade, often allowing a mission to "move money forward" to pay for development costs at the expense of data collection and analysis time during the operations phase. This happened notably in the Discovery Program on Genesis; efforts were made in the early part of the decade to take this option off the table and protect the science return of the Discovery missions. It remained an issue with respect to science descopes, removing scientific instrumentation from the payload, or observation time from operations, to pay for overruns in development, whether the overruns originated from an element of the science payload or an engineering subsystem. Given the choice to non-confirm or terminate the mission, to allow it to exceed its cost cap, or to descope a science instrument—for some managers, the last choice was often the path of least resistance. After all, descoping an instrument could be seen as both a solution to the cost overruns and a punishment. This was not one of the more inspiring aspects of the program, but in a cost-constrained environment that did not allow missions to exceed their cost cap, this option was preferable to non-confirmation or termination of the entire mission.

The third criticism was certainly valid. It played out in an interesting way. With cost and schedule constraints fixed and risk one of the primary selection factors, not all mission concepts or investigations were on equal footing at proposal. A mission to a particular comet, for example, may be ideal for one set of Announcement of Opportunity parameters, but changes in the "launch by" date or significant delay in the release of the AO could make the original trajectory unusable. The team could often torque the proposal to fit into the constraints of the new AO, but the resulting plan would have been placed in a higher-risk category and therefore become un-selectable. Cost and schedule constraints, coupled with a desire for lower-risk missions, constrained the choice of science investigations in the Discovery Program.

The availability of small, low-cost launch vehicles was and remained a difficult parameter for proposers developing mission concepts for Discovery in its first twenty years. At one point, the program faced the option of extending NASA's contract for Delta II expendable launch vehicles to accommodate a single launch; Discovery would have to pay not only for the launch vehicles desired, but also the launch pad and "standing army" costs of required personnel up to the last launch date—including times when no Discovery mission was being readied for launch. This option was prohibitive on a long-term basis, and it temporarily threw the program into crisis. Because of the phase-out of the Delta II rocket at NASA, proposers to the 2010 AO were able

---

8 Ibid.

to propose missions using three larger launch vehicles: the Delta IV, the Atlas V, and the Falcon 9. The only catch was that as the NASA launch services contract was not finalized when they proposed, proposers would have to keep their designs compatible for all three shrouds, masses, and power constraints, or discuss their rationale for proposing to a use a particular launch vehicle (see Requirement 88 of the 2010 Announcement Opportunity).

In the early years of the Discovery Program, the use and development of new technologies was a supporting objective. As this report made clear, however, its pairing with scientific objectives was not always an ideal match. For a new technology to be ready to launch on a mission with a 35-month development phase, its expected development time would need to be considerably shorter. This required the initial development of these technologies to occur well before the proposal of any individual mission proposing its use.

This "reliance on non-mission funds (e.g., Planetary Instrument Definition and Development Program, or PIDDP)," was an accepted aspect of the program, and PIDDP was funded appropriately, making a wide range of selections of technologies that later were incorporated into NASA flight missions.[9] The stated goal of the PIDDP program was always "to define and develop instruments or instrument components to the point where the instruments may be proposed in response to future announcements of flight opportunity without additional extensive technology development."[10] When that report was written, and for several years afterward, this was the case. PIDDP provided funding for the development of instruments at low technology readiness levels (1–3), including "feasibility studies, conceptual design, and laboratory breadboarding (but not brass-boarding) of critical components and complete instruments," and Discovery proposals were encouraged to propose new technologies, as shown in the following excerpt, identical in the 1998 and 2000 Discovery AOs:[11]

> *Supporting Objective 2: Encourage the use of new technologies to achieve program objectives and foster their transfer into the private sector.*
>
>> *The inclusion of new technologies to achieve performance enhancements and to reduce total mission cost is encouraged in Discovery proposals. Proposals that include new technologies should pay especially careful attention to technology development plans and/or risk mitigation approaches. The use of new technologies will enable more*

---

9   Ibid.; NASA. (1998, 5 February). *Research Opportunities in Space Science 1998*, NRA 98-OSS-03. Planetary Instrument Definition and Development Program. Appendix A 3.5.

10 NASA. (1998, 5 February). *Research Opportunities in Space Science 1998*, NRA 98-OSS-03. Planetary Instrument Definition and Development Program. Appendix A 3.5.

11 NASA. (2003). *Research Opportunities in Space Science 2003*. Planetary Instrument Definition and Development Program. Appendix A.2.11.

aggressive and exciting scientific objectives to be pursued. The teaming of industry, university, and government is meant to foster an environment conducive to technology development, utilization, and commercialization.[12]

However, the changing risk tolerance at NASA, precipitated in part by four FBC mission failures (Lewis, the Wide-Field Infrared Explorer, Mars Polar Lander, and Mars Climate Orbiter), would lead to the deletion of this supporting objective for the program and also in the 2004 AO. In its place was a much harsher demand of technology readiness, using the agency-wide definitions:

2004: "Investigations proposing new technology, i.e., technologies having a technology readiness level (TRL) less than 7 (see TRL Definitions in the DPL), will be penalized for risk if adequate backup plans to ensure success of the mission are not described." All proposals would be required to include a "Description of the proposed plan for bringing each of the identified items to a minimum of TRL 6, defined as "system/subsystem model or prototype demonstration in a relevant environment, space, or ground" by Confirmation Review (CR) at the end of Phase B (include discussion of simulations, prototyping, systems testing, life testing, etc., as appropriate)."[13]

The 2006 Announcement of Opportunity had the exact same wording of this requirement, with a slight change to the first sentence, where the flight requirement was relaxed to "less than 6."[14] By the end of the decade, the expectation was even more stringent: "Proposed investigations are generally expected to have mature technologies, specifically all technologies at a technology readiness level (TRL) of six or higher."[15]

However, PIDDP still allowed only the development of instruments through technology readiness levels 1 to 3 (breadboarding, but not brass-boarding) until the release of the 2008 Research Opportunities in Space and Earth Science (ROSES). This caused quite a problem for proposers in the early and middle parts of the decade, as they struggled to continue instrument development without the support of a NASA Supporting Research and Technology program. Astrobiologists and Mars scientists had mid-level technology readiness level programs, the argument went, but the other planetary scientists did not, and they were at a disadvantage. As they realized this to be true, the expansion of PIDDP or the addition of a mid-technology readiness level technology program was discussed and advocated for by the Discovery Program Scientist, who also managed PIDDP for a time; the Discovery Program Manager at NASA Headquarters; and others, but approval would not be granted until 2008.

---

12   NASA. (1998). Discovery Announcement of Opportunity. See also: NASA. (2000). Discovery Announcement of Opportunity.

13   NASA. (2004). Discovery Announcement of Opportunity.

14   NASA. (2006). Discovery Announcement of Opportunity.

15   NASA. (2010). Discovery Announcement of Opportunity.

Meanwhile, the Discovery Program still had to plan and release AOs under its current constraints and within the environment of Office of Space Science and NASA in the early days of the twenty-first century.

CURRENT NEEDS VS. FUTURE PLANS: THE 2002 AO

The 2000 AO selection process was the last to go smoothly for quite some time. The program was not able to hold program-level reserves, due to a difficult budget environment and the OSS philosophy that project overruns should be solved "within the Division," making funds interchangeable for planetary projects. Any reserve held was held at the division level, and there were many claims on the small amount of funds available in any given year. The delays imposed on Dawn and Kepler due to insufficient funds at time of selection had been funded by this time, but additional funds were still required for the additional layer of management imposed as the mission team complied with the Associate Administrator's direction to add NASA Goddard Space Flight Center or the Jet Propulsion Laboratory as the management institution. CONTOUR was getting ready for launch, and frequent management changes at the program level may have lessened the traceability of needs signaled in previous years.

Dave Jarrett, who led the Discovery Program Office, continued ably at the NASA Management Office at JPL, assisted by Kate Wolf on financial affairs, but he became additionally taxed with frequent trips to the East Coast to help MESSENGER as it became apparent that the project was in financial trouble. As MESSENGER's project manager, Max Peterson, retired, expecting his deputy to step up and fill in, his deputy likewise became overwhelmed, leaving the project after a particularly taxing trip to a West Coast supplier. The replacement project manager took a "clean slate" approach, buckling down with cost charts and outstanding needs to determine what would be required to bring the mission to the launch pad. Jarrett spent many hours with the project preparing their request to NASA Headquarters—a request for which they were not fully financially prepared. MESSENGER ultimately went to NASA Headquarters requesting additional funds. Deep Impact followed, their own requests ready and waiting.

Unfortunately, NASA Headquarters had no program-level reserve with which to fulfill requests. Any additional funding granted the projects came out of a line labeled "Futures," which Nancy C. Porter and Susan Niebur of the Discovery Program guarded staunchly; it was this line that would determine when the next Discovery Announcement of Opportunity could be released. The draft 2002 AO sat on Niebur's desk through the five requests for additional funding from the projects in 2002–2003, progressively buried under iterations of the Discovery Program spreadsheet and the diminishing outyears of the Futures budget line that made it impossible to release. Each conference or community meeting brought questions about the subsequent AO release, and each meeting saw Niebur, Jay T. Bergstralh, or Colleen Hartman of the Planetary Science Division reply that the AO could not be released until there was sufficient funding in the outyears to support an appropriate mission profile. The AO was pushed to late 2002, then 2003, and then canceled altogether.

The budget overruns had not gone unnoticed. After yet another request for additional funding, Ed Weiler, the Associate Administrator of the Science Mission Directorate, showed great frustration during a monthly meeting of NASA center representatives and NASA Headquarters personnel. He pushed back from the table, looked the center representatives in the eye, and declared that these constant requests would not be tolerated on future missions. The trouble is, he said, that the missions don't carry enough reserves. From that point forward, each mission would be required to carry 25 percent reserves at confirmation.

The news surprised even the Discovery personnel in the room. Niebur, who had just been speaking with Dawn management, worried about the missions in the pipeline. Before she could speak up, Weiler turned to Hartman and other Solar System Exploration Division managers seated behind her and repeated the policy: All future AOs will require 25 percent reserves at proposal and at confirmation. Niebur worried that this could adversely affect missions already struggling to stay within their budgets; she spoke up, forgetting for a moment that she was the youngest in the room and junior staff were not encouraged to speak when Weiler was interacting with center directors and their designees. So she asked if this applied to missions in formulation, hoping that he would issue an exemption for Dawn and Kepler and the Explorer projects proposed under one set of rules and now being faced with living by another. Weiler refused to grant any exceptions. All missions should be proposed with and maintain a level of 25 percent reserves by confirmation.

Clearly, Dawn and Kepler had some work to do. The program executives and scientists returned to their cubicles and offices and called their projects. This new edict would affect all missions that had not yet passed confirmation, and there would be no exemptions available for the newest Discovery missions as there was no argument that they were not prone to the same cost risks as their immediate predecessors, MESSENGER and Deep Impact.

Discovery's troubles were reported in the press, and the postponement of the 2002 Announcement of Opportunity was noted by SpaceNews:

> MESSENGER's problems also prompted a number of changes in the way NASA manages its Discovery class missions, the most immediate being a postponement of a competition to select the next round of moderate-cost space science missions. When that competition finally goes forward, the selected missions will be required to hold 25 percent of their budgets in reserves to better deal with the kinds of technical and schedule challenges the MESSENGER team

encountered. While a 5 percent or 6 percent overrun is not considered serious enough to
automatically trigger a program termination review, MESSENGER's budget troubles stand
out because it is the first Discovery class spacecraft not to be completed within the cost cap.[16]

This was not technically true, as Genesis had also required additional funds in operations to compensate for the funds that had been moved forward to compensate for technical needs, but the fiction remained "common knowledge" in the community for years afterward.

NASA Headquarters personnel continued to work toward a release as soon as possible—that is, as soon as the program's budget profile allowed it. Potential proposers and planetary scientists believed it would happen, as did program management.[17] That the 2002 AO would be canceled altogether was unexpected.

Delays in AO release impacted the public sharing of lessons learned, as each AO was typically followed by a formal Lessons Learned Workshop open to the community of scientists, project managers, business managers, and new business representatives from industry and other partners. Since the AO was delayed to 2004, the workshop was delayed as well, causing a large gap between public workshops. A program-only retreat, not affected by the imminent release of an AO, would be held in 2003.

NEW FRONTIERS

By this time, the Space Studies Board and hand-picked experts in solar system science had created the first planetary science Decadal Survey outlining the state of the field and the recommendations for flight projects in the next decade: "New Frontiers in the Solar System." Discovery was recommended as the top priority in small solar system flight missions, and the New Frontiers mission line was created for medium-size missions, at about twice the cost cap of Discovery. The survey noted, "Given Discovery's highly successful start, the SSE Survey endorses the continuation of this program, which relies on Principal Investigator leadership and competition to obtain the greatest science return within a cost cap. A flight rate of no less than one launch every 18 months is recommended."[18]

The report praised Discovery's structure and performance, saying:

The success of the Discovery Program, exemplified by the Near Earth Asteroid Rendezvous
(NEAR) mission, Lunar Prospector, and Mars Pathfinder, has convinced even the most

---

16   Berger, B. (2003, 22 September). "MESSENGER Busts Cost Cap, Prompting Changes to NASA's
       Discovery Program." *SpaceNews.* 1–3.

17   "Fayetteville prof making progress on space project." (2002, 28 November). The Associated Press;
       Whitehouse, D. (2003, 24 April). "Bunker buster missiles aim at moon." BBC News.

18   National Research Council. (2003). *New Frontiers in the Solar System: An Integrated Exploration
       Strategy.* National Academies Press: Washington, DC, *http://nap.nationalacademies.org/10432*, p. 2.

hardened skeptic that small, relatively low-cost missions can effectively address significant scientific goals. The discipline of Discovery's competitive selection process has been particularly effective in eliminating ill-conceived concepts and has resulted in a richness of mission goals that few would have thought possible a decade ago. The planetary science community's enthusiastic support for Discovery has led to calls for the competitive acquisition of all flight projects…. Competition is seen as a vehicle to increase the scientific richness of flight missions and, perhaps of equal importance, as a device to constrain the large costs associated with flying robotic missions to the planets.[19]

The report also praised the education and public outreach efforts associated with Discovery missions, stating that the requirement for each mission to devote 1 percent to 2 percent of the mission budget exclusively to education and public outreach, along with the tradition of leveraging resources from other organizations identified by the mission team, has been very effective; all planetary missions of the time, including Deep Impact, MESSENGER, CONTOUR, and Stardust, had extensive education and public outreach activities. "Most planetary scientists agree that the current funding levels of 1 to 2 percent are about right within the [solar system exploration] program," said the report, and the mission education and public outreach programs serve as models for solar system exploration engagement in general, working much more effectively than the "supplemental" outreach awards for individual research grants, reviewed separately and without a mission connection.[20] This one percent, however, would not last long, as the number would be drastically reduced by upper management by the time of the next Announcement of Opportunity.

Staffing Up: Changes in Program Management

The MESSENGER overruns highlighted issues within the project but also within the management of missions overall. While each mission had an assigned program executive and program scientist at NASA Headquarters, all missions reported to a single program manager at the NASA Management Office at JPL, Dave Jarrett. The needs of MESSENGER were tremendous during this time period, and Jarrett worked so well and so often with the team out there that he had trouble also being alert to changes and imminent overruns on other projects, such as Deep Impact.[21]

Program reviews had shown as early as the late 1990s that the Discovery project management office was insufficiently staffed. Study after study revealed that to staff the office in a similar fashion to the Explorers Program Office at Goddard Space Flight

---

19   Ibid.

20   Ibid.

21   Niebur, S. (2009, May 14). Personal interview with D. Jarrett and Kate Wolf. Located in "Discovery Program" file, NASA Historical Reference Collection, History Division, NASA Headquarters, Washington, DC.

Center, which had been operating for many years due to the earlier incarnations of Explorer projects, an independent Discovery Program Office should be staffed with approximately 17 people—a far cry from the NASA Management Office at JPL, composed essentially of Jarrett and Wolf.

Fittingly, it was the November 2002 report of the standing Program Independent Review Team for Discovery that documented those numbers and pushed for changes from outside the program, again expressing the urgency to NASA Headquarters management. Faced with program overruns and threats of additional overruns on multiple projects, NASA Headquarters listened.

The Independent Review Team, charged with regular assessment of the technical and programmatic plans for accomplishing program objectives in accordance with the Program Commitment Agreement (i.e., AO process and release rate, checks and balances, lessons learned, program budget, risks to program budget, level of project cost cap), including assessing program risks and mitigations, was also asked to examine strengths and weaknesses of the approach to cost control, program-level and project-level technical reviews, and near-term actions that could strengthen the program. After attending several project reviews, interviewing program and project personnel, and conducting a review of the NASA Management Office, the Independent Review Team concluded that the Discovery Program continued to meet its commitments and objectives, with the work of the Discovery Program Office supplemented by Project Integrated Action Teams staffed by experts (most of whom continued from their original involvement with the projects during the myriad Technical, Management, Cost, Outreach [TMCO] reviews). And this is where it got interesting: The Independent Review Team characterized project cost control assurance by the program as a mixed bag. While they judged the cost analysis element of the TMCO process as providing a good assessment of a proposed project's cost realism and risk—and in addition, stated that Integrated Action Team assessments at decision gates could provide good updates—they found the primary problem with maintaining cost control was inadequate staffing: "Current Program Office staffing level does not provide necessary ongoing insight into and evaluation of flight project technical performance or cost and schedule control." At NASA Headquarters, "Program Executives have no technical support." In all, "program staffing is inadequate to assure low risk implementation of missions that do not have GSFC, JPL, or APL as the implementing organization." When briefed, Weiler immediately authorized adding four full-time employees at the NASA Management Office.[22]

To obtain parity with the Explorers Program Office at Goddard, however, the Discovery Program would have to add more than 17 full-time equivalents to the

---

22   Report of the Program Independent Review Team. (2002, 19 November).

NASA Management Office. Playing by Weiler's rules of solving problems within the program, the funding for these new contractors or civil servants would have to come out of the Discovery Program itself.

Senior Office of Space Science management would take these recommendations and work to implement them in a reasonable and effective manner, augmenting personnel and proficiencies at the program office. Changes were suggested, initiated, and discarded frequently during this time period, with the origins and justification behind each iteration not always publicly apparent.

The first solution was to hire an independent organization, Aerospace Corporation, which had done analysis work on a number of NASA programs and projects over the years. That relationship dissolved, however, and JPL took ownership of the Discovery Program Office, appointing John McNamee, a veteran of multiple flight projects, as manager. There were obvious conflicts of interest, as McNamee's line management stood to benefit from future Discovery missions. (McNamee reported indirectly to Charles Elachi, the Director of JPL.) This did not sit well with the broader planetary science community.

Reducing Risk: Evaluating Past Performance

As costs grew in the early part of the second decade of Discovery on flight project after flight project, management at NASA Headquarters realized that costs could be controlled only so much during a mission's development, integration, and test stages. Problems had to be caught early. But even the pre-PDR interventions seemed inadequate to the task of addressing projects at risk of growing out of control, as Deep Impact had demonstrated, coming back for additional resources early on. The Dawn team, in addition, had trouble meeting their requirements in time for PDR.

Preproposal evaluation of past performance of management institutions was proposed time and time again, but even this would prove unsatisfactory, as NASA's procurement office pointed out: Everyone has had overruns. If evaluators had been provided with the full details of past performance on NASA contracts, all experienced players would have had major weaknesses, and only new players—those without any management experience of flight projects—could compete. The results would have had a devastating effect on these one-off, mission-unique requirements, and the agile management techniques that they required. After a great deal of work in 2002 to 2004, the proposal to evaluate past performance of management institutions was dropped, and the 2004 Announcement of Opportunity was released.

In April 2004, NASA charged both the National Research Council and the National Academy of Public Administration with studying PI-led missions in the hopes of understanding financial overruns in several of the PI-led mission lines. The Discovery AO, however, could not wait.

Implementing Change: The 2004 AO

Finally, on 16 April, NASA Headquarters released the 2004 Announcement of Opportunity, almost four years after the previous one. The 25 percent reserve requirement was added, and the cost cap increased to $360 million (Fiscal Year 2004 dollars)—the maximum available within the "futures" line in the Discovery Program budget.

The AO had been rewritten substantially since 2000, with greater attention to incorporating lessons learned over the past five years to avoid recurrences of the problems incurred during implementation of previous missions. New requirements had been added—such as the staffing requirement of a deputy project manager—and additional financial reserves were now mandated. Investigations were now required to publish their data and analysis in peer-reviewed scientific literature—a change since the Stardust days, as management realized that the mission was not obligated to deliver NASA-funded mission science. Moreover, each mission was required to deliver data to the Planetary Data System. After some discussion, missions were again required to propose a full set of education and public outreach activities at 1 percent to 2 percent of NASA cost. To combat the bait-and-switch tactics that some perceived in the 1998 competition, and the frequent personnel changes in Deep Impact leadership, the AO required that the project manager be named at proposal, and his or her qualifications would be evaluated as part of the Technical-Management-Cost evaluation. Missions were to launch by 31 December 2009.

The Discovery Program held an AO Preproposal Conference in Washington, DC, on 23 April 2004, to provide a direct interface to the community, as well as AO clarification to assure high-quality proposals. Andy Dantzler, the Division Director of the Planetary Science Division, and Susan Niebur, the Discovery Program Scientist, had a message to send. Both Niebur's first and last slides emphasized the importance of properly scoping mission investigations and accounting for adequate reserve: "Mission investigations must be appropriately scoped. Mission proposals must include adequate reserve. Remember the value to the taxpayers."[23]

The new parameters were introduced, explained, and emphasized, as Niebur and Dantzler also emphasized the importance of scoping investigations to fit within the cost cap, proposing only the science that could be done for the available dollars. The 25 percent reserve requirement was announced, justified, and clarified: All projects must show at least a 25 percent reserve at proposal, through the end of Phase A (selection) and Phase B (confirmation).

The AO included new opportunities to involve other scientists, such as the Guest Observer program made popular by Kepler and astrophysical missions; the opportunity to propose Participating Scientist Programs at proposal that could be chosen for

---

23   Niebur, S. (2004, April 23). "Discovery AO Highlights and Science Evaluation." Slides. Susan Niebur's personal collection.

later implementation; and the option to propose data analysis programs to encourage community use of the data during and after operations. Other ways to involve taxpayers at large included the use of education and public outreach programs and Small Disadvantaged Business contracting.

Project management options had been opened up again and were not limited to NASA Goddard Space Flight Center and JPL. In fact, project management was no longer limited to NASA centers, leveling the field for funded research and development centers, universities, and industry partners. The AO was management-centric, with the new requirement of a named project manager at proposal who would continue on to manage the project during formulation and implementation.

Management approaches were codified, as all missions would be required to adhere to NPR 7120.5B for approval to progress to the implementation phase. In the 1998 and 2000 AOs, NPR 7120.5A NASA Program and Project Management Processes and Requirements had been introduced to proposers; the AO stated that it "may be used as a reference in defining a team's mission approach," while reiterating that "[m]ission teams have the freedom to use their own processes, procedures, and methods, and the use of innovative processes is encouraged when cost, schedule, and technical improvements can be demonstrated."[24] In the 2004 AO, however, the words had changed, with the team now given "responsibility and authority to accomplish the entire mission investigation by utilizing innovative approaches to stay within the strict cost and schedule limits of the program, as long as fundamental principles for sound management, engineering, and safety and mission assurance (e.g., those listed in NPR 7120.5B and referenced in Section 5.3.1) are not compromised."[25]

New language added to the 2004 AO also included a change in the degree of expected oversight of projects. Whereas in the 2000 AO, "the major responsibility for the selected investigation rests with the investigation team, which will have a large degree of freedom to accomplish its proposed objectives within the stated constraints with only essential NASA oversight" and "NASA oversight and reporting requirements will be limited to only that which is essential to assure science investigation success in compliance with committed cost, schedule, performance, reliability, and safety requirements," in 2004, the essential NASA oversight had morphed into more ominous language, made necessary by the multiple cost overruns and late parts deliveries in the missions in development at that time: "NASA intends to maintain a significant degree of insight into mission development."[26]

New types of Missions of Opportunity would be allowed in the 2004 AO. In addition to the established opportunity to propose an instrument to launch as part of a foreign

---

24   NASA. (2004). Discovery Announcement of Opportunity.

25   Ibid.

26   Ibid.

mission, separately competed, for the first time institutions could propose mission extensions. This was implemented in lieu of establishing a senior review process for the Solar System Exploration Division, such as existed in the Heliophysics and Astronomy and Physics Divisions. Ideas for mission extensions and new ways to use existing spacecraft for new scientific investigations were percolating in the community, and this would be an avenue for proposing in an open and competitive environment, evaluated to the same standards as new mission investigations by technical-management-cost. A compliance checklist was also introduced for the first time, to help proposers ensure that they had addressed the AO requirements.

Despite all these changes, the principles of the program had not changed. The AO solicited small self-contained planetary mission investigations that would result in new science discoveries. Discovery Program missions were not fishing expeditions to new planetary targets, but carefully designed scientific investigations. The evaluation process would be a two-step evaluation by both science and technical-management-cost reviewers. The evaluation factors had not changed significantly, and the additional selection factors remained the same: cost and reserve, education and public outreach, and small and disadvantaged business commitment. Proposers were strongly encouraged to limit the number of co-investigators to the bare minimum, to allow sufficient availability of qualified scientists to serve as science reviewers.

NASA expected to select three missions to perform concept studies during a six-month Phase A funded at a cost of up to $1 million.[27] Proposals would be due 16 July 2004. The agency ultimately received eighteen such proposals—the smallest number ever for the program—and categorization, steering, and selection committees at NASA Headquarters evaluated each on scientific, technical, management, and cost criteria.[28]

On 2 February 2005, NASA Headquarters made a shocking announcement: for the first time in the history of the Discovery and Explorer Programs, NASA had selected no proposals to proceed to the competitive concept study phase. The now-more-rigorous review cycle and selection process had found weaknesses with each proposal; none had met the high standards of the program in all areas of scientific merit; technical, management, and cost; and program balance. The press release did not detail the reasons for a non-selection but did promise an imminent opportunity to repropose in a less-constrained environment: "We are looking forward to the March release of the Discovery 12 AO that will provide greater flexibility commensurate with the technical complexities associated with Discovery class experiments," said Dantzler, recently promoted to acting director of the Solar System Exploration Division.[29]

---

27   Niebur, S. (2004, 23 April). "Discovery AO Highlights and Science Evaluation." Slides.

28   NASA. (2005, 2 February). "NASA Selects Moon Mapper for Mission of Opportunity." NASA news release 05-037.

29   Ibid.

The non-selection was a hard lesson for Discovery proposers. Each team was debriefed in person at NASA Headquarters, learning about their own mission's shortcomings when judged against the requirements in the AO. After the announcement, the results were challenged, and a letter was written by Senator Barbara Mikulski to NASA Deputy Administrator Fred Gregory. A study later absolved the Science Mission Directorate of any wrongdoing and confirmed the results. There would be no mission selected in this round of Discovery.

FIFTH TIME'S THE CHARM: DISCOVERY AND NEW FRONTIERS PROGRAM OFFICE AT MSFC

Meanwhile, after months of active discussion, the Discovery and New Frontiers Program Office was established at Marshall Space Flight Center, a neutral center for the proposing community. The office quickly staffed up to a total of seventeen people that first year, with other technical experts available onsite for specialist reviews and assistance as requested. NASA Headquarters responded by adding layers of documentation, no longer constrained by the workforce available when the office consisted of only Jarrett and Wolf. "We were 'better, faster, cheaper,'" recalled Jarrett. "If there is something you don't need to do, you don't do it. You don't just build documentation as prescribed and at the time it wasn't prescribed."[30]

Program scientist Michael New added: "On a day-to-day basis, the mission managers at the program office are the ones who are almost daily, if not hourly, [in] contact with the [project managers and] sometimes the PIs." A project in development could expect weekly teleconferences with the program executive, Program Scientist, and D&NFPO, in addition to the PI. The Discovery and New Frontiers Program Office advocated risk-based insight and oversight, with the ability to be hands-on and provide assistance or additional review in the face of problems. "One of the things they've been able to tap into is the large body of [Exploration Systems Mission Directorate] [and Space Operations Mission Directorate] engineers at Marshall who decide they're a little tired of working on projects that either will never see the light of day or won't see the light of day until they're retired." At the D&NFPO, however, engineers could get a broad view of the program and "see multiple missions go through their entire

---

30   Niebur, S. (2009, 14 May). Personal interview with D. Jarrett and Kate Wolf. Located in "Discovery Program" file, NASA Historical Reference Collection, History Division, NASA Headquarters, Washington, DC; Niebur, S. (2009, 4 September). Personal interview with L. Johnson. Located in "Deep Impact" file, NASA Historical Reference Collection, History Division, NASA Headquarters, Washington, DC.

life cycle. And they really liked that. They like seeing a mission go from a concept study to launch, operations and then go to another one. It gives them a real charge to go through this whole life cycle. Those are really attractive features for recruitment."[31]

Increasing the Cost Cap: The 2005 AO (Plan)

The Office of Program Analysis and Evaluation review into the 2004 evaluation delayed the next AO, planned for March 2005. When March, April, and May came and went, proposers again became anxious. On 13 June, Andy Dantzler gave an interview to *Aerospace Daily* outlining parameters for the upcoming AO, including an increase in cost cap from $360 million to $450 million—a figure even higher than Discovery's companion program, Mars Scout. In this interview, he acknowledged that the AO had been delayed by an internal review to ensure that "all the processes are in place, make sure everything is fair." He also admitted problems with the 2004 AO requirements, such as the oft-disputed budget profile that had frustrated proposers and even the program scientist, saying that the AO "kind of forced proposers to propose things not the way they would like to, creating a lot of the problems that we've seen, a lot of overruns, a lot of early problems. The new AO takes care of that by relieving a lot of those restrictions."[32]

While not new in this AO, proposers showed a great deal of interest in the upcoming opportunity to propose a new science mission for spacecraft completing their prime mission. The Deep Impact flyby spacecraft, which had a high-resolution multispectral camera, an 11.8-inch-aperture telescope, an infrared spectrometer, and a medium-resolution camera, was still intact after its impactor collided with Comet Tempel 1. Community members were encouraged to write proposals to the upcoming AO, and every effort was made to release the AO as soon as the internal investigation into the 2004 AO non-selection was complete. The appropriate evaluation criteria were determined to be similar to criteria used in previous Discovery Program AOs, with the addition of the appropriateness of the proposed investigation for the available hardware and consumables. The opportunity to reuse Deep Impact was well known, since it had recently completed its prime mission and had been put in a holding orbit in the inner solar system, "making the task of tracking and communicating with it easier," said Dantzler, but "the spacecraft is being offered as-is."[33]

---

31   Niebur, S. (2009, 10 December). Personal interview with M. New. Located in "Discovery Program" file, NASA Historical Reference Collection, History Division, NASA Headquarters, Washington, DC.

32   Discovery Preproposal Conference Transcript. (2004, 23 April); Morris, J. (2005, 13 June). "Discovery Program to release revamped AOA." *Aviation Week's Aerospace Daily & Defense Report*, 214(51).

33   NASA. (2005, 20 July). "NASA Announces Deep Impact Future Mission Status." Press release.

The opportunity to reuse other spacecraft would be riskier, as completed missions were turned off and allowed to drift through the solar system after their fuel had been expended. The Stardust spacecraft, still in operation, would have less than a quarter of its hydrazine remaining when it returned to Earth; the prime mission would not be sacrificed to increase the probability of reuse.[34] This limitation did not deter proposers, though, including the Stardust team, who were busy preparing not only for launch, but for the proposal of their extended mission concept, Scar Quest, a proposal to send Stardust to observe the gash that Deep Impact had created in the comet.[35] Overlap between the teams was strong. The Deep Impact team proposed as DIXI, and the Stardust team proposed as Stardust NExT, with the addition of Deep Impact alumni Michael A'Hearn, Mike Belton, Karen Meech, Ken Klaasen, Jay Melosh, Peter Schultz, Jessica Sunshine, Peter Thomas, and Joe Veverka. Another team would propose to reuse the Deep Impact spacecraft as well: the EPOCH team of extrasolar planet hunters, led by L. Drake Deming at NASA Goddard Space Flight Center.

New Competition: The 2006 AO

By the time the 2005—now 2006—AO was released, the climate at NASA had changed again. No longer the hot new program, Discovery was now a Solar System Exploration Division mainstay. NASA management in the positions of division director, Associate Administrator, and Administrator had changed, however, and the President's new agenda to return to the Moon and Mars was driving New Starts and initiatives across the agency. NASA's renewed emphasis on these human spaceflight plans worried many proposers, concerned how this would affect open competition such as Discovery, but the community was assured that all missions would compete on equal footing and according to the established ground rules laid out in the AO.[36]

The cost cap had seen a significant increase—the first in three years—to $425 million (Fiscal Year 2006). The mission cost profile and all associated references were removed. Proposers could propose any distribution of funding in the years post-selection; if the Planetary Science Division could not afford the proposed outlay in a given fiscal year, the decision would have to be made to move money between programs, move money between fiscal years, or not select that mission.

Phase A was increased to seven months and $1.2 million. The historical limit of 36 months of development was removed in response to analysis that the program was over-constrained and that the strict three-year development cycle eliminated targets that fell between AOs. Missions still were required to meet a "launch by" date, but the date was extended to cover most potential targets and missions, with a longer actual

---

34   Clark, S. (2005, 12 October). "Robotic comet explorers could be given new lives." *Spaceflight Now.*

35   Erickson, J. (2006, 16 March). "Colorado craft could return to the stars." *Rocky Mountain News.*

36   NASA. (2006). Discovery Announcement of Opportunity.

window ending on 1 October 2013. Although the 2004 AO budget profile had additional dollars available for Phase B formulation, the 2006 AO reinstated the limit on expenditures prior to confirmation at its previous value of 25 percent.

The Discovery Program goals were revised and updated to more accurately reflect the current goals and desired outcomes of the program, as the original goals were overtaken by events and the faster, better, cheaper language no longer accurately reflected the management expectations of the program. The program now would "provide frequent flight opportunities for high-quality, high-value scientific investigations that can be accomplished under a not to exceed cost cap," with the following outcomes:

- Advancement in scientific knowledge and exploration of the elements of our solar system and other planetary systems;
- Addition of scientific data, maps, and other products to the Planetary Data System archive for all scientists to access;
- Announcement of scientific progress and results in the peer-reviewed literature, popular media, scholastic curricula, and materials that can be used to inspire and motivate students to pursue careers in science, technology, engineering, and mathematics;
- Expansion of the pool of well-qualified Principal Investigators and Project Managers for implementation of future missions in Discovery and other programs, through current involvement as CoIs and other team members; and
- Implementation of technology advancements proven in related programs.[37]

All requirements in the new NPR 7120.5C, including the use of Earned Value Management and Cost Analysis Data Requirement reporting, were made requirements for Discovery mission proposals and plans. Draft Level 1 requirements were requested in an attempt to set them early and have them truly drive the missions as envisioned, rather than layered on top of the mission as late as the Preliminary Design Review, as in the case of Dawn. Without firm and steady requirements, the trade space remained fluid and decisions may have been made based on different understandings of the mission drivers. AO requirements for sample return, orbital debris, program and project management, communications link budget design data, and page count were updated.

The program's education and public outreach commitment was drastically reduced to 0.25–0.50 percent of the NASA Science Mission Directorate cost, excluding launch vehicles. Participating scientist programs, data access programs, and guest observers

---

37   NASA. (2014). "Discovery Program Goals." Downloaded from *http://discovery.larc.nasa.gov/ dpgoals.html*.

were encouraged at no cost to the missions' cost caps. Review by the NASA Independent Verification and Validation Facility in West Virginia was still required, but costs were not included in this AO.

Student collaborations, science enhancement opportunities, and technology demonstration opportunities were added to the AO as the new Associate Administrator, Mary Cleave, put her own stamp on the process. Between the completion and approval of the draft AO and its release, several months passed while the budget became available. Susan Niebur had resigned from the position of program scientist but was not replaced until just before the AO release. During that time, several changes were made, including the insertion of a new concept: the student collaboration. Michael New remembers this being a problem when he first assumed the role vacated by Niebur: "That turned out to be an issue when we started figuring out how we were going to evaluate against the AO criteria, because the words used to describe student collaborations and their evaluation criteria were not consistent with the language in the rest of the AO." Because the Discovery Program was unclear in its definition of what a student collaboration was, what its goals should be, and whether its goals should be linked to the scientific goals of the mission, evaluation became an issue. "Some teams embraced it wholeheartedly," said New. "There was one team that even had their student collaboration write their section, and it was great. At the site visit, they actually had the students present [that part of the presentation]. They really embraced the whole concept."[38] Student collaborations had been a successful part of the New Horizons mission launching that year, and so the opportunity was seen as a positive enhancement to the next generation of NASA missions.

Science enhancement and technology demonstration opportunities included innovative new instruments, investigations, technology, hardware, and software to be demonstrated on either the flight system or ground system during mission development and operations. By making them clearly separable from the proposed baseline investigation and the performance floor from selection onward, NASA could fund those options without adding unacceptable risk to a mission's ability to meet its science requirements. The Discovery AO NNH06ZDA001O was released on 3 January 2006.

At February's preproposal conference, the Discovery and New Frontiers Program Office briefed proposers on the first results from their cost study, with these additional "areas to watch" recommendations:

- Software: Test beds and Fault Protection/Autonomy;
- Integrated Project Schedule;

---

38   Niebur, S. (2009, 10 December). Personal interview with M. New. Located in "Discovery Program" file, NASA Historical Reference Collection, History Division, NASA Headquarters, Washington, DC.

- Heritage Hardware;
- Workforce roll off for launch, Optimistic Test Schedules, V&V [Verification and Validation]; and
- Vendor assumptions, both in the areas of experience and insight/oversight requirements.[39]

Discovery proposals were due 5 April 2006.

NRC Assessment: Reports on PI-Led Missions in the Space Sciences

Though the National Research Council Space Studies Board's report, "Principal-Investigator-Led Missions in the Space Sciences," and the National Academy of Public Administration's report, "PI Led Missions in Space Science," had both been published in quick succession almost four months earlier, NASA's response was muted, as it was already on the path for a Discovery AO release as announced in Federal Business Opportunities earlier that fall.[40] No community discussion of policy changes could be held with an open or pending solicitation in the program.

Once the Discovery proposals were submitted, however, the NASA Science Mission Directorate hosted an event for community discussion of the recommendations and of lessons learned. The Lessons Learned Workshop for PI-Led Planetary Science Missions in Crystal City, Virginia, was held on 11 April 2006. Speakers included representatives of the technical-management-cost review process, the Integrated Action Teams, Science Mission Directorate science management, NASA and ESA international relations, implementing institutions (JPL, Goddard, APL, and Ames), PI institutions (University of Washington, University of Arizona, Carnegie Institution, Southwest Research Institute), and major contractors (Ball, Southwest Research Institute, JPL, Malin Space Science Systems, Lockheed Martin).[41] The workshop was broadly applicable to the Explorer, Discovery, Mars Scout, and New Frontiers PI-led programs, and the lessons learned were collected over the review of 657 proposals to these programs from 1996 to 2005.[42] The technical-management-cost lessons learned were illuminating, including the most common specific weaknesses over the set of programs. These were shared with the community in the hopes that future proposers would give the issues extra attention,

39 NASA. (2006, 2 February). "Discovery and New Frontiers Program Office: Some Lessons Learned," presented at the Discovery Preproposal Conference, Washington, DC.

40 National Research Council. *Committee on Principal-Investigator-Led Missions in the Space Sciences, National Research Council Principal-Investigator-Led Missions in the Space Sciences.* (2006). National Academies Press: Washington, DC. 132; National Academy of Public Administration. (2005). *Principal Investigator Led Missions in Space Science.*

41 NASA. (2006, 11 April). "Agenda: Lessons Learned Workshop for PI-Led Planetary Science Missions."

42 Perry, R. (2006, 11 April). "TMC lessons learned from PI-led planetary science missions." Presentation.

reducing future weaknesses in both proposals and projects. Brad Perry of the Science Mission Directorate, and colleagues, also wrote an accompanying white paper, "to reduce the learning curve for new proposers, and to improve the overall quality and maturity of all proposals submitted."[43]

In addition, a new National Research Council committee on PI-led missions in the space sciences had been convened and charged with six items: assessing the selection process and objectives; examining the roles, relationships, and authority among members of past PI-led teams, where members were defined as institutions; identifying lessons learned from scientific and technical performance of past missions; analyzing factors contributing to mission cost overruns; identifying opportunities for knowledge transfer to new PIs and sustained technical management expertise; and identifying lessons learned, recommending practices and incentives for improving the overall conduct of future PI-led missions. The resultant report had 15 findings and 15 recommendations. While the recommendations were largely either adopted (2, 6, 7, 8, 13, 14, and 15) or rejected (1, 3, 4, 5, 9, 10, and 11) in the first five years after the report was issued, many of the findings remained relevant. The 15 findings are reproduced as follows:

Principal-Investigator-Led Missions in the Space Sciences Findings:

1. ***Proposals and Reviews:*** *The PI-led mission selection process could be made more efficient and effective, minimizing the burden on the proposer and the reviewer and facilitating the selection of concepts that become more uniformly successful projects.*

2. ***Concept Study:*** *The still-competitive but already funded concept study stage (Phase A) of selected, short-listed PI-led missions is the best stage for the accurate definition of the concept details and cost estimates needed to assist in final selection.*

3. ***Proposals and Reviews:*** *Community-based studies of science opportunities and priorities can be used to focus AO proposals on specific topics of great interest and to guide the choices of selection officials.*

4. ***The Proposing Team Experience and Leadership (PI & PM)*** *is critical to mission success. Programs can emphasize the importance of experience in their selections and create opportunities for prospective PIs and PMs to gain such experience.*

5. ***Technology Readiness:*** *As a rule, PI-led missions are too constrained by cost and schedule to comfortably support significant technology development.... Regular technology development opportunities managed by PI-led programs could lead to a technology pipeline that would help to enable successful mission selection and implementation.*

---

43   Perry, R., et al. (2006, 21 February). "Lessons learned from Technical, Management, and Cost Review of Proposals: A Summary of 10 years' experience in reviewing competitively selected proposals for new science missions." Presentation.

6. **Funding Profiles** *represent a special challenge for PI-led missions because they are planned at the mission concept stage with the goals of minimizing costs and achieving schedules. However, like all NASA missions, PI-led missions are subject to the availability of NASA funding, annual NASA budgetary cycles, and agency decisions on funding priorities, all of which can disrupt the planned funding profiles for PI-led missions.*

7. **International contributions** *have an important positive impact on the science capabilities of PI-led missions but are faced with an increasingly discouraging environment, in part due to ITAR. In addition, logistic difficulties associated with foreign government budgetary commitments and the timing of proposals and selections persist. The result is both real and perceived barriers to teaming and higher perceived risk for missions including international partners.*

8. **The program offices** *can play a critical positive role in the success of PI-led missions if they are appropriately located and staffed, and offer enabling infrastructure for projects and NASA Headquarters from the proposal through the implementation stages.*

9. **NASA oversight of PI-led missions,** *as well as of all missions, increased following a string of mission failures in the late 1990s and is again increasing following the Columbia shuttle disaster. Some of the added oversight, and especially the style of that oversight, appears excessive for robotic missions as small as the PI-led missions. Increases in oversight also strain project resources and personnel to the point of adding risk rather than reducing it.*

10. **Program Oversight:** *There is confusion about the processes in place for adjusting PI-led mission cost caps and schedules to accommodate oversight requirements introduced after selection.*

11. **The threat of cancellation** *in a termination review is no longer an effective way of keeping PI-led missions within their cost caps, because few missions have been canceled as a result of exceeding their cost caps. Nevertheless, a termination review is taken seriously because it reflects negatively on project management performance and raises the possibility of science descopes. [Other] project leaders need to be made aware of problems that lead to termination reviews so that they can avoid them.*

12. **Descopes:** *High-impact decisions such as descopes made by NASA outside the termination review process undermine a PI's authority and can cause a mission to lose science capability.*

13. **Technical and Programmatic Failures:** *Lessons learned from experience in both PI-led and other missions can be extremely valuable for reducing risk and inspiring ideas about how to do things better. Much useful lessons-learned documentation is available on the Web but is not collected in a coherent library or directory. A modest effort by the program offices to locate these distributed documents, provide a centralized Web site containing links, and advertise its existence would allow these lessons to be more widely used.*

14. *The leaders of PI-led missions occasionally find they must* **replace a manager** *or a key team member to reach their goals. While the cost and schedule impacts of such a major change must be considered, a change in project management needs to be allowed if it is for the good of the mission. The PI should make all final decisions on project management personnel.*

15. ***The summary cost and schedule performance records*** *for PI-led and other missions are not kept in a consistent way, making external comparative analyses difficult. Science activities on PI-led missions seem to be competitive with those on core missions to the extent that the data sets are made available and science analysis is supported.*[44]

Some of the conclusions were outdated before the report was published, such as this statement: "The Discovery Program Office has been relocated on more than one occasion and is in a state of flux, which has led to difficulties for some Discovery missions."[45] As a result of this flux, the D&NFPO had already been established at Marshall Space Flight Center, where it remained for subsequent years.

Other conclusions exposed the crux of the problem and a large part of the reason that the studies were commissioned in the first place: "The committee was unable to obtain the kind of moderately detailed [cost] data that would normally be expected to be readily available for NASA's own internal use or for an analysis of historical trends." The problems weren't just in PI-led missions, however. "The information that could be obtained on cost and schedule performance in PI-led missions indicated that they face the same cost growth drivers as core or strategic missions but that any such growth in PI-led missions is more visible within NASA because the cost caps are enforced so much more strictly. The cost growth, in percent, of PI-led missions is in any case documented as being, on average, less than that for core missions. The perception of a cost growth problem specific to PI-led mission lines is thus not supported by the records."[46] This was not surprising to many inside the program; it was, indeed, a source of frustration when directed missions with much higher costs overran significantly more, but the harsh adherence to cost caps enabled the Discovery Program and others like it to accomplish more than just a single directed mission, ending when the fuel (or dollars) ran out. By enforcing cost caps for each mission in development, future missions were protected. If the program had become lax in its attention to cost, it would face scrutiny and possibly cancellation, forcing the Planetary Science Division to propose each new mission separately to congress as a New Start—a very difficult process with the outcome anything but certain. No, by simply adhering to the Discovery Program principles of cost-capped missions, short development times, and focused science, they could initiate new missions approximately every two years, without congressional approval, whenever the "futures" budget supported the release of another AO.

---

44   National Research Council. *Committee on Principal-Investigator-Led Missions in the Space Sciences, National Research Council Principal-Investigator-Led Missions in the Space Sciences.* (2006). National Academies Press: Washington, DC. 132.

45   Ibid.

46   Ibid.

The committee also "found that potentially valuable lessons learned in both the technical and management areas of PI-led missions are neither easily located nor widely discussed despite being resources of which every PI-led mission leader should be aware."[47] This had been addressed earlier in the decade in part with the creation of an online Lessons Learned Archive for Discovery, but the lack of written reports from most Lessons Learned Workshops inhibited archival, and the lack of incentive for proposers to absorb lessons from experienced mission leadership inhibited its use.

Termination reviews, particularly those faced by missions such as MESSENGER, came under strict scrutiny:

The committee learned that termination reviews are no longer regarded as mission-threatening, because very few missions have been canceled even though some PI-led (and most core) missions do grow beyond their initial cost cap. Moreover, canceling a mission after substantial investment has been made is not reasonable if the mission has no fatal technical issues or additional cost or schedule requirements. However, a PI-led mission is more vulnerable than a core mission to cancellation or descopes because its cost cap was a key factor in its winning the competition. The committee considers termination reviews as an effective management tool for missions that overrun their cost caps, provided that both NASA and the project teams recognize that such reviews raise the prospect of NASA Headquarters–mandated changes to the mission capability. Lessons learned from these reviews should be used to inform other active PI-led program and project leaders.[48]

The National Academy of Public Administration study, meanwhile, was charged by NASA with providing an in-depth analysis of cost growth and relevant management aspects of PI-led missions. This study produced eight findings and associated recommendations. The first described the program's "characteristics and limitations [25 percent minimum unencumbered reserve level, focus on end-to-end mission costs, high science return favored over lower cost and schedule risks, slowly adjusted cost caps, 20 percent maximum cost growth in Phase A] that encourage the submission of optimistic basic mission cost proposals for science missions."[49]

The second stated that the 25 percent reserve mandate "operate(s) as a disincentive for the proposer to provide more realistic baseline cost estimates and an assessment of the appropriate level of reserves." This was seen at NASA Headquarters as a somewhat curious statement, although it must have reflected the spirit of proposers consulted. From the program perspective, the 25 percent reserve mandate was a final check that a minimum level of reserves had been met for each phase of the program. The 25 percent

---

47   Ibid.

48   Ibid.

49   National Research Council 2006. *Principal-Investigator-Led Missions in the Space Sciences.* Washington, DC: The National Academies Press. *https://doi.org/10.17226/11530*, p. 110.

reserve level had been set in response to several missions in development simultaneously exceeding their bids by amounts significantly over their reserve posture and the corresponding need to protect the program from similar overruns in the future. Projects were still expected to provide realistic costs in both Step 1 and 2 proposals, to assess the appropriate level of reserves per project element, and to discuss the budget reserve strategy, including budget reserve levels as a function of mission phase.[50]

The third finding, "PIs are expected to provide leadership and management, but most lack the requisite skills," could be seen as insulting, but it was indicative of a change in the implementation of Discovery and Explorer missions, which required a great deal more hands-on management than imagined in the early days of the program's establishment. In 1992, the PI's role was to manage the science; by 2006, the PI also was charged with full responsibility for "the execution of the investigation within the committed cost and according to the committed schedule," a codification of the implications in AOs as far back as 2000 indicating that PIs "must be prepared to recommend project termination when, in the judgment of the PI, the successful achievement of established minimum science objectives, as defined in the proposal as the performance floor, is not likely within the committed cost and schedule reserves." Perhaps since this clause had not been exercised before 2002, the full impact of its statement had not been tested, but certainly after that, PIs had to take a more hands-on role to avoid bringing their project in for termination or deleting instruments in order to achieve the mission within the committed cost and schedule reserves. This realization would indeed require a "fundamental understanding of the elements of project control," as discussed in the last clause of the third finding, but it certainly wasn't the way that the Discovery founders, including Wes Huntress, envisioned or managed the program in the 1990s.[51]

The fourth finding, "The costs incurred by proposers in responding to AOs has [sic] been identified as a potential limiting factor by the proposal teams as to whether they will respond to future AOs" and that "NASA does not possess good information on the costs incurred by proposers in responding to an AO," was certainly true but was thought by NASA Headquarters to be ameliorated by increases in Phase A study funding in 2004, 2006, and 2010.[52] The common wisdom was that initial proposal costs had to be undertaken by the proposing organizations; if a potential Discovery team didn't have $1 million or so between them for proposing costs, they would be

50   NASA. (2006). Discovery Announcement of Opportunity.

51   Niebur, S. (2009, 13 March). Personal interview with W. Huntress. Located in "Wes Huntress" file, NASA Historical Reference Collection, History Division, NASA Headquarters, Washington, DC.

52   National Academy of Public Administration. (2005). Principal Investigator Led Missions in Space Science.

hard-pressed to manage a mission costing 300 times that. NASA was prohibited by the Federal Acquisition Regulation from funding preproposal costs, so this was seen as a necessary cost of doing business.

The fifth finding encouraged NASA to focus additional attention on the cost, schedule, and funding risks to a project at confirmation and to determine "whether the cost estimate reflects the level of design maturity and the related constraints."[53]

The sixth finding encouraged all involved to carefully consider the financial implications of the changing risk environment at NASA in establishing cost estimates for future mission proposals.

The seventh finding gave guidance on termination reviews, noting that "the forecasts given to decision makers of the costs required to complete the missions were consistently understated. Also, the decision official is not provided with high/mid/low confidence engineering estimates of the costs-to-go, and parametric cost-estimating tools are not used to provide comparative cost estimates." These additional requirements could be implemented in future termination reviews.[54]

The eighth and last recommendation was damning for the record-keepers and provides an instructive point for those reading the analyses of the first two decades of Discovery found in this book and in later reports: "The recorded costs for PI-led science missions understate the true amount of the costs required to execute these missions." The study also reported internal cost growth of each of the Discovery missions, comparing the C/D estimate (without reserves) to the actual costs in such a way that would indicate the appropriate level of reserves or extent of overrun, but the numbers do not correlate with numbers reported in either of NASA's 2008 to 2010 studies, so the reports are difficult to reconcile.[55]

This study brought to light some interesting facts not otherwise codified, such as the understatement of costs-to-go at termination reviews, but unfortunately those lessons had already been learned informally after the Deep Impact and MESSENGER termination and continuation reviews at NASA.[56]

Three Competing Concept Studies

In parallel with the consideration of the findings of these two reports, evaluation of the 2006 proposals continued. After rigorous science and technical-management-cost evaluations, NASA announced the AO results on 30 October 2006. "The science

---

53   Ibid.

54   Ibid.

55   Ibid.

56   Ibid. "NASA could gain useful information from proposers by requiring them to address a specific list of 'cost risk subfactors.' [Such as the list presented by JPL management to the NAPA study team.] The NASA evaluation team could use the responses to these subfactors as a consistent basis of comparison among proposals."

community astounded us with the creativity of their proposals," said Mary Cleave, the Associate Administrator of the Science Mission Directorate.[57] From a set of 24 proposals, NASA selected three missions for $1.2 million in concept studies: the Origins Spectral Interpretation, Resource Identification and Security (OSIRIS) mission to return asteroid regolith samples; the Vesper mission to study the atmosphere of Venus; and the Gravity Recovery and Interior Laboratory (GRAIL) mission to study the interior structure and history of the Moon.[58]

The $415 million OSIRIS mission would orbit the 580-meter-wide near-Earth asteroid RQ36 for 300 days at a very low altitude of 100 meters and return samples of asteroid regolith for study on Earth.[59] "We're going to an object that is a remnant of a planet's formation," said Dante Lauretta, OSIRIS Deputy PI and associate professor of lunar and planetary science at the University of Arizona's Lunar and Planetary Laboratory. "This is really pristine material, and one of the mission's goals is to keep it that way."[60] The samples would be scooped up by a spring-loaded robotic arm briefly touching the surface of RQ36, capturing the dirt in a sample return canister behind the arm's trapdoor, and bouncing back like a pogo stick, heading back to Earth after the third scooping opportunity. The canister would be released as the spacecraft approached Earth in 2017, parachuting to Utah's Dugway Proving Grounds, a favorite landing spot of NASA's sample return missions. The long period of mission operations before sample return prompted the OSIRIS team to adopt a management structure that, like Dawn, involved the Deputy PI very closely in the management work but, unlike Dawn, stated explicitly that the Deputy PI would eventually succeed the PI. "I'll be 71 when the samples come back," said Michael Drake, the OSIRIS Principal Investigator. "You not only want to make sure your mission is successful, but make sure the next generation [of scientists] is coming along." Drake intentionally composed the team of both senior and junior scientists able to do the work.[61] Mission management would be located at NASA's Goddard Space Flight Center.[62]

Vesper, a Venus chemistry and dynamics orbiter, would drop a probe into the atmosphere of Venus and orbit the planet for 486 days, enough time for Venus to rotate exactly twice. NASA had not been back to Venus since the days of Magellan,

57   NASA. (2006, 30 October). "NASA Announces Discovery Program Selections." NASA news release 06-342.

58   NASA. (2007, 11 December). "New NASA Mission to Reveal Moon's Internal Structure and Evolution." NASA news release 07-274.

59   Steigerwald, B., and Lori Stiles. (2007, 9 March). "Proposed Mission Will Return Sample from Near-Earth Object." NASA press release.

60   Sorenson, D. (2006, 1 November). "NASA picks UA mission to asteroid as a finalist." *Arizona Daily Star.*

61   Shiga, D. (2006, 1 November). "Deep Impact's blurry camera may study exoplanets." *New Scientist.*

62   Niebur, S. (2009, August). "Principal Investigators and Mission Leadership." *Space Policy, https:// www.sciencedirect.com/science/article/pii/S0265964609000538?via%3Dihub*, 181–186.

and scientists of the time were eager to investigate the composition and dynamics of its atmosphere—a wild, swirling mess of clouds of sulfuric acid, with "vortices of spinning clouds resembling twin hurricanes, side by side," at both north and south poles of the planet. The thick atmosphere covering the hot, waterless planet (at 92 times Earth's pressure) is rich with carbon dioxide, a compound that should be broken down by sunlight into carbon monoxide and oxygen. Because it exists still as carbon dioxide, however, scientists are intrigued by what in the atmosphere might be preventing its dissolution and what unknown chemistry may exist on a planet with very similar size, gravity, and bulk composition to that of Earth. "The big mystery Vesper will help answer is how these two similar worlds ended up with such different outcomes," explained PI Gordon Chin of NASA Goddard, which would also be the managing institution.[63]

GRAIL, led by Maria Zuber, head of the Department of Earth, Atmospheric and Planetary Sciences at the Massachusetts Institute of Technology (MIT), would study the interior structure of the Moon using high-quality gravity field mapping conducted by twin satellites launched on a single launch vehicle. The satellites claimed heritage from the 100-kilogram Experimental Satellite System-11 (XSS-11) microsatellite developed by Lockheed Martin under the Air Force Research Laboratory's Experimental Satellite System's Micro Satellite Flight Demonstration Program and launched a year earlier, on 11 April 2005.[64] GRAIL's main instrument would be a Ka-band Lunar Gravity Ranging System built at the Jet Propulsion Laboratory with significant heritage from the twin Gravity Recovery and Climate Experiment satellites launched in March 2002. The mission boasted no new technology.[65] JPL would manage the GRAIL mission.

NEW DISCOVERY MISSION: GRAIL

By the time the concept studies were submitted to NASA and reviewed by the technical-management-cost evaluators, NASA Science Mission Directorate management had changed again. Alan Stern, the new Associate Administrator, announced the selected Discovery mission at a full meeting of the American Geophysical Union on 11 December 2007. A press release followed the next morning with details about GRAIL, which had been selected for flight. For $375 million, GRAIL would launch two spacecraft on a single Delta 7920H-10 rocket and orbit the Moon in a low, 50-kilometer polar orbit for three months, mapping its gravity field in exquisite detail. The selection of GRAIL was in line with the agency's renewed emphasis on sending humans to the Moon by 2020 and then to Mars, as announced by President George W. Bush at NASA Headquarters on 14 January 2004. Stern confirmed that this was an important contribution when

---

63   NASA. (2006, 24 November). "Vesper Mission Could Explore Earth's Fiery Twin." News release.

64   Air Force Research Laboratory (2011, September). "Fact sheet: XSS-11 micro satellite."

65   Taylor, R. (2009). "Preparing for an NPR 7120.5D Life-Cycle Review." Presentation.

he announced the selection of this "low risk" mission, saying, "GRAIL also offers to bring innovative Earth studies techniques to the moon as a precursor to their possible later use at Mars and other planets."[66]

Knowing the gravity field to such a high degree of certainty would enable scientists to understand the Moon's interior structure better than ever before. This knowledge might reveal subsurface structures and, indirectly, the thermal history of the Moon and its evolution.[67] "After the three-month mission is completed, we will know the lunar gravitational field better than we know Earth's," explained Zuber, the mission PI, to the media shortly after selection.[68] It would be valuable information for any future lunar landings.[69] The gravity data would also enable lunar studies from formation to evolution, and even the very stability of the Moon's orbit.

GRAIL's primary science objectives were to determine the structure of the lunar interior from crust to core and to further the understanding of its thermal evolution. To achieve these goals, GRAIL would take measurements and the GRAIL science team would conduct six lunar science investigations:

- Map the structure of the crust & lithosphere.
- Understand the Moon's asymmetric thermal evolution.
- Determine the subsurface structure of impact basins and the origin of mascons.
- Ascertain the temporal evolution of crustal brecciation and magmatism.
- Constrain deep interior structure from tides.
- Place limits on the size of the possible inner core.[70]

A secondary objective of the mission was to extend knowledge gained from the Moon to the terrestrial planets: Mercury, Venus, Earth, and Mars.

The winning GRAIL concept did have a student collaboration—an education and public outreach component led by co-investigator Sally Ride. Even this student collaboration had strong heritage: Ride's successful EarthKam program on the International Space Station. Up to five MoonKam camera heads on each spacecraft would be operated by students from a separate MoonKam Operations Center—a collaboration of middle school students selecting targets and high school students performing operations under Ride's

---

66 NASA. (2007, 11 December). "New NASA Mission to Reveal Moon's Internal Structure and Evolution." NASA news release 07-274.

67 Fillion, R. (2007, 14 December). "Lockheed lands lunar mission." *Rocky Mountain News.*

68 Chandler, D. (2007, 14 December). "MIT to lead ambitious lunar mission." News release.

69 Shiga, D. (2007, 14 December). "NASA spacecraft to study moon's lumpy interior." *New Scientist.*

70 NASA. (N.d.). "GRAIL Science objectives and Investigations." Downloaded from *http://moon. mit.edu/objectives.html.*

direction. "Interestingly enough," noted Michael New, "the science goals of GRAIL are not really related at all to any science that would be done by the student collaboration, because GRAIL is a gravity retrieval mission, and the imaging is completely unrelated."[71]

The project manager was Dave Lehman, who also had served in that role on the technology demonstration mission Deep Space 1. Gregg Vane of JPL called him "very successful. That's the caliber of person we're looking to put on a competed mission as the project manager."[72] Co-investigators were similarly seasoned, with specific experience in Earth and planetary gravity mapping investigations. Moreover, the project scientist, mission system manager, and instrument manager on GRAIL had recently had the same roles on GRACE.

GRAIL proceeded to development, with the start of Phase B in January 2008 quickly followed by its Project Mission System Review in April. The next major gate would be November's Preliminary Design Review. GRAIL wasted no time, setting out a detailed schedule in preparation for the latter review that began almost immediately, headed by a review captain, Randall Taylor, GRAIL Project Acquisition Manager, rather than the project manager. Taylor would later call the following tasks absolutely critical when preparing for a life-cycle review:

- Establish the standing review board, and your relationship with it, six months in advance;
- Draft the Terms of Reference early;
- Negotiate the scope of review (any special assessments), pre-review documentation deliveries (including schedule), and participation of standing review board members in project internal reviews;
- Establish a review organization with clear roles and responsibilities;
- Identify all required activities and have a detailed schedule;
- Determine how to handle reviews prior to the Preliminary Design Review, gate products, presentation materials, IT, and logistics; and
- Leverage institutional resources and learn from other projects.[73]

---

71 Niebur, S. (2009, 10 December). Personal interview with M. New. Located in "Discovery Program" file, NASA Historical Reference Collection, History Division, NASA Headquarters, Washington, DC.

72 Niebur, S. (2009, 22 March). Personal interview with G. Vane. Located in the "Discovery Program" file, NASA Historical Reference Collection, History Division, NASA Headquarters, Washington, DC.

73 Taylor, R. (2009). "Preparing for an NPR 7120.5D Life-Cycle Review." Presentation. See also R. L. Taylor, "Reducing NPR 7120.5D to practice: Preparing for a life-cycle review," *2009 IEEE Aerospace conference*, Big Sky, MT, USA, 2009, pp. 1–12, doi: 10.1109/AERO.2009.4839721.

As the mission marched toward its Preliminary Design Review, GRAIL held thirteen formal element inheritance reviews, covering all spacecraft subsystems and all instrument assemblies; a flight system inheritance review in July; and an additional alternative avionics inheritance review in August. Each of these reviews, and the later ones, included board reports and responses from the project. Just as these inheritance reviews were completed, reviews before the Preliminary Design Review began. The 20-element Preliminary Design Review and technical interchange meetings addressed requirements, verification and validation, mission design and navigation, all spacecraft subsystems, and all instrument assemblies. It wrapped up with a top-level assessment of the instrument at the payload Preliminary Design Review in November 2008.[74]

The mission confirmation review (Key Decision Point-C) was held in January 2009, followed by the risk management peer review in April and May's mission operations system peer review, which showed that the project had answered the driving issues from the Preliminary Design Review.[75] The system CDR in November 2009 showed that the mass and power margins were tighter and that the project was managing them closely. The top project risk was considered the launch vehicle, as GRAIL was scheduled to fly on the last Delta II. The total duration of the mission, including cruise, would be just 270 days, starting at launch on 8 September 2011.

Repurposing Spacecraft: Extended Missions and New Science Investigations

The 2006 AO also resulted in selections of three extended missions—new science investigations using the existing hardware on the Stardust and Deep Impact spacecraft. Deep Impact, with its telescope, proved particularly rich in opportunities after the completion of its prime mission, the impact of Comet Tempel 1. At one point, seven distinct proposals were in preparation for submission to NASA Headquarters for review. Of those submitted to the 2006 AO, two proposals were selected. The Deep Impact eXtended Investigation of Comets (DIXI) was selected to fly by a second comet, photograph the nucleus, and provide additional material for scientists to perform a comparative study of the comets observed by Stardust and Deep Impact. The Extrasolar Planet Observations and Characterization (EPOCH) mission was also selected, to operate while the spacecraft was in transit to the second comet, all the while searching for the first Earth-sized planets around nearby stars with Deep Impact's high-resolution camera.

Meanwhile, the Stardust NExT mission, reusing the Stardust spacecraft, would revisit Comet Tempel 1 after its closest solar approach and identify changes since Deep

---

74   Ibid.
75   NASA. (2009, June). "Discovery and New Frontiers News." 8.

Impact's encounter in 2005. Two of the three PIs selected to lead these extended missions had previous experience as Discovery PIs, and the third had Explorer experience; management of these missions of opportunity was thus expected to require minimal oversight. Each concept study was funded at $250,000, and each was eventually selected for implementation as an extended mission.[76]

Alan Stern, Associate Administrator of the Science Mission Directorate, summed up the opportunities to return to a comet, fly by a new comet, and search for small planets around stars with large known planets, saying: "These mission extensions are as exciting as it gets."[77] By reusing spacecraft that have completed their prime mission, "it's an effective way to get more science done with our budget. Often this gives you more bang for the buck by providing important new science for very little additional cost. With these extensions, we're going to get two new comet visits and a search for extrasolar planets for about 15 percent of the cost that either of the Stardust and Deep Impact missions took to build."[78] Or, as Michael Belton, the deputy PI of Deep Impact and co-investigator on the DIXI and Stardust NExT proposals, put it, "If you've got it, use it."[79]

Evaluating Missions of Opportunity Like Full Missions: The 2006 AO Evaluation

"It was a huge amount of work," said Michael A'Hearn, the PI of Stardust NExT, "given that we had to do a proposal and a Concept Study Report, a Phase A study for a mission in Phase E, and then a site visit." A'Hearn compared the two-step proposal process to Cassini's extended mission proposal, saying, "I think we did *far* more work than Cassini did for its extended mission."[80]

The combination of the Deep Impact and Stardust teams for the Stardust NExT study was a clever solution to a difficult problem: managing two extended missions for a fixed period of time for less than $35 million. Efficiencies were realized by combining not just the co-investigators, but also the project management, led by Tim Larson; education and public outreach, led by Aimee Meyer Whalen; administrative functions;

---

76   NASA. (2006, 30 October). "NASA Announces Discovery Program Selections." NASA news release 06-342.

77   Malik, T. (2007, 12 July). "NASA probes get new mission." *Florida Today*.

78   Alers, P. (2007, 30 August). "Space, Science, and the Bottom Line." *Nature*, 448(978).

79   Erickson, J. (2006, 16 March). "Colorado craft could return to the stars." *Rocky Mountain News*.

80   Niebur, S. (2009, 11 March). Personal interview with M. A'Hearn. Located in "Deep Impact" file, NASA Historical Reference Collection, History Division, NASA Headquarters, Washington, DC; Niebur, S. (2009, 4 September). Personal interview with L. Johnson. Located in "Deep Impact" file, NASA Historical Reference Collection, History Division, NASA Headquarters, Washington, DC.

and JPL oversight. "We basically told them here from [NASA] Headquarters that for us to be able to approve both these missions, you guys really need to consolidate your operations closely to cut down the cost," said Lindley Johnson, the program executive.[81]

Reducing Risk to the Program: PI Experience Rule

Despite the best efforts of NASA and the planetary science community, flight project costs continued to grow. The Associate Administrator's edict that divisions solve their own financial problems had not contained costs. Nor had the efforts of several division directors. Nor had the implementation of a minimum of 25 percent reserve for all current and future missions (indeed, it caused some missions like Dawn *additional* troubles). Scientific instruments were thrown overboard to compensate for industry delays, and mission operations budgets were slashed to pay for overruns. Replans of current missions seemed to provide solutions, but in the end, costs continued to grow. Nearly everyone was frustrated, and NASA would have to introduce new ideas or lose credibility with the scientific community and with Congress over the definition of Discovery as a cost-capped program.

Less than a month after Alan Stern assumed the role of Associate Administrator of the Science Mission Directorate, he made a major policy change to all PI-led mission lines. Each proposing PI, Stern said, must have proven experience delivering a previous flight project in a leadership role. PIs without experience leading a small flight mission or an instrument development team on a larger flagship mission would be disqualified from even *proposing* a future mission to the Discovery, Mars Scout, New Frontiers, or Explorer mission lines. The community did not have to wait long for the official language, codified in an announcement of the upcoming SMEX AO: "A proposal PI for this AO must have demonstrated sufficient experience to successfully lead a SMEX mission by having held a key position (PI, PS, Deputy PI, Deputy PS) for a space project (orbital or suborbital or deep space, mission or experiment or instrument) that has launched."[82]

The official policy further defined the required level of experience by mission class and duration. Discovery proposers were required to demonstrate "at least two years of experience in a lead role [responsibilities of a PI, PM, PS, or Deputy PI/PM/PS] for an orbital or deep space mission or instrument that will be launched prior to AO downselection." In addition, since "leading a spaceflight mission [is] one of the

---

81   Ibid.

82   NASA. (2007, 24 April). "Explorer Program Announcement of Opportunity."

most difficult jobs in the world," with this policy the Science Mission Directorate also established for the first time a mandatory post-selection training program for all PIs, including those already selected and leading missions in the program.[83]

The new preproposal requirements for formal demonstration of PI experience posed a problem. Very few PIs had led a mission before because of the extended time scales required for comprehensive mission development. After attaining doctorates, proposing PIs typically spent many years performing independent research and possibly serving as a co-investigator on one or more missions, and then submitting a series of unsuccessful proposals to competitive AOs, leading to successful selection of a mission with the scientist as PI. The series of proposals was key: in the Discovery Program, seven of the nine competitively selected missions in the first twenty years of the program were first proposed in some form in 1992 and 1994. The need for successive proposals over a decade further lengthened the time elapsed between PhD and selection as a PI. No studies then existed on the typical age or experience level of a PI, but anecdotal evidence was overwhelming: this rule would exclude most of the field.

While no one denied that the charge to design, develop, implement, and operate a space or Earth science mission on time and on budget encompassed many tasks and skillsets, some began to dispute, first quietly and then louder, whether previous experience in the leadership role was necessary for a proposing PI. Sean Solomon, the MESSENGER PI, acidly noted at a Planetary Science Subcommittee meeting that this rule would mean that only he, of all the PIs who had led Discovery missions, would be considered formally qualified to lead.

The PI experience rule, as it came to be called, also had the effect, if not necessarily the intent, of barring younger investigators and almost all women from submitting proposals, due to their lack of previous experience in these specific science leadership positions, despite mission experience as members of the science team in numbers more proportionate to their representation in the field as a whole. The policy undervalued the contribution of a co-investigator, who might have been responsible for the design and delivery of an instrument, completion of a scientific investigation, mission operations, and coordinating supporting observations from ground-based telescopes or other space assets, without providing any avenue for these co-investigators or other scientists to become qualified under the new definition.

After a hue and cry, and a change of Associate Administrators at NASA, the explicit experience requirement was not included in the 2008 "standard AO," a document proposed for use by all PI-led mission lines. The expectation of *extensive* experience, however, remained, as did confusion about what "experience" was considered suf-

---

83   NASA. (2007, 20 November). "SMD Policy: Experience Requirements for Mission Principal Investigators." Approved by Stern on 15 January 2008. Revised policy document approved 19 February 2008.

ficient, how to obtain such experience, and what an aspiring PI might do to increase the odds of selection in the future. The 2010 AO stated: "The commitment, spaceflight experience, and past performance of the PI and of the implementing institutions will be assessed against the needs of the investigation," and implemented the modified requirement as follows:

> Requirement 42. Proposals shall identify the management positions that will be filled by key management team members. These positions shall include, as a minimum, the PI, PM, Project Systems Engineer (PSE), and, where appropriate, the PS and partner leads. For management positions for which key management team members are named (including the PI and PM per Requirement 39 and Requirement 40), proposals shall describe the qualifications and experience of those team members who occupy those positions [and]…shall demonstrate that the described qualifications and experience are commensurate with the technical and managerial needs of the proposed investigation.[84]

The flexibility inherent in this text was an improvement over the 2007 requirement, but it replaced absolutes with ambiguity. The reader might have been left wondering whether there was an unwritten rule that adequate spaceflight experience included positions in the key roles as mandated the year before. In the absence of direction, there was no clear confirmation that, for example, experience as a deputy project scientist or as a co-investigator on several successful missions would be considered sufficient. The reader was left with uncertainty about the agency's expectations and criteria for PI experience, evaluated by the science panel and technical-management-cost review.

This uncertainty led to broader questions of PI experience, such as acceptable career stage and expected previous participation on missions, as well as questions of adequate opportunity for newer scientists to gain such pre-PI experience.

Adding Capability: DSMCE Mission Studies

At the conclusion of the Discovery 2006 AO cycle (and his first month in office), Stern set in motion a new initiative to encourage the community to think proactively about missions that could be submitted to future New Frontiers and Discovery AOs. Stern approached Division Director Jim Green about initiating a series of mission studies, to be paid for out of the Associate Administrator's own budget reserve. While the list of allowable targets for New Frontiers specified in the 2003 National Research Council report had aged and become less relevant in the face of the council's next study, internal Planetary Science Division discussions over the summer identified an additional benefit to mission studies: the ability to study the potential impact of new technologies

---

84   NASA. (2010). Discovery Announcement of Opportunity.

such as Advanced Stirling Radioisotope Generators on Discovery mission concepts.[85] Stern agreed to fund this kind of study at the 50 percent level and told the division to make it happen before the October meeting of the American Astronomical Society Division of Planetary Sciences.

Less than three weeks later, the Discovery and Scout Mission Capabilities Expansion (DSMCE) NASA Research Announcement was prepared, announced at the Discovery@15 Workshop, and released on the NASA Solicitation and Proposal Integrated Review and Evaluation System (NSPIRES). While the Discovery Program Scientist and Program Executive may have remained unconvinced of the merit of expanding the Discovery Program's parameters to include ASRGs and other new technologies, the studies proceeded under the direction of Curt Niebur, who had recently run a series of mission studies at this level, including the "Billion Dollar Box" study of Saturn missions, the Comet Surface Sample Return study, and various studies of future outer planet flagship missions. Although scientists and engineers were given no notice that the opportunity was coming, proposals were due a mere 60 days after the announcement. NASA received 40 proposals on 20 November—a rate that Curt Niebur called a "tremendous response" to this first Discovery-size mission study call in 15 years. Nine were selected and given $200,000 to $300,000 each—the full amount that each had proposed for the six-month studies.[86]

The DSMCE studies were evaluated by scientists from the planetary science community and mission designers from NASA Ames Research Center, the Jet Propulsion Laboratory, Goddard Research Center, and Aerospace Corporation. The evaluations showed that although the missions were all near the top of the DSMCE cost cap ($450 million, Fiscal Year 2008 dollars), most of the concepts would be implementable within Discovery constraints. In accordance with the study ground rules, information about each mission concept was posted on the web in both abstract and fact sheet format. Consequently, there was now some evidence that opening up the Discovery mission line to Advanced Stirling Radioisotope Generators and other new technologies would expand the trade space available for future mission proposals.

FAMILY REUNION: DISCOVERY@15

The Discovery Program held a program-wide Lessons Learned Workshop titled "Discovery at 15: Looking Backward, Looking Forward" (also called "Discovery@15") on 19–20 September 2007. It was held in Huntsville, Alabama, home of the Discovery Program Office, by then a 17-person office staffed with engineers and managers working

---

85   Beebe, R., et al. (2008) *Opening New Frontiers in Space: Choices for the Next New Frontiers AO.* Washington, DC: National Academies Press. 82.

86   Niebur, S. (2011, 19 March). Personal interview with C. Niebur.

toward the program's success. The agenda was filled with speakers from every mission and every aspect of program management. PIs introduced each mission or mission of opportunity; project managers spoke about mission development. Evaluators, NASA officials, and curation specialists gave cross-program perspectives. Education and public outreach plans were thoroughly discussed by both program and project personnel. The sessions were generally open and good-natured, and they were beneficial for the nearly 200 scientists and mission managers in attendance. Paul Gilbert, Discovery Program Manager, called it "a family reunion."[87]

Meanwhile, back at NASA Headquarters, a formal process was instituted to create and use a standard AO across all the Earth and space science divisions, guided by three main principles:

Any simplified AO must still enable [these] outcomes: (1) Maintain the ability for NASA to evaluate the science merit (through science peer review) to guide selection. (2) Maintain the ability for NASA to evaluate the feasibility of proposed missions (through TMC review) to guide selection. (3) Ensure that mission teams are ready to successfully conduct Phase A mission concept studies if they are selected.[88]

The standard AO would have clear and consistent requirements and standard reporting formats, and it would eliminate much guesswork as to what the program scientist was asking in any particular paragraph. Over the ten-plus years of PI-led missions in the Discovery, Explorer, Mars Scout, and Earth mission lines, the AOs had tended toward clunky amalgamates of requirements rather than the easy-to-understand requests for data that they were intended to be. Each program incorporated its own lessons learned after each proposal cycle, adding requirements as made sense in order to provide the most accurate evaluation and assessment of potential cost risk. In turn, the data submitted to satisfy these requirements grew and were more fully evaluated, and the next round of reviewers requested an even more detailed level of data. The cycle continued to the point where the claim frequently was made—by proposers and evaluators alike—that a Step 1 proposal now contained the information that NASA used to ask for in Step 2.

Over the next year, NASA Headquarters and the Earth and Space Science Support Office at Langley Research Center convened a number of public meetings for community scientists, managers, and frequent technical-management-cost reviewers to attend and discuss the level and number of potential requirements in this standard AO. Meetings were held in conjunction with the annual Division of Planetary Science and American Astronomical Society conferences that year. Michael New, the program

---

87   Spires, S. G. (2007, 18 September). "Space conference also reunion." *The Huntsville Times.*
88   Stern, A. (2007, 17 December). "NASA Solicitation: Simplifying NASA Announcements of Opportunity—SMD." Solicitation Number: NNH07ZDA001O.

scientist, and Paul Hertz, the chief scientist in the Science Mission Directorate and later head of the Astrophysics Division, participated in the planning and the meetings themselves, along with Brad Perry of the Science Support Office; Jay Bergstralh, the chief scientist of the Solar System Exploration Division (and former Discovery program scientist); and others—all space science veterans of the Discovery Program and review process. Among them were Lisa May, who had worked Explorers from both proposal and review sides, and Cindy Bruno, who had served as Science Support Office Explorer lead at Langley. The study was co-chaired by Hertz and Perry.

The first stand-alone meeting was the Discovery, Mars Scout, and Small Explorer (SMEX) Lessons Learned Workshop, held at the Grand Hyatt Hotel at Dallas–Ft. Worth Airport on 28–29 February. At this workshop, Hertz, New, and Perry outlined current plans for AOs and their evaluation, as well as a "Quick List" of options. Speakers lined up to deliver 10-minute presentations with five minutes for discussion. Six proposers were on the agenda to discuss AO requirements, covering everything from cost and schedule data to letters of commitment and the time reserved for launch services.[89]

The next month, Hertz led an open session at the Lunar and Planetary Science Conference in Houston, TX, on 13 March to brief that community on the plan and gather community input. These sessions and others were followed by the AO Cost and Schedule Lessons Learned Workshop on 17 April, where Hertz opened with an overview of the AO simplification process and options, including the following three straightforward objectives for the process: "1) Simplify the proposal process to the extent possible to eliminate any unnecessary rules/requirements in the AO, and streamline the way that scientific and technical information is provided to NASA, 2) Reduce or eliminate the amount of work that the proposing team has to do over and above what they would have to do anyway to have a credible response, and 3) Revise the AO/evaluation/selection process, as required, to reduce overall burden to the proposing community, the reviewing community, and NASA while maintaining or improving the present quality." This meeting was to be a true exchange of perspectives, with proposers responding to ideas suggested by the evaluators, and evaluators responding to proposers on the content, format, and appropriate level of detail to require. NASA suggested four metrics for each suggested change: 1) Will it reduce work for the proposer? 2) Will it maintain NASA's ability to evaluate and select? 3) What is the downside risk? and 4) Is it a good idea?[90] After this introduction, technical-management-cost reviewers and proposers responded to suggestions from the February workshop and presented some of their own.

---

89   SMD AO Simplification Workshop. 28–29 February 2008. See *https://web.archive.org/web/20111015145949/http://soma.larc.nasa.gov/AO-LL-FinalAgenda.html* (accessed on 11 May 2023).

90   Hertz, P. (2008, 17 April). "AO Simplification Overview." Presentation at AO Simplification Cost and Schedule Workshop in Dallas, TX.

Mike Stancati of SAIC referenced a 2007 study of 24 recent Science Mission Directorate flight projects in several mission classes and management modes, noting that 21 of the projects had cost growth (22 percent on average, and up to 98 percent over and above plan including reserve), for a combined impact of $2 billion on the Science Mission Directorate's $9 billion mission portfolio.[91] Two-thirds of the projects showed a substantially increased rate of internal cost growth after Critical Design Review. In addition, 19 missions had significant schedule slips of five to 42 months each. Technical-management-cost's challenge, the study reported, was to analyze each proposal's basis of cost estimate, design heritage, project reserve, and project plans and to create an independent cost model for comparison of stated costs in each area to identify cost threats and mitigations, answering this core question: "Does the project have enough resources to do what they propose?" Stancati's final point went right to the heart of the initial issues on Kepler, when he noted that currently the proposer must "deal with any funding profile limits imposed by HQ budget reality," proposing that NASA both eliminate funding profile constraints in future AOs and relax the cost cap. Preempting NASA Headquarters' inevitable response that there are nearly always constraints on future funding, and that eliminating the stated profile would just postpone the release of future AOs, Stancati added: "Don't have the money? Then don't start!!"[92]

While this would be a simple solution, the budget reality that those outside NASA Headquarters may not have realized is that program reserve is the first to get "swept up" by budget analysts, division directors, and others looking for uncommitted money to rescue a development project from overruns in the current fiscal year. Larger sums attract more attention, and Discovery AOs had been postponed on several occasions over the second decade of the Discovery Program, including 2002, 2003, 2004, 2005, and 2009. If the program could always wait to have unlimited amounts of cash on hand, requiring no specific funding profile, release would typically be delayed time and again, and the money swept up betweentimes. After further discussion (and the passage of another four years), NASA Headquarters released the 2010 AO without a specific annual funding profile.

Technical-management-cost evaluator Bob Kellogg of the Aerospace Corporation provided additional perspective, reminding proposers that the overall goal of the evaluation is the ability to tell the selection official whether the proposed mission concept is mature enough to be executable within mission constraints. Cost model results, always an issue of concern with proposers, are primarily used as indicators of areas that need to be more closely examined. Discrepancies between models and proposed

---

91   Perry, B. (2010, 29 April). "SMD Cost/Schedule Performance Study." Presentation to the PIF-2. Downloaded from *http://www.nasa.gov/pdf/457672main_PI2_SMD_Cost_Schedule_perry.pdf.*

92   Stancati, M. (2008, 17 April). "TMC Resource Evaluation." Presentation at AO Simplification Cost and Schedule Workshop in Dallas, TX.

costs at lower levels can signal that a subsystem is immature, or an operations plan does not account for all the elements. The proposal is the team's chance to educate technical-management-cost on the proposed approach; the cost tables support the design's maturity. With this understanding, the basis of estimate gains importance as a further demonstration that the proposed cost is adequate to cover development, and the proposal is mature enough to know the cost with sufficient certainty. Grassroots estimates, analogies, and level-of-effort estimates indicate different assumptions about the project, and results of cost models or independent estimates can show how the project addresses any discrepancies. Agreements are good, but disagreements can be useful as well, if the basis for any difference is carefully discussed. As for heritage, Kellogg said, "All proposals claim extensive heritage in technical sections. If heritage is valid, then cost of heritage systems should provide a good sanity check on proposed costs. This is very convincing when it is done well." A thorough discussion of heritage should include "cost of heritage item, discuss any significant technical or program-matic differences, and provide a rationale for the proposed cost." Kellogg also echoed Stancati's request for removing AO funding profiles and a minimum reserve level and added three other recommendations from the cost team: keep funded schedule reserve separate from cost reserves, add detail for projected cost and mass savings for any descopes (and during what project stage those savings would be realized), and remove education and public outreach plans from Step 1 proposals, as they are "not a discriminator."[93] History, however, would argue with the last point; the education and public outreach plan was indeed a discriminator in 1994 for the selection of Stardust over its closest competitor.

Mark Jacobs from SAIC, also a technical-management-cost reviewer, made the argument that the AO simplification process should not reduce the concept definition requirements of a proposal. Indeed, NASA's emphasis on better cost performance would require *more* thorough definition of the baseline design. "Science objectives drive the entire implementation plan," he said, and "cost is entirely dependent on the techni-cal and management approach. Omitting technical/management definition details to simplify the process could seriously compromise independent cost assessments."[94]

Jacobs then made a striking claim, saying: "Recent attempts to improve cost per-formance rely on higher reserve level requirements, although past history shows cost reserves typically do not offset issues with early estimates," and he supported it with a slide showing that while CONTOUR and MESSENGER grew less than 20 percent

93   Kellogg, B. (2008, 17 April). "Proposed Budget: Evaluator's View." Presentation at AO Simplification Cost and Schedule Workshop in Dallas, TX.

94   Jacobs, M. (2008, 17 April). "No Cost AO." Presentation at NASA Cost and Schedule Lessons Learned Workshop. Downloaded from *http://soma.larc.nasa.gov/StandardAO/PDFDallasPresentations/%5B4%5DJacobs_goals.pdf*.

during development, Deep Impact grew 28 percent, Genesis grew almost 45 percent, and Dawn grew over 60 percent, excluding external impacts despite generally increasing levels of reserves.[95]

Note that the core problem in Discovery and related programs had historically been that although aerospace costs kept growing, management of these missions had become more complex and subject to more external pressures, and the stores of flight spares were becoming depleted. The planetary science community had not yet found a way to execute these small planetary missions or plan in this new environment.

Furthermore, although cost models were typically quoted with accuracy plus or minus 20 percent, no PI-led mission yet had come in at the –20 percent level. Actual costs were typically +20 percent or higher, even when external impacts were excluded. To minimize growth, Jacobs suggested understanding flight hardware at the component level, particularly when subsystems or instruments were modified versions or amalgams of previously flown hardware, and, in addition, remaining aware of significant management and organizational cost drivers, including experience of all partners, the availability of test facilities, parts quality requirements, conflicts with other projects under development by the same organization, and risk mitigation plans.[96]

Violet Barghe-Sharghi, a technical-management-cost schedule evaluator from Aerospace, showed the group several examples of sample schedules from previous Step 1 proposals and discussed their use, including the utility of "random (self-chosen) elements" of the schedule discussion. A list of requirements and "desirements" followed, and while she urged NASA Headquarters to more clearly specify the schedule requirements and a certain level of granularity, she also urged proposers to reflect in their proposal any cross-strapping of their implementation approach to their reported schedules, including 1) basis of estimates for the schedule elements; 2) the addition of schedule impacts to the areas of risk management, descope, and long-lead items; and 3) a rationale for the amount and placement of funded schedule reserves. Acknowledging that some of these requests reflected Step 2 criteria, she requested that the Step 1 schedule requirements be at the summary level of the Step 2 schedule details—a significant change.[97]

After the workshops were complete, the AO Simplification Team issued an interim white paper of draft decisions, noting that they had

> solicited broadly for suggestions and ideas from the proposing and reviewing communities. This solicitation includes (i) setting up a dedicated website and email address, (ii) issuing NSPIRES and FBO announcements, (iii) conducting town meetings at major science conferences, (iv) holding two Lessons Learned Workshops for the proposing community (scheduled

---

95   Ibid.

96   Ibid.

97   Barghe-Sharghi, V. (2008, 17 April). "Proposed Schedule: Evaluator's View." Presentation at AO Simplification Cost and Schedule Workshop in Dallas, TX.

for after SMEX proposal submission), (v) holding a virtual Lessons Learned Workshop for the reviewing community (scheduled for after completion of SMEX proposal evaluation), (vi) requesting coordinated input from GSFC and JPL, and (vii) participating in an AO requirements review with a group of proposers. The Team has also worked with stakeholders to simplify and streamline various interfaces including proposal submission, international participation, launch services, space communications, procurement, and legal. The AO Simplification Team has received more than 500 suggestions for changes.[98]

Widespread community involvement resulted in significant revisions, including numbered requirements to improve traceability and increase efficiency for both proposers and reviewers. Since proposers no longer had to guess which AO statements were requirements (previous AOs had typically—but not always—used the word "shall" to denote requirements), teams could focus on answering the numbered requirements. Their resulting proposals would be more clearly responsive to the AO requirements, enabling a more straightforward technical-management-cost review. Fewer hours of work on both sides would translate to less investment required to create—and to review—a Discovery proposal.

In addition to a new standard AO, NASA released templates for the Step 1 Proposal Evaluation Plan and Guidelines and Criteria for the Phase A Study, two documents that theretofore had been edited (and released, in the case of the latter) with each AO. Making these documents publicly available even between AO releases increased transparency and ease of preparation for both the proposing and reviewing communities, as would be seen in the 2010 AO.

PREDICTING RISK:
SSO EVALUATES THE EVALUATIONS

Several years earlier, the Space Science Office had performed a study of technical-management-cost risk ratings over the history of the PI-led Discovery, New Frontiers, UNEX, SMEX, and MIDEX competitions from 1996 to 2005. The results of that study were reported to NASA Headquarters and published in written form without mission-specific detail.[99] This lack of detail, likely intended to protect proposers and mission teams, unfortunately impeded the usefulness of the report. Fortunately, the data were revisited later and the data published more fully, in both white paper and briefing (PowerPoint) form, with some very interesting tables.

---

98   NASA. (2008, 31 May). "Announcement of Opportunity (AO) Simplification White Paper: Draft Decisions."

99   Perry, R., et al. (2006, 21 February). "Lessons learned from Technical, Management, and Cost Review of Proposals: A summary of 10 years' experience in reviewing competitively selected proposals for new science missions." White paper.

In the aggregate, the proposals from 2006 to 2009 were more likely to have received major weaknesses and higher risk ratings from technical-management-cost reviews (TMC) than the proposals initially studied. This finding was attributed to the increased expertise and depth of investigation in TMC assessments of the instrument development and operation plans, even though additional major weaknesses were detected in all areas (cost, systems engineering, schedule) except management. The 2006–2009 proposals were also less likely to be rated Low Risk; only about 30 percent received that rating at Step 1.[100]

Common causes of major weaknesses in TMC reviews across all Science Mission Directorate programs from 1996 to 2009 included overstatement of heritage and maturity; inadequate definition, traceability, and flow-down of requirements; technical margins (particularly in mass and power); cost reserve; complexity of instruments or operations; attitude control and pointing; and—particularly in the case of Discovery projects—implementing new technology.

Common causes of major weaknesses based on data from 783 Step 1 proposals:[101]

Technical design margins for flight system and payload:

- 119 [22 percent of proposals] had one or more major weaknesses on mass margins;
    - Insufficient description to allow independent verification of the claimed mass margin;
    - Heritage masses didn't account for potential design modifications;
    - No clearly stated mass margin (none given, conflicting statements, confusion between contingency and margin), characterized as both failure to follow AO directions and deliberate proposal puffery;
    - Low mass margin; or
    - Missing and undersized elements (e.g., launch vehicle payload adapter) create immediate lien on claimed margin.

---

100   Perry, R. (2010, 29 April). "Step 1 & 2 Lessons Learned Study: Presentation to the PIF-2." Presentation to the second Principal Investigator (PI) Team Masters Forum. Downloaded from *http://www.nasa.gov/pdf/457658main_PI2_Lessons_Learned_perry.pdf.*

101   Perry, R., et al. (2006, 21 February). "Lessons learned from Technical, Management, and Cost Review of Proposals: A summary of 10 years' experience in reviewing competitively selected proposals for new science missions." White paper. See also Perry, R. (2010, 29 April). "Step 1 & 2 Lessons Learned Study: Presentation to the PIF-2." Presentation to the second Principal Investigator (PI) Team Masters Forum. Downloaded from *http://www.nasa.gov/pdf/457658main_PI2_Lessons_Learned_perry.pdf.*

- 68 [13 percent of proposals] had a major weakness on power/energy margins, for similar reasons; also, power margin was not always calculated against the most critical or demanding operating mode;
- 53 had major weaknesses on data handling and communications links; and
- Other common major weaknesses [less than 5 percent of proposals] were found regarding propellant, thermal design margins, volume margin, radiation protection factor, and other factors.

Cost: 261 proposals overall [33 percent] had a cost-related major weakness, including in cost-reserve. Of the 124 proposals [16 percent] with a cost-reserve-related major weakness, most fell into the following categories:

- Reserve below the stated AO requirement for overall level or by project phase;
- Existing liens against reserve;
- Reserve too low to cover cost threats, as identified by proposer or TMC analysis; or
- Reserves phased too late in the funding profile to be available when the schedule of activity suggested the need.

Instruments: ~255 proposals [32 percent] had an instrument-related major weakness:

- Complex, new design;
- Inadequate or inconsistent description and detail;
- Weak heritage claims;
- Integration and accommodations, such as a mismatch between stated instrument requirements and known bus capacity;
- Integration and test program; end-to-end verification testing;
- Pointing performance; or
- Detector contamination.

Systems Engineering: ~235 proposals with a related major weakness [30 percent]

- Science requirements and flow-down to instruments, payload accommodations, and flight systems (more common in earlier AOs);
- Project-wide systems engineering responsibility;
- Credible plans for success; or
- Underestimates of the cost of this function.

Management: 203 major weaknesses [26 percent]

- Low time commitments for essential members of the core management team;
- Confusing organization roles and responsibilities;
- Unclear lines of authority; or
- Missing commitment letters and/or endorsements from institutions and international partners.

Schedule detail and (funded) margins: 130+ with major weaknesses [17 percent]

- Inadequate detail presented for TMC evaluation;
- No reserve or inadequate reserve;
- Too ambitious or success-oriented for what needs to be done, especially during ATLO; or
- Unrealistic timing of key milestones.

Complex Operations: 64 proposals [8 percent] with complex operational requirements—for payload, observing sequence, landers, etc.

Interestingly, the number of proposals having a major weakness of any kind in Step 1 exceeded the number of missions rated Low Risk, which seems contradictory, as an evaluation ground rule had been that only major weaknesses affect the risk. No explanation for this was given. The paper noted recent improvements in the area of systems requirements and flow-down, perhaps in response to more detailed requirements in the AO and the additional requirement of a traceability matrix.

Proposers selected to perform a Concept Study Report were encouraged to specifically address the Step 1 weaknesses identified *for their proposal*; the study explicitly noted that most of the proposing teams later to be selected for implementation directly addressed the identified weaknesses and attempted to alleviate the reviewers' concerns in their Step 2 Concept Study Report. Seventy-nine full mission Concept Study Reports were studied; common causes of major weaknesses are tabulated below.[102]

---

102   Ibid.

Technical weaknesses:

- Requirements definition, traceability, and flow-down [17 percent];
- Verification [15 percent], often correlated with major weaknesses in requirements, system complexity, or design maturity;
- Heritage [15 percent], including overstatement of the benefits or inaccurate accounting for modifications;
- Mass Margin [9 percent];
- Thermal [7 percent], many of these at the instrument level;
- Optics/Focal Plane [7 percent], particularly overstatement of performance of instrument optics;
- Low Maturity/technology readiness levels [6 percent], particularly of instruments; and
- Attitude determination and control [6 percent].

Management major weaknesses:

- Key individuals [36 percent], including lack of relevant experience, limited project manager history of flight project accountability, and low time commitments;
- Schedule [27 percent]: incomplete schedule, inadequate or inappropriately placed schedule reserve, inadequate definition (or complete lack) of critical path;
- Management plans [19 percent], particularly risk management;
- Systems engineering [16 percent], often reflecting inconsistency among project elements; and
- Descope definition [3 percent], often associated with overstatement of heritage or TRL.

Cost major weaknesses:

- Inadequate cost reserve [36 percent], often the result of increased definition in the design and implementation in Phase A; also associated with low maturity and/or heritage major weaknesses;
- Cost [32 percent] significantly different from independent cost estimates, often due to a dispute in the proposer's underlying assumptions in areas such as technical performance, TRLs, or heritage;
- Basis of estimate [20 percent] inadequate; and
- Credibility [12 percent] or relevance of supporting cost data.

A relatively small percentage of proposals received improved risk ratings in Step 2. An equal number stayed the same or got worse. This may be explained in part by more detailed review and less "benefit of the doubt" given to proposers at Step 2.

SALMON AO

The first Stand Alone Missions of Opportunity (SALMON) AO was released in 2008, with proposals due in December. After five months of review, two of the eight proposed investigations were funded as Discovery Program Missions of Opportunity to be flown on future ESA missions.

The Lander Radioscience (LaRa) on ExoMars, a radio science investigation, would have used the onboard X-band transponder provided by Belgium and NASA's Deep Space Network to measure variances in the orientation and rotation of Mars in space. During normal operations, a signal would have been sent from Earth to the ExoMars lander, bounced back by LaRa, and returned to Earth. The measured frequency of the signal would have been shifted relative to the initial signal due to the Doppler effect as Mars moves relative to Earth.

These measurements would have been used to study the interior of Mars and, on the surface, the sublimation/condensation process of carbon dioxide as it moved between the atmosphere and the ice caps with the seasons. The PI was William Folkner of JPL; the investigation would have included no instrument and would have cost approximately $6.6 million.

The second chosen was the STart from a ROtating FIeld mass spectrOmeter (STROFIO), a mass spectrometer designed to launch aboard ESA's BepiColombo mission in 2013 and study the atoms and molecules that make up Mercury's atmosphere—part of the Search for Exospheric Refilling and Emitted Natural Abundances (SERENA) experiment (which included three other sensors).[103]

2010 AO

As the decade came to a close, NASA prepared a new AO for release in January, then July 2010. NASA-wide changes since the 2006 AO included the implementation of NPR 7120.5D, issued on 9 March 2007. This NPR "focused on institutionalizing the processes by which NASA formulates and implements space flight programs and

---

103 NASA. (2009, 18 May). "NASA Selects Future Projects To Study Mars And Mercury." NASA News Release.

projects, provided a standardized life cycle review process that is built around the key decision points, formalized the technical authority, dissenting opinion resolution, and waiver processes, and streamlined the document."[104]

Michael Griffin ended his nearly four-year term as NASA Administrator, stepping down on 20 January 2009, at the start of President Obama's administration. Associate Administrator Alan Stern had served from April 2007 to April 2008; Associate Administrator Weiler was in charge again, and a number of policies reverted to those in effect during his previous term as Associate Administrator.

The Discovery Program had not substantially changed since the 2006 AO, but "a large number" of changes were made to the draft AO, "including both policy changes and changes to proposal submission requirements."[105] The draft AO (NNH10ZDA003J), based on the new NASA Science Mission Directorate Standard AO, was released 7 December 2009, with a $425 million (FY 2010) cost cap not including launch vehicle, contributions, or specific NASA-developed technologies discussed in the AO.

Proposers should be aware of the following major changes in this AO from the previous Discovery Program AO in 2006 (NNH06ZDA001O).

- The cost of standard launch services is <u>not</u> included within the cap on the PI-Managed Mission Cost (Section 4.3.1), but mission-unique launch services and the differential cost of more capable LVs [Launch Vehicles] than the standard LV will be included in the PI-Managed Cost (Section 5.9.2).
- The Discovery Program requirement that returned space-exposed hardware be curated and that the costs for such curation be included in the PI-Managed Mission Cost has been added (Section 5.1.5.4)[.]
- Proposals may designate a Project Manager Alternate. At selection and subject to the approval of NASA, the Alternate may be named as the Project Manager (Section 5.3.2).
- The minimum reserve level of 25% is now assessed against the Phase A-E cost (Section 5.6.3) rather than the Phase A-D cost.
- Proposal of investigations enabled by the use of Advanced Stirling Radioisotope Generators (ASRGs) is allowed (Section 5.9.3). ASRGs are provided as Government Furnished Equipment (GFE).
- New propulsion technology has been developed by NASA and is available for infusion into Discovery missions (Section 5.9.3).

---

104   NASA. (2012, 14 August). "NASA Space Flight Program and Project Management Requirements." NPR 7120.5E. *https://nodis3.gsfc.nasa.gov/npg_img/N_PR_7120_005E_/N_PR_7120_005E_.pdf.*

105   NASA. (2009). DRAFT Announcement of Opportunity: Discovery 2010. *https://nspires.nasaprs.com/external/viewrepositorydocument/cmdocumentid=214565/solicitationId=%7BCEE916F8-B142-2611-6CE0-399BCEDA3B3E%7D/viewSolicitationDocument=1/Discovery%2010%20DRAFT%20RELEASE.pdf.*

- Investigations focused on Mars are allowed (Section 2.2).
- Missions of Opportunity investigations are no longer solicited through the Discovery AO. Missions of Opportunity investigations may be solicited through the Stand Alone Mission of Opportunity Notice (SALMON) AO at a future date.
- Letters of Commitment are not required from Co-investigators. However, all proposal team members must commit to the proposal through NSPIRES (Section 5.8.1.3).[106]

Changes in the final AO, as compared to the draft AO, included an extension of the no-later-than launch date from 31 December 2016 to 31 December 2017, as well as:

- The role of NASA Marshall Space Flight Center in the AO process is explicitly described (Section 4.1.2) as is the role of NASA Centers in public affairs for selected missions (Section 4.1.3).
- The costs associated with National Environmental Protection Act (NEPA) compliance, Nuclear Launch Safety Approval (NLSA) compliance, and nuclear launch services for missions proposing to use ASRGs are reduced to a firm, fixed cost of $20M (FY10) (Section 5.2.4.4).
- The requirement for justifying the use of a frequency other than Ka-band for science data return is clarified (Section 5.2.5).
- The latest allowable Launch Readiness Date (LRD) is December 31, 2017 (Section 5.9.1).
- Launch vehicles in the "medium" and "high" performance classes with 4m fairings have been added as options (Section 5.9.2).
- Proposed missions are required to be compatible with three families of launch vehicles: Atlas V, Delta IV, and Falcon 9 (Section 5.9.2).
- The minimum requirements for taking advantage of technology-infusion cost cap incentives are detailed in a new document in the Program Library entitled *In-Space Propulsion Technologies Minimum Demonstration Requirements (Section 5.9.3)*.
- Missions to the Martian surface are not required to carry the *Electra-lite* UHF radio package (Section 5.9.4).[107]

---

106   Ibid.
107   NASA. (2010). Announcement of Opportunity: Discovery 2010.

Michael New said: "We are allowing the use of RTGs, radioisotope power systems, in this Discovery area, which is a first for Discovery. It's almost a first for the agency in the sense that this will be the first widely competed PI-led mission to use nuclear power systems."[108]

There were four primary changes to the AO. The insertion of Advanced Stirling Radioisotope Generators was so new that a clarification amendment was issued on 13 July asking ten additional questions on the cover page to be answered "yes," "no," or "possibly." Then, two additional questions were also added to ease the assignment of proposals to TMC experts in radioactive power sources. A third set of amendments was released just three weeks before the due date, requesting additional technical trajectory information, including solar electric propulsion–specific assumptions, models, and operations concept to be included. The due date was delayed a week to accommodate this late request. Proposals closed on 10 September 2010. NASA received 28 proposals.[109]

The announcement of the selected missions was delayed due to a series of Continuing Resolutions by Congress; the selection would not be made until the enactment of a Fiscal Year 2011 budget for NASA. While this made good sense as a national policy, it would make it difficult for proposal teams to stay together and available.

Ultimately, by including options for advanced technologies, the Discovery Program had been expanded to include more complex missions and missions to planets beyond the asteroid belt.

STUDYING COST GROWTH: REPORTS

In July 2008, three NASA study groups briefed the Planetary Science Subcommittee on their findings in parallel cost studies conducted by the Discovery and New Frontiers Program Office, the Space Science Office, and NASA Headquarters. The Discovery and New Frontiers Program Office, led by Paul Gilbert, studied five recent missions from its program in order to better understand the cost growth of missions since Genesis, using the official cost numbers from the proposal, Concept Study Report, and Preliminary Design Review, with additional information from Cost Analysis Data Requirement results, milestone review products at the Critical Design Review, the System Implementation Review, the Operations Readiness Review, the Mission Readiness Review, project status reports, and program budget exercises. Results were briefed to the community at the 2006 Discovery Lessons Learned Workshop, a July 2008 Planetary Science Subcommittee meeting, and full results were written up in 2010.

---

108   Niebur, S. (2009, 10 December). Personal interview with M. New. Located in "Discovery Program" file, NASA Historical Reference Collection, History Division, NASA Headquarters, Washington, DC.

109   Green, J. (2010, 8 March). Presentation at the 2011 Lunar and Planetary Science Conference.

This study was much more thorough in its methodology; the Discovery and New Frontiers Program officials performing the study met in person with representatives from the program management and project officials. Program management and analysis officials included NASA Headquarters Program Executives, Discovery and New Frontiers Program Office mission managers, budget analysts, and people involved in TMC. Project representatives included PIs, project managers, budget analysts, and representatives of the home institution. (The inclusion and role of the latter were not explained.)

The cost growth figures for the missions were released. The last six missions included were Deep Impact, MESSENGER, Kepler, Dawn, New Horizons, and GRAIL. As in the CADRe study in the previous section, the data did not exclude the effects of programmatic changes implemented as NASA became increasingly less tolerant of risk. The study noted that the numbers did include the changes implemented to address the NASA Integrated Action Team recommendations, the change to accommodate a 25 percent reserve level, and the change to incorporate full cost accounting within NASA. As this book has discussed, there were other decisions that impacted the missions, such as lack of cash flow forcing the postponement of start dates of studies or mission formulation (i.e., Dawn and Kepler). This study did not address the effects of these changes and excluded any conclusions that could be drawn from programmatic or division-level changes.

Early briefings discussed mission-specific and overall issues identified by the study:

…technology challenges; longevity engineering issues; higher than anticipated ($1M/year) implementation costs of the NASA Integrated Action Team recommendations; higher than expected development costs for science instruments (exceeding preliminary design estimate by $18 million during Phase C/D in one instance (with the problem attributed to a contractor)); and lack of a revalidated vendor quote since the Concept Study Report (CSR) estimate. Another project had start-stop issues due to the events of September 11, 2001. In other instances, a project had three different PMs during Phase C/D; a contractor never had prime responsibility; a contractor had no primary system-level planetary experience; and in one project, the PI and PM expended reserves at a high rate during Phase C/D.[110]

At the 2008 briefing, the D&NFPO made a surprising conclusion: "one cannot perform credible estimates in the early stage of a project."[111]

In addition, it reported that this was "a NASA-wide problem for missions, [attributed to] maturity of Phase A concepts, optimistic key assumptions (heritage, personnel sharing and multi-tasking), and perhaps competitive pressures." Also, "programs and

---

110   Planetary Science Subcommittee. (2008, 2–3 July). Report from the NAC PSS meeting at Goddard Space Flight Center.

111   Ibid.

projects were not tracking or mitigating risks identified in the Phase A competitive review process, such as upper stage certification, or hidden costs for nuclear compliance processing."[112]

By 2010, the Discovery and New Frontiers Program Office was able to draw nine conclusions from this study that they could use to better manage missions at the program or project level. These conclusions could be summarized as optimistic heritage and technology assumptions, insufficient project insight into contractor performance, inadequate planning for mission operations, inadequate mission replans, inadequate Integrated Master Schedules, inadequate time and effort planned to execute fault protection and autonomy, ineffective management structure and unclear roles and responsibilities, project team inexperience, and inadequate consideration of senior-level expert review team findings.[113]

Because these findings are so significant, the conclusions are explained further in the following figure, the executive summary of this report:

Executive Summary

In order to improve cost and schedule performance, the Discovery and New Frontiers (D&NF) Program Office studied life cycle cost (LCC) and schedule growth for five missions. The goal was to identify the underlying causes for the cost overruns and schedule delays, and to develop practical mitigations to assist D&NF projects in identifying potential risks and controlling the associated impacts to proposed mission costs and schedules. The study found nine systemic issues involving project management and systems engineering that were the primary contributors to LCC and schedule growth:

1. *Optimistic hardware/software inheritance and technology readiness assumptions caused cost and schedule growth in the detailed design and development phases (Phases C/D) for all five missions studied.*

2. *Insufficient project management and technical insight into contractor performance resulted in poor communications, schedule delays, and technical problems that were manifested as cost overruns in three missions.*

3. *Inadequate planning for operations (Phase E) resulted in significant LCC impacts in four missions.*

4. *Mission replans were inadequate, and significant changes to mission scope, schedule, or funding profiles were not sufficiently understood or analyzed, resulting in unexpected cost increases and schedule delays in three missions.*

---

112   Ibid.

113   Barley, B., et al. (2010, February). "Improving the life cycle cost management of planetary missions: Results from the Life Cycle Cost Growth Study performed by the Discovery and New Frontiers Program Office at NASA Marshall Space Flight Center." Presentation.

5. *Projects demonstrated problems developing and maintaining Integrated Master Schedules (IMSs); problems stemming from inadequate IMSs were seen in four missions.*

6. *The complexity drivers for fault protection and autonomy (FPA) capabilities are not well understood and projects underestimated the time and effort required to complete FPA development in four missions.*

7. *Ineffective management structure and unclear roles and responsibilities resulted in cost and schedule impacts to three of the five missions studied. Issues resulting from the management structure compounded the effects of other project issues, such as overly optimistic heritage or technology assumptions, inadequate project schedules, and inadequate planning or replans. The management structure issues were exacerbated by project team member inexperience.*

8. *Team players with limited experience in planetary mission development were a significant contributor to project management issues resulting in cost over-runs. Project team inexperience was a direct factor in only two of the missions studied, however it also contributed to other problems cited within this study.*

9. *Many of the technical and project management drivers for LCC escapes were identified as issues (weaknesses, risks, concerns, or findings) during one or more of the mandated NASA project reviews, but there was insufficient follow-through to address (mitigate or refute) the panel's conclusions and recommendations.*

The study also made three observations:

1. *The collection, analysis, and synthesis of the study data was much more intensive than anticipated, primarily due to the lack of official, formal program and project historical documentation.*

2. *The D&NF programs, as well as NASA as a whole, need to address the credibility of project cost estimates, including independent cost evaluations.*

3. *The majority of the underlying causes are embedded in the project approach during the concept study (Phase A) and preliminary design (Phase B) phases, but the actual cost or schedule impacts typically are not experienced until late in the development or operations phases (Phases D and E).*[114]

The most surprising result was that none of these findings were new. All the findings had been reported over the years as project management and systems engineering issues; good project management and systems engineering practices had been iden-

---

114   Life Cycle Cost Growth Study for the Discovery and New Frontiers Program Office—Final Report 2010.

tified addressing each of the findings. However, the study concluded that problems remained, and additional attention was required to control or eliminate these problems and contain the resulting impacts to project costs and schedules.[115]

Although the Planetary Science Subcommittee in July 2008 called for these results to be incorporated into a PI Handbook, no such product exists to date.

As part of this study, the program office also codified their definition of mission success in three parts: "delivering mission science to the PI (meeting the Level 1 Requirements), ensuring the implementing organization's success in delivering the spacecraft on cost and schedule (meeting the launch date and cost cap), and meeting the program launch frequency requirement for science missions."[116]

Inherent Optimism and Cost and Schedule Growth

A 2008 study of ten NASA Science Mission Directorate missions found that the average cost growth was 76 percent over programmatic reserves and that the average schedule growth over and above reserves was 26 percent when the final cost was compared to the cost established at the beginning of Phase B. The study did not identify a common root cause of this growth beyond "the inherent optimism in initial concept designs due to competitive pressures," stating that this optimism could cause underestimation of mass, power, data rate, complexity, and other technical specifications—which then would lead to underestimation of cost. This underestimation, coupled with success-oriented schedules implemented to meet a launch window, control overall costs, and/or to obtain science quickly, could lead to cost and schedule growth.[117]

The study was later expanded to 20 missions to quantify the effect of inherent optimism in early conceptual designs on cost and schedule growth of NASA Science Mission Directorate missions. Cost at selection—the Cost Analysis Data Requirement (CADRe) numbers submitted with the CSR—was compared with cost at Preliminary Design Review, Critical Design Review, and launch to quantify mission growth over time and compare it to industry guidelines. Overall results showed the following life-cycle growth: 37 percent in mass, 41 percent in power, 56 percent in cost, 38 percent in schedule. Discovery missions included in the study were Genesis, Deep Impact,

---

115 Barley, B., et al. (2010, February). "Improving the life cycle cost management of planetary missions: Results from the Life Cycle Cost Growth Study performed by the Discovery and New Frontiers Program Office at NASA Marshall Space Flight Center." Presentation. See also Clardy, D. (2010, 9–10 February). "Improving Life-Cycle Cost Management of Spacecraft Missions." Presentation at the 2010 NASA Program Management Challenge in Houston, TX.

116 Barley, B., et al. (2010, February). "Improving the life cycle cost management of planetary missions: Results from the Life Cycle Cost Growth Study performed by the Discovery and New Frontiers Program Office at NASA Marshall Space Flight Center." Presentation.

117 Freaner, C., et al. (2008, 15–16 May). "An assessment of the inherent optimism in early conceptual designs and its effect on cost and schedule growth." Presentation at the 2008 SSCAG/SCAF/EACE Joint International Conference in Noordwijk, The Netherlands.

MESSENGER, Dawn, and Kepler. Of the seven planetary missions (Mars Reconnaissance Orbiter, Lunar Reconnaissance Orbiter, and New Horizons were also studied; Kepler was classified as an Astrophysics mission), six experienced 28 percent or more growth in cost. Two had 85 percent or more growth in power, two had about 27 percent growth in power, and two had less than 10 percent growth in power (one showed no data). As for cost growth, three planetary missions showed just less than 40 percent cost growth, one had about 25 percent cost growth, two had a little more than 15 percent cost growth, and one was less than 10 percent. This growth, while unfortunate, was dwarfed by the growth in Earth-orbiting missions (five Astrophysics, five Earth Science, and three Heliophysics, considered as a group) in development during the same decade. Four Earth-orbiting missions doubled their Phase B cost, and five more missions had more than 60 percent cost growth. Only two of the 13 experienced 25 percent or less growth in cost.[118]

The weakness of many CADRe cost studies of the time was the absence of *reasons* for cost growth. Sometimes numbers can be misleading—and nowhere was this more the case than in the early days of Dawn and Kepler, when institutional and management changes caused the costs committed at the start of Phase B to be almost meaningless in the face of changes in institutional burden and the layering of an additional management institution at no fault of the project. These factors, and factors such as additional costs incurred to comply with the NASA Integrated Action Team recommendations for the earlier missions such as Genesis, Deep Impact, and MESSENGER, were essential to understand and track before making sweeping statements. This study notwithstanding, it was not at all clear that missions like Dawn were underscoped; instead, there were not sufficient reserves or commitment to proposed costs on the part of the managing institutions involved. Numbers alone do not tell the whole story.

Comparisons were also made between the individual missions and types of missions in schedule growth. Taken as a whole, the set of 20 missions showed 38 percent schedule growth. Seven Earth-orbiting missions had growth at about the 50 percent level or greater. Another four Earth-orbiting and two planetary missions had greater than 30 percent schedule growth. Only two planetary missions had 10 percent or less schedule growth, with the remaining three between 15 and 30 percent. But the study may not account for program-directed changes, such as the effects of the late start for both Dawn and Kepler after the 2000 selection, when the money to start Phase B was not available as predicted. Indeed, while schedule growth was a real problem for Astrophysics, Earth Science, and Heliophysics missions, it tended to be less of an issue for planetary and Discovery missions with fixed launch windows. Schedule growth of planetary missions was typically constrained by launch windows, but when

118   Freaner, C., et al. (2010, 9–10 February). "Conceptual design optimism, cost and schedule growth effects." Presentation at the 2010 NASA Program Management Challenge in Houston, TX.

a launch window was missed, such as was foreseen during the development of Deep Impact, cost growth was commensurate with a year of development costs, unless other arrangements such as early delivery to the Cape were made explicitly with approval of the delayed launch date. The study did show unexpected growth for the missions after the Preliminary Design Review, but the numbers for post-PDR growth were not made publicly available.

Meanwhile, studies by the Space Science Office were based on detailed analyses of data at key milestones ("Project Milestone Performance History") for 24 missions, both directed and PI-led, across the Science Mission Directorate.[119] Recommendations conveyed to the Planetary Science Subcommittee included the following:

...more emphasis on detailed technical design concepts, more rigor in process of generating early cost estimates, more conservatism in base estimates, and advocating options for extending Phases A and B whenever possible. To compensate for internal and external impacts, projects must develop a credible baseline plan, keep the funding profile constraints out of the AO, avoid redirection from SMD, become educated on EVM [Earned Value Management] and verify that projects are applying it. In order to curtail instrument cost growth, projects must address the weaknesses of current NASA tools for early estimation of science instrument costs and require a variety of baseline instrument estimates (using analogies, parametric models and grass roots estimates). For general cost performance improvement, it was recommended that NASA hold budget reserves at the program level. The key internal factors for cost growth were identified as over-optimism in early formulation and instrument development complexity, and the external factors were identified as launch and budget instability. Practices that improved performance of missions were the presence of ample reserves, best project managers, and best management practices.[120]

The Role of Leadership in Small Missions

NASA's Discovery mission line demonstrated in its first two decades that with careful planning, flexible management techniques, and a commitment to cost control, small space science missions could be built and launched at a fraction of the price of strategic missions. Many credit management techniques such as co-location, early contracting for long-lead items, and a resistance to scope creep, but it is also important to examine what may have been the most significant variable in small mission implementation: the roles and the relationship of the Principal Investigator, who was responsible to NASA for the success of the mission, and the project manager, who was responsible for delivering the mission to NASA.

---

119   Perry, R. (2010, 29 April). "SMD Cost/Schedule Performance Study: Presentation to the PIF-2." Downloaded from *http://www.nasa.gov/pdf/457672main_PI2_SMD_Cost_Schedule_perry.pdf.*

120   Bruno, C. (2008, 2–3 July). "SSO Studies of Mission Cost Drivers." Documented in the NAC PSS Meeting Report.

This book concludes here, with a report on a series of 55 oral histories with PIs, project managers, co-investigators, system engineers, and senior management from nearly every competitively selected Discovery mission launched in the program's first two decades. These figures shared the definition and evolution of their roles and offered revealing insights.[121] There are as many ways to define the Principal Investigator and project manager relationship as there are missions, and the subtleties in the relationship often provide new management tools not practical in larger missions.

---

121   Originally published as Niebur, S. M. (2010) "Principal investigators and project managers: Insights from Discovery." *Space Policy.* 1–11.

CHAPTER 9

Insights from Discovery

THE ROLE OF THE PRINCIPAL INVESTIGATOR

Traditionally, the PI has been a senior scientist responsible for the delivery of the science from a mission or instrument. The PI led the science team and definition and development of the science instruments but left the spacecraft design and development to engineers at NASA centers, federally funded research and development centers, and industry.

New mission lines started or rescoped in the early 1990s, however, introduced a new paradigm, charging the PI with responsibility for the delivery of the entire mission, from design to decommissioning, including all aspects of project management and scientific success.[1] The intent was sincere, and the ideas were radical. Scientists were charged with composing teams that would design, build, and operate whole missions and analyze the data returned within a predefined overall budget. Management restrictions were lifted, and the teams were given flexibility to design their management structure as best served the mission, with minimal oversight from NASA Headquarters.

---

1   NASA Office of Space Science. (1992, November). *Discovery Program Handbook*.

The procurement process became one of buying scientific investigations, rather than instruments, and this change increased the focus on obtaining usable scientific results. The missions were cost-capped in order to increase the frequency of flight in the program. The cost constraints increased the possibility that unrestrained increases in engineering growth on a mission could require compensatory decreases in the capability for science return. To combat this, the role of the principal scientist was elevated above the project manager. The Office of Space Science at NASA had taken a chance on a new way of implementing missions, with Wes Huntress, then–Associate Administrator, saying, "We've turned the old way of doing business upside down."[2]

Definition

From the first announcement of these new PI-led programs, the PI was responsible for managing the planning, development, and execution of the mission, from selecting the team members to defining roles and responsibilities.[3] The PI served as a new kind of manager, responsible for meeting and reporting on cost and schedule objectives, even though he or she did not have matrix or line institutional authority over a single engineer. Due to the inherent difficulties of a scientist managing technical work at a federally funded research and development center or NASA center as much as three thousand miles away, early reviewers of the program strongly recommended that the management authority be delegated to a project manager, but this decision, like all other project design decisions, was left up to the PI by NASA Headquarters.[4]

Evolution

The first competitive selections for new missions in the Discovery Program allowed PIs the freedom to construct their management teams as they saw fit. This encouraged the use of innovative techniques customized for the smaller teams that must work together creatively to design and build a small mission for an even smaller cost cap. Subsequent selections included greater constraints, as lessons were learned and best practices identified, but the responsibility was still left in the hands of the PI.

The first PI-led mission, Lunar Prospector, was led by a scientist who had been looking for a way to fly his mission to the Moon for years, seeking and obtaining funding from the Department of Defense and the short-lived Space Exploration Initiative.

---

2   NASA Office of Space Science. (1995, July). "NASA's Discovery Program: Solar System Exploration for the Next Millennium."

3   NASA Office of Space Science. (1992, November). *Discovery Program Handbook*.

4   NASA. (1991, September). "Discovery Cost and Management Team Report." As cited in the NASA Small Planetary Mission Plan, Report to Congress, April 1992; NASA Office of Space Science. (1994, 4 August). "AO: Discovery Missions." NASA AO 94-OSS-03.

This PI was involved in all phases and stages of design and development of the mission, leading his team with assurance through the many stages required for successful mission implementation.[5]

Later missions were characterized not by a single driving personality, but by the teamwork found to be essential between the PI and the project manager. Each mission teaming of Principal Investigator and project manager found their own balance, and each made the mission work in their own way. On CONTOUR and Genesis, the PIs remained deeply involved, traveling to the implementing organization several times a month to review progress and participating in change control boards, discussions of concern, and regular staff meetings as needed. The Stardust PI, in contrast, delegated implementation responsibility almost entirely to the project management organization, making himself available by telephone for questions about how engineering changes would affect the intended science. In nearly every case where the PI delegated more responsibility to the project manager, the project manager rewarded that trust with exemplary performance. Where this failed, however, the results were significant: both Deep Impact and MESSENGER, for example, experienced crises in project management and large overruns in 2002–2003, nearly ten years after the Discovery Program began.

During this time, Deep Impact, largely built by an engineering team in Colorado with a West Coast project manager and an East Coast PI, suffered from insufficient oversight of subcontractors. This problem deteriorated to the crisis point, requiring replacement of the project manager and a change in management style. The PI began spending increased amounts of time onsite with the prime contractor, getting to know its engineering culture and inviting informal questions in the hallway. Once the PI took these steps and the new project manager spent more time onsite managing the prime contractor and checking on the progress of subcontractors, the project turned around and delivered a successful spacecraft and spectacular science.

In the case of MESSENGER, technical challenges such as late deliveries coincided with an unexpected change in project management as the original project manager retired and his deputy disappeared, not returning to work after a particularly challenging trip to an underperforming subcontractor. The implementing organization was left scrambling, and the new project manager began a fresh costing effort that determined that the mission was in far greater trouble than imagined. This manager worked closely with the PI and NASA management to bring the mission back on track, and, after several infusions of additional funding, it went on to become one of NASA's greatest successes.

As PIs delegated more and more responsibility to project managers, increasingly the roles returned to those of the pre-Discovery era, where the project manager was

---

5   Binder, A. (2005). *Against All Odds.* Tucson: Ken Press.

in charge of delivering a mission and the PI was responsible for the science. NASA Headquarters was slow to acknowledge this reality, however, holding the PIs of the later missions responsible for errors in manufacturing, subcontractor oversight, and costs that had grown far beyond the mission cost cap. The Deep Impact, MESSENGER, Dawn, and Kepler PIs were held responsible for cost growth in heated meetings at NASA Headquarters. Each was directed eventually to perform a replan with the project where the science could still be accomplished within the agreed-upon constraints. This admittedly strange outcome, where a university professor was held responsible for cost overruns, tank qualifications, late delivery of parts, and changes at some of the largest aerospace corporations in the country, was a direct effect of the innovation heralded some years earlier, at the beginning of the program.

The Kepler mission, which had suffered from delays, management changes, and cost difficulties for years, had even been reclassified as a strategic mission for Astrophysics instead of a Discovery mission subject to firm cost caps. Then the Kepler mission exceeded its cost cap again in 2007, and NASA reacted strongly. The agency demoted the Kepler PI to a science PI, removing some of the responsibility for the mission from his shoulders. NASA insisted on a total rewiring of the organization's management structure as well, with the project manager, deputy project manager, transition manager for operations, and chief engineer at the top and the science PI and project scientist in subordinate roles. This unusual step was not repeated in the first two decades of Discovery.

The 2010 Discovery Program AO solicited proposals for investigations led by a single PI "with full responsibility for its scientific integrity and for its execution within committed cost and schedule," albeit with stronger language reinforcing essential NASA oversight "to ensure that the implementation is responsive to the requirements and constraints of the Discovery Program."[6]

REFLECTIONS OF THE PIs

During a series of individual oral history interviews performed in 2009 as part of this NASA-funded research, each mission PI was asked to reflect on his or her own lessons learned and identify one thing he or she wished he or she had known before proposing a small planetary mission to the Discovery Program. Almost without exception, the PI was surprised to be asked such a question, often protesting that he or she would not change a thing, or that he or she was completely prepared for such a role. More than once, a PI responded that the answer was irrelevant, as he or she would never have listened to such advice or warnings when caught up in the first flush of proposing.

---

6   NASA Science Mission Directorate. (2009. 7 December). "Draft AO: Discovery 2010." NASA AO NNH10ZDA003J.

However, as the discussions continued, these senior scientists revealed hints of doubt and an openness to considering what they might have done differently. The responses provide a window into nagging regrets in some cases, while in others the PI admitted that he or she had had no idea of the magnitude of the challenge that lay ahead.

Perhaps prompted by the 2007 discussion of screening requirements proposed for future PIs, every PI brought up the importance of experience.[7] The CONTOUR PI had served in key science roles on NEAR and the Galileo imaging team, for example, and he emphasized the reliability of past performance in previous instrument deliveries as being predictive of performance leading a mission team, despite the difference in scope. He stopped short of requiring previous experience, however, recognizing that a lack of previous executive experience is not a fatal flaw, but something that can be remedied by earlier exposure through roles such as deputy PI or deputy project scientist. Increased exposure creates more qualified PIs who can then be trusted more completely to deliver mission success.

Remembering the incredible diversity of sample substrates deployed on the spacecraft and the intense preparation each required, the PI of Genesis might have taken greater care with scheduling so very many deliverables for the science co-investigators, particularly himself and his project scientist, in the same time frame in 2000. Perhaps it would have been wiser to be somewhat less ambitious, he reflected. This sentiment is interesting in the context of the outcome of the mission, where, according to his project scientist, the very diversity of the materials enhanced the science that could be salvaged after its crash landing.

The PIs of Deep Impact and MESSENGER had remarkably similar sentiments about the grand challenge of leading a multi-hundred-million-dollar mission as a university professor or researcher. The former expected to lead the science while the project manager made the mission happen, which, the PI admitted, was a misconception. The challenges of coming up to speed on managing contracts, managing engineers, and monitoring technical progress at contractor facilities went far beyond his expectations. In his case, he ended up with additional business management duties because of a transfer of contract management intended to save on overhead charges. Universities charge significantly less overhead on large contracts than government labs or federally funded research and development centers, so contract administration may be moved in order to cut costs when money is tight. Unfortunately for the project staff, lower overhead means fewer resources available to assist, and the PI and his team end up doing much more of the work themselves (at a greater real cost, but lower financial cost, to the mission).

---

7   Niebur, S. (2009). "Principal Investigators and Mission Leadership." *Space Policy*, vol. 25. 181–186.

Much of this contract management work on Deep Impact involved unexpected travel to contractor facilities. Demands for travel ballooned from roughly quarterly to monthly at the start of the design phase. The increased demands paid off, however, and the PI brightened as he talked about the rewards of being present and bringing science to the engineers on the ground. Their tremendous enthusiasm encouraged him, and he delighted in talking to them formally and in hallway conversations. In fact, it was the informal conversations in the hallways that contributed strongly to the team's effectiveness, as the engineers asked to understand more about the science driving their requirements, about the goals of the mission, and about routine administrative details as well. It was a small thing, but the importance of being there was soon evident, as, for all the questions that came up informally, not once was the PI contacted by the engineers with similar questions by phone. The take-away lesson from this PI was straightforward: spend time with the engineering team doing the work.

The MESSENGER PI also invoked the broad scope of the role, noting that practical knowledge and experience in engineering, subsystem engineering, systems engineering, and project management, particularly of the kind gained by previous participation on flight missions, was an important component of an ideal preparation. The exact nature of the previous experience required was not immediately clear to either PI, however; they and others questioned whether serving as a co-investigator was sufficient or even helpful, although both agreed that previous exposure, of the casual everyday kind that one gets working on a project with or in proximity to another PI, would be extremely beneficial.

The PI of Dawn, another of the middle-era missions, also strongly recommended selecting future mission leaders with significant previous experience and a commitment to being present at the contractor site. He encouraged greater understanding of the political and social context in which management decisions are made. He worried that perhaps a greater attention to the appearance of progress, as well as progress itself, would have made his mission appear more favorable to NASA management. Like other scientists located near their management institution or prime contractor (a coincidence that Genesis and MESSENGER were also able to leverage), he made it a priority to attend weekly engineering staff meetings and participate in reviews. It was on the question of reserves, however, that he spoke the longest, discussing the importance of "stated reserves" and what he called "hidden reserves"—concealed "from everybody including your staff."[8] He continued, encouraging bookkeeping a high level (30–50 percent) of nonessential items, those you can later descope without affecting the program.

---

8   Niebur, S. (2009, 24 March). Personal interview with C. Russell. Located in "Dawn" file, NASA Historical Reference Collection, History Division, NASA Headquarters, Washington, DC.

The Dawn PI also emphasized the point that no mission exists in a vacuum. Missions that encounter unexpected technical issues and overrun effectively "punished" other missions with additional reviews and requirements meant to stave off a recurrence of the same issue.[9] These changes require additional robust reserves accessible only to the project at hand, and not others in the same institution or program, to carry the project through a difficult period.

Dawn's Deputy PI spoke about the double-edged sword of requirements definition, a task not fully appreciated until much later, when the team was being held to account. Properly defining requirements—useful for the engineers and scientists alike—can guide the mission throughout development; it was a task with which that mission had trouble from the very beginning. Over-defining the requirements could cause the expenditure of significant resources unnecessarily. Under-defining the requirements could cause contractors to provide hardware insufficient to take scientific measurements with appropriate precision—or even work at all in the harsh environment of space.

The Kepler PI also found that there was a lot to learn, stating that scientists simply do not have the necessary experience. However, he continued, people at the NASA centers (for example) have a great deal of experience and are trained to handle such difficult tasks as requirements definition and reserve management. It is quite possible for a PI to rely on the implementing institution to handle the day-to-day management of a mission and all that it entails. The daily task of mission management is tremendous, requiring constant attention, 100 hours a week, leading him to say, "I probably wouldn't have done this had I known how much work it would be, how long it would take, all the obstacles to be overcome, and all the frustration to be endured."[10]

Time and again in interviews with project scientists, deputy project scientists, and co-investigators, science team members lauded the PIs of Discovery for their unwavering commitment to the science. These scientists stayed focused on mission goals, ensuring the delivery of the science to the community even as they struggled to manage missions threatening to grow out of control, often employing innovative approaches that required a great deal of additional, unexpected time and energy commitment. The Genesis PI, for example, proposed and received a funded analysis period for the Genesis scientists after the samples were returned, counting it as an official part of the mission; all other missions, including Stardust, which also returned samples to Earth, ended abruptly with the end of spacecraft operations. In another example, the PI on Deep Impact learned to spend substantial amounts of time onsite with the contractor during development, away from his own research and the students he was expected to teach at the university. The MESSENGER PI pushed his team to publish papers

---

9   Ibid.

10   Niebur, S. (2009, 16 December). Personal interview with W. Borucki. Located in "Kepler" file, NASA Historical Reference Collection, History Division, NASA Headquarters, Washington, DC.

without delay, reading every paper and conference abstract, and garnering special issues of *Science* for every planetary flyby, well before the spacecraft even achieved Mercury Orbit Insertion. The Kepler PI spent decades working to make his mission a success. These PIs worked day and night for many years to ensure mission success.

Insights from the Project Managers

These efforts did not go unrecognized by the project managers. In their formal oral history interviews, the project managers were also asked to identify the characteristics or skills that are important for a good PI. While a few reiterated points they had made earlier while discussing mission challenges, others credited the level of involvement of the PI who they had worked with, and how it contributed to mission development.[11]

The CONTOUR project manager for design and development named decisiveness, fairness, and taking a stand against scope creep (the temptation to add capabilities after design) as top qualities for a PI. It is very difficult for a scientist leading a team of scientists to resist recommending or approving small engineering tweaks that promise great increases in the science return. The temptation to improve the mission during development is present in every mission, often accompanied by pressure from the science team also invested in mission success. A good PI keeps careful watch on his or her payload, resisting changes in instruments that deviate significantly from the requirements in either direction, as small changes in scope can have disastrous effects on mission budgets. The CONTOUR PI also was described as a good listener, allowing new ideas from all sorts of sources, taking them into account while remaining focused on the carefully plotted next steps to mission success.

Stardust's PI was focused on the science return of the mission and delegated the day-to-day work of management to the project manager. He understood the engineering enough, as the first project manager put it, that he felt it best to delegate its management and trust that he would be consulted on tough issues. Both project managers appreciated that, cajoling him occasionally to join them at certain meetings or travel to the implementing organization to review progress. The second project manager spoke just as highly of him as the first, calling him a gem who gave the project manager all the freedom he needed to get the job done. By delegating the contract management, cost and technical oversight, and mission planning to the project manager and his implementing organization, the PI was free to keep working on his own science, to serve on community panels, to give public talks, and to do interviews in support of the mission. He sparked interest in the mission by being present in another way—not at the engineering level, but at the level of public engagement.

---

11   Niebur, S. (2011, 19 March). Personal interview with C. Niebur.

On MESSENGER, the PI was deeply involved in the implementation of the mission, asking the right questions, keeping abreast of developments, and being onsite as necessary. The project manager for most of the development called him a first-class scientist, very knowledgeable about the current status of development and cognizant of others' roles as well. On cost and technical issues, the PI stood back to let the engineering team get the job done, an approach the project manager praised effusively. Since the PI could not be onsite every minute, the institution relied on an experienced project scientist for day-to-day oversight of the science and nuances in the written requirements. The MESSENGER team was not the only one to employ a project scientist or team member at the project manager's institution, but it was one of the most visible.

The Deep Impact PI was praised by the project manager who got the mission to the launch pad. The project manager respected the PI's decision to be a silent presence in the engineering meetings, always present, never interfering. The scientist was available, and he let the team know that, but he didn't obstruct the engineers from doing the work that had to be done. A good PI has a positive outlook, motivating the team when necessary and trusting them to build the right instruments or spacecraft on time, on cost, under his high-level direction, but not with constant interference. A project manager on Deep Impact's extended mission, EPOXI, noted that the Principal Investigator was hands-on with NASA Headquarters and with the management of the federally funded research and development center implementing the mission, in ways that the project team could not be. Both the PI and this project manager had significant previous mission experience, dating back to the mid-1970s and Comet Halley as well as European and Soviet missions, and they had a good relationship of mutual respect in part because of this experience and common background.

The Dawn project manager praised the PI for holding the line, refusing to let requirements creep during development even as his instrument scientists pushed him to do more. That commitment to requirements made implementation of the project easier, eliminating the burden of major readjustments to engineering hardware and design that could have caused major problems in development.

Former Discovery Program Manager Jarrett explained the requirements well when he described the ideal PI as "not just an expert in his particular scientific field, but the ability to comprehend spacecraft design, trajectory design, and the technical side of putting a mission together as well as the budgetary aspects of it."[12]

---

12   Niebur, S. (2009, 14 May). Personal interview with D. Jarrett and Kate Wolf. Located in "Discovery Program" file, NASA Historical Reference Collection, History Division, NASA Headquarters, Washington, DC.

THE ROLE OF THE PROJECT MANAGER

The project manager of a Discovery mission has in theory only the responsibilities delegated to him or her by the PI. In practice, however, the project manager must oversee the design, formulation, integration, testing, and preparation for launch of a spacecraft that may cost over half a billion dollars at launch. The role of a project manager is a challenging one, encompassing skills as varied as technical insight; cost containment; institutional advocacy; and the management, directly or indirectly, of the efforts of up to a thousand people per mission.

Definition

At first, the Discovery Program did not define the role of project manager, leaving it up to the PI to define. The first AO, however, did note that the project manager should oversee the technical implementation of the mission and that the project manager should have sufficient role and experience to meet the technical needs of the investigation.[13]

Evolution

The loose definition of the project manager's role solidified over time, and requirements were added for the project manager to be named, for the role to be clearly defined in the proposal, and eventually for NASA to approve the project manager at each major milestone review. Principal Investigators were strongly encouraged at later points in the program to name a deputy program manager or an alternate project manager at the time of proposal. These stricter requirements or recommendations arose as a result of lessons learned from previous missions.

In the early missions, it was not uncommon for the same project manager to take a mission from proposal to launch. Stardust, for example, had that continuity, which enabled the mission leadership to keep tight rein on requirements and fight scope creep. In later missions, however, project managers, named as part of the proposing team, began to disappear after selection, to be replaced by unexpected players. In response, NASA required PIs to name the project manager at proposal. Project managers' qualifications were carefully reviewed by technical-management-cost reviewers before selection, and NASA concurrence was required before a personnel change at this level.

The role of the project manager came under additional scrutiny after the 1999 failures of the Mars Climate Orbiter and Mars Polar Lander, even though these missions were not part of the Discovery Program. NASA immediately introduced reviews where none had been before, adding layers of people to look at the mission reports and expanding the NASA Program Guideline for Program and Project Management

---

13   NASA Office of Space Science. (1994, 4 August). "AO: Discovery Missions." NASA AO 94-OSS-03.

(NPG 7120) to include greater institutional oversight of mission development. NASA also increased review of the definition of the role of the project manager in its rigorous pre-selection evaluations.

Later missions recognized that some technical challenges in the changing landscape of the aerospace industry might be insurmountable for even a very highly qualified project manager, and the centers began to replace PMs with those of complementary expertise at key trouble points in a mission. For example, when a project struggled with late subsystem deliveries, a more aggressive manager with a "boots on the ground" philosophy for contractor oversight was appointed, and the climate of the mission development changed drastically. After this change in management style, the team successfully delivered the spacecraft to the launch pad, leading even the previous manager to conclude that his replacement had been the right decision.

Project managers began to change more often and with less provocation. One PI chuckled ruefully at the reflection as he enumerated the eight project managers he had worked with sequentially from proposal to extended mission. To combat this revolving door while encouraging the leadership of project managers with the appropriate style as times and circumstances require, NASA added a new requirement for approval of the project manager not just at selection, but at each major milestone review. By the 2010 AO, the project manager was explicitly charged with overseeing the technical and programmatic implementation of the project and working "closely with the PI in order to ensure that the mission meets its objectives within the resources outlined in the proposal."[14]

REFLECTIONS OF THE PROJECT MANAGERS

Each project manager was also asked to reflect on lessons learned. The project managers were asked to identify one thing they wished they had known before working on their first small planetary mission. The responses ranged from specific wishes for additional testing of spacecraft systems and subsystems to insights about managing offsite contractors separated by significant distances.

On Genesis, much of the spacecraft had high heritage from Stardust, and arguments were made that some of the testing required for other missions was unnecessary for this one, selected early on, while Discovery was still in faster, better, cheaper mode. If it had been selected later, it might have been subject to more rigorous testing; as it was, no one required a system-level test of the capsule, and none was performed. As it turned out, the similarity was an oversimplification. At the detailed design level, it was a different box, and the analogy arguments broke down. Missions selected later were

---

14   NASA Science Mission Directorate. (2009, 7 December). "Draft AO: Discovery 2010." NASA AO NNH10ZDA003J.

much more reluctant to claim direct heritage, and the review boards repeatedly extolled the merit of this decision, particularly in cases where a technology or system had not yet flown. Another remnant of the earlier era, when Discovery was a grand experiment in possibilities, was the removal of requirements that critical areas of spacecraft design be built with multiple safeguards. It was not uncommon for mechanisms to be "single string," without a built-in backup in case part of the mechanism failed. Genesis would have benefited from a second redundant technique—not just redundancy in parts—for sensing deceleration upon Earth return, for example. Safeguards like that, not deemed essential in the earlier era, were reintroduced over time.

Through formulation, design, development, and testing, the CONTOUR project manager echoed the Genesis experience; she added that one of the key things she liked about Discovery is that managers are forced to make decisions in short time frames and not let matters remain unresolved. The constraints force project managers to be even more proactive in addressing potential issues, as there is little time built in to correct problems that have gone on too long. Experienced project managers know to keep vigilant for potential issues, not letting optimism about the mission distract them, and for that reason, experience is important. Even small issues can have large consequences if not rapidly resolved. CONTOUR's early financial difficulties also highlighted the importance of selecting savvy project managers with experience in costing and replanning space missions.

The second MESSENGER project manager reiterated the point about carefully scheduling or agreeing to delivery dates. The initial bid must be planned carefully, and the project manager should be involved at proposal so that he or she can not only enforce the words in the proposal, but also carry through with the intent, with full knowledge of the assumptions and context. Both project managers emphasized the importance of teamwork at all levels, including making sure that everyone down to the most peripheral contributor knows that their contribution is part of the success. As the second project manager put it, "I know the guy that loads the spacecraft on the truck and takes it down to the Cape."[15] Close-knit teams ensure critical crosstalk between the engineers, the scientists, and the managers. Scientists are often found talking to engineers on campus, and vice versa. This collaboration is both spurred on by and contributes to an overall excitement about the pending data return.

The Dawn mission, managed on the opposite coast and in a different engineering culture, ran into trouble in part because faraway contractors did not make satisfactory progress on technical deliveries, and the team did not realize the full extent of the problem in time. The second project manager faulted his trust in the contractor to deliver on its promises; the third project manager then acknowledged that trust was

---

15   Niebur, S. (2009, 27 July). Personal interview with D. Grant. Located in the "MESSENGER" file, NASA Historical Reference Collection, History Division, NASA Headquarters, Washington, DC.

not sufficient in this case. He frequently traveled 3,000 miles to the contractor to watch over the final stages of integration and testing. To overcome delays and uncertainty, project management had to return to pre-Discovery models in some sense, and the manager or his deputy had to be onsite essentially until the spacecraft was complete. Both these project managers now are firm believers in the benefits of project management spending significant time onsite at subcontractors' locations, even though planning for such oversight may strain the lean budget of small missions.

Communication was deemed critical in many interviews, with project managers from MESSENGER to Deep Impact to Dawn talking about the importance of in-person discussions. The second Dawn manager, for example, advocated setting up "really, really flat lines of communication," being visible to every member of the team, and having all-hands meetings several times a year.[16] The program managers and the PIs enthusiastically recommended sharing not just the technical triumph with the team, but also the excitement of bringing home data that would be the key to new science in solar system exploration.

Insights from the PIs

At the end of each interview, the PI was asked to identify the characteristics or skills important for a good project manager. This is a role that had been discussed repeatedly within management institutions; funding agencies; and organizations such as APPEL, the Academy of Program/Project and Engineering Leadership at NASA; and yet the reflections here, collected in 2009, provide a new dimension of such discourse. The PIs were given the opportunity to discuss what they had learned about the role of the project manager over the course of the development of their missions, just as the PMs had been asked to talk about the role of the PI.

Each PI defined the role of project manager, agreed to the appointment of said project manager, and was responsible for the work of the project manager, and yet most were somewhat humbled by the fact that, in the end, it was the project manager who really had the power and skills to deliver a working spacecraft to the launch pad. The Genesis PI dealt with this dichotomy by recognizing that the project manager was very capable of delivering the mission and respecting his authority to do so, staying with the project to understand and concur on every major decision. The project manager knows what to do and does it, and the PI looks for insight into his or her decisions and confirms them. In the words of one, "You delegate, but you don't walk away." He

---

16   Niebur, S. (2009, 12 August). Personal interview with T. Fraschetti. Located in "Dawn" file, NASA Historical Reference Collection, History Division, NASA Headquarters, Washington, DC.

also appreciated the second project manager's ability to "tell it like it is"—to effectively lay out the problems and the proposed mitigating strategies, and to sell the preferred option to the senior management and the team.[17]

After a first proposal that failed, the MESSENGER PI was convinced of the importance of selecting the right project manager. He insisted on approving the potential project manager before any subsequent proposal, selecting for certain skills, including communication. He valued a rapport with his project manager and insisted on someone who worked well with his own engineers, put together credible budgets, understood risk, and had the experience to see the project to completion.

Dawn began formulation with a less experienced project manager who had delivered a small payload on the Mars Polar Lander several years earlier, but never a full mission. The PI insisted that he needed a project manager with greater experience, and, after a difficult Preliminary Mission and Systems Review, the project manager was replaced with a more experienced manager. The second project manager was then lauded as a real leader, one who commanded respect from the engineers but was also available for questions and guidance.

The Kepler PI valued insight as a top priority for project managers. The project manager needs to know what every technical lead is doing during instrument development, to understand and perhaps to be deeply involved in every test, and to engage appropriate staff to realistically estimate schedule and cost for each task independently of the contractor.

The CONTOUR PI appreciated honesty in a project manager, requiring him to act aboveboard at all times, not promising different outcomes to different stakeholders. Hard work was essential, of course, as was respect from the team assembled both for their individual qualifications and ability to collaborate. In fact, he emphasized that the most important qualification is not an individual one, but how well the project manager and PI can work together.

Teamwork

The roles of PI and project manager do not exist independently but are interwoven with reciprocal responsibilities. As previously demonstrated, each team in Discovery's first two decades was free to define its own division of labor at proposal but was then required to live within those constraints. The PIs and project managers often talked about teamwork and how they relied on each other to fulfill their respective responsibilities. Their duties varied, but one thing never changed: commitment to the success of the mission.

---

17   Niebur, S. (2009, 24 March). Personal interview with D. Burnett. Located in "Genesis" file, NASA Historical Reference Collection, History Division, NASA Headquarters, Washington, DC.

PI and Project Manager Perspectives

One project manager, who worked on three missions, said that he was "blessed with three very good PIs." From the project manager perspective, a PI's working knowledge of NASA Headquarters and the lead NASA center on a mission could be valuable, and, likewise, being able to work with the highest level of an institution's management is essential. The ability to stand up to a center Director or their assistants and say "no" is appreciated by a project manager who may not have such freedom.[18]

The CONTOUR PI had the advantage of decades of experience leading planetary missions and serving on science teams. When defining roles and choosing his approach to management, he purposefully struck a balance between the "PI who gets involved in everything and makes life miserable for the investigator and for all the people who work with him" and the PI who disappears into the background between selection and data return. Precisely because he wanted to be involved, he made a particular effort to find excellent people whom he could trust to work independently but who also would trust him enough to turn back for help when needed. He agreed to take on issues at NASA Headquarters, for instance, and to weigh in on technical issues when asked. Weekly conference calls helped the team work together between the monthly in-person meetings. The PI added, "I tried very hard not to get in the way of people who knew what they were doing," as he complimented his team over and over again, as well as the team he had worked with as an instrument lead on NEAR, one of the first Discovery missions, implemented before the Principal Investigator mode.[19] The relationship between the top technical and top scientific experts on the team is essential, and they must be well matched, he said, adding that he always insisted that the two should be able to select each other and that institutions not force relationships between personalities that do not work well together. Successful implementation of a mission within such tight constraints takes an extremely close relationship. Others, including funding agencies and managing institutions, must honor this as well, however, and he did note that one of the most significant activities for his mission—the Mishap Investigation Board after the failure of CONTOUR's solid rocket motor burn 42 days after launch—was conducted entirely without the involvement of the PI. Because of his close relationship with his team, however, he continued to receive information about the review, even without any contact from the board.

The Genesis project managers were recognized by the PI for going out of their way to meet the science team and get to know them and what was important to their research.

---

18   Niebur, S. (2009, 4 September). Personal interview with T. Duxbury. Located in "Stardust" file, NASA Historical Reference Collection, History Division, NASA Headquarters, Washington, DC.

19   Niebur, S. (2009, 10 September). Personal interview with J. Veverka. Located in the "CONTOUR" file, NASA Historical Reference Collection, History Division, NASA Headquarters, Washington, DC.

On this mission, the science team was rarely involved with the engineers because of their disparate duties, but project managers before and after landing made efforts to travel and meet the science teams at their meetings and planetary science conferences.

Project managers emphasized the role of teamwork and a well-defined project management relationship over and over in interviews. The Stardust project manager during development reviewed several possible types of relationships, such as the more traditional model where science co-investigators or a science working group pressure the PI to increase scope, the PI does, and then the project manager must push back to stay within cost and schedule constraints. This tension can create an "us versus them" mentality, and traditional issues such as poor communication and competing requirements can threaten to derail the project.

In Discovery, however, the PI/project manager relationship was established differently, and this redefinition not only empowered the PI, but it also empowered the project manager because he or she no longer reported only to his or her own line management, but also to an outside senior scientist who reported directly to NASA Headquarters for the success of his or her mission. Wise project managers could leverage this relationship to push the project forward in the face of adversity. A good team could not only implement spacecraft development more effectively but also answer management queries from all levels faster, without delaying project progress. Project managers would help PIs understand center management concerns, and PIs could intervene when outside influences threatened the project. The two would work together and build a trust that would allow each to perform their own roles but work together as a team when difficulties arose.

Science benefits when a champion is established outside of the existing engineering structure that has the power to redirect the project back on track as necessary. The project managers recognized this, even writing protection clauses into proposals that required the PI's approval before the spending of one penny of reserve. These gates introduced checks and balances into the system, reducing the possibility that engineering overruns would erode the science return without careful consideration and approval by the primary science stakeholder. The interjection of a PI at this point in the system caused the project managers to think twice about cutting the science budget and to resist such cuts if pressured, even directed, by their own line or center management.

Project managers who have worked with multiple Discovery PIs spoke highly of all of them, contrasting their different styles. One gave the project manager the freedom he needed to get the job done. Others were more hands-on in the day-to-day development. In every case, any decisions with potential impact on the mission design and subsequent performance were discussed thoroughly with the PI, with the project manager laying out a suggested direction, while reminding the PI that he had the power to overrule him using the structures and review boards in place. That power was rarely used, but everyone appreciated the possibility that they might not agree and briefed each other thoroughly.

As the PI on CONTOUR brought forth proposed changes, the project manager detailed the impact that each would have on the spacecraft, and together they struck compromises that improved the science without increasing scope. Both kept tight rein on scope and how it affected the program budget. Their weekly conversations were wide-ranging and supplemented by phone calls as needed, both with the project manager and with instrument developers. This open communication enhanced their teamwork, and the project manager was not threatened by the PI also directing instrument developers at her institution.

Tight collaboration between scientists, engineers, and managers such as that exhibited on MESSENGER fed forward into excitement about engineering challenges met and anticipated data return, on all sides, making conflicts more negotiable. When scientists and engineers are used to working together in a culture and a problem arises, they have a common language and mutual respect that make issue resolution more straightforward and more effective. No one throws issues to the other side of the fence because everyone is already sitting at the table. Everyone's contributions are well defined and valued, all in support of the successful launch and data return. This collaborative atmosphere increases the willingness of team members to take direction and implement decisions, since they have a greater understanding of the efforts of people on other sides of the interface.

The second Dawn project manager came to the project after much of the formulation work had been done, but he fit into the mission smoothly due to his two decades of experience working with scientists and engineers at a federally funded research and development center. As a deputy director for the Engineering and Science Directorate before joining Dawn, he spoke the language of both sides, appreciating science as well as the engineering that it took to obtain groundbreaking science results. It was this respect for science and scientists that gained the respect of the PI, and they worked together to heal the rifts left in the team after the systems requirements definition failures highlighted at the program mission and systems review. The two were able, quickly, to address the mass, power, and budget problems, facing them as a team rather than leaders of opposing sides. Working together, they harnessed their resources to proceed in a unified direction and keep the mission from being canceled.

The next Dawn project manager, who appeared at another critical juncture, agreed that the working relationship between the project manager and PI was essential. The PI needs to know when not to interfere in the engineering, and the project manager needs to honor the science requirements. This project manager had also been the project manager on Deep Impact just before launch, and he appreciated that the Deep Impact

PI or his representative was so often silently supporting the engineering meetings, ready to answer questions, but never interfering, and he praised that as a wonderful relationship that helped them get to launch.

On Deep Impact, the PI who had been so adamant about the importance of being onsite with the engineers was equally adamant that, on his visits to the contractor, he was not managing the mission but letting the project manager manage. It was on these visits that he learned another important lesson when working with distributed teams: despite written and unwritten agreements, confusion can arise when two groups use the same word to indicate different requirements or procedures. In his case, a lot of additional work was required to satisfy both parties that the implementation of the mission testbeds was sufficient to predict mission success. Project managers, PIs, and subcontractors must understand differences in culture and not only use the same words but ensure that the words being used mean the same thing to all parties.

No relationship is static, however, and the replacement of the project manager can cause difficulty in maintaining the forward momentum of a mission. The deputy PI of Dawn talked about the danger of losing continuity as project managers are changed and the inherent difficulty in maintaining priorities through personnel changes. As new project managers take charge, they tend to reprioritize to accomplish ambitious goals with small budgets and limited staff; it is then up to other members of the team to explain the assumptions inherent in the mission design, the approach, and the expectations.

Teamwork is essential all up and down the line, of course, but the project managers interviewed reinforced the importance of well-defined roles and responsibilities and communication. The second MESSENGER project manager pushed this point, saying that he had spent significant time thinking about the people necessary for mission work, particularly in the systems engineering function. "If you've got the right people then the work is heaven," he said in an interview. "If you've got the wrong people, it's hell."[20] The perfect match of skills, capabilities, and approach is difficult to define but well worth the initial investment. This project manager made it a point to get the best people on the team and to take care of them. He recognized that people are what make a spacecraft work and that the right person in the right job makes the work go much more smoothly. To get the most out of this match, a project manager must understand the engineers' needs and assign the work accordingly. Knowing what each engineer does, what approaches he or she prefers, and what he or she really loves doing helps eliminate outside distractions and contribute to mission success. Seemingly small details, like inviting the most junior engineers to the parties, rotating critical test

---

20   Niebur, S. (2009, 27 July). Personal interview with D. Grant. Located in the "MESSENGER" file, NASA Historical Reference Collection, History Division, NASA Headquarters, Washington, DC.

engineers out and sending them home for an occasional weekend with their families at home, and holding events for families all contribute to the engineers' happiness and reinforce the total dedication required in the crunch.

These relationships are not formed in a vacuum, but typically during the first of the key project activities required by the Discovery Program: the proposal. The CONTOUR project manager described this experience as an intense period of work in which many hundreds of thousands of dollars are spent and many people are exhausted, but the effort pays off in well-designed missions and teams that are ready to work together from the start. Not only are the roles of PI, project manager, mission system engineer, and the rest defined during proposal, but they are tested under stress; team members come to understand each other's strengths and how their team will solve the problems that invariably arise. Team members take on complementary roles and trust each other to accomplish defined tasks. While proposals consume large amounts of resources, the time and energy spent on this task set the tone for future collaboration critical to mission success.

Management Perspectives

A discussion of how PIs and project managers see their roles individually and with respect to each other would not be complete without a few comments from those in program leadership over the years. Each mission has a program executive and program scientist at NASA Headquarters who maintain cognizance of the mission and respond to issues raised by the project or their own management. Another pair, the Discovery Program executive and Discovery Program scientist, propose policy modifications and oversee the selection of future missions. All of these scientists and executives report to their division director. The NASA Associate Administrator for the Science Mission Directorate, who oversees all, is the selecting official.

Wes Huntress, former NASA Associate Administrator and the de facto founder of the Discovery Program, spoke passionately about the relationship as it had been envisioned at the start, saying, "You don't hold the PI responsible for everything; he's head of science," and that the project manager does the best he can to implement the mission as the PI designed it, with all significant decisions made with the PI at the head of the table.[21]

A key player in a federally funded research and development center—and a former PI himself on a non-Discovery mission—explained that mission planning often begins with a discussion of the prospective roles and planned interaction. The initial conditions are set at the time of proposal, with ongoing dialogue through the years as the

---

21   Niebur, S. (2009, 13 March). Personal interview with W. Huntress. Located in "Discovery Program" file, NASA Historical Reference Collection, History Division, NASA Headquarters, Washington, DC.

contexts change. This partnership is critical, and the institution puts a high premium on making a good match between the PI and project manager for new missions, in large part because a well-founded relationship and close-knit team make addressing future problems possible before they become crises requiring the attention of senior-level management and the costs that those incur.

The former head of the Space Department at another institution heavily engaged in the design, development, and implementation of Discovery missions—a scientist who has sent instruments to every planet in the solar system—agreed that the partnership is key, but the leadership of the PI is critical in the successful implementation of a mission, and his or her authority should be respected. When asked about the concept that a PI should stay out of the way of the implementing engineers, he called such an assertion "damn arrogant" and shortsighted for those interested in maximizing the science return within available resources.[22]

A program executive charged with the oversight of the Dawn and New Horizons missions at NASA Headquarters cautioned that project managers need to be receptive to requests from all sides without taking comments as direction. Communication is critical, but the project manager that is accommodating to everyone—or no one—may become distracted from achieving the defined requirements. Mission success often hangs on the willingness of project managers to listen to other ideas and the judgment to know when to push back on the customer or team when appropriate, asking for clarification, explaining the effect of such a change on other spacecraft systems, providing technical data that show the change to be unwise, and standing up to management when necessary. Judgment is a key quality necessary in a program manager, as he decides whom to trust, how much to verify, and whether a change can be accommodated without losing sight of the requirements necessary for mission success.

Another program executive discussed the challenges of PI management of missions that can exceed a half-billion dollars. Missions that struggle require additional management resources, and sometimes different arrangements. On Kepler, repeated financial overruns during development caused the mission to be redefined from a small, focused Discovery mission to a strategic mission for the astrophysics community, and the role of the PI was later downgraded in acknowledgment of the increased attention required by the project manager and senior management. The project manager was replaced with another experienced engineer then working in senior management, and she reported directly to the center Director. This brought an increased gravitas that a scientist working several levels down at another institution did not, and could not, have.

---

22   Niebur, S. (2009, 24 September). Personal interview with T. Krimigis. Located in the "Discovery Program" file, NASA Historical Reference Collection, History Division, NASA Headquarters, Washington, DC.

Several people who previously held the positions of Discovery Program Scientist and Discovery Program Executive were also interviewed as part of this series of interviews in 2009. All agreed that well-defined roles and responsibilities, teamwork, and a commitment to success are critical. One former program executive emphasized the power of the project manager to maintain cognizance of the status of all the pieces and players required for successful delivery of the spacecraft as a whole. Project managers should be encouraged to delegate responsibility such that they can act as a kind of coach, monitoring progress and looking for areas that need extra attention in the project, while maintaining awareness of developments external to the project that may affect mission success. Thoughtful communication with the team, the contractor, his or her management, the program officer, and NASA officials is essential; "feeding the management dragon" appropriately will keep issues at the proper level, rather than burying the issue and hoping for success or raising the issue too quickly, when additional resources may create more interference than assistance.[23] It is recognized as a strength, he said, to identify issues that are beyond the capability of the project to resolve and to call for additional resources to help determine the best course of action.

When asked what makes a good project manager, former Discovery Program Manager Jarrett said,

> Someone who's able to see the future, someone who is a very flexible individual who can roll with the punches as problems come in. You will always have funding issues where contractors don't come in within budget or suppliers' costs go up. You've got to know how to handle your reserve strategy to do that. You need to be able to juggle schedules to be able to account for problems and things you need to go fix. You don't necessarily need to fully understand the scientific aspects of the mission, but you need to have an appreciation of them. An understanding of them is even better. And you have to have the people skills to be able to deal with the whole realm of the community from the NASA bureaucrats to the scientist who has his one little piece of data or her piece of data that they want to get. You have to really comprehend the significance of that.... And again, it's a team effort between the PI and the project manager in order to accomplish the whole thing. There's got to be a balance.[24]

Gregg Vane of the Jet Propulsion Laboratory emphasized the importance of teamwork, saying, "If the Project Manager and PI aren't really a close-knit team, it makes it virtually impossible to come to agreement as to how to deal with the issues. Which

---

23   Niebur, S. (2009, 4 September). Personal interview with L. Johnson. Located in "Deep Impact" file, NASA Historical Reference Collection, History Division, NASA Headquarters, Washington, DC.

24   Niebur, S. (2009, 14 May). Personal interview with D. Jarrett and Kate Wolf. Located in "Discovery Program" file, NASA Historical Reference Collection, History Division, NASA Headquarters, Washington, DC.

means it becomes a crisis for some senior-level management at JPL or at [NASA] Headquarters, and the cost of fixing it is much greater. We think it's essential. It's a requirement, really. We have to feel confident that both parties will be comfortable working with each other."[25]

LESSONS LEARNED

Much was learned in the first twenty years after the first Discovery proposal about the nuances inherent in an arrangement that places a senior scientist at the head of an extremely large team of engineers at a NASA center, a federally funded research and development center, and aerospace contractors. Individuals, teams, and programs have all collected lessons learned and incorporated them into future missions to varying degrees. It is the intent of this chapter not to replace but to add to these conversations by conveying a sense of the reflections shared by the PIs, project managers, and management executives as interviewed by a colleague. Every Discovery mission is unique, and yet there are clearly some common strengths. The PI must remain cognizant of development milestones and challenges and be onsite at key reviews and as much other time as feasible, given the other demands on a mission leader and internationally known scientist. The project manager must understand the nature of the PI's commitment and be comfortable with implementing the design of the mission independently, within the science requirements defined at proposal or shortly thereafter. Both parties must make substantial efforts at communication in weekly conference calls, in monthly meetings, in quarterly reviews, and as issues arise that may affect the science return of the mission. These principles are largely universal and have been used to define roles and responsibilities over the first two decades of Discovery.

There are, however, less obvious lessons to learn here about how a project evolves. Contractor oversight may require "boots on the ground" by both the PI and the project manager, to varying degrees and at various times during a mission. The ideal project manager skill set is not constant, varying with mission design and with mission phase. In some cases, a project requires a different management style in different phases of design and development. Communication choices adequate during design may be insufficient when the hardware is being built and contractors approaching deadlines. Projects should be willing to change approach as the demands of the project change, with the full understanding that changes in project management will tax the entire

---

25   Niebur, S. (2009, 22 March). Personal interview with G. Vane. Located in the "Discovery Program" file, NASA Historical Reference Collection, History Division, NASA Headquarters, Washington, DC.

team, including the PI, who must ensure that the new management fully understands not just the science requirements but the assumptions implicit therein. Change is not a panacea, but it may be a necessary kick-start to the successful completion of a mission.

Principal Investigator

PIs can employ varied management styles, but each must be available to the mission as needed and be willing to act, within the project or with more senior management, when the success of the mission is threatened. Because it is so difficult to determine the origin of a crisis, the PI must maintain a keen insight into the progress of the project and be ready to act appropriately. PIs must understand rudimentary aspects of project management, including effective requirements definition, allocation of cost and schedule reserves, systems engineering, and determination of the full impact of potential trades. A PI must be fair, reasonable, decisive, slow to anger, and careful to consider the impact of any decision on the mission and the personnel involved. A good PI resists scope creep, listens to team members, takes decisive action, and effectively represents the mission to NASA Headquarters, center management, the science community, and the media.

Experience is critical for both PIs and project managers, although there is no clear consensus on what experience would adequately prepare a person to lead a half-billion-dollar mission. All experience, from that of a co-investigator to an instrument developer to a leader of teams, is helpful, and each must be evaluated with the management expectations in mind. It is particularly critical that mission leaders have delivered projects or instruments on time in the past and that they have employed appropriate support for the scheduling function in mission development to minimize the impact of late deliveries, the end result of many, many technical troubles. Some systems engineering experience would aid in evaluating project plans.

PIs would be well served to have worked closely with engineering teams at the proposed NASA center or federally funded research and development center in the past, to understand the engineering culture there, to know and have good relationships with center management, to be able to push back on new demands from all sides, and to stand up for the project when unfairly affected by failures, delays, or overruns on other projects at the center. The PI must also, of course, have the experience to understand when the project is being punished unfairly for another's mistakes, and when the new regulations reflect new insights into program and project management that will aid the project in its quest for mission success. An effective PI is aware of the daily challenges but does not interfere with the project manager's implementation style unless it is adversely affecting mission progress.

Project Manager

Former project managers have identified challenges of managing within Discovery's constraints on cost and schedule. Key among them are selecting the right level of testing, appropriately relying on heritage, considering when to move beyond "single string" to redundancy in parts and technique, and monitoring scheduled deliveries from subcontractors to detect problems well in advance. Project managers must be vigilant, decisive, open, and honest while accurately conveying to the PI and upper-level management the severity of any given technical challenge. Teamwork is essential, and a good project manager not only knows the status of scheduled development and testing, but the principals involved, how they work, and what motivates them to deliver on time and on budget.

A good project manager likely has systems engineering experience under his or her belt and may have managed smaller missions or subsystems on previous missions. Experience managing contracts, understanding costs, and discovering potential problems early directly enables both PMs and PIs to do their job more thoroughly and effectively.

PIs say that they value the following characteristics in a project manager: honesty, capability, availability, insight, straight talk, experience, reputation, teamwork, financial acumen, scheduling experience, commitment, independence, and a good understanding of risk. They also require a rapport that makes them comfortable with delegating the engineering of their project, knowing that they will be called in to discuss any critical problems or those that may affect the science return. This rapport allows the team to focus on solving technical problems as they arise in the most direct way possible. Effective project managers in Discovery appreciate the science return of the missions that they design and build; PIs value the engineering breakthroughs that make it possible. A mission team that is designed and implemented with effective communication between the scientists and engineers creates a culture in which problems can be solved more quickly, more effectively, and with less stress on the team as they move to mitigate the effects and get back on schedule. Regular communication (formal, informal, and social) reinforces this sense that the implementers are all one team, rather than a team of scientists and a team of engineers as in the models predating Discovery.

Projects that require PI approval before spending reserves or making significant trades introduce checks and balances into the engineering culture from *outside* the system, reducing the possibility of engineering issues eroding the science return without careful consideration and approval by the primary science stakeholder. This does more than bring one scientist into the conversation; it introduces a wedge whereby the science *community* now has leverage into the project in ways that did not exist before principal-investigator-led missions. When engineering challenges threaten to erode the science return, the science community—represented by the PI—now is empowered to stand up and interject the implications of such modifications into the discussion and to stop overdesign or unnecessary improvements in the proposed design that would then take resources from operations. As mission after mission in the Discovery Program has shown, the era of cutting operations budgets to increase margins of certainty is over. In the end, despite the disparate mission designs, science goals, and team organizations, nearly all the PIs and project managers agreed on one principle. The PI/project manager responsibilities can be divided many ways, but those two people must be able to trust each other, to act in the best interest of the project, and to act as a team. If the mission is not executable within the constraints that NASA and each mission team have defined, the rest is simply theory.

The Job of a Lifetime

Every Discovery PI interviewed called his or her role the best job they ever had. In an interview in 2003, Wes Huntress, former Associate Administrator of NASA, said: "I think the Discovery Program has been an enormous success. It's the thing I'm most proud of.... I have no disappointments in it at all, except for this one loss that we've had, but that's the business we're in. It's a risky business, and that's going to happen."[26]

The first 20 years of Discovery missions included spectacular successes and difficult times, right along the learning curve that accompanies any new initiative. Through it all, the individuals and organizations involved persevered, using the constraints introduced by the crisis du jour in creative ways to implement their missions and the hardware required to reach the scientists' dreams. By planning far ahead, manipulating constraints, being present, and coming up with innovative ways to approximate the results of much larger, deeper, more well-funded programs, the people of Discovery designed, built, and launched amazing spacecraft on their quests to explore other planets, comets, asteroids, the Sun, and planets around other stars.

NASA's Discovery Program has been a grand experiment, implemented by some of the greatest scientists, engineers, and managers of our time. To continue its success, NASA must learn from the past and share both the trials and the joys of robotic spaceflight with generations to come. The students of today will be the PIs of tomorrow.

---

26   Wright, R. (2003, 9 January). Personal interview with W. Huntress. Located in "Wes Huntress" file, NASA Historical Reference Collection, History Division, NASA Headquarters, Washington, DC.

AFTERWORD

By Curt Niebur

The project that led to this book began as a straightforward endeavor to document the history of the Discovery Program while it was still fresh. And who better, concluded the NASA History Office after reviewing her proposal, than Susan Niebur, the person who had recently run the program? But it was the stories Susan uncovered while researching that history that ignited her passion and lengthened the straightforward history book—and lengthened it, and lengthened it more. Because the most amazing things about NASA's missions aren't the discoveries, or the destinations, or even the science. It's the stories. And those stories are about people.

Spacecraft don't build themselves, budget spreadsheets don't spend funds, and policies are not self-executing. People do all of those things, and every single person has a story about how she did it and what she felt while doing it. NASA, like all government bureaucracies, tends to bury the individual and her story in favor of impersonal rules and policies and processes. Susan never lost her focus on the individual, and after leaving NASA, she was free to put the people and their stories front and center. After her death in 2012, the hundreds and hundreds of pages of stories languished, waiting for someone to undertake the task of editing them down to a book with the proper balance of historical narrative, stories, and length. NASA and David Brown ultimately undertook that effort. The final book is a product of a diverse team effort, just like everything NASA undertakes.

Not all stories are happy ones. Sometimes they aren't even true (though they are always true to the storyteller!). But all stories have value. They teach us. They motivate us. They make us stronger, smarter, and humbler. Stories make us better people. Susan knew this truth, and her hope was that this book and its stories would help its readers. Because her ultimate goal had always been to help people.

And after all, who doesn't love a good story?

Acronym List

AA	Associate Administrator
AAS	American Astronomical Society
ACE	Advanced Composition Explorer
ACME	Asteroid, Comet, Moon Explorers
AGU	American Geophysical Union
AMBR	Advanced Material Bi-propellant Rocket
AO	Announcement of Opportunity
APL	Applied Physics Laboratory of Johns Hopkins University
APS	Alpha Particle Spectrometer (on Lunar Prospector)
APXS	Alpha Proton X-ray Spectrometer (on Mars Pathfinder)
ARC	Ames Research Center
ARR	Assembly, Test, and Launch Operations Readiness Review
ASI	Agenzia Spaziale Italiana (Italy)
ASI/MET	Atmospheric Structure Instrument/Meteorology Package (on Pathfinder)

ASPERA-3	Analyzer of Space Plasma and Energetic Atoms (on Mars Express)
ASRG	Advanced Stirling Radioisotope Generator
ASU	Arizona State University
ATLO	Assembly, Test, and Launch Operations
AU	astronomical unit
AXAF	Advanced X-Ray Astrophysics Facility, later Chandra
BATC	Ball Aerospace and Technology Corporation
BMDO	Ballistic Missile Defense Organization
C&DH	Command and Data Handling
CA	Confirmation Assessment
CADRe	Cost Analysis Data Requirement
CCD	charge-coupled device
CDR	Conceptual Design Review; Critical Design Review
CESAR	Comet Earth Sample and Return
CfA	Harvard-Smithsonian Center for Astrophysics
CFI	CONTOUR Forward Imager
CIDA	Comet Impact Dust Analyzer (on CONTOUR); Cometary and Interstellar Dust Analyzer (on Stardust)
CIW	Carnegie Institute of Washington
CNR	Comet Nucleus Rendezvous
Co-I	Co-Investigator
COMPLEX	Committee on Planetary Exploration
CONTOUR	COmet Nucleus TOUR
COROT	Convection Rotation and planetary Transits
COTS	Commercial Off The Shelf
CR	Confirmation Review
CRAF	Comet Rendezvous Asteroid Flyby Return
CRISP	CONTOUR Remote Imaging SPectrograph
CRR	Capability and Requirements Review
CSSR	Comet Surface Sample Return
CZT	Cadmium-Zinc Telluride (detectors on Dawn's GRaND)
D&NFPO	Discovery and New Frontiers Program Office
DAP	Data Analysis Program
DARA	Deutsche Agentur für Raumfahrtangelegenheiten
DAVINCI	Deep Atmosphere Venus Investigation of Noble gases, Chemistry, and Imaging

DFMI	Dust Flux Monitor Instrument
DGE	Doppler Gravity Experiment (on Lunar Prospector)
DIXI	Deep Impact eXtended Investigation (proposed mission of opportunity)
DLLSG	Discovery Lessons Learned Steering Group
DLR	Institut für Planetenforschung of the Deutsches Zentrum für Luft-und Raumfahrt (Berlin)
DPI	Deputy Principal Investigator
DPM	Deputy Project Manager; Discovery Program Manager
DPO	Discovery Program Office
DPS	American Astronomical Society's Division of Planetary Sciences
DSMCE	Discovery and Scout Mission Capabilities Expansion
DSWG	Discovery Science Working Group
ECF	Early Career Fellow
ELV	Expendable Launch Vehicle
EOM	End of Mission
EPO	Education and Public Outreach
EPOCh	Extrasolar Planet Observations and Characterization
EPOXI	Extrasolar Planet Observations and Characterization (EPOCh) and Deep Impact eXtended Investigation (DIXI)
ESA	European Space Agency
ESSP	Earth System Science Pathfinder; Earth System Science Program
ESSSO	Earth and Space Science Support Office (at LaRC)
ETRR	Environmental Test Readiness Review
FAR	Federal Acquisition Regulation
FBC	faster, better, cheaper
FBO	Fixed-Base Operator
FC	Framing Camera
FISTA	Flying Infrared Signature Technologies Aircraft
FPA	Fault Protection and Autonomy
FRR	Flight Readiness Review
FTE	Full-Time Equivalent
FY	Fiscal Year
GAO	Government Accountability Office
GAS	Get Away Specials
GEM	Genesis Electron
GFE	Government Furnished Equipment

GIM	Genesis Ion Monitor
GO	Guest Observer Program
GPMC	Governing Program Management Council
GR/NS	Gamma Ray and Neutron Spectrometer
GRACE	Gravity Recovery and Climate Experiment
GRAIL	Gravity Recovery and Interior Laboratory
GRaND	Gamma Ray and Neutron Detector (on Dawn)
GRS	Gamma Ray Spectrometer (on Lunar Prospector)
GSFC	Goddard Space Flight Center
HEAO-2	High Energy Astrophysics Observatory 2, later Einstein Observatory
HER	Halley–Earth Return
HIM	Halley Intercept Mission
HRD	High Rate Detector
HST	Hubble Space Telescope
HZ	Habitable Zone
I&T	Integration and Test
IAT	Independent Assessment Team
ICE	Independent Cost Estimate
IDP	Interplanetary Dust Particle
IDS	Interdisciplinary Scientist (on Galileo)
IIR	Independent Implementation Review
IMP	Imager for Mars Pathfinder (instrument); Interplanetary Monitoring Platform (series of satellites)
IMS	Integrated Master Schedules
INAF	Instituto Nazionale Di Astrofisica (Italy)
INSIDE Jupiter	Interior Structure and Internal Dynamical Evolution of Jupiter (proposed)
InSight	Interior exploration using Seismic Investigations, Geodesy and Heat Transport
IPAO	Independent Project Assessment Office
IR	Inheritance Review
IRT	Independent Review Team
ISAS	Institute of Space and Astronautical Science (Japan)
ISIS	International Satellites for Ionospheric Studies (series of satellites)
ISP	Interstellar Particle
ISRO	Indian Space Research Organisation

ISS	International Space Station
ITAR	International Traffic in Arms Regulations
JHU	Johns Hopkins University
JPL	Jet Propulsion Laboratory
JSC	Johnson Space Center
KASC	Kepler Asteroseismic Science Consortium
KDP	Key Decision Point
KREEP	potassium, rare earth elements, and phosphorus
KSC	Kennedy Space Center
LANL	Los Alamos National Laboratory
LaRa	Lander Radioscience
LaRC	Langley Research Center
LCC	Life Cycle Costs
LDEF	Long Duration Exposure Facility
LGRS	Lunar Gravity Ranging System
LLIS	Lessons Learned Information System
LLNL	Lawrence Livermore National Laboratory
LM	Lockheed Martin
LMA	Lockheed Martin Astronautics
LPSC	Lunar and Planetary Sciences Conference
LRD	Launch Readiness Date
LRR	Launch Readiness Review
M^3	Moon Mineralogy Mapper
MAG	Magnetometer
MAG/ER	Magnetometer/Electron Reflectometer (on Lunar Prospector)
MBAR	Main Belt Asteroid Rendezvous
MDR	Mission Definition Review
MDRA	Mission Definition and Requirements Agreement
MEGANE	Mars-moon Exploration with GAmma rays and NEutrons
MER	Mars Exploration Rovers
MESSENGER	MErcury Surface, Space ENvironment, GEochemistry, and Ranging
MIB	Mishap Investigation Board
MIDEX	Medium-Sized Explorer
MIT	Massachusetts Institute of Technology
MMR	Monthly Management Review
MMX	Martian Moons eXploration

MO	Mission of Opportunity (formerly MOO)
MO&DA	Mission Operations and Data Analysis
MOWG	Mission Operations Working Group
MPS	Max Planck Institut für Sonnensystemforschung (Germany)
MRO	Mars Reconnaissance Orbiter
MRR	Mission Readiness Review
MS	IR Mapping Spectrometer
MSFC	Marshall Space Flight Center
MSI	MultiSpectral Imager (on NEAR)
MSL	Mars Science Laboratory
MSSS	Malin Space Science Systems
MSX	Midcourse Space Experiment (Department of Defense mission)
NAC	NASA Advisory Council
NAPA	National Academy of Public Administration
NASA	National Aeronautics and Space Administration
NEAR	Near Earth Asteroid Rendezvous
NEPA	National Environmental Protection Act
NEXT	NASA's Evolutionary Xenon Thruster; New Exploration of Tempel 1
NGIMS	Neutral Gas and Ion Mass Spectrometer (on CONTOUR)
NIAT	NASA Integrated Action Team
NIS	Near-Infrared Spectrometer (on NEAR)
NLR	NEAR Laser Rangefinder
NLSA	Nuclear Launch Safety Approval
NLT	No Later Than
NMO	NASA Management Office
NPD	NASA Policy Directive
NPG	NASA Procedures and Guidelines
NPR	NASA Procedural Requirement
NRA	NASA Research Announcement
NRC	National Research Council
NRL	Naval Research Laboratory
NS	Neutron Spectrometer (on Lunar Prospector)
NSPIRES	NASA Solicitation and Proposal Integrated Review and Evaluation System
NSTAR	NASA Solar Technology Application Readiness
OAST	Office of Aeronautics and Space Technology

OCO	Orbiting Carbon Observatory
OIG	Office of Inspector General
OMB	Office of Management and Budget
ONR	Office of Naval Research
ORR	Operations Readiness Review
OSC	Orbital Sciences Corporation
OSIRIS	Origins Spectral Interpretation, Resource Identification and Security
OSS	Office of Space Science
OSSA	Office of Space Science and Applications
OTTR	Ocean-going Transportable Test and Evaluation Resource (tracking ship)
PA	Program Analyst (at NASA Headquarters)
PCA	Program Commitment Agreement
PDR	Preliminary Design Review
PDS	Planetary Data System
PE	Program Executive (at NASA Headquarters)
PETR	Post-Environmental Test Review
PI	Principal Investigator
PIDDP	Planetary Instrument Definition and Development Program
PIR	Program Implementation Review
PM	Program Manager (at NASA Headquarters); Project Manager (at APL, JPL, or GSFC)
PMC	Program Management Council
PMDAP	Planetary Mission Data Analysis Program
PMSR	Preliminary Mission and Systems Review
POP	Program Operating Plan
PPS	Planetary Protection Subcommittee
PS	Program Scientist (at NASA Headquarters); Project Scientist (at APL or JPL)
PSG	Project Science Group
PSI	Planetary Science Institute
PSLV	Polar Satellite Launch Vehicle
PSP	Participating Scientist Program
PSS	Planetary Science Subcommittee (of the NAC)
QuikScat	Quick Scatterometer
R&A	Research and Analysis

RECON	Rendezvous with a Comet Nucleus
RPS	Radioisotope Power Systems
RS	Radio Science
RY	Real-Year (dollars)
SAIC	Science Applications International Corporation
SALMON	Stand-ALone Mission of Opportunity Notice
SAO	Smithsonian Astrophysical Observatory (at Harvard)
SASF	Spacecraft Activity Sequence File
SDB	Small Disadvantaged Business
SDIO	Strategic Defense Initiative Organization
SE	Systems Engineer
SEI	Space Exploration Initiative
SERENA	Search for Exospheric Refilling and Emitted Natural Abundances
SETI	Search for Extraterrestrial Intelligence
SIR	System Implementation Review
SIR-C	Spaceborne Imaging Radar-C
SIRTF	Space Infrared Telescope Facility, later Spitzer Space Telescope
SJI	San Juan Capistrano Research Institute
SMD	Science Mission Directorate
SMEX	Small Explorer
SOCCER	Sample of Comet Coma Earth Return
SOFIA	Stratospheric Observatory for Infrared Astronomy
SOMA	Science Office for Mission Assessments (at LaRC)
SR&T	Supporting Research and Technology
SRB	Standing Review Board
SRC	Sample Return Capsule
SRR	System Requirements Review
SSAC	Solar System Advisory Committee
SSB	Space Studies Board (of the NRC)
SSE	Solar System Exploration (Division)
SSEC	Solar System Exploration Committee
SSED	Solar System Exploration Division
SSES	Solar System Exploration Subcommittee (of the SSAAC)
SSO	Science Support Office (at LaRC)
Stardust NExT	Stardust New Exploration of Tempel 1 (mission of opportunity)
STA	Sample Tray Assembly (on Stardust)
STROFIO	STart from a ROtating FIeld mass spectrOmeter

STScI	Space Telescope Science Institute
SWG	Science Working Group
SwRI	Southwest Research Institute
SWSR	Solar Wind Sample Return (mission concept)
THEMIS	Time History of Events and Macroscale Interaction during Substorms
TIE	Twin Ion Engines produced for the Galactic Empire's combat fleet
TIM	Technical Interchange Meeting
TLA	Three Letter Acronym
TMC	Technical, Management, and Cost Review
TMCO	Technical, Management, Cost, and Outreach Review
TOPS	Toward Other Planetary Systems
TOR	Terms of Reference
TRL	Technology Readiness Level
UARS	Upper Atmosphere Research Satellite
UCLA	University of California, Los Angeles
UHF	Ultra-High Frequency
USGS	United States Geological Survey
UTTR	Utah Test and Training Range
V&V	Verification and Validation
VERITAS	Venus Emissivity, Radio science, InSAR, Topography & Spectroscopy
VESAT	Venus Environmental Satellite (proposed mission)
VESPER	Venus Sounder for Planetary Exploration (proposed mission)
VEXAG	Venus Exploration Analysis Group
VIR	Visible and Infrared Imaging Spectrometer
VIRTIS	Visible and Infrared Thermal Imaging Spectrometer
WBS	Work Breakdown Structure
XRS-GRS	X-Ray/Gamma Ray Spectrometer (on NEAR)
XSS-11	EXperimental Satellite System-11

Note: Aladdin, Lunar Prospector, Mars Pathfinder, NetLander, Genesis, Stardust, Suess–Urey, Deep Impact, Dawn, Kepler, Space Lab, Kuiper Airborne Observatory, Ulysses, and Uhuru are names of missions but not acronyms.

APPENDIX B
Further Reading

NEAR

Bell, Jim, and Jacqueline Mitton. *Asteroid Rendezvous: NEAR Shoemaker's Adventures at Eros*. Cambridge University Press, 2002.

McCurdy, Howard E. *Low-Cost Innovation in Spaceflight: The NEAR Earth Asteroid Rendezvous (NEAR) Shoemaker mission*. Monographs in Aerospace History, number 36, 2005.

Russell, C. T., ed. *The Near-Earth Asteroid Rendezvous Mission*. Reprinted from Space Science Reviews, vol. 82, nos. 1–2, 1997.

Mars Pathfinder

Muirhead, B. K., and W. L. Simon. (1999) *High Velocity Leadership: The Mars Pathfinder Approach to Faster, Better, Cheaper*. Harper Business, HarperCollins.

Pritchett, P. (1998) *The Mars Pathfinder Approach to "Faster-Better-Cheaper:" Hard Proof from the NASA/JPL Pathfinder Team on How Limitations Can Guide You to Breakthroughs*. Pritchett & Associates.

Shirley, Donna. (1998) *Managing Martians*. Broadway Books.

Lunar Prospector

Binder, Alan B. (2005) *Lunar Prospector: Against All Odds*. Ken Press.

Stardust and Stardust NExT

Atkins, Ken. "Stardust: The rewards of commitment, care, and communication." *ASK Magazine* 23:14–17, 2006.

Atkins, Kenneth L., Bredt D. Martin, Joseph M. Vellinga, and Rick A. Price. "Stardust: Implementing a New Manage-to-Budget Paradigm," Proceedings of the Fourth IAA Conference on Low Cost Spacecraft, Johns Hopkins University, May 2–5, 2000, also recorded in *Acta Astronautica* 52:87–97, 2003. Available online at *http://www.sciencedirect.com*.

Atkins, Kenneth L. "How to plan and manage reserves effectively," IEEE paper #1292, 2004 IEEE Aerospace Conference, 8–12 March, 2004, Big Sky, MT.

Brownlee et al. "Comet 81P/Wild 2 under a microscope," and following papers in *Science* special section, vol. 314: 1711–1739, 15 December 2006.

Brownlee, D. E., P. Tsou, J. D. Anderson, M. S. Hammer, R. L. Newburn, Z. Sekanina, B. C. Clark, F. Horz, M. E. Zolensky, J. Kissel, J. A. M. McDonnell, S. A. Sandford, and A. J. Tuzzolino, "Stardust: Comet and interstellar dust sample return mission," *JGR* 108, no. E10, 8111–8125, 2003, and the following instrument papers in that issue of *JGR*.

"Stardust at Comet Wild 2": *Science* special section, vol. 304, no. 5678: 1701–1856, 18 June 2004.

Genesis

Roberts, Barney B., and Richard B. Bennett, "Risk Management for the NASA/JPL Genesis Mission: A Case Study," 30 August 2000, available online from *http://www.futron.com/resources.xml?page=4#tabs-1*.

Russell, C. T., ed., *The Genesis Mission*. Kluwer Academic Publishers. Reprinted from *Space Science Reviews*, vol. 105, nos. 3–4, 2003.

Williams, Kenneth E. "Overcoming Genesis Mission Design Challenges," IAA-L-0603P 2004.

CONTOUR

CONTOUR Mishap Investigation Board (2003). *CONTOUR Mishap Investigation Board Report*.

Deep Impact and EPOXI

A'Hearn, Michael F., and Michael R. Combi, eds. *Deep Impact at Comet Tempel 1*. Reprinted from *Icarus*, vol. 191, no. 2S, 2007.

Russell, C. T., ed. *Deep Impact Mission: Looking Beneath the Surface of a Cometary Nucleus.* Springer. Reprinted from *Space Science Reviews,* vol. 117, nos. 1–2, 2005.

MESSENGER

Domingue, D. L., and C. T. Russell, eds. *The MESSENGER mission to Mercury.* Springer. Reprinted from *Space Science Reviews,* vol. 131, nos. 1–4, 2007.

Science special issues 2008, 2009, 2010.

Dawn

Rayman, M. D., et al. "Dawn: A mission in development for exploration of main belt asteroids Vesta and Ceres," *Acta Astronautica* 58: 605–616, 2006.

Russell, C. T., et al. "Dawn: A Journey In Space and Time," *Planet. Space Sci.* 52: 465–489, 2004.

Lessons Learned

Bearden, D. A. (2003). "A complexity-based risk assessment of low-cost planetary missions: When is a mission too fast and too cheap?" *Acta Astronautica,* vol. 52, no. 2–6.

Discovery Program Goals (2005). Online at *http://discovery.larc.nasa.gov/dpgoals. html.*

Discovery Program Handbook 1992. Solar System Exploration Division, Office of Space Science, NASA Headquarters.

Discovery Program Workshops (16–20 November 1992, 13–15 April 1993, 14–15 June 1995, 30 January 1998, 23–24 February 2000, 24 July 2002, 2 February 2006, 6–7 April 2006, 24 July 2002, September 2007); some available online at the Discovery Program Acquisition Web site: *http://discovery.larc.nasa.gov/ lessonslearned.html.*

McCurdy, H. E. (2001). *Faster, Better, Cheaper: Low Cost Innovation in the US Space Program.* Johns Hopkins University Press. Baltimore, MD.

Perry, R. B., and D. G. Pelaccio (2003). "Considerations and Lessons Learned in Implementing Effective, Low-Cost, Unmanned Space Exploration Missions." Space Technology & Applications International Forum (STAIF-2003, Albuquerque, New Mexico, February 2003).

Perry, R. B., J. R. Rogers, and M. L. Stancati (2006). "Lessons Learned from Technical, Management, and Cost Review of Proposals." Online at *http://discovery.larc. nasa.gov//discovery/PDF_FILES/TMC_Paper_21Feb06.pdf.*

—————

The NASA History Series

REFERENCE WORKS, NASA SP-4000

Grimwood, James M. *Project Mercury: A Chronology*. NASA SP-4001, 1963.

Grimwood, James M., and Barton C. Hacker, with Peter J. Vorzimmer. *Project Gemini Technology and Operations: A Chronology*. NASA SP-4002, 1969.

Link, Mae Mills. *Space Medicine in Project Mercury*. NASA SP-4003, 1965.

Astronautics and Aeronautics, 1963: Chronology of Science, Technology, and Policy. NASA SP-4004, 1964.

Astronautics and Aeronautics, 1964: Chronology of Science, Technology, and Policy. NASA SP-4005, 1965.

Astronautics and Aeronautics, 1965: Chronology of Science, Technology, and Policy. NASA SP-4006, 1966.

Astronautics and Aeronautics, 1966: Chronology of Science, Technology, and Policy. NASA SP-4007, 1967.

Astronautics and Aeronautics, 1967: Chronology of Science, Technology, and Policy. NASA SP-4008, 1968.

Ertel, Ivan D., and Mary Louise Morse. *The Apollo Spacecraft: A Chronology, Volume I, Through November 7, 1962*. NASA SP-4009, 1969.

Morse, Mary Louise, and Jean Kernahan Bays. *The Apollo Spacecraft: A Chronology, Volume II, November 8, 1962–September 30, 1964*. NASA SP-4009, 1973.

Brooks, Courtney G., and Ivan D. Ertel. *The Apollo Spacecraft: A Chronology, Volume III, October 1, 1964–January 20, 1966*. NASA SP-4009, 1973.

Ertel, Ivan D., and Roland W. Newkirk, with Courtney G. Brooks. *The Apollo Spacecraft: A Chronology, Volume IV, January 21, 1966–July 13, 1974*. NASA SP-4009, 1978.

Astronautics and Aeronautics, 1968: Chronology of Science, Technology, and Policy. NASA SP-4010, 1969.

Newkirk, Roland W., and Ivan D. Ertel, with Courtney G. Brooks. *Skylab: A Chronology*. NASA SP-4011, 1977.

Van Nimmen, Jane, and Leonard C. Bruno, with Robert L. Rosholt. *NASA Historical Data Book, Volume I: NASA Resources, 1958–1968*. NASA SP-4012, 1976; rep. ed. 1988.

Ezell, Linda Neuman. *NASA Historical Data Book, Volume II: Programs and Projects, 1958–1968*. NASA SP-4012, 1988.

Ezell, Linda Neuman. *NASA Historical Data Book, Volume III: Programs and Projects, 1969–1978*. NASA SP-4012, 1988.

Gawdiak, Ihor, with Helen Fedor. *NASA Historical Data Book, Volume IV: NASA Resources, 1969–1978*. NASA SP-4012, 1994.

Rumerman, Judy A. *NASA Historical Data Book, Volume V: NASA Launch Systems, Space Transportation, Human Spaceflight, and Space Science, 1979–1988*. NASA SP-4012, 1999.

Rumerman, Judy A. *NASA Historical Data Book, Volume VI: NASA Space Applications, Aeronautics and Space Research and Technology, Tracking and Data Acquisition/ Support Operations, Commercial Programs, and Resources, 1979–1988*. NASA SP-4012, 1999.

Rumerman, Judy A. *NASA Historical Data Book, Volume VII: NASA Launch Systems, Space Transportation, Human Spaceflight, and Space Science, 1989–1998*. NASA SP-2009-4012, 2009.

Rumerman, Judy A. *NASA Historical Data Book, Volume VIII: NASA Earth Science and Space Applications, Aeronautics, Technology, and Exploration, Tracking and Data Acquisition/Space Operations, Facilities and Resources, 1989–1998*. NASA SP-2012-4012, 2012.

No SP-4013.

Astronautics and Aeronautics, 1969: Chronology of Science, Technology, and Policy. NASA SP-4014, 1970.

Astronautics and Aeronautics, 1970: Chronology of Science, Technology, and Policy. NASA SP-4015, 1972.

Astronautics and Aeronautics, 1971: Chronology of Science, Technology, and Policy. NASA SP-4016, 1972.

Astronautics and Aeronautics, 1972: Chronology of Science, Technology, and Policy. NASA SP-4017, 1974.

Astronautics and Aeronautics, 1973: Chronology of Science, Technology, and Policy. NASA SP-4018, 1975.

Astronautics and Aeronautics, 1974: Chronology of Science, Technology, and Policy. NASA SP-4019, 1977.

Astronautics and Aeronautics, 1975: Chronology of Science, Technology, and Policy. NASA SP-4020, 1979.

Astronautics and Aeronautics, 1976: Chronology of Science, Technology, and Policy. NASA SP-4021, 1984.

Astronautics and Aeronautics, 1977: Chronology of Science, Technology, and Policy. NASA SP-4022, 1986.

Astronautics and Aeronautics, 1978: Chronology of Science, Technology, and Policy. NASA SP-4023, 1986.

Astronautics and Aeronautics, 1979–1984: Chronology of Science, Technology, and Policy. NASA SP-4024, 1988.

Astronautics and Aeronautics, 1985: Chronology of Science, Technology, and Policy. NASA SP-4025, 1990.

Noordung, Hermann. *The Problem of Space Travel: The Rocket Motor.* Edited by Ernst Stuhlinger and J. D. Hunley, with Jennifer Garland. NASA SP-4026, 1995.

Gawdiak, Ihor Y., Ramon J. Miro, and Sam Stueland. *Astronautics and Aeronautics, 1986–1990: A Chronology.* NASA SP-4027, 1997.

Gawdiak, Ihor Y., and Charles Shetland. *Astronautics and Aeronautics, 1991–1995: A Chronology.* NASA SP-2000-4028, 2000.

Orloff, Richard W. *Apollo by the Numbers: A Statistical Reference.* NASA SP-2000-4029, 2000.

Lewis, Marieke, and Ryan Swanson. *Astronautics and Aeronautics: A Chronology, 1996–2000.* NASA SP-2009-4030, 2009.

Ivey, William Noel, and Marieke Lewis. *Astronautics and Aeronautics: A Chronology, 2001–2005.* NASA SP-2010-4031, 2010.

Buchalter, Alice R., and William Noel Ivey. *Astronautics and Aeronautics: A Chronology, 2006.* NASA SP-2011-4032, 2010.

Lewis, Marieke. *Astronautics and Aeronautics: A Chronology, 2007.* NASA SP-2011-4033, 2011.

Lewis, Marieke. *Astronautics and Aeronautics: A Chronology, 2008*. NASA SP-2012-4034, 2012.

Lewis, Marieke. *Astronautics and Aeronautics: A Chronology, 2009*. NASA SP-2012-4035, 2012.

Flattery, Meaghan. *Astronautics and Aeronautics: A Chronology, 2010*. NASA SP-2013-4037, 2014.

Siddiqi, Asif A. *Beyond Earth: A Chronicle of Deep Space Exploration, 1958–2016*. NASA SP-2018-4041, 2018.

Management Histories, NASA SP-4100

Rosholt, Robert L. *An Administrative History of NASA, 1958–1963*. NASA SP-4101, 1966.

Levine, Arnold S. *Managing NASA in the Apollo Era*. NASA SP-4102, 1982.

Roland, Alex. *Model Research: The National Advisory Committee for Aeronautics, 1915–1958*. NASA SP-4103, 1985.

Fries, Sylvia D. *NASA Engineers and the Age of Apollo*. NASA SP-4104, 1992.

Glennan, T. Keith. *The Birth of NASA: The Diary of T. Keith Glennan*. Edited by J. D. Hunley. NASA SP-4105, 1993.

Seamans, Robert C. *Aiming at Targets: The Autobiography of Robert C. Seamans*. NASA SP-4106, 1996.

Garber, Stephen J., ed. *Looking Backward, Looking Forward: Forty Years of Human Spaceflight Symposium*. NASA SP-2002-4107, 2002.

Mallick, Donald L., with Peter W. Merlin. *The Smell of Kerosene: A Test Pilot's Odyssey*. NASA SP-4108, 2003.

Iliff, Kenneth W., and Curtis L. Peebles. *From Runway to Orbit: Reflections of a NASA Engineer*. NASA SP-2004-4109, 2004.

Chertok, Boris. *Rockets and People, Volume I*. NASA SP-2005-4110, 2005.

Chertok, Boris. *Rockets and People: Creating a Rocket Industry, Volume II*. NASA SP-2006-4110, 2006.

Chertok, Boris. *Rockets and People: Hot Days of the Cold War, Volume III*. NASA SP-2009-4110, 2009.

Chertok, Boris. *Rockets and People: The Moon Race, Volume IV*. NASA SP-2011-4110, 2011.

Laufer, Alexander, Todd Post, and Edward Hoffman. *Shared Voyage: Learning and Unlearning from Remarkable Projects*. NASA SP-2005-4111, 2005.

Dawson, Virginia P., and Mark D. Bowles. *Realizing the Dream of Flight: Biographical Essays in Honor of the Centennial of Flight, 1903–2003*. NASA SP-2005-4112, 2005.

Mudgway, Douglas J. *William H. Pickering: America's Deep Space Pioneer*. NASA SP-2008-4113, 2008.

Wright, Rebecca, Sandra Johnson, and Steven J. Dick. *NASA at 50: Interviews with NASA's Senior Leadership*. NASA SP-2012-4114, 2012.

Project Histories, NASA SP-4200

Swenson, Loyd S., Jr., James M. Grimwood, and Charles C. Alexander. *This New Ocean: A History of Project Mercury*. NASA SP-4201, 1966; rep. ed. 1999.

Green, Constance McLaughlin, and Milton Lomask. *Vanguard: A History*. NASA SP-4202, 1970; rep. ed. Smithsonian Institution Press, 1971.

Hacker, Barton C., and James M. Grimwood. *On the Shoulders of Titans: A History of Project Gemini*. NASA SP-4203, 1977; rep. ed. 2002.

Benson, Charles D., and William Barnaby Faherty. *Moonport: A History of Apollo Launch Facilities and Operations*. NASA SP-4204, 1978.

Brooks, Courtney G., James M. Grimwood, and Loyd S. Swenson, Jr. *Chariots for Apollo: A History of Manned Lunar Spacecraft*. NASA SP-4205, 1979.

Bilstein, Roger E. *Stages to Saturn: A Technological History of the Apollo/Saturn Launch Vehicles*. NASA SP-4206, 1980 and 1996.

No SP-4207.

Compton, W. David, and Charles D. Benson. *Living and Working in Space: A History of Skylab*. NASA SP-4208, 1983.

Ezell, Edward Clinton, and Linda Neuman Ezell. *The Partnership: A History of the Apollo-Soyuz Test Project*. NASA SP-4209, 1978.

Hall, R. Cargill. *Lunar Impact: A History of Project Ranger*. NASA SP-4210, 1977.

Newell, Homer E. *Beyond the Atmosphere: Early Years of Space Science*. NASA SP-4211, 1980.

Ezell, Edward Clinton, and Linda Neuman Ezell. *On Mars: Exploration of the Red Planet, 1958–1978*. NASA SP-4212, 1984.

Pitts, John A. *The Human Factor: Biomedicine in the Manned Space Program to 1980*. NASA SP-4213, 1985.

Compton, W. David. *Where No Man Has Gone Before: A History of Apollo Lunar Exploration Missions*. NASA SP-4214, 1989.

Naugle, John E. *First Among Equals: The Selection of NASA Space Science Experiments*. NASA SP-4215, 1991.

Wallace, Lane E. *Airborne Trailblazer: Two Decades with NASA Langley's 737 Flying Laboratory*. NASA SP-4216, 1994.

Butrica, Andrew J., ed. *Beyond the Ionosphere: Fifty Years of Satellite Communications*. NASA SP-4217, 1997.

Butrica, Andrew J. *To See the Unseen: A History of Planetary Radar Astronomy*. NASA SP-4218, 1996.

Mack, Pamela E., ed. *From Engineering Science to Big Science: The NACA and NASA Collier Trophy Research Project Winners*. NASA SP-4219, 1998.

Reed, R. Dale. *Wingless Flight: The Lifting Body Story*. NASA SP-4220, 1998.

Heppenheimer, T. A. *The Space Shuttle Decision: NASA's Search for a Reusable Space Vehicle*. NASA SP-4221, 1999.

Hunley, J. D., ed. *Toward Mach 2: The Douglas D-558 Program*. NASA SP-4222, 1999.

Swanson, Glen E., ed. *"Before This Decade Is Out…" Personal Reflections on the Apollo Program*. NASA SP-4223, 1999.

Tomayko, James E. *Computers Take Flight: A History of NASA's Pioneering Digital Fly-By-Wire Project*. NASA SP-4224, 2000.

Morgan, Clay. *Shuttle-Mir: The United States and Russia Share History's Highest Stage*. NASA SP-2001-4225, 2001.

Leary, William M. *"We Freeze to Please": A History of NASA's Icing Research Tunnel and the Quest for Safety*. NASA SP-2002-4226, 2002.

Mudgway, Douglas J. *Uplink-Downlink: A History of the Deep Space Network, 1957–1997*. NASA SP-2001-4227, 2001.

No SP-4228 or SP-4229.

Dawson, Virginia P., and Mark D. Bowles. *Taming Liquid Hydrogen: The Centaur Upper Stage Rocket, 1958–2002*. NASA SP-2004-4230, 2004.

Meltzer, Michael. *Mission to Jupiter: A History of the Galileo Project*. NASA SP-2007-4231, 2007.

Heppenheimer, T. A. *Facing the Heat Barrier: A History of Hypersonics*. NASA SP-2007-4232, 2007.

Tsiao, Sunny. *"Read You Loud and Clear!" The Story of NASA's Spaceflight Tracking and Data Network*. NASA SP-2007-4233, 2007.

Meltzer, Michael. *When Biospheres Collide: A History of NASA's Planetary Protection Programs*. NASA SP-2011-4234, 2011.

Conway, Erik M., Donald K. Yeomans, and Meg Rosenburg. *A History of Near-Earth Objects Research*. NASA SP-2022-4235, 2022.

Gainor, Christopher. *Not Yet Imagined: A Study of Hubble Space Telescope Operations*. NASA SP-2020-4237, 2020.

Niebur, Susan M., with David W. Brown, ed. *NASA's Discovery Program: The First Twenty Years of Competitive Planetary Exploration*. NASA SP-2023-4238, 2023.

Center Histories, NASA SP-4300

Rosenthal, Alfred. *Venture into Space: Early Years of Goddard Space Flight Center*. NASA SP-4301, 1985.

Hartman, Edwin P. *Adventures in Research: A History of Ames Research Center, 1940– 1965.* NASA SP-4302, 1970.

Hallion, Richard P. *On the Frontier: Flight Research at Dryden, 1946–1981.* NASA SP-4303, 1984.

Muenger, Elizabeth A. *Searching the Horizon: A History of Ames Research Center, 1940–1976.* NASA SP-4304, 1985.

Hansen, James R. *Engineer in Charge: A History of the Langley Aeronautical Laboratory, 1917–1958.* NASA SP-4305, 1987.

Dawson, Virginia P. *Engines and Innovation: Lewis Laboratory and American Propulsion Technology.* NASA SP-4306, 1991.

Dethloff, Henry C. *"Suddenly Tomorrow Came…": A History of the Johnson Space Center, 1957–1990.* NASA SP-4307, 1993.

Hansen, James R. *Spaceflight Revolution: NASA Langley Research Center from Sputnik to Apollo.* NASA SP-4308, 1995.

Wallace, Lane E. *Flights of Discovery: An Illustrated History of the Dryden Flight Research Center.* NASA SP-4309, 1996.

Herring, Mack R. *Way Station to Space: A History of the John C. Stennis Space Center.* NASA SP-4310, 1997.

Wallace, Harold D., Jr. *Wallops Station and the Creation of an American Space Program.* NASA SP-4311, 1997.

Wallace, Lane E. *Dreams, Hopes, Realities. NASA's Goddard Space Flight Center: The First Forty Years.* NASA SP-4312, 1999.

Dunar, Andrew J., and Stephen P. Waring. *Power to Explore: A History of Marshall Space Flight Center, 1960–1990.* NASA SP-4313, 1999.

Bugos, Glenn E. *Atmosphere of Freedom: Sixty Years at the NASA Ames Research Center.* NASA SP-2000-4314, 2000.

Bugos, Glenn E. *Atmosphere of Freedom: Seventy Years at the NASA Ames Research Center.* NASA SP-2010-4314, 2010. Revised version of NASA SP-2000-4314.

Bugos, Glenn E. *Atmosphere of Freedom: 75 Years at the NASA Ames Research Center.* NASA SP-2014-4314, 2014. Revised version of NASA SP-2000-4314.

No SP-4315.

Schultz, James. *Crafting Flight: Aircraft Pioneers and the Contributions of the Men and Women of NASA Langley Research Center.* NASA SP-2003-4316, 2003.

Bowles, Mark D. *Science in Flux: NASA's Nuclear Program at Plum Brook Station, 1955–2005.* NASA SP-2006-4317, 2006.

Wallace, Lane E. *Flights of Discovery: An Illustrated History of the Dryden Flight Research Center.* NASA SP-2007-4318, 2007. Revised version of NASA SP-4309.

Arrighi, Robert S. *Revolutionary Atmosphere: The Story of the Altitude Wind Tunnel and the Space Power Chambers.* NASA SP-2010-4319, 2010.

Wallace, Lane E., and Christian Gelzer. *Flights of Discovery: 75 Years of Flight Research at NASA Armstrong Flight Research Center*. NASA SP-2021-4309. Revised version of NASA SP-2007-4318.

General Histories, NASA SP-4400

Corliss, William R. *NASA Sounding Rockets, 1958–1968: A Historical Summary*. NASA SP-4401, 1971.

Wells, Helen T., Susan H. Whiteley, and Carrie Karegeannes. *Origins of NASA Names*. NASA SP-4402, 1976.

Anderson, Frank W., Jr. *Orders of Magnitude: A History of NACA and NASA, 1915–1980*. NASA SP-4403, 1981.

Sloop, John L. *Liquid Hydrogen as a Propulsion Fuel, 1945–1959*. NASA SP-4404, 1978.

Roland, Alex. *A Spacefaring People: Perspectives on Early Spaceflight*. NASA SP-4405, 1985.

Bilstein, Roger E. *Orders of Magnitude: A History of the NACA and NASA, 1915–1990*. NASA SP-4406, 1989.

Logsdon, John M., ed., with Linda J. Lear, Jannelle Warren Findley, Ray A. Williamson, and Dwayne A. Day. *Exploring the Unknown: Selected Documents in the History of the U.S. Civil Space Program, Volume I: Organizing for Exploration*. NASA SP-4407, 1995.

Logsdon, John M., ed., with Dwayne A. Day and Roger D. Launius. *Exploring the Unknown: Selected Documents in the History of the U.S. Civil Space Program, Volume II: External Relationships*. NASA SP-4407, 1996.

Logsdon, John M., ed., with Roger D. Launius, David H. Onkst, and Stephen J. Garber. *Exploring the Unknown: Selected Documents in the History of the U.S. Civil Space Program, Volume III: Using Space*. NASA SP-4407, 1998.

Logsdon, John M., ed., with Ray A. Williamson, Roger D. Launius, Russell J. Acker, Stephen J. Garber, and Jonathan L. Friedman. *Exploring the Unknown: Selected Documents in the History of the U.S. Civil Space Program, Volume IV: Accessing Space*. NASA SP-4407, 1999.

Logsdon, John M., ed., with Amy Paige Snyder, Roger D. Launius, Stephen J. Garber, and Regan Anne Newport. *Exploring the Unknown: Selected Documents in the History of the U.S. Civil Space Program, Volume V: Exploring the Cosmos*. NASA SP-2001-4407, 2001.

Logsdon, John M., ed., with Stephen J. Garber, Roger D. Launius, and Ray A. Williamson. *Exploring the Unknown: Selected Documents in the History of the*

U.S. Civil Space Program, Volume VI: Space and Earth Science. NASA SP-2004-4407, 2004.

Logsdon, John M., ed., with Roger D. Launius. *Exploring the Unknown: Selected Documents in the History of the U.S. Civil Space Program, Volume VII: Human Spaceflight: Projects Mercury, Gemini, and Apollo*. NASA SP-2008-4407, 2008.

Siddiqi, Asif A., *Challenge to Apollo: The Soviet Union and the Space Race, 1945–1974*. NASA SP-2000-4408, 2000.

Hansen, James R., ed. *The Wind and Beyond: Journey into the History of Aerodynamics in America, Volume 1: The Ascent of the Airplane*. NASA SP-2003-4409, 2003.

Hansen, James R., ed. *The Wind and Beyond: Journey into the History of Aerodynamics in America, Volume 2: Reinventing the Airplane*. NASA SP-2007-4409, 2007.

Hogan, Thor. *Mars Wars: The Rise and Fall of the Space Exploration Initiative*. NASA SP-2007-4410, 2007.

Vakoch, Douglas A., ed. *Psychology of Space Exploration: Contemporary Research in Historical Perspective*. NASA SP-2011-4411, 2011.

Ferguson, Robert G. *NASA's First A: Aeronautics from 1958 to 2008*. NASA SP-2012-4412, 2013.

Vakoch, Douglas A., ed. *Archaeology, Anthropology, and Interstellar Communication*. NASA SP-2013-4413, 2014.

Asner, Glen R., and Stephen J. Garber. *Origins of 21st-Century Space Travel: A History of NASA's Decadal Planning Team and the Vision for Space Exploration, 1999–2004*. NASA SP-2019-4415, 2019.

Launius, Roger D. *NACA to NASA to Now: The Frontiers of Air and Space in the American Century*. NASA SP-2022-4419, 2022.

Monographs in Aerospace History, NASA SP-4500

Launius, Roger D., and Aaron K. Gillette, comps. *Toward a History of the Space Shuttle: An Annotated Bibliography*. Monographs in Aerospace History, No. 1, 1992.

Launius, Roger D., and J. D. Hunley, comps. *An Annotated Bibliography of the Apollo Program*. Monographs in Aerospace History, No. 2, 1994.

Launius, Roger D. *Apollo: A Retrospective Analysis*. Monographs in Aerospace History, No. 3, 1994.

Hansen, James R. *Enchanted Rendezvous: John C. Houbolt and the Genesis of the Lunar-Orbit Rendezvous Concept*. Monographs in Aerospace History, No. 4, 1995.

Gorn, Michael H. *Hugh L. Dryden's Career in Aviation and Space*. Monographs in Aerospace History, No. 5, 1996.

Powers, Sheryll Goecke. *Women in Flight Research at NASA Dryden Flight Research Center from 1946 to 1995.* Monographs in Aerospace History, No. 6, 1997.

Portree, David S. F., and Robert C. Trevino. *Walking to Olympus: An EVA Chronology.* Monographs in Aerospace History, No. 7, 1997.

Logsdon, John M., moderator. *Legislative Origins of the National Aeronautics and Space Act of 1958: Proceedings of an Oral History Workshop.* Monographs in Aerospace History, No. 8, 1998.

Rumerman, Judy A., comp. *U.S. Human Spaceflight: A Record of Achievement, 1961–1998.* Monographs in Aerospace History, No. 9, 1998.

Portree, David S. F. *NASA's Origins and the Dawn of the Space Age.* Monographs in Aerospace History, No. 10, 1998.

Logsdon, John M. *Together in Orbit: The Origins of International Cooperation in the Space Station.* Monographs in Aerospace History, No. 11, 1998.

Phillips, W. Hewitt. *Journey in Aeronautical Research: A Career at NASA Langley Research Center.* Monographs in Aerospace History, No. 12, 1998.

Braslow, Albert L. *A History of Suction-Type Laminar-Flow Control with Emphasis on Flight Research.* Monographs in Aerospace History, No. 13, 1999.

Logsdon, John M., moderator. *Managing the Moon Program: Lessons Learned from Apollo.* Monographs in Aerospace History, No. 14, 1999.

Perminov, V. G. *The Difficult Road to Mars: A Brief History of Mars Exploration in the Soviet Union.* Monographs in Aerospace History, No. 15, 1999.

Tucker, Tom. *Touchdown: The Development of Propulsion Controlled Aircraft at NASA Dryden.* Monographs in Aerospace History, No. 16, 1999.

Maisel, Martin, Demo J. Giulanetti, and Daniel C. Dugan. *The History of the XV-15 Tilt Rotor Research Aircraft: From Concept to Flight.* Monographs in Aerospace History, No. 17, 2000. NASA SP-2000-4517.

Jenkins, Dennis R. *Hypersonics Before the Shuttle: A Concise History of the X-15 Research Airplane.* Monographs in Aerospace History, No. 18, 2000. NASA SP-2000-4518.

Chambers, Joseph R. *Partners in Freedom: Contributions of the Langley Research Center to U.S. Military Aircraft of the 1990s.* Monographs in Aerospace History, No. 19, 2000. NASA SP-2000-4519.

Waltman, Gene L. *Black Magic and Gremlins: Analog Flight Simulations at NASA's Flight Research Center.* Monographs in Aerospace History, No. 20, 2000. NASA SP-2000-4520.

Portree, David S. F. *Humans to Mars: Fifty Years of Mission Planning, 1950–2000.* Monographs in Aerospace History, No. 21, 2001. NASA SP-2001-4521.

Thompson, Milton O., with J. D. Hunley. *Flight Research: Problems Encountered and What They Should Teach Us*. Monographs in Aerospace History, No. 22, 2001. NASA SP-2001-4522.

Tucker, Tom. *The Eclipse Project*. Monographs in Aerospace History, No. 23, 2001. NASA SP-2001-4523.

Siddiqi, Asif A. *Deep Space Chronicle: A Chronology of Deep Space and Planetary Probes, 1958–2000*. Monographs in Aerospace History, No. 24, 2002. NASA SP-2002-4524.

Merlin, Peter W. *Mach 3+: NASA/USAF YF-12 Flight Research, 1969–1979*. Monographs in Aerospace History, No. 25, 2001. NASA SP-2001-4525.

Anderson, Seth B. *Memoirs of an Aeronautical Engineer: Flight Tests at Ames Research Center: 1940–1970*. Monographs in Aerospace History, No. 26, 2002. NASA SP-2002-4526.

Renstrom, Arthur G. *Wilbur and Orville Wright: A Bibliography Commemorating the One-Hundredth Anniversary of the First Powered Flight on December 17, 1903*. Monographs in Aerospace History, No. 27, 2002. NASA SP-2002-4527.

No monograph 28.

Chambers, Joseph R. *Concept to Reality: Contributions of the NASA Langley Research Center to U.S. Civil Aircraft of the 1990s*. Monographs in Aerospace History, No. 29, 2003. NASA SP-2003-4529.

Peebles, Curtis, ed. *The Spoken Word: Recollections of Dryden History, The Early Years*. Monographs in Aerospace History, No. 30, 2003. NASA SP-2003-4530.

Jenkins, Dennis R., Tony Landis, and Jay Miller. *American X-Vehicles: An Inventory — X-1 to X-50*. Monographs in Aerospace History, No. 31, 2003. NASA SP-2003-4531.

Renstrom, Arthur G. *Wilbur and Orville Wright: A Chronology Commemorating the One-Hundredth Anniversary of the First Powered Flight on December 17, 1903*. Monographs in Aerospace History, No. 32, 2003. NASA SP-2003-4532.

Bowles, Mark D., and Robert S. Arrighi. *NASA's Nuclear Frontier: The Plum Brook Research Reactor*. Monographs in Aerospace History, No. 33, 2004. NASA SP-2004-4533.

Wallace, Lane, and Christian Gelzer. *Nose Up: High Angle-of-Attack and Thrust Vectoring Research at NASA Dryden, 1979–2001*. Monographs in Aerospace History, No. 34, 2009. NASA SP-2009-4534.

Matranga, Gene J., C. Wayne Ottinger, Calvin R. Jarvis, and D. Christian Gelzer. *Unconventional, Contrary, and Ugly: The Lunar Landing Research Vehicle*. Monographs in Aerospace History, No. 35, 2006. NASA SP-2004-4535.

McCurdy, Howard E. *Low-Cost Innovation in Spaceflight: The History of the Near Earth Asteroid Rendezvous (NEAR) Mission.* Monographs in Aerospace History, No. 36, 2005. NASA SP-2005-4536.

Seamans, Robert C., Jr. *Project Apollo: The Tough Decisions.* Monographs in Aerospace History, No. 37, 2005. NASA SP-2005-4537.

Lambright, W. Henry. *NASA and the Environment: The Case of Ozone Depletion.* Monographs in Aerospace History, No. 38, 2005. NASA SP-2005-4538.

Chambers, Joseph R. *Innovation in Flight: Research of the NASA Langley Research Center on Revolutionary Advanced Concepts for Aeronautics.* Monographs in Aerospace History, No. 39, 2005. NASA SP-2005-4539.

Phillips, W. Hewitt. *Journey into Space Research: Continuation of a Career at NASA Langley Research Center.* Monographs in Aerospace History, No. 40, 2005. NASA SP-2005-4540.

Rumerman, Judy A., Chris Gamble, and Gabriel Okolski, comps. *U.S. Human Spaceflight: A Record of Achievement, 1961–2006.* Monographs in Aerospace History, No. 41, 2007. NASA SP-2007-4541.

Peebles, Curtis. *The Spoken Word: Recollections of Dryden History Beyond the Sky.* Monographs in Aerospace History, No. 42, 2011. NASA SP-2011-4542.

Dick, Steven J., Stephen J. Garber, and Jane H. Odom. *Research in NASA History.* Monographs in Aerospace History, No. 43, 2009. NASA SP-2009-4543.

Merlin, Peter W. *Ikhana: Unmanned Aircraft System Western States Fire Missions.* Monographs in Aerospace History, No. 44, 2009. NASA SP-2009-4544.

Fisher, Steven C., and Shamim A. Rahman. *Remembering the Giants: Apollo Rocket Propulsion Development.* Monographs in Aerospace History, No. 45, 2009. NASA SP-2009-4545.

Gelzer, Christian. *Fairing Well: From Shoebox to Bat Truck and Beyond, Aerodynamic Truck Research at NASA's Dryden Flight Research Center.* Monographs in Aerospace History, No. 46, 2011. NASA SP-2011-4546.

Arrighi, Robert. *Pursuit of Power: NASA's Propulsion Systems Laboratory No. 1 and 2.* Monographs in Aerospace History, No. 48, 2012. NASA SP-2012-4548.

Renee M. Rottner. *Making the Invisible Visible: A History of the Spitzer Infrared Telescope Facility (1971–2003).* Monographs in Aerospace History, No. 47, 2017. NASA SP-2017-4547.

Goodrich, Malinda K., Alice R. Buchalter, and Patrick M. Miller, comps. *Toward a History of the Space Shuttle: An Annotated Bibliography, Part 2 (1992–2011).* Monographs in Aerospace History, No. 49, 2012. NASA SP-2012-4549.

Ta, Julie B., and Robert C. Treviño. *Walking to Olympus: An EVA Chronology, 1997–2011*, vol. 2. Monographs in Aerospace History, No. 50, 2016. NASA SP-2016-4550.

Gelzer, Christian. *The Spoken Word III: Recollections of Dryden History; The Shuttle Years*. Monographs in Aerospace History, No. 52, 2013. NASA SP-2013-4552.

Ross, James C. *NASA Photo One*. Monographs in Aerospace History, No. 53, 2013. NASA SP-2013-4553.

Launius, Roger D. *Historical Analogs for the Stimulation of Space Commerce*. Monographs in Aerospace History, No. 54, 2014. NASA SP-2014-4554.

Buchalter, Alice R., and Patrick M. Miller, comps. *The National Advisory Committee for Aeronautics: An Annotated Bibliography*. Monographs in Aerospace History, No. 55, 2014. NASA SP-2014-4555.

Chambers, Joseph R., and Mark A. Chambers. *Emblems of Exploration: Logos of the NACA and NASA*. Monographs in Aerospace History, No. 56, 2015. NASA SP-2015-4556.

Alexander, Joseph K. *Science Advice to NASA: Conflict, Consensus, Partnership, Leadership*. Monographs in Aerospace History, No. 57, 2017. NASA SP-2017-4557.

Electronic Media, NASA SP-4600

Remembering Apollo 11: The 30th Anniversary Data Archive CD-ROM. NASA SP-4601, 1999.

Remembering Apollo 11: The 35th Anniversary Data Archive CD-ROM. NASA SP-2004-4601, 2004. This is an update of the 1999 edition.

The Mission Transcript Collection: U.S. Human Spaceflight Missions from Mercury Redstone 3 to Apollo 17. NASA SP-2000-4602, 2001.

Shuttle-Mir: The United States and Russia Share History's Highest Stage. NASA SP-2001-4603, 2002.

U.S. Centennial of Flight Commission Presents Born of Dreams — Inspired by Freedom. NASA SP-2004-4604, 2004.

Of Ashes and Atoms: A Documentary on the NASA Plum Brook Reactor Facility. NASA SP-2005-4605, 2005.

Taming Liquid Hydrogen: The Centaur Upper Stage Rocket Interactive CD-ROM. NASA SP-2004-4606, 2004.

Fueling Space Exploration: The History of NASA's Rocket Engine Test Facility DVD. NASA SP-2005-4607, 2005.

Altitude Wind Tunnel at NASA Glenn Research Center: An Interactive History CD-ROM. NASA SP-2008-4608, 2008.

A Tunnel Through Time: The History of NASA's Altitude Wind Tunnel. NASA SP-2010-4609, 2010.

Conference Proceedings, NASA SP-4700

Dick, Steven J., and Keith Cowing, eds. *Risk and Exploration: Earth, Sea and the Stars.* NASA SP-2005-4701, 2005.

Dick, Steven J., and Roger D. Launius. *Critical Issues in the History of Spaceflight.* NASA SP-2006-4702, 2006.

Dick, Steven J., ed. *Remembering the Space Age: Proceedings of the 50th Anniversary Conference.* NASA SP-2008-4703, 2008.

Dick, Steven J., ed. *NASA's First 50 Years: Historical Perspectives.* NASA SP-2010-4704, 2010.

Billings, Linda, ed. *50 Years of Solar System Exploration: Historical Perspectives.* NASA SP-2021-4705, 2021.

Societal Impact, NASA SP-4800

Dick, Steven J., and Roger D. Launius. *Societal Impact of Spaceflight.* NASA SP-2007-4801, 2007.

Dick, Steven J., and Mark L. Lupisella. *Cosmos and Culture: Cultural Evolution in a Cosmic Context.* NASA SP-2009-4802, 2009.

Dick, Steven J. *Historical Studies in the Societal Impact of Spaceflight.* NASA SP-2015-4803, 2015.

Index